Distinction
2000

ATSU

Distinction 2000

新しい英単語学習の始まり。

大学受験や専門領域で使用されるアカデミックな英語と、日常会話や
ビジネスで使用されるプラクティカルな英語を、立体的に、最高のバ
ランスで育て上げ、様々な場面で通用する確固たる語彙力を築き上げ
ることを目的とした Distinction 2000 は、あなたの英単語学習を改革
する、全く新しい英単語帳です。

これまでの英単語帳は、「こんな英文どこで使うの？」と疑問に思っ
てしまうような、非常に堅く、非実用的な例文で溢れているものばか
りでした。一方、実用的な英単語帳となると、簡単な表現・フレーズ
集が多く、確固たる語彙力を鍛えるのには不向きでした。

しかし、英語は複数の軸を持つ、立体的なものです。アカデミックな
英語も、実用的な英語も、同様に重要なのです。異なる軸を最高のバ
ランスでまとめ上げ、立体的な英語力を鍛えるために作り上げた英単
語帳、それが Distinction 2000 です。本書を使って、一緒に最高の英
単語学習をつくりあげていきましょう。

Contents

目次

The Authors

著者紹介

ATSU （西方 篤敬）

オーストラリア国立大学会計学修士を成績優秀で修了した後、オーストラリア、メルボルンにて世界4大会計事務所の一つ Deloitte トーマツに入社。アメリカ、イギリス、日系など幅広いグローバル監査案件に従事し、多様な会計実務経験を蓄積。同社クライアントマネージャーを経て、登録者数50万人を超える YouTube チャンネルを軸とした英語学習メディア Atsueigo をプラットフォームとし、合同会社 Westway を設立して独立。TOEIC 990点満点、TOEIC SW 400点満点、英検1級、IELTS Academic 8.5点、TOEFL iBT 114点、Versant 80点満点、元米国公認会計士・豪州勅許会計士、オーストラリア永住権保持。著書にDistinction I、II、III、IV、V、Structures、Vocabularist がある。

Atsueigo.com   🐦 / 📷 @Atsueigo   ▶ Atsueigo

上記書籍は著者サイトでのみ販売。

Andrew Huang

オーストラリア、メルボルン育ち。モナッシュ大学卒（商学）。卒業後はDeloitteトーマツ メルボルン事務所に勤務し、現在はオーストラリア最大の通信会社テルストラの投資戦略部門にてシニア財務アナリストとして活躍している。豪州勅許会計士。

Micah Judish

アメリカ合衆国、カリフォルニア州オレンジ出身。カリフォルニア州立大学卒（経営学）。Deloitteトーマツ サンフランシスコ事務所、サクラメント事務所、メルボルン事務所に勤務した後、アメリカ最大の衣料品リテーラーの一つであるギャップにシニア財務アナリストとして参画。現在はロンドンのアーンスト・アンド・ヤングにてアシスタントマネージャーとして活躍している。米国公認会計士。

Kino Tsumori

アメリカ合衆国、カリフォルニア州ロサンゼルス出身。ニューヨーク育ち。17歳で早稲田大学教育学部英語英文学科に入学。卒業後は公立中学、私立高校、東進ビジネススクールにて講師を歴任。現在は神田外語学院で講師として勤務する傍ら、DistinctionシリーズやAtsueigoハイスクールなど、その他の英語教育活動にも積極的に携わっている。TOEIC満点。国際バカロレア教員資格保持。

Colin O'Brien

アメリカ合衆国、オレゴン州ポートランド出身。ロヨラメリーマウント大学卒（会計学）。卒業後はロサンゼルスのDeloitteトーマツで勤務し、現在は同社のメルボルン事務所にてクライアントマネージャーとして活躍している。米国公認会計士。

Brooke Lathram-Abe

アメリカ合衆国、テネシー州メンフィス出身。ライス大学卒（統計・数学・数量経済分析）。ミシガン大学大学院修士課程修了（アジア研究）。 これまで多数の書籍・報告書などの校閲・校正・翻訳を担当。

Nick Norton

アメリカ合衆国、カリフォルニア州サンフランシスコ出身。サンフランシスコ大学卒（日本学）。英語教育番組にも多数出演（NHK、フジテレビ、日本テレビ、TBS）。英語講師、翻訳家としても活躍している。上智大学大学院グローバル・スタディーズ研究科在学中。

Mark Welch

イギリス、マンチェスター出身。ニューカッスル大学卒（言語学）。卒業後は日本の様々な英会話スクールにて英語講師を務める。現在は観光業界に特化したマーケティング会社で活躍している。

Ann Lethin

アメリカ合衆国、アラスカ州アンカレジ出身。アラスカ大学卒（生物学、言語学）。英文翻訳者としての豊富な経験を有し、これまで多数の書籍・論文・報告書の翻訳を担当。現在は翻訳ライターをする傍ら、英文校閲・校正者としても活躍している。

Vinay Murthy

アメリカ合衆国、カリフォルニア州ロサンゼルス出身。ブラウン大学卒（映画学）。ナレーター・声優として、TVCM、英語教材、アニメ、ゲームソフト、ドキュメンタリー番組吹き替えなど、様々なナレーションに携わる。

Karen Haedrich

アメリカ合衆国、メイン州キタリー出身。ハミルトン・カレッジ卒（クリエイティブライティング）。日本ではナレーター、ライターとして活躍している。

基本構成

Distinction 2000 は、経済、音楽、環境や政治、AIなど、合計40のトピックから構成されています。40 ものトピックを用意した背景には、幅広い分野に触れることで視野を広げ、英語力を身につけたその先まで描けるような一冊にしたい、という想いがあります。本書で少しでも、自らの将来観を育む機会を提供できればと思っています。

各トピックは、3つのセクションから構成されています。

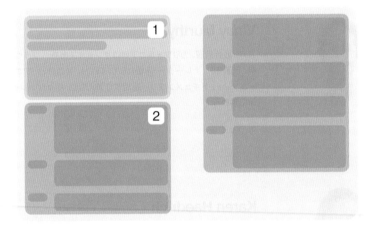

1 **アカデミックセクション**　　　Ac Academic

1つ目は、アカデミックな英語に焦点を当てたセクションです。このセクションは、大学受験や専門分野でよく出会うタイプの例文と、それを左から右に図式化したイラストで構成されています。このイラストの目的は、「英語脳」をつくり上げることにあります。英語を話すための学習を行う際、日本語から英語に変換するのではなく、イメージや感覚から英文をアウトプットすることで、日本語を介在させない英語学習を実現します。これを繰り返し行うことで、ネイティブと同じように、英語を英語で考える「英語脳」を構築することができます。比較的難易度の高い例文も収録されているため、英語初心者の方は次のプラクティカルセクションから取り組むのがおすすめです。

② **プラクティカルセクション**

2つ目は、日常会話やビジネスで使用される、プラクティカルな英語に焦点を当てています。1つ目のアカデミックセクションにある英文から重要単語を7つ取り上げ、用法や関連語を掲載するだけでなく、各単語が実際にどのように使われるのかを、ネイティブが使う自然な例文で表現しています。

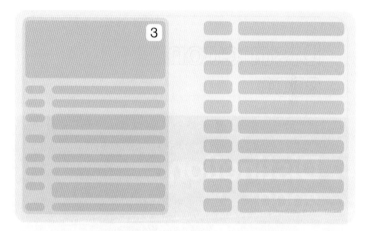

③ **スナップショットセクション**

3つ目は、日常会話やブログ記事、ニュース、雑誌、図鑑など、今後英語を実際に使用していく上で出会うさまざまな場面を切り取ったセクションです。多様なシーンで柔軟に対応できる英語力を、よりいっそう高めてくれます。

こだわり抜いたカバーデザイン

美しいカバーデザインは、モチベーショナルな英単語学習をサポートしてくれます。これまで、カバーデザインが洗練された英単語帳は少なく、無地のカバーをつけたり、カバーを取ったりして使用していた方が多いのではないでしょうか。しかし、書籍の顔とも言うことができるカバーは、それを積極的に、楽しく使っていく上で大きな役割を果たしています。カバーデザインからとことんこだわることで、開く前からワクワクするような一冊に仕上げました。

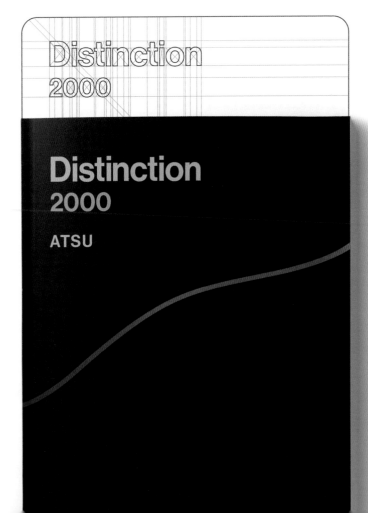

▬ 分かりやすい解説を豊富に

Distinction 2000 には、かゆいところに手が届くていねいな解説が多数収録されています。似た単語の間に存在するニュアンスの違いから、接頭語や接尾語、単語の語源に関するものまで、幅広いタイプの解説を収録することで、常に「納得感」を持ちながら英単語学習を進めることができます。

Example / 例

live in vs be living in

どちらもある場所に住んでいることを表しますが、live in はその場所にこれまでもずっと住んできたというニュアンスを持ち、be living in はその-ing の形から今現在そこに住んでいるというニュアンスが強くなります。そのため、例えば現在一年間の交換留学でアメリカに住んでいる場合、I'm living in the U.S. という方が、その状況をより正確に表す文章になります。

014

æ 音の変化まで考慮したIPA式の発音記号

発音記号には、国際的に幅広く使用されているIPA（国際音声記号）を採用し、関連語から句動詞まで、すべての収録英単語に発音記号を掲載しました。さらに、発音記号は音の変化や脱落も考慮されています。例えば give it a shot（試してみる）という表現は、発音記号通りに書くと [gɪv ɪt ə ʃɑːt] と4語が独立した発音になりますが、実際にネイティブが発音すると [gívɪtəʃɑːt] となり、まるで1語のように聞こえます。Distinction 2000 ではこうしたフレーズや句動詞の発音記号には音の変化・脱落を考慮した修正を加え、発音記号通りに読むだけでネイティブの音に近づけるように設計しました。

C/U 可算·不可算名詞の表記

すべての名詞に、その英単語が数えられるか、数えられないかを示す、可算·不可算記号が表記されています。可算·不可算の概念は、日本語にはない、英語を学ぶ上でとても重要な概念です。しかし、ほとんどの英単語帳はこの可算·不可算について言及していません。その結果、英語学習者はこの重要性を理解したあと、再度自分で可算·不可算について調べ直すという、非常に大きなムダが発生しています。可算·不可算の感覚を磨き上げ、効率的な英単語学習を実現しましょう。

超自然なネイティブ音声

ネイティブの「超」自然な音声を、すべての英単語、そして例文に収録しています。英単語帳に付属する音声は、ネイティブが実際に話すときと比べて、全体の抑揚や各単語の発音が誇張される傾向にあり、実際にネイティブに話しかけると「なんかいつものと違う」と感じたことがある方も多いのではないでしょうか。Distinction 2000 に付属する音声は、スピード、抑揚、音の繋がり、そして脱落まで、すべてにこだわり、完全なナチュラル音声を再現しました。聞いていると、まるでネイティブが本当に隣で話しているかのように感じられる音声をイメージしています。また、少しスピードを落としたネイティブ音声も用意しているので、どんな方でも安心して学習することができます。

本書の表記ルール

品詞	V[I]	自動詞	N[S]	単数扱い名詞
	V[T]	他動詞	N[P]	複数扱い名詞
	[PV]	句動詞	N[Prop.]	固有名詞
	Adj.	形容詞	Prep.	前置詞
	Adv.	副詞	Cnj.	接続詞
	N[C]	可算名詞	Pron.	代名詞
	N[U]	不可算名詞	Phr.	慣用句

略語

sth	something – 「物・事」の略	
sb	somebody – 「人」の略	
do	動詞の原形	
doing	動名詞または現在分詞	
one's	文の主語に呼応した代名詞の所有格 (my, your, his, her, their, its, our)	

※例えば deep inside one's heart (心の奥底で) の例文 …deep inside her heart she loves me.では、deep inside one's heart が含まれる文章の主語 she に呼応した所有格 her が使われています。

sb's	その状況下で意味している人の所有格

※例えば sb's type (〜の (好みの) タイプ) の例文 …she's actually not really my type.では、sb's typeが含まれる文章の主語は she ですが、その状況下の発言者であるIの所有格 my が使われています。

記号

⟷	反意語 (ほぼ反対の意味・用法)
＝/≒	同義語 (ほぼ同じ意味・用法) /類義語
( )	省略可能なもの
【 】	必ずtheが付くもの/頭文字が大文字 (小文字) になる場合
adjective	形容詞
that+sentence	that 節 (補語、目的語の位置にあるthat節のthatは省略可能)
▶	関連語
■	以下に例文があることを示す
<英>	イギリス英語

発音記号・アクセント　　[´] 第一アクセント　　[`] 第二アクセント

本書では原則として一般米語 (General American)、国際音声記号 (IPA) に準拠。

英単語の覚え方

効果的な英単語の覚え方について理解しよう

英単語の覚え方についてしっかりと理解すれば、大量の英単語もスムーズに覚えることができます。ここでは、英単語の覚え方を戦略と戦術の2つのフェーズに分けて説明します。戦略は、英単語を覚えるという目標を達成するための全体的なアプローチ、方向性のことです。これを理解することで、ブレのない、一貫した英単語学習をすることができます。戦術は、具体的な手段やテクニックのことです。これを使えば Distinction 2000 を使った学習はもちろん、今後のどんな英単語学習も効果的に行うことができます。

 英単語を覚えるための戦略

英単語を覚えるための戦略は、高い回転率を維持することです。一つ一つの単語にじっくり時間をかけるのではなく、短期間の中で、何度も何度もDistinction 2000を回転させることで、着実に英単語を覚えることができます。

「ものすごい時間をかけて1周したけど、確認したら半分も覚えられていなかった」という経験はありませんか？それは、記憶力が悪いからではありません。人の脳はそもそも復習しないと忘れるようにできています。これは、ドイツの心理学者ヘルマン・エビングハウスによる研究によっても科学的に証明されています。この実験をもとに、人の記憶は適切なタイミングで復習をすると定着率がよくなることもわかっています。

 Active Recall

Active Recall を見るだけで、いつ、どこを復習すべきか一目でわかる

Distinction 2000 には、記憶の忘却パターンを考えて設計された、Active Recall
が付いています。Active Recall を使えば、自分でどのタイミングでどこを復習すべ
きか考えなくても、簡単に最適化された英単語学習を進めることができます。一日
1チャプター学習し、Active Recall 通りに復習すれば、たった2か月ですべての英単
語に6回も出会うことができます。

CH. 3, 6, 9	=	Review Chapter 3, 6, 9 before you proceed any further.	次のチャプターに進む前に チャプター3、6、9を復習

Active Recall の具体的な使い方は pg. 18 を参照してください。

英単語を覚えるための戦術

たった3つの戦術で、英単語は覚えることができます。所要時間は1語**30–60秒**。
「高い回転率」を意識して、サクサクと進めていきましょう。

---

1 英単語を見て意味を確認する (3–5秒)

はじめに、英単語の意味を確認しましょう。このとき、日本語訳をそのまま覚えようと
するのではなく、その意味の先にあるイメージや感覚を大事にしましょう。例えば、
organized という英単語を覚えるとき、「組織的な」という日本語の丸暗記を行うので
はなく、「組織的な」という言葉の奥にある「何かが一貫性を持って整理されているイ
メージ」を強く意識します。こうすることで、より感覚的に英語を捉えられるようになり
ます。

英語と日本語は異なる言語です。いつまでも日本語と英語の間を行ったり来たりして
いては、素早く英語を理解し、発信できるようにはなりません。この「イメージ・感覚」を
英単語学習の段階から意識するだけで、英語と日本語の変換という悪い癖を回避し、
英語を英語で理解する「英語脳」をつくり上げることができます。

2　意味をイメージしながら発音する（7–10秒）　

次に、英単語のイメージ・感覚を頭に思い浮かべながら、発音記号に沿って数回発音しましょう。実際に発音して音で覚えれば、聞いたときに理解できるだけでなく、話したときに相手に伝わるようになります。ゴロ合わせで覚えたり、カタカナ英語で覚えたりすると、見たらわかるけど聞き取れない、発音したときに通じないといった問題が起きます。発音をちょっと意識するだけで、そんな問題からも解放されます。しっかりと発音を意識した英単語学習を進めていきましょう。

3　英単語を使って文をつくる（45–50秒）

最後に、英単語を使って文章をつくり、何度も気持ちを込めて発音してみましょう。中学英語レベルの、簡単な英文でも大丈夫です。Distinction 2000には実践的な例文が掲載されているので、それを参考にすることもできます。3つの戦術の中で一番時間がかかるものなので、完璧を求めず、時間が経過したら次の単語に移りましょう。このステップは覚えた英単語を使えるようになることが主な目的です。最初は、1つ目と2つ目の戦術がしっかりできていれば、特に大きな問題はありません。

復習の方法（Active Recall の使い方）

英単語の学習が終わったら、定期的に復習をして、記憶の定着を高めましょう。復習のタイミングと範囲は、Active Recall が教えてくれます。復習時に行うことはとっても簡単。英単語を見て、覚えられていればさっと目を通すだけ。覚えられていなければ、その場で1つ目と2つ目の戦術を行いましょう。3つ目の戦術は、時間に余裕がある場合だけ行いましょう。復習のときに、覚えられていなくても大丈夫。何度も何度も同じ英単語に出会うことで、記憶の定着は確実に高まります。Active Recall を使いながら、繰り返し学習していきましょう。必ず覚えられるようになります。

よくある質問

最初から関連語や用法等も一緒に覚えた方がいいの？

収録単語のほとんどが初見の場合、最初は見出し語だけで十分です。一番重要なの
は、**高い回転率を維持して、サクサクと進む**ことです。時間や気持ちに余裕がなけれ
ば、まずは見出し語に取り組むことを優先し、学習の中で少しずつ関連語等も確認しま
しょう。これまでに英語学習経験がある方は、最初から関連語や用法、そしてその例文
などにも目を通し、英単語学習を加速させていきましょう。

たくさん意味がある英単語を覚えるときのコツは？

複数の意味が掲載されている場合、それらに共通した核となる感覚、コアイメージが
ないか探ってみましょう。例えば、organized には「組織的な；整理された、（人が）きち
んとした」という3つの意味が掲載されていますが、どれも「何かが一貫性を持って整
理されているイメージ」が存在します。このコアイメージをしっかりと掴めば、複数の意
味をすべて丸暗記することなく、**柔軟に英単語の意味を解釈し、実践的に使える**ように
なります。

おすすめの学習プランは？

Distinction 2000 では、2か月（60日間）で完結する学習プランをご提案します。プラン
内容はいたってシンプル。毎日、新しいチャプターを1つと Active Recall が教えてくれ
るチャプターを復習するだけです。これを忠実に行うことで、一定の間隔で各英単語に
合計6回も出会うことができます。40日間かけてすべてのチャプターが終わったら、残り
の20日間は復習のみを行います。復習プランは pg. 527 に掲載されています。

アカデミックセクションの英文とイラストの使い方は？

英単語が覚えられてきたら、左上のアカデミックセクションにもチャレンジしてみましょ
う。比較的難易度の高いアカデミックな英文を、できるだけ訳さず、左から右に何度も
読み返すことで、高度な読解力を育てることができます。そして、英文の意味が理解でき
たら、次はイラストだけを見てその英文を想起し、口から出す練習をしましょう。イラスト
は、英文を左から右に図式化しています。**日本語を介さずに英語をアウトプットする**練
習をすることで、英語を英語で考える「英語脳」を構築することができます。

発音記号

æ

聞き取れる、伝わる英語力を育てましょう

発音記号に沿って英単語を覚えるだけで、相手の英単語がもっと聞き取りやすく、伝わりやすくなります。間違った発音で英単語学習を進めると、英語を聞いたとき、知っている英単語ですら聞き取れなくなってしまいます。英語を話すとき、発音記号から大きく異なる発音では、相手もあなたの英語を理解するのに苦労するでしょう。英単語は、将来の自分の英語の土台になります。この土台をつくり上げる段階からしっかりと発音記号に沿って学習することで、あなたの将来の英語力は驚くほど向上します。

発音記号を覚えるのはあっという間

発音記号は誰でも簡単に覚えることができます。発音記号のほとんどが、アルファベットと同じ、もしくは少し変化しただけです。たくさんあるように見えても、実際に覚える作業はほんの少し。これまで覚えたことがない、もしくは自信がないという方は、まとまった時間を取ってすべて覚えてしまいましょう。そうすることで、圧倒的に効率化された英単語学習をすることができます。

母音 (Vowels)

Long Vowels（長母音）		
発音記号	**この音を含む単語例**	**発音の仕方**
[iː]	deal, keen, peak	日本語の「イー」とほぼ同じ音です。
[ɑː]	mark, October, solve	日本語の「アー」の音に近く、唇を自然に開いた状態で発音します。アクセントが無い時は「ア」と短い音になります。
[ɔː]	border, foreign, store	日本語の「オー」に近い音です。アメリカ英語では [r] が続くことがほとんどです。
[uː]	boost, due, suit	日本語の「ウー」の音に近く、リラックスした状態から唇を丸めて発音します。
[ɜː]	certain, earn, purpose	「アー」という曖昧な音で、口をあまり開かず発音します。アメリカ英語では必ず [r] が続き、合わせて発音します。

Short Vowels（短母音）		
[ɪ]	bill, fit, include	リラックスした状態で出す「イ」の音で、喉の奥から出します。アクセントがある時の方が若干音が長くなります。
[æ]	attack, ban, fad	「アとエの中間音」とよく言われる音で、リラックスして口を大きめに開き、喉の奥を使って「ア」と発音します。[m] か[n] が後に続くときは [æə] のように弱い [ə] が続き（例：man＝マァン）、[ŋ] が続く時は [eɪ] の音に変わる（例：thanks＝セインクス）傾向にあります。
[ʊ]	book, childhood, Europe	リラックスした状態で出す「ウ」の音で、喉の奥から出します。アクセントがある時の方が若干音が長くなります。
[ʌ]	blood, crust, uncover	口はあまり開けず、とてもリラックスした状態で「ア」と発音します。アクセントがある時の方が若干音が長くなります。
[ə]	accept, occur, reason	シュワ（schwa）と呼ばれる音で、口はあまり開けず、とてもリラックスした状態で「ア」と弱く発音します。常にアクセントがつかない母音で、とても曖昧な音になります。
[e]	fresh, help, smell	日本語の「エ」とほぼ同じ音です。
[i]	coffee, merely, pity	日本語の「イ」とほぼ同じ音です。
[u]	actual, ritual, visual	日本語の「ウ」の音に近く、リラックスした状態から唇を丸めて発音します。

Diphthongs（二重母音）		
[eɪ]	able, operate, place	リラックスした状態で「エィ」という音を出します。アクセントがある時の方が若干音が長くなります。
[aɪ]	might, idea, time	リラックスした状態で「アィ」という音を出します。アクセントがある時の方が若干音が長くなります。
[ɔɪ]	cuboid, employ, noise	リラックスした状態で「オィ」という音を出します。アクセントがある時の方が若干音が長くなります。
[aʊ]	allow, hometown, loud	リラックスした状態で「アゥ」という音を出します。アクセントがある時の方が若干音が長くなります。
[oʊ]	focus, go, solo	リラックスした状態で「オゥ」という音を出します。アクセントがある時の方が若干音が長くなります。

子音 (Consonants)

発音記号	この音を含む単語例	発音の仕方
[p]	poor, reception, tip	唇で空気をせき止め「プッ」と弾きます。喉を振動させない無声音です。
[b]	book, hub, subject	[p] と同じ要領で発音しますが、喉を振動させる有声音です。
[t]	edit, internal, treat	日本語の「タ」とほぼ同じポジションで空気をせき止め、勢いよく弾いて解放します。喉を振動させない無声音です。また、本書では [d] の音に変化する可能性のあるものは [t] で表しています。(pg. 27) 参照。
[d]	award, deep, edit	[t] と同じ要領で発音しますが、喉を振動させる有声音です。
[k]	key, shaken, track	舌の根元を口蓋 (上あご) につけて空気をせき止め、勢いよく「ク」と解放します。喉を振動させない無声音です。
[g]	glad, legal, colleague	[k] と同じ要領で発音しますが、喉を振動させる有声音です。
[f]	favor, often, thief	上の前歯が下唇の裏側に軽く触れる状態で日本語の「フ」と同じ要領で発音します。喉を振動させない無声音です。
[v]	positive, revise, vital	[f] と同じ要領で発音しますが、喉を振動させる有声音です。
[θ]	theory, method, width	舌の先を上下の歯に軽く当て、その隙間から息を出します。喉を振動させない無声音です。
[ð]	rather, smooth, though	[θ] と同じ要領で発音しますが、喉を振動させる有声音です。
[s]	cease, skill, waste	上下の歯の間から「ス」と空気を出すことで発音します。喉が振動しない無声音です。
[z]	buzzword, praise, result	[s] と同じ要領で発音しますが、喉を振動させる有声音です。
[ʃ]	crash, mention, sharp	日本語の「シ」と同じ要領で空気を出すことで発音し、[s] よりも舌が盛り上がります。喉が振動しない無声音です。
[ʒ]	pleasure, treasure, vision	[ʃ] と同じ要領で発音しますが、喉を振動させる有声音です。
[h]	ahead, history, horizon	日本語のハを発音するときと同じ要領で発音する無声音で、唇、口の開き方、舌の動かし方は音に影響しません。
[tʃ]	breach, choose, chore	日本語の「チ」と同じ要領で少し勢いをつけて発音します。
[dʒ]	budget, generate, wage	[tʃ] と同じ要領で発音しますが、喉を振動させる有声音です。
[m]	esteem, move, vitamin	両唇を軽く合わせた状態で喉を振動させることで発音します。口を閉じているため、自然と鼻から音が出る鼻音になります。
[n]	control, name, return	日本語のナ行を発音するときと同じ舌の位置で喉を振動させ発音します。息が舌にせき止められるので、自然と鼻から息が出る鼻音になります。
[ŋ]	link, swing, training	日本語で「ンガ」と素早く言った時のように舌の奥で喉を塞いだ状態で n の音をつくるイメージです。[n] のときと異なり舌先は上の歯茎に当たりません。また sing であれば舌先を上の歯茎につけずに「シン」と発音します。舌の奥で喉を塞ぐため、自然と鼻から息が出る鼻音になります。
[l]	formal, literally, novelist	[l] には2種類の発音があります。1つ目は発音記号上の母音の前に来るもの (例：like) で、Light L と呼ばれます。これは舌先を上前歯の裏側につけて発音します。2つ目は発音記号上の母音の後に来るもの (例：people) で、Dark L と呼ばれます。この時は口をあまり開かず、リラックスした状態で舌先を下前歯の裏側につけて暗い発音をします。
[r]	right, work, weather	口をリラックスさせた状態で喉の奥で発音します。犬が「グルルルル」と鳴いた時に似たガラガラした音になります。舌を少し巻く、もしくは舌を少し後ろ側に移動し、盛り上がる状態をつくることで発音します。
[j]	graveyard, yet, young	日本語の「ヤ」行の音で、喉の奥から発音します。舌は盛り上がりそのまま口の上に軽く触れ、そこから息を押し出すような感じになります。
[w]	sweet, war, world	口にかすかな隙間を残して「ゥワ」と弾くような音を喉の奥から発音します。

句動詞について

句動詞（phrasal verbs）とは、work out（解決する）、line up（用意する）といった「動詞＋副詞/ 前置詞」によって構成され、1つの動詞のように機能する表現を指します。句動詞は以下のように3つに分類することが可能です。

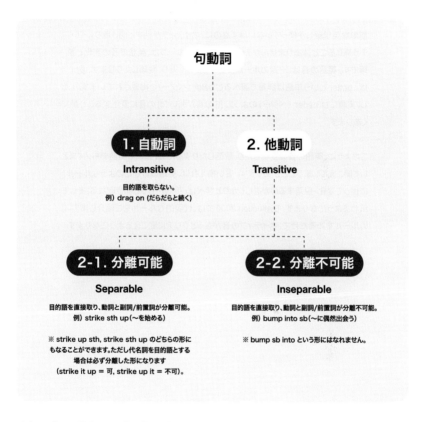

本書では「2-1. 他動詞 – 分離可能」に該当する句動詞は strike sth up のように目的語を表す sth もしくは sb を必ず動詞と副詞/前置詞の間に表記しています。ゆえに bump into sb のように、目的語が副詞/前置詞の後に表記されている場合は、その句動詞は「2-2. 他動詞 – 分離不可能」に該当することを意味します。

音の変化と脱落の法則 UX

簡単なルールを知るだけで、ネイティブの音がもっとクリアに

簡単な英単語しか使っていないはずなのに、ネイティブが話すと聞き取りにくい。そう感じることはありませんか？その大きな原因の一つは、英語の音の変化と脱落です。英語の音は、一定のルールに従って変化したり、脱落したりします。例えば、better という単語は辞書で調べると béter（ベター）と掲載されています。しかし、実際には béder（ベダー）のように [t] の音が弱い [d] の音に変化することがよくあります。

このように、英語の音は変化したり、脱落したりするため、簡単な英語でもノイズとして聞こえてしまうことがあります。言い換えれば、英語の音がどのようなルールに従って変化・脱落するのかをしっかりと学べば、英語がもっと聞き取れる、そして伝わるようになります。Distinction 2000 では、代表的なルールをご紹介します。このルールを知るだけで、ネイティブの音がもっとクリアに聞こえるようになります。

 Liaison (Linking)

リエゾン(liaison)、あるいはリンキング(linking)とは、音と音が「繋がること」を意味しています。複数の単語が並んでいる場合、1つ目の単語の「最後の音」と次の単語の「最初の音」が繋がって音が変化する、という現象が英語ではよく見られます。ここでは、4つのケースに分けて見ていきましょう。

1　子音と母音が連結するパターン　　　　*Consonant* + *Vowel*

1語目の「最後の音」が子音で、次に続く語の「最初の音」が母音のとき、つなぎ目が連結して「1つの音」として発音されることがあります。

例1) my name is [maɪnéɪmɪz]

例2) strike up [straɪkʌ́p]

例3) fade out [feɪdáʊt]

2　子音と子音が連結するパターン　　　　*Consonant* + *Consonant*

1語目の「最後の音」が子音で、次に続く語の「最初の音」も子音であるとき、発音時の口のポジションが似ていれば連結(1語目の最後の子音が脱落)することがあります。

例1) not too [nɑ(t) tuː] (全く同じ子音が続くときは口のポジションが同じであるため)

例2) right there [raɪ(t) ðer] (t と ð の発音時の口のポジションが近いため)

例3) sit down [sɪ(t) daʊn] (t と d の発音時の口のポジションが近いため)

3　母音と母音が連結するパターン　　　　*Vowel* + *Vowel*

1語目の「最後の音」が母音で、次に続く語の「最初の音」も母音であるとき、つなぎ目の部分に[w] や [y] といった音が生じることがあります。[w] や [y] のどちらが続くかは1語目の最後の音を発音するときの口のポジションで自然と決まってきます。

例1) go away [góʊ(w)əwéɪ] (oʊ の発音時の口のポジションが w に近いため)

例2) tidy up [taɪdi(y)ʌ́p] (i の発音時の口のポジションが y に近いため)

例3) play on words [pléɪ(y)ɑn wɜːrdz] (ɪ の発音時の口のポジションが y に近いため)

4　T, D or Z とY が連結するパターン　　　　*T,D,Z* + *Y__*

1語目の「最後の音」が [t, d, z] のいずれかの子音で、次に続く語の「最初の音」が [y] であるとき、以下のように音が変化します。

[t] + [y] = [tʃ]　　|　　[d] + [y] = [dʒ]　　|　　[z] + [y] = [ʒ]

次のページでいくつか例をみていきましょう。

$$[t] + [y] = [t\int]$$ $$[d] + [y] = [d\math３]$$ $$[z] + [y] = [\math３]$$

例1) can't you [kǽntʃu]　　例1) did you [dídʒu]　　例1) how's your [háʊʒʊər]

例2) want you [wάntʃu]　　例2) would you [wʊ́dʒu]　　例2) where's your [wérʒʊər]

例3) let you [létʃu]　　例3) could you [kʊ́dʒu]　　例3) says you're [séʒʊr]

Reduction

リダクション (reduction) は、音の「脱落」とも言われ、スペリング上では確かに存在しているにもかかわらず「発音されなくなる音」、あるいは「極めて弱く発音されるようになる音」のことです。リダクションは種類がかなり多いので、以下、いくつか有名なリダクションの例を見ていきましょう。

1　and のリダクション [ænd] → [ən]

例1) bread and butter [brédən bʌ̌ţər]

例2) nice and easy [náɪsən díːzi]

2　for のリダクション [fɔr] → [fər]

例1) break for lunch [breɪk fər lʌntʃ]

例2) good for you [gʊd fər juː]

3　to のリダクション [tuː] → [tə]

例1) up to you [ʌ́ptə juː]

例2) thanks to him [θǽŋks tə hɪm]

4　of のリダクション [ʌv] → [əv]

例1) out of it [áʊdəvɪt]

例2) unheard of [ənhɜ́ːrdəv]

NOTE: 音が脱落するかどうかは「スピーカー本人が強調したいと考えているかどうか」にも左右されます。つまり、文章の中でその英単語が重要であればはっきりと発音し、さほど重要でなければリダクションしやすいのです。例えば bread and butter であれば、「パンだけじゃなくて、バターも！」というように強調したい場合には bread AND butter [bred ænd bʌ̌ţər] というように ænd をしっかりと発音する可能性もあります。ですから、「and ＝ 脱落」という風に覚えるのではなく、臨機応変に対応するようにしましょう。

 Flapping

フラッピング (flapping) とは、語中の [t] が [d] のように発音される現象を指します。ゆえにこの現象は語頭の [t] には起きません。また、本書ではフラッピングする [t] の音を [t̬] で表しています。フラッピングはパターンが少ないので、サクッと覚えることができます。

フラッピングの2つの条件

1. [t] が母音に挟まれていること
2. [t] の音を含む音節にアクセントが置かれていないこと

以上2つの条件を満たすと、語中の [t] の音が濁って [d] のように発音されます。

フラッピングされる単語 (フレーズ) の例

例1) water [wɑ́ːt̬ər]

例2) later [léɪt̬ər]

例3) better [bét̬ər]

water は「ウォーダー」、later は「レイダー」、better は「ベダー」というように [t] の音が濁り [d] の音になります。フラッピングとはこの現象を指します。上の2つの条件に当てはまらなければ、基本的にはフラッピングは起きません。また、イギリス英語の発音ではフラッピングが起きにくく、water は「ウォータ」、later は「レイタ」、better は「ベタ」というように、[t] をしっかりと立てて発音します。本書は基本的にアメリカ英語に基づいていますが、英語が話される地域によってはこれらのルールが適用されない場合があることも理解しておきましょう。

移民・移住
Immigration

Most immigrants move to foreign countries either for better employment opportunities and income or for an improved living environment.

While many immigrants relocate to be better off financially, research suggests that the movement of labor between borders also improves the stability of the global economy and helps it to flourish.

It is argued that this is because immigrants bring diverse and scarce skills and abilities to the countries to which they immigrate. They also fulfill the eternal demand for unskilled labor in these countries.

As an illustration, Australia has supported the view that the liberty of movement is a core and innate human rights principle rather than a privilege. Thanks to this, the country has prospered economically.

1 Most immigrants move to foreign countries either for better employment opportunities and income or for an improved living environment.

移民の大半は、より良い雇用機会や所得増、あるいは住環境の改善を求め、他国へ渡る。

₁ immigrant
[íməgrənt]
☐☐☐☐☐☐

N[C] 移民、移住者

Because I also moved to this country not too long ago, I understand the struggles that new **immigrants** face.
(僕もこの国に移ってからそんなに経ってないから、新しい移民にどんな苦労があるかは理解できるよ。)

▶ **immigrate** [íməgreɪt] V[I] （外国から〜へ）移住する、他国に移る （into/to sth）

I have to do a lot of paperwork in order to **immigrate** to Australia.
(オーストラリアに移住するためにたくさん書類の記入をしないといけないんだ。)

⟷ **emigrate** [éməgreɪt] （〜から）他国に移住する （from sth）

▶ **migrate** [máɪgreɪt] V[I] （国内外を）移住する；（鳥などが）移動する

▶ **immigration** [ìməgréɪʃən] N[U] 移住、移民、入国；入国審査

at **immigration** （入国審査で）

⟷ **emigration** [èməgréɪʃən] N[C/U] （他国への）移住

immigrate vs emigrate どちらも migrate（移住する）に接頭語が付いた形です。immigrate の im- は「中に」という意味があるため「外国から移住する」、emigrate の e- には「外に」という意味があるため「（自国などから）他国に移住する」という意味になります。

₂ move
[mu:v]
☐☐☐☐☐☐

V[I] 移動する、動く；引っ越す V[T] を移動させる、動かす；を感動させる

Can you help me **move** this couch over there?(このソファーあそこに動かすの手伝ってくれない？)
I was so **moved** by the film. （その映画みてすごい感動したよ。）

▶ **movement** [mú:vmənt] N[C/U] 動き、移動 N[C] （社会的な）運動

The ballet performance was very impressive. All of their **movements** were so smooth.
(あのバレエは素晴らしかったな。全ての動きがすごいスムーズだったよ。)

₃ foreign
[fɔ́:rən]
☐☐☐☐☐☐

Adj. 海外の、外国の；なじみのない

Learning **foreign** languages is very hard but really rewarding.
(外国語を勉強するのはものすごい難しいけど、本当にそれだけの価値はあるよ。)

a **foreign** language（外国語）　　a **foreign** country（外国）

▶ **foreigner** [fɔ́:rənər] N[C] 外国人

I've lived in the U.S. for so long I sometimes feel like a **foreigner** in Japan.
（アメリカにもう長く住んでるから、日本にいるとたまに自分が外国人なんじゃないかって感じになるよ。）

---

4 **either**
[íːðər]
[áɪðər]
☐☐☐☐☐☐

Cnj.（either A or B の形で）A あるいは B、A もしくは B

At a competitive consulting firm, you will **either** climb the ranks **or** leave.
（競争の激しいコンサル会社では、昇進するか辞めるかどっちかだよ。）

Pron.（肯定文で）どちらか、どちらでも；（否定文で）どちらも

Either is fine.（どっちでもいいよ。）　I don't like **either** of them.（どっちも好きじゃないなぁ。）

Adv.（否定文で）〜でもない　= **also** [ɑ́ːlsoʊ]　= **too** [tuː]

Tim hates vegetables, but he doesn't like meat **either**. I wonder what he eats.
（ティムって野菜が嫌いなんだけど、肉も好きじゃないんだ。何食べてるんだろう。）

Adj.（肯定文で）どちらの〜でも；（否定文で）どちらの〜も

either way（どちらにせよ）

---

5 **income**
[ínkʌm]
☐☐☐☐☐☐

N[C/U] 所得、収入

I just had a kid, so I'll need another source of **income**.
（子供ができたから、収入源がもう一つ必要だな。）

a high/low **income** earner（高所得者 / 低所得者）

---

6 **improved**
[ɪmprúːvd]
☐☐☐☐☐☐

Adj. 改善された、向上した

Eating and sleeping well are prerequisites for **improved** quality of life.
（よく食べてよく寝ることは QOL の改善に必要なことだよ。）

▶ **improve** [ɪmprúːv] V[I] 良くなる、向上する V[T] を改善する、向上する

Wow, your English has really **improved**!（おぉ、英語めちゃくちゃ上手くなったね！）

▶ **improvement** [ɪmprúːvmənt] N[C/U] 改善、向上 N[C] 改善点

Since I started doing yoga every day, I've seen a massive **improvement** in sleep
quality.　（ヨガを毎日やり始めてからめっちゃ睡眠の質が上がった。）

---

7 **environment**
[ɪnváɪrənmənt]
☐☐☐☐☐☐

N[C/U] 環境　**N[S]** 自然環境【the -】

Everybody is quitting because of the toxic work **environment**.
（劣悪な職場環境のせいでみんな辞めていってるんだ。）

▶ **environmental** [ɪnvàɪrənméntl] Adj. 環境の

environmental problems（環境問題）

▶ **environmentally** [ɪnvàɪrənméntəli] Adv. 環境的に

environmentally friendly（環境に優しい）

2 While many immigrants relocate to be better off financially, research suggests that the movement of labor between borders also improves the stability of the global economy and helps it to flourish.

多くの移民は経済的な豊かさを求めて他国に移る一方で、研究では、労働力が国家間を移動すると、世界経済の安定と繁栄にもつながると示唆されている。

---

8 financially

[faɪnǽnʃəli]

▢▢▢▢▢▢

Adv. 経済的に、金銭的に、財政的に

I'm aiming to be **financially** independent by the time I turn forty.
(40 歳までに経済的に独立することを目指してるんだよね。)

▶ **financial** [faɪnǽnʃəl] Adj. 金融の、財務の、金銭的な　N[P] 財務諸表、財務結果【-s】

▶ **finance** [fáɪnæns] N[U] 金融、財務、財政、融資　V[T] に融資する

the global **financial** crisis（世界金融危機）

---

9 suggest

[səʤést]

▢▢▢▢▢▢

V[T] を示唆する；を提案する、勧める

Aaron **suggested** a book for me, so I'm going to get my hands on it tonight.
(アーロンが僕にある本をお勧めしてくれたから、今夜読み始める予定なんだ。)

My coach **suggested** that I drink 30 glasses of milk a day, but I think that's impossible.
(コーチに牛乳を一日グラス 30 杯飲んだ方がいいって提案されたんだけど、さすがにそれは無理でしょ。)

▶ **suggestion** [səʤésʧən] N[S/U] 示唆　N[C] 提案、勧め

Do you have any **suggestions** for lunch?（どこかランチで良いところあるかな？）

---

10 labor

[léɪbər]

▢▢▢▢▢▢

N[U] 労働力、労働、（集合的に）労働者；陣痛、分娩

Our **labor** costs are way too high at the moment, so we shouldn't hire any more people.
(いまうちの人件費はめちゃくちゃ高いから、これ以上人は雇わない方がいいよ。)

manual **labor**（肉体労働、単純労働）　　skilled **labor**（熟練労働）

■ **a labor of love**（（報酬のためでなく好きでする）仕事）

If you want to be a good teacher, you should see your job as **a labor of love**.
(良い先生になりたいんだったら、その仕事が好きじゃないとね。)

V[I] 労働する

▶ **laborious** [ləbɔ́:riəs] Adj. 多くの時間と労力を必要とする

a **laborious** task（大変な仕事）

▶ **laboriously** [ləbɔ́:riəsli] Adv. 苦労して

---

11 **border**
[bɔ́:rdər]
☐☐☐☐☐☐

N[C] 国境、境界 **V[T]** に隣接する

Will building a wall between the U.S. and Mexico really help with **border** protection?
（アメリカとメキシコの間に壁を建設するのって、本当に国境警備の役に立つのかな？）

▶ **borderless** Adj. 国境のない
[bɔ́:rdərləs]

▶ **borderline** N[S] 境目 Adj. ぎりぎりの
[bɔ́:rdərlaɪn]

We are constantly on the **borderline** between breaking up and being together.
（俺ら、別れるか別れないかいつもぎりぎりのとこにいるんだよね。）

---

12 **stability**
[stəbíləti]
☐☐☐☐☐☐

N[U] 安定性 ↔ **instability** [ɪnstəbíləti] N[C/U] 不安定

I thought about moving to Paris next month, but I need some **stability** in my life right now.
（来月パリに移ろうとも思ったんだけど、今はちょっと生活に安定が必要なんだ。）

▶ **stable** [stéɪbəl] Adj. 安定した ↔ **unstable** [ʌnstéɪbəl] 不安定な

The Wi-Fi isn't **stable** here.（ここの Wi-Fi は安定してないよ。）

▶ **stably** [stéɪbli] Adv. 安定して、安定的に

▶ **stabilize** [stéɪbəlaɪz] V[T] を安定させる V[I] 安定する

▶ **stabilization** [stèɪbələzéɪʃən] N[U] 安定化

---

13 **economy**
[ɪká:nəmi]
☐☐☐☐☐☐

N[C] 経済、景気；経済国 **N[U]** 節約

I wonder if India's **economy** will ever be bigger than China's.
（インド経済が中国経済より大きくなることなんてあるのかな。）

▶ **economic** [i:kəná:mɪk] Adj. 経済の、金銭的な

The **economic** situation in Italy is not great at the moment.
（今イタリアの経済状況はあんまり良くないんだよ。）

▶ **economical** [i:kəná:mɪkəl] Adj. 経済的な、節約できる

an **economical** car（燃費が良い車）

▶ **economics** [i:kəná:mɪks] N[U] 経済学、経済（状態）

---

14 **flourish**
[flə́:rɪʃ]
☐☐☐☐☐☐

V[I] 繁栄する、栄える、花開く = **prosper** [prá:spər]

It's really important to have good mentors if you want your career to **flourish**.
（キャリアを花開かせたいなら良いメンターを持つことがすごい重要だよ。）

▶ **flourishing** [flə́:rɪʃɪŋ] Adj. 繁栄している = **prosperous** [prá:spərəs]

接頭語 flo(u)r-「花」を意味する接頭語で、そこから、「花のように咲く＝繁栄する」という意味になります。他には floral（花の）、flour（小麦粉＝小麦の花）があります。

3 It is argued that this is because immigrants bring diverse and scarce skills and abilities to the countries to which they immigrate. They also fulfill the eternal demand for unskilled labor in these countries.

これは、移民が移住先の国に、多様で、なおかつその国に不足しているスキルや能力を持ち込むからだと言われている。また、移民はその国に絶えず存在する単純労働の需要も満たしてくれる。

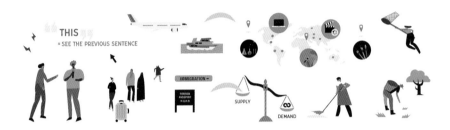

---

15 **argue**
[á:rgju:]
□□□□□□

V[I/T]（〜だと）主張する（that + sentence）

V[I]（〜について）言い争う（over/about sth）

Let's stop **arguing** about where to go for dinner and just flip a coin to decide.
(夕飯どこ行くか言い争うのはやめて、もうコイン投げて決めちゃお。)

▶ **argument** N[C/U] 議論、口論
[á:rgjəmənt]

▶ **argumentative** Adj. なんでも議論したがる
[à:rgjəméntətɪv]

Joe and Kim are having an **argument** again.（ジョーとキム、また喧嘩してるよ。)

The less you respond to **argumentative** people, the happier your life will be.
(なんにでも議論をふっかけてくるような人は相手にしないほうが、人生ハッピーだよ。)

---

16 **scarce**
[skers]
□□□□□□

Adj. 不足している、乏しい、まれな

Quality political leaders are a bit **scarce** these days.
(質の良い政治リーダー、最近あんまりいないなぁ。)

▶ **scarcely** [skérsli] Adv. ほとんど〜ない　**= hardly** [há:rdli]

Scarcely anybody uses a flip phone these days.（最近ガラケーはほぼ誰も使ってないよ。)

▶ **scarcity** [skérsəti] N[S/U] 不足、希少性　**scarcity** value（希少価値）

---

17 **skill**
[skɪl]
□□□□□□

N[C/U] スキル、能力

I think my accounting **skills** will come in handy when I start my own business.
(僕の会計スキルは、自分のビジネスを始める時に役立つと思う。)

▶ **skilled** [skɪld] Adj. 熟練した、特殊技能を持つ　a **skilled** worker（熟練労働者）

▶ **skillful** [skɪlfəl] Adj. 熟練した、上手な　▶ **skillfully** [skɪlfəli] Adv. 巧みに、上手に

It takes a lot of practice to become a **skillful** surfer.
(上手なサーファーになるにはたくさん練習が必要だよ。)

18 **ability**
[əbíləṭi]
☐☐☐☐☐☐

N[C/U] （〜する）能力（to do） ↔ **inability** [ìnəbíləṭi] 無力

How can I improve my **ability** to make people laugh? I'm so boring!
（どうやったら人を笑わせる能力を高められるの？俺、めっちゃつまんないんだ）

▶ **able** [éɪbəl] Adj.（〜することが）できる（to do） ↔ **unable** [ʌnéɪbəl] できない

I wasn't **able** to answer the question that my teacher asked me.
（先生にされた質問、答えられなかった。）

▶ **enable** [ɪnéɪbəl] V[T] が（〜）できるようにする（to do）、を可能にする

This website **enables** people to earn a full-time income online.
（このサイトを使えばオンラインでフルタイムの収入を稼ぐことができるようになるんだ。）

▶ **disability** N[C/U] 身体障害
[dìsəbíləṭi]

▶ **disable** V[T] に障害を与える
[dɪséɪbəl]

skill vs **ability** どちらも似ていますが、skill は習得するもの、ability は生まれつきのものという感覚があります。しかし、実際には区別なしに使用したり、両方並べて使用したりすることも多くあります。

---

19 **fulfill**
[fʊlfíl]
☐☐☐☐☐☐

V[T] （約束や要求）を満たす、果たす

I finally got to **fulfill** my childhood dream of driving a Ferrari yesterday!
（フェラーリを運転するっていう子供のころからの夢を、昨日ついに実現させたんだ！）

▶ **fulfilled** Adj. 満足した、充足感のある
[fʊlfíld]

▶ **fulfilling** Adj. 充実した
[fʊlfílɪŋ]

Watching the sunset makes me feel **fulfilled**. （日が落ちるのを見ると満たされた気持ちになるよ。）

▶ **fulfillment** [fʊlfílmənt] N[U] （約束や要求を）満たすこと；満足感

---

20 **eternal**
[ɪtə́:rnəl]
☐☐☐☐☐☐

Adj. 常に存在する、永遠の、不変の

My love for you is **eternal**. （僕の君への愛は永遠さ。）

▶ **eternally** Adv. 永久に、いつまでも
[ɪtə́:rnəli]

▶ **eternity** N[U] 永久、永遠
[ɪtə́:rnəṭi]

I'm **eternally** grateful to you. （君にはいつまでも感謝しているよ。）

---

21 **demand**
[dɪmænd]
☐☐☐☐☐☐

N[U] 需要 **N[C]** 要求 **V[T]** を要求する、必要とする

The **demand** for AI professionals has ballooned over the past few years.
（AI の専門家に対する需要はここ数年で急増したんだ。）

■ **in demand** （需要がある）　　　　supply and **demand** （供給と需要）

Bilingual people are **in high demand** in Japan. （バイリンガルの人は日本ですごい需要あるよ。）

▶ **demanding** [dɪmændɪŋ] Adj. 要求値の高い；負担の大きい

This course is very **demanding**. I have to finish three assignments in a couple of
months. （このコースの要求値めちゃくちゃ高いよ。2 か月で 3 つの課題を終わらせないといけないんだ。）

4 As an illustration, Australia has supported the view that the liberty of movement is a core and innate human rights principle rather than a privilege. Thanks to this, the country has prospered economically.

例えば、オーストラリアでは、移動の自由は特権ではなく、根幹的かつ生来的な人権の原則であるという考えが支持されてきた。それにより、この国は経済的に成功することができたのだ。

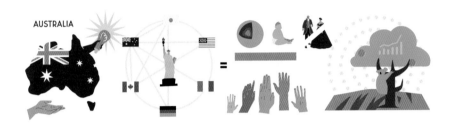

---

22 support

[səpɔ́:rt]

□□□□□□

V[T] を支持する、支える ; を裏付ける　**N[U]**　支持、支援

I want to **support** you, but your argument doesn't make sense at all.
(君のこと支持したいけど、主張が完全に意味不明だよ。)

▶ **supportive** [səpɔ́:rʈɪv] Adj.（〜に）協力的な（of sth/sb）

Her husband was really **supportive** after the baby was born.
(彼女の旦那さんは赤ちゃんが生まれてからはとても協力的だったんだ。)

▶ **supportively** Adv. 協力的に　　▶ **supporting** Adj. 裏づけとなる ; 脇役の
[səpɔ́:rʈɪvli]　　　　　　　　　　　　　[səpɔ́:rʈɪŋ]

---

23 liberty

[líbərʈi]

□□□□□□

N[U]　自由　= **freedom** [frí:dəm]

This company will give you the **liberty** to work from anywhere in the world.
(この会社は世界のどこからでも自由に働かせてくれるよ。)

the Statue of **Liberty**（自由の女神）　■ take the **liberty** of doing（勝手に〜する）

Just to let you know, I **took the liberty of** canceling your flight.
(一応知らせておくけど、フライト勝手にキャンセルしといたから。)

▶ **liberal** Adj. 自由主義の、リベラルな　　◆ **conservative** 保守主義の
[líbərəl]　　　　　　　　　　　　　　　　[kənsə́:rvəʈɪv]

When people say they have left-wing views, that means they have **liberal** views.
(「私は左翼的な思想だ」と言う人がいた場合、それは自由主義的な考えを持ってるという意味だよ。)

▶ **liberally** [líbərəli] Adv. 気前よく、寛大に　▶ **liberalism** [líbərəlɪzəm] N[U] 自由主義

▶ **liberate** V[T] を自由にする、解放する　▶ **liberation** N[U] 自由化、解放
[líbəreɪt]　　　　　　　　　　　　　　[lìbəréɪʃən]

This famous musician says that music can **liberate** your mind from anxiety and other problems.
(この有名なミュージシャンいわく、音楽とは不安とか色々な問題から心を解放してくれるものらしい。)

24 **core**
[kɔ:r]

☐☐☐☐☐☐

Adj. 根幹となる、中心的な　**N[C]** 中心部、核心；（果物の）芯

What kind of **core** skills do you need to become an astronaut?
（宇宙飛行士になる上で、最も重要なスキルは何ですか？）

V[T] （果物の芯）を取る

This video explains how to **core** an apple.（この動画では、りんごの芯の取り方を説明してるよ。）

25 **innate**
[ɪnéɪt]

☐☐☐☐☐☐

Adj. 生来的な、生まれながらの

Is perfect pitch **innate**?（絶対音感って生まれつきかな？）

▶ **innately** [ɪnéɪtli] Adv. 生まれつき

You seem **innately** destined to be an artist. Your painting is just amazing.
（君って生まれつきアーティストになる運命だったのかもね。絵がとにかく最高。）

26 **right**
[raɪt]

☐☐☐☐☐☐

N[C] 権利　**N[S]** 右　**Adj.** 右の；正しい ⟷ wrong [rɔ́ːŋ] 間違った

Adv. 右に；すぐに

Just because you have the **right** to speak your mind doesn't mean that you should.
（思ってることをはっきり言う権利があるからといって、そうした方が良いわけじゃない。）

human **rights**（人権）　　I'll be **right** back.（すぐ戻るよ）

V[T] を正しい位置に戻す、改善する

27 **principle**
[prínsəpəl]

☐☐☐☐☐☐

N[C] 原則、原理　**N[C/U]** 行動規範、主義

You should know the seven **principles** of business success before you start your own business.（自分のビジネスを始める前に、ビジネス成功の 7 つの原則くらいは知っとくべきだよ。）

■ in **principle**（原則として、おおむね）　　basic **principles**（基本原則）

I agree with the plan **in principle**, but I'm not sure if it's actually feasible.
（その計画にはおおむね同意していますが、実際それが実現可能かどうかは分かりません。）

28 **privilege**
[prívəlɪdʒ]

☐☐☐☐☐☐

N[C/U] 特権、特典；光栄

I get a lot of **privileges** working here, so I'm going to stick around for a bit.
（ここで働いてると色んな特典があるから、もうしばらくいるつもり。）

■ have the **privilege** of doing（～する機会に恵まれる）

I'm so pleased to **have the privilege of** work**ing** with a smart person like you.
（あなたみたいな優秀な人と働ける機会に恵まれてとても嬉しいです。）

▶ **privileged** [prívəlɪdʒd] Adj. 特権を持つ、恵まれた；光栄な

I don't think students from a **privileged** background have an advantage in getting into university.（恵まれた環境で育った学生が大学に入る上で有利だとは思わないな。）

Woman Hey, my friend mentioned that you just moved here from Sweden. It's a pretty courageous move. Are you finding it difficult to adjust?

Man It's actually been pretty straightforward. I'll confess I was a bit stressed about meeting new people, but everyone has been incredibly friendly and authentic. The only thing I've noticed is that the road rules are a bit peculiar, and people pronounce things weirdly. But so far, so good.

Woman That's really good to hear. Whereabouts are you going to live?

Man I've just found a decent place out in the suburbs, so I'm going to move in next week once I sign the contract and get some furniture. It's nothing fancy, but it'll just be temporary until I can ponder and decide whether I should take the plunge and migrate permanently.

女性 ねぇ、友達から聞いたんだけど、スウェーデンから引っ越して来たばっかりなんでしょ？すごい勇気あるね。慣れるの大変？

男性 実際結構楽だよ。正直、知らない人に初めて会わなきゃいけないのはちょっとストレスだったけど、みんなめちゃくちゃフレンドリーで信用できる人ばっかりだしね。唯一気づいたのは、交通ルールがちょっと独特なことと、みんなの発音が変っていうくらいかな。でも、今のところ良い感じ。

女性 良かった。どの辺に住む予定なの？

男性 郊外にそこそこ良い感じの家を見つけたから、契約書サインして、家具も買って、来週にはもう引っ越そうかなって。しゃれた場所ってわけじゃないけど、思い切って永住するかどうかじっくり考えて決めるまでのただの仮住まいだしね。

---

29 **mention**
[ménʃən]

▢▢▢▢▢▢

V[T] と言う、について言及する **N[C/U]** 言及

Don't **mention** it.（感謝の言葉に対して）どういたしまして。

---

30 **courageous**
[kəréɪdʒəs]

▢▢▢▢▢▢

Adj. 勇気のある、勇敢な = **brave** [breɪv]

▶ **courageously** [kəréɪdʒəsli] Adv. 勇気を持って

▶ **courageousness** [kəréɪdʒəsnəs] N[U] 勇敢さ ▶ **courage** [kɜ́:rɪdʒ] N[U] 勇気

have the **courage** to do 〜する勇気がある

---

31 **adjust**
[ədʒʌ́st]

▢▢▢▢▢▢

V[I]（〜に）慣れる、順応する (to sth)；調節される **V[T]** を調節する

▶ **adjustment** [ədʒʌ́stmənt] N[C/U] 順応；調節 ▶ **adjustable** [ədʒʌ́stəbəl] Adj. 調節できる

---

32 **confess**
[kənfés]

▢▢▢▢▢▢

V[T] と正直に言う、を認める **V[I]** 自白する、白状する

▶ **confession** [kənféʃən] N[C] 認めること；自白、白状

---

33 **stressed**
[strest]

▢▢▢▢▢▢

Adj.（〜に）ストレスを感じた (about sth) = **stressed out** [strèst áʊt]

▶ **stress** [stres] N[U] ストレス N[C] ストレスの要因 V[T] を強調する、に重点を置く

▶ **stress sb out** [stres aʊt] [PV] 〜にストレスを与える

▶ **stressful** [strésfəl] Adj. ストレスの多い

---

34 **authentic**
[ɑ:θéntɪk]

▢▢▢▢▢▢

Adj. 信用できる、本物の

▶ **authenticity** [ɑ̀:θentísəti] N[U]（作品などが）本物であること；信憑性

▶ **authenticate** [ɑ:θéntəkeɪt] V[T] を鑑定する、証明する

▶ **authentication** [ɑ̀:θentəkéɪʃən] N[U] 鑑定、証明

---

35 **notice**
[nóʊtɪs]

▢▢▢▢▢▢

V[T] に気づく **N[U]** 通知、予告；注目 **N[C]** 掲示

without **notice**（予告なしで）

▶ **noticeable** [nóʊtɪsəbəl] Adj. 目立つ ▶ **noticeably** [nóʊtɪsəbli] Adv. 目立って

---

36 **peculiar**
[pɪkjú:ljər]

▢▢▢▢▢▢

Adj. 独特な；変な、変わった

▶ **peculiarity** [pɪkjù:liérəti] N[C] 特性；奇妙さ

▶ **peculiarly** [pɪkjú:ljərli] Adv. 独特に；変に

---

37 **pronounce**
[prənáʊns]

▢▢▢▢▢▢

V[T] を発音する

▶ **pronunciation** [prənʌ̀nsiéɪʃən] N[C/U] 発音

▶ **pronounced** [prənáʊnst] Adj. 目立った、顕著な

スペルと発音注意！　動詞は pronounce、名詞は pronunciation で、発音も異なります。

---

38 **weirdly**
[wírdli]

▢▢▢▢▢▢

Adv. 変に、奇妙に

▶ **weird** [wɪrd] Adj. 変な ▶ **weirdo** [wírdoʊ] N[C] 変な人

▶ **weirdness** [wírdnəs] N[U] 奇妙さ

39 decent
[díːsənt]
☐☐☐☐☐

Adj. そこそこの、まずまずの；きちんとした、礼儀正しい
▶ **decently** [díːsəntli] Adv. まともに；きちんと、礼儀正しく

---

40 place
[pleɪs]
☐☐☐☐☐

N[C] 家、場所　**V[T]** を置く
Do you want to come to my **place**?（家来る？）

---

41 suburb
[sʌ́bɜːrb]
☐☐☐☐☐

N[C] 郊外
▶ **suburban** [səbɜ́ːrbən] Adj. 郊外の

---

42 sign
[saɪn]
☐☐☐☐☐

V[I/T]（～に）サインする、署名する　**N[C]** 合図；兆し；記号；標識
▶ **signature** [sígnətʃər] N[C] サイン、署名　N[U] 署名すること　Adj. 特徴的な、看板の
a **signature** dish（看板メニュー、名物料理）
▶ **signify** [sígnəfaɪ] V[T] を意味する、表す

---

43 contract
N.[káːntrækt]
v.[kəntrækt]
☐☐☐☐☐

N[C] 契約書　**V[I]** 契約する
V[I]（筋肉が）収縮する　**V[T]** に感染する
▶ **contractor** [káːntræktər] N[C] 請負業者、契約者

---

44 fancy
[fǽnsi]
☐☐☐☐☐

Adj. 豪華な、高級な；変わった
nothing **fancy**（大したことないもの）

---

45 temporary
[témpəreri]
☐☐☐☐☐

Adj. 一時的な、（仕事が）短期の
▶ **temporarily** [témpərerəli] Adv. 一時的に

---

46 ponder
[páːndər]
☐☐☐☐☐

V[I/T]（～を）じっくりと考える
▶ **ponderous** [páːndərəs] Adj.（話し方などが）重々しい
▶ **ponderously** [páːndərəsli] Adv. 重々しく
▶ **ponderousness** [páːndərəsnəs] N[U] 重々しさ

---

47 plunge
[plʌndʒ]
☐☐☐☐☐

N[C] 飛び込むこと、落下、急落　**V[I]**（場所などに）突っ込む、急落する
take the **plunge** and do（思い切って～する）
▶ **plunger** [plʌ́ndʒər] N[C]（詰まった排水管などを直す）ラバーカップ

---

48 migrate
[máɪgreɪt]
☐☐☐☐☐

V[I] 移住する、移動する
▶ **migrant** [máɪgrənt] N[C] 移住者、移民；渡り鳥
▶ **migration** [maɪgréɪʃən] N[C/U] 移動、移住　▶ **migratory** [máɪgrətɔːri] Adj. 移動性の

言語学
Linguistics

Linguistics is the scientific inquiry into and study of language. It involves the analysis of language form and meaning as well as language in context.

Traditionally, linguistics endeavors to analyze language by studying and comparing the elements of sound and meaning. This process has subsequently led to the division of linguistics into various disciplines including phonetics, semantics, syntax, and pragmatics.

Given its scientific nature, the field of linguistics is descriptive and neutral and does not attach subjective value judgments to the features or use of language.

The study of the different accents and dialects of English spoken by communities within the United Kingdom offers a prime example of this attitude. No way of speaking is held by linguists to be superior, acceptable, or correct.

1

Linguistics is the scientific inquiry into and study of language. It involves the analysis of language form and meaning as well as language in context.

言語学は、言語を科学的に調査・研究する学問である。その中には、文脈における言語の分析だけでなく、言語の形式や意味の分析も含まれる。

---

49 linguistics
[lɪŋgwístɪks]
☐☐☐☐☐☐

N[U] 言語学

I studied **linguistics** in college, but that doesn't mean I'm fluent in a second language.
（大学で言語学を勉強したけど、だからといって第二言語を流暢に話せるわけじゃないよ。）

▶ **linguistically** Adv. 言語学的に、言語学上　▶ **linguistic** Adj. 言語学の、言語に関する
[lɪŋgwístɪkli]　　　　　　　　　　　　　　　[lɪŋgwístɪk]

▶ **linguist** [lɪ́ŋgwɪst] N[C] 言語学者

---

50 scientific
[sàɪəntífɪk]
☐☐☐☐☐☐

Adj. 科学的な、科学の

I know it doesn't sound very **scientific**, but I feel that five minutes of exercise a day is more than enough.　（科学的に正しいかは微妙だけど、一日 5 分の運動で十分だと思う。）

▶ **scientifically** [sàɪəntífɪkli] Adv. 科学的に

There are a lot of **scientifically** proven benefits of protein intake.
（プロテインの摂取には科学的に証明された利点がたくさんあるよ。）

▶ **science** [sáɪəns] N[U] 科学 N[C] 自然科学　▶ **scientist** [sáɪəntɪst] N[C] 科学者

---

51 inquiry
[ínkwəri]
☐☐☐☐☐☐

N[C/U] 調査　**N[C]** 質問、問い合わせ

I think there should be a thorough **inquiry** into those shady restaurants downtown.
（街中にあるあの怪しいレストランの数々は徹底的に調査されるべきだと思うよ。）

■ make an **inquiry** (about sth) （（～について）問い合わせる）

I **made an inquiry about** the product yesterday, but I haven't got a reply yet.
（昨日その商品について問い合わせしたんだけど、まだ返信は来てないよ。）

▶ **inquire** [ɪnkwáɪr] V[I/T] （～について）尋ねる、問い合わせる （about sth/sb）

---

52 language
[læŋgwɪdʒ]
☐☐☐☐☐☐

N[U] 言語；言葉遣い　**N[C]** （特定の国や地域の）言語

I'm always so impressed by people who speak more than one **language**.
（複数の言語を話せるひとってすごいなぁっていつも思うよ。）

53 form
[fɔːrm]

N[U]　（表現の）形式　N[C/U]　形、形状　N[C]　記入用紙

Could you please fill out this application **form**?（この応募用紙に記入していただけますか？）

V[I]　形を成す　V[T]　を形づくる、形成する

▶ **formation** [fɔːrméɪʃən] N[U] 成り立ち、形成 N[C] 形態

I learned about the **formation** and evolution of the Solar System today.
（今日は太陽系の形成と進化について学んだよ。）

54 meaning
[míːnɪŋ]

N[C/U]　意味　N[U]　（人生などの）意義

I love this artist's work because it has so much **meaning**, but in a really subtle way.
（このアーティストの作品にはたくさんの意味が込められてるんだけど、それが本当に控えめな感じですごい好きなんだ。）

▶ **mean** [miːn] V[T] を意味する

Can you explain what that actually **means**?（それ実際どういう意味か説明してくれない？）

■ **mean** to do（〜するつもりである）

It was a joke! I didn't **mean to** hurt your feelings.
（冗談だって！傷つけるつもりはなかったんだ。）

■ **mean** it（本気で言う）

Don't say you love me if you don't **mean it**.
（本気じゃないなら愛してるなんて言わないで。）

▶ Adj. 意地悪な

You're so **mean**.（お前本当に意地悪だな。）

55 context
[káːntekst]

N[C/U]　文脈、状況、背景、コンテクスト

Can you give me some **context** behind why you suddenly want a new phone?
（なんで急に新しい携帯欲しいってなってるのかもうちょっと状況説明してくれない？）

■ take sth out of **context**（〜を文脈を無視して解釈する）

The star was saying her comments were **taken out of context**.
（その有名人は自分のコメントが文脈を無視して解釈されたって言ってたよ。）

▶ **contextual** Adj. 文脈上の、背景の　▶ **contextually** Adv. 文脈的に、背景的に
　[kəntékstʃuəl]　　　　　　　　　　　　[kəntékstʃuəli]

2 Traditionally, **linguistics** endeavors to analyze **language** by studying and comparing the elements of sound and meaning. This process has subsequently led to the division of linguistics into various disciplines including phonetics, semantics, syntax, and pragmatics.

伝統的に、言語学は音声と意味の要素を研究・比較することで言語の分析を試みる学問であるが、その後このプロセスは、音声学や意味論、統語論、語用論といったさまざまな専門分野に分裂していった。

---

56 traditionally
[trədíʃənəli]
☐☐☐☐☐☐

Adv. 伝統的に、昔から

My family **traditionally** uses only handmade ornaments on our Christmas tree.
(うちの家庭では昔からクリスマスツリーに手作りの飾りしか使わないんだ。)

▶ **traditional** Adj. 伝統的な、昔ながらの
[trədíʃənəl]

▶ **tradition** N[C/U] 伝統、慣習
[trədíʃən]

a **traditional** Japanese breakfast（伝統的な日本の朝食）

You should be respectful of the local culture and **traditions** when you are in a foreign country.（外国にいるときはその地域の文化と伝統に敬意を払うべきだよ。）

breakfast/lunch/dinner は可算 or 不可算？ 基本的に不可算名詞ですが、traditional や nice などの形容詞が付いて具体的になると可算名詞扱いになります（例：a nice lunch, a wonderful dinner）。

---

57 endeavor
[ɪndévər]
☐☐☐☐☐☐

V[I] （〜しようと）試みる、努力する（to do） N[U] 努力 N[C] 試み

I'll **endeavor** to get back to you by tomorrow morning.
(明日の朝までにはなんとしてでも返事できるように努力するよ。)

endeavor vs effort どちらも「努力」を意味しますが、effort が単純に「努力をすること」を表すのに対し、endeavor は「どんな困難があっても何か大きなゴールを達成しようと努力する」というニュアンスがあります。

---

58 analyze
[ǽnəlaɪz]
☐☐☐☐☐☐

V[T] を分析する

Can you get Ryan to **analyze** these stock market patterns for me?
(この株式市場のパターンをライアンに分析してもらうことってできる？)

▶ **analysis** [ənǽləsɪs] N[C/U] 分析、解析（複数形：analyses）

How did your data **analysis** go? What did you find out?（データ分析どうだった？何か分かった？）

▶ **analytics** [ænəlíṭɪks] N[U] パターンを分析すること、アナリティクス

▶ **analytical** [ænəlíṭɪkəl] Adj. 分析の
▶ **analytically** [ænəlíṭɪkli] Adv. 分析的に

▶ **analyst** [ǽnəlɪst] N[C] 分析者、アナリスト

an **analytical** tool（分析ツール）　　a security **analyst**（証券アナリスト）

59 compare
[kəmpér]
☐☐☐☐☐☐

V[T] を（〜と）比べる(to/with sth/sb)；を（〜に）例える(to sth/sb)

This website makes it so much easier to **compare** insurance policies between different companies.（このサイトを使えば異なる会社の保険内容の比較がものすごい簡単になるよ！）

V[I]（〜に）匹敵する（to/with sth/sb）

sth doesn't/can't **compare** (to/with sth)（は（〜には）及ばない）

beyond **compare***（比べものにならない）

* この用法では N[U] 扱いですが、基本的に名詞単体で使われることはありません。

▶ **comparable** Adj.（〜と）比較できる、（〜に）匹敵する ⟷ **incomparable** 無比の
[ká:mpərəbəl]   (to/with sth/sb)   [ɪnká:mpərəbəl]

▶ **comparison** [kəmpérɪsən] N[C/U] 比較

in **comparison** (to/with sth)（（〜と）比べて） make a **comparison** between A and B（A と B を比べる）

▶ **comparative** [kəmpérətɪv] Adj. 比較の ▶ **comparatively** [kəmpérətɪvli] Adv. 比較的に

---

60 element
[éləmənt]
☐☐☐☐☐☐

N[C] 要素、成分；（化学の）元素、単体

No matter how safe they try to make it, skydiving always has an **element** of risk.
（どれだけ安全にしようとしてもスカイダイビングには常にリスク要素はあるよ。）

▶ **elementary** [èləméntəri] Adj. 初歩的な、基本の；小学校の

▶ **elemental** Adj. 基本的な、要素の、成分の ▶ **elementally** Adv. 基本的に
[èləméntl]   [èləméntli]

---

61 sound
[saʊnd]
☐☐☐☐☐☐

N[C/U] 音、音声 **Adj.** 健康な；（眠りが）深い；堅実な

Hey George, can you do something about that horrible **sound** coming out of the speakers?（ねぇジョージ、あのスピーカーから出てるヒドい音なんとかできないの？）

a **sound** sleep（深い眠り）   a **sound** investment（安定した投資）

V[I]（〜に / 〜のように）聞こえる、思える（adjective/like sth）

That **sounds** fantastic.（（何かを聞いて）それ最高だね。） **Sounds** good!（いいね！）

sound like（（聞いた感じ）〜のようだ） It **sounds** like a good idea.（良い考えだね。）

感覚を表す単語については pg.472 のスナップショットを参照。

---

62 division
[dɪvíʒən]
☐☐☐☐☐☐

N[C/U] 分裂、分割 **N[C]** 部門 **N[U]** 割り算

The Berlin Wall was a physical **division** between East and West Germany.
（ベルリンの壁は東西ドイツを物理的に分割するものだったんだ。）

multiplication（掛け算）   addition（足し算）   subtraction（引き算）

the sales **division**（販売部門） J.League **Division** 2（J2 リーグ（J リーグの 2 部））

▶ **divide** [dɪváɪd] V[T] を分ける、分割する；(数) を（〜で）割る (by sth) V[I] 分かれる

⟷ **multiply** [mʌ́ltəplaɪ] V[T] に（〜を）掛ける (by sth)

▶ **divisible** [dɪvízəbəl] Adj. 割り切れる

数学にまつわる表現については pg. 406 のスナップショットを参照。

3 Given its scientific nature, the field of linguistics is descriptive and neutral and does not attach subjective value judgments to the features or use of language.

科学的な性質から、言語学の分野は記述的かつ中立的であり、言語の特徴や用法について主観的な価値観に基づく判断をすることはない。

---

63 given
[gívən]

Prep. 〜を考えると、考えて（sth/that + sentence） **= considering**
[kənsídərɪŋ]

Given that you're late again, you're buying drinks tonight.
（また遅刻したんだし、今夜の飲みはあなたの奢りね。）

通常、前置詞は直後に名詞をとりますが、given は that + sentence もとることができます。

---

64 nature
[néɪtʃər]

N[C/U] 性質、本質　**N[U]** 自然

I want to believe that it's human **nature** to be kind rather than selfish.
（人間の本質は親切であることであって、自分勝手であることじゃないって信じたいよ。）

▶ **natural** Adj. 自然な、天然の；生まれつきの　　◆▶ **unnatural** 不自然な
[nætʃərəl]　　　　　　　　　　　　　　　　　　　　[ʌnnætʃərəl]

a **natural** disaster（自然災害）　　do **natural** makeup（自然なメイクをする）

---

65 descriptive
[dɪskríptɪv]

Adj. 記述的な、説明的な

Harry Potter is so **descriptive** that I can easily picture the story in my mind.
（ハリーポッターってすごい具体的に描かれているから、ストーリーを簡単に頭に描写できるよ。）

▶ **describe** V[T] を言い表す、描写する　▶ **description** N[C/U] 説明、描写
[dɪskráɪb]　　　　　　　　　　　　　　　　　[dɪskrípʃən]

It's hard to **describe** how I'm feeling right now.（今の気持ちを言い表すのは難しいよ。）

This YouTube video doesn't have a **description**.（この YouTube 動画は説明がないんだ。）

■ beyond **description**（言葉では言い表せない）

How important you are to me is **beyond description**.
（あなたが私にとってどれだけ重要かなんて言葉では言い表せないよ。）

---

66 neutral
[nú:trəl]

Adj. 中立的な、どっちつかずの　**N[C]** 中立者

I tried to keep a pretty **neutral** face, but she could still tell I was lying.
（無表情でいようと結構頑張ったんだけど、それでもあの子は私が嘘をついてるって分かったみたい。）

■ gender-**neutral**（性別不問の）

I heard **gender-neutral** toys are becoming common in the U.S. and Western Europe.
（性別不問のおもちゃはアメリカと西欧では普通になってきてるらしいよ。）

▶ **neutrality** [nu:trǽləṭi] N[U] 中立状態

---

67 attach
[ətǽtʃ]
□□□□□□

V[T] を（〜に）与える、くっつける、添付する（to sth）

Sorry, I forgot to **attach** the slides.（ごめん、スライド添付するの忘れちゃった。）

⬅➡ **detach** [dɪtǽtʃ] を（〜から）取り外す（from sth）

▶ **attached** [ətǽtʃt] Adj. 添付の、付属の；（〜に）愛着が湧いた（to sth/sb）

I'm so **attached** to this huge plush toy that my grandma gave me when I was three.
（3歳の時におばあちゃんがくれたこの巨大なぬいぐるみ、ものすごい愛着があるんだ。）

▶ **attachment** N[C] 添付ファイル、付属品 N[C/U] 愛着、愛情 N[U] 取り付け
[ətǽtʃmənt]

The email **attachment** is missing!（あのメールの添付ファイルがない！）

attached = 愛着？ attached には「くっついた」という意味があり、そこから派生して「物や人にくっついている＝愛着がある」という意味に派生しています。このように、全く違う意味に見えてもコアとなる感覚・イメージは一緒であることが多く、これを意識すると複数の意味も覚えやすくなります。

---

68 judgment
[dʒʌ́dʒmənt]
□□□□□□

N[C] 判断、決断、意見 **N[U]** 判断力 **N[C/U]** （法）判決

■ pass **judgment** on sth（〜に判断を下す、批判的になる）

You can't **pass judgment on** something you've never done before.
（自分がやったことないことに対して批判的になっちゃだめだよ。）

in sb's **judgment**（〜の意見では）

▶ **judge** [dʒʌ́dʒ] V[I/T]（〜を）判断する N[C] 裁判官

judging from/by sth（〜から判断すると）

▶ **judgmental** [dʒʌdʒméntl] Adj. なんでもすぐ判断するような、すぐ批判的になる

You haven't even met him yet, right? Don't be so **judgmental**.
（まだ彼に会ってすらいないんでしょ？そんなすぐになんでも判断しちゃだめよ。）

スペル注意！ judgement(-al) も可。

---

69 feature
[fíːtʃər]
□□□□□□

N[C] 特徴、特性；顔だち；特集記事

There are no distinctive **features** on this trail, so people get lost here all the time.
（この道には明確な特徴がないから、みんないつもここで迷っちゃうんだ。）

V[T] を特集する；を主役にする、出演させる

The Japanese work environment will be **featured** on the show.
（その番組で日本の労働環境が特集されるよ。）

▶ **featured** [fíːtʃərd] Adj. 特集された、主演の ▶ **featureless** [fíːtʃərləs] Adj. 特徴のない

4 The study of the different accents and dialects of English spoken by communities within the United Kingdom offers a prime example of this attitude. No way of speaking is held by linguists to be superior, acceptable, or correct.

イギリスの地域ごとに異なる英語のアクセントや方言の研究は、こうした考え方の最たる例を示している。言語学者らは、どの話し方が優れている、受け入れられる、または正しいといった判断を一切していない。

---

70 **accent**
[ǽksənt]
☐☐☐☐☐☐

N[C] アクセント

I can't tell where Michael is from because his **accent** is so unique.
（マイケルってアクセントがユニークだからどこ出身なのか分かんないなぁ。）

▶ **accentuate** [əksén tʃuert] V[T] を強調する

She **accentuated** her look with a beautiful diamond necklace and low-key earrings.
（彼女は美しいダイヤのネックレスと控えめなイヤリングで自分の見た目を強調した。）

---

71 **dialect**
[dáɪəlekt]
☐☐☐☐☐☐

N[C/U] 方言

Isn't it curious that there are so many different **dialects** spoken in a small country like Japan? （日本みたいな小さい国ですごい色んな方言が話されてるって興味深くない？）

speak a **dialect** （方言を話す）

---

72 **community**
[kəmjúːnə ti]
☐☐☐☐☐☐

N[C] 地域社会、共同社会、コミュニティ

Building an online **community** from scratch is not as difficult as it seems.
（一からオンラインコミュニティをつくるのはそこまで難しくないよ。）

community service （地域奉仕）

---

73 **the United Kingdom**
[ðə jʊnàɪt̬ɪd kíŋdəm]
☐☐☐☐☐☐

N[Prop.] イギリス、英国

The United Kingdom consists of England, Scotland, Wales, and Northern Ireland.
（イギリスはイングランド、スコットランド、ウェールズ、北アイルランドから成っている。）

（略称）the U.K. （正式名称）United Kingdom of Great Britain and Northern Ireland
（グレートブリテン及び北アイルランド連合王国）

▶ **British** [brít̬ʃ] Adj. イギリスの　N[P] イギリスの人たち【the -】

You sound so **British**. （君イギリス人みたいな話し方するね。）

▶ **Brit** [brɪt] N[C] イギリス人

Is he a **Brit**? His accent sounds American.（彼ってイギリス人なの？アクセントがアメリカ人に聞こえるけど。）

the U.K. vs **Great Britain**　どちらも「イギリス、英国」を意味するためによく使われる単語ですが、厳密に言えば the U.K. のみがイギリス全体を表す単語です。Great Britain はイングランド、スコットランド、ウェールズの３つから成るイギリス最大の島を指し、北アイルランドを含んでいません。

---

74 **example**
[ɪgzǽmpəl]
□□□□□□

N[C] 例、手本

I think Japanese food is a good **example** of cuisine that doesn't need spice to taste awesome.（日本食ってスパイスを使わなくても最高においしい料理の良い例だと思うんだよね。）

for **example**（例えば）= for instance

▶ **exemplify** [ɪgzémpləfaɪ] V[T] の良い例である

Rolex watches **exemplify** enduring craftsmanship.（ロレックスの時計は不朽の職人技の良い例だ。）

(as) **exemplified** by sth（〜を例にして）

▶ **exemplary** [ɪgzémpləri] Adj. 模範的な

an **exemplary** student（模範となるような学生）

---

75 **attitude**
[ǽt̬ətuːd]
□□□□□□

N[C/U]（〜に対する）考え方、姿勢、態度（to/toward sth）

You have such a great **attitude** toward learning new things!
（あなたの新しいことを学ぶことに対する姿勢は素晴らしい！）

■ take the **attitude** that + sentence（〜という態度を取る）

The student **took the attitude that** the class was a waste of time.
（その学生、授業は時間の無駄みたいな態度を取ったんだ。）

---

76 **correct**
[kərékt]
□□□□□□

Adj. 正しい　V[T] を正す、直す、訂正する

It's so hard to pick the **correct** answer when all the options are so similar.
（こんなに選択肢が全部似てると、どれが正解か選ぶのものすごい大変だよ。）

▶ **correctly** [kəréktli] Adv. 正しく

▶ **correctness** [kəréktnəs] N[U] 正しさ

I can't pronounce some words **correctly**.（いくつか正しく発音できない単語があるんだ。）

▶ **correction** [kərékʃən] N[C/U] 訂正、修正

make a **correction**（訂正する）

Woman   I'm trying to learn Danish, but there's a ridiculous number of ways to learn languages nowadays. Should I use an app, attend formal lessons at a language institute, or live in the country?

Man   The most sensible approach depends on your objective and how much you already know. Are you aspiring to be fluent?

Woman   As a priority, I want to speak basic Danish so I can strike up a conversation with my relatives and not sound stupid. I haven't tried acquiring a new language before, but I'm pretty optimistic because I have Danish parents.

Man   In that case, it's preferable for you to move to Denmark and steadily soak in the language, even if it costs you a fortune. You don't need to learn to spell, and I assure you that this is the quickest way to expand your vocabulary, improve your grammar, and become fluent.

女性   デンマーク語を学ぼうと思ってるんだけど、最近とんでもない数の言語学習法があるよね。アプリを使うか、ちゃんとしたレッスンを語学学校で受けるか、それともその国に住むか、どれが良いと思う？

男性   目標とか、既にどれくらい知識があるかによって一番賢いアプローチは変わると思うけど、ペラペラを目指してるの？

女性   まず優先順位としては、簡単なデンマーク語を話せるようになりたいんだよね。親戚と会話を始められて、かつおバカに聞こえないように。これまで新しい言語を習得しようとしたことはないんだけど、両親がデンマーク人だから結構楽観的なんだよね。

男性   それなら、ものすごいお金がかかったとしても、デンマークに引っ越して、ずっとデンマーク語に浸った方がいいと思う。スペルは学ばなくてもいいだろうし、これが語彙を増やして、文法も向上させて、ペラペラになる一番早い方法だと思うよ。

77 ridiculous
[rɪdíkjələs]

Adj. とんでもない、ばかげた

▶ **ridiculously** [rɪdíkjələsli] Adv. ばかばかしいほど、信じられないほど

▶ **ridiculousness** [rɪdíkjələsnəs] N[U] ばかばかしさ

78 nowadays
[náʊədeɪz]

Adv. 最近は、今日では　= **these days** [ðí:zdeɪz]

What are young people interested in **nowadays**? (最近の若い人って何に興味があるのかな？)

79 institute
[ínstətu:t]

N[C] 機関、研究所、学会　V[T] (制度など) を制定する

▶ **institution** [ìnstətú:ʃən] N[C] 機関、団体；制度；施設　N[U] 制定

▶ **institutional** [ìnstətú:ʃənəl] Adj. 機関の；制度化された；施設の

▶ **institutionalize** [ìnstətú:ʃənəlaɪz] V[T] を施設に入れる；を制度化する

80 sensible
[sénsəbəl]

Adj. 賢い、分別のある

▶ **sensibly** [sénsəbli] Adv. 賢明に、分別よく　▶ **sensibleness** [sénsəbəlnəs] N[U] 賢明さ

▶ **sensibility** [sènsəbíləti] N[U] 感性　▶ **sensibilities** [sènsəbílətiz] N[P] 感情

81 depend
[dɪpénd]

V[I] (〜に) よる、次第である (on sth/sb)
(〜を) 頼りにする、当てにする (on sth/sb)

It **depends** on you. (それは君次第だよ。)

▶ **dependence** [dɪpéndəns] N[U] 依存、頼ること

82 aspire
[əspáɪr]

V[I] (〜することを) 目指す、熱望する (to do)

▶ **aspiration** [æspəréɪʃən] N[C/U] 熱望、野心　▶ **aspiring** [əspáɪrɪŋ] Adj. 野心のある、意欲的な

83 fluent
[flú:ənt]

Adj. (外国語などが) ペラペラの、流暢な (in sth)

▶ **fluently** [flú:əntli] Adv. ペラペラに、流暢に　▶ **fluency** [flú:ənsi] N[U] (〜の) 流暢さ

84 priority
[praɪɔ́:rəti]

N[C] 優先すべきこと　N[S/U] 優先

a top **priority** (最優先事項)　a high/low **priority** (優先度の高い / 低いもの)

▶ **prioritize** [praɪɔ́:rətaɪz] V[T] を優先する、に優先順位をつける　V[I] 優先順位を決める

▶ **prioritization** [praɪɔ̀:rətəzéɪʃən] N[U] 優先順位をつけること

85 strike sth up
[straɪkʌ́p]

[PV] (会話や関係など) を始める　= **start** [stɑ:rt]

Do you know a good app that I can use to **strike up** an online friendship?
(オンラインで人と仲良くなれるような良いアプリ知らない？)

86 stupid
[stú:pɪd]

Adj. ばかな、頭の悪い、愚かな

▶ **stupidly** [stú:pɪdli] Adv. ばかみたいに、愚かに

▶ **stupidity** [stu:pídəti] N[U] ばかであること、頭の悪いこと　N[C/U] 愚行

87 optimistic
[ὰ:ptəmístɪk]

Adj. 楽観的な、楽天的な、(考えなどが) 甘い　↔ **pessimistic** [pèsəmístɪk]

▶ **optimistically** [ὰ:ptəmístɪkəli] Adv. 楽観的に、楽天的に

▶ **optimist** [ά:ptəmɪst] N[C] 楽観的な人、楽天家

88 preferable
[préfərəbəl]

Adj. (〜よりも) より良い、好ましい (to sth)

▶ **preferably** [préfərəbli] Adv. できれば、なるべく

▶ **preference** [préfərəns] N[C/U] (〜に対する) 好み、望み (for sth)

89 steadily
[stédəli]

Adv. ずっと、絶え間なく；徐々に、着実に

▶ **steady** [stédi] Adj. 絶え間ない；徐々の、着実な　V[I] 安定する　V[T] を安定させる

▶ **steadiness** [stédinəs] N[U] 着実、安定

90 soak
[soʊk]

V[I] (〜に) 浸る、つかる (in sth)　V[T] を浸す、つける；をずぶぬれにする

▶ **soaked** [soʊkt] Adj. (〜で) ずぶぬれの (with/in sth)

soaked to the bone/skin (雨などで) びしょぬれになった)

91 cost
[kɑ:st]

V[T] (金額) がかかる；を犠牲にする　N[C/U] 費用；犠牲　N[P] 経費【-s】

cost (sb) sth ((〜に) 〜がかかる)

▶ **costly** [kά:stli] Adj. (値段が) 高い、お金のかかる

92 fortune
[fɔ́:rtʃu:n]

N[S] 大金　N[C] (個人の) 財産、資産　N[U] 富；運

▶ **fortunate** [fɔ́:rtʃənət] Adj. 運のよい、幸運な　↔ **unfortunate** [ʌnfɔ́:rtʃənət] 運の悪い、不幸な

▶ **fortunately** [fɔ́:rtʃənətli] Adv. 幸い、運よく　↔ **unfortunately** [ʌnfɔ́:rtʃənətli] 運悪く、不幸にも

93 spell
[spel]

V[I/T] (〜の) スペルを書く、(〜を) つづる　N[C] 呪文、魔法；しばらくの間

▶ **spelling** [spélɪŋ] N[C] スペル、つづり　N[U] つづり方

94 assure
[əʃúr]

V[T] に保証する、(勝利など) を確実なものにする

assure sb of sth/that + sentence (〜に〜を保証する)

▶ **assurance** [əʃúrəns] N[C/U] 保証　N[U] 自信、確信

▶ **assured** [əʃúrd] Adj. 確実な、保証された；自信に満ちた

95 vocabulary
[voʊkǽbjəleri]

N[U] 語彙

many vocabularies は間違い？　一つ一つの単語は word であり、その集合体のことを vocabulary と呼びます。ゆえに、「たくさんの語彙」と言いたい時は、many vocabularies とは言えず、a large/ wide vocabulary と言います。

96 grammar
[grǽmər]

N[U] 文法

▶ **grammatical** [grəmǽtɪkəl] Adj. 文法上の；文法的に正しい

▶ **grammatically** [grəmǽtɪkli] Adv. 文法的に

It's **grammatically** correct but sounds a bit weird. (文法的には正しいけど少し変な感じがする。)

Chapter

03

人類学
Anthropology

The purpose of anthropology is mainly to shed light on the origins and development of humans. It includes the study of how the emergence of humans is related to the development of other primates such as apes and monkeys.

While many disciplines have trended toward dissolving into increasingly confined areas of specialization, anthropology has maintained its status as a fusion of humanity-related studies, investigating manifold fields including commerce, linguistics, and archaeology.

For instance, the anthropological study of money has extended our understanding of the shifting role of currency throughout history, therefore assisting in predicting the impact of burgeoning currencies such as Bitcoin and Ethereum on commercial transactions.

This example illustrates how obtaining a more complete and cohesive view of humanity offers perspective on our current condition and helps us foresee where we are heading. For this reason, the value of anthropology should not be underestimated.

1 The purpose of anthropology is mainly to shed light on the origins and development of humans. It includes the study of how the emergence of humans is related to the development of other primates such as apes and monkeys.

人類学の目的は、主に人類の起源や進化を解明することである。その中には、人類の出現が類人猿やサルといった他の霊長類の進化とどのように関連しているのかという研究も含まれている。

---

⁹⁷ **purpose**
[pə́ːrpəs]

N[C] 目的、意図　**N[U]** （目標への）決意、意識

The whole **purpose** of this meeting is to give everyone an opportunity to share their ideas.
（この会議の目的は、みんなが意見を共有する場を設けることだよ。）

■ on **purpose**（意図的に、故意に）

Did you do that **on purpose** or by accident?
（それって意図的にやったの？それとも単純に間違えただけ？）

■ for the **purpose** of doing（～することを目的として）

I went to the seminar **for the purpose of** finding a new job.
（新しい仕事を見つける目的で、そのセミナーに参加したんだ。）

a sense of **purpose**（目的意識）

---

⁹⁸ **anthropology**
[æ̀nθrəpɑ́ːlədʒi]

N[U] 人類学、人間学

My school offered a course in Christian **anthropology**.
（私の学校にはキリスト教人間学のコースがあったんだ。）

▶ **anthropological** [æ̀nθrəpəlɑ́ːdʒɪkəl] Adj. 人類学の

---

⁹⁹ **mainly**
[méɪnli]

Adv. 主に

Products sold in Japan are **mainly** made in China.
（日本で売られている商品の大部分は中国で生産されているよ。）

▶ **main** [meɪn] Adj. 主な

The **main** themes of this movie are love and revenge.
（この映画の主なテーマは愛と復讐なんだ。）

100 **shed**
[ʃed]
☐☐☐☐☐☐

V[T] （光や熱）を放つ、発する；（血や涙）を流す

■ **shed** light (on sth)（（～を）解明する、明らかにする、光を放つ）

The documentary **shed light on** the issue of poverty in developing countries.
（あのドキュメンタリーは発展途上国における貧困問題を明らかにしたんだ。）

■ **shed** tears/blood（涙 / 血を流す）

It's not worth **shedding tears** for such a dishonest guy.
（あんな不誠実な男には涙を流す価値もないよ。）

V[I] （葉や毛が）落ちる、抜け落ちる

V[T] （葉や毛）を落とす；（不要なもの）を取り除く、削る；（服）を脱ぎ捨てる

Trees **shed** their leaves during the fall simply because they don't need them anymore.
（秋に木が葉っぱを落とすのは、単純にもう葉っぱが必要なくなるからだよ。）

N[C] 小屋

---

101 **include**
[ɪnklúːd]
☐☐☐☐☐☐

V[T] を（～に）含む、含める（in sth）

I'm very disappointed that this sushi bento doesn't **include** pickled ginger.
（この寿司弁当、ガリが入ってなくてめっちゃがっかり。）

◆ **exclude** [ɪksklúːd] を含まない、（～から）除外する（from sth）

▶ **including** Prep. ～を含めて　　◆ **excluding** ～を除いて
[ɪnklúːdɪŋ]　　　　　　　　　　　　　[ɪksklúːdɪŋ]

▶ **included** [ɪnklúːdɪd] Adj. （～に）含まれた（in sth）

Is tax **included** in the price?（税金は価格に含まれてますか？）

▶ **inclusive** [ɪnklúːsɪv] Adj. （～を）含んだ（of sth）；誰でも受け入れる

Our company is trying to build a more **inclusive** and diverse workplace culture.
（うちの会社は、もっとみんなを受け入れるような、多様な職場風土をつくろうとしているんだ。）

▶ **inclusion** N[U] 含めること　　◆ **exclusion** N[C/U] 排除
[ɪnklúːʒən]　　　　　　　　　　　　[ɪksklúːʒən]

---

102 **primate**
[práɪmeɪt]
☐☐☐☐☐☐

N[C] 霊長類；大司教

She conducts research on non-human **primates**, such as gorillas and orangutans.
（彼女はゴリラとかオランウータンみたいな人間以外の霊長類の研究をしてるんだって。）

---

103 **ape**
[eɪp]
☐☐☐☐☐☐

N[C] 類人猿　**V[T]** をまねる

Chimpanzees are considered to be one of the smartest **apes**.
（チンパンジーが類人猿の中で一番賢いって言われてるよ。）

primates はサル（monkeys）、原猿（prosimians）、類人猿（apes）、ヒト（humans）を全て合わせたグループのことで、その中で最も進化したものが類人猿です。現存する類人猿はオランウータン（orangutan）、チンパンジー（chimpanzees）、ゴリラ（gorillas）、テナガザル（gibbons）の四類と言われています。

2 While many disciplines have trended toward dissolving into increasingly confined areas of specialization, anthropology has maintained its status as a fusion of humanity-related studies, investigating manifold fields including commerce, linguistics, and archaeology.

多くの学問分野は、狭い専門領域にますます枝分かれしていく傾向にある中、人類学は人類に関連する研究を融合させた地位を維持し、商学、言語学、考古学といった、多様な分野の調査を行っている。

---

104 trend
[trend]
☐☐☐☐☐☐

V[I] （～の）傾向にある（toward sth）；トレンド入りする、流行る

How can I search for hashtags that are **trending**?
（流行ってるハッシュタグってどうやって調べられるの？）

N[C] 傾向、動向；流行、トレンド

Singapore abolished school exam rankings. I think this is going to become a global **trend**.
（シンガポールでは学校の試験の順位記載を廃止したんだけど、これは世界的なトレンドになると思うよ。）

economic **trends**（経済動向）　　fashion **trends**（ファッショントレンド）

▶ **trendy**［tréndi］Adj. 流行している、トレンドの　N[C] トレンドを追う人

I love going to **trendy** new restaurants every now and then.
（たまに流行りのレストランに行くのがすごい好きなんだ。）

---

105 dissolve
[dɪzáːlv]
☐☐☐☐☐☐

V[I] （～の中に）溶ける（into sth）

How can I make sugar **dissolve** into this iced tea?
（どうやったらこのアイスティーに砂糖を溶かすことができるかな？）

V[T] を溶かす；を解散する

Japan's Prime Minister has **dissolved** the Lower House of Parliament.
（日本の首相は衆議院を解散した。）

▶ **dissolution**［dìsəlúːʃən］N[U]（組織の）解散、解体；（契約の）解消

The **dissolution** of nation-states is often violent.
（国民国家の解体は暴力的であることが多いんだ。）

106 confined
[kənfáɪnd]
☐☐☐☐☐☐

Adj. 狭い、限られた、制約のある

I feel sorry for my pet turtles being in this **confined** space, so I'm going to buy a bigger aquarium.
(ペットの亀をこんな狭い場所に閉じ込めておくのはかわいそうだから、もっと大きい水槽を買う予定だよ。)

▶ **confine** [kənfáɪn] V[T] を（〜に）制限する、限定する、監禁する、閉じ込める (to sth)

I'm **confining** myself to the library today to study for the exam I have tomorrow.
(明日の試験に向けて勉強するために今日は図書館にこもってるんだ。)

▶ **confinement** [kənfáɪnmənt] N[U] 制限、限定、監禁

---

107 status
[stéɪṭəs]
☐☐☐☐☐☐

N[C/U] 地位、立場；状況

The role and **status** of women in Japanese society is an ongoing topic of debate, but at a fundamental level I don't think roles and status should be determined by gender.
(日本社会における女性の役割と地位はずっと議論され続けているトピックだけど、そもそも役割や地位って性別で決められるべきじゃないと思う。)

high/low **status** (高い / 低い地位)   the financial **status** (財政状況)

---

108 fusion
[fjúːʒən]
☐☐☐☐☐☐

N[C/U] 融合 **N[U]** （原子などの）融合 ↔ **fission** [fíʃən] 分裂

California Rolls are like a **fusion** of American and Japanese food.
(カリフォルニアロールはアメリカと日本の食べ物を融合した感じかな。)

▶ **fuse** V[I]（〜と）融合する (with sth)；(熱で) 溶ける
[fjuːz] V[T] を融合させる；を (熱で) 溶かす

---

109 investigate
[ɪnvéstəgeɪt]
☐☐☐☐☐☐

V[I/T] （〜を）調査する、調べる

The police are currently **investigating** the apartment where the homicide occurred.
(警察は今まさに殺人が起きたアパートを捜査してるとこ。)

▶ **investigation** [ɪnvèstəgéɪʃən] N[C] 調査、捜査 N[U] 調査すること

▶ **investigator** [ɪnvéstəgeɪṭər] N[C] 調査員、捜査官

---

110 manifold
[mænəfoʊld]
☐☐☐☐☐☐

Adj. 多様な、多数の

There are **manifold** advantages to studying English.
(英語の勉強にはたくさんのメリットがあります。)

3 For instance, the anthropological study of money has extended our understanding of the shifting role of currency throughout history, therefore assisting in predicting the impact of burgeoning currencies such as Bitcoin and Ethereum on commercial transactions.

例えば、お金に関する人類学的な研究は、歴史とともに変化し続ける貨幣の役割について、私たちの理解を広げてきた。そしてそれによって、ビットコインやイーサリアムといった急成長を見せる通貨が商取引に与える影響を予想する上でも役立っている。

---

111 extend
[ɪksténd]

V[T] を広げる、引き延ばす、延長する；（気持ち）を伝える、述べる

We will **extend** the Q&A session to cover everyone's questions.
（みなさんの質問に答えるために、Q&A セッションを延長します。）

extend one's thanks/gratitude (to sb)（(〜に) ありがとう / 感謝の気持ちを伝える）

extend one's condolences (to sb)（(〜に) お悔やみを言う）

V[I] （空間や時間が）広がる、続く、伸びる

▶ **extension** N[C/U] 拡張、延長　N[C] 内線；拡張子　N[P] （髪の）エクステ【-s】
[ɪksténʃən]

A good tennis racket should feel like an **extension** of your arm.
（良いテニスラケットっていうのはまるでそれが腕の延長であるかのように感じるはずだよ。）

▶ **extended** [ɪksténdɪd] Adj. 長期の　▶ **extendable** [ɪksténdəbəl] Adj. 延長可能な

an **extended** vacation（長期休暇）

---

112 shifting
[ʃíftɪŋ]

Adj. 変化し続ける、絶えず変化する

We have to be agile and flexible so we can meet the **shifting** demands of customers.
（顧客の変わり続ける需要に対応できるようにするために、私たちは俊敏かつ柔軟でないといけない。）

▶ **shift** V[I] 変化する、移る、シフトする　V[T] を変化させる、移す
[ʃíft] N[C] 変化、転換；(仕事の) シフト

■ on the day/night **shift**（昼 / 夜のシフトが入っている）

I'm **on the night shift** tomorrow.（明日は夜のシフトが入ってるんだ。）

113 **currency**
[kə́:rənsi]
□□□□□□

N[C/U] 通貨、貨幣　**N[U]** （言葉や表現の）普及

I think that paper **currency** will be replaced by digital **currency** soon.
（僕は紙の通貨はすぐにデジタル通貨に代わると思ってるよ。）

domestic/foreign **currency**（国内通貨 / 外貨）

---

114 **assist**
[əsíst]
□□□□□□

V[I] （〜の）役に立つ、（〜するのを）手伝う（in/with sth）

V[T] が（〜するのを）助ける、力を貸す（in/with sth）

Can you **assist** me with booking flights?（飛行機予約するの手伝ってくれない？）

N[C] （スポーツの）アシスト

▶ **assistance** N[U] 援助、手伝い　　▶ **assistant** N[C] アシスタント、助手
　[əsístəns]　　　　　　　　　　　　　　　[əsístənt]

---

115 **predict**
[prɪdíkt]
□□□□□□

V[T] を予想する、予測する、予言する

Even though Japan has experienced many earthquakes, it's still not easy to **predict** when the next one will come.
（日本はたくさん地震を経験しているけど、それでも次の地震がいつ起きるか予想するのは難しいんだ。）

predict that + sentence（〜だと予想する）　　be **predicted** to do（〜すると予想されている）

▶ **prediction** [prɪdíkʃən] N[C/U] 予想、予測、予言

Making a **prediction** about the stock market is pretty difficult.
（株式市場の予測を立てるのはなかなか難しいよ。）

▶ **predictable** Adj. 予想通りの、予測可能な　⬌ **unpredictable** 予測できない
　[prɪdíktəbəl]　　　　　　　　　　　　　　　　［ ʌnprɪdíktəbəl]

▶ **predictably** Adv. 予想通りに　　▶ **predictability** N[U] 予測可能性
　[prɪdíktəbli]　　　　　　　　　　　　[prɪdíktəbíləti]

語根 dict 「言う」という意味の語根で、前もって（= pre）言う（=dict）ことから「予想する」という意味になります。他には contradict（矛盾する）、dictate（書きとらせる）などがあります。

---

116 **burgeoning**
[bə́:rdʒənɪŋ]
□□□□□□

Adj. 急成長する、急増する

The key to sports brands staying competitive is taking advantage of the **burgeoning** e-sports industry.
（スポーツブランドが競争力を維持できるかどうかは急成長中の e スポーツ業界をうまく利用できるかにかかってる。）

▶ **burgeon** [bə́:rdʒən] V[I] 急成長する；芽生える、発芽する

I'm expecting coat sales to **burgeon** as the weather gets colder.
（外が寒くなるにつれて、コートの売り上げはきっと急激に上がっていくと思うよ。）

---

117 **transaction**
[trænzǽkʃən]
□□□□□□

N[C] 取引　**N[U]** 業務

The **transaction** fee is minimal if you withdraw money from an ATM run by your bank.
（ご自身の銀行の ATM で引き出せば取引手数料を最小限に抑えることができます。）

▶ **transact** [trænzǽkt] V[I] （〜と）取引する（with sth/sb）　V[T] （取引など）を行う

4 This example illustrates how obtaining a more complete and cohesive view of humanity offers perspective on our current condition and helps us foresee where we are heading. For this reason, the value of anthropology should not be underestimated.

こうした例は、人類についてより完璧でまとまりのある考えを手に入れることで、私たちの現状を大局的にとらえ、今後の予想もできるようになることを示している。そしてそれゆえ、人類学の真価を過小評価すべきではない。

---

118 complete
[kəmplí:t]
☐☐☐☐☐☐

Adj. 完璧な、完全な ↔ **incomplete** [ìnkəmplí:t] 不完全な

He went to the hair salon to get a **complete** makeover.
（彼は美容室に行ってガラっとイメチェンしたんだ。）

V[T] を完了する、を完成させる

▶ **completely** [kəmplí:tli] Adv. 完全に

Sorry, I **completely** forgot about the meeting. （ごめん、会議のこと完全に忘れてた。）

▶ **completion** [kəmplí:ʃən] N[U] 完成、完了

---

119 cohesive
[koʊhí:sɪv]
☐☐☐☐☐☐

Adj. まとまりのある、団結力のある

I don't mind writing an essay, but whether I can write a **cohesive** one is a different story.
（エッセイを書くのは好きだけど、まとまりのあるものを書けるかはまた別の話だよ。）

▶ **cohesiveness** [koʊhí:sɪvnəs] N[U] まとまり、団結

▶ **cohesion** [koʊhí:ʒən] N[U] 団結、結合

---

120 offer
[á:fər]
☐☐☐☐☐☐

V[T] を提供する　**V[I/T]** （ものや援助を）申し出る　**N[C]** 申し出

My university **offered** me a scholarship for my first two years, which made things so much easier. （うちの大学、最初の2年間は奨学金を出してくれたからそのおかげでかなり色々と楽になったよ。）

Thank you for **offering** to help. （助けたいって言ってくれてありがとう。）

▶ **offering** [á:fərɪŋ] N[C] 贈り物；株式公開；奉納物；作品

■ **a peace offering** （仲直りをするためにあげるプレゼント）

I gave Cindy some flowers as **a peace offering**. （仲直りするために、シンディーにお花をあげたんだ。）

---

121 **perspective**
[pərspéktɪv]

□□□□□□

N[U] 大局、全体像；遠近法   **N[C]** 見方、視点、考え方、観点

I prefer hanging out with people who have different **perspectives**.
（僕は違った視点を持ってる人と付き合う方が好きだなぁ。）

from sb's/sth's **perspective** = from the **perspective** of sth/sb （〜の観点から、から見ると）

put sth in **perspective** （広い視野を持って〜を見る）

---

122 **foresee**
[fərsíː]

□□□□□□

V[T] を予想する、予見する、予測する

I **foresee** you getting married by the time you're thirty.
（君は大体 30 歳までには結婚しそうだね。）

▶ **foresight** [fɔ́ːrsaɪt] N[U] 先見の明

■ have the **foresight** to do （〜する先見の明がある）

I **had the foresight to** sell all my stocks right before the global financial crisis.
（僕には先見の明があって、世界金融危機が起きる直前に株を全部売ってたんだ。）

▶ **foreseeable** [fɔːrsíːəbəl] Adj. 予測できる、予測可能な

■ in/for the **foreseeable** future （近い将来 / しばらくは）

I'm leaving Japan **for the foreseeable future**. （しばらく日本を離れる予定だよ。）

↔ **unforeseeable** [ʌnfɔːrsíːəbəl] 予測できない、予期できない

an **unforeseeable** consequence （予期せぬ結果）

接頭語 fore- 「前に、先に」を意味する接頭語で、そこから、「前を見る＝予想する」という意味になります。他には forecast（予測する）、foreshadow（前兆になる）などがあります。

---

123 **head**
[hed]

□□□□□□

V[I] （〜に）向かう、進む、行く (to/toward sth)

Let's drop off our stuff at the hotel and **head** to the beach! （荷物ホテルに置いてビーチ行こうよ！）

N[C] 頭、頭部；代表、長   **N[S]** （単位としての）人、匹、頭

Use your **head**! （頭使えよ！）   a department **head** （部門長）

N[U] （コインの）表 【-s】 ↔ **tails** [teɪlz] （コインの）裏

Heads or tails? （（コインを投げて）表と裏、どっちにする？）

---

124 **underestimate**
V. [ʌndəréstəmeɪt]
N. [ʌndəréstəmət]

□□□□□□

V[T] を過小評価する   **N[C]** 過小評価

Never **underestimate** the power of teamwork. （チームワークの力をなめちゃいけないよ。）

↔ **overestimate** を過大評価する / 過大評価
V. [òʊvəréstəmeɪt] N. [òʊvəréstəmət]

▶ **underestimation** N[C/U] 過小評価   ↔ **overestimation** 過大評価
[ʌndərèstəméɪʃən]   [òʊvərèstəméɪʃən]

Drone Technology Uncovers Secrets of Hidden Tribes

With advancements in drone technology in recent years, it has become more feasible to locate isolated, **native** tribes **situated** in **tropical** rainforests, such as the Amazon. It is also much less **intrusive** and **conspicuous** to observe and study these populations.

This **approach** of using sophisticated **mobile** surveillance technology is beneficial for a number of reasons.

Firstly, costs of exploration are drastically reduced. Due to the logistical and resourcing difficulties of **embarking** on **expeditions** in the **wilderness**, the cost of these missions can **prohibit persevering** with exploration.

Secondly, minimizing the **visibility** of researchers reduces the danger and risk which researchers are **prone** to being subjected to. **Furthermore**, stealth research allows these tribes, who have **presumably** not had any **encounters** with modern civilization, to continue living in **solitude**. This also increases the **chance** of their culture being studied without disruption and leads to the **uncovering** of new insights.

ドローン技術が隠れた民族の秘密を明らかにする

近年、ドローン技術が進歩したおかげで、アマゾンなどの熱帯雨林に住む、孤立した先住民族の存在を突き止めることが容易になりました。それによって、そうした人々の観察・研究も、これまでと比べてずっと立ち入らない、目立たない方法でできるようになっています。

高性能のモバイル監視技術を利用したこの方法は、さまざまな理由で役に立ちます。

まず、調査にかかるコストが劇的に削減されます。未開の地の探索に乗り出す際の物資輸送や資源確保の問題によって、こうした任務におけるコストは忍耐強く調査を続ける上で妨げとなる可能性があります。

次に、研究者が人目につく可能性を最小限に抑えることで、研究者自身がさらされやすい危険やリスクが軽減されます。さらに、人目につかないよう密かに研究することで、おそらく現代文明に遭遇したことのない先住民族は、隔絶された生活を続けることができます。こうすることで、先住民族の文化を何の妨げもなく研究できる可能性が高まり、新たな洞察の発見にもつながります。

125 native
[néɪṭɪv]
□□□□□□

Adj. 先住の、土着の；自国の、故郷の；母語の；その土地固有の

sb's **native** language（〜の母語）　a **native** speaker（ネイティブスピーカー）

N[C] 現地の人、その土地の人、固有の動植物

126 situated
[sítʃueɪṭɪd]
□□□□□□

Adj.（〜に）ある、位置している（in sth）　= located [lóʊkeɪṭɪd]

▶ **situate** [sítʃueɪt] V[T] を置く、位置づける

127 tropical
[trá:pɪkəl]
□□□□□□

Adj. 熱帯の、熱帯地方の

(a) **tropical** rainforest（熱帯雨林）

▶ **tropic** [trá:pɪk] N[C] 回帰線；熱帯地方【the -s】

128 intrusive
[ɪntrú:sɪv]
□□□□□□

Adj. 立ち入った、出しゃばりの、押しつけがましい

▶ **intrusion** [ɪntrú:ʒən] N[C/U] 侵入、侵害　▶ **intruder** [ɪntrú:dər] N[C] 侵入者、邪魔者

▶ **intrude** [ɪntrú:d] V[I]（〜に）立ち入る、押し入る（on/into sth）

129 conspicuous
[kənspíkjuəs]
□□□□□□

Adj. 目立つ、顕著な　↔ **inconspicuous** [ìnkənspíkjuəs] 目立たない

Tim's pink jacket made him very **conspicuous**.（ティムはピンクのジャケットで目立ってたよ。）

▶ **conspicuously** [kənspíkjuəsli] Adv. 目立って

▶ **conspicuousness** [kənspíkjuəsnəs] N[U] 目立つこと

130 approach
[əpróʊtʃ]
□□□□□□

N[C] 方法、アプローチ；要請、打診；接近

V[T] に取り組む　**V[I/T]**（〜に）近づく、（〜に）接近する

▶ **approachable** [əpróʊtʃəbəl] Adj. 近づきやすい、親しみやすい

131 mobile
[móʊbəl]
□□□□□□

Adj. モバイルの、携帯式の、可動式の、移動式の

▶ **mobility** [moʊbíləṭi] N[U] 流動性、移動性

a **mobile** (phone)（携帯電話、スマホ）〈英〉　= a cell (phone)〈米〉

132 embark
[ɪmbá:rk]
□□□□□□

V[I]（〜に）乗り出す、（船や飛行機に）乗り込む（on sth）

V[T]（船や飛行機に荷物）を積み込む

▶ **embarkation** [èmbɑ:rkéɪʃən] N[C/U] 乗船、搭乗；積み込み

133 expedition
[èkspədíʃən]
□□□□□□

N[C] 探索、探検、遠征

Our group went on an **expedition** to Mexico for our research.
（うちのグループはリサーチのために、メキシコに探検に行ったんだ。）

134 wilderness
[wíldərnəs]
□□□□□□

N[C] 未開の地、荒野

▶ **wild** [waɪld] Adj. 未開の、荒れ果てた；野生の；乱暴な

a **wild** animal（野生動物）

135 prohibit
[prəhíbɪt]
□□□□□□

V[T] を妨げる；を禁止する　**= forbid** [fərbíd]　**= ban** [bæn]

prohibit sb from doing （～が～するのを禁止する）

▶ **prohibitive** [prouhíbəṭɪv] Adj. 禁止するための；（値段が）ひどく高い

▶ **prohibitively** [prouhíbəṭɪvli] Adv. ひどく、法外に

▶ **prohibition** [pròuɪbíʃən] N[C/U] 禁止

---

136 persevere
[pə̀:rsəvír]
□□□□□□

V[I] （～を）忍耐強く続ける （with/in sth）

▶ **perseverance** [pə̀:rsəvírəns] N[U] 忍耐、不屈の努力

---

137 visibility
[vìzəbíləṭi]
□□□□□□

N[U] 人目につきやすいこと、視認性、視界

▶ **visible** [vízəbəl] Adj. 目に見える　▶ **visibly** [vízəbli] Adv. 目に見えて

I put beauty cream on my skin every day, but there's no **visible** change.
（肌に毎日美容クリーム塗ってるんだけど、目に見える変化はないんだ。）

---

138 prone
[proʊn]
□□□□□□

Adj. （～） しやすい、しがちな （to sth/to do）

---

139 furthermore
[fɜ́:rðərmɔ:r]
□□□□□□

Adv. さらに、そのうえ

---

140 presumably
[prɪzú:məbli]
□□□□□□

Adv. おそらく、多分

▶ **presume** [prɪzú:m] V[I/T] （～と） 推定する、（～ではないかと） 思う

▶ **presumption** [prɪzʌ́mpʃən] N[C] 推測、仮定　▶ **presumptive** [prɪzʌ́mptɪv] Adj. 推測上の

---

141 encounter
[ɪnkáʊnṭər]
□□□□□□

N[C] 遭遇、出会い　**V[T]** に遭遇する、出会う

I **encountered** a homeless guy wearing a Louis Vuitton jacket on the street. What the hell. （道でヴィトンのジャケットを着てるホームレスの人に出会ったんだ。なんてことだ。）

---

142 solitude
[sá:lətu:d]
□□□□□□

N[U] 孤独

in **solitude** （他と交わらずに、一人で）

▶ **solitary** [sá:ləteri] Adj. 孤独の、一人の　▶ **solitarily** [sɑ:lətérəli] Adv. 孤独に、一人で

---

143 chance
[tʃæns]
□□□□□□

N[C/U] 可能性　**N[C]** 機会　**N[U]** 偶然

chances are + that sentence （多分～だ）　■ by **chance** （偶然にも）

I ran into my ex **by chance** at the café. So awkward.
（偶然カフェで元カノに会ったんだ。ほんと気まずい。）

---

144 uncover
[ʌnkʌ́vər]
□□□□□□

V[T] を発見する、発掘する、明らかにする；のふたを取る

Chapter

04

考古学
Archaeology

Archaeology is the study of historical human activity through the recovery, inspection, and analysis of material remains that are usually concealed, such as graves, tools, and pottery.

At a practical level, archaeology usually involves the surveying of sites and the removal, analysis, and preservation of fragile recovered items. The analysis typically relies on cross-disciplinary research that often sheds light on ancient civilizations.

Stonehenge, for example, one of the first archaeological discoveries, was especially critical for providing an understanding about a now-extinct ancient society, for which no written records or documentation exist.

Therefore, this discipline is very important in furthering our visual understanding of the way ancient humans lived, engaged, and interacted. It also shows us how this ancient history has shaped our lives today.

1 Archaeology is the study of historical human activity through the recovery, inspection, and analysis of material remains that are usually concealed, such as graves, tools, and pottery.

考古学は、墓や道具、陶器など、大抵は明らかにされていない有形の遺跡を修復・調査・分析することで人間の歴史的な活動を研究するものである。

145 archaeology
[ὰ:rkiɑ́:ləʤi]

☐☐☐☐☐☐

N[U]　考古学

I want to work in **archaeology**. It'll give me a lot of opportunities to travel abroad.
(考古学の分野で仕事をしたいんだ。外国を旅できる機会がたくさんあるからね。)

▶ **archaeological** Adj. 考古学の
[ὰ:rkiəlɑ́:ʤɪkəl]

▶ **archaeologist** N[C] 考古学者
[ὰ:rkiɑ́:ləʤɪst]

接頭語 arch-　「最初の、古い」という意味の接頭語で、他には archaic（古風な）などがあります。

146 activity
[æktívəṭi]

☐☐☐☐☐☐

N[C/U]　活動

Let's pick an **activity** to do after work tomorrow!
(明日仕事終わりに何するか決めようよ！)

▶ **active** [ǽktɪv] Adj. 活発な、積極的な　⟷　**inactive** [ɪnǽktɪv] 活発でない

He's very **active** on social media.（彼は SNS ですごい活発なんだ。）

▶ **actively** [ǽktɪvli] Adv. 活発に、積極的に

147 recovery
[rɪkʌ́vəri]

☐☐☐☐☐☐

N[S/U]　修復、回復、復帰

Saturday night was pretty wild, so I spent most of Sunday in **recovery** mode.
(土曜の夜は結構やばかったから、日曜はほぼほぼずっと回復モードで過ごしたよ。)

▶ **recover**　V[I]（正常な状態に）戻る；（風邪や病気から）回復する（from sth)
[rɪkʌ́vər]　V[T]（損失や失ったもの）を取り戻す、回復する

I've finally **recovered** from my cold.（やっと風邪が治ったよ。）

148 inspection
[ɪnspékʃən]

☐☐☐☐☐☐

N[C/U]　調査、検査、点検

I really hate it when teachers do random bag and locker **inspections**.
(先生が鞄とロッカーの抜き打ち検査するのマジ嫌い。)

▶ **inspect** [ɪnspékt] V[T] を調査する、検査する、点検する

---

149 **material**
[mətíriəl]

Adj. 有形の、物質的な；重大な

The meeting went on for a good few hours, but there was no **material** outcome.
（会議はかなりの時間続いたんだけど、具体的な成果は何もなかったよ。）

N[C/U] 物質、素材、材料、生地　**N[U]** 題材

I can't tell what **material** this jacket is made of, but it feels amazing!
（このジャケット、素材は何か分からないけど感触が最高！）

N[U] ネタ、題材

Can you teach me the best way to collect **material** for blog posts?
（ブログのネタ集めの一番いい方法教えてくれない？）

---

150 **conceal**
[kənsíːl]

V[T] を（見えないところに）隠す、秘密にする

We need to **conceal** that hole in the wall before the landlord notices.
（家主に気づかれる前にあの壁の穴隠さなきゃね。）

▶ **concealer** [kənsíːlər] N[C/U] コンシーラー（シミなどを隠すことから）

---

151 **grave**
[greɪv]

N[C] 墓　**Adj.** 重大な、深刻な、危機的な

My pet hamster died last week, so I dug a small **grave** for it.
（先週ペットのハムスターが死んじゃったから、小さなお墓を掘ってあげたんだ。）

The country's economy is facing a **grave** situation, but the government seems to have no idea how to fix it.
（その国の経済は危機的な状況にあるけど、政府はどうやって立て直せば良いのか全くわかっていないみたい。）

▶ **graveyard** [gréɪvjɑːrd] N[C] 墓地

2 At a practical level, archaeology usually involves the surveying of sites and the removal, analysis, and preservation of fragile recovered items. The analysis typically relies on cross-disciplinary research that often sheds light on ancient civilizations.

実際の考古学では、通常、遺跡の調査や、壊れやすい修復品を取り出し、分析・保存する作業が含まれている。一般的に、分析の際は学際的な研究に頼ることになり、これが多くの場合古代文明の解明につながる。

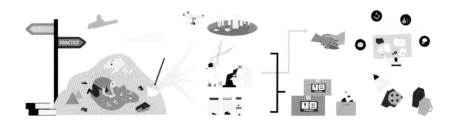

---

152 **survey**
V1. [sərvéɪ]
V2./N. [sɜ́:rveɪ]
▢▢▢▢▢▢

V[T] を調査する；に関して世論調査をする

N[C] 調査；世論調査

More than 90% of people **surveyed** say they spend over five hours a day on their phone. (調査を受けた 90%以上の人が一日 5 時間以上携帯を使ってるって答えてるんだ。)

▶ **surveillance** N[U] 監視　　▶ **surveyor** N[C] 測量技師
　 [sərvéɪləns]　　　　　　　　 [sərvéɪər]

Hey, do you think that **surveillance** camera is watching us?
(ねぇ、あの監視カメラ、私たちのこと見てると思う？)

---

153 **site**
[saɪt]
▢▢▢▢▢▢

N[C] 遺跡；会場、場所、敷地；サイト

This looks like a great **site** for camping. (ここはテントを張るのに最高の場所だね。)

■ **on site** (現場で)　　◀▶ **off site** (現場外で)

She's working **on site** today. (彼女は今日現場で働いてるよ。)

on site は活動が通常行われる場所にいること、off site はその場所以外にいることを意味します (例：普段会社のオフィスで働いている人は、オフィスで働くことは work on site、それ以外の場所では work off site に)。

---

154 **removal**
[rɪmúːvəl]
▢▢▢▢▢▢

N[U] 取り除くこと、除去、削除

I put acne **removal** cream on my face this morning. (今朝顔にニキビ除去クリーム塗ったよ。)

▶ **remove** [rɪmúːv] V[T] を取り除く、除去する、削除する

Do you know how to **remove** a tag from a photo I'm tagged in?
(どうやってタグ付けされた写真からタグ削除するか知ってる？)

接頭語 re- 「再び」という意味の接頭語で、再び (= re) 動かす (= move) から「〜を除去する」という意味になり、他には repeat (繰り返す) や retry (もう一度やってみる) があります。

155 **preservation**
[prèzərvéɪʃən]

□□□□□□

N[U]　保存、保護、保全

The **preservation** of these books will become impossible if we don't fix the air conditioning.（空調を直さないとこの書籍の保存は不可能だよ。）

▶ **preserved** [prɪzɔ́:rvd] Adj. 保存された、漬物にされた

preserved vegetables（野菜の漬物）

▶ **preservative** Adj. 保存力のある、防腐効果のある　N[C/U] 保存料、防腐剤
[prɪzɔ́:rvətɪv]

no **preservatives**（保存料無添加）　　　a wood **preservative**（木材防腐剤）

preservation vs **conservation**　環境を守るという意味での「保護」を意味する単語にconservationがありますが、若干ニュアンスが異なります。environmental preservation は自然を人間による利用から完全に守ることを意味し、environmental conservation は天然資源の採掘などは継続しながらも、人間と自然の関係を持続可能にしようとすることを意味します。

156 **fragile**
[frǽdʒəl]

□□□□□□

Adj.　壊れやすい、もろい、虚弱な

My luggage is super **fragile**, so try not to throw it around too much.
（私の荷物はものすごい壊れやすいから、あんまり振り回したりしないでね。）

▶ **fragility** [frədʒíləti] N[U] 壊れやすさ、もろさ、虚弱さ

157 **rely**
[rɪláɪ]

□□□□□□

V[I]　（〜に）頼る、信頼する（on/upon sth/sb）

I don't want to **rely** on my parents for money.（親にお金のことで頼りたくない。）

▶ **reliance** [rɪláɪəns] N[U] 頼りにすること　▶ **reliability** [rɪlàɪəbíləti] N[U] 信頼性

We're developing artificial intelligence that can quickly assess the **reliability** of data.
（私たちはデータの信頼性を素早く評価できるような人工知能を開発中なんです。）

▶ **reliable** Adj. 信頼できる、頼りにできる　⬌ **unreliable** 信頼できない
[rɪláɪəbəl]　　　　　　　　　　　　　　　　　　　　　 [ʌnrɪláɪəbəl]

Japanese cars are extremely **reliable**.（日本製の車はものすごい信頼できるよ。）

158 **research**
N1. [rí:sɜ:rtʃ]
V./N2. [rɪsɔ́:rtʃ]

□□□□□□

N[U]　研究、調査　V[I/T]　（〜を）研究する、調査する（into sth）

■ do some **research** (on sth)（（〜について）少し調べる）

I need to **do some research on** China before I travel there next year.
（来年旅行に行く前に少し中国のこと調べなきゃ。）

▶ **researcher** [rɪsɔ́:rtʃər] N[C] 研究者

3 Stonehenge, for example, one of the first archaeological discoveries, was especially critical for providing an understanding about a now-extinct ancient society, for which no written records or documentation exist.

例えば、最初の考古学的発見の一つであるストーンヘンジは、今や消滅してしまって文献記録や文書も残っていない古代社会について理解を深める上で特に重要な存在となった。

---

159 especially
[ɪspéʃəli]

Adv. 特に、とりわけ

I find it **especially** annoying when people who are late don't apologize.
（私は特に遅れた時に謝らない奴にイラっとする。）

▶ **special** [spéʃəl] Adj. 特別な

---

160 critical
[krít̮ɪkəl]

Adj. 非常に重要な ;（～に）批判的な（of sth/sb）;危機的な

Breakfast is very **critical** for my brain to function.
（朝ごはんは自分の脳を働かせるためにかなり重要なんだよね。）

▶ **critically** [krít̮ɪkli] Adv. 非常に ; 批判的に ; 危機的に

critically injured（重体である） a **critically** acclaimed book（批評家による評価が高い本）

▶ **critic** [krítɪk] N[C] 批評家、評論家 ; 批判する人

▶ **critique** N[C]（文芸作品などの）批評   ▶ **criticism** N[C/U] 批評、批判
[krɪtíːk]   [krít̮ɪsɪzəm]

▶ **criticize** [krít̮ɪsaɪz] V[I/T]（～を）批判する

Stop **criticizing** yourself. Stay positive!（自分のこと批判するの止めなよ。ポジティブにいこう！）

---

161 provide
[prəváɪd]

V[T] を与える、供給する

■ **provide** A with B, B for A, B to A（B を A に与える）

I'll **provide** you **with** instructions later, so don't worry.
（後でちゃんと指示を与えるから心配しないで。）

■ **provided** (that + sentence)（もし～なら、～という条件で）

You may go to the party **provided that** you are home by 11.
（11 時までに帰ってくるならパーティに行ってもいいよ。）

▶ **provider** [prəváɪdər] N[C] 供給者、接続業者、プロバイダー

an internet **provider**（インターネット接続業者）

熟語の覚え方　provide A with B といった熟語を覚えるときは、呪文のようにこれを何度も唱えるのではなく、provide you with information のように実際に何か具体的な言葉を入れて練習すると覚えやすく、かつどちらが A でどちらが B かといった混乱も自然に避けることができます。

---

162 **extinct**
[ɪkstíŋkt]
☐☐☐☐☐☐

Adj. 消滅した、絶滅した

■ become/go **extinct**（絶滅する）

I find it fascinating that we still don't know how the dinosaurs **became extinct**.
（恐竜がどうやって絶滅したか未だに分かっていないなんて、魅力的だなぁ。）

▶ **extinction** [ɪkstíŋkʃən] N[U] 消滅、絶滅

■ in danger of **extinction**（絶滅の危険がある）

There are many species currently **in danger of extinction**.（現在多くの種に絶滅の危険がある。）

---

163 **society**
[səsáɪəʈi]
☐☐☐☐☐☐

N[C/U] 社会、世間　**N[C]** （学校などの）サークル

Of course there's crime, but by and large, our **society** is pretty peaceful.
（もちろん犯罪はあるけど、全体的にみれば私たちの社会は結構平和だよ。）

▶ **social** [sóʊʃəl] Adj. 社会の、社会的な、社交的な

▶ **socially** [sóʊʃəli] Adv. 社会的に、社交的に

▶ **sociable** Adj. 社交的な　◀▶ **unsociable** 非社交的な
　　[sóʊʃəbəl]　　　　　　　　　　[ʌnsóʊʃəbəl]

▶ **socialize** [sóʊʃəlaɪz] V[I] （人と社交的に）付き合う（with sb）V[T] を社交的にする

---

164 **record**
N. [rékərd]
V. [rɪkɔ́:rd]
☐☐☐☐☐☐

N[C/U] 記録；業績　**V[T]** を記録する；を録音する、録画する

Ichiro is a legend. He broke the Major League **record** for the number of hits in a season in 2004.（イチローは伝説だよ。2004 年にはメジャーのシーズン安打記録を更新したんだ。）

on **record**（記録された）　set a **record**（記録をつくる）

▶ **recording** [rɪkɔ́:rdɪŋ] N[C] 録音、録画 N[U] 録音すること、録画すること

発音注意！　record は名詞と動詞で発音が違うので注意。名詞は第一音節に、動詞は第二音節にアクセントがあります。

---

165 **documentation**
[dà:kjəmentéɪʃən]
☐☐☐☐☐☐

N[U] 文書、資料、文書化

Did the bank really ask you for all that **documentation** just to prove your age?
（年齢確認のためだけに、ほんとに銀行がそんなにたくさんの資料を提出しろって言ってきたの？）

▶ **document** N[C] 文書、書類　V[T] を記録する、記載する
　　N. [dá:kjəmənt]　**V.** [dá:kjəment]

4 Therefore, this discipline is very important in furthering our visual understanding of the way ancient humans lived, engaged, and interacted. It also shows us how this ancient history has shaped our lives today.

そのため、考古学という学問は、古代の人々がどのように生活・関与・交流したかを、より視覚的に理解する上で非常に重要である。また、この古代の歴史が、今日の私たちの生活をどのように形成したのかも示してくれる。

---

166 further

[fɜ́ːrðər]

□□□□□□

V[T] をいっそう促進する、発展させる

What kind of training do I need to do to **further** my career?
(キャリアをより発展させるためにはどんなトレーニングをしたらいいかな？)

Adv. さらに、もっと、より遠くへ

I really want to **further** improve my English!（本当にもっと英語力上達させたい！）

Adj. さらなる、よりいっそうの

Should you need any **further** information, please do not hesitate to contact me.
（さらに情報が必要であれば、遠慮なくご連絡ください。）

further vs **farther** 「より遠くへ」という意味を持つ似た単語に farther があります。2つの違いは、farther は「距離が遠い」を意味する far から来ていることからも分かるように「物理的な距離」を表す時に使われ（How much farther is it to the convenience store? コンビニまであとどれくらい？）、一方で further は「抽象的な距離」を表します。この区別はネイティブも間違えることがあります。

---

167 visual

[víʒuəl]

□□□□□□

Adj. 視覚的な　**N[P]** （写真や映像などの）視覚的なもの【-s】

There are three types of learners: **visual** learners, verbal learners, and experiential learners.
（学習者には3つのタイプがあるんだ。視覚で学ぶタイプ、聞いて学ぶタイプ、そして実際に経験して学ぶタイプ。）

You should add more **visuals** to your slides.
（もうちょっとスライドにグラフとかそういうの入れた方がいいよ。）

▶ **visually** Adv. 視覚的に
[víʒuəli]

▶ **visualize** V[T] を思い浮かべる、をイメージする
[víʒuəlaɪz]

If you can **visualize** it, you can actualize it.（イメージできるなら、それは実現できるってことだよ。）

168 **ancient**
[éɪnʃənt]

Adj. 古代の、とても古い   **N[P]** 古代人【the -s】

This car's absolutely **ancient**, so I don't really feel safe driving it.
(この車めちゃくちゃ古いから、運転しててあんまり安全な感じしないんだよね。)

---

169 **human**
[hjúːmən]

N[C] 人、人間   **Adj.** 人間の、人間らしい

I swear, sometimes I think Joe gets along better with pets than **humans**.
(マジでさ、たまにジョーって人間よりもペットとの方が仲良くなれるんじゃないかって思う。)

We're only **human**. We all make mistakes. (私達はただの人間なんだから、誰だってミスはするよ。)

▶ **humane** Adj. 人道的な、(人として) 思いやりのある   ◀▶ **inhumane** 非人道的な、残虐な
[hjuːméɪn]   [ìnhjuːméɪn]

inhumane treatment (非人道的な扱い)

▶ **humanity** [hjuːmǽnəti] N[U] 人類；人としての性質

human vs **person**   human は他の動物と区別した「人」という意味で、生物学的な人のニュアンス
を持ちます。故に、普段の生活でたくさんの人のことを a lot of humans ということは基本的にはあり
ません。一方で person（複数形：people）は普段会話で私たちがよく使う「人」の意味を持ちます。ま
た、哲学の分野でも person を使用します。

---

170 **engage**
[ɪngéɪdʒ]

V[I] （〜と）関与する、付き合う（with sb）；（〜に）参加する（in sth）

V[T] を従事させる、参加させる   ◀▶ **disengage** [dìsɪngéɪdʒ] を解放する

His lectures are chaotic. The students are not **engaged** at all.
(彼の授業はカオスだよ。学生が全然参加してない。)

▶ **engagement** N[C] 婚約、約束；関わり   ▶ **engaged** Adj. 婚約した；従事した
[ɪngéɪdʒmənt]   [ɪngéɪdʒd]

Wo finally got **engaged**. (私たちついに婚約しました。)

---

171 **interact**
[ìntərǽkt]

V[I] （〜と）交流する、（相互に）作用する（with sth/sb）

It's really interesting to see how the coach **interacts** with his team.
(コーチがチームとどうやって交流してるか見るのは本当に面白いよ。)

▶ **interaction** N[C/U] 交流, 相互作用   ▶ **interactive** Adj. 双方向の、相互作用する
[ìntərǽkʃən]   [ìntərǽktɪv]

an **interactive** workshop (双方向的なワークショップ)

---

172 **shape**
[ʃeɪp]

V[T] を形成する、形づくる、整える

I seriously need to learn how to **shape** my eyebrows. They're a mess right now.
(ほんとに眉毛の整え方勉強しないと。今すごくぐちゃぐちゃなんだよね。)

N[C/U] 形   **N[U]** （健康などの）状態

a round **shape** (丸い形)   in good/bad **shape** (体調が良い / 悪い)

■ take **shape** (具体化する、形になる)   in **shape** (健康的な、良い体型の)

My ideas are starting to take **shape**!   ◀▶ out of **shape** (運動不足の)
(自分のアイディアが形になってきた！)

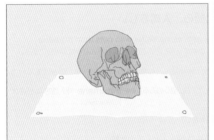 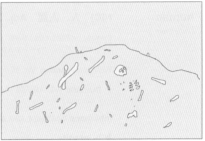

The last couple weeks were pretty exhausting. Our team attended an annual archaeology conference held in Germany, which was exceptional. We then moved to Peru for site excavation the following day. However, we couldn't start our work right away because the permits were still pending approval when we arrived. What a nightmare!

Thankfully, they were finally approved about a week ago, and the result of our excavation has been fairly amazing so far. We found piles of scattered bones with fragments of clothing in the middle of a royal tomb (see the picture above). This could be a victim of human sacrifice or some other tragedy with a higher death toll.

Excavation is a slow, delicate task, so we estimate that we have found roughly half of the bones buried at this site.

We'll give you guys more updates as we make progress, so look out for the next post.

ここ2、3週間は結構しんどかったです。僕のチームはドイツで開催された年に一度の考古学会議に出席して、それは素晴らしかったんですが、その後翌日には遺跡発掘のため、ペルーに移動。しかし、到着したときは許可がまだ承認待ちで、すぐに作業を開始できず。本当に悪夢でした！

幸い、約1週間前に許可がおりまして、今のところ発掘の結果は中々良い感じです。王族の墓の真ん中ではバラバラになった骨の山がいくつか見つかり、衣類の破片も一緒に見つかっています（上の写真参照）。もしかするとこれは人身御供か、多数の死者が出た何らかの悲劇の犠牲者かもしれません。

発掘は時間のかかる、慎重を要する作業で、ここまでで遺跡に埋まっている骨の約半分ほどを発見したと見積もっています。

進捗があればまたアップデートするので、次の投稿もお見逃しなく。

173 exhausting
[ɪgzɑ́:stɪŋ]

Adj.（疲れて）しんどい、ひどく疲れた

▶ **exhausted** [ɪgzɑ́:stɪd] Adj. 疲れきった；（資源などが）使い尽くされた

I'm **exhausted**.（めっちゃ疲れた。）

▶ **exhaust** [ɪgzɑ́:st] V[T] を疲れ果てさせる；を使い尽くす　N[U] 排気ガス　N[C] 排気管

---

174 annual
[ǽnjuəl]

Adj. 年に一度の、年次の

▶ **annually** [ǽnjuəli] Adv. 年に一度、毎年

▶ **biannual** [baɪǽnjuəl] Adj. 年に二度の　= **semiannual** [sèmaɪǽnjuəl]

---

175 conference
[kɑ́:nfərəns]

N[C] 会議

a **conference** call（電話会議）

---

176 exceptional
[ɪksépʃənəl]

Adj. 素晴らしい、優れた；例外的な

▶ **exceptionally** [ɪksépʃənəli] Adv. 格別に、非常に；例外的に

▶ **exception** [ɪksépʃən] N[C] 例外

without **exception**（例外なく）

---

177 excavation
[èkskəvéɪʃən]

N[C/U] 発掘

▶ **excavate** [ékskəveɪt] V[I/T]（〜を）発掘する

---

178 permit
[pərmít]

N[C] 許可（証）　V[T] を認める；を実現可能にする

if time **permits**（もし時間があれば）　= time permitting

▶ **permission** [pərmíʃən] N[U] 許可、認可

---

179 pending
[péndɪŋ]

Prep. 〜を待つ間、〜の間　Adj. 未解決の、申請中の

My visa is still **pending**.（ビザがまだ申請中なんだよね。）

---

180 result
[rɪzʌ́lt]

N[C] 結果　V[I]（〜が原因で）起きる（from sth）

as a **result** of sth（〜の結果）　**result** in sth（〜という結果になる）

---

181 amazing
[əméɪzɪŋ]

Adj. 素晴らしい、驚くべき

▶ **amazingly** [əméɪzɪŋli] Adv. 驚くほど

▶ **amaze** [əméɪz] V[T] をびっくりさせる

▶ **amazed** [əméɪzd] Adj.（〜に）驚いた（at/by sth/sb）

---

182 pile
[paɪl]

N[C] 山　≒ **stack** [stæk]

V[T] を積み上げる　= **pile sth up** [paɪlʌ́p]

183 scattered
[skǽṭərd]

□□□□□□

Adj. バラバラの、散らばった

▶ **scatter** [skǽṭər] V[T] をまき散らす　V[I] 散らばる

▶ **scattering** [skǽṭərɪŋ] N[C] （〜の）点在（of sth）

184 fragment
N. [frǽgmənt]
v. [frǽgment]

□□□□□□

N[C] 破片　**V[I]** 分裂する　**V[T]** を分裂させる

▶ **fragmentation** [frægmentéɪʃən] N[U] 分割、分裂

▶ **fragmented** [frægméntɪd] Adj. 崩壊した

185 tomb
[tu:m]

□□□□□□

N[C] 墓

▶ **tombstone** [túːmstoʊn] N[C] 墓石

186 victim
[víktəm]

□□□□□□

N[C] 犠牲者、被害者、犠牲

▶ **victimize** [víktəmaɪz] V[T] を犠牲者にする

▶ **victimization** [vìktəməzéɪʃən] N[U] 犠牲にすること

187 sacrifice
[sǽkrəfaɪs]

□□□□□□

N[C/U] いけにえ、犠牲　**V[T]** を犠牲にする

human **sacrifice**（人身御供、人間をいけにえとすること）

188 tragedy
[trǽdʒədi]

□□□□□□

N[C/U] 悲劇、惨事

▶ **tragic** [trǽdʒɪk] Adj. 悲惨な　▶ **tragically** [trǽdʒɪkli] Adv. 悲惨に

189 toll
[toʊl]

□□□□□□

N[C] 死者数、けが人の数；通行料、使用料

a death **toll**（死亡者数）

190 task
[tæsk]

□□□□□□

N[C] 作業、タスク

191 roughly
[rʌfli]

□□□□□□

Adv. 約、大体、ざっと；荒く

I spend **roughly** $5 a day on coffee.（私は一日大体5ドルくらいコーヒーに使うんだ。）

▶ **rough** [rʌf] Adj. 大体の；荒い、ざらざらした

▶ **roughen** [rʌfən] V[I] ざらざらになる　V[T] をざらざらにする

192 bury
[béri]

□□□□□□

V[T] を埋める、埋葬する

▶ **burial** [bériəl] N[C/U] 埋葬

Chapter

05

芸術
Art

In essence, the majority of art consists of three classical branches: painting, sculpture, and architecture.

More broadly speaking, the definition of art also includes the deliberate production, compiling, and publication of music, film, dance, literature, and interactive media.

As typified by the debate over graffiti's classification as either art or vandalism, whether or not something is classified as art is often the subject of controversy, particularly in contemporary times. Indeed, some people proclaim that the definition of art is too vague.

This persistent ambiguity in classifying something as art is amplified by subtle differences in what people find aesthetically pleasing and how strictly they define the term.

1 **In** essence, **the** majority **of** art consists of **three** classical branches: painting, sculpture, **and architecture.**

基本的に、芸術の大部分は 3 つの古典的な分野から構成されている。それは、絵画、彫刻、建築である。

majority

---

¹⁹³ **essence**
[ésəns]
☐☐☐☐☐☐

N[U] 本質、根底 **N[C/U]**（植物などの）エッセンス、エキス

The **essence** of a good wine is its ability to age well.（良いワインの本質はその熟成能力にある。）

in **essence**（基本的に、本質的に）　　■ of the **essence**（最も重要な）

Time is **of the essence**.（スピード（時間）が最も重要だよ。）

▶ **essential** Adj.（〜に）/（〜するのに）絶対不可欠な、最も重要な (to/for sth) / (to do)；本質的な
[isénʃəl]

Food is **essential** to life.（食べ物は生命維持に欠かせない。）

Play is **essential** for children's development.（遊ぶことは子供の発育には欠かせない。）

▶ **essentially** [isénʃəli] Adv. 基本的に、本質的に

---

¹⁹⁴ **majority**
[mədʒá:rəti]
☐☐☐☐☐☐

N[S] 大部分、大半、過半数

■ the **majority** (of sth/sb)（（〜の）大部分）

I don't want to go to the beach, but I'll follow **the majority**.
（僕はビーチに行きたくないけど、まぁみんなに合わせるよ。）

◆▶ **minority** N[S] 少数、少数派 N[U] 未成年　▶ **minorities** N[P] 少数民族
[maɪnó:rəti]　　　　　　　　　　　　　　　　[maɪnó:rətiz]

There are a number of ethnic **minority** groups that live in China.
（中国にはたくさんの少数民族が住んでいるんだ。）

▶ **major** [méɪdʒər] Adj. 主な、重要な　N[C]（大学の）専攻

a **major** cause（主な原因）　　　What's your **major**?（大学で何を専攻してるの？）

◆▶ **minor** [máɪnər] あまり重要でない / 未成年者；副専攻

a **minor** problem（あまり重要でない問題）

In Australia, a person under the age of 18 is considered a **minor**.
（オーストラリアでは 18 歳未満の人が未成年とされるんだ。）

195 art
[ɑːrt]

N[U] 芸術、美術、アート　N[P]（歴史や文学などの）人文科学 [-s]

I don't understand modern **art** at all. Am I missing something?
（モダンアートって全然理解できない。なんか見逃してるだけかな？）

▶ **artistic** Adj. 芸術の、芸術的な　　▶ **artistically** Adv. 芸術的に
[ɑːrtístɪk]　　　　　　　　　　　　　　　　[ɑːrtístɪkli]

I think she is **artistically** talented.（彼女って芸術センスに長けてるんだよなぁ。）

▶ **artist** [ɑ́ːrtɪst] N[C] 芸術家、アーティスト

---

196 consist of sth
[kənsístəv]

[PV]　〜から構成される、成る

= **be composed of sth** [biː kəmpóʊzdəv]

= **be made up of sth** [biː meɪdʌ́pəv]

The best hamburgers always **consist of** good quality meat and fresh ingredients.
（最高のハンバーガーはいつも良質なお肉とフレッシュな材料からできてるんだ。）

consist in sth（（本質的なものが）〜に存在する）

---

197 classical
[klǽsɪkəl]

Adj. 古典的な；（音楽などが）クラシックの

I enjoy listening to **classical** music every now and again.（たまにクラシック音楽を聞くのが好き。）

▶ **classic** [klǽsɪk] N[C] 傑作、名作　Adj. 傑作の；典型的な；素晴らしい

Harry Potter is a **classic.**（ハリーポッターは傑作だ。）　　　a **classic** song（傑作曲）

---

198 branch
[bræntʃ]

N[C]　分野；枝；部門；支店

It took me way too long to pick which **branch** of economics to study.
（経済学のどの分野を勉強するか決めるのにとんでもなく時間かかった。）

V[I]　枝分かれする、分岐する

■ **branch** out (into sth)（（〜を）新しく始める）

The tech company has **branched out into** making wearables.
（そのテクノロジー企業はウェアラブル端末の生産を新しく始めた。）

---

199 sculpture
[skʌ́lptʃər]

N[C/U]　彫刻、彫刻作品

I know this **sculpture**. It's *The Thinker*, right?（この彫刻知ってる。『考える人』だよね？）

▶ **sculpt** [skʌlpt] V[I] 彫刻を作る　V[T] を（〜から／〜に）彫刻する（out of/into sth）

Hey look! I **sculpted** this cute dinosaur out of clay.（見て！この可愛い恐竜、粘土から作ったよ。）

▶ **sculpted** [skʌ́lptəd] Adj.（顔立ちなどが彫刻のように）美しい、整った

Oh my god, he's so good-looking. I think he has a perfectly **sculpted** face.
（ヤバっ、あいつ本当にイケメンだなぁ。完璧に整った顔してると思う。）

▶ **sculptural** [skʌ́lptʃərəl] Adj. 彫刻的な　　▶ **sculptor** [skʌ́lptər] N[C] 彫刻家

2 More broadly speaking, the definition of art also includes the deliberate production, compiling, and publication of music, film, dance, literature, and interactive media.

広い意味では、芸術の定義の中には、音楽、映画、ダンス、文学、インタラクティブメディアなどを意図的に制作・編集・出版することも含まれる。

---

200 broadly
[brɔ́ːdli]
☐☐☐☐☐☐

Adv. 広く、大まかに、大体

The website says that TOEFL scores are most **broadly** accepted in foreign universities. （サイトによると TOEFL の点数は海外の大学で最も広く受け入れられているんだって。）

broadly speaking （広い意味では、広く言えば）

▶ **broad** [brɔ́ːd] Adj. （幅や範囲が）広い、大まかな　◄► **narrow** [nérou] 狭い

This oversized T-shirt makes me look so **broad**.
（このオーバーサイズの T シャツ着るとすごい肩幅広く見えるんだよね。）

▶ **broaden** [brɔ́ːdn] V[I] 広くなる　V[T] を広げる　▶ **breadth** [bredθ] N[C/U] 幅、横幅

I want to travel the world to **broaden** my mind. （自分の視野を広げるために世界中を旅したいんだ。）

---

201 definition
[dèfɪníʃən]
☐☐☐☐☐☐

N[C] 定義　**N[U]** （写真や映像の）鮮明度

You say you want to be rich, but what's your **definition** of rich?
（金持ちになりたいって言うけど、金持ちの定義は何？）

▶ **define** [dɪfáɪn] V[T] を定義する、明確にする

Machine learning software is often **defined** as a program whose performance improves with experience.
（機械学習ソフトウェアは、経験と共にパフォーマンスが改善するプログラムだとよく定義される。）

▶ **definitely** Adv. 確実に、絶対に　◄► **indefinitely** 無期限に、不確定に
　[défənətli]　　　　　　　　　　　[ɪndéfənətli]

You should **definitely** follow this guy on Instagram. His photos are amazing.
（この人、インスタ絶対フォローした方がいいよ。彼の写真マジで最高。）

▶ **definite** [défənət] Adj. 確実な　◄► **indefinite** [ɪndéfənət] 無期限の、不確定の

▶ **definitive** [dɪfínətɪv] Adj. 最終的な、決定的な

a **definitive** answer （最終的な答え）　make a **definitive** decision （最終的な決定をする）

202 **deliberate**

Adj. [dɪlíbərət]
V. [dɪlíbəreɪt]

□□□□□□

Adj. 意図的な、故意の

That was a **deliberate** foul! How is that not a red card?
（あれ意図的なファールじゃん！なんでレッドカードじゃないの？）

take **deliberate** action（よく考えた上で行動する）

V[I/T] （～を）熟考する、（陪審員が）審議する

The jurors **deliberated** for about two hours.（陪審員は約2時間審議した。）

▶ **deliberately** [dɪlíbərətli] Adv. わざと、意図的に；慎重に

I'm pretty sure the article misinterpreted the truth **deliberately** to attract public attention.（その記事、きっと世間の関心を集めるためにわざと間違って真実を解釈したんだよ。）

▶ **deliberation** [dɪlìbəréɪʃən] N[U] 熟考；慎重さ N[P] 審議【-s】

203 **compile**

[kəmpáɪl]

□□□□□□

V[T] （資料など）を編集する、集める、作成する

I'm **compiling** a list of my favorite bubble tea shops.
（お気に入りのタピオカティー屋さんのリストを作成中。）

▶ **compilation** [kà:mpəléɪʃən] N[C] 編集物 N[U] 編集すること

204 **publication**

[pʌ̀bləkéɪʃən]

□□□□□□

N[U] 出版、公表、発行 N[C] 出版物

Do you think that the **publication** of newspapers will still occur in the future?
（新聞って将来もまだ発行されてると思う？）

▶ **publish** V[I/T]（～を）出版する、公開する、発行する   ▶ **publisher** N[C] 出版社
[pʌ́blɪʃ]   [pʌ́blɪʃər]

We finally **published** a book online.（ついに本をオンラインで出版した。）

205 **literature**

[líṭərəṭʃər]

□□□□□□

N[U] 文学、文学作品；文献

My favorite type of **literature** is detective fiction.（お気に入りの文学作品のタイプは推理小説です。）

▶ **literary** [líṭəreri] Adj. 文学の   ▶ **literate** [líṭərət] Adj. 読み書きができる

literary knowledge（文学の知識）   **literate** people（読み書きができる人）

▶ **literacy** [líṭərəsi] N[U] 読み書きの能力；（ある特定の分野で必要になる）知識

Over the last six decades or so, the global **literacy** rate has increased by more than 40%.
（ここ60年ほどで、世界の識字率は40%以上増加した。）

▶ **literal** [líṭərəl] Adj. 文字通りの   ▶ **literally** [líṭərəli] Adv. 文字通り、本当に

literal translation   Man, I **literally** have no friends except you.
（直訳）   （ねぇ、俺マジでお前以外友達いないよ。）

206 **media**

[mí:diə]

□□□□□□

N[S/P] メディア、媒体；（TV、ネット、新聞等）マスメディア【the -】

I hate how **media** companies these days focus on clicks and views rather than quality.
（最近のメディア会社って質よりもクリック数とか閲覧数にフォーカスしてて嫌。）

the national **media**（全国メディア）   attract **media** attention（メディアの注目を集める）

3 As typified by the debate over graffiti's classification as either art or vandalism, whether or not something is classified as art is often the subject of controversy, particularly in contemporary times. Indeed, some people proclaim that the definition of art is too vague.

ただ、特に現代では、グラフィティをアートと破壊行為のどちらに分類すべきかという議論によく見られるように、あるものを芸術として分類するかどうかをめぐってよく論争が起きている。実際、芸術の定義が曖昧過ぎるという意見もある。

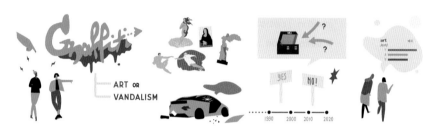

ART or VANDALISM

207 **classify**
[klǽsəfaɪ]
□□□□□□

V[T] を（〜に）分類する（into sth）

I don't get how they **classified** this as being French food.
（何がどうなったらこれがフランス料理に分類されたのか理解不能。）

V[T] （情報や文書など）を機密扱いにする

The government **classified** the documents.（政府はその文書を機密扱いにした。）

▶ **classification** [klæsəfəkéɪʃən] N[U] 分類すること　N[C] 分類、区分、カテゴリー

▶ **classifiable** [klǽsəfaɪəbəl] Adj. 分類可能な

208 **controversy**
[kɑ́:ntrəvɜ:rsi]
□□□□□□

N[C/U] 論争、議論

I secretly love all the drama and **controversy** that's currently happening at work.
（今職場で起きてるドラマと論争、実は結構楽しんでるんだよね。）

▶ **controversial** [kɑ̀:ntrəvɜ́:rʃəl] Adj. 物議をかもす、議論の的になる

Religion can be such a **controversial** topic, so you should be careful when talking about it.（宗教はものすごい物議をかもすこともある話題だから、話すときは気を付けた方が良いよ。）

209 **particularly**
[pərtíkjələrli]
□□□□□□

Adv. 特に、とりわけ　= in particular　= especially
[ɪn pərtíkjələr]　[ɪspéʃəli]

I don't like reptiles, and I find snakes **particularly** creepy.
（爬虫類は好きじゃないし、特にヘビは気持ち悪い。）

▶ **particular** Adj. 特有の、独特の；（〜についての好みが）うるさい (about sth)
[pərtíkjələr]　N[P] 詳細【-s】

Some Japanese English learners are very **particular** about pronunciation.
（日本人の英語学習者には発音にものすごいうるさい人がいる。）

210 contemporary
[kəntémpəreri]
☐☐☐☐☐☐

Adj. 現代の；（〜と）同時代の、同時期の（with sth/sb）

I've gotten into **contemporary** music recently, and I'm addicted to it.
（最近現代音楽にはまり始めて、今じゃもう中毒になってるよ。）

N[C] （誰かと）同じ時代に生きていた人（of sb）

John Fletcher was a **contemporary** of William Shakespeare.
（ジョン・フレッチャーはウィリアム・シェイクスピアと同じ時期に生きていた。）

▶ **contemporaneous** [kəntèmpəréɪniəs] Adj.（〜と）同時代の、同時期の（with sth）

▶ **contemporaneously** [kəntèmpəréɪniəsli] Adv.（〜と）同時代に、同時期に

contemporary vs **contemporaneous** どちらも「同時期の」という意味を持ちますが、contemporary は人や小規模の団体が同時期に活発に活動していたことを表し（例：Beethoven and Mozart were contemporary musicians.）、contemporaneous は出来事、社会運動、傾向などが同時期に起きていたことを表します（例：The rise of rock and roll was contemporaneous with the economic growth of the 1950s.）。

211 time
[taɪm]
☐☐☐☐☐☐

N[P] （歴史上の）時代、年代【the -s】 **N[U]** 時間、時

I think we live in pretty interesting **times**.（僕たちってかなり面白い時代に生きていると思う。）

ancient **times**（古代）　medieval **times**（中世）　modern **times**（現代）

N[C/U] （一定の）期間；時期 **N[C]** 〜回 **V[T]** の時間を測る

a long **time**（長い間）　a good **time**（to do）（（〜するのに）いい時期）

▶ **timely** [táɪmli] Adj. タイムリーな　▶ **timing** [táɪmɪŋ] N[C/U] タイミング

a **timely** topic（タイムリーな話題）　in a **timely** manner（すみやかに、タイミング良く）

with perfect **timing**（完璧なタイミングで）

212 proclaim
[proʊkléɪm]
☐☐☐☐☐☐

V[T] を公言する、宣言する、明白に示す

Of course the lawyer's going to **proclaim** her client's innocence.
（もちろん弁護士はクライアントの無罪を明白に示すだろうね。）

▶ **proclamation** [prà:kləméɪʃən] N[C/U] 宣言、発表

the Emancipation **Proclamation**（奴隷解放宣言*）
*1863年1月にアメリカ合衆国大統領であったリンカーンが命じた宣言

接頭語 pro-「前へ」という意味の接頭語で、「前へ（= pro）発言する（= claim）」から「公言する、宣言する」という意味になります。他には proceed（前に進む）や prolong（引き延ばせる）などがあります。

213 vague
[veɪg]
☐☐☐☐☐☐

Adj. 曖昧な、ぼんやりした

I only have a **vague** idea of what I want to do in the future.
（将来何したいかに関してはぼんやりした考えしかないんだよね。）

▶ **vaguely** Adv. 曖昧に、なんとなく、ぼんやりと　▶ **vagueness** N[U] 曖昧さ
[véɪgli]　　　　　　　　　　　　　　　　　　　[véɪgnəs]

I **vaguely** remember my childhood.（子供の時のことはなんとなく覚えてるよ。）

4 This persistent ambiguity in classifying something as art is amplified by subtle differences in what people find aesthetically pleasing and how strictly they define the term.

こうした、あるものを芸術として分類する際に常に伴う曖昧さは、人が何に対して美的な喜びを覚えるか、そして芸術という言葉をどれくらい厳密に定義するかといった、微妙な違いによって増幅してしまう。

---

214 **persistent**
[pərsístənt]

Adj. いつまでも続く、しつこい

George is way too **persistent** with his personal questions.
（ジョージはプライベートな質問をしつこくしすぎ。）

▶ **persistently** [pərsístəntli] Adv. いつまでも、しつこく

My ex **persistently** texts me. So annoying. (元カノがしつこくメッセージ送ってくる。めっちゃうざい。)

▶ **persist** V[I] ずっと続く；しつこく〜する ▶ **persistence** N[U] 粘り強さ、こだわり
　[pərsíst]　　　　　　　　　　(in doing)　　　[pərsístəns]

Persistence pays off. （粘り強さは報われる。）

---

215 **ambiguity**
[æmbɪgjúːəti]

N[U] 曖昧さ、不明確さ　**N[C]** 曖昧な表現・言葉

The **ambiguity** of my role at work really demotivates me.
（職場での自分の役割の曖昧さのせいで本当にモチベ下がる。）

▶ **ambiguous** [æmbígjuəs] Adj. 曖昧な、多義的な

▶ **ambiguously** [æmbígjuəsli] Adv. 曖昧に、多義的に

ambiguous vs **vague**　どちらも「曖昧な」という意味を持ちますが ambiguous は具体的ではあるものの複数の異なる意味で解釈ができるものを指します。例えば Look at the dog with one eye. という文章は「あの目が一つしかない犬を見て」とも「片目であの犬を見て」とも捉えることができ、これは vague ではありませんが ambiguous な文章と言えます。一方 vague は He is very tall. のような、背が高いと言ってもどれくらい高いのか不明瞭な程度の曖昧さを意味します。この二つはネイティブも混同することがあります。

---

216 **amplify**
[æmpləfaɪ]

V[T] を増幅させる、増大する；を詳述する

Social media **amplifies** the influence of celebrities a lot.
（ソーシャルメディアは有名人の影響力をものすごい増幅させるんだ。）

▶ **amplification** N[U] 増幅、増大
[æmpləfəkéɪʃən]

▶ **amplifier** N[C]（音楽用の）アンプ、増幅器
[æmpləfaɪər]

---

217 subtle
[sʌ́tl]
☐☐☐☐☐☐

Adj. 微妙な、わずかな、さりげない

■ in a **subtle** way/manner（さりげなく）

Nancy's really good at throwing shade **in a subtle way**.
（ナンシーってさりげなく人の悪口を言うのが本当に上手だよね。）

Silver accessories are a nice way to introduce color **in a subtle manner**.
（シルバーのアクセサリーはさりげなく色を足せる良い方法だと思う。）

▶ **subtly** [sʌ́təli] Adv. 微妙に、わずかに、さりげなく

▶ **subtlety** [sʌ́tl̩ti] N[U] 微妙さ　N[C] 微妙な点、微妙なニュアンス、繊細さ

the **subtleties** of language（言語の微妙なニュアンス）

発音注意！ subtle には b が入っていますがこの b は発音しません。他にも debt（借金）や doubt（疑う）など t の前の b を発音しないケースがあるため注意しましょう。

---

218 pleasing
[plíːzɪŋ]
☐☐☐☐☐☐

Adj. 喜びを与える、心地よい

I'm not usually a heavy metal kind of person, but when I'm angry I suddenly find it very **pleasing**.（普段へビメタ聞くタイプじゃないんだけど、怒ってるときに聞くと急に心地よくなるんだよね。）

▶ **please** [pliːz] V[T] を喜ばせる、満足させる　Adv. お願いします、どうか

Please give me two minutes.（2分下さい。）

▶ **pleasure** [pléʒər] N[U] 喜び、楽しさ　N[C] 楽しみ

---

219 strictly
[stríktli]
☐☐☐☐☐☐

Adv. 厳密に、厳しく

Smoking is **strictly** prohibited in this area.（このエリアでの喫煙は厳しく禁止されています。）

▶ **strict** [strɪkt] Adj. 厳密な、厳しい　▶ **strictness** [stríktnəs] N[U] 厳密さ、厳しさ

---

220 term
[tɜːrm]
☐☐☐☐☐☐

N[C] 言葉、用語

Is there a **term** to describe what you're doing right now?
（あなたが今やってることを表す言葉はありますか？）

N[C] 期間、学期

in the long/short **term**（長期的 / 短期的には）

N[P] 条件【-s】

terms of employment（雇用条件）　　**terms** and conditions（諸条件、契約条件）

■ in **terms** of sth（〜の点で、〜の点から）　be on good **terms**（with sb）（（〜と）良い間柄で）

You should view the financial results **in terms of** profit.
（財務情報は利益の点から見た方がいいよ。）

MoAM x 100

Picasso
+Monet

To **celebrate** our gallery's 100 year **anniversary**, we have **plenty** of **splendid** exhibitions **lined up** for you over the next year. Here are two that we have organized so far.

Picasso JAN - MAR   For three months, the largest-ever collection of Picasso's **legendary** works will take up **residence** at our gallery. The pieces will span his entire career, from the Blue Period, characterized by the use of a **vivid** cool pallet, to his **iconic** abstract works.

Monet MAY - AUG   In May, we will be transforming and **furnishing** a **carved**-out section of the gallery. The **aesthetics** of this **luxurious** space will **evoke** a sense of tranquility and complement the Monet exhibition. This exhibition will **comprise** paintings from the late period of the artist's life. Paintings **crafted** during this period **depict** the idyllic garden of his Giverny house and **sealed** his status as the world's most **eminent** Impressionist artist.

Register your interest for these exhibits now to avoid disappointment.

MoAM Modern Art Museum

ギャラリー100周年を祝って、来年は数多くの素晴らしい展示会をみなさまにご用意しております。現時点では以下２つをご用意しております。

ピカソ 1月 - 3月   3か月間、ピカソの伝説的な作品の過去最大のコレクションがわたしたちの美術館の住人となります。作品は、鮮やかな寒色が特徴的な「青の時代」のものから、象徴的な抽象画まで、彼の生涯にわたります。

モネ 5月 - 8月   5月には、ギャラリーの彫刻がほどこされた区域を変貌させ、整備いたします。贅沢なスペースの美しさが心を落ち着かせ、モネ展を引き立ててくれることでしょう。本展覧会はモネ後期の作品群からなる予定です。この時代に制作されたジヴェルニーの自宅の牧歌的な庭を描いた絵画は、世界で最も著名な印象派画家としてのモネの地位を確実なものとしました。

これらの展示会にご興味がある方は、お見逃しのないよう今のうちにお申し付けください。

221 **celebrate**
[séləbreɪt]

V[T] を祝う　V[I] お祝いする

▶ **celebration** [sèləbréɪʃən] N[U] お祝い、祝賀　N[C] 祭典、祝賀会　N[C/U] 称賛

▶ **celebratory** [sèləbréɪṭəri] Adj. お祝いの

---

222 **anniversary**
[ænəvə́:rsəri]

N[C] 周年、記念日

a wedding **anniversary**（結婚記念日）

---

223 **plenty**
[plénṭi]

N[U] たくさん　Adv. 大いに、とても

plenty of sth/sb（たくさんの〜）

▶ **plentiful** [plénṭɪfəl] Adj. 豊富な、有り余るほどの

---

224 **splendid**
[spléndɪd]

Adj. 素晴らしい

▶ **splendidly** [spléndɪdli] Adv. 素晴らしく

---

225 **line sth up**
[laɪnʌ́p]

[PV] を用意する、手配する

▶ **line-up** N[C] [láɪnəp]（商品の）ラインアップ；レギュラー選手；顔ぶれ

---

226 **legendary**
[lédʒənderi]

Adj. 伝説的な、伝説上の

▶ **legend** [lédʒənd] N[C/U] 伝説　N[C] 伝説的な人

You're a **legend**!（お前、最高！）

---

227 **residence**
[rézədəns]

N[U] 居住　N[C] 住宅

take up **residence**（仕人となる、居を定める）

▶ **resident** [rézədənt] N[C] 住民　Adj. 居住している

▶ **residential** [rèzədénʃəl] Adj. 住宅の、居住の

▶ **reside** [rɪzáɪd] V[I]（〜に）居住する（in sth）

---

228 **vivid**
[vívɪd]

Adj. 鮮やかな、鮮明な

▶ **vividly** [vívɪdli] Adv. 鮮やかに、鮮明に

▶ **vividness** [vívɪdnəs] N[U] 鮮やかさ、鮮明さ

---

229 **iconic**
[aɪká:nɪk]

Adj. 象徴的な、偶像的な

▶ **icon** [áɪkɑ:n] N[C] 象徴、偶像

---

230 **furnish**
[fə́:rnɪʃ]

V[T] に（家具などを）備え付ける（with sth）；（情報など）を提供する

▶ **furniture** [fə́:rnɪtʃər] N[U] 家具

▶ **furnished** [fə́:rnɪʃt] Adj. 家具付きの

I'm looking for a **furnished** apartment.（家具付きのアパート探してる。）

231 carve
[kɑːrv]

V[T] を彫る、彫刻する

carve sth out（〜を彫刻する）

▶ **carving** [kɑ́ːrvɪŋ] N[U] 彫刻　N[C] 彫刻作品

---

232 aesthetics
[esθéṭɪks]

N[U] 美学

▶ **aesthetic** [esθéṭɪk] Adj. 美しい、美学の　N[C] 美意識、美的センス

an Instagram **aesthetic**（（フィードなどにおける）インスタの美的センス）

▶ **aesthetically** [esθéṭɪkli] Adv. 美的に、美学的に

---

233 luxurious
[lʌɡʒúriəs]

Adj. 贅沢な、豪華な

▶ **luxuriously** [lʌɡʒúriəsli]Adv. 贅沢に　▶ **luxuriousness** [lʌɡʒúriəsnəs] N[U] 贅沢さ

▶ **luxury** [lʌ́kʃəri] N[U] 贅沢　N[C] 贅沢品

Why are **luxury** fashion brands so expensive?（高級ファッションブランドってなんでこんな高いの？）

---

234 evoke
[ɪvóʊk]

V[T]（感情など）を呼び起こす、引き起こす、誘い出す

▶ **evocative** [ɪvɑ́ːkəṭɪv] Adj.（感情を）呼び起こすような

▶ **evocation** [ìːvəkéɪʃən] N[C/U] 呼び起こすこと、喚起

---

235 comprise
[kəmpráɪz]

V[T] から成る；を構成する、占める

---

236 craft
[kræft]

V[T] を制作する　N[C] 工芸；（専門的な）技能

▶ **craftsman** [kræftsmən] N[C] 職人　▶ **craftsmanship** [kræftsmənʃɪp] N[U] 職人技

---

237 depict
[dɪpíkt]

V[T] を描く、表現する　= **portray** [pɔːrtréɪ]

▶ **depiction** [dɪpíkʃən] N[C/U] 描写、表現

---

238 seal
[siːl]

V[T] を確実なものにする、決定的にする；をふさぐ、密閉する

⟷ **unseal** [ʌnsíːl] を開封する

N[C]（封をするための）シール；公印；アザラシ

▶ **sealed** [siːld] Adj. 密閉された

---

239 eminent
[émənənt]

Adj. 著名な、有名な

▶ **eminently** [émənəntli] Adv. 著しく　▶ **eminence** [émənəns] N[U] 著名、卓越

---

240 register
[rédʒəstər]

V[T] を表明する　V[I/T]（〜を）登録する　V[I]（〜の）記憶に残る（with sb）

register one's interest（興味があると表明する）

▶ **registration** [rèdʒəstréɪʃən] N[C/U] 登録

06

建築
Architecture

Architecture is the process and outcome of planning, designing, and constructing buildings as well as other artificial structures.

Architectural styles differ widely among various geographical locations as a result of the influence of history, culture, and climate.

It is interesting to note that structures have become much more complex over the last few decades, reflected in the remarkable increase in the number of spectacular and magnificent buildings with regionally specific designs. This is exemplified by buildings such as The Shard in London.

Some of the key causes behind this increased complexity are advancements in energy, building materials, and construction methods, and workers becoming more proficient.

1

Architecture **is the** process **and** outcome **of** planning**, designing, and** constructing **buildings as well as other** artificial structures**.**

建築とは、建物や人工建造物の計画、設計、建設の過程と、その結果のことである。

241 architecture
[ɑ́ːrkətektʃər]

N[U]　建築、建築学、建築様式

Wow! This is the coolest **architecture** I've ever seen. (うわ！こんなカッコいい建築見たことない。)

▶ **architectural** Adj. 建築の、建築学の
[ɑ̀ːrkətéktʃərəl]

▶ **architect** N[C] 建築家、建築士
[ɑ́ːrkətèkt]

242 process
[prɑ́ːses]

N[C]　過程、プロセス、工程

The **process** behind making beer is actually really interesting.
(ビール製造の裏にある過程って実際めちゃくちゃ面白いよ。)

V[T]　を処理する、（食品など）を加工する

■ in the **process** of doing（〜しようとしているところ）

I'm **in the process of** buying a new house. (新しい家を買おうとしているところなんだよね。)

processed food（加工食品）

▶ **procession** [prəséʃən] N[C/U]（人の）行列

a wedding **procession**（婚礼の行列）

243 outcome
[áʊtkʌm]

N[C]　結果、結末

I don't care how you do it as long as you achieve the right **outcome**.
(ちゃんとした結果を達成できるなら別にどうやっても良いよ。)

244 plan
[plæn]

V[I/T]　（〜を）計画する、予定する

■ **plan** for sth（〜に向けて予定を立てる）

Planning for our Kyoto trip is taking ages because I have to do all of it myself.
(京都旅行の計画立てるのすごい時間かかってる。全部自分でやらないといけないからね。)

■ **plan** to do sth/on doing（〜する予定だ、〜するつもりだ）

I'm **planning to** study in Australia next year. (来年はオーストラリアで勉強する予定。)

N[C]　計画、予定；見取り図

make a **plan** for a trip（旅行の計画を立てる）　　　go according to **plan**（計画通りにいく）

▶ **planner** [plǽnər] N[C] 計画する人、プランナー；スケジュール帳

▶ **planned**　Adj. 計画された、予定された　　↔ **unplanned**　計画外の、予定外の
　[plǽnd]　　　　　　　　　　　　　　　　　[ʌnplǽnd]

a daily **planner**（(日別の) スケジュール帳）　　a **planned** economy（計画経済）

---

245 **construct**
[kənstrʌ́kt]
☐☐☐☐☐☐

V[T]　を建設する、構築する　　↔ **deconstruct** [di:kənstrʌ́kt] を解体する

You need to show me how you want the website to look before I can **construct** it.
（サイト構築する前にどういう感じのサイトにしてほしいか言ってもらう必要があるよ。）

▶ **constructive** [kənstrʌ́ktɪv] Adj. 建設的な、前向きな

I appreciate your **constructive** feedback.（建設的なフィードバックをくれて本当にありがとう。）

▶ **constructively** [kənstrʌ́ktɪvli] Adv. 建設的に

▶ **constructor** N[C] 建設者、建設業者　　▶ **construction** N[U] 建設、工事 N[C] 建造物
　[kənstrʌ́ktər]　　　　　　　　　　　　　[kənstrʌ́kʃən]

under **construction**（建設中の）

---

246 **artificial**
[ɑ̀:rtəfíʃəl]
☐☐☐☐☐☐

Adj.　人工的な、人造の、模造の

I hate playing soccer on this **artificial** grass because it's so slippery in the rain.
（この人工芝、雨の日はすごい滑るからここでサッカーするの本当に嫌いなんだよね。）

artificial intelligence (AI)（人工知能）　　**artificial** flowers（造花）

▶ **artifice** [ɑ́:rtəfɪs] N[C/U] 策略、ずるさ

by **artifice**（巧妙な策略によって）

---

247 **structure**
[strʌ́ktʃər]
☐☐☐☐☐☐

N[C]　建造物、建物　**N[C/U]**　構造、骨組み、構成

Our new organizational **structure** is too complicated for me to understand.
（うちの新しい組織構造、複雑すぎて私には理解できないよ。）

V[T]　を構成する、組み立てる

a well-**structured** movie（構成がよくできた映画）

▶ **structural**　Adj. 構造上の、構成の　▶ **restructure**　V[T]（〜を）再構築する、作り直す
　[strʌ́ktʃərəl]　　　　　　　　　　　[ri:strʌ́ktʃər]

This building has many **structural** defects, such as cracks on the walls and water seepage.　（この建物、壁のひび割れとか水漏れとか構造上の欠陥がたくさんある。）

▶ **restructuring** [ri:strʌ́ktʃərɪŋ] N[C/U]（組織などの）再構築、再編成

リストラは和製英語？　日本で「人の解雇」を意味するリストラですが、これは再構築を意味する restructuring から来ている和製英語で、英語において解雇という意味はありません。しかし、実際会社 の restructuring は人員削減を伴うことが多く、間接的にそれを意味することはあります。

2 Architectural styles differ widely among various geographical locations as a result of the influence of history, culture, and climate.

建築様式は歴史や文化、気候の影響を受けるため、結果として地理的な位置による差が非常に大きい。

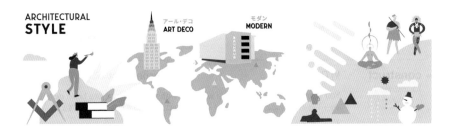

ARCHITECTURAL STYLE

アール・デコ ART DECO

モダン MODERN

---

248 differ

[dífər]

▢▢▢▢▢▢

V[I] （〜と）異なる、違う（from sth/sb）

How does this car **differ** from last year's model? (この車って去年のとどう違うの？)

▶ **different** [dífərənt] Adj. （〜と）異なった、違った（from sth/sb）

▶ **differently** [dífərəntli] Adv. 異なって、違って

There are quite a few words that Brits and Americans say **differently**.
(イギリス人とアメリカ人が違った言い方をする言葉はかなりたくさんある。)

▶ **difference** [dífərəns] N[C/U] 違い、相違

make a big **difference** (to sth) ((〜に) 大きな違いを生む)

---

249 geographical

[dʒìəgræfíkəl]

▢▢▢▢▢▢▢

Adj. 地理的な　= **geographic** [dʒìəgræfɪk]

The only **geographical** difference between these two areas is their elevation.
(この二つの地域の唯一の地理的な違いは高度です。)

▶ **geography** [dʒiɑ́:grəfi] N[U] 地理、地理学

---

250 location

[loʊkéɪʃən]

▢▢▢▢▢▢

N[C/U] 位置、場所

Can you send me the **location** of the karaoke place?(そのカラオケの場所送ってくれない？)

▶ **locate** [lóʊkeɪt] [loʊkéɪt] V[T] を見つける、に設置する　V[I] 本拠地を置く

Can anyone help me **locate** autosaved files?
(誰か自動保存されたファイル見つけるの手伝ってくれたりしない？)

■ **be located** (in/near sth) ((〜に / 〜の近くに) 位置している、ある)

Our office **is located in** New York. (私たちのオフィスはニューヨークにあります。)

▶ **local** [lóʊkəl] Adj. 地元の、現地の　N[C] 地元の人、現地の人

I went to a **local** school.
(私は地元の学校に行ったんだ。)

This restaurant is popular with **locals**.
(このレストランは地元の人に人気があるんだ。)

▶ **locally** [lóʊkəli] Adv. 地元で、現地で

251 influence
[ínfluəns]
☐☐☐☐☐☐

N[C/U] 影響　N[C] 影響を与えるもの・人

■ have an **influence** (on sth)（(〜に) 影響を与える）

That teacher **had a** significantly positive **influence on** my life.
（あの先生は自分の人生にものすごく良い影響を与えてくれたんだ。）

V[T] に影響を与える

be **influenced** (by sth)（(〜に) 影響を受ける）

▶ **influential** Adj. 影響力のある、有力な
[ìnfluénʃəl]

▶ **influencer** N[C] 影響力のある人
[ínfluənsər]　インフルエンサー

---

252 history
[hístəri]
☐☐☐☐☐☐

N[C/U] 歴史　N[U] 歴史学

To me, **history** just seems like a jumble of names and events.
（自分にとっては歴史ってただ名前と出来事がごちゃまぜになってるようにしか見えない。）

N[U] 過去のこと、過去の人　N[C] 経歴、履歴

I'm not seeing Ben anymore. He's **history**.（ベンとはもう付き合ってないよ。もう過去の人。）

a career/medical **history**（職歴 / 病歴）　sb's browser/browsing **history**（(〜の) 閲覧履歴）

▶ **historical** Adj. 歴史的な、過去の
[hıstɔ́ːrɪkəl]

▶ **historic** Adj. 歴史上重要な
[hıstɔ́ːrɪk]

historical data（過去のデータ）　**historic** buildings（歴史上重要な建物）

---

253 culture
[kʌ́ltʃər]
☐☐☐☐☐☐

N[C/U] 文化　N[U]（細菌や細胞の）培養　V[T] を培養する

Japan has a fascinating **culture** unlike any other.
（日本は他とは違った魅力的な文化を持っている。）

▶ **cultural** [kʌ́ltʃərəl] Adj. 文化的な　▶ **culturally** [kʌ́ltʃərəli] Adv. 文化的に

▶ **cultured** Adj. 教養のある　↔ **uncultured** 教養のない
[kʌ́ltʃərd]　　　　　　　　　[ʌnkʌ́ltʃərd]

a **cultural** exchange program（文化交流プログラム）　a **cultured** person（教養のある人）

---

254 climate
[kláɪmət]
☐☐☐☐☐☐

N[C/U] 気候　N[C]（特定の時代に存在する）風潮、環境

I don't mind the heat, but I can't stand cold **climates**.（暑いのは大丈夫だけど、寒い気候は無理。）

climate change（気候変動）

a tropical/temperate/dry/cold **climate**（熱帯 / 温帯 / 乾燥 / 寒冷気候）

▶ **acclimatize** [əkláɪmətaɪz] V[I]（(〜に) 慣れる（to sth）　V[T] を慣れさせる

= **acclimate** [ǽkləmeɪt]

3

It is interesting to note that structures have become much more complex over the last few decades, reflected in the remarkable increase in the number of spectacular and magnificent buildings with regionally specific designs. This is exemplified by buildings such as The Shard in London.

そして興味深いことに、建築構造はここ数十年で一層複雑化してきており、これは地域ごとに独自のデザイン性を持つ、見事で壮大な建物が著しく増えてきていることに表れている。こうした建物の例には、ロンドンの「ザ・シャード」などがある。

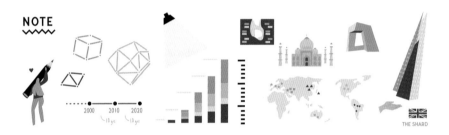

---

255 note
[noʊt]
□□□□□□

V[T] に気付く、注目する；に言及する

I think it's pretty important to **note** that not everything happens how you want it to happen.
(何でも自分の思い通りにいくわけじゃないことに気付くのは、結構大事だと思う。)

it is interesting to note that + sentence   as (is) noted above
(〜であることは興味深い)   (上記のように)

N[C] 手紙；注釈；音、音符　**N[P]** メモ、記録【-s】

■ take **notes**（メモを取る）

Do you think I should **take notes** during an interview?
(面接中ってノート取った方が良いと思う？)

▶ **notable** Adj. 注目に値する、有名な   ▶ **notably** Adv. 特に、顕著に
[nóʊṭəbəl]   [nóʊṭəbli]

Natsume Soseki is one of the most **notable** writers in Japan.
(夏目漱石は日本で最も有名な作家の一人だよ。)

---

256 complex
Adj. [kɑːmpléks]
N. [kɑ́ːmpleks]
□□□□□□

Adj. 複雑な、複合の　⟷ **simple** [símpəl] シンプルな、単純な

Don't you think Andrew has a really **complex** and unique personality?
(アンドリューは本当に複雑でユニークな個性を持ってると思わない？)

N[C] 複合施設；嫌悪感、強迫観念

a shopping **complex**（ショッピングセンター（= a shopping mall, a shopping center））

▶ **complexity** N[U] 複雑なこと   ▶ **complexities** N[P] 複雑さ
[kəmpléksəṭi]   [kəmpléksəṭiz]

257 decade
[dékeɪd]
☐☐☐☐☐☐

N[C] 10 年間

I've been doing the same boring job for almost a **decade** now.
(同じつまらない仕事を続けて、もうかれこれ 10 年。)

100 年間は century [séntʃəri]、1000 年間は millennium [mɪléniəm] と言います。

---

258 remarkable
[rɪmáːrkəbəl]
☐☐☐☐☐☐

Adj. 著しい、注目すべき、驚くべき

Finishing a marathon in three hours is good but not really **remarkable**.
(マラソンを 3 時間で完走するのは立派だけど、別に注目に値するようなものでもない。)

▶ **remarkably** [rɪmáːrkəbli] Adv. 著しく、目立って、驚くほど

Your dad looks **remarkably** young for 60. (君のお父さん、60 歳にしては驚くほど若く見えるよ。)

▶ **remark** [rɪmáːrk] V[I/T] （意見などを）述べる、発言する（on sth） N[C] 意見、発言

His **remarks** are unacceptable. (彼の発言は受け入れられないよ。)

---

259 spectacular
[spektǽkjələr]
☐☐☐☐☐☐

Adj. 見事な、目を見張るような、素晴らしい、華やかな

The rooms at that new five-star hotel are **spectacular**. (あの新しい 5 つ星ホテルの部屋、華やかだよ。)

spectacular economic growth (目覚ましい経済成長)

a **spectacular** view (目を見張るような景色)

▶ **spectacularly** [spektǽkjələrli] Adv. 見事に、素晴らしく、華やかに

a **spectacularly** beautiful city (素晴らしく美しい街)

▶ **spectacle** [spéktəkəl] N[C/U] 見ごたえのある光景 N[C] 見せ物、ショー

The show was a **spectacle**. (ショーは見ごたえがあったよ。)

■ make a **spectacle** of oneself ((視線を集めて) 恥をかく)

She **made a spectacle of herself** by screaming at the waiters.
(彼女はウェイターにあたって恥をかいたんだ。)

▶ **spectator** [spektéɪtər] N[C] （ショーなどの）観客、見物人

---

260 magnificent
[mæɡnífəsənt]
☐☐☐☐☐☐

Adj. 壮大な、雄大な、見事な、（質などが）素晴らしい

The new speakers I got over the weekend sound **magnificent**.
(週末に買った新しいスピーカー、音質がすごく良いんだ。)

That was a **magnificent** goal! (見事なゴールでした！)

▶ **magnificently** Adv. 壮大に、見事に   ▶ **magnificence** N[U] 壮大さ、雄大さ
  [mæɡnífəsəntli]   [mæɡnífəsəns]

---

261 regionally
[ríːdʒənəli]
☐☐☐☐☐☐

Adv. 地域的に

This curry shop uses only fresh, **regionally** produced ingredients.
(このカレー屋さんは地元の新鮮な食材のみを使ってるんだ。)

▶ **regional** [ríːdʒənəl] Adj. 地域の、地方の ▶ **region** [ríːdʒən] N[C] 地域、地方

Champagne is one of the main wine growing **regions** of France.
(シャンパーニュはフランスの主要なワイン生産地域の一つです。)

4 Some of the key causes behind this increased complexity are advancements in energy, building materials, and construction methods, and workers becoming more proficient.

このように建築構造の複雑さが増した主な原因としては、エネルギー、建築資材、建築方法の進歩、そして熟練労働者が増えたことなどが挙げられる。

262 **key**
[ki:]
☐☐☐☐☐☐

Adj. 主要な、重要な、鍵となる

Laura's really the **key** person on this project.
(ローラはこのプロジェクトで本当に重要な人なんだよね。)

N[C] 鍵、キー；（音の）調

■ the **key** (to sth)（（〜を実現するための）鍵）

Learning a lot of vocabulary is **the key to** improving your English.
(たくさんの語彙を学ぶことが英語力を上げるための鍵だよ。)

263 **cause**
[kɑːz]
☐☐☐☐☐☐

N[C/U] 原因、理由、要因 **N[C]** 主義、主張、運動

What's the root **cause** of global warming?（地球温暖化の根本的な原因って何？）

cause and effect（因果関係） for a good **cause**（大義名分の下で、正当な理由で）

V[T] を引き起こす

■ **cause** sb trouble（〜に迷惑をかける） **cause** sth/sb to do（sth/sb に〜させる）

Sorry to **cause** you a lot of **trouble**.（たくさん迷惑かけてごめんね。）

▶ **causal** [kɑ́ːzəl] Adj. 因果関係がある、原因となる

a **causal** relationship between A and B（A と B の因果関係）

because の語源 会話の中では because の意味で cause を使うことも多く、この時の発音は [kəz] となります。

264 **increase**
V. [ɪnkríːs]
N. [ínkriːs]
☐☐☐☐☐☐

V[T] を増やす、上げる **V[I]** 増える、上がる

Sorry, I won't be able to **increase** your wages this year.（ごめん、今年は君の賃金上げられないいわ。）

My electricity bill has **increased** by about 20%.（電気代が 20% くらい上がったよ。）

N[C/U] 増加、上昇

an **increase** of 15% （15%の増加）   an **increase** in sales （売上の増加）

↔ **decrease** を減らす / 減る / 減少、低下
V. [dɪkríːs] **N.** [díːkriːs]

▶ **increasing** [ɪnkríːsɪŋ] Adj. ますます多くの

An **increasing** number of people are now using the internet to find jobs.
（ますます多くの人が仕事探しにネットを使っている。）

▶ **increasingly** [ɪnkríːsɪŋli] Adv. ますます

---

265 **advancement**
[ədvǽnsmənt]
☐☐☐☐☐☐

N[C/U] 進歩、発展、前進   **N[U]** （キャリアの）昇進

Opportunities for career **advancement** only come up if you have the right qualifications. （キャリアを前進させる機会は、適切な資格を持ってる場合にのみやってくる。）

▶ **advance** V[I] 進歩する、前進する   ▶ **advanced** Adj. 進歩した；上級の
[ədvǽns]   V[T] を前進させる、促進する   [ədvǽnst]

an **advanced** course （上級者向けコース）

---

266 **energy**
[énərdʒi]
☐☐☐☐☐☐

N[U] エネルギー、元気、活力

Misato brings really good **energy** to the team.
（ミサトはチームに本当に良い活力をもたらしてくれるよ。）

▶ **energetic** [ènərdʒétɪk] Adj. エネルギッシュな、活動的な

This band is so **energetic**. （このバンドってすごいエネルギッシュだよね。）

▶ **energize** [énərdʒaɪz] V[T] にエネルギーを与える、を元気づける

I feel **energized** when I hear this song. （この曲聞くと元気になる。）

---

267 **method**
[méθəd]
☐☐☐☐☐☐

N[C] 方法、方式、手段、メソッド

Mike told me that he'd found the perfect **method** to pick up girls, but he failed right in front of me. （マイクが女の子をナンパする完璧な方法を見つけたって言ってたんだけど、目の前で失敗してた。）

▶ **methodology** N[C/U] 方法論   ▶ **methodical** Adj. 順序立った、整然とした
[mèθədáːlədʒi]   [məθáːdɪkəl]

---

268 **proficient**
[prəfíʃənt]
☐☐☐☐☐☐

Adj. 熟練した、堪能な、上手な

Can you give me some tips on how to become more **proficient** in English?
（どうやったらもっと英語がうまくなるかアドバイスくれない？）

▶ **proficiently** [prəfíʃəntli] Adv. 熟練して、堪能に、上手に

▶ **proficiency** [prəfíʃənsi] N[U] 熟練、熟達

language **proficiency** （言語熟達度）

FROM EYESORE TO MUST-SEE:
THE EIFFEL TOWER'S TRANSFORMATION

The world-renowned Eiffel Tower, located in Paris, France, is named after Gustave Eiffel, whose company designed and constructed the tower. Construction commenced in 1887 and was completed in 1889, and it remained the tallest man-made structure in the world until it was surpassed by the Chrysler Building, built in 1930. It was initially held by numerous critics to be an eyesore and a calamity, but this resistance gradually faded over time. Today, it is cherished, being widely praised as a national treasure and acknowledged as a perpetual and iconic symbol of France's outstanding art, culture, and industrial might. Much of the fame and prestige it commands is derived from its instantly-recognizable silhouette, along with other notable features such as a three-tiered structure, wrought-iron construction, and lattice pattern.

目障りから必見へ:
エッフェル塔の変貌

フランス・パリに位置する世界的名所、エッフェル塔は、塔の設計および建設を手掛けた会社の代表ギュスターヴ・エッフェルにちなんで名付けられた。建設は1887年に開始され、1889年に完成。1930年に建設されたクライスラー・ビルディングに抜かれるまで、世界で最も高い人工建造物であり続けた。建設当時は目障り、悲惨だと数々の批判を受けたが、こうした反発の声は時間と共に徐々に薄れていった。今日では、エッフェル塔は大切にされており、国宝級のものとして広く称賛され、フランスの極めて優れた芸術、文化、産業力の恒久的かつ象徴的なシンボルとして認識されている。エッフェル塔が集める名声と威信の多くは、すぐにそれと分かるようなシルエットと、3層構造、錬鉄製の建造物、そして格子模様といった注目すべき特徴に由来している。

269 renowned
[rɪnáʊnd]
☐☐☐☐☐☐

Adj. 有名な

world-**renowned**（世界的に有名な）

▶ **renown** [rɪnáʊn] N[U] 有名、名声

---

270 name
[neɪm]
☐☐☐☐☐☐

V[T] に名前をつける

name A after B（B にちなんで A に名前をつける）　　**name** A B（A に B という名前をつける）

N[C] 名前

---

271 commence
[kəméns]
☐☐☐☐☐☐

V[I] 開始する、始まる　**V[T]** を開始する、始める

▶ **commencement** [kəménsmənt] N[U] 開始　N[C/U] 卒業式

---

272 surpass
[sərpǽs]
☐☐☐☐☐☐

V[T] を超える、より優れている

I'm proudest when my students **surpass** me.

（生徒が自分を超えた時、僕は最高に誇らしく感じるんだ。）

---

273 numerous
[núːmərəs]
☐☐☐☐☐☐

Adj. 数多くの、たくさんの

Tokyo attracts **numerous** tourists every year.（東京は毎年たくさんの旅行客を引き付けるんだ。）

---

274 eyesore
[áɪsɔːr]
☐☐☐☐☐☐

N[C] 目障りなもの、見たくないもの

Japan's above-ground power lines are such an **eyesore**.

（日本の地上の電線、目障りなんだよなぁ。）

---

275 calamity
[kəlǽməṭi]
☐☐☐☐☐☐

N[C/U] 悲惨なこと、災難

▶ **calamitous** [kəlǽmətəs] Adj. 悲惨な

▶ **calamitously** [kəlǽmətəsli] Adv. 悲惨なほどに

---

276 resistance
[rɪzístəns]
☐☐☐☐☐☐

N[U] 反対、抵抗

▶ **resist** [rɪzíst] V[I/T]（〜に）抵抗する　V[T]（欲しいもの）を我慢する

▶ **resistant** [rɪzístənt] Adj. 抵抗する；耐性のある

▶ **irresistible** [ìrəzístəbəl] Adj.（感情が）抑えきれない；非常に魅力的な

---

277 gradually
[grǽdʒuəli]
☐☐☐☐☐☐

Adv. 徐々に、次第に

▶ **gradual** [grǽdʒuəl] Adj. 徐々の

---

278 fade
[feɪd]
☐☐☐☐☐☐

V[I]（次第に）消えていく、（色が）あせる、（力が）衰える

= **fade away** [féɪdəwéɪ]

V[T]（色）をあせさせる、（力）を衰えさせる

▶ **fade out** [feɪdáʊt] [PV]（恋愛関係が）自然消滅する

279 cherish
[tʃérɪʃ]
V[T] を大切にする、大事にする
▶ **cherished** [tʃérɪʃt] Adj. 大切な

280 praise
[preɪz]
V[T] (〜に対して) を称賛する、ほめる (for sth)
I feel uncomfortable when I get **praised** too much.
(私、褒められすぎるとなんか嫌な感じするんだよね。)
N[U] 称賛、ほめ言葉

281 treasure
[tréʒər]
N[C/U] 宝物　N[P] 貴重な品々【-s】　V[T] を大切にする
▶ **treasury** [tréʒəri] N[C] 宝庫　N[U] 財務省【the- T】
▶ **treasurer** [tréʒərər] N[C] 会計係

282 acknowledge
[əkná:lɪdʒ]
V[T] を (〜として) 認識する (as sth)、認める
▶ **acknowledged** [əkná:lɪdʒd] Adj. 広く認められた
▶ **acknowledgment** [əkná:lɪdʒmənt] N[C/U] 認識、承認；謝辞、感謝の言葉

283 perpetual
[pərpétʃuəl]
Adj. 恒久の、永遠の；絶え間ない
▶ **perpetually** [pərpétʃuəli] Adv. 絶え間なく

284 outstanding
[àʊtstǽndɪŋ]
Adj. 極めて優れた、傑出した；未払いの
▶ **outstandingly** [àʊtstǽndɪŋli] Adv. 著しく、傑出して

285 might
[maɪt]
N[U] 力
▶ **mighty** [máɪti] Adj. 強力な；(打撃や音が) 凄まじい

286 fame
[feɪm]
N[U] 名声
rise to **fame** (有名になる)　**fame** and fortune (富と名声)

287 prestige
[presti:ʒ]
N[U] 威信、高い評判
▶ **prestigious** [prestídʒəs] Adj. 権威ある、一流の、名門の
a **prestigious** university (名門大学)

288 command
[kəmǽnd]
V[T] (尊敬など) を集める；を命じる；(軍隊) を指揮する
V[I] 命じる；指揮する
N[U] 指揮　N[C] 命令；(言語などの) 運用能力
have a good **command** of sth ((言語など) が上手に使える)

⟳ CH. 3,6

Chapter

07

舞台芸術
Performing Arts

Performing arts are a type of art typically enacted in front of live audiences and delivered by performers using their voices or bodies. Examples include theater, dance, and opera.

While it is often believed that we need to attend specialized schools to learn performing arts, educational opportunities are now easy to pursue at most secondary schools and universities.

This increase in accessibility is in response to research that suggests that performing arts offer many benefits to students, in spite of the fact that they may not lead directly to employment opportunities.

For instance, studies have indicated that students often find that performing arts allow them to freely express emotions that they might otherwise feel uncomfortable revealing.

1 Performing **arts are a** type **of art** typically enacted **in front of live** audiences **and** delivered **by performers using their voices or bodies. Examples include** theater**, dance, and opera.**

舞台芸術は通常、観客の前で生披露される芸術の一種で、パフォーマーが声や体を使って行うものである。例としては、演劇、舞踏、オペラなどがある。

289 perform
[pərfɔ́ːrm]
□□□□□□

V[I/T] （〜を）演じる、披露する；（仕事などを）行う、実行する

He's going to **perform** a new song tonight! I'm so hyped!
（彼は今夜新曲を披露するんだ！マジで興奮してる！）

performing arts （舞台芸術）

He **performed** very poorly during his probation period.
（彼の試用期間中のパフォーマンスはひどいものだった。）

▶ **performer** [pərfɔ́ːrmər] N[C] 演者、役者；仕事をする人

a good/strong/high **performer**　◆━▶　a poor/weak/low **performer**
（仕事ができる人）　　　　　　　　　　　（仕事ができない人）

▶ **performance** N[C] 上演、演技、演奏　N[C/U] パフォーマンス、成績、実績
[pərfɔ́ːrməns]

Let's analyze the financial **performance** of Google and Apple.
（グーグルとアップルの財務成績を分析してみよう。）

接頭語 per-　「完璧に、徹底的に」という意味の接頭語で、「完璧に（＝ per）形作る（＝ form）」から「演じる、演奏する」という意味になります。他には perfect（完璧な）、pervasive（蔓延した）などがあります。

---

290 type
[taɪp]
□□□□□□

N[C] 種類、タイプ　**N[C]** 活字、文字　**N[U]** 字体、書体

I'm learning a lot from working with different **types** of people.
（色んなタイプの人と働くことで多くのことを学んでいるよ。）

■ sb's **type** （〜の（好みの）タイプ）

I'm attracted to this girl, but she's actually not really **my type**.
（この女の子に惹かれてるんだけど、実際そんなに俺のタイプじゃないんだ。）

V[I/T] （〜をキーボードで）タイプする、打ち込む

■ **type** sth in （〜を入力する）　　　**type away** （一生懸命タイプする）

Can you **type in** your password?（自分のパスワード入力してくれる？）

291 typically
[típɪkli]

Adv. 通常は、普通は、典型的に

I **typically** take the train to work in the morning but just felt like cycling today.
（普段は朝電車で通勤するんだけど、今日は自転車の気分だったんだよね。）

▶ **typical** [típɪkəl] Adj. 典型的な、よくある ▶ **typify** [típəfaɪ] V[T] の典型となる

Worrying too much about making mistakes is a **typical** problem when learning a new language.（ミスすることを心配しすぎちゃうことは、新しい言語を学ぶときによくある問題だよ。）

■ **typical** of sth/sb（〜にとって典型的な、らしい、よくある）

Did John change jobs again? That's so **typical of** him.
（ジョンまた仕事変えたの？本当に彼らしいね。）

292 enact
[ɪnǽkt]

V[T] を演じる；(法律など) を制定する

I hope they **enact** this ban on smoking on the street soon.
（この路上喫煙禁止条例、早く制定されてほしいなぁ。）

▶ **enactment** [ɪnǽktmənt] N[C] 法令 N[U]（法律などの）制定

293 audience
[áːdiəns]

N[C] 観客、観衆、視聴者

I don't mind speaking in front of small crowds, but big **audiences** make me nervous.
（少人数の前で話すのは別にいいけど、大勢の前だと不安になるんだよなぁ。）

接頭語 audi-「音の」という意味の接頭語で、他には audio（音声の）、audition（オーディション）などがあります。

294 deliver
[dɪlívər]

V[T] (演技や演説など) を行う；を提供する、与える；の出産を手伝う

This video gave me a lot of tips for **delivering** a great speech.
（この動画は最高のスピーチをするための秘訣をたくさん教えてくれたんだ。）

The midwife **delivered** three babies last night.
（あの助産師さんは昨夜3人の赤ちゃんの出産を手伝ったんだ。）

V[I/T] （〜を）配達する、届ける

I sent this parcel last Thursday, but I can't check if it's actually been **delivered**.
（この小荷物先週の木曜日に送ったんだけど、実際に配達されたか確認できないんだよね。）

▶ **delivery** [dɪlívəri] N[C/U] 配達；分娩 N[U]（サービスなどの）提供；演説（のやり方）

The pizza **delivery** driver forgot my drinks again.   a **delivery** room
（あのピザの配達員、また飲み物忘れたんだよ。）   （分娩室）

▶ **deliverer** [dɪlívərər] N[C] 配達員；救世主、救助人

295 theater
[θíːətər]

N[U] 演劇 **N[C]** 劇場、映画館、シアター

Is that new movie playing in **theaters** already?（その新しい映画ってもう映画館でやってるの？）

▶ **theatrical** Adj. 演劇の、大げさな ▶ **theatrically** Adv. 劇みたいに、大げさに
[θiǽtrɪkəl]   [θiǽtrɪkli]

2 While it is often believed that we need to attend specialized schools to learn performing arts, educational opportunities are now easy to pursue at most secondary schools and universities.

舞台芸術を学ぶには専門的な学校に通う必要があると思われる一方で、今では大半の高校や大学でその教育機会を簡単に求めることができる。

---

296 **believe**
[bɪlíːv]
□□□□□□

V[I/T] （〜だと）思う、（〜を）信じる

I know it's hard to **believe**, but it's true. (信じられないとは思うけど、本当なんだ。)

- **believe** in sth/sb
  （〜の存在を信じる；（力や能力を）信じる）

- **believe** it or not
  （信じられないかもしれないけど）

Do you **believe** in UFOs?
(UFO って信じる？)

Believe it or not, this beautiful model is my girlfriend.
(信じられないかもしれないけど、この美人モデル、俺の彼女なんだ。)

Seeing is **believing**. (百聞は一見に如かず。)

▶ **belief** N[C/U] 信じること、信念、信条
  [bɪlíːf]

▶ **believer** N[C] 信者、信じる人
  [bɪlíːvər]

- beyond **belief** （信じられないほど）

London is a lovely city, but it gets cold **beyond belief** during winter.
(ロンドンは美しい街だけど、冬には信じられないほど寒くなるんだ。)

think vs **believe** どちらも「思う」と訳されることが多い単語ですが、believe は「信じる」という意味があるところから、確信度が強く、よく考えた後でそう思ったというニュアンスがあります。

---

297 **attend**
[əténd]
□□□□□□

V[T] に通う　V[I/T] （〜に）出席する

I'm sure plenty of people will **attend** your event tonight.
(きっとたくさんの人が今夜のイベントに出席してくれるよ。)

attend to sth/sb （〜に注意を払う、耳を傾ける；対処する）

▶ **attendance** [əténdəns] N[C/U] 出席、出勤、出席者数

- take **attendance** （出席を取る）

The lecturer **takes attendance**, but a lot of students just have their friends sign in on their behalf. (あの講師は出席取るんだけど、学生の多くが友達に代理で記入してもらってる。)

▶ **attendant** [əténdənt] N[C] 乗務員、接客係　▶ **attendee** [ətendíː] N[C] 出席者

flight **attendant** = cabin crew （客室乗務員）

298 specialized
[spéʃəlaɪzd]
☐☐☐☐☐☐

Adj. 専門的な、特殊な

I strongly recommend you go to graduate school if you want further **specialized** knowledge in a particular area.
(特定の分野で専門的な知識をもっと身につけたいんだったら大学院に行くことを強く勧めるよ。)

▶ **specialize** [spéʃəlaɪz] V[I] (〜を) 専攻する、専門にする (in sth)

If you want to **specialize** in accounting, you will first require a qualification.
(もし会計を専門にしたいんだったら、まず資格を取らなきゃいけないよ。)

▶ **specialization** N[C/U] 専門化、専門分野 ▶ **specialist** N[C] (〜の) 専門家 (in sth)
[spèʃələzéɪʃən]   [spéʃəlɪst]

299 educational
[èdʒəkéɪʃənəl]
☐☐☐☐☐☐

Adj. 教育の、教育的な

I like watching shows that are **educational**.
(僕は教育番組を見るのが好き。)

▶ **educationally** [èdʒəkéɪʃənəli] Adv. 教育的に ▶ **education** [èdʒəkéɪʃən] N[U] 教育

Living and working overseas is the best kind of **education**.
(海外で生活して働くことこそ最高の教育の一つだよ。)

▶ **educate** V[T] を教育する   ▶ **educated** Adj. 教育を受けた、教養のある
[édʒəkeɪt]   [édʒəkeɪtɪd]

We **educate** our staff thoroughly to maintain the quality of our customer service.
(我々は顧客サービス品質を維持するために、スタッフを徹底的に教育しています。)

He's well-**educated** but earns nothing. (彼は良い教育を受けてるんだけど、収入はゼロなんだ。)

300 pursue
[pərsú:]
☐☐☐☐☐☐

V[T] を追い求める、追求する

I know I shouldn't **pursue** Tina, but I'm in love with her.
(ティナのこと追い求めるべきじゃないのは分かってるんだけど、それでも彼女のことが大好き。)

▶ **pursuit** [pərsú:t] N[C] 追求 N[C/U] 追跡

in **pursuit** of sth (〜を求めて)

301 secondary
[sékənderi]
☐☐☐☐☐☐

Adj. 第二の、二次的な；あまり重要でない

I broke up with my girlfriend because my happiness was only ever a **secondary** concern to her, while she was my whole world.
(彼女にとって俺の幸せは二の次でしかなかったから、別れたよ。彼女は俺の全てだったのに。)

a **secondary** school (高校 *)
* 小学校と大学の間にある (=第二の) 学校を意味し、アメリカでは主に高校、もしくは中高を指します。

▶ **secondarily** [sèkəndérəli] Adv. 二次的に

302 university
[jù:nəvə́:rsəṭi]
☐☐☐☐☐☐

N[C/U] 大学

I didn't do much actual studying at **university**, but it was the best time of my life.
(大学では勉強自体はそんなにしなかったけど、人生で最高の時間だったよ。)

3 This increase in accessibility is in response to research that suggests that performing arts offer many benefits to students, in spite of the fact that they may not lead directly to employment opportunities.

舞台芸術を学んだからといって、就職の機会には直接繋がらないかもしれないにもかかわらず、このように舞台芸術に手が届きやすくなった背景には、舞台芸術が生徒に多くのメリットをもたらすという研究結果があるからだ。

---

303 **accessibility**
[əksèsəbíləṭi]
☐☐☐☐☐☐

N[U]　手の届きやすさ、近づきやすさ、アクセスのしやすさ

Building a train line to the airport will really improve **accessibility**.
(空港まで路線を引いたら、すごくアクセスが良くなるだろうね。)

▶ **access** [ǽkses] N[U] アクセス、接近　V[T] (場所) に入る、アクセスする

gain/get **access** to sth
(〜に接近する、アクセスする)

■ have **access** to sth
(〜を利用できる、アクセスがある)

Do you **have access to** this website? It's asking for a password.
(このサイトにアクセスできる？パスワード要求してくるんだけど。)

▶ **accessible** [əksésəbəl] Adj. (〜にとって) 入手しやすい、近づきやすい (to sb)

---

304 **benefit**
[bénəfɪt]
☐☐☐☐☐☐

N[C/U]　メリット、利益、便益、ためになること

You get no **benefit** from Robert's misery, so why are you so happy about it?
(君はロバートの不幸から何の利益も得られないのに、何がそんなに嬉しいわけ？)

V[T] の利益になる、ためになる　**V[I]** (〜から) 利益を得る (from sth)

▶ **beneficial** [bènəfíʃəl] Adj. 利益になる、有益な、ためになる

▶ **beneficially** [bènəfíʃəli] Adv. 有益に

---

305 **in spite of**
[ɪnspáɪṭəv]
☐☐☐☐☐☐

Prep.　〜にもかかわらず　= despite [dɪspáɪt]

John is a friendly and talkative guy **in spite of** his appearance.
(ジョンは見かけによらずフレンドリーでおしゃべりなやつなんだ。)

---

306 **fact**
[fækt]
☐☐☐☐☐☐

N[C/U]　事実

■ **in fact** (実際は)　the **fact** that + sentence (〜ということ、〜という事実)

The handbag looks like leather, but it's **in fact** canvas.
(あのハンドバッグレザーに見えるけど実際はキャンバス素材だよ。)

■ as a matter of fact（実は、実際のところ）   ■ a **fact** of life（人生の現実）

As a matter of fact, we are dating.
（実は、僕たち付き合ってるんだ。）

Everyone gets old. It's just **a fact of life**.
（みんな歳を取る。それが現実だよ。）

▶ **factual** [fǽktʃuəl] Adj. 事実に基づく   ▶ **factually** [fǽktʃuəli] Adv. 事実上

Social media is full of information that isn't **factual**.（SNSは事実に基づかない情報でいっぱいだよ。）

---

307 **directly**
[dəréktli]
[dàɪréktli]
☐☐☐☐☐☐

Adv. 直接に、直接的に

Are you going **directly** to the hotel, or are you going to pick up some food first?
（ホテルに直接行く？それともまずご飯買ってく？）

▶ **direct** Adj. 直接的な；直行の V[T] を監督する；を（〜に）向ける (to sth/sb)
[dərékt] [dàɪrékt]

Ben is very **direct**, but he's not a bad person.（ベンはすごい直接的に物を言う人だけど、悪い人じゃないよ。）

▶ **direction** N[C] 方向、方角 N[P] 指示；行き方【-s】 N[U] 監督
[dərékʃən] [dàɪrékʃən]

■ a sense of **direction**（方向感覚）   in the **direction** of sth（〜の方向に）

I have no **sense of direction**.（俺、方向感覚が全然ないんだよね。）

I accidentally gave someone the wrong **directions** this morning. I feel a bit guilty.
（今朝誰かに間違った道を教えちゃったんだ。ちょっと罪悪感。）

▶ **director** [dəréktər] [dàɪréktər] N[C] ディレクター、監督；取締役；部長

---

308 **employment**
[ɪmplɔ́ɪmənt]
☐☐☐☐☐☐

N[U] 就職、雇用、雇用率

The new factory is going to provide many people with **employment** opportunities.
（その新しい工場はたくさんの人に雇用機会を提供する予定だ。）

in **employment**（就職している、雇用されている）

↔ **unemployment** [ʌnɪmplɔ́ɪmənt] 失業、失業者数、失業率

▶ **employ** [ɪmplɔ́ɪ] V[T] を雇う；を用いる   ▶ **employer** [ɪmplɔ́ɪər] N[C] 雇用主

▶ **employed** [ɪmplɔ́ɪd] Adj. 雇われた ↔ **unemployed** [ʌnɪmplɔ́ɪd] 仕事のない

▶ **employee** [ɪmplɔ́ɪì:] [ìmplɔ́ɪì:] N[C] 従業員

---

309 **opportunity**
[à:pərtú:nəţi]
☐☐☐☐☐☐

N[C/U] 機会、チャンス

Studying in the UK is a great **opportunity** for me to learn English.
（イギリスで勉強することは私にとって英語を学ぶ最高の機会なんだ。）

take/miss an **opportunity**（機会を掴む / 逃す）

▶ **opportunist** [à:pərtú:nɪst] N[C] ご都合主義者、日和見主義者

I thought she was a friend, but she was actually an **opportunist** contacting me only when she needed something.（彼女は友達だと思ってたけど、実際は必要な時だけ連絡してくるご都合主義者だった。）

▶ **opportunistic** Adj. ご都合主義的な   ▶ **opportunism** N[U] ご都合主義、日和見主義
[à:pərtu:nístɪk]   [à:pərtú:nɪzəm]

4 For instance, studies have indicated that students often find that performing arts allow them to freely express emotions that they might otherwise feel uncomfortable revealing.

例えば、研究によると、生徒たちは、普段なら抵抗を感じてあらわにできないような感情でも、舞台芸術を通してであれば自由に表現できると感じることが多いと示唆されている。

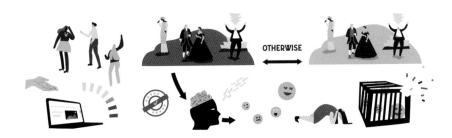

---

310 allow
[əláʊ]
☐☐☐☐☐☐

V[T] が（〜するのを）可能にする、許可する、許す（to do）

I love how my new job **allows** me to work from anywhere in the world.
(僕の新しい仕事、世界中のどこからでも働かせてくれるところがすごい好き。)

▶ **allowance** [əláʊəns] N[C] 許容量；手当、お小遣い

baggage/luggage **allowances** (手荷物許容量)

▶ **allowable** [əláʊəbəl] Adj. 許容可能な、許される

let vs allow vs permit これらは3つとも「許可する」という意味を持ち、どれも基本的な意味は一緒です。唯一の違いはそのフォーマルさにあり、let が最もカジュアル、permit が最もフォーマル、そして allow がその中間的なフォーマルさを持つ表現になります。

---

311 freely
[fríːli]
☐☐☐☐☐☐

Adv. 自由に

I just want to live life **freely**. (私はただ人生を自由に生きたいだけなんだ。)

▶ **free** [fríː] Adj. 自由な、無料の ▶ **freedom** [fríːdəm] N[C/U] 自由

for **free** (無料で)

have the **freedom** to do (〜する自由がある) **freedom** of speech (表現の自由)

---

312 express
[ɪksprés]
☐☐☐☐☐☐

V[T] を表現する、表す

■ **express** oneself (自分の考えを表現する、自己表現する)

Hannah only seems to be able to **express herself** properly when she's singing.
(ハナって歌ってるときだけちゃんと自己表現できるっぽいよな。)

Adj. 急行の、速達の **N[C]** 急行 **N[U]** 速達

Can you send it to me by **express** mail? (それを私に速達で送ってくれない？)

▶ **expression** [ɪkspréʃən] N[C/U] 表現 N[C] 表情；言い回し、(言葉の) 表現

I've never heard that **expression** before. What does it mean?
(その表現聞いたことないなぁ。どういう意味？)

▶ **expressive** [ɪksprésɪv] Adj. 表情豊かな、感情表現が豊かな

an **expressive** face　　　　She's a very **expressive** person.
(表情豊かな顔)　　　　　　(彼女は感情表現が豊かな人なんだ。)

▶ **expressively** [ɪksprésɪvli] Adv. 表情豊かに

---

313 **emotion**
[ɪmóʊʃən]

N[C/U] 感情

I wish my mom was better at keeping her **emotions** under control.
(母さん、もうちょっと感情をうまくコントロールできたら良いんだけどなぁ。)

▶ **emotional** [ɪmóʊʃənəl] Adj. 感情的な　▶ **emotionally** [ɪmóʊʃənəli] Adv. 感情的に

Why do you get so **emotional**? Let's keep calm and discuss.
(なんでそんな感情的になるの？落ち着いて議論しようよ。)

---

314 **otherwise**
[ʌ́ðərwaɪz]

Adv. さもなければ、そうしないと

You'd better take notes; **otherwise**, you'll forget and ask me again.
(メモ取った方がいいよ、じゃないと忘れてまた僕に聞いてくるから。)

---

315 **uncomfortable**
[ʌnkʌ́mfərtəbəl]

Adj. 抵抗がある、気まずい、心地良くない

Oh my god, my new chair is so **uncomfortable**.
(いやもうマジで、俺の新しい椅子めちゃくちゃ座り心地悪いんだけど。)

↔ **comfortable** [kʌ́mfərtəbəl] 快適な、心地良い

The couch at home is really fluffy and **comfortable**, so I often fall asleep when I'm
lying on it. (うちの家にあるソファ、ものすごいフカフカで快適だから、横になってるとよく寝ちゃう。)

▶ **uncomfortably** [ʌnkʌ́mfərtəbli] Adv. 心地悪く

↔ **comfortably** [kʌ́mfərtəbli] 心地よく

▶ **comfort** [kʌ́mfərt] N[U] 快適さ、安らぎ　N[C/U] 慰め，慰安　V[T] を慰める

---

316 **reveal**
[rɪvíːl]

V[T] をあらわにする、明らかにする、暴露する

If you ever betray me, I'll **reveal** your secrets to the world.
(俺のこと裏切ったら、お前の秘密を世の中に暴露するからな。)

▶ **revelation** N[U] 明らかになること、暴露　N[C] 意外な新事実、明らかになったこと
　　[rèvəléɪʃən]

Some **revelations** about his private life have damaged his reputation.
(彼のプライベートが明らかになったことで、彼の評判は傷ついた。)

▶ **revealing** [rɪvíːlɪŋ] Adj. 露出の多い；(隠れていたことを) 明らかにする

a **revealing** dress (露出の多いドレス)　a **revealing** fact ((物事を) 明らかにする事実)

Man	You go ahead and find our seats, and I'll order some snacks. Is there anything you want in particular?
Woman	I'm on a really painful diet right now, so maybe just water. By the way, what's the situation with your colleague? Should we wait for him, or are we meeting inside?
Man	He's actually running a bit late, so he can work it out himself. He's usually pretty reliable, so the traffic must be miserable. It'd be a shame if he missed the start.
Woman	Yeah, the public transport options around here are a nightmare. There'll be plenty of advertisements anyway, so he can probably afford to be a few minutes late. See you inside.

男性	先行って席見つけといてよ。俺は軽食を注文しとくから。なんか特にほしいものある？
女性	今めっちゃつらいダイエットしてるから、私は水だけで大丈夫かな。てか、そういえば同僚の人、どうなってるの？待った方がいいかな？それとも中で会う？
男性	実はあいつちょっと遅れてるんだよね。だから、彼は自分で何とかするよ。いつもはかなり信頼できるやつだから、渋滞が悲惨なんだろうね。最初の部分見逃したら残念だね。
女性	そうだね。この辺、公共交通機関の選択肢も全然ないしね。まぁ広告も多いだろうし、きっと数分遅れても大丈夫だよ。じゃあ中でね。

317 **go ahead**
[góʊ(w)əhéd]
□□□□□□

[PV]（～より）先に行く（of sb）；（～を）実行する（with sth）
Phr.（許可を求められて）どうぞ
▶ **go-ahead** [góʊ(w)əhed] N[S] ゴーサイン、許可【the -】
give sb the **go-ahead** (to do)（～に（～する）ゴーサインを出す）

---

318 **order**
[ɔ́:rdər]
□□□□□□

V[I/T]（～を）注文する **V[T]** を命じる **N[C]** 注文；命令 **N[U]** 秩序
take sb's **order**（～の注文を聞く）
N[C/U] 順番
in **order**（順番に） put sth in **order**（～を順番に並べる）

---

319 **snack**
[snæk]
□□□□□□

N[C] 軽食 **V[I]**（～を）軽食に食べる（on sth）

---

320 **painful**
[péɪnfəl]
□□□□□□

Adj. つらい、苦しい；痛い = **sore** [sɔ:r]
▶ **painfully** [péɪnfəli] Adv. 痛いほど、つらいほど ▶ **painkiller** [péɪnkìlər] N[C] 痛み止め

---

321 **diet**
[dáɪət]
□□□□□□

N[C] ダイエット **N[C/U]** 食事、食生活 **V[I]** ダイエットする
Adj. ダイエット用の
be/go on a **diet**（ダイエットをしている / する）
N[U]（日本の）国会【the- D】
▶ **dietary** [dáɪəteri] Adj. 食事の
dietary restrictions/requirements（（アレルギーや宗教上の理由で）食べられないもの）

---

322 **situation**
[sìtʃuéɪʃən]
□□□□□□

N[C] 状況、事態
What's the **situation** with sth/sb（～の状況はどうなってるの？）
▶ **situational** [sìtʃuéɪʃənəl] Adj. 状況の、場面の

---

323 **colleague**
[kɑ́:li:g]
□□□□□□

N[C] 同僚 = **coworker** [kòʊwə́:rkər]

---

324 **wait**
[weɪt]
□□□□□□

V[I]（～を）待つ（for sth/sb, on sth）；後になる **N[S]** 待つこと
It can **wait** till tomorrow.（明日になっても大丈夫だよ。）
Sorry for the long **wait**.（長らく待たせてごめんね。）
▶ **await** [əwéɪt] V[T] を待つ

---

325 **meet**
[mi:t]
□□□□□□

V[T] に会う；にばったり会う；（基準や要求値）を満たす **N[C]** 競技会
Nice to **meet** you.（初めまして。） Nice **meeting** you.（お会いできて良かったです。）
上記の表現は初めて会う（会った）人に対して使う表現で、以前にも会ったことがある人に対しては Nice to see you. や Nice seeing you. を使います。

326 actually
[ǽktʃuəli]

Adv. 実は、実際は

▶ **actual** [ǽktʃuəl] Adj. 実際の　▶ **actualize** [ǽktʃuəlaɪz] V[I/T]（〜を）実現する

---

327 run late
[rʌnléɪt]

Phr.（予定時刻より）遅れる、遅刻する

Are you ready yet? We're **running late**.（準備まだなの？ 遅れてるんだよ。）

---

328 work (sth) out
[wɜ́:rkáʊt]

[PV] を解く、解決する；（work out の形で）うまくいく；運動をする

= **exercise** [éksərsaɪz]

---

329 reliable
[rɪláɪəbəl]

Adj. 信頼できる、当てにできる

▶ **reliability** [rɪlàɪəbíləți] N[U] 信頼性　▶ **rely** [rɪláɪ] V[I]（〜に）頼る（on/upon sth/sb）

▶ **reliance** [rɪláɪəns] N[U]（〜への）依存（on/upon sth/sb）

---

330 miserable
[mízərəbəl]

Adj. ひどい、悲惨な、惨めな

▶ **miserably** [mízərəbli] Adv. ひどく、惨めに　▶ **misery** [mízəri] N[C/U] 惨めさ

---

331 shame
[ʃeɪm]

N[C] 残念なこと　　N[U] 恥ずかしい思い、恥

That's a **shame**.（それは残念だね。）　**Shame** on you!（恥を知れ！）

▶ **shameful** [ʃéɪmfəl] Adj. 恥ずべき

---

332 miss
[mɪs]

V[T] を見逃がす、聞き取れない；がいなくて寂しい　V[I] 標的を外す

I **miss** you!（君がいなくて寂しいよ！）

▶ **missing** [mísɪŋ] Adj. 見つからない、行方不明の

---

333 option
[á:pʃən]

N[C] 選択肢、選択

▶ **optional** [á:pʃənəl] Adj. 選択の、任意の

▶ **opt** [ɑ:pt] V[I]（〜を / 〜することを）選ぶ（for sth/to do）

---

334 nightmare
[náɪtmer]

N[C] 悪夢、ひどい状況

All my contact info just disappeared. What a **nightmare**!（連絡先全部消えた。悪夢だ。）

---

335 advertisement
[ædvɜ:rtáɪzmənt]

N[C] 広告、宣伝　= **ad** [æd]

▶ **advertise** [ædvərtaɪz] V[I/T]（〜を）広告する

▶ **advertising** [ædvərtaɪzɪŋ] N[U] 広告すること、広告業

---

336 afford
[əfɔ́:rd]

V[T]（can を伴って）（〜する）余裕がある、（〜しても）大丈夫（to do）
を許容できる；を（金銭的に）買うことができる

▶ **affordable** [əfɔ́:rdəbəl] Adj.（価格が）手ごろな、良心的な

↻ CH. 1, 4, 7

音楽
Music

Music is indispensable to people around the world because of its significant role in celebrations, social gatherings, entertainment, and religious customs.

While music is undoubtedly important in every part of the world, what constitutes music is a polarizing topic that continues to be the subject of debate.

For example, rap music drew a large amount of criticism when it first emerged due to its violent and aggressive lyrics and unfamiliar melody.

This kind of controversy commonly surrounds newer genres of music, as the perception of genres when they first emerge tends to be mixed, leading to delayed mainstream acceptance.

1 Music is indispensable to people around the world because of its significant role in celebrations, social gatherings, entertainment, and religious customs.

音楽は、祝いの席、社交的な集まり、娯楽、そして宗教上の慣習において重要な役割を果たすことから、世界中の人々にとって不可欠な存在になっている。

---

337 indispensable
[ìndɪspénsəbəl]

Adj. （〜にとって）不可欠な、絶対に必要な（to/for sth）

That player is important to the club but not **indispensable**.
（あの選手はクラブにとって重要だけど、絶対に欠かせないというわけではないね。）

↔ **dispensable** [dɪspénsəbəl] 必ずしも必要でない

---

338 significant
[sɪgnífəkənt]

Adj. 重要な、大きな、意味がある

Andrew, you made a **significant** contribution to the creation of this book.
（アンドリュー、君はこの本の制作に大きく貢献してくれたよ。）

▶ **significantly** [sɪgnífəkəntli] Adv. 大いに、かなり

Social media has **significantly** changed the way we communicate.
（SNS ってかなりコミュニケーションの方法を変えたよね。）

▶ **significance** [sɪgnífəkəns] N[U] 重要性、意味

---

339 role
[roʊl]

N[C] 役割；役 ＝ **part** [pɑːrt]

■ play a **role**（役割を果たす；役を演じる）

Instagram **plays a** key **role** in the advertising strategy of many companies.
（インスタは多くの会社の広告戦略において重要な役割を果たしている。）

---

340 celebration
[sèləbréɪʃən]

N[C] 祝いの席、祝賀会、パーティ　**N[U]** 祝賀、祝い

I think I'm going to keep my birthday **celebrations** low-key this year.
（今年の誕生日のお祝いは控えめにしておこうと思ってる。）

in **celebration** of sth（〜を祝福して）

▶ **celebrate** [séləbreɪt] V[I/T]（〜を）祝う

My friend and I are **celebrating** the launch of our new website on Friday! Do you want to come?　（金曜日に友達と一緒に新しいウェブサイトの開設祝いするんだけど、来る？）

341 gathering
[ɡǽðərɪŋ]
☐☐☐☐☐☐

N[C] 集まり、集会 **N[U]** 集めること、収集

There was a small **gathering** at my place last night.（昨晩私の家で小さな集まりがあった。）

a social **gathering**（社交的な集まり）

▶ **gather** [ɡǽðər] V[T] を集める V[I] 集まる

I've been trying to **gather** ideas for my new project.
（新しいプロジェクトのためにアイディアを集めようとしているんだよね。）

gather speed（スピードを上げる）   **gather** momentum（勢いを増す）

A crowd began to **gather** in front of the stadium way before the concert started.
（コンサートが始まるずっと前から群衆がスタジアムの前に集まり始めたんだよ。）

342 entertainment
[entərtéɪnmənt]
☐☐☐☐☐☐

N[C/U] 娯楽、もてなし

I think people watch the news for **entertainment** more than information.
（みんなニュースは情報としてじゃなくて娯楽として見てると思うよ。）

entertainment expenses（接待費、交際費）

▶ **entertain** [entərtéɪn] V[T] を楽しませる V[I/T]（〜を）もてなす

I want to become a comedian because I love **entertaining** people and making them
laugh.（人を楽しませて笑わせるのが好きだからコメディアンになりたい。）

▶ **entertaining** Adj. 愉快な N[U] もてなし   ▶ **entertainer** N[C] エンターテイナー
　[entərtéɪnɪŋ]　　　　　　　　　　　　　　　　　　[entərtéɪnər]

343 custom
[kʌ́stəm]
☐☐☐☐☐☐

N[C/U] 慣習、しきたり **N[P]** 税関【-s】

There are a lot of unique **customs** in China that you won't find in other countries.
（中国には他の国にはないたくさんのユニークな慣習があるよ。）

■ at **customs**（税関で）   a **customs** officer（税関職員）

I think it'd be safer to declare these snacks **at customs**.
（このお菓子、税関で申告した方が安全だと思うよ。）

Adj. カスタムの、特注の

custom software（特注のソフトウェア）

▶ **customary** Adj. 習慣的な   ▶ **customarily** Adv. 通常、通例
　[kʌ́stəmeri]　　　　　　　　　[kʌ̀stəmérəli]

■ It is **customary** to do sth（〜するのが習慣である、普通のことである。）

It's customary for Americans **to** shake hands when they meet someone.
（誰かに会ったときに握手をするのは、アメリカ人にとっては普通のことだよ。）

2 While music is undoubtedly important in every part of the world, what constitutes **music is a** polarizing topic **that** continues **to be the subject of** debate.

音楽が世界中のあらゆる地域で重要なものであることは疑う余地もないが、音楽とはどのようなものであるのかというトピックについては、大きく意見が分かれ、論争が尽きない。

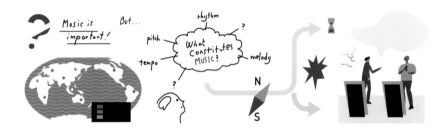

---

344 undoubtedly
[ʌndáʊṭɪdli]
☐☐☐☐☐☐

Adv. 疑う余地もなく、明らかに

This is **undoubtedly** the best bubble tea I've ever had.
（これは明らかに今まで飲んだ中で最高のタピオカティーだな。）

▶ **doubt** [daʊt] V[T] を疑う、怪しいと思う　N[C/U] 疑い、疑念

Rob promised that he'd clean up his desk today, but I **doubt** he'll do it.
（ロブが今日絶対デスクを片付けるって言ってたけど、怪しいな。）

no **doubt**（きっと）　without **doubt**（間違いなく）

▶ **doubtful** [dáʊtfəl] Adj. 疑わしい　▶ **doubtfully** [dáʊtfəli] Adv. 疑わしげに

I'm a bit **doubtful** about it.（それ、ちょっと疑わしいなって思うんだよね。）

---

345 part
[pɑːrt]
☐☐☐☐☐☐

N[C] 地域、地区；部品；役　N[C/U] 部分、一部

It's really easy to tell which **part** of Japan you're from because of your dialect.
（君、方言があるから日本のどこ出身なのか本当にすぐに分かるよ。）

■ in **part**（部分的に）

My boyfriend doesn't eat chicken **in part** because he has a chicken as a pet.
（私の彼氏、ペットにニワトリを飼っていることもあって鶏肉食べないんだよね。）

▶ **partly** [pɑ́ːrtli] Adv. 部分的に

It's **partly** cloudy today.（今日は部分的に曇っている。）

---

346 constitute
[kɑ́ːnstətuːt]
☐☐☐☐☐☐

V[T] とみなされる、を構成する、から成る

It's hard to explain exactly what **constitutes** a good song, but I know when I hear one.
（良い曲とはどんなものかと正確に説明するのは難しいけど、私は聞けばすぐにわかるよ。）

▶ **constituent** [kənstítʃuənt] N[C] 構成要素；有権者　Adj. 構成する

Caffeine is the main **constituent** of drinks such as tea and coffee.
（カフェインはお茶とかコーヒーの主な構成成分だよ。）

▶ **constitution** [kà:nstətúːʃən] N[C] 憲法；構成

The **Constitution** of Japan（日本国憲法）

---

347 polarize
[póʊləraɪz]

▢▢▢▢▢▢

V[T] を二極化させる　**V[I]**　二極化する

I feel like America is more politically **polarized** than ever.
（アメリカはこれまで以上に政治的に二極化しているような気がする。）

▶ **polar** [póʊlər] Adj. 極地の、南極の、北極の　　▶ **pole** [poʊl] N[C] 極；棒

a **polar** bear（ホッキョクグマ）　　　the North/South **Pole**（北極 / 南極）

---

348 topic
[tá:pɪk]

▢▢▢▢▢▢

N[C]　トピック、題材

I find robotics to be a really interesting **topic**, but I'm not sure everybody else does.
（個人的にはロボティクスはすごい面白いトピックだと思うけど、他のみんながどう思うかは分からないなぁ。）

---

349 continue
[kəntínjuː]

▢▢▢▢▢▢

V[I]　続く　**V[T]**　を続ける、継続する

I'm really sorry, but I need to go now. Can we **continue** this chat later?
（本当に申し訳ないんだけど、もう行かなきゃ。この話また後で続けても良い？）

■ **continue** doing/to do（〜し続ける）

I'm sad about losing the game, but I just need to **continue** to move forward.
（試合に負けたのは悲しいけど、それでもただただ前に進み続けないといけないんです。）

▶ **continuous** Adj. 継続的な、連続した　　▶ **continuously** Adv. 継続的に、途切れなく
　　[kəntínjuəs]　　　　　　　　　　　　　　　　[kəntínjuəsli]

Continuous effort is the key to unlocking your potential.
（継続的な努力こそがポテンシャルを解き放つ上で最も重要なことなんだ。）

▶ **continuance** [kəntínjuəns] N[C/U] 継続　　▶ **continuity** [kà:ntənúːəti] N[U] 継続性

---

350 debate
[dɪbéɪt]

▢▢▢▢▢▢

N[C/U]　論争、議論、討論

I'm not good at winning **debates**, so I'll take the minutes.
（討論に勝つのは得意じゃないから、私は議事録を取るね。）

V[I/T]　（〜について）議論する、討論する；（〜について）迷う、考える

▶ **debatable** [dɪbéɪtəbəl] Adj. 議論の余地がある

It's **debatable** whether singing is a learnable skill or not.
（歌唱力が学習可能なスキルなのかどうかには議論の余地がある。）

▶ **debater** [dɪbéɪtər] N[C] 討論者

debate vs **argument** vs **discussion**　どれも「議論」という意味を持ちますが、debate は日本語の「ディベート」のイメージからも想像できるようにフォーマルで知的な議論を意味します。argument はよりカジュアルで、ネガティブなニュアンスを含むことが多く、喧嘩と訳されることもあります。discussion は協力的かつ中立的に対話をし、意見交換や決定をすることを意味します。

3 For example, rap music drew a large amount of criticism when it first emerged due to its violent and aggressive lyrics and unfamiliar melody.

例えば、ラップミュージックが世に登場した当初は、歌詞が暴力的かつ攻撃的で、メロディーも馴染みのないタイプのものだったために、大きな批判を集めた。

351 draw
[drɑ:]
☐☐☐☐☐☐

V[T] を引き付ける

Is he wearing a watch on both wrists to **draw** attention to himself?
（彼って注目されるために両手首に時計してるのかな？）

■ **draw** a conclusion（結論を導く）　　　**draw** sb's eyes（〜の目を引き付ける）

You can't **draw a conclusion** without listening to everyone's opinion.
（みんなの意見を聞かないで結論を導くなんてダメだよ。）

V[I] 絵を描く　V[T] を描く

Wow! You can **draw** really well!（おぉ！絵描くのすごい上手なんだね！）

▶ **drawing** [drɔ́ːɪŋ] N[C] 描画、線画　N[U] 絵を描くこと

352 amount
[əmáʊnt]
☐☐☐☐☐☐

N[C/U] 量、額

■ a large/huge **amount** (of sth)（ものすごい量 / 額（の〜））

I wanted to go to a university in the States, but I decided not to because it was going to cost **a huge amount of** money.
（アメリカの大学行きたかったんだけど、ものすごい額のお金がかかりそうだったからやめちゃった。）

V[I] （数や額が）合計で（〜に）なる（to sth）；（〜）同然になる（to sth）

353 violent
[váɪələnt]
☐☐☐☐☐☐

Adj. 暴力的な、激しい；（嵐などが）猛烈な；（色が）強烈な

This may be a dumb question, but do you think all zombies are **violent**? There might be nice and kind ones, right?
（バカな質問かもしれないけど、ゾンビってみんな暴力的だと思う？すごい優しい奴もいるかもしれないでしょ？）

▶ **violence** [váɪələns] N[U] 暴力；威力　　▶ **violently** [váɪələntli] Adv. 暴力的に

Scott is a strong man, but he'd never resort to **violence**.
（スコットは強い男だけど、決して暴力に頼ったりしないんだ。）

domestic **violence**
（家庭内暴力、DV）

354 aggressive
[əgrésɪv]
☐☐☐☐☐☐

Adj. 攻撃的な、積極的な

I much prefer jazz to rock. Rock is way too **aggressive** for me.
（ジャズの方がロックよりずっと好きかな。ロックは私には攻撃的すぎるよ。）

▶ **aggression** [əgréʃən] N[U] 攻撃性；（他国への）武力侵略

I just don't believe that playing violent video games increases **aggression** in young people.（暴力的なテレビゲームをすることで若者の攻撃性が高まるなんてただただ信じられないんだよなぁ。）

an act of **aggression** （侵略行為）

▶ **aggressively** [əgrésɪvli] Adv. 攻撃的に、積極的に

▶ **aggressiveness** [əgrésɪvnəs] N[U] 攻撃性、積極性

355 lyrics
[lírɪks]
☐☐☐☐☐☐

N[P]　歌詞

I'm not great at remembering **lyrics**, so I usually just make them up.
（歌詞覚えるの得意じゃないから、いつも適当に歌ってるよ。）

▶ **lyricist** [lírəsɪst] N[C] 作詞家

This random guy on TV said Michael Jackson was a good singer but not a good **lyricist**. Who does he think he is?
（テレビに出てるよく分かんないやつが、マイケル・ジャクソンは良い歌手だったけど良い作詞家ではなかったって言ってた。何様なんだろう。）

356 unfamiliar
[ʌnfəmílijər]
☐☐☐☐☐☐

Adj.（〜にとって）馴染みのない（to sb）

This song is **unfamiliar** to me. （この曲は聞いたことないなぁ。）

■ be **unfamiliar** with sth/sb （〜のことはよく知らない）

I'm pretty **unfamiliar with** this area, so I might need you to show me around.
（このエリアはあんまり知らないから、ちょっと君に案内してもらわないといけないかも。）

↔ **familiar** [fəmílijər] 馴染みのある、見覚えのある、聞き覚えのある

▶ **familiarize** [fəmíljəràɪz] V[T] を（〜に）慣れさせる（with sth/sb）

It took some time to **familiarize** myself with this new phone.
（この新しい携帯に慣れるのにしばらくかかったよ。）

接頭語 un-　「否定」を意味する接頭語で、よく知っている（= familiar）という形容詞を否定して「よく知らない」という意味になります。他には unsuccessful（うまくいかない）や unfortunate（不運な）があります。

357 melody
[mélədi]
☐☐☐☐☐☐

N[C]　メロディー、曲；旋律

This song has a great **melody**, but I don't like the singer's voice.
（この曲、メロディーはすごい良いけど歌手の声が嫌いだな。）

▶ **melodious** [məlóʊdiəs] Adj. 美しいメロディーの

The moment I heard his **melodious** voice, I fell in love.
（彼のメロディーのように美しい声を聞いた瞬間惚れたわ。）

▶ **melodiously** [məlóʊdiəsli] Adv. 美しいメロディーで

4 This kind of controversy commonly surrounds newer genres of music, as the perception of genres when they first emerge tends to be mixed, leading to delayed mainstream acceptance.

こうした論争は一般的に、新たに生まれた音楽のジャンルをめぐって起こるが、それは、そのジャンルが出現したときの認識には大抵ばらつきがあり、主流として受け入れられるまでに時間がかかるからである。

---

358 **commonly**
[kά:mənli]

Adv. 一般的に、広く

Why aren't 2000 yen notes more **commonly** used?
(2000 円札ってどうしてもっと一般的に使われてないんだろう？)

▶ **common** Adj. 一般的な、よくある；共通の　◆ **uncommon** まれな、珍しい
[kά:mən]　　　　　　　　　　　　　　　　　　[ʌnkά:mən]

common knowledge （一般常識）

▶ **commonality** [kὰ:mənǽləţi] N[C/U] 共通性、共通点

Even though we come from many places and cultures, we all share human **commonalities**. （私たちは色んな場所や文化から来てるけど、みんな人間としての共通点を持っているよ。）

359 **genre**
[ʒά:nrə]

N[C] ジャンル

I listen to various **genres** of music like jazz, rock, and pop.
（私はジャズとか、ロックとか、ポップとか、色んなジャンルの音楽を聞くよ。）

360 **perception**
[pərsépʃən]

N[C] 認識、見方　N[U] 知覚、感覚

There's a **perception** that Adam's a slacker, but he's really just efficient.
（アダムは怠けものだって見方をされてるけど、彼は本当に効率が良いだけなんだよ。）

▶ **perceive** [pərsíːv] V[T] を知覚する、に気づく、（物事）をとらえる

Did you know that different animals **perceive** time at different speeds?
（動物によって時間の進み方が異なる速度で知覚されるって知ってた？）

▶ **perceptive** Adj. 洞察力のある　▶ **perceptiveness** N[U] 洞察力、理解力
[pərséptɪv]　　　　　　　　　　　　　　　　　[pərséptɪvnəs]

▶ **perceptible** [pərséptəbəl] Adj. 知覚できる

361 **emerge**
[ɪmə́:rdʒ]
☐☐☐☐☐☐

V[I]　（〜から）出現する、現れる（from sth）

Details and rumors are finally starting to **emerge** about the new PlayStation.
（新しいプレステに関する情報と噂がついに出始めてる。）

▶ **emergence** N[U] 出現　　　　▶ **emergency** N[C/U] 緊急、非常（事態）
　[ɪmə́:rdʒəns]　　　　　　　　　　　　[ɪmə́:rdʒənsi]

the **emergence** of life on Earth（地球における生命の出現）　　in case of **emergency**（緊急時には）

---

362 **mixed**
[mɪkst]
☐☐☐☐☐☐

Adj.　（評価や意見などが）ばらついた、さまざまな；混合の

I've heard **mixed** things about that restaurant, but let's give it a try anyway.
（そのレストランについては良いこと悪いこと色々聞いたことがあるけど、とりあえず試してみよう。）

▶ **mix**　[mɪks]　V[T] を（〜と / 〜に）混ぜる（with/in sth）　V[I]（〜と / 〜に）混ざる（with/in sth）
　　　　　　　　N[S] 混合　N[C/U]（ケーキなどの）素

Mash the bananas and then **mix** in the yogurt.（バナナをすりつぶして、ヨーグルトと混ぜて下さい。）

■ **mixed** up（混乱した）

The teacher said the next class will be on the 29th, but that's Sunday, right? I think he's **mixed up** about the dates.
（先生、次の授業は 29 日って言ってたけど、それ日曜日じゃない？日にち混乱してると思う。）

▶ **mixture**　[mɪkstʃər] N[C] 混合物、混ぜたもの　N[U] 混合すること

Tagalog is like a **mixture** of Malay, Spanish, and English.
（タガログ語はマレー語、スペイン語、そして英語を混ぜ合わせたようなものだよ。）

---

363 **delayed**
[dɪléɪd]
☐☐☐☐☐☐

Adj.　遅れた、遅延した

I'm getting **delayed** reactions on my computer, so I'm going to uninstall some of my unused programs.
（パソコンの反応が遅いから、使っていないプログラムをいくつかアンインストールしようと思うんだ。）

▶ **delay**　V[T] を遅らせる、先延ばしにする　V[I] ぐずぐずする　N[C/U] 遅れ、遅延
　[dɪléɪ]

Don't **delay** the inevitable. You'll have to do it anyway.
（避けられないことを先延ばしにするの止めなよ。どうせやんなきゃいけないんだから。）

■ without **delay**（すぐに、ただちに）

I love how these Bluetooth headphones connect **without delay**.
（この Bluetooth ヘッドフォン、すぐに接続されるからすごく良いんだ。）

---

364 **mainstream**
[méɪnstri:m]
☐☐☐☐☐☐

Adj.　主流の、メインストリームの　　**N[U]**　主流派【the -】

Veganism is becoming more **mainstream** around the world.
（菜食主義は世界中でますますメインストリームになってきている。）

Woman I **picked up** a guitar last week and started trying to teach myself how to play. **Turns out**, it's a bit harder than I **expected**. I've **poured** so much time and effort into it, but I still haven't learned a single song yet.

Man Speaking from experience, you do need to show some **patience**. Learning **from scratch** can be a bit **overwhelming**, and it can take a while to build up some **confidence**. Have you ever played any other instrument, or is this your first one?

Woman I played a bit of piano and did a bit of drumming for the marching band, but it's not really **helping** me **make sense** of the guitar. I **assume** you're **busy** after work today, but would you be **willing** to give me a few **tips** at some **point**?

Man Bring it in tomorrow morning. I'll **postpone** my meeting and help you out a little bit then. You won't transform into a guitar god **overnight**, but I should be able to make you a bit less **awful**.

女性 先週ギター始めて、独学で弾こうとしてるんだ。でも分かったんだけど、ちょっと予想してたよりも難しいんだよね。時間もいっぱい注ぎ込んで努力もすごいしたのに、まだ1曲も弾けるようになってないし。

男性 俺の経験だけど、ちょっと辛抱強さが必要なんだよね。ゼロから学ぶのはちょっと大変かもしれないし、それなりの自信をつけるには時間がかかったりするしね。他に楽器は弾いたことあるの？それともこれが初めて？

女性 ピアノはちょっと弾いてたことがあって、マーチングバンドでドラムも少しやってた。でも、それがギターの理解に役立つって感じはないかなあ。今日仕事終わった後忙しいとは思うんだけど、どこかでちょっとアドバイスもらえたりしない？

男性 明日の朝持ってきなよ。ミーティングあるけど延期して、ちょっと手伝ってあげる。急にギターの神みたいに変身するのは無理だけど、ちょっとましにするくらいならできるはずだから。

365 **pick sth up**
[pɪkʌ́p]

[PV] （習い事や趣味）を始める；を持ち上げる

---

366 **turn out**
[tɜ́:rnáʊt]

[PV] （〜であることが）分かる、判明する **(to be sth/adjective)**

What he was saying **turned out** to be true. （彼の言っていたことが本当だと判明した。）

it **turns out** that + sentence（〜であることが分かる）

---

367 **expect**
[ɪkspékt]

V[T] を予想する、期待する

expect (sth/sb) to do sth（（〜が）〜することを予想する、期待する）

▶ **expected** [ɪkspéktɪd] Adj. 予想される ↔ **unexpected** [ʌ̀nɪkspéktɪd] 思いがけない

▶ **expectation** [èkspektéɪʃən] N[C/U] 見込み、予想、期待

▶ **expectancy** [ɪkspéktənsi] N[U] 見込み

life **expectancy**（推定寿命）

---

368 **pour**
[pɔːr]

V[T] を注ぐ **V[I/T]** （雨が）激しく降る

Oh no, it's **pouring** outside. （うわっ、外すごい雨降ってるじゃん。）

---

369 **patience**
[péɪʃəns]

N[U] 辛抱強さ、我慢

▶ **patient** N[C] 患者 Adj. 辛抱強い、我慢強い ↔ **impatient**（待たされて）いらいらした
   [péɪʃənt]   [ɪmpéɪʃənt]

▶ **patiently** [péɪʃəntli] Adv. 辛抱強く

---

370 **from scratch**
[frəmskrǽtʃ]

Phr. ゼロから、最初から、一から

Did you make this curry **from scratch**? （このカレー、一から作ったの？）

---

371 **overwhelming**
[òʊvərwélmɪŋ]

Adj. 大変な、圧倒的な

▶ **overwhelm** [òʊvərwélm] V[T] を圧倒する、打ちのめす

▶ **overwhelmingly** [òʊvərwélmɪŋli] Adv. 圧倒的に

---

372 **confidence**
[kɑ́:nfədəns]

N[U] （〜に対する）自信、信頼、確信 **(in sth/sb)**

Have **confidence**. You can do it. （自信持ちなよ。君ならできる。）

▶ **confident** [kɑ́:nfədənt] Adj. 自信のある、確信のある

▶ **confidently** [kɑ́:nfədəntli] Adv. 自信を持って

---

373 **help**
[help]

V[I/T] （〜を）助ける、手伝う **V[I]** 役に立つ

■ **help** sb (to) do/with sth（〜が〜するのを手伝う）

Can you **help** me **do** my homework? （私の宿題手伝ってくれない？）

374 make sense
[meɪkséns]

Phr. 理解できる、分かる

That **makes sense**.（なるほどね。）

---

375 assume
[əsú:m]

V[T] と思う、見なす、仮定する　= suppose [səpóʊz]

（負債や責任）を引き受ける

▶ **assumption** [əsʌ́mpʃən] N[C] 思い込み、仮定　▶ **assuming** [əsú:mɪŋ] Cnj. 〜と仮定して

---

376 busy
[bízi]

Adj.（〜で / 〜するのに）忙しい（with sth/doing）

Mom, later. I'm **busy** playing a video game.（母さん、後にして。ゲームで忙しいから。）

---

377 willing
[wílɪŋ]

Adj.（〜しても）かまわない、（進んで〜する）気がある（to do）

◆ **unwilling** [ʌnwílɪŋ] 気の進まない、（〜を）したがらない（to do）

▶ **willingly** [wílɪŋli] Adv. 自発的に　▶ **willingness** [wílɪŋnəs] N[U] 自発性

---

378 tip
[tɪp]

N[C] アドバイス、助言；先端；チップ

Can you give me some **tips**?（アドバイスもらえないかな？）

V[I] 傾く　V[T] を傾ける　V[I/T]（〜に）チップを渡す

---

379 point
[pɔɪnt]

N[C] 時点、地点；点、ポイント；問題点　N[U] 意味、目的

at some **point**（いつか）　What's the **point**?（それ意味あるの？）

V[I]（〜を）指さす（at/to/toward sth/sb）

V[T] を（〜の方向に）向ける

▶ **point sth out** [pɔ́ɪn(t)áʊt] [PV] 〜を指摘する

---

380 postpone
[poʊstpóʊn]

V[T] を延期する　= put sth off [pʊtɑ́:f]

▶ **postponement** [poʊstpóʊnmənt] N[C/U] 延期

---

381 overnight
[òʊvərnáɪt]

Adv. 急に、突然、一晩で；夜通し

Adj. 急な、突然の；夜通しの

---

382 awful
[ɑ́:fəl]

Adj. ひどい、最悪な

This coffee tastes **awful**.（このコーヒーめっちゃ不味い。）

▶ **awfulness** [ɑ́:fəlnəs] N[U] ひどさ

↻ CH. 2, 5, 8

文学
Literature

Until recently, all books and documents in wide circulation were accepted as literature and considered to have artistic merit, particularly in Western Europe.

After the 18th century, the definition was revised to refer to imaginative writing that appeals to respected academics on account of its superior or tremendous quality.

Although many famous and admired literary figures, such as Shakespeare and Arthur Conan Doyle, are European, there have been many well-known and important authors around the world who should not be ignored.

Influential writers outside of Europe, such as Murasaki Shikibu and Sun Tzu, have had lasting impacts on the development of culture and art both locally and on a global scale and are appreciated worldwide.

1 Until recently, all books and documents in wide circulation were accepted as literature and considered to have artistic merit, particularly in Western Europe.

最近まで、特に西ヨーロッパでは、広く流通している書籍や文書は全て文学として受け入れられ、芸術的な価値があるとみなされていた。

WILLIAM SHAKESPEARE
HAMLET
SHERLOCK HOLMES
ARTHUR CONAN DOYLE

---

383 recently
[ríːsəntli]

Adv. 最近、近頃

Have you been back home **recently**?（最近実家帰った？）

▶ **recent** [ríːsənt] Adj. 最近の、近頃の

These are his **recent** photos on Instagram.（これがインスタにある彼の最近の写真。）

---

384 book
[bʊk]

N[C] 書籍、本　N[P] 会計簿、帳簿【-s】

I'd heard great things about this **book**, but I'm finding it pretty boring so far.
（この本最高だって聞いてたんだけど、今のところかなり退屈。）

V[I/T]　（〜を）予約する

Our event on Saturday is fully **booked**.（土曜日に行う僕らのイベントは予約で一杯だよ。）

▶ **booking** [bʊkɪŋ] N[C]（ホテルやチケットの）予約　= **reservation** [rèzərvéɪʃən]

Can I make a **booking** online with my credit card?（クレジットカードでオンライン予約できますか？）

---

385 circulation
[sàːrkjəléɪʃən]

N[U] 流通、循環；血行　N[S] 発行部数

How can this watch be limited edition if there are thousands in **circulation** already?
（この時計、既にものすごい数が出回ってるのにどうして限定版なんだろう？）

The Wall Street Journal has a global **circulation** of more than two million.
（『ウォール・ストリート・ジャーナル』は全世界で 200 万部を超える発行部数を誇る。）

▶ **circulate** [sàːrkjəleɪt] V[I] 循環する　V[T] を循環させる

You should learn how money **circulates** if you want to better understand the logic of monetary policy.（金融政策のロジックをよりよく理解したいならお金がどう循環するか学んだ方が良いよ。）

The heart pumps all day to **circulate** blood around the body.
（心臓は血液を身体中に循環させるために一日中ポンプとしての役割を果たしているんだ。）

---

386 accept
[əksépt]

V[I/T]　（〜を）受け入れる、受け取る

Do you **accept** credit cards?（クレジットカード使えますか？）

▶ **acceptable** Adj. 受け入れられる；満足できる ⟷ **unacceptable** 受け入れられない
[əkséptəbəl]   [ʌnəkséptəbəl]

Being late is **unacceptable** in Japan.（遅刻は日本では許されないよ。）

▶ **acceptance** [əkséptəns] N[U] 受け入れ、承諾

---

387 **consider**
[kənsídər]
☐☐☐☐☐☐

V[T] は（〜すると）みなす (to do sth)；を思いやる
V[I/T] （〜を）よく考える

I'm **considering** a few options for dinner tonight.（今夜のディナーにはいくつか候補を考えてるよ。）

▶ **considerate** [kənsídərət] Adj.（〜に対して）思いやりを持つ（of sb）

Be **considerate** of others.（他人を思いやりなさい。）

▶ **consideration** [kənsìdəréɪʃən] N[U] 考慮；思いやり N[C] 考慮すべきこと

■ take sth into **consideration**（〜を考慮する）= take sth into account

I think the interviewer will **take** your experience as a manager **into consideration**.
（面接官は君のマネージャーとしての経験を考慮してくれると思うよ。）

▶ **considerable** [kənsídərəbəl] Adj.（大きさや額が）かなりの、ものすごい

a **considerable** amount of time（ものすごい量の時間）

▶ **considerably** [kənsídərəbli] Adv. かなり、ものすごく

You know what, I'm attracted to a person **considerably** older than me. She's 95 now.
（ちょっと聞いて、自分よりものすごい年上の人に惹かれてるんだよね。彼女は今95歳なんだ。）

▶ **considering** [kənsídərɪŋ] Prep. 〜を考慮すると（sth/that + sentence）

---

000 **merit**
[mérɪt]
☐☐☐☐☐☐

N[U] 価値 N[C] 長所、利点

I think his ideas have **merit**.（彼のアイディアは価値があると思うよ。）

■ based on **merit**（実績に基づいて）

I wonder if Jun got promoted **based on merit** or because he's buddies with the manager.
（ジュンの昇進って実績に基づいたものだったのかな、それともマネージャーと友達だったからなのかな。）

V[T] に値する = deserve [dɪzɜ́:rv]

■ **merit** attention（注目に値する）

There are a lot of people in the world that **merit** more attention.
（世界にはもっと注目されるべき人がたくさんいるよ。）

---

389 **Europe**
[júrəp]
☐☐☐☐☐☐

N[Prop.] ヨーロッパ

The next time I visit **Europe**, I'm definitely spending longer than a month there.
（次ヨーロッパに行くときは絶対1か月以上は滞在する予定だよ。）

▶ **European** [jùrəpí:ən] Adj. ヨーロッパの N[C] ヨーロッパ出身の人

the **European** Union（欧州連合）

▶ **euro** [júroʊ] N[C] ユーロ通貨（=€, EUR）

2 After the 18th century, the definition was revised to refer to imaginative writing that appeals to respected academics on account of its superior or tremendous quality.

18世紀以降、その定義は見直された。文学は、優れた、素晴らしい品質で立派な研究者を惹きつける、独創的な書物を指すようになったのだ。

390 revise
[rɪváɪz]

V[T] を見直す、修正する、改訂する

I've **revised** the itinerary to include Turkey and Croatia as well.
(トルコとクロアチアも入れるために、旅程表を改訂しました。)

▶ **revision** N[C/U] 修正、改訂
[rɪvíʒən]

▶ **revised** Adj. 修正された、改訂された
[rɪváɪzd]

I need to make some **revisions** to my thesis.
(論文にいくつか修正を加えなきゃ。)

the third **revised** edition of sth
(〜の第三改訂版)

391 imaginative
[ɪmǽdʒənət̬ɪv]

Adj. 独創的な、想像力豊かな

Steven's films are always **imaginative** and fun. (スティーブンの映画っていつも独創的で面白いんだ。)

▶ **imagine** V[T] を想像する、心に描く
[ɪmǽdʒɪn]

▶ **image** N[C] イメージ、画像、像
[ímɪdʒ]

Anything you can **imagine** can become reality if you put your mind to it.
(しっかりと努力をすれば、想像できることはなんでも現実のものにできるんだ。)

I have a clear **image** in my mind of what I want to look like.
(どんな見た目になりたいか、心の中に明確なイメージがある。)

▶ **imaginary** Adj. 想像上の、架空の
[ɪmǽdʒəneri]

▶ **imaginable** Adj. 想像できる、考えられる
[ɪmǽdʒənəbəl]

▶ **imagination** [ɪmǽdʒənéɪʃən] N[C/U] 想像、想像力

beyond **imagination** (想像を超える)

392 appeal
[əpíːl]

V[I] （〜を）惹きつける（to sb）；（〜に）訴える、懇願する（to sb）

This leather jacket doesn't really **appeal** to me.
(このレザージャケット、個人的にはそんなに魅力を感じないなぁ。)

appeal to the Supreme Court (最高裁判所に上告する)

N[C] 訴え、懇願　N[C/U] 上訴　N[U] 魅力

▶ **appealing** [əpíːlɪŋ] Adj. 魅力的な ↔ **unappealing** [ʌnəpíːlɪŋ] 魅力的でない

That color is really **appealing**. Can I get that one?
（あの色すごい魅力的ですね。あれもらえますか？）

---

393 **respected**
[rɪspéktɪd]

Adj. 立派な、評判の良い、尊敬された

You'll probably pay more attention if a **respected** celebrity tells you exactly the same thing that I just did, right?
（今僕が言ったのと全く同じことを尊敬されるような有名人が言ったらきっともっとちゃんと聞くんでしょ？）

▶ **respect** [rɪspékt] V[T] を尊敬する、尊重する　N[U] 尊敬、尊重；関連 N[C] 点、事項

respect oneself（自分を大事にする）　**respect** sb's feelings/the law（〜の気持ち / 法律を尊重する）

pay **respect** to sth/sb（〜に敬意を表す）　　with **respect** to/in **respect** of sth（〜に関して）

▶ **respectful** [rɪspéktfəl] Adj. （他人に対して）敬意を表す、礼儀正しい

▶ **respectfully** [rɪspéktfəli] Adv. 敬意を表して、礼儀正しく

▶ **respectable** Adj. ちゃんとした、きちんとした　▶ **respectably** Adv. ちゃんと、きちんと
　[rɪspéktəbəl]　　　　　　　　　　　　　　　　　　[rɪspéktəbli]

▶ **respective** [rɪspéktɪv] Adj. それぞれの　▶ **respectively** [rɪspéktɪvli] Adv. それぞれ

---

394 **superior**
[səpíriər]

Adj. （〜より）優れた（to sth/sb）、上から目線の　N[C] 上の人、上司

Is flying really **superior** to taking the train?（電車乗るより飛行機の方が本当に良いの？）

↔ **inferior** [ɪnfíriər]（〜より）劣った（to sth/sb）/ 下の人、劣った人

You don't have to feel **inferior** to returnees. Your English will be better than theirs if you keep working on it.　（帰国子女に劣等感を感じる必要なんてないよ。やり続ければ君の英語は彼らより良くなるよ。）

▶ **superiority** N[U] 卓越、優越　↔ **inferiority** 劣等、粗悪
　[səpìrió:rəṭi]　　　　　　　　　　　　[ɪnfìrió:rəṭi]

a sense of **superiority/inferiority**（優越感 / 劣等感）

---

395 **tremendous**
[trɪméndəs]

Adj. 素晴らしい、とてつもなく大きい

Surfing in Hawaii was such a **tremendous** experience.
（ハワイでのサーフィンは本当に素晴らしい経験だったよ。）

▶ **tremendously** [trɪméndəsli] Adv. とてつもなく

---

396 **quality**
[kwáːləṭi]

N[U] 品質　N[C] 性質　Adj. 質の良い ↔ **quantity** [kwáːnṭəṭi] N[C/U] 量

The **quality** of these shoes is incredible.（この靴の品質は信じられないくらい良いよ。）

▶ **qualitative** [kwáːləteɪṭɪv] Adj. 質的な、定性的な ↔ **quantitative** [kwáːnṭəteɪṭɪv] 量的な

a **qualitative** analysis（定性分析）

▶ **qualitatively** [kwáːləteɪṭɪvli] Adv. 質的に ↔ **quantitatively** [kwáːnṭəteɪṭɪvli] 量的に

It's not easy to measure happiness **quantitatively**.（幸福を定量的に測るのは簡単じゃない。）

3 Although **many** famous **and** admired **literary** figures, **such as Shakespeare and Arthur Conan Doyle, are European, there have been many** well-known **and important** authors **around the world who should not be** ignored.

シェークスピアやアーサー・コナン・ドイルなど、有名でなおかつ評価も高い作家の多くはヨーロッパ人だが、それ以外にも、知名度もあり、重要な存在で無視できない作家は世界中に大勢いる。

---

397 although
[ɑːlðóʊ]

Cnj. 〜だが、〜にもかかわらず　　= **even though** = **though**
　　　　　　　　　　　　　　　　　[íːvən ðoʊ]　　　 [ðoʊ]

Although we're running late, we should still get there before the show starts.
（予定よりは遅れてるけど、それでもショーが始まる前には着くはずだよ。）

although vs **even though** vs **though**　この3つはどれも同じ意味を持ち、どれも文頭と文中で使用することができます。また、唯一 though だけ文末で使用することができ、「〜だけどね」という意味でカジュアルな場面でもとてもよく使われます（例：The quality of this bag is really good! It's very expensive though. このバッグの質はものすごい良いよ！すごい高いけど）。

---

398 famous
[féɪməs]

Adj. 有名な　◆→ **infamous** [ínfəməs] 悪名高い、評判が悪い

I have a love-hate relationship with being **famous**.
（有名になることに関しては大好きな面もあるけど、そうでない面もあるなぁ。）

▶ **famously** [féɪməsli] Adv. よく知られているように　　▶ **fame** [feɪm] N[U] 名声

rise to **fame**（有名になる）　　**fame** and fortune（名声と富）

---

399 admire
[ədmáɪr]

V[T]　を高く評価する、称賛する；を鑑賞する

I really **admire** how patient you are with David.（そんなにデイビッドのこと我慢できるなんてすごいね。）

The museum was packed with people **admiring** the Mona Lisa.
（ミュージアムは『モナ・リザ』を鑑賞する人でいっぱいだった。）

▶ **admiring** [ədmáɪrɪŋ] Adj. 称賛の気持ちを表す

▶ **admiration** N[U] 称賛、感心　　▶ **admirer** N[C] 崇拝者、ファン
　　[ædməréɪʃən]　　　　　　　　　　　[ədmáɪrər]

---

400 figure
[fígjər]

N[C]　人物；体型、スタイル；数字；（本の）図

Steve is a really popular business **figure**, so you should try to make friends with him.
（スティーブはビジネス界ではとても人気のある人物だし、友達になっておいた方がいいよ。）

a literary **figure**（作家） a public **figure**（有名人）

This model has a perfect hourglass **figure**.
（このモデル、くびれてて完璧なスタイルしてるなぁ。）

Why doesn't this **figure** agree with the report?（なんでこの数字あのレポートと合わないの？）

V[T]　を計算する；と考える

- **figure** sth out（〜を理解する、解決する）

I can't **figure out** why I can't get a girlfriend.（なんで僕には彼女ができないのか理解できないよ。）

---

401 well-known
[wèl nóʊn]
☐☐☐☐☐☐

Adj. 知名度のある、よく知られた

Michael Phelps is a pretty **well-known** swimmer, so I'm surprised you haven't heard of him.（マイケル・フェルプスは結構知名度のある水泳選手だから、君が聞いたことないなんて驚き。）

well + 過去分詞　well は過去分詞について「よく（広く）〜された」という意味になります。well-known の他には well-written（よく書かれた）、well-accepted（広く受け入れられた）などがあります。

---

402 author
[á:θər]
☐☐☐☐☐☐

N[C] 作家、著者

My favorite **author** right now is Haruki Murakami from Japan.
（今私が一番好きな作家は日本の村上春樹なんだ。）

V[T]　を執筆する、著す

He has **authored** more than 100 books.（彼は 100 冊以上本を執筆してきた。）

---

403 ignore
[ɪɡnɔ́:r]
☐☐☐☐☐☐

V[T]　を無視する

I'm so sorry, I didn't mean to **ignore** you yesterday.
（本当にごめん、昨日は別に君のこと無視するつもりはなかったんだよ。）

▶ **ignorance** [íɡnərəns] N[U] 知らないこと、無知

Ignorance is bliss.（知らぬが仏。）

▶ **ignorant** [íɡnərənt] Adj. 無知な

David is so **ignorant**. I feel like I have to explain every little thing to him.
（デイヴィッドって本当無知だよな。どんな小さいことも全部説明しなきゃいけないみたいな感じなんだ。）

4 Influential writers outside of Europe, such as Murasaki Shikibu and Sun Tzu, have had lasting impacts on the development of culture and art both locally and on a global scale and are appreciated worldwide.

ヨーロッパ以外で大きな影響力を持つ作家、例えば紫式部や孫子などは、それぞれの国のみならず世界規模で後世の文化や芸術の発展に影響を与え続け、世界中で高く評価されている。

---

404 **lasting**
[lǽstɪŋ]
▢▢▢▢▢▢

Adj. 長続きする

The war had a **lasting** impact on my grandpa. (戦争は、おじいちゃんへ長期的な影響を及ぼした。)

▶ **last** [læst] V[I] 続く、長持ちする　Adj. 最後の　Adv. 最後に　N[U] 最後【the -】

If you want to make your battery **last** longer, you should minimize the number of apps running in the background.
(バッテリー長持ちさせたいんだったら、後ろで動いてるアプリの数を最小限にした方がいいよ。)

I managed to catch the **last** train. (なんとか終電乗れたよ。)

The **last** thing I want to do is sth (〜だけはしたくない)　at **last** (ついに)

last but not least (これも重要なことなのですが)

▶ **lastly** [lǽstli] Adv. 最後に

---

405 **impact**
N. [ímpækt]
V. [ɪmpǽkt]
▢▢▢▢▢▢

N[C] 影響、影響力　**N[U]** 衝撃

■ make an **impact** (影響を与える)　have an **impact** on sth (〜に影響を与える)

Working at a smaller company is great because I feel like I'm actually **making an impact**.
(小さい会社で働くと自分が実際に影響を与えている感じがしてすごい良いよ。)

Glass screen protectors protect your phone from **impact**.
(ガラス製の画面保護シートは携帯を衝撃から守ってくれるよ。)

V[I/T] （〜に）影響を与える

This movie **impacted** my personality a lot. (この映画、自分の性格にものすごい影響を与えたよ。)

▶ **impactful** [ɪmpǽktfəl] Adj. 影響力の強い、インパクトのある

I find that Apple commercials are always **impactful** and punchy.
(アップルの広告はいつもインパクトがあって力強いなぁと思うんだ。)

▶ **impacted** [ɪmpǽktɪd] Adj. (歯が歯茎に) 埋伏した

I'm seeing my dentist on Tuesday because I have an **impacted** wisdom tooth.
(親知らずが埋もれてるから今週の火曜日に歯医者さんに診てもらうんだ。)

406 development
[dɪvéləpmənt]
▯▯▯▯▯▯

N[U] 発展、発達、進歩 **N[C]** 情勢、（事態の）進展

Personal **development** and continuous learning are much more important to me than how much I get paid.
（自己啓発と継続学習は自分にとっていくら払ってもらえるかよりもずっと重要だよ。）

▶ **develop** [dɪvéləp] V[I] 発展する、発達する　V[T] を発展させる；を開発する

▶ **developing** [dɪvéləpɪŋ] Adj. 発展途上の ▶ **developed** [dɪvéləpt] Adj. 発展した

a **developing/developed** country（発展途上国 / 先進国）

---

407 global
[glóʊbəl]
▯▯▯▯▯▯

Adj. 世界的な、グローバルな

My teacher said if China collapses, it won't be a China problem, but a **global** issue.
（先生が、もし中国が崩壊したらそれは中国だけの問題じゃなくて世界的な問題になるって言ってたよ。）

▶ **globally** [glóʊbəli] Adv. 世界的に、グローバルに

▶ **globe** [gloʊb] N[S] 地球、世界【the -】　N[C] 地球儀

around **the globe**（地球上で、世界中で）

▶ **globalization** [glòʊbələzéɪʃən] N[U] グローバル化

▶ **globalism** N[U] グローバリズム　　　　◆ **isolationism** 孤立主義
　[glóʊbəlɪzəm]　　　　（地球全体を一つの共同体とみる考え方）　[àɪsəléɪʃənɪzəm]

---

408 scale
[skeɪl]
▯▯▯▯▯▯

N[S/U] 規模　**N[C]** 階級；目盛り；音階；うろこ　**N[C/U]** 縮尺

I need to work out how to market my products on a larger **scale**.
（もっと大きい規模で自分の商品をマーケティングする方法を考えないといけないな。）

on a **scale** of one to five（五段階評価で（5が最高、1が最低））

N[C] はかり

---

409 appreciate
[əpríːʃieɪt]
▯▯▯▯▯▯

V[T] を高く評価する；を感謝する；を理解する　**V[I]** 価値が上がる

I really **appreciate** your help!（手伝ってくれて本当に感謝してるよ！）

■ would **appreciate** it if + sentence（〜してくれると嬉しいです）

I **would appreciate it if** you could get back to me as soon as possible.
（できるだけ早くお返事いただけると嬉しいです。）

The USD has **appreciated**.（米ドルの価値が上がった。）

▶ **appreciation** [əpríːʃiéɪʃən] N[U] 評価；感謝；理解；値上がり

▶ **appreciative** [əpríːʃəṭɪv] Adj. 目の肥えた；（〜に）感謝している（of sth）

▶ **appreciatively** [əpríːʃəṭɪvli] Adv. 感謝して

---

410 worldwide
[wɔ́ːrldwaɪd]
▯▯▯▯▯▯

Adv. 世界中で、世界的に　**Adj.** 世界中の、世界的な

This site's great because it offers free shipping **worldwide**.
（このサイト、世界中どこでも送料無料だから最高。）

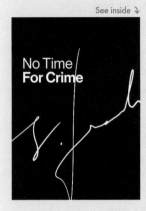

No Time For Crime

by **S. J. Holm** (Author)

★★★★☆

ⓐ Andrew   *January 15, 2018*

No Time for Crime, the much-anticipated novel in S. J. Holm's riveting fiction series *Criminal Minds*, easily exceeds expectations. As the third novel in the series, *No Time for Crime* continues to follow the crime-solving adventures of charming super-sleuth Henry Buckley. In a departure from the well-worn format of the previous two novels, the storyline finds our protagonist attempting to solve a puzzling murder in a destination outside of his home continent. Inserting Henry into a new backdrop, along with the sheer unpredictability of the plot, serves to keep things fresh.

Moreover, this novel explores yet more interesting dimensions of Henry's character.

While it drags on in parts, the exquisite writing, as well as the ample character development witnessed throughout, never ceases to be compelling and makes this a supremely rewarding read.

S. J. ホルムの素晴らしいフィクションシリーズ「Criminal Minds」の待望の新作小説「No Time for Crime」は、期待をはるかに上回るものだった。シリーズ3作目となる「No Time for Crime」では、今回も魅力的な名探偵ヘンリー・バックリーが犯罪捜査のために冒険を繰り広げる。前2作の使い古されたフォーマットから脱却し、主人公ヘンリーは生まれ育った大陸を離れ、訪れた目的地で不可解な殺人事件の解決に乗り出す。ヘンリーが新たな状況に置かれ、筋立てが全く予測不可能なおかげで、新鮮みもある。

さらに、この小説ではヘンリーというキャラクターの興味深い側面がよりいっそう引き出されている。

冗長なところもあるが、極めて美しい文章と、全編を通じて見られる登場人物の十分な成長によって、心をつかんで離さない、非常に読み応えのある一冊になっている。

411 **riveting**
[rívəṭɪŋ]
□□□□□□

Adj. 素晴らしい、わくわくするような

▶ **rivet** [rívɪt] V[T] を（〜に）くぎ付けにする（on/to sth/sb）；をびょうで留める

---

412 **fiction**
[fíkʃən]
□□□□□□

N[U] フィクション、小説　N[C/U] 作り話

▶ **fictional** [fíkʃənəl] Adj. 想像上の、架空の

---

413 **series**
[síri:z]
□□□□□□

N[C] シリーズ、一連

a **series** of sth（一連の〜、連続する〜）

▶ **serial** [síriəl] Adj. 連続の

---

414 **adventure**
[ədvéntʃər]
□□□□□□

N[C/U] 冒険

▶ **adventurous** [ədvéntʃərəs] Adj. 冒険的な

▶ **adventurously** [ədvéntʃərəsli] Adv. 冒険的に

▶ **adventurer** [ədvéntʃərər] N[C] 冒険家

---

415 **charming**
[tʃá:rmɪŋ]
□□□□□□

Adj. 魅力的な

▶ **charm** [tʃa:rm] N[U] 魅力　N[C] 呪文；お守り、飾り、チャーム
V[T] を魅了する；に魔法をかける

---

416 **departure**
[dɪpá:rtʃər]
□□□□□□

N[C] 脱却　N[C/U] 出発、出国、発車　↔ **arrival** [əráɪvəl] 到着

▶ **depart** [dɪpá:rt] V[I]（〜から / 〜へ）出発する（from/for sth）　V[T] を出発する

---

417 **format**
[fɔ́:rmæt]
□□□□□□

N[C] フォーマット、体裁、型、形式　V[T] の体裁の整える

Is there a way to download images in PDF **format**?

（画像を PDF 形式でダウンロードする方法ってあるかな？）

---

418 **puzzling**
[pʌ́zlɪŋ]
□□□□□□

Adj. 不可解な

▶ **puzzle** [pʌ́zəl] V[T] を悩ませる　N[C] 不可解なこと、謎；パズル

▶ **puzzled** [pʌ́zəld] Adj. 困惑した、戸惑った

---

419 **murder**
[mə́:rdər]
□□□□□□

N[C/U] 殺人、殺害　V[T] を殺害する

attempted **murder**（殺人未遂）　commit a **murder**（殺人を犯す）

▶ **murderer** [mə́:rdərər] N[C] 殺人犯

▶ **murderous** [mə́:rdərəs] Adj. 残虐な　▶ **murderously** [mə́:rdərəsli] Adv. 残虐に

---

420 **destination**
[dèstənéɪʃən]
□□□□□□

N[C] 目的地、行き先

▶ **destined** [déstɪnd] Adj.（〜）行きの（for sth）；（〜する / 〜の）運命にある（to do/for sth）

▶ **destiny** [déstɪni] N[C] 運命　N[U] 運命の力

421 continent
[ká:nṭənənt]

☐☐☐☐☐☐

N[C] 大陸

What **continent** is Jamaica in?（ジャマイカってどの大陸に入るの？）

▶ **continental** [kà:nṭənént̩l] Adj. 大陸の

---

422 insert
v. [ɪnsə́:rt]
n. [ínsə:rt]

☐☐☐☐☐☐

V[T] を（～に）差し込む、挿入する（in/into sth）
N[C] 折り込み広告；挿入されたもの

▶ **insertion** [ɪnsə́:rʃən] N[U] 挿入

---

423 sheer
[ʃɪr]

☐☐☐☐☐☐

Adj. 全くの、完全な

■ by **sheer** luck（完全な運で）

He said he got the job **by sheer luck**, but I think luck comes from hard work.
（彼は完全に運でその仕事を手に入れたって言ってたけど、運は努力から来るものだと思うんだ。）

---

424 plot
[plɑ:t]

☐☐☐☐☐☐

N[C]（話の）筋；陰謀、策略；（土地などの）区画　**V[I]** たくらむ
V[T] の筋立てを練る；(データ) をグラフに記入する

▶ **plotter** [plɑ́:ṭər] N[C] 陰謀者

---

425 dimension
[dɪménʃən]

☐☐☐☐☐☐

N[C] 側面、局面、次元　**N[P]** 寸法【-s】

▶ **dimensional** [dɪménʃənəl] Adj. ～次元の

I'm so bad at sketching three-**dimensional** objects.（立体の物スケッチするの本当に下手なんだ。）

---

426 drag on
[drǽɡán]

☐☐☐☐☐☐

[PV] だらだらと続く、だらだら長引く

The meeting **dragged on** for a while.（あのミーティングは長い間だらだら続いたよ。）

---

427 exquisite
[ɪkskwízɪt]

☐☐☐☐☐☐

Adj. 極めて美しい、実に素晴らしい

The food at the restaurant was **exquisite**.（あのレストランでの食事、実に素晴らしかったよ。）

▶ **exquisitely** [ɪkskwízɪtli] Adv. 非常に

---

428 ample
[ǽmpəl]

☐☐☐☐☐☐

Adj. 十分な、豊富な

ample evidence/time（十分な証拠 / 時間）

▶ **amplify** [ǽmpləfaɪ] V[T]を増やす、増幅する　▶ **amplification** [ǽmpləfəkéɪʃən] N[U]増幅

---

429 witness
[wítnəs]

☐☐☐☐☐☐

V[T] を目にする、目撃する；の証人になる　**N[C]** 目撃者；証人

▶ **eyewitness** [áɪwitnəs] N[C] 目撃者

---

430 cease
[si:s]

☐☐☐☐☐☐

V[T]（～するの）をやめる、中止する（to do/doing）　**V[I]** 終わる、やむ

without **cease***（絶え間なく）

* この用法では N[U] 扱いですが、基本的に名詞単体で使われることはありません。

▶ **ceasefire** [sí:sfaɪr] N[C] 停戦、休戦

伝記
Biography

Biographies usually narrate in detail a person's experience of events that have occurred in their life and often include analyses of the subject's personality.

Information used for writing biographies can be sourced from oral history, online articles, interviews, diaries, letters, and so forth.

On the other hand, autobiographies are compiled and written primarily based on interviews with the subject, with minimal use of other sources.

Therefore, while autobiographies can attract complaints for lacking accuracy and an objective perspective, they can be some of the most insightful and interesting books.

1 Biographies **usually** narrate in detail a person's experience of events that have occurred in their life and often include analyses of the subject's personality.

伝記は通常、ある人物が人生で経験した出来事を詳細につづったもので、その人物の性格についての分析を含んでいるものが多い。

431 biography
[baɪάːɡrəfi]
□□□□□□

N[C] 伝記　**N[U]** 伝記文学

Your life would make such a great **biography**, and you're not even thirty yet.
（君の人生はものすごい伝記になりそうだね。まだ 30 歳にもなってないのに。）

▶ **biographical** [bàɪoʊɡrǽfɪkəl] Adj. 伝記の、（ある人の）人生についての

▶ **biographer** [baɪάːɡrəfər] N[C] 伝記作家、他人の人生ストーリーを書く人

432 narrate
[nəréɪt]
[néreɪt]
□□□□□□

V[I/T] （〜を）つづる、物語る、（〜の）ナレーションをする

Morgan Freeman could **narrate** a history book, and I would still find it interesting.
（モーガン・フリーマンって歴史の本ですらナレーションできそうだよね。しかもそれでも面白そう。）

▶ **narrative** [nérətɪv] N[C] 物語　N[U] 話術　Adj. 物語の

I want to write a personal **narrative** on my blog!（自分のブログで個人的な物語を書きたい！）

▶ **narration** N[C/U] ナレーション　　　▶ **narrator** N[C] ナレーター、語り手
　[neréɪʃən]　　　　　　　　　　　　　　　 [néreɪtər]

433 detail
[dɪtéɪl]
[díːteɪl]
□□□□□□

N[U] 詳細、細かいこと　**N[C]** （個々の）細部、詳細

My new camera captures so much **detail** and color.　　　　　in **detail**
（私の新しいカメラは細部とか色をものすごくよく捉えてくれるんだ。）　（細かく）

My boyfriend keeps asking me to explain every single **detail** of what I was doing yesterday.（私の彼氏、昨日何してたか細かいことまで全部説明してってずっと聞いてくるんだけど。）

N[P] （〜に関する）詳細情報（of sth）【-s】

Please DM me and I'll give you more **details**!（DM してくれたら詳細教えます！）

▶ **detailed** [díːteɪld] Adj. 詳細な、詳しい

detailed information（詳細な情報）

434 **experience**
[ɪkspíriəns]
☐☐☐☐☐☐

N[U] （仕事や人生の）経験、体験　**N[C]** （具体的な）経験、体験

Diving with the sharks off the coast of South Africa was such an amazing **experience**!
（南アフリカの沖合でサメと一緒にダイビングしたのは最高の経験だったよ！）

In my **experience**, people don't really care what others do.
（自分の経験的に、人って周りがやることはそんな気にしてないよ。）

V[T] を経験する、体験する

I **experienced** a lot of difficulty finding a job in the UK.（UKでの職探しでたくさんの苦労を経験した。）

▶ **experienced** Adj. 経験豊富な　　　　　　◀▶ **inexperienced** 経験の浅い
　[ɪkspíəriənst]　　（経験による）知識が豊富な　[ìnɪkspíriənst]

Jacob is an **experienced** teacher. （ジェイコブは経験豊富な先生だよ。）

▶ **experiential** [ɪkspìriénʃəl] Adj. 経験に基づく

experiential learning （経験に基づく学習）

435 **event**
[ɪvént]
☐☐☐☐☐☐

N[C] 出来事、事件、イベント

I love this city because there's usually some kind of **event** happening over the weekend. （この街、週末は基本的に何かしらイベントをやっているから大好きなんだ。）

■ in the **event** that + sentence/of sth （〜という / 〜の場合には）

In the event of an emergency, please put on your own oxygen mask before assisting others. （緊急時には他の人を助ける前にまずは自分の酸素マスクを着用してください。）

▶ **eventful** Adj. 波乱万丈な　　　◀▶ **uneventful** （面白いことなどが）特に何もない
　[ɪvéntfəl]　　　　　　　　　　[ʌnɪvéntfəl]

an **eventful** life　　　My trip to Paris was **uneventful**.
（波乱万丈な人生）　　　（パリ旅行では特に何も面白いことは起きなかった。）

436 **occur**
[əkə́:r]
☐☐☐☐☐☐

V[I] （出来事などが）起こる、発生する

We should install security alarms to stop further robberies from **occurring**.
（これ以上強盗が起きないようにセキュリティアラームを設置するべきだね。）

■ It **occurred** to me that + sentence （〜だとふと思った）

It just **occurred to me that** I should study English for my future.
（自分の将来のために英語を勉強すべきだってふと思った。）

▶ **occurrence** [əkə́:rəns] N[C] 出来事　N[U] （出来事などの）発生

437 **life**
[laɪf]
☐☐☐☐☐☐

N[C/U] 人生；生活；命；（物の）寿命　**N[U]** 生命、生き物

I don't mean to brag, but my **life** is great right now.（自慢じゃないけどさ、私の人生今最高なんだ。）

life expectancy （平均寿命）　　　Is there **life** on Mars? （火星に生命って存在するの？）

▶ **lively** Adj. 生き生きした、活発な　▶ **alive** Adj. 生きている；存続した
　[láɪvli]　　　　　　　　　　　　[əláɪv]

a **lively** city （活気ある街）　　　Keep hope **alive**. （希望を捨てるなよ。）

2 Information **used for writing biographies can be** sourced **from** oral **history,** online articles, **interviews, diaries,** letters, and so forth.

伝記を書く際に利用される情報源としては、オーラルヒストリー、インターネット上の記事、インタビュー、日記、手紙などがある。

A Biography eBook
by Samuel Richards

---

438 information N[U] 情報
[ìnfərméɪʃən]

This book has really good **information**, but parts of it are a bit too detailed.
（この本って本当に良い情報載ってるんだけど、いくつかちょっと細かすぎる部分があるんだよね。）

▶ **informative** [ɪnfɔ́ːrmət̬ɪv] Adj. 役立つ情報が豊富な

This book was very **informative**. It was absolutely worth my time.
（この本は本当に役立つ情報が豊富で、確実に読む価値があったよ。）

▶ **informed** [ɪnfɔ́ːrmd] Adj. 情報に精通した ⟷ **uninformed** [ʌ̀nɪnfɔ́ːrmd] 無知の

I'll keep you **informed**. （随時お知らせしますね。）

▶ **inform** [ɪnfɔ́ːrm] V[T] に（〜について）知らせる (of/about sth)

John **informed** me of some changes made to our plan yesterday.
（ジョンが昨日いくつかのプラン変更について知らせてくれたよ。）

■ **inform** sb (that + sentence) （（〜だと）〜に知らせる）

I was **informed that** the cute cow's name is "Hamburger."
（あの可愛い牛の名前「ハンバーガー」なんだってさ。）

▶ **informational** [ìnfərméɪʃənəl] Adj. 情報に関する、情報を含む

an **informational** interview/conversation （自分が望んでいる職種に就いている人と話をすること）

「二つの情報」と言いたいときは？　information は不可算名詞のため、具体的な数を表すときは piece(s) of を使用します。そのため、「二つの情報」というときは two pieces of information と言います。

---

439 source V[T] を仕入れる、調達する　N[C] 源；原因；情報源
[sɔːrs]

I need to **source** some new ingredients for the restaurant.
（あのレストランのためにいくつか新しい材料を調達しないといけないんです。）

a **source** of energy （エネルギー源）

▶ **outsource** [áʊtsɔːrs] V[I/T] （〜を）外注する

440 **oral**
[ɔ́:rəl]
□□□□□□

Adj. 口頭の、口述の、口の ↔ **written** [rítn] 文書の、書かれた

I'll give an **oral** presentation in front of the class tomorrow. (明日クラスの前で口頭プレゼンするんだ。)

oral history（オーラルヒストリー *）　*関係者から直接話を聞き取り、過去の情報を集め記録すること

an **oral** contract（口頭契約、口約束）

▶ **orally** [ɔ́:rəli] Adv. 口頭で、口で

---

441 **online**
[ɑ́:nlaɪn]
□□□□□□

Adj. インターネット上の、オンラインの

What's your favorite free **online** game?（無料のオンラインゲームで好きなの何？）

Adv. インターネット上で、オンラインで

I hate going to the shops, so I try to buy things **online** whenever I can.
（お店に行くの嫌いだから、できるだけオンラインで買うようにしてるよ。）

↔ **offline** [ɑ̀:flа́ɪn] オフラインの／オフラインで

---

442 **article**
[ɑ́:rt̬ɪkəl]
□□□□□□

N[C] 記事、論文；(a, the などの) 冠詞；品目；(法的な契約書などの) 条項

I read a really cool **article** about virtual reality the other day.
（この前仮想現実についてのめちゃくちゃ良い記事読んだんだ。）

I'll teach you how to write a blog **article** that will go viral.
（バズるブログ記事の書き方、教えてあげるよ。）

It's no exaggeration to say that using **articles** is the hardest part of English grammar.
（冠詞の使い方は英文法で一番難しいと言っても過言じゃないよ。）

---

443 **letter**
[létər]
□□□□□□

N[C] 手紙；文字

I can't remember the last time a friend sent me a **letter**.
（最後に友達から手紙もらったのがいつかなんて思い出せないよ。）

Do you know why 'A' is the first **letter** of the alphabet?
（A がどうしてアルファベットの最初の文字なのか知ってる？）

---

444 **and so forth**
[əndsóʊfɔ:rθ]
□□□□□□

Phr. 〜など、〜とか = **and so on** [əndsóʊɑ:n]

Having a good education helps you get a good job, earn more money, **and so forth**.
（良い教育を受けると良い仕事を得たり、もっとお金を稼いだりするのに役立つよ。）

3 On the other hand, autobiographies are compiled and written primarily based on interviews with the subject, with minimal use of other sources.

一方、自伝の編集と執筆は、主に対象者へのインタビューを基に行われ、それ以外の情報源の利用は最小限にとどめられる。

ON THE OTHER HAND

---

445 on the other hand
[ɑ́:nðìʌðərhǽnd]
☐☐☐☐☐☐

Phr. 一方で、他方では

I enjoy warm-weather vacations. My husband, **on the other hand**, only wants to go skiing.
(私は暖かいところでの休暇が好きなんだけど、夫はその一方でスキーしか行きたがらないのよ。)

---

446 autobiography
[ɑ̀:təbaɪɑ́:grəfi]
☐☐☐☐☐☐

N[C] 自伝、自叙伝　N[U] 自伝文学

I think Michelle Obama's fascinating, so I'm going to read her **autobiography**.
(ミシェル・オバマは魅力的だなって思うから、彼女の自伝を読もうと思ってるんだ。)

▶ **autobiographical** Adj. 自伝的な
[ɑ̀:təbàɪəgrǽfɪkəl]

▶ **autograph** N[C]（有名人などの）サイン
[ɑ́:təgræf]

---

447 primarily
[praɪmérəli]
☐☐☐☐☐☐

Adv. 主に

I'm **primarily** responsible for the cooking and gardening at home.
(自分は家では主に料理とガーデニング担当なんだ。)

▶ **primary** [práɪmeri] Adj. 最も重要な；初等の

a **primary** school(小学校＜英＞) ＝ an elementary school ＜米＞

▶ **prime** [praɪm] Adj. 第一の、主要な；最上級の　N[S] 最盛期、全盛期

prime Kobe beef（最高品質の神戸牛）　a **prime** minister（首相、内閣総理大臣）

in one's **prime**（今が全盛期の）　past one's **prime**（全盛期を過ぎた）

---

448 base
[beɪs]
☐☐☐☐☐☐

V[T] を（〜に）基づかせる(on sth)；の本拠地を（〜に）置く(in sth)

■ be **based** on/in sth（〜に基づいている / 〜に本拠地を置いた）

Are Ryan's stats actually **based on** anything, or did he just pluck them out of thin air?
(ライアンの統計って実際なんかに基づいてるの？それともテキトーかな？)

I **based** my decision on your advice.（君のアドバイスを基に決断したよ。）

The company is **based** in Tokyo.（その会社は東京に拠点を置いている。）

N[C] 基盤、基礎、土台；基地

a military **base** (軍事基地)

▶ **basic** [béɪsɪk] Adj. 基礎的な、基礎の、基本的な N[P] 基礎、基本 【-s】

basic training (基礎トレーニング)　　Let's get back to the **basics**.(基本に戻ろう。)

▶ **basis** [béɪsɪs] N[C] 基礎、根拠（複数形：bases）

■ on the **basis** of sth（〜に基づいて）　on a + adjective + **basis**（〜の基準で）

In Australia, it is unlawful to discriminate **on the basis of** age, disability, or race.
(オーストラリアでは年齢、障害、人種に基づいて差別することは違法なんだよ。)

on a yearly/monthly/weekly/daily **basis** (毎年 / 毎月 / 毎週 / 毎日)

on a regular **basis** (定期的に)　　on a voluntary **basis** (ボランティアで)

---

449 **interview**
[ínṭərvjuː]
▯▯▯▯▯▯

N[C] インタビュー、面接、取材

I'm pretty sick of doing job **interviews**. (仕事の面接やるのもう結構だるいよ。)

V[T] にインタビューをする、を面接する　V[I] 面接を受ける

I **interviewed** this Japanese guy, and his English was pretty good.
(この日本人は私が面接したんだけど、彼の英語は中々良かったよ。)

I **interviewed** for a new job about a week ago, but I haven't heard back yet.
(一週間前くらいに新しい仕事の面接を受けたんだけど、まだ何も返事来てないんだ。)

▶ **interviewer** N[C] インタビュアー、面接官　⟷　**interviewee** 面接を受ける人
　　　[ínṭərvjuːər]　　　　　　　　　　　　　　　　[ínṭərvjuiː]

---

450 **subject**
N./Adj. [sʌ́bdʒekt]
v. [səbdʒékt]
▯▯▯▯▯▯

N[C] 話の対象となる人（物）；話のトピック；科目、教科

My favorite **subjects** at school were science and math. (学校で好きだった教科は科学と数学だよ。)

change the **subject** (話題を変える)

Adj. 〜に影響を受ける可能性がある(to sth)；〜を条件として(to sth)

I quickly made a to-do list, but it's **subject** to change.
(やることリストを簡単に作ったんだけど、これは変わる可能性があるよ。)

Everything is 300 yen here, **subject** to availability. (ここは全部 300 円ですよ、在庫限りです。)

V[T] を（〜に）さらす（to sth）

---

451 **minimal**
[mínəməl]
▯▯▯▯▯▯

Adj. 最小限の、最低の　⟷　maximal [mǽksəməl] 最大限の、最高の

I only do a **minimal** amount of practice right before an important match.
(大事な試合の直前は最小限の練習しかしないんだよね。)

▶ **minimize** V[T] を最小限にする、最小化する　⟷　**maximize** を最大化する
　　　[mínəmaɪz]　　　　　　　　　　　　　　　　[mǽksəmaɪz]

▶ **minimum** Adj. 最小限の、最低の　N[C] 最小　⟷　**maximum** 最大限の / 最大限
　　　[mínəməm]　　　　　　　　　　　　　　　　[mǽksəməm]

▶ **minimalism** [mínəməlɪzəm] N[U] ミニマリズム

4 **Therefore, while autobiographies can** attract complaints **for** lacking accuracy **and an** objective **perspective, they can be some of the most** insightful **and** interesting **books.**

そのため自伝は、正確さや客観的な視点に欠けるとの不満を招くことがあるが、極めて本質を突いた面白い本にもなり得る。

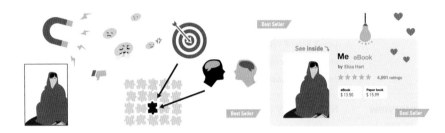

---

452 **attract**
[ətrǽkt]
☐☐☐☐☐☐

V[T] を招く；を惹きつける、魅了する

I'll be honest, the only reason I changed my hairstyle is to **attract** Hiroki's attention.
（正直な話、髪型を変えたのはヒロキの注意を引くためだけなんだ。）

Most people can tell if they're **attracted** to someone in the first 30 seconds after they meet.
（大体の人が会って30秒でその人に惹かれてるかどうかが分かる。）

▶ **attractive** [ətrǽktɪv] Adj. 魅力的な

an **attractive** offer（魅力的なオファー）　physically **attractive**（（その人の）見た目が魅力的な）

▶ **attractiveness** [ətrǽktɪvnəs] N[U] 魅力的であること

▶ **attraction** [ətrǽkʃən] N[S/U]（性的な）魅力　N[C] 見どころ、名所、アトラクション

Hearst Castle is one of the top-rated tourist **attractions** in California.
（ハースト・キャッスルはカリフォルニアで最も評価の高い観光名所の一つですよ。）

---

453 **complaint**
[kəmpléɪnt]
☐☐☐☐☐☐

N[C/U] 不満、不平、苦情

I'm pretty relieved that there haven't been many **complaints** about customer service this month.（今月は顧客サービスに関する苦情があんまり来てないから結構安心してるよ。）

▶ **complain** [kəmpléɪn] V[I]（〜について）不満を言う、不平を言う（about sth）

Stop **complaining**.（文句言うのやめなよ。）

---

454 **lack**
[læk]
☐☐☐☐☐☐

V[T] を欠く、が足りない

Most of these new movies coming out **lack** imagination.
（この新しい映画のほとんどは想像性に欠けているわ。）

Mark completely **lacks** any common sense. I mean, why would you use your phone in the bathroom?（マークって本当常識ないよね。いや、だって普通トイレで携帯使わないでしょ？）

N[S/U]　（〜の）欠乏、不足（of sth）

a **lack** of money（金欠）　a **lack** of sleep（睡眠不足）

---

455 **accuracy**
[ǽkjərəsi]
☐☐☐☐☐☐

N[U]　正確さ、精度

Can you teach me how to improve my passing **accuracy**?　　　with **accuracy**
（パスの正確さ上げる方法教えてくれないかな？）　　　　　　　　　　（正確に）

▶ **accurately** [ǽkjərətli] Adv. 正確に、正しく

This photo **accurately** shows how I feel right now.
（この写真、自分の今の気持ちを正確に表してるよ。）

▶ **accurate** [ǽkjərət] Adj. 正確な　　**⟷ inaccurate** [ɪnǽkjərət] 不正確な

---

456 **objective**
[əbdʒéktɪv]
☐☐☐☐☐☐

Adj. 客観的な ⟷ subjective [səbdʒéktɪv] 主観的な　　**N[C]　目標**

It's hard to be **objective** about my boyfriend's cooking.
（彼氏の料理に対して客観的になるなんて難しいよ。）

Let's set some **objectives** so you can achieve your goals. （ゴール達成の為にいくつか目標を立てよう。）

▶ **objectively** [əbdʒéktɪvli] Adv. 客観的に　**⟷ subjectively** [səbdʒéktɪvli] 主観的に

objectively speaking（客観的に言って）

▶ **objectivity** [àːbdʒektívəti] N[U] 客観性 **⟷ subjectivity** [sʌbdʒektívəti] 主観性

---

457 **insightful**
[ɪnsáɪtfʊl]
☐☐☐☐☐☐

Adj. 本質を突いた、洞察に満ちた

Colin and I had a very deep and **insightful** conversation yesterday.
（コリンと私は昨日ものすごく深くて洞察に満ちた会話をしたんだ。）

▶ **insight** [ínsaɪt] N[C/U] 洞察、洞察力

---

458 **interesting**
[íntrɪstɪŋ]
☐☐☐☐☐☐

Adj. 面白い、興味深い

I know it's hard, but can you at least act like what he's saying is **interesting**?
（大変なのは分かるけどさ、最低でも彼の言ってること面白いと思ってる雰囲気出してくれない？）

▶ **interest** [íntrɪst] N[S/U] 興味、関心　N[C] 趣味 N[U] 面白み　　V[T] に興味を持たせる

have an **interest** (in sth)（（〜に）興味がある）　lose **interest** (in sth)（（〜への）興味を失う）

just out of **interest**（ちょっと興味本位で聞きたいんだけど）

This ad doesn't **interest** me.（この広告には興味ないな。）be **interested** (in sth)（（〜に）興味がある）

▶ N[U] 利子、利息、金利

an **interest** rate（利子率）　　earn **interest** income（利息収入を得る）

▶ N[C/U] 利益、利害（関係）

a conflict of **interest**（利益相反行為）　　a vested **interest**（既得権益）

▶ **interestingly** [íntrɪstɪŋli] Adv. 興味深いことに、面白いことに

Hi guys, my name is Stella, and I've just arrived here from San Francisco. Since I'm new, I thought it'd be a good idea to **introduce** myself **briefly**.

I've spent most of my life in California, but I was born in London. However, my family moved to New York when I was three and to San Francisco not too long after that.

As a kid, I enjoyed **exercise** and being outdoors. During my **adolescence**, I managed to **convince** my parents to let me travel around America **solo**. **Slightly** after that, I spent **approximately** six months in Europe where, as **fate** would have it, I became **enthusiastic** about engineering. All the **excellent** European machinery, **monuments**, and roads really **impressed** me. They **released** a passion inside of me to build **stuff**.

Since I'm not sure how long I'm **sticking** around for, I'm **desperate** to explore as much of this city as possible. I'd love some **advice** for cool things to do or things that would make life more **convenient**.

みなさんこんにちは。ステラです。サンフランシスコから来たばかりです。新しく来たので、簡単に自己紹介した方が良いかなと思いました。

人生のほとんどをカリフォルニアで過ごしてきたんですけど、生まれはロンドンです。でも、3歳の時に家族がニューヨークに引っ越して、それから少しして、サンフランシスコに引っ越しました。

子供の時は、運動したり、外にいたりするのが好きでした。思春期には、親をなんとか説得して、アメリカ中を一人旅させてもらいました。それから少しして、ヨーロッパで大体半年くらい過ごして、そこで運命の巡り合わせで、工学に夢中になりました。ヨーロッパの素敵な機械とか、遺跡とか、道路とか、全部本当に感動しました。そこで、何かを建設したいっていうパッションが自分の中にあふれたんです。

どれくらいここに居続けるか分からないので、とにかくこの街をできるだけ探索したいなと思っています。やって楽しいこととか、生活がもっと便利になるようなこととか、何か良いアドバイスがあれば、教えてくれると嬉しいです。

459 **introduce**
[ìntrədúːs]

V[T] を紹介する；を導入する

▶ **introduction** [ìntrədʌ́kʃən] N[C/U] 紹介 N[U] 導入　N[C] 前書き

▶ **introductory** [ìntrədʌ́ktəri] Adj. 入門の、前書きの

460 **briefly**
[bríːfli]

Adv. 簡単に、手短に；少しの間；要するに

▶ **brief** Adj. 簡単な、手短な；短い　V[T] に（〜に関して）要点を伝える（on/about sth）
[briːf]

461 **exercise**
[éksərsaɪz]

N[C/U] 運動、エクササイズ　N[C] 練習、練習問題
V[I] 運動する　V[T] を運動させる；を行使する；を働かせる

462 **adolescence**
[ædəlésəns]

N[U] 思春期

▶ **adolescent** [ædəlésənt] Adj. 思春期の　N[C] 思春期の人

463 **convince**
[kənvíns]

V[T] を説得する、納得させる　= persuade [pərswéɪd]

▶ **convinced** [kənvínst] Adj. 納得した；確信した

▶ **convincing** [kənvínsɪŋ] Adj. 説得力のある、納得のいく

464 **solo**
[sóʊloʊ]

Adv. 一人で　Adj. 一人で行う、ソロの　N[C] 独奏、ソロ

Is Egypt good for a **solo** traveler?（エジプトって一人旅に良いのかな？）

465 **slightly**
[sláɪtli]

Adv. 少し、わずかに

▶ **slight** [slaɪt] Adj. わずかな

466 **approximately**
[əprɑ́ːksəmətli]

Adv. 大体、約

▶ **approximate** Adj. 大体の　V[I]（〜に）近くなる（to sth）　V[T] に近い
Adj. [əprɑ́ːksəmət] *V.* [əprɑ́ːksəmeɪt]

▶ **approximation** [əprɑ̀ːksəméɪʃən] N[C] 概算、近いもの

467 **fate**
[feɪt]

N[C/U] 運命

as **fate** would have it（運命の巡り合わせで）

468 **enthusiastic**
[ɪnθùːziǽstɪk]

Adj.（〜に）夢中になった、熱狂的になった（about sth）

▶ **enthusiastically** [ɪnθùːziǽstɪkli] Adv. 夢中で、熱狂的に

▶ **enthusiasm** [ɪnθúːziæzəm] N[U] 夢中、熱狂　N[C] 夢中になっているもの

469 **excellent**
[éksələnt]

Adj. 素敵な、素晴らしい、優秀な

▶ **excellence** [éksələns] N[U] 優秀さ

▶ **excel** [ɪksél] V[I]（〜において）優れている（in/at sth）

470 monument
[mɑ́ːnjəmənt]
□□□□□□

N[C] 遺跡；記念建築物、記念碑

▶ **monumental** [mɑ̀ːnjəméntl̩] Adj. 記念の；とてつもない

---

471 impress
[ɪmprés]
□□□□□□

V[T] を（〜で）感動させる、に（〜で）良い印象を与える（with sth）
V[I] 良い印象を与える

▶ **impressive** [ɪmprésɪv] Adj. 印象的な

▶ **impression** [ɪmpréʃən] N[C] 印象；思い込み；物まね

under the **impression** that + sentence（〜と思い込んだ）

---

472 release
[rɪlíːs]
□□□□□□

V[T] を放つ、解放する；を公表する

Yoga helps me **release** stress.（ヨガやるとストレス発散になるんだよね。）

N[S/U] 解放　N[U] 放出；公表、リリース、発売

N[C]（メディアを通じた）発表

---

473 stuff
[stʌf]
□□□□□□

N[U] もの　V[T] を（〜に）詰め込む（in sth）、に（〜を）詰め込む（with sth）

▶ **stuffed** [stʌft] Adj. いっぱい詰まった：お腹がいっぱいの；剥製の

I'm **stuffed**.（お腹いっぱい。）

---

474 stick
[stɪk]
□□□□□□

V[I] 動かない；（〜に）くっつく（to sth）；（〜に）刺さる（in/into sth）
V[T] を（〜に）くっつける（on/to sth）　N[C] 小枝；棒；つえ

▶ **stick around** [stɪkəráʊnd] [PV] 少し居る、近くにいる

▶ **sticker** [stíkər] N[C] ステッカー

---

475 desperate
[déspərət]
□□□□□□

Adj. とにかく（〜したい）（to do）；必死の、絶望的な、自暴自棄の

▶ **desperately** [déspərətli] Adv. とにかく；必死で

I **desperately** want a girlfriend.（死ぬほど彼女欲しい。）

▶ **desperation** [dèspəréɪʃən] N[U] 必死、自暴自棄

---

476 advice
[ədváɪs]
□□□□□□

N[U] アドバイス、助言

Can you give me some **advice**?（ちょっとアドバイスくれない？）

▶ **advise** [ədváɪz] V[I/T]（〜に）アドバイスする、助言する

---

477 convenient
[kənvíːniənt]
□□□□□□

Adj. 便利な、都合の良い

What time is **convenient** for you?（何時が都合良い？）

▶ **conveniently** [kənvíːniəntli] Adv. 都合良く

▶ **convenience** [kənvíːniəns] N[U] 便利さ　N[C] 便利なもの

Chapter

11

地理学
Geography

Contrary to popular belief, geography not only involves the study of the Earth's surface but also encompasses the study of its inhabitants, cultures, climate, and phenomena such as natural disasters.

As geography weaves together several related but contrasting themes, to make this discipline more systematic and transparent, it is often split into two branches: physical geography and human geography.

Physical geography, the study of the natural world, includes the examination of processes and spatial patterns that make up the atmosphere, soil, vegetation, water, the animal world, and landforms.

In human geography, on the other hand, human activity is of paramount importance. The field covers topics such as agricultural systems, urban systems, transportation, settlements, and the distribution and composition of populations.

1 Contrary to popular belief, geography not only involves the study of the Earth's surface but also encompasses the study of its inhabitants, cultures, climate, and phenomena such as natural disasters.

一般的に考えられていることとは反対に、地理学には地表の研究だけではなく、その地域の住民や文化、気候、自然災害などの現象についての研究も含まれている。

---

478 contrary
[ká:ntreri]
☐☐☐☐☐☐

Adj. (〜と) 反対に、逆の (to sth)　**N[U]**　反対【the -】

What you're telling me is **contrary** to what I learned at school, so I'm going to have to verify it. (君が今言ってること、私が学校で習ったことと全然違うから、ちょっと確かめないとなぁ。)

■ on the **contrary** (それどころか、それとは反対に、むしろ)

I don't think she wanted to create a problem. **On the contrary**, I believe she was trying to help you.(彼女は問題を引き起こしたかったわけじゃないと思うよ。むしろ君を助けようとしてたんだと思う。)

■ to the **contrary** ((修飾する言葉の後について) 反対の)

Even though many experts say that fasting is not good for your health, the researcher found evidence **to the contrary**.
(多くの専門家が断食は健康によくないと言っているけど、その研究者はそれとは反対の証拠を見つけたんだ。)

▶ **contrarily** [kəntrérɪli] Adv. 反対に、逆に

---

479 earth
[ɜ́:rθ]
☐☐☐☐☐☐

N[S/U] 地球【the -】= Earth　**N[U]** (空や海と対比して) 地面【the -】；土壌

I just can't believe some people still think that the **earth** is flat.
(地球が平面だと思ってる人が未だにいるなんて信じられないよ。)

▶ **earthy** [ɜ́:rθi] Adj. 土のような、土臭い；気取らない

▶ **earthly** [ɜ́:rθli] Adj. 地球の、(天国に対して) 地上の

an **earthy** smell (土のにおい)

the earth vs **Earth** vs **the Earth**　頭文字が小文字の earth は「地球」を意味するときは必ず the が付きます (the earth)。また、地球を固有名詞として扱う場合、Earth のように頭の e を大文字にします。この時、Earth は惑星としての地球というイメージが強くなります。通常、固有名詞には人の名前 (例：Bob, Sarah 等) と同様 the などの冠詞は付けませんが、Earth は例外的に the Earth となるパターンを持ちます (Earth との意味の違いはありません)。

---

480 surface
[sɜ́:rfɪs]
☐☐☐☐☐☐

N[C] 表面、面　**Adj.** 表面の；うわべだけの

I had to wear special shoes on stage because it was such a slippery **surface**.
(表面がすごい滑りやすかったから、ステージでは特別な靴を履く必要があったんだ。)

on the **surface**（表面上は）　　　come/rise to the **surface**（表面化する）

V[I] 水面に浮上する；（問題などが）表面化する　**V[T]** を舗装する

The pod of orcas **surfaced** a few miles off the coast. It was amazing.
（オルカの群れが岸から数マイル離れたところで水面に浮上したんだ。すごかったよ。）

---

481 **encompass**　**V[T]** を含む、包む、取り囲む
[ɪnkʌ́mpəs]

□□□□□□

"Japanese cuisine" **encompasses** a lot of different food, so you're going to need to be more specific.　（「日本料理」にはたくさんの異なる料理が含まれるから、もっと具体的に言わないと。）

---

482 **inhabitant**　**N[C]** 住民、居住者（同じ意味を持つ単語に habitant がありますが、こちらの方がずっと一般的です。）
[ɪnhǽbɪtənt]

□□□□□□

I wonder who the original **inhabitants** of this forest were.
（もともとこの森に住んでた人って誰なんだろう。）

▶ **inhabit** [ɪnhǽbɪt] V[T] に住む、生息する

These small islands are **inhabited** by only a few species of animals.
（この小さな島には数種類の動物しか住んでいないんだ。）

▶ **uninhabited** [ʌ̀nɪnhǽbətɪd] Adj. 無人の

an **uninhabited** island（無人島）

▶ **inhabitable** Adj. 居住に適した　　　◀▶ **uninhabitable** 居住に適さない
　[ɪnhǽbɪt̬əbəl]　　　　　　　　　　　　　　[ʌ̀nɪnhǽbət̬əbəl]

▶ **habitat** [hǽbətæt] N[C] 生息地、すみか

▶ **habitation** [hæ̀bətéɪʃən] N[U] 居住　N[C] 居住地

This house doesn't have a roof, windows, or even doors. It's obviously unfit for human **habitation**.（この家は屋根も窓も無いし、ドアだって無いじゃん。明らかに人が住めるような場所じゃないよ。）

---

483 **phenomenon**　**N[C]** 現象、事象（複数形：phenomena）
[fənɑ́ːmənɑːn]

□□□□□□

The popularity of K-Pop groups in Japan has become a big social **phenomenon**.
（日本での K-Pop グループの人気は大きな社会現象になってるよ。）

N[C] 天才的な人、ものすごく成功している人、驚くべきもの（複数形：-s）

Freddie Mercury was a **phenomenon**.（フレディ・マーキュリーは天才だったよ。）

▶ **phenomenal** Adj. 素晴らしい、驚異的な　▶ **phenomenally** Adv. 驚くほど
　[fənɑ́ːmənəl]　　　　　　　　　　　　　　[fənɑ́ːmənəli]

This novel is just **phenomenal**!（この小説は本当に素晴らしい！）

---

484 **disaster**　**N[C/U]** 災害、悲惨なこと；大失敗
[dɪzǽstər]

□□□□□□

The event wasn't a **disaster**, but it definitely could've been better.
（イベントは大失敗ではなかったけど、絶対もっとよくできたと思うんだよね。）

▶ **disastrous** Adj. 悲惨な　　　　　▶ **disastrously** Adv. 悲惨に
　[dɪzǽstrəs]　　　　　　　　　　　　　　[dɪzǽstrəsli]

2 As geography weaves together several related but contrasting themes, to make this discipline more systematic and transparent, it is often split into two branches: physical geography and human geography.

地理学は、いくつかの関連性があると同時に対照的でもあるテーマを織り交ぜたものであるため、この学問分野をより体系的で分かりやすいものにするために、自然地理学と人文地理学の2つに分けられることが多い。

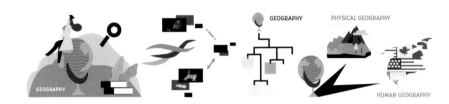

---

485 **weave**
[wiːv]

V[T] を織る、編む　**V[I]** 織物を織る；縫うように進む　**N[C]** 織り方

I've been told that this shirt is really expensive because it was **woven** in Italy using some special technique. （このシャツはイタリアで特別な技術を使って織られてるからものすごい高いんだって。）

■ **weave** in and out of traffic（車の隙間を縫うように進む）

He kept **weaving in and out of traffic**, but he still couldn't get much further ahead.
（彼はずっと車の間を縫うように運転していったんだけど、それ以上前に進むことはできなかったんだ。）

▶ **weaving** [wiːvɪŋ] N[U] 織ること　▶ **weaver** [wiːvər] N[C] 織り手、織物職人

---

486 **several**
[séverəl]

Adj. いくつかの、数個の

We've been dating for **several** years now, so I'm planning to propose soon.
（もう何年も付き合ってるから、そろそろプロポーズしようと思ってる。）

---

487 **contrasting**
[kəntræstɪŋ]

Adj. 対照的な

You should use **contrasting** colors like black and yellow if you want to attract people's attention.（人に注目してもらいたいなら、黒と黄色みたいに対照的な色を使った方が良いよ。）

▶ **contrast**
　　N. [kɑ́ːntræst] N[C/U]（比較したときの）対照、差異　N[U]（明暗の）コントラスト
　　V. [kəntræst] V[T] を（〜と）対比する（with sth/sb）V[I]（〜とは）対照的である（with sth/sb）

It's really interesting to see the **contrast** between traditional and modern culture in Japan.
（日本の伝統的な文化と現代の文化が対照的で面白いね。）

The saltiness of the meat really **contrasts** with the sweetness of the sauce. I think it's delicious.　（このお肉の塩気はソースの甘味とのコントラストがあって、僕は美味しいと思うな。）

488 theme
[θi:m]

N[C] テーマ、題材

Long hours seem to be a recurring **theme** in these employee surveys, so we should look into why that is.
（従業員アンケートで長時間労働がよく書かれてるみたいだから、なぜなのか調べた方がいいね。）

▶ **thematic** Adj. テーマの
[θi:mǽtɪk]

▶ **thematically** Adv. テーマ的には
[θi:mǽtɪkli]

---

489 systematic
[sìstəmǽtɪk]

Adj. 体系的な、組織的な

The police did a **systematic** search of the city, but still couldn't find the gunman.
（警察は街を計画的に捜索したんだけど、それでも武装した犯人を見つけることができなかったんだ。）

▶ **systematically** [sìstəmǽtɪkli] Adv. 体系的に、組織的に

Why are you so awesome at explaining things logically and **systematically**?
（君ってどうしてそんなに物事を論理的かつ体系的に説明するのが上手なの？）

▶ **system** [sístəm] N[C] システム、体系、制度

the solar **system**（太陽系）   the immune **system**（免疫系）

---

490 transparent
[trænspérənt]

Adj. 明白で分かりやすい；透明な

The sea in Cebu was so **transparent** that I could see fish swimming from the beach.
（セブの海はめちゃくちゃ透明だったから、ビーチから魚が泳いでるのが見えたんだ。）

transparent（透明な）   translucent（半透明の）   opaque（不透明の）
[trænspérənt]   [trænslú:sənt]   [oupéɪk]

▶ **transparency** [trænspérənsi] N[U] 透明性 ⟷ **opacity** [oupǽsəti] 不透明性

I understand we need **transparency** in our relationship, but I don't think that justifies checking my messages secretly.
（俺たちの関係にもっと透明性が必要だっていうのは分かるけど、だからと言ってこっそり俺のメッセージをチェックしても良いってわけじゃないだろ。）

---

491 split
[splɪt]

V[T] を分ける、分裂させる、割る **V[I]** が分かれる、分裂する、割れる

This cake is too big for me. Let's **split** it in half.
（このケーキ、俺には大きすぎるよ。半分に分けよう。）

■ **split up**（手分けをする）   **split** (sth) **down the middle**（（〜を）真っ二つに分ける）

Let's **split up** and find our missing cat.（手分けしていなくなっちゃったネコを探そう。）

▶ **splitting** [splɪtɪŋ] Adj. (痛みや音が) 割れるような、裂けるような

3 **Physical geography, the study of the natural world, includes the** examination **of processes and** spatial patterns **that make up the** atmosphere, soil, vegetation, water, the animal world, and landforms.

自然地理学は、自然界についての研究で、大気や土壌、植生、水文、動物界、地形に関するプロセスや、空間パターンの調査が含まれるものである。

PHYSICAL GEOGRAPHY

---

492 **examination**
[ɪgzæmənéɪʃən]
☐☐☐☐☐☐

N[C/U] 調査、検査、考察 N[C] 診察；試験 = **exam** [ɪgzæm]

We need to give the app a proper **examination** before we release it.
（アプリは正式にリリースする前にちゃんとチェックしないとね。）

under **examination**（調査中の）

▶ **examine** [ɪgzæmɪn] V[T] を調査する、考察する；に試験を課す；を診察する

I think we've got to **examine** this issue as soon as possible.
（この問題はできるだけ早く調査しないといけないと思うよ。）

▶ **examiner** [ɪgzæmɪnər] N[C] 試験官 ▶ **examinee** [ɪgzæməni:] N[C] 受験者

---

493 **spatial**
[spéɪʃəl]
☐☐☐☐☐☐

Adj. 空間の、空間的な = **spacial** [spéɪʃəl]

He's great at a lot of sports because he has excellent **spatial** awareness.
（彼は空間認識能力に長けてるから、どんなスポーツもできるんだ。）

▶ **space** N[C] 空き；行間 N[U] 空間；宇宙、大気圏外 (the space とはならないので注意)
[speɪs]

We've got to make some **space** for the new TV. It's really huge.
（新しいテレビのためにスペース作らないとね。本当に巨大だから。）

正：I want to go to **space**.
誤：I want to go to *the* **space**.

▶ **spacious** [spéɪʃəs] Adj. 広々とした、開放感のある

Now that we have twins, we need a more **spacious** living room.
（双子ができたからもっと広いリビングが必要だね。）

▶ **spaciously** Adv. 広々と ▶ **spaciousness** N[U] 広さ、広大さ
[spéɪʃəsli]　　　　　　　　　　　　[spéɪʃəsnəs]

494 pattern
[pǽtərn]
☐☐☐☐☐☐

N[C]　パターン、模様、柄

I love the **patterns** on your suit!（そのスーツの柄めちゃくちゃ良いじゃん！）

▶ **patterned** [pǽtərnd] Adj. 模様のある、柄のある

Should we buy plain or **patterned** carpet?
（カーペット、無地と柄入りどっち買った方が良いかな？）

a floral **pattern**/floral-**patterned**（花柄 / 花柄の）

polka dots/polka-dot（ドット柄 / ドット柄の）　stripes/striped（ストライプ / ストライプ柄の）

ボーダー T シャツなどの「ボーダー」は和製英語で、英語では striped が使用されます。また、striped は縦横どちらのしま模様も指すことができます。

495 atmosphere
[ǽtməsfɪr]
☐☐☐☐☐☐

N[S]　（地球の）大気【the -】　N[C]　（天体の）大気；（部屋の）空気

Auroras are caused by a particular type of particle being emitted into the Earth's upper **atmosphere**.（オーロラは地球の大気の上の方にある特定の種類の粒子が放出されることで起きるんだ。）

N[C/U]　ムード、雰囲気

This bar has a great **atmosphere**, which is why I love coming here.
（このバーはムードが素敵だから、ここに来るのが大好きなんだ。）

▶ **atmospheric** [ætməsférɪk] Adj. 大気の；雰囲気のある

atmospheric music（雰囲気のある音楽）

496 soil
[sɔɪl]
☐☐☐☐☐☐

N[C/U]　土壌、土　V[T]　を（泥などで）汚す

Will this cactus grow in any kind of **soil**?（このサボテンってどんな土でも育つの？）

▶ **soiled** [sɔɪld] Adj.（泥などで）汚れた

Oh my god, I will never get used to changing **soiled** diapers.
（はぁ、汚れたオムツを交換するの全然慣れない。）

497 vegetation
[vèdʒətéɪʃən]
☐☐☐☐☐☐

N[U]　植生、（集合的に）植物

The **vegetation** in this part of the woods is quite unique.
（林のこの辺に生息する植物はかなり特殊なんだ。）

▶ **vegetable** [védʒtəbəl] N[C] 野菜；植物人間

▶ **vegetate** [védʒəteɪt] V[I] 何もしないでダラダラ過ごす

498 landform
[lǽndfɔːrm]
☐☐☐☐☐☐

N[C]　地形

The **landforms** on Mars indicate that water once traveled across the planet.
（火星の地形をみると、かつては水が流れていたことが分かる。）

4

In human geography, on the other hand, human activity is of paramount importance. The field covers topics such as agricultural systems, urban systems, transportation, settlements, and the distribution and composition of populations.

一方、人文地理学では、人の活動が最も重視される。この分野で扱われるテーマには、農業システム、都市システム、交通輸送、集落、そして人口の分布と構成などがある。

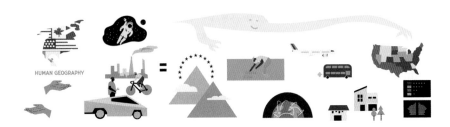

HUMAN GEOGRAPHY

---

499 paramount
[pérəmaʊnt]

Adj. 最重要の

Getting this part done quickly is absolutely **paramount** to the success of the project.
（この仕事を早く終わらせることは、プロジェクトの成功においてものすごい重要だよ。）

sth of **paramount** importance（最重要の〜）

---

500 cover
[kʌ́vər]

V[T] を取り扱う；を（〜で）覆う（with sth）；を報道する；を保険対象とする

We've **covered** a lot of topics today, so I'm going to pause for a few minutes to let you reflect.（今日はここまでたくさんのトピックを扱ったし、みんなちょっとここで止まって復習してみようか。）

N[C] カバー；表紙　**N[P]** 寝具【the -s】

judge a book by its **cover**（見た目で判断する）

▶ **coverage** [kʌ́vərɪdʒ] **N[U]** 報道；保険；（ネットなどの）受信可能範囲

I can't trust media **coverage** anymore because it's often distorted.
（メディアの報道はよく歪められてるからもう信用できないよ。）

You shouldn't **judge a book by its cover**.（人は見た目で判断しちゃいけないよ。）

---

501 agricultural
[æɡrəkʌ́ltʃərəl]

Adj. 農業の

I think it's critical for the future of poor countries that we continue to develop and improve **agricultural** technologies.（貧しい国の将来にとって、農業技術の継続的な発展と向上は必要不可欠だと思う。）

▶ **agriculture** [æɡrəkʌ́ltʃər] **N[U]** 農業、農学

One way for Japanese **agriculture** to survive is for scientists and farmers to create unique products like square watermelons and Yubari King.
（日本の農業が生き残る方法の一つは、科学者と農家が四角いスイカや夕張キングメロンのようなユニークな商品を作ることだよ。）

502 **urban**
[ə́:rbən]
☐☐☐☐☐☐

Adj. 都市の、都会の ↔ rural [rúrəl] 田舎の

I personally prefer **urban** life over rural life.
〈個人的には田舎暮らしより都会暮らしのほうが好きだなぁ。〉

▶ **urbane** [ɜːrbéɪn] Adj. あか抜けた、洗練された、上品な

He's lived in New York for eight years, but he doesn't have an **urbane** manner.
〈彼はニューヨークに8年くらい住んでるけど、全然あか抜けてないんだよね。〉

▶ **urbanely** [ɜːrbéɪnli] Adv. あか抜けて、洗練されて、上品で

▶ **urbanization** [ə̀:rbənəzéɪʃən] N[U] 都市化、都会化

---

503 **transportation**
[træ̀nspərtéɪʃən]
☐☐☐☐☐☐

N[U] 交通輸送、交通機関

■ public **transportation** （公共交通機関）   a means of **transportation** （交通手段）

Public transportation in Tokyo is really confusing because there are so many different lines. 〈東京の公共交通機関は、めっちゃたくさん路線が通ってるから、すごい混乱するよ。〉

▶ **transport** V[T] を運ぶ、輸送する N[U] 運送、輸送
V. [trænspɔ́:rt] *N.* [trǽnspɔ:rt]

▶ **transportable** [trænspɔ́:rtəbl] Adj. 輸送可能な

---

504 **settlement**
[sétlmənt]
☐☐☐☐☐☐

N[C] 集落 N[C/U] （紛争などの）解決、和解 N[U] （負債などの）返済

Did you know that more than 500 indigenous groups lived in Australia before British **settlement**? 〈イギリスが入植する前、オーストラリアには500以上の先住民族が住んでたって知ってた？〉

▶ **settle** V[T] を解決する；を決定する；に入植する；（胃や神経）を落ち着かせる
[sétl] V[I] （物事が）落ち着く；（胃や神経が）落ち着く

settle in （（環境などに）慣れる、落ち着く） **settle** down （（決まった場所などに住んで）落ち着く）

settle (on) a date （日程を決定する） **settle** a dispute/the matter （紛争 / 問題を解決する）

We've finally **settled** all our debts. 〈僕らはついに全借金を返済したんだ。〉

↔ **unsettle** [ʌnsétl] V[T] を動揺させる

---

505 **distribution**
[dìstrɪbjúː ʃən]
☐☐☐☐☐☐

N[C/U] 分布 N[U] 分配、配分；流通

I worry that the **distribution** of wealth is becoming increasingly uneven.
〈富の分配がどんどん偏ってきていることが心配なんだよね。〉

▶ **distribute** [dɪstríbjuːt] V[T] を（〜に）分配する、配布する （to sth/sb）

He'll **distribute** the tickets to each of you, so please wait in line.
〈彼がチケットを一人一人に配布いたしますので、列になってお待ちください。〉

▶ **distributor** [dɪstríbjuːt̬ər] N[C] 流通業者、卸売業者、販売代理店

He owns the largest **distributor** of sports equipment in Asia.
〈彼はアジア最大のスポーツ用品の流通企業を所有しているんだ。〉

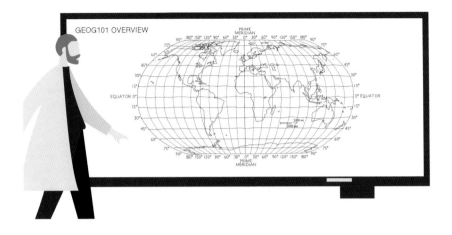

Hello **folks**. Welcome to GEOG101 – Introduction to World Geography. **Curious** what's going to be covered today? Maybe feeling a bit anxious? Don't stress, I'm going to give you a bit of a **refresher** today to help you **conquer** your anxiety before diving into the more academic side of geography.

So, we'll **outline** the elements that make up this map of the world which you all know and love. Hopefully I'm covering some ground you already know here, but the world map has **vertical** lines called lines of **longitude** connecting the North and South Poles and **horizontal** lines called lines of **latitude**. The horizontal line running through the middle separating the Northern and Southern **hemispheres** is called the **equator**.

We have seven continents (North America, South America, Asia, Europe, Africa, Australia, and Antarctica), and five **oceans** (the Pacific, **Atlantic**, Indian, Arctic, and Southern Oceans). Here is some historical trivia for you: these continents used to be **merged** together as one supercontinent called "Pangea."

みなさんこんにちは。GEOG101 – 世界地理入門へようこそ。今日の内容がどんなものか気になっていますか？それともちょっと不安かな？まぁそんなにストレスを感じなくても大丈夫。今日は地理学のもっとアカデミックな側面を見ていく前に、簡単なおさらいをして、そんな不安を克服しましょう。

それでは、まずはこのみなさんご存じ、そして大好きな世界地図の要素から、簡単にまとめていきますね。みなさんきっともう知ってることだとは思いますが、まず世界地図には北極と南極を結ぶ経線と呼ばれる垂直な線と、緯線と呼ばれる水平な線があります。また、北半球と南半球を隔てて真ん中を横切って走っている線は赤道と呼ばれています。

そして、北アメリカ、南アメリカ、アジア、ヨーロッパ、アフリカ、オーストラリア、南極の7つの大陸と、太平洋、大西洋、インド洋、北極海、そして南極海の5つの大洋があります。ここで少し歴史的な雑学があります。これらの大陸は元々全て一緒にくっついていて、「パンゲア」と呼ばれる超大陸だったんですよ。

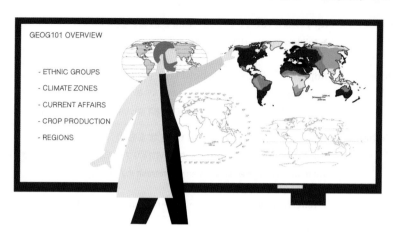

In this course, we're going to explore this map through many different lenses such as ethnic groups, climate zones, current affairs, agriculture and crop production, and regions including countries, states, counties, provinces, prefectures, you name it.

At first glance, these may appear a bit disconnected. However, in fact, they are all closely associated with each other. After you learn all this, you'll be able to see the world from many different angles. Let's move on to the next slide.

このコースでは、民族や気候帯、時事問題、農業、作物生産、そして国、州、郡、省、県といった地域など、ありとあらゆる多様な観点からこの地図を見ていきます。

一見、これらには関連性がないように見えるかもしれません。しかし、実際にこれらは全て密接に関連し合っているのです。これらを全て学習すれば、世界をさまざまな異なる角度からとらえることができるようになることでしょう。それでは次のスライドに移りましょう。

506 folk
[foʊk]

N[P] みなさん、人々【-s】　Adj. 民族の、民族伝承の

▶ **folklore** [fóʊklɔːr] N[U] 民族伝承

---

507 curious
[kjʊ́riəs]

Adj. (〜が) 気になる (about sth)；好奇心の強い

I'm **curious** about this new novel. (この新しい小説、気になるなぁ。)

▶ **curiosity** [kjʊ̀riɑ́səţi] N[S/U] 好奇心　N[C] 珍しいもの　out of **curiosity** (好奇心から)

---

508 refresher
[rɪfréʃər]

N[C] おさらい、再教育、思い出させるもの

▶ **refresh** [rɪfréʃ] V[I] リフレッシュする　V[T] をリフレッシュさせる；を思い出させる

When was his birthday again? Can you **refresh** my memory?
(彼の誕生日いつだったっけ？思い出させてくれない？)

▶ **refreshed** [rɪfréʃt] Adj. リフレッシュした　▶ **refreshing** [rɪfréʃɪŋ] Adj. リフレッシュするような

---

509 conquer
[kɑ́ːŋkər]

V[T] を克服する；を征服する

conquer one's fears (恐怖心を克服する)

▶ **conqueror** [kɑ́ːŋkərər] N[C] 征服者　▶ **conquest** [kɑ́ːŋkwest] N[S/U] 征服

---

510 outline
[áʊtlaɪn]

V[T] をまとめる、の要点を述べる；の輪郭を描く　N[C] 概要；輪郭

---

511 vertical
[vɜ́ːrţəkəl]

Adj. 垂直な　N[C] 垂直線

▶ **vertically** [vɜ́ːrţəkli] Adv. 垂直に

---

512 longitude
[lɑ́ːndʒətuːd]

N[C/U] 経度

lines of **longitude** (経線)

▶ **longitudinal** [lɑ̀ːndʒətúːdɪnəl] Adj. 経度の

---

513 horizontal
[hɔ̀ːrɪzɑ́ːnt̬l]

Adj. 水平な、横の　N[C] 水平線

▶ **horizontally** [hɔ̀ːrɪzɑ́ːnt̬əli] Adv. 水平に、横に

▶ **horizon** [həráɪzən] N[S] 地平線、水平線【the -】　N[P] 視野【-s】

broaden sb's **horizons** (〜の視野を広げる)

---

514 latitude
[lǽţətuːd]

N[C/U] 緯度

lines of **latitude** (緯線)

▶ **latitudinal** [lǽţətúːdɪnəl] Adj. 緯度の

---

515 hemisphere
[héməsfɪr]

N[C] 半球；脳半球

the Northern/Southern **Hemisphere** (北 / 南半球)

516 **equator**
[ɪkwéɪṱər]

☐☐☐☐☐☐

N[U] 赤道【the -】

▶ **equatorial** [èkwətɔ́:riəl] Adj. 赤道の、赤道付近の

---

517 **ocean**
[óʊʃən]

☐☐☐☐☐☐

N[C] 大洋 N[S] 海【the -】

---

518 **Atlantic**
[ətlǽnṱɪk]

☐☐☐☐☐☐

N[S] 大西洋【the -】 = the Atlantic Ocean Adj. 大西洋の

---

519 **merge**
[mɜ:rdʒ]

☐☐☐☐☐☐

V[T] を結合させる、合併させる V[I] (〜と)結合する、合併する (with sth)

▶ **merger** [mɜ́:rdʒər] N[C] 結合、合併

mergers and acquisitions（合併と買収、M&A）

---

520 **ethnic**
[éθnɪk]

☐☐☐☐☐☐

Adj. 民族の N[C] 民族の一員

▶ **ethnically** [éθnɪkli] Adv. 民族的に ▶ **ethnicity** [eθnísəṱi] N[C/U] 民族性

---

521 **affair**
[əfér]

☐☐☐☐☐☐

N[P] 情勢、事情【-s】 N[C] 浮気

current **affairs**（時事） have an **affair** (with sb) ((〜と) 浮気する)

---

522 **crop**
[krɑːp̬]

☐☐☐☐☐☐

N[C] 作物、農作物、収穫高 V[I] 収穫できる

V[T] (動物が牧草など) を食べる；(髪) を短く切る；を切り取る

▶ **cropped** [krɑːpt] Adj. (髪を) 短く切られた；ショート丈の

---

523 **county**
[káʊnṱi]

☐☐☐☐☐☐

N[C]（アメリカの）郡

---

524 **province**
[prɑ́:vɪns]

☐☐☐☐☐☐

N[C] 省、州、県 N[P] 地方【-s】

▶ **provincial** [prəvínʃəl] Adj. 省の、州の、県の；地方の

---

525 **prefecture**
[prí:fektʃər]

☐☐☐☐☐☐

N[C]（日本やフランスの）県

---

526 **you name it**
[jʊnéɪmɪt]

☐☐☐☐☐☐

Phr. ありとあらゆるものを、何でも

I love all kinds of food. **You name it**.（食べ物はどんなものも大好き。何でもだよ。）

527 **glance**
[glæns]
☐☐☐☐☐☐

N[C] ちらっと見ること　**V[I]**（〜を）ちらっと見る（at sth）

at first **glance**（一見したところ、最初は）　at a **glance**（一目見ただけで）

528 **associate**
V. [əsóʊʃieɪt]
Adj./N. [əsóʊʃiət]
☐☐☐☐☐☐

V[T] を（〜と）関連づける（with sth）　**V[I]**（人と）付き合う

This article says there are some specific genes **associated** with intelligence.
（この記事によると、知能に関連した特定の遺伝子があるんだって。）

Adj. 準〜、副〜　**N[C]** 関係者

an **associate** professor（准教授）

529 **angle**
[ǽŋgəl]
☐☐☐☐☐☐

N[C] 角度、角　**V[I]** ある角度に向く　**V[T]** に角度をつける

12

↻ CH. 1, 5, 8, 11

歴史
History

History is an umbrella term that refers to past events as well as the discovery, collection, presentation, and interpretation of information and evidence relating to these events.

While not immediately apparent, one of the most important reasons for studying history is that the events of the past and the activities of our ancestors are crucial for understanding the present and may indicate what the future holds.

For example, leaders seeking to understand previous military disputes among European nations and minimize the risk of future disputes formed the European Union to improve relationships between these nations.

This illustrates that by developing our knowledge and awareness of the links between historical events, and focusing on avoiding mistakes that were made in the past, we are able to refrain from repeating them.

1 **History is an umbrella term that** refers **to** past **events as well as the** discovery, collection, presentation, **and** interpretation **of information and** evidence relating to these events.

歴史は包括的な言葉で、過去の出来事と、それに関わる情報と証拠の発見や収集、提示、解釈を指す。

---

530 **refer**
[rɪfɜ́ːr]
□□□□□□

V[I] （〜を）指す、（〜に）言及する、（〜を）参照する（to sth/sb）

Can you add page numbers to the documents so that I know which part you're **referring** to?（どの部分のことを言ってるか分かるように書類にページ番号追加してくれない？）

■ **refer** to A as B（A を B と呼ぶ）

Japan is often **referred to as** a smoker's paradise.（日本は喫煙者の楽園だとよく言われている。）

V[T] を（〜に）紹介する

▶ **reference** [réfərəns] N[C/U] 言及　N[U] 参照、参考　N[C] 参考文献；推薦、推薦者

for your **reference**（参考までに）　　in/with **reference** to sth/sb（〜に関して、〜を参照して）

Could you write a **reference** letter for me?（私に推薦状を書いてもらえませんか？）

---

531 **past**
[pæst]
□□□□□□

Adj. 過去の　**Prep.** 〜を過ぎて　**N[S]** 過去【the -】

Don't let **past** events stop you from challenging new things.
（過去の出来事にとらわれて新しいことに挑戦しないってのはやめなよ。）

It's five **past** three.（3時5分です。）　I walked **past** a friend today.（今日友達とすれ違ったんだ。）

You shouldn't think too much about what's happened in **the past**.
（過去に起きたことについては考えすぎない方が良いよ。）

in **the past**（昔は、過去に）　　at present（現在は）　　in the future（将来に）

---

532 **discovery**
[dɪskʌ́vəri]
□□□□□□

N[C/U] 発見

I made a few great **discoveries** at the flea market over the weekend.
（週末のフリーマーケットでいくつか良いもの発見したんだ。）

▶ **discover** V[T] を発見する；だと分かる　　▶ **discoverer** N[C] 発見者
[dɪskʌ́vər]　　　　　　　　　　　　　　　　[dɪskʌ́vərər]

What I love most about traveling is being able to **discover** delicious new dishes.
（旅行で一番好きなことは美味しいご飯を新しく見つけられることなんだ。）

533 **collection**
[kəlékʃən]

N[C/U] 収集、回収 N[C] 収集品、コレクション；募金 N[C/U] (税金などの) 徴収

Ben's shoe **collection** is absolutely insane. (ベンの靴コレクションはマジで狂ってるよ。)

▶ **collect** [kəlékt] V[T] を集める、回収する、徴収する、(年金など) を受け取る

I don't know why, but I love **collecting** comic books.
(なんでか分からないけど、漫画を集めるのが大好き。)

▶ **collective** Adj. 集団的な、共同の   ▶ **collectively** Adv. 集団で、共同で
[kəléktɪv]   [kəléktɪvli]

collective action (集団行動)

▶ **collectivism** N[U] 集団主義   ◆ **individualism** 個人主義
[kəléktəvɪzəm]   [ìndəvídʒuəlɪzəm]

534 **presentation**
[prèzəntéɪʃən]

N[U] 提示、提出 N[C/U] 言い方、見せ方；授与 N[C] 発表、プレゼン

When is your **presentation**? (君のプレゼンはいつ？)

You should get a haircut before your date. **Presentation** is very important.
(デートの前に髪切った方がいいよ。自分をどう見せるかはものすごい大事だからね。)

▶ **present** V[T] を示す、提示する；を贈る；を発表する
V. [prɪzént]   Adj. 出席している、存在している；現在の
Adj./N. [prézənt] N[C] プレゼント N[S] 現在 【the -】

Please **present** this QR code to the reception staff.
(この QR コードを受付の人に提示してください。)

The whole family was **present** at the wedding party.   a birthday **present**
(ウェディングパーティには家族みんなが出席していたよ。)   (誕生日プレゼント)

▶ **presence** [prézəns] N[U] 存在 N[S] 存在感

535 **interpretation**
[ɪntɜːrprətéɪʃən]

N[C/U] 解釈

This blogger's **interpretation** of the news is a breath of fresh air.
(このブロガー、ニュースに対する解釈が斬新なんだよな。)

▶ **interpret** [ɪntɜːrprɪt] V[T] を (~だとして) 解釈する (as sth) V[I/T] (~を) 通訳する

While his constant texting could be a sign of love, it could be **interpreted** as
something more sinister.
(彼が常にメッセージしてくるのは愛の印かもしれないけど、もっと危険なものとも解釈できるかも。)

▶ **interpreter** [ɪntɜːrprətər] N[C] 通訳者

536 **evidence**
[évədəns]

N[U] 証拠、証言

I can't go and report that John stole something if I don't have any **evidence**.
(証拠もないのにジョンがなんか盗んだなんて報告しに行けないよ。)

▶ **evident** [évədənt] Adj. 明白な、明らかな

It's **evident** you're angry because your face is turning red.
(君顔が赤くなってるから怒ってるって明らかに分かるよ。)

2 While **not** immediately apparent, **one of the most important** reasons **for studying history is that the events of the past and the activities of our** ancestors **are** crucial **for understanding the present and may** indicate **what the future holds.**

すぐには分からないかもしれないが、歴史を学ぶ最も重要な理由の一つは、過去の出来事と私たちの祖先の活動は、現在について理解する上で極めて重要で、未来に起きる出来事を示してくれる可能性があることだ。

---

537 **while**
[waɪl]
☐☐☐☐☐☐

Cnj. ～だが；～している間に　= **whilst** [waɪlst]（よりフォーマル）

While I understand Eiken Grade-1 is very difficult, I don't think it's impossible to pass it.
（英検1級がすごい難しいのは分かってるけど、合格が不可能だとは思ってないよ。）

While you were out drinking and partying, I was at home studying hard.
（君が外で飲んでパーティしている間、私は家で頑張って勉強してたよ。）

N[S] しばらくの間【a -】

---

538 **immediately**
[ɪmíːdiətli]
☐☐☐☐☐☐

Adv. すぐに、即座に；すぐ近くに；直接に

■ **immediately** before/after（～の直前 / 直後に）

I'm going to a concert tonight, so I have to go home **immediately after** work.
（今夜はコンサートに行くから、仕事の後はすぐ家に帰らないといけないんだ。）

▶ **immediate** [ɪmíːdiət] Adj. 即時の、緊急の；隣接した；直属の

sb's **immediate** boss（～の直属の上司）　　the **immediate** future（近い将来）

▶ **immediacy** [ɪmíːdiəsi] N[U] 即時性；臨場感

---

539 **apparent**
[əpérənt]
☐☐☐☐☐☐

Adj. すぐに分かる、明らかな

It's becoming **apparent** that Ben has no idea what he's doing.
（ベンは自分で何をやっているのか分かってないということがドンドン明らかになってきたよ。）

▶ **apparently** [əpérəntli] Adv. 明らかに

語根 par, pear　「見える」という意味の語根で、他には appear（現れる）や transparent（透明な）などがあります。

540 **reason**
[ríːzən]
☐☐☐☐☐☐

N[C/U] 理由   N[U] 理性；道理、理屈

Is there a **reason** why you dyed your hair pink? (髪の毛ピンクに染めたのには何か理由あるの？)

■ for some **reason**（なぜか、何かしらの理由で）   **reason** for sth（〜の理由）

For some reason, she doesn't like me. (なぜか彼女は私のこと好きじゃないんだって。)

■ the **reason** why + sentence（〜である理由）

The reason why I'm so tired now is because the dog barked all night, and I couldn't sleep. (今めちゃくちゃ疲れてるのは、夜犬がずっと吠えてて寝られなかったからなんだ。)

▶ **reasonable** [ríːzənəbəl] Adj. 合理的な；(値段などが) 手頃な；(水準や結果が) まぁまぁの

Do you think it's **reasonable** to ask for a pay raise this time, given my performance?
(自分のパフォーマンスを考慮した上で、今回昇給のお願いするのって理に適ってると思う？)

↔ **unreasonable** [ʌnríːzənəbəl] 合理的でない、理不尽な

▶ **reasonably** Adv. 合理的に   ↔ **unreasonably** 不合理に
[ríːzənəbli]   [ʌnríːzənəbli]

▶ **reasoned** [ríːzənd] Adj. 道理に基づいた、筋の通った

▶ **reasoning** [ríːzənɪŋ] N[U] 論理、推理

541 **ancestor**
[ǽnsestər]
☐☐☐☐☐☐

N[C] 祖先、先祖 ↔ descendant [dɪséndənt] 子孫

The coolest thing about this DNA test is that it tells me who my **ancestors** were.
(この DNA テストの最高なところは自分の先祖が誰か教えてくれることなんだよね。)

▶ **ancestral** [ænséstrəl] Adj. 祖先の、先祖の

▶ **ancestry** [ǽnsestri] N[C/U] (集合的に) 祖先、先祖、家系

ancestral knowledge (先祖の知恵)

542 **crucial**
[krúːʃəl]
☐☐☐☐☐☐

Adj.（〜にとって）極めて重要な（for/to sth）

This part of the lecture is really **crucial**, so you should pay attention.
(レクチャーのこの部分はものすごい重要だから、注意して聞いた方がいいよ。)

543 **indicate**
[índəkeɪt]
☐☐☐☐☐☐

V[T] を示す、表す

Do you think that these stats **indicate** that a recession is coming?
(この統計データ、これから不景気になることを示してると思う？)

▶ **indication** [ìndəkéɪʃən] N[C/U] 兆候、しるし、表れ

I'm sure Jim was nervous when he was making that speech, but he gave no **indication**.
(ジムはあのスピーチしてる時緊張してたはずなのに、全然そんな感じしなかったんだ。)

▶ **indicator** [índəkeɪtər] N[C] 指標、(あることを) 示すもの

▶ **indicative** [ɪndíkətɪv] Adj. (〜を) 示した、表した (of sth)

Dark clouds are not necessarily **indicative** that there will be a big storm.
(黒い雲は必ずしも大きな嵐が来ることを示しているわけではないよ。)

3 For example, leaders seeking to understand previous military disputes among European nations and minimize the risk of future disputes formed the European Union to improve relationships between these nations.

例えば、欧州諸国の間で起きた過去の軍事紛争について理解し、将来紛争が起きるリスクを最小限にとどめようとしていた各国の指導者は、互いの関係を改善するために欧州連合を設立した。

---

544 **leader**
[líːdər]
□□□□□□

N[C] 指導者、リーダー

Warren Buffett is one of the **leaders** I really look up to.
(ウォーレン・バフェットは私が本当に尊敬してるリーダーの一人なんだ。)

▶ **leadership** [líːdərʃɪp] N[U] リーダーシップ、統率力；指導者の地位

▶ **lead** [líːd] V[T] を（〜に）導く（to sth）；を率いる　V[I]（〜に）通じる（to sth）
　　　　　　　N[S] 先頭、首位　Adj. 主な

■ **lead** to sth（（結果など）をもたらす、引き起こす）　■ **lead** the way（案内する、（目的地まで）連れていく）

There is no doubt that working long hours can **lead to** physical illness.
(長時間労働は間違いなく体の病気を引き起こすよ。)

Can you **lead the way**?（案内してくれない？）

---

545 **seek**
[síːk]
□□□□□□

V[T] を求める、探し求める

■ **seek** to do（〜しようとする）

I like how John always **seeks to** clarify the issue.（ジョンの常に問題を明確にしようとするところが好き。）

▶ **seeker** [síːkər] N[C]（しばしば複合語で）探し求める人

job **seekers**（求職者）　　asylum **seekers**（亡命希望者）

---

546 **understand**
[ʌndərstǽnd]
□□□□□□

V[T] を理解する、が分かる　**V[I]** 理解できる

I'm trying to **understand** how blockchain works, but it's not really sinking in.
(ブロックチェーンがどうやって機能してるのか理解しようとしてるんだけど、なんかしっくりこない。)

▶ **understanding** [ʌndərstǽndɪŋ] N[S/U] 理解　N[C] 合意　Adj. 理解のある

Thank you for your **understanding**.　　a tacit **understanding**
(ご理解いただきありがとうございます。)　　(暗黙の了解)

▶ **understandable** [ʌndərstǽndəbəl] Adj. 理解できる；（行動などが）無理もない

It's **understandable** why you would think I lied, but I definitely didn't.
（私が嘘ついたって思うのも理解できるけど、私は絶対に嘘は言ってないよ。）

---

547 **previous**
[príːviəs]
☐☐☐☐☐☐

Adj. 以前の、前の

Did you like working for your **previous** boss?（前の上司と働くの好きだった？）

▶ **previously** [príːviəsli] Adv. 以前に、前に

We tried to vlog in Indonesia **previously**, but the internet in the area wasn't great.
（前にインドネシアでVLOGしようとしたんだけど、そのエリアはネット環境があんまり良くなかったんだよね。）

---

548 **military**
[míləteri]
☐☐☐☐☐☐

Adj. 軍事の、軍隊の　N[S] 軍隊【the -】

Do you think the U.S. will ever actually take **military** action against North Korea?
（アメリカって北朝鮮に対していつか本当に軍事行動とると思う？）

This K-Pop star has finally returned from the **military**.
（この K-Pop スターはついに軍隊から戻ってきた。）

▶ **militarized** Adj. 軍事化した、武装された　◀▶ **demilitarized** 非武装の
　[mílətəraɪzd]　　　　　　　　　　　　　　　　　[diːmílətəraɪzd]

a **militarized** border（軍事境界線）　the **demilitarized** zone（非武装地帯）

---

549 **dispute**
[dɪspjúːt]
☐☐☐☐☐☐

N[C/U] 紛争、議論、論争　V[I/T]（～について）論争する

■ in **dispute**（疑わしい、論争中で）

Her ability is not **in dispute**.（彼女の能力に疑いはないよ。）

▶ **disputable** [dɪspjúːṭəbəl] Adj. 疑わしい、議論の余地のある

There were some **disputable** decisions by the referee during the game.
（その試合中、いくつかレフリーによる疑わしい判定があったんだよね。）

▶ **disputed** [dɪspjúːṭɪd] Adj. 紛争中の；争点となっている

---

550 **future**
[fjúːtʃər]
☐☐☐☐☐☐

N[S] 将来、未来【the -】

In the **future**, I want to be a YouTuber known all over the world.
（将来は世界中に知られるユーチューバーになりたいんだ。）

■ what the **future** holds（将来何が起きるか）　■ in the **future**（将来に）= in **future** <英>

Nobody knows **what the future holds**.（将来何が起きるかは誰にも分からない。）

What do you want to be **in the future**?（将来何になりたいの？）

N[C]（具体的な）将来　N[S] 明るい未来、将来性

Don't worry, you have a **future**.（心配しないで。あなたには明るい未来が待ってるから。）

N[P] 先物（取引）【-s】　Adj. 将来の、未来の

▶ **futuristic** [fjùːtʃərístɪk] Adj. 未来的な

4 This *illustrates* **that by developing our** knowledge **and** awareness **of the** links **between historical events, and** focusing **on avoiding** mistakes **that were made in the past, we are able to** refrain **from repeating them.**

これが示しているのは、過去の事象間の関連性に対する理解と認識を深め、過去の過ちの回避に重点的に取り組むことで、同じ過ちを繰り返さないで済むということである。

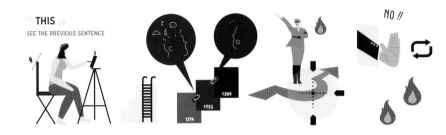

---

551 illustrate
[íləstreɪt]
☐☐☐☐☐☐

V[I/T] （～を）例示する、説明する

Let me draw a diagram to **illustrate** my point. （自分の言いたいことを説明するために図を描くね。）

▶ **illustration** [ìləstréɪʃən] N[C/U] 例、実例　N[C] 挿絵、イラスト

▶ **illustrative** [ɪlʌ́strətɪv] Adj. （～の）例となる、説明の役に立つ（of sth）

---

552 knowledge
[nάːlɪdʒ]
☐☐☐☐☐☐

N[U] 理解、知識

My **knowledge** of Japanese history used to be great, but it's a bit rusty now.
（昔は日本史の知識すごかったんだけどさ、今はちょっとさびついちゃってるよ。）

to the best of my **knowledge** （私の知っている限りでは）

▶ **knowledgeable** [nάːlɪdʒəbəl] Adj. （～について）知識が豊富な（about sth）

Our guide was very **knowledgeable**. He told us so many fun facts about the shrine.
（ガイドさんは本当に知識が豊富だったんだ。その神社にまつわる面白いことをたくさん教えてくれたよ。）

▶ **knowledgeably** [nάːlɪdʒəbli] Adv. 知識が豊富な感じで

The teacher always speaks **knowledgeably**. （あの先生いつも知識豊富そうな感じで話すよね。）

---

553 awareness
[əwérnəs]
☐☐☐☐☐☐

N[S/U] 認識、意識、自覚　⟷ **unawareness** [ʌnəwérnəs] 気づいていないこと

It's important to have **awareness** of how your body language makes others feel.
（自分のボディーランゲージが周りの人をどういう気持ちにさせるのか自覚しておくのは大事だよ。）

▶ **aware** [əwér] Adj. （～を）認識している、（～に）気づいている（of sth）

⟷ **unaware** [ʌnəwér] （～に）気づいていない（of sth）

554 link
[lɪŋk]
□□□□□□

N[C] 関連性；連携；（サイトの）リンク V[T] を結びつける

I accidentally clicked on a sketchy **link**.
（なんか怪しいリンク間違ってクリックしちゃった。）

▶ **linkage** [líŋkɪdʒ] N[C] 関連性 N[C/U]（人や組織の）結びつき、連携

The **linkages** between rising global temperatures and climate change are really obvious.　（世界の気温上昇と気候変動の関連性はものすごい明らかだよ。）

---

555 focus
[fóʊkəs]
□□□□□□

V[I] （〜に）重点的に取り組む、焦点を合わせる（on sth）

One simple way to relieve stress is to **focus** only on what you can control.
（ストレスを和らげる簡単な方法の一つは、自分がコントロールできることだけにフォーカスすることなんだ。）

V[T] の焦点を（〜に）合わせる（on sth） N[C] 焦点、中心
N[U] （注意などの）集中

▶ **focused** [fóʊkəst] Adj.（〜に）集中した（on sth/sb）

Stay **focused** on your goals, and you will reach them eventually.
（目的に向かって集中し続ければ、最終的にそこにたどり着くことができるよ。）

▶ **focal** [fóʊkəl] Adj. 焦点の

a **focal** point（焦点）

---

556 mistake
[mɪstéɪk]
□□□□□□

N[C] 過ち、間違い、ミス

■ make a **mistake**（ミスをする）

It's okay to **make mistakes**, as long as you learn from them.
（ミスしたっていいんだよ、そこから学習する限りはね。）

■ by **mistake**（誤って、間違って）

Here's your pen. I took it **by mistake**.（これ君のペン。間違って取っちゃった。）

▶ **mistaken** [mɪstéɪkən] Adj. 間違った、誤解した、勘違いした

If I'm not **mistaken**, watermelon is not a fruit.
（私の間違いでなければ、スイカは果物じゃないですよ。）

▶ **mistakenly** [mɪstéɪkənli] Adv. 間違って、誤って、勘違いして

ミスは和製英語？　日本語ではよく「失敗」の意味でミスという言葉を使いますが、英語でミス（miss）は単体で「〜を逃す」という意味の動詞になり（例：I missed the train.）、失敗の意味はありません。

---

557 refrain
[rɪfréɪn]
□□□□□□

V[I] （〜するのを）控える（from doing）

Please **refrain** from smoking on the plane.（飛行機では喫煙をお控えください。）

Although Genghis Khan is an incredibly well-known and infamous historical figure, there is ironically much mystery surrounding many of his significant life events.

For instance, it is commonly accepted that he was born as Temüjin around 1162. However, there are few written records regarding his early life, and these contradict each other or omit details. Having said that, we know a formative incident that definitely occurred was Temüjin being detained by an enemy tribe around 1177. Following his escape, he amassed allies and ascended to the position of khan of the Mongols in 1187. However, he was quickly defeated by his enemy Jamukha.

By 1206, he had somehow returned to power with the title of Genghis Khan, uniting the roaming Mongol tribes into an obedient, mounted army. In his capacity as khan, he performed the remarkable feat of forging what would become the largest-ever contiguous empire.

The cause of his death in 1227 is unknown. It has been attributed to various causes such as fever, a horse riding accident, and battle wounds.

チンギス・カンは非常に有名で、悪名も高い歴史上の人物だが、皮肉にも彼の人生における重要な出来事の多くについては謎が多い。

例えば、彼が1162年頃に生まれ、テムジンという名を与えられたことは一般に受け入れられているが、彼の若い頃に関して書かれた記録はほとんどなく、あったとしても矛盾するか、詳細が省かれている。とは言え、1177年頃にテムジンが敵の部族に拘束されたことは確実であり、彼の成長に重要な影響を与えた出来事であることが分かっている。敵のもとから逃れると、彼は仲間を集め、1187年にはモンゴルのカンの地位に上りつめるも、それからすぐに敵対していたジャムカに敗れた。

彼は1206年までにチンギス・カンの称号で何とかして権力を取り戻し、放浪していたモンゴルの諸部族を従順な騎兵隊にまとめ上げた。そしてカンの立場で、史上最大の領域を持つ帝国を築き上げるという驚くべき偉業を達成したのだ。

1227年に亡くなったが、死因は不明である。熱病、落馬事故、戦傷など、さまざまな原因が挙げられている。

558 **ironically**
[aɪrɑ́:nɪkli]
☐☐☐☐☐☐

Adv. 皮肉にも

▶ **ironic** [aɪrɑ́:nɪk] Adj. 皮肉な

▶ **irony** [áɪrəni] N[U] 皮肉　N[C/U] 予想と異なること

---

559 **omit**
[oʊmít]
☐☐☐☐☐☐

V[T] を（〜から）省く、除外する（from sth）

Ben was **omitted** from the starting line-up.（ベンはスタメンから外されたんだ。）

▶ **omission** [oʊmíʃən] N[C/U] 省略、脱落

---

560 **detain**
[dɪtéɪn]
☐☐☐☐☐☐

V[T] を拘束する、勾留する

▶ **detention** [dɪténʃən] N[C/U] 拘束、勾留

---

561 **enemy**
[énəmi]
☐☐☐☐☐☐

N[C] 敵

the **enemy** within（内部の敵）

---

562 **escape**
[ɪskéɪp]
☐☐☐☐☐☐

N[C/U]（〜からの）逃亡、脱走、脱出（from sth/sb）　N[S] 逃避

an **escape** from reality（現実逃避）

V[I/T]（〜から）逃げる（from sth/sb）

▶ **escaped** [ɪskéɪpt] Adj. 逃げた　▶ **escapee** [ɪskèɪpí:] N[C] 脱獄者、脱走者

---

563 **ally**
[ǽlaɪ]
☐☐☐☐☐☐

N[C] 仲間、協力者；同盟国　V[T] に（〜と）同盟を結ばせる（with）

ally oneself with sb（〜と同盟を結ぶ）

▶ **allied** [ǽlaɪd] Adj. 同盟関係にある、連合国の

▶ **alliance** [əláɪəns] N[C/U] 同盟、提携、連合

---

564 **ascend**
[əsénd]
☐☐☐☐☐☐

V[I]（〜まで）上り詰める、出世する、上昇する（to sth）　V[I/T]（〜を）登る

↔ **descend** [dɪsénd]（〜を）下る

▶ **ascending** [əséndɪŋ] Adj. 上昇的な　↔ **descending** [dɪséndɪŋ] 降下的な

in **ascending/descending** order（小さい / 大きい順に）

---

565 **defeat**
[dɪfí:t]
☐☐☐☐☐☐

V[T] を負かす、破る；を困らせる　N[C] 負け、敗北、敗戦

This math question has **defeated** me.（この数学の問題は無理だわ。）

▶ **defeated** [dɪfí:tɪd] Adj. 敗北した；挫折した、へこんだ

---

566 **return**
[rɪtɜ́:rn]
☐☐☐☐☐☐

V[I]（〜に / 〜から）戻る、帰る（to/from sth）　N[S] 戻ること、帰ること
V[T] を戻す；を返す、返品する、返却する　N[C/U] 返品、返却；利益

in **return** (for sth)（(〜の) 見返りに）

▶ **returnee** [rɪtɜ̀:rní:] N[C] 帰国子女、帰還者

567 title
[táɪṭl]
□□□□□□

N[C] 称号、敬称；タイトル、題名；肩書き、職名　N[U] 所有権

▶ **titled** [táɪṭld] Adj. タイトルが付いた

be **titled** sth（〜というタイトルが付いている）

---

568 unite
[juːnáɪt]
□□□□□□

V[T] をまとめる、団結させる

▶ **united** [juːnáɪṭɪd] Adj. 統一された、団結した　▶ **unity** [júːnəṭi] N[U] 統一、団結、結束

---

569 roam
[roʊm]
□□□□□□

V[I/T]（〜を）放浪する、うろつく

■ **roam** around (sth)（(〜を) うろつく）

I'm serious. I saw lions **roaming around** on the streets in South Africa.
（本当だって。南アフリカでライオンが道をうろついてるのを見たんだ。）

▶ **roamer** [róʊmər] N[C] 放浪者

---

570 obedient
[oʊbíːdiənt]
□□□□□□

Adj. 従順な、服従した

▶ **obediently** [oʊbíːdiəntli] Adv. 従順に　▶ **obedience** [oʊbíːdiəns] N[U] 従順さ、服従

---

571 mounted
[máʊnṭɪd]
□□□□□□

Adj. 騎馬の、馬に乗った

▶ **mount** [maʊnt] V[I/T]（〜の上に）乗る　V[I] 高まる　V[T] (活動)を開始する　N[C] 山、丘

---

572 capacity
[kəpǽsəṭi]
□□□□□□

N[S] 立場；能力　N[C/U] 収容能力、容量

in one's **capacity** as sth（〜の立場で、〜の資格で）

---

573 feat
[fiːt]
□□□□□□

N[C] 偉業、離れ業

perform a **feat**（偉業を成し遂げる）

---

574 empire
[émpaɪr]
□□□□□□

N[C] 帝国

the Roman **Empire**（ローマ帝国）

▶ **emperor** [émpərər] N[C] 皇帝、天皇　▶ **empress** [émprəs] N[C] 女帝、皇后

---

575 fever
[fíːvər]
□□□□□□

N[C/U] 熱病、発熱、熱　N[U] フィーバー、熱狂

have a **fever**（熱がある）

▶ **feverish** [fíːvərɪʃ] Adj. 熱っぽい、熱のある；熱狂した

---

576 accident
[ǽksədənt]
□□□□□□

N[C] 事故、交通事故、災難；偶然の出来事

▶ **accidental** [æksədénṭl] Adj. 偶然の

▶ **accidentally** [æksədénṭli] Adv. 偶然に、うっかりと

---

577 wound
[wuːnd]
□□□□□□

N[C] 負傷、けが　V[T] を傷つける

▶ **wounded** [wúːndɪd] Adj. 負傷した、傷ついた

Chapter

13

哲学
Philosophy

Philosophers are dedicated to contemplating the fundamental nature of existence, reality, knowledge, values, reason, and mind. Their aim is to raise and answer difficult and challenging questions.

For instance, one of the most fiercely debated and enduring philosophical riddles was first posed in ancient times and relates to the question of whether humans have morality inherently or it is learned.

While classical scholars such as Charles Darwin tended to argue more in favor of inherent morality, contemporary research increasingly reinforces the idea that morality is largely acquired after birth, which accounts for the variability in what is considered to be moral behavior.

Although some find the contemplation and discussion of questions such as these to be boring and frustrating, most acknowledge that philosophy promotes clear, mature thinking about a wide range of obscure issues.

1 Philosophers **are** dedicated **to** contemplating **the fundamental nature of existence, reality, knowledge, values, reason, and** mind**. Their aim is to** raise **and answer** difficult **and** challenging **questions.**

哲学者は、存在や実在、知識、価値、理性、精神そのものの本質についてひたすら熟考する。その目的は、難しくも興味深い問いを提起し、答えることにある。

---

578 **philosopher**
[fɪlάːsəfər]
□□□□□□

N[C] 哲学者；物事を深く考える人

Don't you think his super logical way of speaking makes him sound a bit like a **philosopher** sometimes? （彼って超ロジカルな話し方のせいでたまにちょっと哲学者みたいに聞こえると思わない？）

▶ **philosophy** [fɪlάːsəfi] N[U] 哲学　N[C] （特定の哲学者の）哲学、人生哲学、哲学観

My **philosophy** on life is to stop worrying about things that won't matter in a year from now. （僕の人生哲学は、今から一年後にどうでもよくなっていることに関しては心配しないことなんだ。）

▶ **philosophical** Adj. 哲学の；（嫌なことなどに対して）怒ったりしない、冷静な
[fìləsάːfɪkəl]

---

579 **dedicated**
[dédəkeɪ̯tɪd]
□□□□□□

Adj. （〜に）献身的な、ひたむきな、熱心な（to sth）；専用の

I'm **dedicated** to this project, but I'm not going to put in the extra hours if nobody else is. （僕はこのプロジェクトに全力を捧げてるけど、他のみんながそうじゃないなら残業するつもりはないよ。）

be **dedicated** to doing （ひたすら〜する、〜に専念する）

a **dedicated** computer （専用コンピューター）

▶ **dedicate** [dédəkeɪt] V[T] を（〜に）捧げる；（時間など）を（〜に）充てる（to sth）

I decided to **dedicate** at least three hours to studying English every day. （毎日最低3時間は英語の勉強に充てることにしたんだ。）

dedicate oneself to sth/sb （〜に専念する、身を捧げる）

▶ **dedication** [dèdəkéɪʃən] N[U] 献身、専念

---

580 **contemplate**
[kάːntəmpleɪt]
□□□□□□

V[I/T] （〜を）熟考する、（将来の行動について）考える

Sometimes I **contemplate** deleting all of my Facebook profile photos. （たまに Facebook のプロフィール写真全部削除しようかなってめっちゃ考える。）

▶ **contemplation** [kὰːntəmpléɪʃən] N[U] よく考えること；瞑想

581 **mind**
[maɪnd]
☐☐☐☐☐☐

N[C/U] 精神、心 N[C] 知性、頭脳；知性のある人

My **mind** is all over the place at the moment, so I need a bit of time to think.
(僕の気持ちは今混乱してるから、ちょっと考える時間が必要なんだ。)

■ on sb's **mind**（〜の気にかかって）   keep/bear sth in **mind**（〜を心に留めておく）

What's **on your mind**?（何か気になってるの？）

V[I/T] （〜を）気にする、いやがる

I don't **mind** working on weekends.（俺は週末に働くのは別に構わないんだ。）

■ Do you **mind** if + sentence?（〜してもいいですか？）

"**Do you mind if** I sit here?"（ここに座っていいですか？）"No, go for it!"（もちろんどうぞ。）

直訳すると「〜することを気にしますか？」となるため、気にしないときは No、気にするときは Yes で回答します。

Mind your own business. = It's none of your business.（余計なお世話だ。）

▶ **mindful** [máɪndfəl] Adj.（〜に）気を配る（of sth/sb）

Be **mindful** of others.（周りに気を配りなよ。）

582 **raise**
[reɪz]
☐☐☐☐☐☐

V[T] を提起する；を上げる；を育てる

Raise your hand if you agree with Nick.（ニックの意見に賛成の人は手を上げてください。）

raise issues/problems/questions   **raise** taxes/salaries/prices
（問題を提起する）   （税率 / 給与 / 価格を上げる）

583 **difficult**
[dífəkəlt]
☐☐☐☐☐☐

Adj. 難しい、困難な；気難しい、頑固な

Is juggling really that **difficult**, or does it just look hard?
（ジャグリングって本当にそんなに難しいの？それともそう見えるだけかな？）

▶ **difficulty** [dífəkəlti] N[U] 困難、苦労；難しさ N[C] 問題

■ have **difficulty** doing（〜するのに苦労する）

After I quit my job, my boss **had difficulty** finding a replacement.
（俺が仕事辞めた後、上司は俺の代わりを見つけるのに苦労してたよ。）

I'm doing my best, but I'm still having financial **difficulties**. Do you have any tips?
（自分の中では精いっぱい頑張ってるつもりなんだけど、まだ財政的に苦しいんだ。アドバイスある？）

584 **challenging**
[tʃǽlɪndʒɪŋ]
☐☐☐☐☐☐

Adj. （難しいが）興味深い、やりがいのある；大変な

I don't find my job interesting because it's not really **challenging**.
（僕の仕事、ちょっと簡単すぎてやりがいがないんだ。）

Studying and working at the same time is **challenging**.（勉強と仕事の両立は大変だよ。）

▶ **challenge** N[C/U] 挑戦、課題 N[C] 抗議、異議
[tʃǽlɪndʒ]   V[T]（人や能力など）をためす；に異議を唱える；（正当性など）について疑う

2 For instance, one of the most fiercely debated and enduring philosophical riddles was first posed in ancient times and relates to the question of whether humans have morality inherently or it is learned.

例えば、最も激しい論争を呼び、今なお答えの出ていない哲学的な難問の一つは、大昔に提起されたもので、それは、人は生まれつき道徳的なのか、それともそれは学習して身に付くものなのかという問いである。

---

585 **fiercely**
[fíɪrsli]
□□□□□□

Adv. 激しく、猛烈に

I'm **fiercely** passionate about growing my business.
（私には自分のビジネスを成長させることに猛烈な情熱があるんです。）

▶ **fierce** [fɪɪrs] Adj. 激しい；（動物などが）獰猛な

a **fierce** battle （激しい戦い）　　a **fierce** storm （激しい嵐）

▶ **fierceness** [fíɪrsnəs] N[U] 激しさ；獰猛さ

---

586 **enduring**
[ɪndʊ́rɪŋ]
□□□□□□

Adj. 永続する、長続きする

This is an **enduring** problem that we're probably not going to solve today.
（この問題は永続的で、今日解決できるってことはきっとないよ。）

an **enduring** peace （恒久的平和）

▶ **enduringly** [ɪndʊ́rɪŋli] Adv. 永続的に、長い間

▶ **endure** [ɪndʊ́r] V[I/T] （〜を）我慢する、耐える　V[I] 存在し続ける

I can't **endure** this pressure anymore! （このプレッシャーにはもう耐えられない！）

▶ **endurance** N[U] 我慢強さ、忍耐力　　　▶ **endurable** Adj. 耐えられる
[ɪndʊ́rəns]　　　　　　　　　　　　　　　[ɪndʊ́rəbəl]

---

587 **riddle**
[rídl]
□□□□□□

N[C] 難問、謎；なぞなぞ　**V[T]** を（弾丸などで）穴だらけにする

■ speak in **riddles** （謎めいたことを言う）

It's really hard to understand Olivia because she's always **speaking in riddles**.
（オリヴィアはいつも謎めいたことを言うから理解するのがめちゃくちゃ大変なんだ。）

▶ **riddled** [rídld] Adj. （〜で）いっぱいの （with sth）

Your website is **riddled** with problems, so let me fix them for you.
(君のウェブサイトは問題だらけだから、直してあげるね。)

---

588 **pose**
[poʊz]

V[T] （質問など）を提起する；（危険や問題など）を引き起こす

The student **posed** a very interesting question.
(その学生はものすごい興味深い質問を投げかけたんだ。)

pose a problem（問題を提起する）　　pose a threat to sth/sb（〜に脅威を与える）

V[T] にポーズをとらせる　**V[I]** （〜のために）ポーズをとる (for sth)

I always struggle to **pose** for pictures. (いつも写真撮る時どういうポーズしようか困っちゃうんだ。)

---

589 **question**
[kwéstʃən]

N[C] 問い、質問、問題、疑問

That's a great **question**, but let me get back to you on it later.
(すごい良い質問なんですけど、その質問にはまた後で回答させて下さい。)

■ out of the **question**（論外、絶対あり得ない）　　sth/sb in **question**（問題となっている〜）

For me, having pasta without Parmesan cheese is **out of the question**.
(僕的には、パスタを粉チーズ無しで食べるとか論外なんだよね。)

V[T] を取り調べる；を疑問に思う

▶ **questionable** [kwéstʃənəbəl] Adj. 疑わしい、いかがわしい

▶ **questionnaire** N[C] アンケート　　▶ **questioner** N[C] 質問者
　　[kwèstʃənér]　　　　　　　　　　　　　　[kwéstʃənər]

---

590 **inherently**
[ɪnhírəntli]

Adv. 生まれつき、生来的に

I'm an **inherently** lazy person. (俺って生まれつき怠け者なんだよね。)

▶ **inherent** [ɪnhírənt] Adj. 生まれながらの、固有の

Is the ability to dance **inherent** or acquired?
(ダンスが上手いのって生まれつきかな？それともあとから習得できるものなのかな？)

---

591 **learn**
[lɜːrn]

V[T] を学習する、習得する　**V[I]** （〜について）学ぶ (about sth)

I want you to understand how important it is to **learn** how to study effectively.
(効果的な勉強法について学ぶことがどれだけ重要か、君に理解してほしいんだ。)

▶ **learning** [lɜːrnɪŋ] N[U] 学習；（勉強によって得られた）知識

learn vs **study** learn は知識やスキルを習得することを意味し、study は何かを暗記したり、授業を受けたり、本を読んだりといった、learn する過程を意味します。ゆえに、study hard と言うことはできますが、learn hard と言うことはできません。

3 While classical scholars such as Charles Darwin tended to argue more in favor of inherent morality, contemporary research increasingly reinforces the idea that morality is largely acquired after birth, which accounts for the variability in what is considered to be moral behavior.

チャールズ・ダーウィンなどの古典的な学者は、どちらかというと人は生まれながらにして道徳的であるという考えを好んで唱える傾向にあったが、現代の研究では、道徳的な行動とされることに関して意見が分かれやすいことから、道徳心の大部分は後天的に身に付くという考えが次第に強まっている。

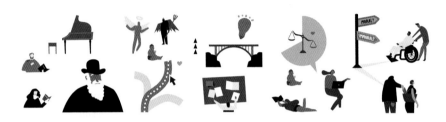

---

592 tend
[tend]
☐☐☐☐☐☐

V[I] （〜する）傾向がある、しがちである（to do）

I **tend** to struggle on high notes nowadays, so I really need to warm up properly before I sing.
（最近は高音が出にくいことが多いから、歌う前にちゃんとウォーミングアップしなきゃな。）

▶ **tendency** [téndənsi] N[C] （〜する）傾向（to do）

She has a **tendency** to exaggerate facts. （彼女は事実を誇張する傾向があるんだ。）

---

593 favor
[féɪvər]
☐☐☐☐☐☐

N[U] 支持、賛成

■ in sb's **favor**（〜に有利に）　　in **favor** of sth（〜に賛成して、〜を好んで）

Being able to speak English will definitely work **in your favor** in Japan.
（日本で英語を話せたら絶対に有利に働くよ。）

N[C] 好意、親切

Could you do me a **favor**? （ちょっとお願いがあるんですけど。）

▶ **favorable** [féɪvərəbəl] Adj. （意見などが）好意的な；好都合な；（利率などが）妥当な

I'm glad my new video received a lot of **favorable** reviews.
（僕の新動画にたくさん良い感じのレビューが来てて嬉しいよ。）

▶ **favorably** [féɪvərəbli] Adv. 好意的に；好都合に

▶ **favorite** [féɪvərət] Adj. お気に入りの、好きな　N[C] お気に入りのもの・人

---

594 reinforce
[ri:ɪnfɔ́:rs]
☐☐☐☐☐☐

V[T] を（〜で）強化する、補強する（with sth）

I'm going to watch this documentary again to **reinforce** my knowledge.
（知識を強化するためにもう一回このドキュメンタリーを見ようと思ってるんだ。）

▶ **reinforcement** [ri:ɪnfɔ́:rsmənt] N[U] 強化、補強　N[P] 援軍【-s】

595 idea
[aɪdíːə]
□□□□□□

N[C] 考え、意見、アイディア **N[S/U]** イメージ

I have lots of great **ideas**, but I need money to make them happen.
（素晴らしいアイディアはたくさんあるんだけど、実際にやるためのお金が必要なんだ。）

I have no **idea** why.（なぜかは分からないよ。）

N[S] 目的、意図

The whole **idea** of using Skype is to save money.（お金を節約したいからこそスカイプ使ってるんだよね。）

▶ **ideal** [aɪdíːəl] Adj. 理想的な N[C] 理想的なもの、理想形

I know the timing isn't **ideal**, but I don't think there's ever a good time to have a baby.
（タイミングはベストではないけど、まぁ赤ちゃんを授かるのに良い時期なんてないしね。）

We argue about small things, but we share the same **ideals**.
（僕たちは小さなことで喧嘩するけど、理想とすることは同じなんだ。）

▶ **ideally** [aɪdíːəli] Adv. 理想的には

---

596 largely
[láːrdʒli]
□□□□□□

Adv. 大部分は、主に

The weather forecast was **largely** correct.（天気予報は大体合ってたね。）

▶ **large** [lɑːrdʒ] Adj. 大きい

---

597 birth
[bɜːrθ]
□□□□□□

N[C/U] 誕生、出生、出産

I've been speaking English pretty much since **birth**, but I performed terribly on my last TOEFL test.（生まれてこの方ほぼずっと英語を話してきたんだけど、TOEFL の試験はズタボロだったわ。）

■ give **birth** to sth/sb（〜を産む）

She gave **birth to** a baby.（彼女赤ちゃん産んだんだって。）

---

598 account
[əkáʊnt]
□□□□□□

V[I] （〜を）説明する、（〜の）理由である（for sth）

How do you **account** for your success?（あなたの成功の理由は何ですか？）

V[I] （部分や割合を）占める（for sth）

College students **account** for about 40% of our customers.
（うちのお客さんの 40% は大学生なんだ。）

N[C] 報告、説明；口座；アカウント

I need to withdraw some money from this **account**.（この口座からお金をいくらか下ろさなきゃ。）

■ on **account** of sth（〜の理由で、〜のため）

He resigned from the company **on account of** his poor health.
（彼は健康状態が悪いことを理由に会社を辞めたんだ。）

▶ **accountable** [əkáʊntəbəl] Adj.（〜に）説明責任がある（for sth）

Part of becoming an adult is being **accountable** for your own actions.
（大人になるということは、自らの行動に対して責任を持つことでもある。）

▶ **accountability** [əkàʊntəbíləti] N[U] 説明責任

4 Although some find the contemplation and discussion of questions such as these to be boring and frustrating, most acknowledge that philosophy promotes clear, mature thinking about a wide range of obscure issues.

こうした問いを熟考し、議論するのは退屈で、いらいらすると思う人もいるが、大半の人は、哲学はさまざまな分かりにくい問題について、明確かつ成熟した思考を促すものであると認めている。

599 discussion
[dɪskʌ́ʃən]
□□□□□□

N[C/U] 議論、話し合い

■ have a **discussion** (about sth) （(〜について) 議論する）

I can't believe we just **had a** three-hour **discussion** and still haven't made a decision.
（僕たち今3時間も議論してまだ決断できてないなんて信じられないよ。）

under **discussion** （議論中の）

▶ **discuss** [dɪskʌ́s] V[T] について議論する、話し合う

Be sure to write a list of the topics we need to **discuss** during the meeting.
（ミーティング中に話さないといけないことはちゃんとリスト化しておいてね。）

discuss about sth は間違い？ discuss は「〜について議論する」という意味の「他動詞 (Transitive Verb)」なので、discuss the issue のように直接目的語を取ります。ゆえに、discuss about という形は間違いです。

600 boring
[bɔ́:rɪŋ]
□□□□□□

Adj. 退屈な、つまらない

This textbook is extremely **boring**, but I'll fail the exam if I don't read it.
（この教科書は死ぬほどつまんないけど、読まないと試験落ちちゃうから。）

▶ **bore** V[T] を退屈させる、うんざりさせる　N[C] 退屈な人　N[S] 退屈なこと、嫌なこと
[bɔːr] V[I/T] （ドリルなどで〜に）穴をあける ,　N[C] 穴

▶ **bored** [bɔːrd] Adj. 退屈した、うんざりした

We went to see a romantic movie, but my girlfriend was so **bored** that she fell asleep after only half an hour.
（恋愛映画一緒に見に行ったんだけど、僕の彼女、飽きて30分くらいで寝ちゃってた。）

▶ **boredom** [bɔ́:rdəm] N[U] 退屈

■ out of **boredom** （やることがなくて、退屈して）

I often eat out of **boredom**. （よく暇になったら食べちゃうんだよね。）

601 frustrating
[fráʊstreɪtɪŋ]

Adj. いらいらする

I don't always get notifications for DMs. It's **frustrating**.
（ダイレクトメッセージの通知来ないときあるんだけど。いらいらするなぁ。）

▶ **frustrate** V[T] をいらいらさせる
[fráʊstreɪt]

▶ **frustrated** Adj. いらいらした
[fráʊstreɪtɪd]

I get a bit **frustrated** when I can't express myself properly in English.
（英語でちゃんと自分を表現できないときちょっといらいらするんだ。）

▶ **frustration** [frʌstréɪʃən] N[C/U] いらいら、不満

---

602 promote
[prəmóʊt]

V[T] を促進する；を宣伝する；を昇進させる

I love how my workplace actively **promotes** work-life balance.
（うちの職場、ワークライフバランスを積極的に推進してるところがすごい好き。）

▶ **promotion** [prəmóʊʃən] N[U] 促進 N[C/U] 宣伝、プロモーション；昇進

▶ **promotional** Adj. 宣伝用の
[prəmóʊʃənəl]

▶ **promo** N[C] 宣伝用動画、プロモビデオ
[próʊmoʊ]

promotional brochure（宣伝用のパンフレット）

---

603 mature
[mətʊ́r]

Adj. 成熟した、大人な；（食べ物や飲み物が）熟した

Kevin is surprisingly **mature**.（ケヴィンって驚くほど大人だよなぁ。）

mature wine（熟成したワイン）　　**mature** cheese（熟成チーズ）

⟷ **immature** [ìmətʊ́r] 未熟な、子供っぽい

V[I] 成熟する、大人になる；熟す；満期に達する　V[T] を成熟させる

▶ **maturely** Adv. 大人の対応で
[mətʊ́rli]

⟷ **immaturely** 未熟に、子供っぽく
[ìmətʊ́rli]

▶ **premature** [pri:mətʊ́r] Adj. 時期尚早の、早過ぎる

a **premature** decision（早まった決断）　　**premature** birth/death（早産 / 早すぎる死）

---

604 obscure
[əbskjʊ́r]

Adj. 分かりにくい、曖昧な；あまり知られていない

I don't remember my password because I made it too **obscure**.
（パスワード分かりにくくしすぎたせいで覚えてないよ。）

V[T] を見えにくくする；を曖昧にする

▶ **obscurely** [əbskjʊ́rli] Adv. 曖昧に

▶ **obscurity** [əbskjʊ́rəti] N[U] 曖昧さ

---

605 issue
[íʃu:]

N[C] 問題；（雑誌などの）号 N[U] 発行 V[T] を発行する

I think I need to understand the **issue** properly before I can even think about making a decision.（決断について考える以前にまずは問題についてちゃんと理解しないといけないと思ってる。）

▶ **issuance** [íʃuəns] N[U] 発行、発布

Man Lately, a few horrible incidents have happened to me that have made me obsessed with the meaning of life. You know, I'm considering perplexing questions like what constitutes a meaningful and rewarding life. I have innumerable questions, none yielding very many answers.

Woman For what it's worth, I subscribe to Plato and Aristotle's view that life flourishes and is given meaning chiefly through continued learning and the application of this learning, rather than through materialism and greed.

Man That's interesting. I understand that continuing to develop personally is pretty important, but I'm inclined to think that the cultivation and nurturing of meaningful relationships and building a better society are critical, which is the premise of Confucius's teachings.

Woman Well, I think if you become an expert in a field that you're passionate about and continue to hone and apply this knowledge, relationships and society at large will blossom.

男性 最近自分にいくつか恐ろしい出来事が起きて、それから人生の意味についてずっと考えてるんだよね。ほら、有意義で、充実した人生とはどういうものなのかみたいな、複雑な疑問について。数えきれないほどの疑問があるんだけど、その答えはあんまり出てないんだ。

女性 これを言って役に立つか分かんないけど、私はプラトンとかアリストテレスの、人生っていうのは物質主義とか貪欲とかじゃなくて、主に継続的な学びとか、その応用を通じて豊かになって、そして意味が生まれるっていう考えが正しいと思ってるんだよね。

男性 面白いね。個人として発達し続けることがかなり重要だっていうのは分かるんだけど、僕はどちらかと言うと、孔子の教義の前提となっている、意味のある関係を深めて、育んで、よりよい社会を築くことがすごい重要だと考えてるかなぁ。

女性 まぁ、自分が情熱を持てる分野に精通して、その知識に磨きをかけて応用し続ければ、人の関わり合いとか社会全体は発展すると思うよ。

606 horrible
[hɔ́:rəbəl]
□□□□□□

Adj. 恐ろしい、ひどい

▶ **horribly** [hɔ́:rəbli] Adv. 恐ろしく、ひどく

I sing **horribly**, but I still love karaoke.（歌はすごい下手だけど、それでもカラオケは大好きだよ。）

607 incident
[ínsɪdənt]
□□□□□□

N[C] 出来事、事件

▶ **incidental** [ìnsɪdénṭl] Adj. (〜に) 付随して起こる、副次的な (to sth)

▶ **incidentally** [ìnsɪdénṭəli] Adv. ちなみに　= **by the way** [bái ðə wéi]

608 obsessed
[əbsést]
□□□□□□

Adj. (〜のこと) ばかり考えた、(〜に) 心を奪われた (with sth)

▶ **obsess** [əbsés] V[I/T] (〜の) 頭から離れない　▶ **obsession** [əbséʃən] N[C] 強迫観念

▶ **obsessive** [əbsésɪv] Adj. (〜に) 異常にこだわった (about sth)

▶ **obsessively** [əbsésɪvli] Adv. 異常にこだわって

609 perplexing
[pərpléksɪŋ]
□□□□□□

Adj. 複雑な、困惑させる、理解に苦しむ

▶ **perplex** [pərpléks] V[T] を困惑させる、悩ませる

▶ **perplexed** [pərplékst] Adj. (〜に) 困惑した (by/about sth)

610 rewarding
[rɪwɔ́:rdɪŋ]
□□□□□□

Adj. 充実した、やりがいのある

▶ **reward** [rɪwɔ́:rd] N[C/U] 報酬　N[C] お礼、ご褒美　V[T] に報酬を与える、ご褒美を与える

be **rewarded** with/by sth (〜で報われる)

611 innumerable
[ɪnú:mərəbəl]
□□□□□□

Adj. 数えきれないほどの

I've made **innumerable** mistakes in my life, but studying English was not one of them.
（人生では数えきれないほどの過ちを犯してきたけど、英語学習においては間違ってなかったんだ。）

612 yield
[ji:ld]
□□□□□□

V[T] (結果や利益) を得る、もたらす；(農産物など) を生産する；を放棄する

V[I] (〜に) 屈する (to sth/sb)　= **give in** (to sth) [gívɪn]

降伏する　= **surrender** [səréndər]　**N[C/U]** 利回り；産出量

613 subscribe
[səbskráɪb]
□□□□□□

V[I] (考えなどを) 正しいと思う、支持する (to sth)

(サービスなどに) 登録する、加入する (to sth)

▶ **subscriber** [səbskráɪbər] N[C] (サービスなどの) 登録者、(定期) 購読者、加入者

▶ **subscription** [səbskrípʃən] N[C/U] 登録、(定期) 購読；会費　N[C] 加入契約

614 chiefly
[tʃí:fli]
□□□□□□

Adv. 主に

▶ **chief** [tʃí:f] Adj. 主要な、最も重要な；最高位の　N[C] 長、最高位の人

615 materialism
[mətíriəlɪzəm]
□□□□□□

N[U] 物質主義

▶ **materialistic** [mətìriəlístɪk] Adj. 物質主義的な

▶ **materialistically** [mətìriəlístɪkli] Adv. 物質主義的に

▶ **materialist** [mətíriəlɪst] N[C] 物質主義者

616 greed
[gri:d]

N[U] 貪欲さ　= **greediness** [grí:dinəs]

▶ **greedy** [grí:di] Adj. 貪欲な、強欲な　▶ **greedily** [grí:dəli] Adv. 貪欲に

617 pretty
[príti]

Adv. かなり、結構；非常に　Adj. かわいい、きれいな

Your profile picture looks **pretty** good.（プロフの写真、結構良い感じだね。）

▶ **prettiness** [prítinəs] N[U] かわいらしさ、きれいさ

618 inclined
[ɪnkláɪnd]

Adj.（〜する）傾向がある、（〜を）しがちな（to do）
　　（〜を）したい気がする（to do）

▶ **incline** [ɪnkláɪn] V[I] 傾く、傾向がある　V[T] を傾ける；を（〜する）気にさせる（to do）

▶ **inclination** [ìnklənéɪʃən] N[C/U] 傾向；（〜したい）という気持ち

619 cultivation
[kʌltəvéɪʃən]

N[U]（関係などの）強化、開拓；耕作、栽培

▶ **cultivate** [kʌltəveɪt] V[T] を耕す、栽培する；（関係など）を深める；（知識）を磨く

▶ **cultivated** [kʌltəveɪtɪd] Adj. 教養のある、知的な；耕された、栽培された

620 nurture
[nə́:rtʃər]

V[T] を育てる、促進する　N[U] 育ち

Do you think personality is the result of nature or **nurture**?
（性格って遺伝の結果だと思う？それとも育った環境かな？）

621 premise
[prémɪs]

N[C] 前提　N[P] 建物、敷地【-s】　V[T] を基礎とする

on the **premises**（建物の中で、敷地内で）

622 expert
[éksp3:rt]

N[C]（〜の）専門家、エキスパート（in/on/at sth）

He says he's an **expert** at surfing, but I have my doubts.
（あいつ、サーフィンめっちゃ上手いって言ってるけど、嘘だと思うわ。）

Adj.（〜に）精通した（in sth）

▶ **expertise** [èksp3:rtí:z] N[U]（〜の）専門知識（in sth）

623 passionate
[pǽʃənət]

Adj.（〜に）情熱的な、熱烈な（about sth）

▶ **passionately** [pǽʃənɪtli] Adv. 情熱的に、熱烈に　▶ **passion** [pǽʃən] N[C/U] 情熱

624 hone
[hoʊn]

V[T]（技術など）を磨く；（ナイフなど）を研ぐ

hone one's skills（腕を磨く、スキルを磨く）

625 blossom
[blá:səm]

V[I] 開花する　N[C/U] 花

▶ **bloom** [blu:m] V[I] 開花する、咲く　N[C/U] 花

come into **bloom**（花が咲き始める）　in full **bloom**（満開の）

🔄 CH. 3, 7, 10, 13

宗教
Religion

There are an astonishing number of religions around the world, but perhaps unsurprisingly, most of the population on earth is said to be affiliated with one of the five dominant religions: Christianity, Islam, Hinduism, Buddhism, or Judaism.

Each religion embraces its own distinct and unique elements, including sacred rituals, sermons, festivals, prayers, and symbols.

For instance, although Christianity and Islam share a common place of origin in the Middle East, Christians regard Jesus as the Son of God, while Muslims believe that Jesus was a holy prophet.

Since there are abundant differences among religions, some argue that it is important to identify similar traits that religions possess to reach scholarly consensus over what constitutes religion.

1 There are an astonishing number of religions around the world, but perhaps unsurprisingly, most of the population on earth is said to be affiliated with one of the five dominant religions: Christianity, Islam, Hinduism, Buddhism, or Judaism.

世界にはとてつもない数の宗教が存在するものの、これは驚くべきことではないかもしれないが、地球上の人口の大半は五大宗教の一つに属していると言われている。それは、キリスト教、イスラム教、ヒンドゥー教、仏教、またはユダヤ教である。

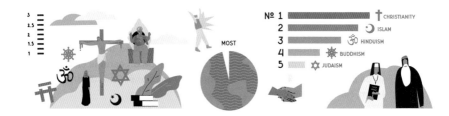

---

626 **astonishing**
[əstá:nɪʃɪŋ]
□□□□□□

Adj. とてつもない、驚くべき

I still find it **astonishing** that he finished reading this book in only one night.
（彼がこの本をたった一晩で読み終えたことに未だに驚いてるよ。）

▶ **astonish** V[T] をびっくりさせる
[əstá:nɪʃ]

▶ **astonishingly** Adv. 驚くべきことに
[əstá:nɪʃɪŋli]

▶ **astonishment** [əstá:nɪʃmənt] N[U] 驚き

To my **astonishment**, my mom didn't scold me for not scoring good marks.
（大変驚くべきことに、母は良い点を取らなかった私のことを叱らなかった。）

---

627 **religion**
[rɪlídʒən]
□□□□□□

N[C/U] 宗教

Don't judge people by their skin color or **religion**.（人を肌の色とか宗教で判断するのはやめようよ。）

▶ **religious** Adj. 宗教上の、宗教的な
[rɪlídʒəs]

▶ **religiously** Adv. 宗教上、まるで宗教のように
[rɪlídʒəsli]

I'm not **religious**.（私は無宗教です。）

I find it interesting how many people follow Apple products **religiously**, even though I'm one of them.（私もその一人なんだけど、人が宗教みたいにアップルの製品をフォローするの、面白いよなぁ。）

---

628 **perhaps**
[pərhǽps]
□□□□□□

Adv. 多分、もしかすると　= **maybe** [méɪbi]

Perhaps we should take lessons before we go skiing.
（多分スキーに行く前にレッスンを受けた方が良いんじゃないかな。）

perhaps vs **maybe**　どちらも「多分」を意味する副詞ですが、perhaps のほうが若干フォーマルな表現です。どちらも約 50% の確率を表すと言われています（その他の可能性を表す副詞については pg. 410 を参照）。

629 unsurprisingly
[ˌʌnsərpráɪzɪŋli]
▢▢▢▢▢▢

Adv. 驚くことではないが ↔ **surprisingly** [sərpráɪzɪŋli] 驚いたことに、驚くほど

Unsurprisingly, Emily's running late again. (やっぱりエミリーはまた遅刻だね。)

▶ **unsurprising** Adj. 驚くほどではない ↔ **surprising** 驚くほどの
[ˌʌnsərpráɪzɪŋ]　　　　　　　　　　　　　　[sərpráɪzɪŋ]

It's **surprising** they are still dating. I thought they would make a terrible couple.
(あの人たちがまだ付き合ってるとか驚き。最悪のカップルになると思ったのに。)

▶ **surprise** [sərpráɪz] V[T] を驚かす　N[C] 驚くべきこと　N[U] 驚き

be **surprised** (at sth/sb, that + sentence, to do) ((〜に) 驚く)　■ come as a **surprise** (驚きである)

His resignation shouldn't **come as a surprise**. His boss has been treating him terribly
for ages. 　(彼の辞職は驚くようなことではないよ。彼に対する上司の扱いはひどかったからね。)

to sb's **surprise** (驚くべきことに)　　　　　in/with **surprise** (驚いて)

630 population
[pàːpjəléɪʃən]
▢▢▢▢▢▢

N[C/U] 人口　N[C] （特定地域の）住民 （の数）、生息数

Japan's **population** is rapidly declining and aging. (日本の人口は急速に減少し、高齢化している。)

▶ **populous** Adj. 人口の多い　▶ **populate** V[T] に住みつく ；(表や記入用紙)を埋める
[pàːpjələs]　　　　　　　　　　　　　　　[pàːpjəleɪt]

Is the most **populous** country China or India? (人口の最も多い国って中国とインドどっち？)

densely **populated** (人口密度の高い)

631 affiliated
[əfílieɪt̬ɪd]
▢▢▢▢▢▢

Adj. （〜に）属している、（〜と）提携している （with sth/sb）

Is this teacher **affiliated** with a particular school, or does he teach at a few?
(この先生はどこか特定の学校に属しているの？それともいくつかの学校で教えてるのかな？)

▶ **affiliation** [əfìliéɪʃən] N[C/U] 加入、提携

▶ **affiliate** *V.* [əfílieɪt] V[I] （〜と）提携する （with sth/sb）　N[C] 支部、系列会社
N. [əfíliət] V[T] を （〜に）提携させる （with sth/sb）

We refuse to **affiliate** with any religious groups. (宗教団体との提携はお断りしてるよ。)

632 dominant
[dάːmənənt]
▢▢▢▢▢▢

Adj. 支配的な、優勢な、優位の

I don't think soccer will become the **dominant** sport in the U.S., but it will certainly grow.
(サッカーがアメリカの主要なスポーツになるとは思わないけど、確実に成長はするだろうね。)

▶ **dominantly** [dάːmənəntli] Adv. 支配的に、優勢に、優位に

▶ **dominate** [dάːməneɪt] V[I/T] （〜を）支配する、（〜で）優位を占める

Lenovo and HP still **dominate** the laptop market.
(レノボと HP は未だにラップトップ市場を支配しているんだ。)

▶ **dominance** N[U] 支配、優勢　▶ **dominating** Adj. 支配的な、優勢な、優位な
[dάːmənəns]　　　　　　　　　　　[dάːməneɪt̬ɪŋ]

dominating vs **dominant** この二つはニュアンスが異なります。dominating は支配して勝利した
い気持ちがあることを表す一方で（例：dominating person 議論などに常に勝利したい人）、dominant
は主要な役割を持つことや大部分を占めることを意味します（例：dominant hand 利き手）。

2 **Each religion** embraces **its own** distinct **and** unique **elements, including** sacred rituals, **sermons, festivals,** prayers, **and** symbols.

そして各宗教は、神聖な儀式や説教、祝祭、祈祷、象徴などを含む、独自で固有の原理を採用している。

---

633 **embrace**
[ɪmbréɪs]

V[T] を採用する、受け入れる　V[I/T] を抱きしめる　N[C] 抱擁

You should **embrace** cultural differences rather than fight them.
（文化の違いは抵抗するよりも受け入れた方がいいよ。）

---

634 **distinct**
[dɪstíŋkt]

Adj. 独自の、独特の、全く異なる；明らかな

I know their logos look very similar, but they're two **distinct** brands.
（ロゴがすごい似てるのは知ってるけど、二つは全く異なるブランドなんだ。）

▶ **distinctive** Adj. 独自の、独特の、特色のある　▶ **distinctively** Adv. 独特に、特徴的に
[dɪstíŋktɪv]　　　　　　　　　　　　　　　　　　　　[dɪstíŋktɪvli]

■ a **distinctive** smell/taste（独特なにおい / 味）

Natto has **a** really **distinctive smell** that a lot of people seem to hate.
（納豆は独特なにおいがあるから、そのせいで嫌いな人が多いみたい。）

▶ **distinction** N[U]（品質や能力の）優秀さ、卓越
[dɪstíŋkʃən]　　N[C/U]（他と異なる）特徴、違い、区別

Use this book to add more **distinction** to your English.
（この本を使って、君の英語をもっと卓越したものにしなよ。）

▶ **distinguish** V[T] を（〜と）区別する（from sth/sb）
[dɪstíŋgwɪʃ]　　V[I]（A と B を）区別する（between A and B）

■ **distinguish** oneself（頭角を現す、卓越する）

If you want to make a lot of money, you need to **distinguish yourself** from the crowd.
（たくさんお金を稼ぎたいなら、大勢の中から頭角を現さないとね。）

Sometimes I can't **distinguish** between dreams and reality.
（私、たまに夢と現実の区別ができなくなることがあるんだ。）

▶ **distinguishable** [dɪstíŋgwɪʃəbəl] Adj. 区別できる、見分けがつく

635 unique
[ju:ní:k]
□□□□□□

Adj. 固有の、独自の、独特の、ユニークな

Alex has a **unique** sense of humor which rubs some people the wrong way.
（アレックスは人をイラっとさせる独特なユーモアのセンスがある。）

▶ **uniquely** Adv. 独特に、ユニークに   ▶ **uniqueness** N[U] 独特さ、ユニークさ
[ju:ní:kli]   [ju:ní:knəs]

---

636 sacred
[séɪkrɪd]
□□□□□□

Adj. 神聖な、聖なる   = holy [hóʊli]

This place is **sacred** to him, so please be careful.
（この場所は彼にとって神聖なところなので、気をつけてくださいね。）

▶ **sacredness** [séɪkrɪdnəs] N[U] 神聖さ

---

637 ritual
[rítʃuəl]
□□□□□□

N[C/U] 儀式

This rugby team has a weird pre-game **ritual**.
（このラグビーチームは試合前の変な儀式があるんだ。）

▶ **ritualistic** [rìtʃuəlístɪk] Adj. 儀式的な、何度も繰り返される

We are studying the **ritualistic** behavior of people with autism.
（私たちは、自閉症の人が何度も繰り返す行動について研究しています。）

▶ **ritualistically** [rìtʃuəlístɪkli] Adv. 儀式的に、何度も繰り返して

The pilot **ritualistically** kisses the plane before he gets on it. So beautiful.
（あのパイロットは毎回飛行機に乗る前に機体にキスをするんだ。素敵。）

---

638 prayer
[prer]
□□□□□□

N[C/U] 祈祷、祈り

I say a **prayer** for your good health every night.（私はあなたの健康のために毎晩お祈りしてるよ。）

▶ **pray** [preɪ] V[I/T]（〜と）祈る

Every August 6th, a lot of people **pray** for the atomic bomb victims at the Hiroshima Peace Memorial Park.
（毎年8月6日は、多くの人が広島平和記念公園で原爆の犠牲者のためにお祈りをするんだ。）

---

639 symbol
[símbəl]
□□□□□□

N[C] 象徴、シンボル；記号

In Japan, the Emperor is a **symbol** of the state and the unity of the people.
（日本では、天皇は国と国民統合の象徴なんだ。）

▶ **symbolic** [sɪmbá:lɪk] Adj.（〜を）象徴する（of sth）、象徴的な

My promotion is purely **symbolic**. I'm not actually getting paid more.
（私の昇進は象徴的なものに過ぎないの。実際、全く給料上がってないし。）

▶ **symbolically** [sɪmbá:lɪkli] Adv. 象徴的に

▶ **symbolize** [símbəlaɪz] V[T] を象徴する

3 For instance, although Christianity and Islam share a common place of origin in the Middle East, Christians regard Jesus as the Son of God, while Muslims believe that Jesus was a holy prophet.

例えば、キリスト教とイスラム教はどちらも中東に共通の起源を持っているが、キリスト教徒はイエスを神の子とみなしているのに対し、イスラム教徒はイエスを神聖な預言者と考えている。

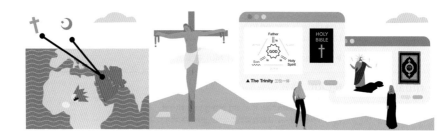

---

640 instance
[ínstəns]

N[C] 例、事例、場合

■ for **instance**（例えば）= for example　　in this **instance**（この場合）

Japanese and Korean languages are similar in many ways. **For instance**, they have a relatively similar grammar structure.
（日本語と韓国語は似ているところが多いんだ。例えば、二つは比較的似た文法構造を持っているよ。）

---

641 share
[ʃer]

V[T] を（〜と）共に持つ、共有する、分け合う（with sb）

How about we order a few dishes to **share**?（いくつか料理頼んでシェアするのはどう？）

V[I] 共有する　　N[C] 分け前、取り分；株；市場占有率

■ sb's (fair) **share**（〜の（平等な）取り分）

Why am I getting the smallest slice of pizza? You have to give me **my fair share**!
（なんで私のピザが一番ちっちゃいの？ちゃんと平等な大きさにしてよ！）

---

642 origin
[ɔ́:rədʒɪn]

N[C/U] 起源、発端；出身、血統

I find theories on the **origins** of the human race fascinating.
（人類の起源をめぐる理論ってすごい面白いなぁって思うよ。）

▶ **original** Adj. 元の、最初の；オリジナルの、独創的な　N[C] 原型、オリジナル
[ərídʒənəl]

All of his artwork is very **original**.（彼の美術作品はみんなすごい独創的なんだ。）

▶ **originally** [ərídʒənəli] Adv. 元々、最初は；独創的に

▶ **originate** [ərídʒəneɪt] V[I]（〜に）由来する、（〜から）始まる (from sth)
V[T] を考え出す

▶ **originality** [ərìdʒənǽləti] N[U] 独創性

643 the Middle East
[ðə mìdəl íːst]
☐☐☐☐☐☐

N[Prop.] 中東

There are so many super-rich people in **the Middle East**.
(中東には超リッチな人がものすごいたくさんいるよ。)

▶ **Middle Eastern** [mìdəl íːstərn] Adj. 中東の　**Middle Eastern** countries (中東諸国)

---

644 regard
[rɪgáːrd]
☐☐☐☐☐☐

V[T] を（〜だと）みなす、考える（as sth/sb）

I **regard** George as my friend, even though he might not feel the same way.
(私はジョージのこと友達だと考えてるよ。彼はそう思ってないかもしれないけど。)

N[U] 観点；注意；敬意、評価

■ in/with **regard** to sth/sb（〜に関して）　■ in this/that **regard**（この／その点に関しては）

I have a few questions **with regard to** the point you have just mentioned.
(君が今言ったことに関していくつか質問があります。)

We will take care of booking your hotels, so you won't have to worry **in that regard**.
(ホテルの予約に関しては我々で手配しますので、その点に関して心配する必要はありません。)

N[P] よろしくの挨拶【-s】

■ give/send my **regards** to sb（〜によろしくお伝えください）

Oh! You are going to Japan to see Junki? **Send my regards to** him.
(おぉ！ジュンキに会いに日本行くの？よろしく伝えておいて。)

▶ **regarding** [rɪgáːrdɪŋ] Prep. 〜に関して

The YouTuber finally made an announcement **regarding** the upcoming event!
(あのYouTuber、ついに次のイベントに関して告知したね！)

regard vs **consider**　どちらも「みなす、考える」という意味で、ニュアンスにもほぼ違いはありません。しかし、基本的にregardはasを後に続けるのに対し、considerはas以外にもthat + sentenceやA to be Bを続けることができます。

---

645 holy
[hóʊli]
☐☐☐☐☐☐

Adj. 神聖な、聖なる　= **sacred** [séɪkrɪd]

Mecca is considered the **holiest** city in Islam.(メッカはイスラム教で最も神聖な街だと考えられてる。)

■ **holy** cow（なんてこった、マジかよ）

Holy cow! How did you manage to finish this massive bowl of ramen in such a short time?　(おいマジかよ！どうやってこんな短い時間でこの巨大ラーメン食べ終わったの？)

---

646 prophet
[práːfɪt]
☐☐☐☐☐☐

N[C] （神の）預言者、（未来の）予言者

His stock market predictions are accurate so often that I think he must be a **prophet**.
(彼の株式市場予想はすごいよく当たるし、彼は予言者に違いない。)

▶ **prophecy** [práːfəsi] N[C] 預言、予言　N[U] 預言能力、予言能力

The seer's **prophecies** have all come true! (あの予言者の予言、全部当たったんだ！)

▶ **prophetic** Adj. 預言的な、予言的な　▶ **prophetically** Adv. 預言的に、予言的に
[prəfétɪk]　　　　　　　　　　　　　　　　　　　　[prəfétɪkli]

4 Since there are abundant differences among religions, some argue that it is important to identify similar traits that religions possess to reach scholarly consensus over what constitutes religion.

宗教間で多くの違いがあるため、宗教を構成しているものについて学術的な統一見解を図るには、異なる宗教が持つ類似した特徴を特定することが重要だという意見もある。

eg dietary restrictions

---

647 **abundant**
[əbʌ́ndənt]
☐☐☐☐☐☐

Adj.（～に）たくさんある、豊富な（in sth）

Birds are really **abundant** in this forest at this time of year.
（この森は毎年この時期になると鳥の数がものすごく増えるんだ。）

▶ **abundantly** Adv. 豊富に、たくさん　　▶ **abundance** N[S/U] 豊富、多数、多量
　[əbʌ́ndəntli]　　　　　　　　　　　　　　[əbʌ́ndəns]

---

648 **identify**
[aɪdéntəfaɪ]
☐☐☐☐☐☐

V[T] を特定する、識別する、見つける

Let's do some exercises to **identify** your hidden strengths and skills.
（君の隠れた強みとスキルを見つけるための演習をいくつかやってみよう。）

▶ **identification** [aɪdèntəfəkéɪʃən] N[U] 特定；身分証（略 ID）

The **identification** of what your problems are is the very first step in the process of improving anything. （何を改善するにも問題が何か特定することが一番最初のステップなんだ。）

Can I see your **identification**, please?（身分証を見せてもらってもいいですか？）

▶ **identity** [aɪdéntəti] N[C/U] 身元；個性、アイデンティティ；同一性

an **identity** crisis（アイデンティティークライシス*、自己喪失）
* 自分は何者かといった疑問により生じる心理的な危機状況のこと

▶ **identical** Adj.（～と）全く同じの（to sth/sb）　▶ **identically** Adv. 全く同じように
　[aɪdéntəkəl]　　　　　　　　　　　　　　　[aɪdéntəkli]

identical twins（一卵性双生児）　　fraternal twins（二卵性双生児）

---

649 **similar**
[símələr]
☐☐☐☐☐☐

Adj.（～と）類似した、似ている（to sth/sb）

Andy and Trent look pretty **similar**, so people often get them confused.
（アンディーとトレントは結構似てるから、みんなよく混同しちゃうんだ。）

▶ **similarly** [símələrli] Adv. 同じように、同様に

Do young people all dress **similarly** nowadays, or is it just me?
（最近の若者ってみんな同じような格好するの？ それともそう思ってるのは私だけかな？）

▶ **similarity** [sɪməlérəṭi] N[S/U] 類似性　N[C] 似ている点

similar vs **alike** vs **identical**　similar は「全く同じではないが似た特徴を持っている」こと、alike は「ほとんど同じ、もしくは全く同じである」こと、identical は「完全に同じである」ことを意味し、左から順に「似ている」「よく似ている」「全く同じの」と訳されることが多い単語です。

---

650 **trait**
[treɪt]

☐☐☐☐☐☐

N[C]　特徴、特性、特質

Integrity is the most important **trait** I look for when hiring employees.
（私が従業員を雇う時に求める最も重要な特性は誠実さだね。）

---

651 **possess**
[pəzés]

☐☐☐☐☐☐

V[T]　を持つ、所有する

I don't **possess** enough knowledge to teach Chinese.
（中国語を教えるだけの十分な知識は持っていません。）

▶ **possessive** [pəzésɪv] Adj.（〜に対して）独占欲の強い（about sth/sb）

My boyfriend is **possessive** and jealous.（私の彼氏は独占欲が強くて嫉妬深いの。）

▶ **possession** [pəzéʃən] N[U] 所有、所持　N[C] 所有物

---

652 **scholarly**
[skáːlərli]

☐☐☐☐☐☐

Adj.　学術的な、学問的な；博識な

George is really **scholarly**, so I don't understand a lot of the words that he uses.
（ジョージってすごい博識だから、彼の使う言葉で分からないのたくさんあるんだ。）

▶ **scholar** [skáːlər] N[C] 学者；博学な人；奨学生

▶ **scholarship** [skáːlərʃɪp] N[C] 奨学金　N[U] 学問、学識

Even if you are from a poor family, you have the option of getting a **scholarship** to study at university.（もし君の家が貧しかったとしても、奨学金をもらって大学で勉強するという選択肢もあるよ。）

---

653 **consensus**
[kənsénsəs]

☐☐☐☐☐☐

N[S/U]　意見の一致、合意

I deliberately talked less to quickly reach a **consensus**.
（早く合意できるように意図的にあまりベラベラしゃべらないようにしたんだ。）

▶ **consensual** [kàːnsénsjuəl] Adj.（契約などが）合意の上の

Was that **consensual**?（それって合意の上だったの？）

▶ **consensually** [kàːnsénsjuəli] Adv. 合意の上で

If we **consensually** manage the company, there should be less risk of ultimate failure.
（みんなが合意の上で会社の経営を行えば、最終的に失敗するリスクが減るはずだよ。）

▶ **consent** [kənsént] N[U] 合意、同意　V[I]（〜に）合意する、同意する（to sth）

with/without (sb's) **consent**（（〜の）合意に基づいて / 合意なしで）

Man   Growing up, my family were very devout Catholics. However, I've become a bit torn in my beliefs. I've seen a multitude of things which make me question the existence of a benevolent, omnipotent entity.

Woman   You're entitled to your beliefs, but how can you look at the world and not believe in a higher being? How can it be so perfect without divine intervention? Besides, we all need a framework for how to live morally and make tough decisions.

Man   I admire your conviction. However, I prefer to follow my conscience and my instincts when I'm faced with tough choices, and not place my faith in a medieval creed.

Woman   It might be a bit naive, but I actually find it quite comforting to lean on my faith when I'm going through a rough patch. It really takes a load off my mind.

男性   僕、すごい敬虔なカトリックの家庭で育ったんだけど、自分の信仰に迷いが出てきたんだよね。いろんなことを目にして、慈悲深い全能なものが存在するっていうことに対して、疑問を抱かざるを得なくなってきているというか。

女性   何を信じるかは自由だけど、この世界を見て、神の存在を信じないなんてできる？神の介入なしにこんなにも完璧な世界が生まれるのかな？それに、私たちにはみんな道徳的に生きて、難しい決断を下すための枠組みが必要だしね。

男性   君の強い信念には感心するよ。でもさ、僕は難しい選択を迫られたときには自分の良心と直感に従いたいんだよね。古くさい教義を信じるんじゃなくて。

女性   ちょっと考えが甘いのかもしれないけど、私はつらい目に遭っているときは、信仰に頼ると結構ほっとするけどね。すごい安心するんだよね。

654 Catholic
[kǽθəlɪk]

N[C] カトリック教徒　**Adj.** カトリックの

▶ **Catholicism** [kəθáːləsɪzəm] N[U] カトリック教

---

655 torn
[tɔːrn]

Adj. 迷った、板ばさみになった

▶ **tear** [ter] V[I] 裂ける　V[T] を引き裂く

---

656 multitude
[mʌ́ltətuːd]

N[C] たくさん、多数

a **multitude** of sth（たくさんの〜）　a **multitude** of reasons（たくさんの理由）

---

657 benevolent
[bənévələnt]

Adj. 慈悲深い、寛大な

▶ **benevolently** [bənévələntli] Adv. 寛大に、慈悲深く

▶ **benevolence** [bənévələns] N[U] 寛大さ、慈悲深さ

---

658 entity
[énṭəti]

N[C]（一つの）存在

a legal **entity**（法人）　a private/public **entity**（民間団体 / 公共団体）

---

659 entitled
[ɪntáɪtld]

Adj.（〜の / 〜する）権利を持った、資格を持った（to sth/to do）

Everyone's **entitled** to their opinion.（みんな自分の意見を持つ権利がある。）

▶ **entitle** [ɪntáɪtl] V[T] に（〜の / 〜する）権利を与える、資格を与える（to sth/to do）

▶ **entitlement** [ɪntáɪtlmənt] N[U]（〜を受け取る）権利、資格（to sth）

---

660 divine
[dɪváɪn]

Adj. 神の、神聖な、（神と言えるくらい）素晴らしい

The band's performance was **divine**.（あのバンドの演奏は神だった。）

▶ **divinity** [dɪvínəti] N[U] 神学、神性

---

661 intervention
[ìntərvénʃən]

N[C/U] 介入、干渉

military **intervention**（軍事介入）　human **intervention**（人の介入）

▶ **intervene** [ìntərvíːn] V[I]（〜に）介入する、干渉する（in sth）

---

662 framework
[fréɪmwɜːrk]

N[C] 枠組み、フレームワーク

within the **framework** of sth（〜の枠組みの中で）

---

663 conviction
[kənvíkʃən]

N[C] 信念；有罪判決　N[U] 確信

▶ **convict** V[T] に（〜の罪で）有罪判決を出す（of sth）　N[C] 受刑者、囚人
V. [kənvíkt] N. [kánvɪkt]

The man was **convicted** of murder.（その男は殺人で有罪判決を受けた。）

▶ **convicted** [kənvíktɪd] Adj. 有罪判決を受けた

664 conscience
[kɑ́:nʃəns]
□□□□□□

N[C/U] 良心

▶ **conscientious** [kà:nʃiénʃəs] Adj. 良心的な

▶ **conscientiously** [kà:nʃiénʃəsli] Adv. 良心的に

▶ **conscientiousness** [kà:nʃiénʃəsnəs] N[U] 良心的なこと

混同注意！ conscience vs consciousness　conscience は「良心」、consciousness [kɑ́:nʃəsnəs] は「意識」を意味します。

---

665 instinct
[ínstɪŋkt]
□□□□□□

N[C/U] 直感、本能

Trust your **instincts**. If it doesn't seem right, don't do it.
（直感を信じなよ。それで正しくなさそうなら、やんなきゃいいんだから。）

▶ **instinctive** [ɪnstíŋktɪv] Adj. 直感的な、本能的な

▶ **instinctively** [ɪnstíŋktɪvli] Adv. 直感的に、本能的に

---

666 faith
[feɪθ]
□□□□□□

N[U] 信じること、信頼、信用、信仰　N[C] 宗教

place/have one's **faith** in sth/sb （〜を信じる、〜に信頼を置く）

▶ **faithful** [féɪθfəl] Adj. 信頼できる、誠実な　▶ **faithfully** [féɪθfəli] Adv. 誠実に

---

667 medieval
[mèdií:vəl]
□□□□□□

Adj. 古くさい；中世の

---

668 creed
[kri:d]
□□□□□□

N[C] 教義、信条

---

669 naive
[naɪí:v]
□□□□□□

Adj. 考えが甘い、うぶな、世間知らずな

▶ **naively** [naɪí:vli] Adv. 無邪気に

---

670 lean
[li:n]
□□□□□□

V[I] （〜に）寄り掛かる、もたれる（on sth）；傾く

lean on sth/sb （〜に頼る、〜にすがる）

V[T] を（〜に）立てかける（against sth）

Adj. 脂肪の少ない、赤身の；引き締まった

I like marbled meat, but I like **lean** meat more.（霜降りの肉も好きだけど、赤身の方が好き。）

---

671 go through a rough patch
[goʊθrú: ərʌ́fpætʃ]
□□□□□□

Phr. つらい目に遭う、ひどい目にあう；倦怠期である

My boyfriend and I are **going through a rough patch**.

（彼氏と私は今倦怠期にあるんだ。）

---

672 load
[loʊd]
□□□□□□

N[C] 重荷、荷物；仕事量　= **workload** [wə́:rkloʊd]

take a **load** off sb's mind （〜を安心させる、〜の重荷を下ろす）

V[I] 荷物を積み込む　V[T] を積む；を読み込む

↻ CH. 4, 8, 11, 14

Chapter

15

心理学
Psychology

While psychology is tough to define in a precise way, it predominantly incorporates the empirical study of the human mind and behavior. It includes studying many aspects of the mind, such as attention, emotion, intelligence, motivation, brain function, and personality.

In practice, psychologists often propose theories that describe human behavior within specific demographic groups. Their ultimate ambition is to help society thrive and progress.

An example of such a theory is Maslow's Hierarchy of Needs, which is a five-tier model that claims that humans are motivated by different levels of needs: physiological needs, the need for safety, the need for love and belonging, the need for esteem, and the need for self-actualization.

As this compelling theory has proven to be immensely useful in many different circumstances, the use of this theory has become prevalent in a variety of fields such as management, marketing, and nursing.

1 While psychology is tough to define in a precise way, it predominantly incorporates the empirical study of the human mind and behavior. It includes studying many aspects of the mind, such as attention, emotion, intelligence, motivation, brain function, and personality.

心理学を正確に定義するのは難しいが、主に人の心と行動に関する実証的な研究を含むものである。そこには、人の注意や感情、知性、動機、脳機能、性格など、心に関するさまざまな側面の研究も含まれている。

---

673 psychology
[saɪkɑ́:lədʒi]

N[U] 心理学

Studying **psychology** helps me understand what my girlfriend is thinking.
（心理学を勉強してると彼女の考えていることがもっとよく分かるようになるんだ。）

▶ **psychological** Adj. 心理的な
[sàɪkəlá:dʒɪkəl]

▶ **psychologically** Adv. 心理的に
[sàɪkəlá:dʒɪkli]

▶ **psychologist** [saɪkɑ́:lədʒɪst] N[C] 心理学者

---

674 tough
[tʌf]

Adj. 難しい；厳しい；たくましい、タフな；（肉などが）固い

Working out is **tough**, but it gets easier once you make it a habit.
（エクササイズをするのは大変だけど、習慣化しちゃえば余裕だよ。）

▶ **toughness** [tʌ́fnəs] N[U] タフさ、丈夫なこと

▶ **toughen** [tʌ́fən] V[T] (基準など) を厳しくする；を強化する

▶ **toughen (sth) up** [tʌ́fənʌ́p] V[PV] たくましくなる；を強くする

---

675 precise
[prəsáɪs]

Adj. 正確な、ぴったりの = exact [ɪgzǽkt]

Your calculations are always so **precise**! How do you do that?
（君の計算っていつも正確だけど、どうやってやってるの？）

▶ **precisely** [prəsáɪsli] Adv. 正確に

Do you remember **precisely** the first time we met?
（僕たちが出会った時のこと、ちゃんと覚えてくれてる？）

▶ **preciseness** [prəsáɪsnəs] N[U] 正確さ = precision [prəsíʒən]

676 **way**
[weɪ]
□□□□□□

N[C] 方法、やり方

There are many **ways** of solving the issue.（その問題を解決する方法はたくさんあるよ。）

in a + adjective + **way**（〜な方法で）

N[C] 方向、方角；道、道順

Which **way** is north?（北ってどっち？）

■ make one's **way**（進む）

Please **make your way** to Platform 9.（9番ホームまでお進みください。）

■ on one's/the **way** (to sth)（（〜に行く）途中で）

I'm **on my way**.（今向かってるよ。）

■ the other **way** around（逆の、逆に）

I didn't dump her! It was **the other way around**!
（俺が彼女を捨てたんじゃない！その逆だよ！）

N[S] 距離、道のり

■ come a long **way**（はるばるやってくる；進歩する）

You've **come a long way**.（よくここまで頑張ったね。）

677 **predominantly**
[prɪdɑ́:mənəntli]
□□□□□□

Adv. 主に、大部分は

Houses in this area are **predominantly** owned by baby boomers.
（この辺の家は主に団塊の世代の人たちによって所有されてるんだ。）

▶ **predominant** [prɪdɑ́:mənənt] Adj. 主な、(他よりも) 優れた

The **predominant** religion in Thailand is Buddhism.（タイの主な宗教は仏教なんだ。）

678 **incorporate**
[ɪnkɔ́:rpəreɪt]
□□□□□□

V[T] を含む、組み込む、取り入れる　V[I/T]（〜を）法人化する

I tried to tell her I have feelings for her by **incorporating** heart emojis in my text.
（彼女に気があることを伝えるためにメッセージにハートの絵文字を入れちゃった。）

▶ **incorporation** [ɪnkɔ̀:rpəréɪʃən] N[U] 組み込むこと、取り入れること；法人化

I think the **incorporation** of young minds in the development of a new product is essential.
（新しい商品の開発には若い人の意見を取り入れることが必要不可欠だと思うよ。）

▶ **incorporated** [ɪnkɔ́:rpəreɪṭɪd] Adj.（会社名の後について）法人の（**= Inc.** [ɪŋk]）

Apple **Inc.**（アップル社）

679 **empirical**
[empírɪkəl]
□□□□□□

Adj. 実証的な、実験に基づく、経験による

I like **empirical** studies much more than theoretical ones.
（僕は論理的な学問よりも実証的な学問のほうが好きだなぁ。）

▶ **empirically** [empírɪkli] Adv. 実証的に、経験的に

2 In practice, psychologists often propose theories that describe human behavior within specific demographic groups. Their ultimate ambition is to help society thrive and progress.

実際には、心理学者は人口統計上の特定層の人の行動を説明する理論をしばしば提唱する。その最終的な野望は、社会の繁栄と進歩を後押しすることにある。

---

680 propose
[prəpóʊz]
☐☐☐☐☐☐

V[T] を提唱する、提案する

You should contribute by actively **proposing** your ideas in meetings.
（会議では積極的に自分のアイディアを提案して貢献した方が良いよ。）

V[I] （〜に）プロポーズする（to sb）　= pop the question

pop the question も「プロポーズをする」という意味の表現ですが、propose よりもカジュアルな表現です。pop は「ポン」と何かを出すイメージで、この時の the question は「結婚してくれるかどうかに関する質問＝プロポーズの言葉」を意味しています。

▶ **proposal** [prəpóʊzəl] N[C]（〜の）提案（for sth）；プロポーズ

▶ **proposed** [prəpóʊzd] Adj. 案の、提案された

a **proposed** agreement（協定案）

---

681 demographic
[dèməgrǽfɪk]
☐☐☐☐☐☐

Adj. 人口統計上の

Japan is going through a big **demographic** shift right now, and it's causing a lot of issues.（日本は今、大きな人口転換を迎えており、たくさんの問題を引き起こしている。）

N[C] （年齢や職業などがほぼ等しい人々から成る）層

I'm only 18, but the majority of my followers belong to the 65+ **demographic**.
（僕はまだ 18 歳だけど、フォロワー層は 65 歳以上がほとんどなんだよね。）

N[U] 人口統計学【-s】　**N[P]** 人口統計データ、人口動態【-s】

▶ **demographically** [dèməgrǽfɪkli] Adv. 人口統計学的に

---

682 group
[gru:p]
☐☐☐☐☐☐

N[C] 層、グループ、集団、群れ

■ a **group** of sth/sb（〜の集団、群れ）

Why are there so many words for **groups of** animals in English?
（なんで英語には動物の群れを表す言葉がこんなにたくさんあるの？）

V[T] を（〜に）分類する（into sth）；を集める　**V[I]** 集まる

- **group** sth/sb **together**（〜をひとまとめにする、を集める）

Can you **group** those books **together**? They're all written by the same author.
（その本全部まとめてくれる？　みんな作者が同じだから。）

---

683 **ultimate**
[ʌ́ltəmət]
□□□□□□

Adj. 最終的な、究極の　**N[U]** 究極のもの【the -】

My **ultimate** goal is to achieve a 990 on the TOEIC test.
（最終的な目標は TOEIC で 990 点満点を取ることなんだ。）

▶ **ultimately** [ʌ́ltəmətli] Adv. 最終的には、結局

Ultimately, it's you who decides what you do.（結局、決めるのは自分だからね。）

▶ **ultimatum** [ʌ̀ltəméɪtəm] N[C] 最終通告

---

684 **ambition**
[æmbíʃən]
□□□□□□

N[C] 野望、夢　**N[U]** 野心、出世欲

My **ambition** is to become a millionaire, even though I only have 300 yen in my wallet right now.　（今現在財布に 300 円しかないけど、僕の野望は億万長者になることなんだ。）

▶ **ambitious** [æmbíʃəs] Adj. 野心的な、熱望して

"Boys, be **ambitious**!" are Dr. Clark's famous words.
（「少年よ、大志を抱け！」はクラーク博士の有名な言葉だよ。）

▶ **ambitiously** [æmbíʃəsli] Adv. 野心的に

---

685 **thrive**
[θraɪv]
□□□□□□

V[I] 繁栄する；（植物などが）良く育つ

This city has **thrived** over the past couple of years, thanks to all the foreign visitors.
（海外からのたくさんの旅行者のおかげで、ここ数年でこの街はかなり繁栄したね。）

▶ **thriving** [θráɪvɪŋ] Adj. 繁盛している

---

686 **progress**
V.[prəgrés]
N.[prɑ́:gres]
□□□□□□

V[I] 進歩する、（物事が）前進する　**N[U]** 進歩、前進

Are you guys **progressing** well?（みんな順調に進んでる？）

- make **progress**（進歩する、前進する）

I **made** a lot of **progress** on my videos over the three-day weekend.
（三連休中に動画制作めっちゃ進んだよ。）

▶ **progressive** [prəgrésɪv] Adj. 革新的な；進行性の；累進的な

a **progressive** idea（革新的な考え）　　a **progressive** disease（進行性の病気）

a **progressive** tax system（累進課税制度）

3 An example of such a theory is Maslow's Hierarchy of Needs, which is a five-tier model that claims that humans are motivated by different levels of needs: physiological needs, the need for safety, the need for love and belonging, the need for esteem, and the need for self-actualization.

そうした理論の一例に、マズローの欲求階層説があり、これは、人がさまざまなレベルの欲求に動機づけられていることを5段階で示したモデルである。その5段階とは、生理的欲求、安全欲求、愛と所属の欲求、承認欲求、そして自己実現欲求である。

---

687 **hierarchy**
[háɪrɑːrki]
☐☐☐☐☐☐

N[C/U] 階層制、ヒエラルキー　**N[U]** （組織などの）支配層

There's a certain **hierarchy** in school, where the popular students dominate the classroom.
（学校には、人気者が教室を支配するという独特なヒエラルキーがあるんだ。）

▶ **hierarchical** Adj. 階層的な、階層制の　▶ **hierarchically** Adv. 階層的に
[hàɪrɑːrkɪkəl]　[hàɪrɑːrkɪkli]

---

688 **need**
[niːd]
☐☐☐☐☐☐

N[C/U] 欲求　**N[S/U]** 必要、要求　**N[P]** 必要なもの、ニーズ【-s】

I think love, food, and sleep are the most fundamental **needs** of human beings.
（僕は愛と食欲と睡眠欲が人間の最も基本的な欲求だと思うんだよね。）

■ sb in **need**（助けが必要な〜）　■ there is no **need** to do（〜する必要はない）

I think people sitting in priority seats should give up their seats for **those in need** without being asked.
（優先席に座ってる人は、必要としている人には頼まれなくても席を譲るべきだと思うよ。）

There's no need to get angry.（怒る必要なんてないよ。）

V[T] を必要とする

need to do（〜する必要がある、しないといけない）

▶ **needed** Adj. 必要とされた　▶ **needy** Adj. 貧しい、飢えた；依存タイプの、重い
[niːdɪd]　[niːdi]

I don't feel **needed** at this company.
（この会社で働いててもあんまり必要とされてる感じがしないんだよな。）

My girlfriend is too **needy** sometimes.（俺の彼女たまに重すぎるんだよな。）

689 **tier**
[tɪr]
☐☐☐☐☐☐

N[C] 段、層

■ top-**tier**（一流の、大手の）   five-**tier**（五つの階層からなる）

I decided against working at a **top-tier** law firm because I care about my work-life balance.
（大手の弁護士事務所では働かないことに決めたんだ。僕はワークライフバランスを大事にしてるからね。）

690 **claim**
[kleɪm]
☐☐☐☐☐☐

V[T] を主張する   **V[I/T]** （～を）請求する   **N[C]** 主張；請求（額）

Some scientists **claim** that drinking wine has health benefits, but I kind of doubt it.
（ワインを飲むと健康に良いって言う科学者がいるけど、なんか信じられないんだよね。）

Tommy makes big **claims** about everything, but he never really backs it up.
（トミーって何でも大きなことを言うけど、それを裏付けるものが全然ないんだよなぁ。）

an insurance **claim**（保険の請求）

▶ **claimant** [kléɪmənt] N[C]（社会保障や保険金の）請求者、申請人

691 **motivate**
[móʊṱəveɪt]
☐☐☐☐☐☐

V[T] を動機づける、のモチベーションを上げる

Ichiro's words **motivate** me to be better.
（イチローの言葉を聞くと、もっと良くなるために頑張ろうと思えるよ。）

▶ **motivated** [móʊṱɪveɪṱɪd] Adj. やる気のある、モチベーションの高い

↔ **unmotivated** [ʌnmóʊṱɪveɪṱɪd] やる気のない

He is one of the most **motivated** students in this class.
（彼はこのクラスの中でもとてもやる気のある生徒の一人なんだ。）

▶ **motivational** Adj. やる気を起こさせる、モチベが上がるような
    [mòʊṱəvéɪʃənəl]

▶ **motivation** [mòʊṱəvéɪʃən] N[U] やる気、モチベーション   N[C] 動機

▶ **motive** [móʊṱɪv] N[C] 動機   Adj. 原動力となる

692 **belonging**
[bɪlá:ŋɪŋ]
☐☐☐☐☐☐

N[U] 所属、帰属   **N[P]** 持ち物、所持品【-s】

After five years, I finally feel a sense of **belonging** to the team.
（５年してやっとこのチームに対する帰属意識が芽生えてきたんだ。）

▶ **belong** [bɪlá:ŋ] V[I]（～の）ものである、属する（to sth/sb）；あるべき場所にある

That book **belongs** to me.（あの本は僕のだよ。）

693 **esteem**
[ɪstí:m]
☐☐☐☐☐☐

N[U] 尊重、尊敬、高い評価

■ self-**esteem**（自尊心）

My brother's hurtful words lowered my **self-esteem**.
（お兄ちゃんにひどいこと言われて自尊心が傷ついた。）

V[T] を尊重する、尊敬する、高く評価する

4 As this compelling theory has proven to be immensely useful in many different circumstances, the use of this theory has become prevalent in a variety of fields such as management, marketing, and nursing.

魅力的なこの理論は、さまざまな状況で非常に有用であることが分かったため、マネジメントやマーケティング、看護などの多様な分野において広く使われるようになった。

---

694 **compelling**
[kəmpélɪŋ]

Adj. (話などが) 魅力的な、人を引きつける ; 説得力のある ; やむを得ない

The way he talks sounds **compelling**, but if you think it through you'll find that what he's saying is actually quite empty.
(彼の話し方には引きつけられるんだけど、よく考えると実際はあんまり中身がないことがわかるんだ。)

▶ **compel** [kəmpél] V[T] に強いる、強制する

■ **compel** sb to do (〜に無理やり〜させる)

I was **compelled to** wear a uniform when I was in high school.
(高校の時は制服を着なきゃいけなかったんだ。)

▶ **compulsion** [kəmpʌ́lʃən] N[U] 強制、無理強い N[C] (〜したい) 衝動 (to do)

---

695 **prove**
[pru:v]

V[I] (〜であることが) 分かる (to do) **V[T]** を証明する

I bought some very cheap Ray-Ban sunglasses, but they **proved** to be fake.
(すごい安いレイバンのサングラス買ったんだけど、偽物だって分かったんだ。)

You say you love me, but can you **prove** it?
(僕のこと愛してるっていうなら、ちゃんと証明してよ。)

■ **prove** sb guilty/innocent (〜が有罪 / 無罪であると立証する)

After hours of investigation, he **was proven innocent**.
(何時間も捜査した結果、彼は無実だと証明された。)

▶ **proven** [prúːvən] Adj. 証明された ▶ **proof** [pruːf] N[C/U] 証明

---

696 **immensely**
[ɪménsli]

Adv. 非常に、とても = **extremely** [ɪkstríːmli]

You were **immensely** helpful in finishing this project. Thanks.
(君がものすごく助けてくれたおかげでプロジェクトを終わらせることができたよ。ありがとう。)

▶ **immense** [ɪméns] Adj. 巨大な、広大な、莫大な

I spent an **immense** amount of time finishing my final thesis.
(卒論を終わらせるのに莫大な時間がかかったよ。)

---

697 **useful**
[júːsfəl]
☐☐☐☐☐☐

Adj. 有用な、役立つ

This app is very **useful** for tracking my fitness activities because it keeps records of my pulse, steps, and calorie consumption.
(このアプリは運動を管理するのにすごく便利なんだ。脈や歩数、カロリー消費を記録してくれるから。)

▶ **usefulness** [júːsfəlnəs] N[U] 有用性

---

698 **circumstance**
[sɚːrkəmstæns]
☐☐☐☐☐☐

N[C] 状況、事情 **N[U]** やむを得ない事態

■ under no **circumstances** (いかなる状況でも～ない)

Under no circumstances should you open the door to strangers.
(どんな状況でも知らない人に対してドアは開けないほうがいいよ。)

▶ **circumstantial** [sɚːrkəmstǽnʃəl] Adj. 状況の

circumstantial evidence (状況証拠)

接頭語 circum- 「周囲」という意味の接頭語で、他には circumlocutory（回りくどい）や circumference（円周）があります。

---

699 **prevalent**
[prévələnt]
☐☐☐☐☐☐

Adj. 広く行き渡った、流行している

Smartphones have become so **prevalent** nowadays that you rarely see people with flip phones. (近頃ほとんどの人がスマホを使ってるから、ガラケーを使う人をほとんど見なくなったね。)

▶ **prevalence** [prévələns] N[U] 普及、流行

The **prevalence** of Starbucks in Japan is crazy. (日本でのスタバの流行は異常なほどだ。)

▶ **prevail** [prɪvéɪl] V[I] (～に) 広がっている (in/among sth)；(～に) 勝つ (over sth)

---

700 **nursing**
[nɚːrsɪŋ]
☐☐☐☐☐☐

N[U] 看護

I studied **nursing** mainly because I wanted to work at a hospital.
(僕は病院で働きたかったから看護を勉強をしたんだ。)

▶ **nurse** [nɜːrs] V[T] を看病する；に授乳する N[C] 看護師

My sister rescued an injured dog and **nursed** it back to health.
(お姉ちゃんはけがをしていた犬を助けて看病して元気にしたんだ。)

I want to be a **nurse** in the future because I like helping people.
(人を助けることが好きだから、将来は看護師になりたいんだ。)

▶ **nursery** [nɚːrsəri] N[C] 保育園、託児所

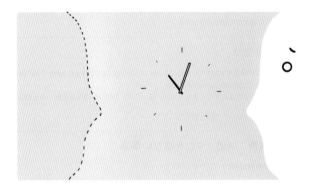

I've been dating a guy for about two months, and he's basically perfect. He's good-looking, smart, and kind. However, he's never punctual. It drives me nuts.

I first asked a female friend for advice. She said that I shouldn't tolerate lateness, even if it ruins our relationship, since there are plenty of fish in the sea.

I guess that's true. I should convey to him that if he continues to be late, then it's over.

I also spoke to a male friend, and he was like, "Maybe lateness is not a virtue, but it's not the worst vice either. Sincerity and spontaneity are more important than superficial politeness in romantic relationships."

I don't know whether he's trying to show off mastery of esoteric language, or I'm just dumb, but I do sort of get his point. I can't expect my boyfriend to be perfect. Love is difficult.

彼とは付き合い始めて約2か月。基本的には完璧。イケメンで、頭もいいし、親切。でも、時間にはものすごいルーズ。頭にきちゃう。

で、まず女友達にアドバイスを求めると、「遅刻に寛容になっちゃだめ。もしそれで関係がだめになったとしてもね。男なんていくらでもいるよ。」って。

まぁ確かにそうだと思う。彼が遅刻するのをやめないなら、もう私たち終わりだよって彼に伝えるべきだよね。

男友達にも話してみると、「まぁ確かに遅刻は美徳ではないかもしれないけど、ひどく不道徳というわけでもないよね。恋愛関係で大事なのは、表面上の礼儀よりも誠実さや自然さなんじゃない?」って。

彼は難しい言葉が使えることをひけらかそうとしてるのか、自分がバカなだけなのか分からないけど、彼が言いたいこともなんとなく分かる。彼氏に完璧を求めちゃいけないってことだよね。恋愛って難しい。

701 date
[deɪt]
☐☐☐☐☐☐

V[I/T] （〜と）付き合う、デートする

Do you think those two are **dating**? （あの二人、付き合ってるのかな？）

V[T] に日付を記入する；の年代を定める **N[C]** デート；日付

go (out) on a **date** (with sb) （（〜と）デートする、付き合う） = go out （with sb）

What's the **date** today? （今日何日だっけ？）

---

702 good-looking
[ɡʊdlʊ́kɪŋ]
☐☐☐☐☐☐

Adj. イケメンの、ルックスの良い、顔立ちの良い

I know he's **good-looking**, but I'm not attracted to him.

（彼がイケメンなのは分かるけど、惹かれないんだよね。）

---

703 punctual
[pʌ́ŋktʃuəl]
☐☐☐☐☐☐

Adj. 時間を守った、時間どおりの

▶ **punctually** [pʌ́ŋktʃuəli] Adv. 時間どおりに ▶ **punctuality** [pʌ̀ŋktʃuǽləti] N[U] 時間厳守

---

704 nuts
[nʌts]
☐☐☐☐☐☐

Adj. 頭のおかしい、気が狂った

drive sb **nuts** （〜の頭をおかしくする） go **nuts** （頭がおかしくなる、気が狂う）

---

705 female
[fíːmeɪl]
☐☐☐☐☐☐

Adj. 女性の、雌の **N[C]** 女性、雌

▶ **feminine** [fémənɪn] Adj. 女性らしい、女性的な

▶ **feminist** [fémənɪst] N[C] フェミニスト ▶ **feminism** [fémənɪzəm] N[U] フェミニズム

---

706 lateness
[léɪtnəs]
☐☐☐☐☐☐

N[U] 遅刻

▶ **late** [leɪt] Adj. 遅刻した、遅い；後半の ▶ **lately** [léɪtli] Adv. 最近

---

707 ruin
[rúːɪn]
☐☐☐☐☐☐

V[T] をだめにする、台無しにする；を破産させる **N[U]** 荒廃、堕落；破産

N[P] 廃墟 【-s】

▶ **ruined** [rúːɪnd] Adj. 台無しになった；廃墟と化した

---

708 fish
[fɪʃ]
☐☐☐☐☐☐

N[C] 魚 **N[U]** 魚肉、魚 **V[I]** （〜を求めて）釣りをする （for sth）

There are plenty of **fish** in the sea. （良い人なんてたくさんいるよ。）

V[T] （場所）で釣りをする

▶ **fishing** [fíʃɪŋ] N[U] 魚釣り、漁業 ▶ **fishy** [fíʃi] Adj. 怪しい

---

709 true
[truː]
☐☐☐☐☐☐

Adj. 本当の、真実の

it is **true** that + sentence （〜は本当だ）

▶ **truly** [trúːli] Adv. 本当に ▶ **truth** [truːθ] N[U] 真実、事実

---

710 convey
[kənvéɪ]
☐☐☐☐☐☐

V[T] を伝える、伝達する

convey one's feelings （自分の感情を伝える）

▶ **conveyance** [kənvéɪəns] N[U] 伝達、輸送

711 male
[meɪl]
☐☐☐☐☐☐

Adj. 男性の、雄の　N[C] 男性、雄

I have two **male** dogs and one female dog.（雄犬を二匹と雌犬を一匹飼ってるんだ。）

▶ **masculine** [mǽskjəlɪn] Adj. 男性らしい、男性的な　= **manly** [mǽnli]

---

712 virtue
[vɚ́ːrtʃu:]
☐☐☐☐☐☐

N[C] 美徳　N[U] 善行

Patience is a **virtue**.（忍耐は美徳だ。）

▶ **virtuous** [vɚ́ːrtʃuəs] Adj. 徳の高い　▶ **virtuously** [vɚ́ːrtʃuəsli] Adv. 道徳心から

---

713 vice
[vaɪs]
☐☐☐☐☐☐

N[C/U] 不道徳、悪徳　Adj. 副〜

a **vice** president（副大統領）

▶ **vicious** [víʃəs] Adj. 悪意のある、意地悪な　▶ **viciously** [víʃəsli] Adv. 意地悪く

---

714 sincerity
[sɪnsérəṭi]
☐☐☐☐☐☐

N[U] 誠実さ、誠意

▶ **sincere** [sɪnsír] Adj. 誠実な、心からの　▶ **sincerely** [sɪnsírli] Adv. 誠実に、心から

---

715 spontaneity
[spɑ̀:ntnéɪəṭi]
☐☐☐☐☐☐

N[U]（行為やふるまいの）自然さ

▶ **spontaneous** [spɑːntéɪniəs] Adj. 自然な

▶ **spontaneously** [spɑːntéɪniəsli] Adv. 自然に

---

716 superficial
[sùːpərfíʃəl]
☐☐☐☐☐☐

Adj. 表面上の、うわべだけの

a **superficial** relationship（うわべだけの関係）

▶ **superficially** [sùːpərfíʃəli] Adv. 表面上は

---

717 politeness
[pəláɪtnəs]
☐☐☐☐☐☐

N[U] 礼儀正しさ

▶ **polite** [pəláɪt] Adj. 礼儀正しい、丁寧な

▶ **politely** [pəláɪtli] Adv. 礼儀正しく、丁寧に

I tried being **polite** to him, but I've run out of patience.
（彼には優しくしてあげてたんだけど、もう我慢できなくなったんだ。）

---

718 romantic
[roʊmǽnṭɪk]
☐☐☐☐☐☐

Adj. 恋愛の、ロマンチックな

▶ **romantically** [roʊmǽnṭɪkli] Adv. 恋愛感情を持って

▶ **romance** [roʊmǽns] N[C] 恋愛関係　N[U] 恋愛感情

---

719 esoteric
[èsətérɪk]
☐☐☐☐☐☐

Adj. とても難しい、難解な

This manual is so **esoteric** I have no idea what it's trying to say.
（このマニュアル難解すぎて何を言おうとしてるか分からないよ。）

---

720 dumb
[dʌm]
☐☐☐☐☐☐

Adj. ばかな

Can I ask you a **dumb** question?（ちょっとばかな質問して良い？）

Chapter

16

社会
Society

A society is a group of people living together in an organized manner, generally characterized by sharing the same sense of cooperation, political authority, territory, and cultural norms.

Typically, societies are culturally homogeneous, but they often contain within them smaller segments of like-minded individuals that form diverse subcultures or "tribes."

One example of such a tribe is the Japanese subculture called "Harajuku style," which is a youth culture that disregards conventional fashion and is typified by people in bold, inventive, and outrageous clothes.

According to some sociologists, these various subcultures function to help maintain the stable equilibrium of society as a whole and are therefore critical elements of a prosperous society.

1 **A society is a group of people living together in an** organized manner, **generally** characterized **by sharing the same sense of** cooperation, political **authority,** territory, **and cultural** norms.

社会とは、組織的に共生する人々の集まりを指し、その一般的な特徴として、同一の連帯感や政治的権力、地域、そして文化的規範を共有していることなどが挙げられる。

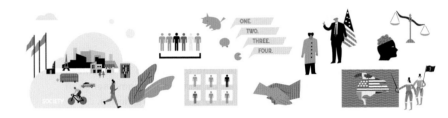

---

721 organized
[ɔ́:rɡənaɪzd]
☐☐☐☐☐☐

Adj. 組織的な；整理された、（人が）きちんとした

I'm really **organized** at work, but my life outside of it is a bit of a mess.
（私は職場ではものすごいきちんとしてるけど、仕事の外ではちょっとだらしないんだ。）

↔ **disorganized** [dɪsɔ́:rɡənaɪzd] 要領の悪い、事前準備がなされていない

▶ **organize** [ɔ́:rɡənaɪz] V[T] を組織する；を整理する、まとめる、計画する

Every year, I **organize** a special trip for my bestie's birthday.
（私は毎年親友の誕生日のために特別旅行を計画するんだ。）

▶ **organization** [ɔ̀:rɡənəzéɪʃən] N[C] 組織、団体　N[U] 組織化；準備、手配

▶ **organizational** [ɔ̀:rɡənəzéɪʃənəl] Adj. 組織の、構造的な

Her **organizational** skills are unmatched.（彼女の物事をまとめるスキルは他に類を見ないよ。）

▶ **organizer** [ɔ́:rɡənaɪzər] N[C]（イベントなどの）主催者

---

722 manner
[mǽnər]
☐☐☐☐☐☐

N[S] やり方、方法；物腰、態度　N[P] 礼儀、マナー【-s】

He had such an awkward **manner**.（彼、ものすごくぎこちない態度だったよ。）

in a + adjective + **manner**（～な方法で）

Eating or drinking on the train is considered bad **manners** in Japan.
（電車で食べたり飲んだりするのは日本ではマナー違反だよ。）

▶ **mannerism** [mǽnərɪzəm] N[C]（話し方などの）癖；（芸術などの）型にはまった表現技法

Your **mannerisms** are so similar to your dad's.（君、お父さんと話し方の癖が本当に似てるよね。）

---

723 characterize
[kérəktəraɪz]
☐☐☐☐☐☐

V[T] を特徴づける；を（～と）みなす（as sth）

Negative people are often **characterized** by frequent job changes.
（ネガティブな人は頻繁に転職すると見なされている。）

▶ **characteristic** [kèrəktərístɪk] Adj. (〜に) 特徴的な (of sth/sb) N[C] 特徴

Improvisation is **characteristic** of jazz music. (即興はジャズの特徴なんだ。)

↔ **uncharacteristic** [ʌnkèrəktərístɪk] Adj. (〜) らしくない (of sb)

▶ **character** [kérəktər] N[C/U] 特徴、特性 N[C] 個性の強い人；キャラクター；(漢字などの) 文字

He's a bit of a **character**. (あの人ちょっと個性強いよな。) Chinese **characters** ((中国の) 漢字)

---

724 cooperation
[koʊàːpəréɪʃən]
☐☐☐☐☐☐

N[U] 協力、協調

I couldn't have done this without your **cooperation**, so thanks again.
(君の協力が無かったらこれは達成できなかったよ。改めてありがとうね。)

a sense of **cooperation** (連帯感)

▶ **cooperative** Adj. 協力的な ▶ **cooperatively** Adv. 協力的に
[koʊàːpərəṭɪv] [koʊàːpərəṭɪvli]

▶ **cooperate** [koʊàːpəreɪt] V[I] (〜と) 協力する (with sth/sb)

混同注意！ **cooperation** vs **corporation** cooperation は「協力」、corporation は「会社」を意味し、発音もそれぞれ [koʊàːpəréɪʃən]、[kɔ̀ːrpəréɪʃən] と異なります。注意しましょう。

---

725 political
[pəlíṭəkəl]
☐☐☐☐☐☐

Adj. 政治的な

The process of allocating classes to teachers can be surprisingly **political**.
(クラスを先生に割り当てる過程は驚くほど政治的になることがあるんだ。)

▶ **politically** [pəlíṭəkli] Adv. 政治的に ▶ **politics** [pá:lətɪks] N[U] 政治 N[P] 政治理念

I'm so sick of workplace **politics**. (社内政治にはうんざりだよ。)

▶ **politician** [pà:lətíʃən] N[C] 政治家

---

726 territory
[térətɔ:ri]
☐☐☐☐☐☐

N[U] 地域 N[C/U] 領土、領域；縄張り

■ come/go with the **territory** ((特定の職場や状況では) つきものである)

People shout at me all the time, but I guess it **comes with the territory** when you work at a call center. (みんな私にいつも怒鳴ってくるけど、まぁコールセンターではこれがつきものなのかもね。)

▶ **territorial** [tèrətɔ́:riəl] Adj. 地域の、領土の a **territorial** dispute (領土問題)

接頭語 **terr-** 「土地」という意味の接頭語で、「土地 (= terr) のある場所 (= itory)」から「地域、領土」という意味になります。他には subterranean (地下の) や terrestrial (地上の) などがあります。

---

727 norm
[nɔ:rm]
☐☐☐☐☐☐

N[P] 規範 【-s】 N[S] 普通なこと 【the -】

Taking vacations overseas has become **the norm** for most of my friends.
(私の友達はほとんど海外で長期休暇を取るのが普通になってるよ。)

▶ **normal** [nɔ́:rməl] Adj. 普通の、正常の ↔ **abnormal** [æbnɔ́:rməl] 異常な

▶ **normally** [nɔ́:rməli] Adv. 普通は、通常は、正常に

Normally we eat dinner at home, but today's my birthday, so my husband's taking me to a fancy restaurant.
(普段は家で夕食を食べるんだけど、今日は私の誕生日だから夫が高級レストランに連れてってくれるんだ。)

2 **Typically, societies are culturally** homogeneous, **but they often** contain **within them smaller** segments **of** like-minded individuals **that form** diverse **subcultures or "**tribes.**"**

一般的に、社会は文化的に同質ではあるが、多くの場合、その社会の中には同じ価値観を共有する個人の小集団が存在し、それが多様なサブカルチャーや「トライブ *」を形成している。

*「〜族、〜系」を意味する集団のこと

---

728 **homogeneous**
[hòʊmoʊdʒíːniəs]

Adj. 同質の、同種の ⟷ **heterogeneous** [hètəroʊdʒíːniəs] 異質の、異種の

We can't treat students as one **homogeneous** mass. They are all different.
(学生を同質の集団として扱っちゃいけないよ。みんな違うんだから。)

接頭語 homo- 「同じ、よく似た」という意味の接頭語で、「同じ (=homo) 種類の (=geneous)」から「同質の」という意味になります。他には homophone（同音異義語）や homosexual（同性愛者の）などがあります。

---

729 **contain**
[kəntéɪn]

V[T] を含む；(感情など) を抑制する、(コストなど) を抑える

I don't eat anything that **contains** gluten, so let's go somewhere else.
(私、グルテン入ってるものは食べないから、どこか他の所に行こうよ。)

▶ **containment** [kəntéɪnmənt] N[U] 抑制、封じ込め

Containment was a foreign policy followed by the U.S. to prevent the spread of communism. (封じ込めは共産主義の拡大を防ぐためにアメリカが行った外交政策のことだよ。)

▶ **container** [kəntéɪnər] N[C] 入れ物、容器、コンテナ

Can I get a **container**? I want to take away our leftovers.
(入れ物もらえますか？食べ残しを持って帰りたいんですけど。)

---

730 **segment**
[ségmənt]

N[C] 区分、部分、セグメント；(番組などの) コーナー

This is my favorite **segment** of the show. (ここ、この番組で好きなコーナーなんだ。)

V[I/T] (〜を) 細分化する

▶ **segmentation** [sègmentéɪʃən] N[U] 分割、区分、セグメンテーション

731 **like-minded**
[làɪkmáɪndɪd]
□□□□□□

Adj. 同じ考えを持った、同じ興味を持った

I know we disagree about some things, but we're generally pretty **like-minded**.
(私たちは意見が合わないこともあるけど、基本的な考え方は一緒だよね。)

---

732 **individual**
[ìndəvídʒuəl]
□□□□□□

N[C] 個人   **Adj.** 個人の、個々の

We'll win only if we play like a team rather than a collection of **individuals**.
(私たちは個々の集まりとしてじゃなく、チームとしてプレーしさえすればきっと勝てる。)

▶ **individually** [ìndəvídʒuəli] Adv. 個別に、一つ一つ

Could you wrap these items **individually** in different colored bags?
(これらの商品を個別に違う色の袋でラッピングしてもらっても良いですか？)

▶ **individualism** [ìndəvídʒuəlɪzəm] N[U] 個人主義

⬌ **collectivism** [kəléktəvɪzəm] 集団主義

---

733 **diverse**
[dɪvə́:rs]
□□□□□□

Adj. 多様な、さまざまな

I love how **diverse** the music is at this bar.
(このバーって色んな種類の曲がかかってるからめちゃくちゃ好きなんだ。)

▶ **diversity** [dɪvə́:rsəti] N[U] 多様性

I think that Japanese people need to acknowledge the importance of racial and gender **diversity**. (日本人は人種と性の多様性が重要であることを認めないといけないと思うよ。)

▶ **diversify** [dɪvə́:rsəfaɪ] V[I/T]（〜を）多様化する　V[I] 多角化する
V[T]（投資）を分散する

I understand that the government should protect farmers from imports to some extent, but I think farmers need to **diversify** their business models.
(政府がある程度農家を輸入品から保護すべきだっていうのは理解できるけど、それでも農家はビジネスモデルを多様化する必要があると思うよ。)

▶ **diversification** [dɪvə̀:rsəfəkéɪʃən] N[U] 多様化、多角化、（投資の）分散

---

734 **tribe**
[traɪb]
□□□□□□

N[C] 部族、種族

It's so fascinating that there are **tribes** in the Amazon that have never come into contact with the outside world.
(アマゾンには外の世界に一切触れたことがない部族がいるなんて魅力的だなぁ。)

▶ **tribal** [tráɪbəl] Adj. 部族の

tribal traditions （部族的な伝統）

3 One example of such a tribe is the Japanese subculture called "Harajuku style," which is a youth culture that disregards conventional fashion and is typified by people in bold, inventive, and outrageous clothes.

そのようなトライブの一例に「原宿系」と呼ばれる日本のサブカルチャーがある。これは、従来のファッションを無視した、大胆で独創的で奇抜な服を着る人々に代表される若者文化のことである。

---

735 **youth**

[ju:θ]

N[C] 若者　N[U] 若さ、若い頃　N[P] 若者たち【the -】

I don't want to waste my **youth** working in a job that makes me unhappy, so I'm going to take a break for a year.
(やってて幸せじゃない仕事で自分の若い頃を無駄にはしたくないから、一年間休みを取るんだ。)

The elderly often say **the youth** of today have bad manners, but I think they were ruder.
(お年寄りの人はよく近頃の若者たちはマナーが悪いって言うけど、あの人たちの方が酷かったと思う。)

▶ **young** [jʌŋ] Adj. 若い、幼い　　▶ **youngster** [jʌ́ŋstər] N[C] 若者、若い人

I'm still considered a **youngster** in my company.
(私はうちの会社の中ではまだ若いと思われてるんだ。)

---

736 **disregard**

[dìsrɪgáːrd]

V[T] を無視する、軽視する　N[S/U] 無視、軽視

Please **disregard** that last message that I sent you.
(私が送った最後のメッセージ、無視してください。)

---

737 **conventional**

[kənvénʃənəl]

Adj. 従来の、慣習的な

It's awesome how Ben challenges **conventional** wisdom by doing his own research.
(ベンって一般的に受け入れられているようなことに対してもちゃんと自分で調べてて偉いよなぁ。)

▶ **conventionally** [kənvénʃənəli] Adv. 慣習的に

▶ **convention** [kənvénʃən] N[C/U] 慣習　N[C] 大会、会議、総会；協定

I think it is only a social **convention** that pink is a girl's color and blue is a boy's one.
(ピンクは女の子の色で、青は男の子の色だという考えは社会的な慣習に過ぎないと思うよ。)

---

738 **fashion**

[fǽʃən]

N[C/U] ファッション、流行

I love your unique **fashion** sense. (君のユニークなファッションセンス、大好き。)

in **fashion**（流行っている）◀▶ ■ out of **fashion**（時代遅れの）

Tattoo tights are **out of fashion** now.（タトゥータイツはもう時代遅れだよ。）

▶ **fashionable** [fǽʃənəbəl] Adj. 流行している、ファッショナブルな

Wearing a cardigan like this was **fashionable** a few years ago but not anymore.
（カーディガンをこんな感じで着るのが数年前流行ってたけど、もう流行ってないね。）

▶ **fashionably** [fǽʃənəbli] Adv. 流行に乗って

---

739 bold
[boʊld]
☐☐☐☐☐☐

Adj. 大胆な、勇敢な；（色や形が）はっきりとした；太字の

You have to be **bold** sometimes and tell people the truth, even if it makes them uncomfortable.
（時には勇気を出して人に真実を伝えないといけないよ。たとえそれがその人を嫌な気持ちにしてもね。）

a **bold** color（はっきりした色）◀▶ a muted color（落ち着いた色）

in **bold**（太字で）

▶ **boldly** [bóʊldli] Adv. 大胆に、勇敢に   ▶ **boldness** [bóʊldnəs] N[U] 大胆さ、勇敢さ

It takes **boldness** to follow your dreams.（夢を追い求めるには勇気が必要だよ。）

---

740 inventive
[ɪnvéntɪv]
☐☐☐☐☐☐

Adj. 独創的な、発明的な

I admire how **inventive** his excuses are.（彼の言い訳はものすごい独創的で感心するよ。）

▶ **inventively** [ɪnvéntɪvli] Adv. 独創的に、発明的に

▶ **inventiveness** [ɪnvéntɪvnəs] N[U] 独創力、発明力

The comedian showed great **inventiveness** during her performance.
（あのお笑い芸人、ものすごい独創力を芸の中で披露したんだ。）

▶ **invent** [ɪnvént] V[T] を発明する

Who **invented** the Internet? That person must be a super genius.
（誰がインターネット発明したの？絶対超天才だよね。）

▶ **invention** [ɪnvénʃən] N[U] 発明   N[C] 発明品

▶ **inventor** [ɪnvéntər] N[C] 発明家

---

741 outrageous
[àʊtréɪdʒəs]
☐☐☐☐☐☐

Adj. 奇抜な、とんでもない；（値段などが）法外な；常軌を逸した

I just saw this guy outside do an **outrageous** triple backflip.
（たった今外でとんでもないトリプルバックフリップをしてる人を見たんだ。）

▶ **outrageously** [àʊtréɪdʒəsli] Adv. 法外に、とんでもなく

The diamond ring in the window is **outrageously** expensive.
（あの展示されてるダイヤモンドの指輪はめちゃめちゃ高価だよ。）

▶ **outrage**　N[U] 憤慨、激怒　N[C] 乱暴な行為、頭にくる行為
[áʊtreɪdʒ]　V[T] を憤慨させる、ひどく怒らせる

My boss was **outraged** by the way the new employee spoke to him.
（うちの上司、新入社員の話し方に対して超怒ってたよ。）

4 According to some sociologists, these various subcultures function to help maintain the stable equilibrium of society as a whole and are therefore critical elements of a prosperous society.

一部の社会学者によると、こうしたさまざまなサブカルチャーは、社会全体が安定したバランスを保つのを助ける働きを担い、それゆえ豊かな社会を築く上で重要な要素になっている。

HARAJUKU STYLE

TATTOOS

PUNK

---

742 **according to**
[əkɔ́:rdɪŋ tù:]
□□□□□□

Prep. 〜によると；〜に応じて、従って

According to Jim, they're flying to New York tomorrow morning.
（ジムによると、彼らは明日の朝ニューヨークに飛び立つんだって。）

according to plan（計画通りに）

▶ **accordingly**［əkɔ́:rdɪŋli］Adv. それに応じて、それに従って；それゆえ

As soon as we receive your instructions, we will follow them **accordingly**.
（指示を受けたらすぐに応じて従います。）

▶ **accord**［əkɔ́:rd］N[C/U] 協定、合意　　▶ **accordance**［əkɔ́:rdəns］N[U] 一致

in **accordance** with sth（〜に従って）

---

743 **various**
[vériəs]
□□□□□□

Adj. さまざまな、多様な

I don't know who sang the original, but this song has been covered by **various** people.
（誰が一番最初に歌ったのか知らないけど、この曲は色んな人にカバーされてるよ。）

▶ **variously**［vériəsli］Adv. さまざまに、色々と

James has been described **variously** as a calm, emotional, and lazy man, so who knows if he's actually a good person.
（ジェームズは冷静だとか、感情的だとか、ダラダラしてるとか、色々言われてるから、彼が実際良い人かは分からないね。）

▶ **vary**　V[I] 異なる、違う、変化する
[véri]　V[T] を変化させる

▶ **variety**［vəráɪəti］N[U] 多様性、変化に富むこと　N[C] 種類

■ a **variety** of sth（さまざまな〜、色々な〜）

I quit my job for **a variety of** reasons.（色んな理由があって仕事を辞めたんだ。）

744 function
[fʌ́ŋkʃən]
☐☐☐☐☐☐

V[I] 働く、機能する N[C/U] 機能 N[C] 催し；関数

My brain doesn't **function** without coffee in the morning.（朝はコーヒー飲まないと頭が動かないんだ。）

I think modern smartphones have too many **functions**. We probably don't even use close to half of them.　（最近のスマホって機能があり過ぎだと思うんだよね。きっと半分も使ってないよ。）

a work **function**（職場の催し）

▶ **functional** [fʌ́ŋkʃənəl] Adj. 機能的な、実用的な

This car isn't the prettiest, but at least it's **functional**.
（この車の見た目は微妙だけど、最低でも機能的ではある。）

▶ **functionally** Adv. 機能的に
[fʌ́ŋkʃənəli]

▶ **functionality** N[U] 機能性
[fʌ̀ŋkʃənǽləţi]

---

745 maintain
[meintéin]
☐☐☐☐☐☐

V[T] を保つ、維持する

It's better to **maintain** your teeth than to fix them.（歯は将来治療するより維持した方がいい。）

▶ **maintenance** [méintənəns] N[U] 維持、メンテナンス

■ high-**maintenance**（（人が）結構面倒な、手間がかかる）

My boyfriend is really **high-maintenance**. I have to send him a message like 100 times a day.（私の彼氏、本当に面倒なんだよ。一日100回くらいメッセージしないといけないんだ。）

---

746 as a whole
[əzəhóʊl]
☐☐☐☐☐☐

Phr. 全体として

Even though we lost, when you look at the game **as a whole**, I think we actually played pretty well.　（負けたけど、試合全体を見れば私たちは実際結構良い試合したと思うよ。）

---

747 therefore
[ðérfɔːr]
☐☐☐☐☐☐

Adv. それゆえ、それを理由として

René Descartes is famous for saying, "I think, **therefore** I am."
（ルネ・デカルトは「我思う、故に我あり」と言ったことで有名だよ。）

---

748 prosperous
[prɑ́ːspərəs]
☐☐☐☐☐☐

Adj. 豊かな、繁栄した、（経済的に）成功した

How did Japan become so **prosperous**?（日本ってどうやってそんなに繁栄したの？）

▶ **prosperously** [prɑ́ːspərəsli] Adv. 繁栄して、裕福に

▶ **prosper** [prɑ́ːspər] V[I] 繁栄する、裕福になる、成功する

I'm putting a lot of effort into growing my Instagram account now, so I'll hopefully **prosper** from it soon.
（インスタを成長させるために今もの凄い努力してるから、そろそろ上手くいったらいいな。）

▶ **prosperity** [prɑːspérəţi] N[U] 繁栄、裕福

The family is finally experiencing a taste of **prosperity** after struggling financially for a long time. I'm very happy for them.
（あの家は長い間金銭的に苦しんだ後、やっと今豊かさを味わえるようになったんだ。私は本当に嬉しいよ。）

接尾語 -ous　prosperous の -ous は「〜に満ちた」という意味の接尾語で、単語を形容詞化する役割を持ちます。同様の接尾語を持つ単語に courageous（勇敢な）、conscious（意識のある）があります。

The Emo Subculture: Reflecting On My Experience

I feel **sorry** for today's kids that live in this **oppressive** and homogenized world without sub-cultures. As a **gift**, I'm taking a **trip** down memory lane back to the early 2000s, when the emo subculture was in full **swing**.

At the start of the decade, I was incredibly **reserved** and mainstream. Soon enough, I became a **rebel grasped** by emo culture. I was all in on the fashion, the music, everything. Like all emos, my daily **outfit** was black **items** only: black jeans, shirts, and sneakers, **complementing** my **dyed** black hair. It seems **absurd** in **retrospect**. I found non-**conformity** in conformity.

I only now **recall** that the bands all sounded the same. At the time, I thought they were **talented geniuses** writing **gloomy masterpieces**. I thought this uniformity made me unique.
My disillusionment with this led to my eventual divorce from emo culture. Maybe the kids aren't missing out after all.

エモサブカルチャー：経験を振り返る

サブカルチャーが存在しない、この過酷で均質化された世界に住む今の子供たちはお気の毒だ。贈り物として、「エモ」サブカルチャーが最も盛り上がった2000年代初頭の思い出をたどってみようと思う。

あの10年が始まった当初、私は非常に控えめで主流派だったのだが、間もなくエモ文化にがっちりと掴まれ、反逆者となってしまった。私は、エモのファッション、音楽、すべてに賭けていた。他のエモの人たちと同じく、私の毎日の服装は黒のアイテムのみで、黒のジーンズ、シャツ、スニーカーが、黒く染めた髪の毛を引き立たせていた。振り返ってみるとばかばかしく思える。私は、同調の中に、非同調を見出していたのだ。

今思えば、エモ・バンドの曲はみんな同じように聞こえた。それでも当時の私は、彼らは憂鬱に満ちた傑作を書く才能のある天才たちだと思い込んでいた。そしてこのエモの画一性こそが、私をユニークにしてくれているのだと思っていた。これに対する幻滅を味わった後、最終的に私はエモ文化から離れてしまった。結局、今の子供たちは何かを逃しているわけではないのかもしれない。

---

749 **sorry**
[sɔ́:ri]
☐☐☐☐☐

Adj. 気の毒に思って、かわいそうに思って（for sb）
（〜を）すまなく思って（for/about sth）
（〜を）残念に思って（about sth/to do）

---

750 **oppressive**
[əprésɪv]
☐☐☐☐☐☐

Adj. 過酷な、弾圧的な
▶ **oppressively** [əprésɪvli] Adv. 過酷に、弾圧的に
▶ **oppressiveness** [əprésɪvnəs] N[U] 弾圧、圧制
▶ **oppression** [əpréʃən] N[U] 弾圧、圧制　▶ **oppressed** [əprést] Adj. 抑圧された

---

751 **gift**
[gɪft]
☐☐☐☐☐☐

N[C] 贈り物、プレゼント、ギフト
▶ **gifted** [gɪftɪd] Adj. 才能のある
a **gifted** child（天才児）

---

752 **trip**
[trɪp]
☐☐☐☐☐☐

N[C] 旅、旅行　**V[I]** つまずく　**V[T]** をつまずかせる
take a **trip** down memory lane（昔を懐かしく思い出す）　go on a **trip**（旅行に行く）

---

753 **swing**
[swɪŋ]
☐☐☐☐☐☐

N[C] （急激な）変化；揺れ；ぶらんこ
V[I] 揺れる；変化する　**V[T]** を揺らす、振る；を変化させる
in full **swing**（最も盛り上がった、真っ最中の）　**swing** a bat（バットを振る）

---

754 **reserved**
[rɪzə́:rvd]
☐☐☐☐☐☐

Adj. 控えめな；予約済みの
▶ **reserve** [rɪzə́:rv] V[T] を予約する、取っておく　N[C/U] 蓄え
▶ **reservation** [rèzərvéɪʃən] N[C] 予約　N[C/U] 懸念、疑い
Did you make a **reservation**?（予約はした？）

---

755 **rebel**
N. [rébəl]
V. [rɪbél]
☐☐☐☐☐☐

N[C] 反逆者　**V[I]** 反逆する、反乱する、反抗する
▶ **rebellion** [rɪbéliən] N[C/U] 反逆、反乱、反抗
▶ **rebelliousness** [rɪbéliəsnəs] N[U] 反逆、反抗
▶ **rebellious** [rɪbéliəs] Adj. 反逆の、反抗的な　▶ **rebelliously** [rɪbéliəsli] Adv. 反抗的に

---

756 **grasp**
[græsp]
☐☐☐☐☐☐

V[T] をしっかりつかむ；を理解する　**N[S/U]** 理解　**N[S]** 握ること
My dad keeps telling me he can't **grasp** the concept of Uber Eats.
（私のお父さんは Uber Eats の概念が理解できないっていつも言ってくるんだ。）

---

757 **outfit**
[áʊtfɪt]
☐☐☐☐☐☐

N[C] 服装（一式）、道具（一式）　**V[T]** に衣服を着せる；に装備を用意する

---

758 **item**
[áɪṭəm]
☐☐☐☐☐☐

N[C] アイテム、品物；品目、項目
▶ **itemize** [áɪṭəmaɪz] V[T] を項目別に分ける　▶ **itemized** [áɪṭəmaɪzd] Adj. 項目別に分けた

222

759 complement
[kά:mpləmənt]

V[T] を引き立たせる、補完する　**N[C]** 引き立たせるもの、補完物；補語

▶ **complementary** [kὰ:mpləméntəri] Adj. 引き立てる、補完するような

760 dyed
[daɪd]

Adj. 染めた

▶ **dye** [daɪ] V[T] を染める

Hey look! I **dyed** my hair purple. （ねぇ見て！髪色を紫に染めてみた。）

761 absurd
[əbsə́:rd]

Adj. ばかげた

Putting Mentos into a bottle of Diet Coke is such an **absurd** idea.
（メントスをダイエットコーラに入れるとかほんとばかな考えだよな。）

▶ **absurdly** [əbsə́:rdli] Adv. ばからしいほど

▶ **absurdity** [əbsə́:rdəti] N[C/U] ばからしさ

762 retrospect
[rétrəspekt]

N[U] 回想

in **retrospect** （振り返ってみれば、今思えば）　= looking back

▶ **retrospective** [rètrəspéktɪv] Adj. 遡及的な

▶ **retrospectively** [rètrəspéktɪvli] Adv. 遡及的に

763 conformity
[kənfɔ́:rməti]

N[U] 同調した行動、規範に従った行動、順応

▶ **conform** [kənfɔ́:rm] V[I] （〜に）同調する （to sth）

764 recall
V./N1. [rikɑ́:l]
N2. [rí:kɑ:l]

V[T] を思い出す；(製品) をリコールする

His face looks familiar, but I can't **recall** his name.
（彼の顔見たことがある気がするけど、名前が思い出せないんだ。）

N[U] 記憶力　**N[C]** （欠陥商品の）リコール

765 talented
[tǽləntɪd]

Adj. 才能のある

▶ **talent** [tǽlənt] N[C/U] 才能　N[C] 才能のある人

766 genius
[dʒí:niəs]

N[C] 天才（の人）　**N[U]** （性質としての）天才

I'm not a **genius**. I just work hard. （俺は天才じゃないよ。努力してるだけ。）

767 gloomy
[glú:mi]

Adj. 憂鬱な、根暗な；薄暗い　↔ **bright** [braɪt] 明るい

▶ **gloomily** [glú:məli] Adv. 憂鬱に　▶ **gloominess** [glú:minəs] N[U] 憂鬱さ

▶ **gloom** [glu:m] N[U] 憂鬱；薄暗さ

768 masterpiece
[mǽstərpi:s]

N[C] 傑作、名作

I watched Frozen for the first time, and it was a real **masterpiece**.
（アナと雪の女王を初めて見たんだけど、本当に傑作だったよ。）

Chapter

17

メディア研究
Media Studies

Media studies refers to the academic discipline that deals with the history, content, and effects of a broad range of mass media. This includes more traditional media such as TV, radio, and newspapers, as well as media that have only existed in recent times, including social media and other web-based media.

Because of its emphasis on critically evaluating media, media studies is becoming increasingly important in a world where the Internet and social media platforms such as Facebook and Twitter have such a strong influence on public opinion.

In fact, much of what is portrayed by social media as being genuine or realistic is often selected carefully and extremely edited.

Given how easy it is for media to shape people's views, a degree of skepticism about how media and communication work is a must-have in our modern society.

1 **Media studies refers to the** academic discipline **that** deals **with the history,** content, **and** effects **of a broad** range **of** mass **media. This includes more traditional media such as TV, radio, and newspapers, as well as media that have only existed in recent times, including social media and other web-based media.**

メディア研究とは、幅広いマスメディアの歴史、内容、そして効果について扱う学問分野で、そこには最近登場したソーシャルメディアやウェブベースのメディアだけでなく、テレビ、ラジオ、新聞といったより伝統的なメディアも含まれている。

Facebook
Twitter

---

769 academic
[ækədémɪk]

Adj. 学問の、学業の **N[C]** 大学教員 **N[P]** 学問【-s】

I found the English taught in schools to be too **academic**.
(学校で教えてもらった英語は学問的過ぎるなぁと思ったよ。)

▶ **academically** Adv. 学問的に、学力的に   ▶ **academia** N[U] 学界、アカデミア
　[ækədémɪkli]　　　　　　　　　　　　　　　　[ækədi:miə]

People who excel **academically** but lack practical skills are often called book-smart.
(学力的に優れてるけど実践的なスキルがない人をよくブックスマートって呼ぶんだ。)

---

770 discipline
[dísəplɪn]

N[C] 分野 **N[U]** 規律、自制、しつけ、訓練

What **discipline** of science did you specialize in?（君は科学のどの分野が専門だったの？）

V[T] をしつける、訓練する

▶ **disciplined** [dísəplɪnd] Adj. 規律正しい、しっかりした、訓練された

The only way I'm going to pass this exam is if I'm **disciplined** enough to stick to my study plan.（僕がこの試験に合格する唯一の方法は、自分を律して、計画通りに勉強をやり抜くことなんだ。）

▶ **disciplinary** [dísəplɪneri] Adj. 懲戒の、訓練の

take **disciplinary** action against sb（〜を懲戒処分にする）

---

771 deal
[di:l]

V[I] （〜を）扱う、処理する、対処する、やり取りする（with sth/sb）

I hate **dealing** with these realtors. They're so shady.
(不動産仲介業者とやり取りするのは嫌だよ。あの人たちすごい怪しいんだ。)

V[I/T] （トランプカードを）配る

N[C] 取引、契約

■ a good/great **deal** (of sth)（かなりの量（の〜））

There is **a great deal** to learn on YouTube.（YouTube って学ぶことがすごいたくさんある。）

▶ **dealer** [díːlər] N[C] 販売業者；麻薬密売人   ▶ **dealing** [díːlɪŋ] N[U] 取引、売買

fair/dodgy **dealing**（公正な / 不正な取引）

---

772 **content**
N. [kántent]
Adj./V. [kəntént]
☐☐☐☐☐☐

N[S/U] 内容、コンテンツ   N[P] （本や雑誌の）内容、項目【-s】

It was a very short video, but it went viral on social media because it covered a lot of important **content**.
（本当に短い動画だったんだけど、重要な内容をたくさんカバーしてたから SNS でバズったんだ。）

a table of **contents**（目次）

Adj.（〜に）満足した（with sth）   V[T] を満足させる

---

773 **effect**
[əfékt]
☐☐☐☐☐☐

N[C/U] 効果、影響

I'm a coffee drinker because I heard it has a good **effect** on my hair. I don't want to go bald. （コーヒーが髪に良いって聞いたから、コーヒーをよく飲んでるんだ。ハゲたくないから。）

■ in **effect**（事実上、実際は；効力のある）   take **effect**（効力を持つ）

This law has been **in effect** for just a couple months, so it's pretty new.
（この法律は施行されてからたった 2 か月だから、結構新しいよ。）

▶ **effective** [əféktɪv] Adj. 効果的な

Is cycling really **effective** for reducing belly fat? Mine is still not going away.
（サイクリングって本当にお腹の脂肪燃やすのに効果的なの？全然減らないんだけど。）

▶ **effectively** [əféktɪvli] Adv. 効果的に；事実上 ▶ **affect** [əfékt] V[T] に影響を与える

Stress can **affect** your health more negatively than anything else.
（ストレスほど健康に悪影響を与えるものはないよ。）

---

774 **range**
[reɪndʒ]
☐☐☐☐☐☐

N[C] （種類の）範囲、幅

The **range** of donuts on sale at the shop down the road is insane.
（この道の先のお店で売ってるドーナッツの種類の数、ものすごいよ。）

■ a **range** of sth（さまざまな種類の〜）

Uniqlo has such **a wide range of** colors to choose from.
（ユニクロは色の選択肢がとても豊富なんだ。）

V[I] （A から B までに）わたる、変動する（from A to B）

Prices **range** from $100 to $800.（価格は 100 ドルから 800 ドルにわたります。）

---

775 **mass**
[mæs]
☐☐☐☐☐☐

Adj. 大衆の、大規模な   N[S] 大きな塊

Don't you think YouTube has made **mass** advertising really cheap and simple?
（YouTube って大衆向けの広告をものすごく安くかつシンプルにしてくれたと思わない？）

2 Because of **its** emphasis on critically evaluating media, media studies is becoming increasingly important in a world where the Internet and social media platforms such as Facebook and Twitter have such a strong influence on public opinion.

メディア批評が重視されるため、メディア研究は、インターネットや、フェイスブック、ツイッターといったソーシャルメディアプラットフォームが世論に強く影響を与える世界において、ますます重要なものになってきている。

---

776 because of
[bɪkɑ́:z əv]
□□□□□□

Prep. 〜のため、のせいで、のおかげで = due to [dú:tu]

Because of the rain, I couldn't go surfing this weekend.
（雨が降ったから週末サーフィンしに行けなかったんだ。）

because of vs **due to** vs **thanks to**　この3つは全て「〜のため、せいで、おかげで」という意味の表現ですが、若干ニュアンスが異なります。because of は日常会話で頻繁に使い、ポジティブな場面でもネガティブな場面でも使うことができます。due to もよく使われる表現ですが、よりフォーマルな場面で好まれる傾向があります。そして、thanks to は thanks という言葉から分かるように「〜のおかげで」というようなポジティブな意味で使われます。

---

777 emphasis
[émfəsɪs]
□□□□□□

N[C/U] 重視、強調、注目

There's been a real **emphasis** on space travel over the last few years.
（ここ数年、宇宙旅行が本当に注目されてきているよ。）

put/place **emphasis** on sth （〜を重要視する）

▶ **emphasize** V[T] を重視する、強調する
[émfəsaɪz]

▶ **emphatic** Adj. 力説した
[emfǽtɪk]

The CEO **emphasized** the importance of crystallizing our strategy before we start the project. （CEOはプロジェクト開始前に戦略を具体化することの重要性を強調した。）

My mom is always very **emphatic** about the need to leave home on time.
（うちの母さん、いつも時間通りに家を出なきゃって力説するんだ。）

▶ **emphatically** [emfǽtɪkli] Adv. 断固として、きっぱりと

---

778 evaluate
[ɪvǽljueɪt]
□□□□□□

V[T] を評価する

I can't believe they're still using attendance rates to **evaluate** students.
（学生を評価するのにいまだに出席率を使ってるなんて信じられないよ。）

▶ **evaluation** [ɪvǽljuéɪʃən] N[C/U] 評価

Basically, palm reading is conducted through the **evaluation** of four lines.
(基本的に手相占いは 4 本の線を評価することで行われる。)

▶ **evaluator** [ɪvǽljueɪtər] N[C] 評価者　　▶ **evaluative** [ɪvǽljueɪt̬ɪv] Adj. 評価による

---

779 **important**
[ɪmpɔ́:rtənt]
▢▢▢▢▢▢

Adj.　重要な、重大な、大切な　↔ **unimportant** [ʌnɪmpɔ́:rtənt] 重要でない

I like the new CEO because he doesn't act like he's more **important** than anybody else.
(新しい CEO、自分が他の人よりも重要であるかのようには振る舞わないから好きだな。)

▶ **importance** [ɪmpɔ́:rtəns] N[U]　重要性、重大さ

▶ **importantly** [ɪmpɔ́:rtəntli] Adv.　重要なことであるが

■ most/more/equally **importantly** (最も / より / 同じく重要なことは)

Most importantly, he's improved his diet. That explains the drop in cholesterol.
(最も重要なのは、彼が食生活を改善したことです。そのおかげで、コレステロールが下がっているんです。)

---

780 **Internet**
[ínt̬ərnet]
▢▢▢▢▢▢

N[S]　インターネット【the I-】　= the internet

■ on **the Internet** (インターネット上で)

Can you look it up **on the Internet** before you ask a question?
(質問する前にまずインターネットで調べてくれる？)

接頭語 inter-　「～の間」を意味する接頭語で、複数の人や団体間で繋がる (= inter) 網 (= net) から生まれた表現です。他には interact (相互作用する) や interview (面接) があります。

---

781 **public**
[pʌ́blɪk]
▢▢▢▢▢▢

Adj.　大衆の、公衆の、公の、公立の　N[S]　一般市民【the -】

This paper says **public** school students outperformed students at private schools in Sweden.
(この論文によるとスウェーデンでは公立の学校に行った生徒の方が私立の生徒よりも成績が良かったんだって。)

■ in **public** (人前で)

It's fine to have those opinions, but maybe don't discuss them **in public**.
(そういう意見を持っても良いけど、人前では話さない方がいいかもね。)

▶ **publicly** [pʌ́blɪkli] Adv.　公に、公然と；政府によって

a **publicly** funded institution (政府が出資した組織)

---

782 **opinion**
[əpínjən]
▢▢▢▢▢▢

N[C]　(～についての) 意見、考え (on/about sth)

What's your **opinion** on universal basic income?
(ユニバーサルベーシックインカムについてはどう思う？)

■ in sb's **opinion** (～の意見では)

In my opinion, the smiley emoji is the most successful artwork of the 20th century.
(俺の意見だけど、スマイリーの絵文字が 20 世紀で一番成功したアート作品だと思う。)

N[U]　(集団が持つ) 意見、見解

public **opinion** (世論)

3 In fact, much of what is portrayed by social media as being genuine or realistic is often selected carefully and extremely edited.

実際、ソーシャルメディアで本物、リアルとして表現されているものの多くは、入念に選ばれて大幅に編集されているものが多い。

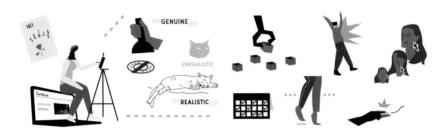

783 **portray**
[pɔːrtréɪ]
☐☐☐☐☐☐

V[T] を表現する、描く

I like these articles. They **portray** a really accurate view of the state of the economy.
（この記事を読むのは楽しいよ。経済状況をすごく正確に表現してるからね。）

▶ **portrayal** [pɔːrtréɪəl] N[C] 描写　▶ **portrait** [pɔ́ːrtrɪt] N[C] 肖像画

My four-year-old kid asked me if the film's **portrayal** of love is real. That's so deep.
（うちの４歳の子がその映画で描かれている愛は本物なのって聞いてきたんだ。深すぎるだろ。）

a **portrait** painter（肖像画家）

784 **genuine**
[dʒénjuɪn]
☐☐☐☐☐☐

Adj. 本物の；誠実な、（感情などが）心からの

I know this bag isn't **genuine** leather, but it looks so nice.
（このバッグのレザー、本物じゃないのは分かってるんだけど、すごい見た目良い感じだよ。）

▶ **genuinely** Adv. 誠実に、心から、純粋に　▶ **genuineness** N[U] 本物であること；誠実さ
[dʒénjuɪnli]　　　　　　　　　　　　　　　　　[dʒénjuɪnnəs]

I'm **genuinely** interested in how you made this cake. Can you teach me?
（どうやってこのケーキ作ったのか純粋に興味があるんだけど、教えてくれない？）

785 **realistic**
[riːəlístɪk]
☐☐☐☐☐☐

Adj. （絵や話が）リアルな、写実的な；現実的な、現実性のある

↔ **unrealistic** [ʌnriːəlístɪk] 非現実的な

I don't think it's **realistic** to expect your teachers to have the answers to all your questions.
（先生が全部の質問に対して答えられると思うのは現実的じゃないと思うよ。）

This humanoid robot is so **realistic**.（このヒューマノイドロボット、すごいリアルだね。）

▶ **realistically** [riːəlístɪkli] Adv. リアルに；現実的に

▶ **realist** [ríːəlɪst] N[C] 現実主義者　↔ **idealist** [aɪdiːəlɪst] 理想主義者

▶ **realism** [ríːəlɪzəm] N[U] リアルさ；現実主義　↔ **idealism** [aɪdiːəlɪzəm] 理想主義

786 **often**
[ɔ́ːfən]

▢▢▢▢▢▢

Adv. 多くの場合、よく、しばしば、頻繁に = **frequently** [fríːkwəntli]

How **often** do you get your hair cut? （どのくらいの頻度で髪切ってる？）

often の t は発音する？　日本の英語教育では often の t を発音しない音で学習することが多いですが、t を発音することもあります。

---

787 **select**
[səlékt]

▢▢▢▢▢▢

V[T] を選ぶ、選択する

When you are ready, please **select** one of the following options.
（ご準備ができましたら、下のオプションから一つお選びください。）

▶ **selective** [səléktɪv] Adj. 選択的な、厳しく選ぶ

The university I most want to attend is **selective**. I'm not sure I'll be accepted.
（僕が行きたい大学は選抜が厳しいから、受かるか分からないよ。）

▶ **selection** [səlékʃən] N[C/U] 選択すること、選択　N[C] 品ぞろえ；選ばれたもの・人

■ have a good **selection** of sth （〜を豊富に取り揃えている）

The shop **has a good selection of** chocolate treats.
（そのお店はチョコレート系のお菓子を豊富に取り揃えている。）

---

788 **extremely**
[ɪkstríːmli]

▢▢▢▢▢▢

Adv. 大いに、非常に、極めて

The event was **extremely** successful, thanks to your help.
（君が助けてくれたおかげでイベントは大成功だったよ。）

▶ **extreme** [ɪkstríːm] Adj. 極端な、極度の　N[C] 極端、極度

■ go to **extremes** （極端な行動をする）

This guy on YouTube filled his bathtub with ice cream. Some people **go to** such **extremes** to get views.
（この YouTube の人、浴槽をアイスクリームでいっぱいにしたんだ。こうやって視聴回数稼ごうとして極端なことする人もいるんだ。）

▶ **extremist** [ɪkstríːmɪst] N[C] 過激派

Islamic **extremists** represent only a tiny minority of Muslims.
（イスラム過激派って、イスラム教徒の内のほんのわずか少数に過ぎないんだよ。）

▶ **extremism** [ɪkstríːmɪzəm] N[U] 過激思想、過激主義

---

789 **edit**
[édɪt]

▢▢▢▢▢▢

V[T] を編集する、修正する　**N[C]** 編集（作業）；校閲

I'll get this document to you once I've finished **editing** these last few bits.
（この最後のわずかな部分を編集し終わったら、このドキュメント渡すね。）

I need to make some **edits** to this video before I can upload it.
（この動画、アップロードする前にいくつか編集しなきゃ。）

▶ **editable** [édɪtəbəl] Adj. 編集可能な　　▶ **editing** [édɪtɪŋ] N[U] 編集

How can I make a PDF **editable**? （どうやったら PDF って編集可能にできるの？）

4 Given how easy it is for media to shape people's views, a degree of skepticism about how media and communication work is a must-have in our modern society.

人の意見がメディアによっていかに簡単に形成されてしまうかを考えても、ある程度疑いの目を持ってメディアとコミュニケーションの仕組みを捉えることは、現代社会において必須である。

---

790 view

[vju:]

□□□□□□

N[C] 意見、考え、見方；眺め

My **view** is that we should spend more time in Spain rather than in Italy.
（僕的にはイタリアよりスペインでもっと時間を過ごすべきだと思うけど。）

■ a world **view**（世界観）　　in sb's **view**（〜の考えでは）

I think I have **a world view** vastly different from other people's, and I'm proud of it.
（僕は他の人と全く違った世界観を持っていると思っていて、それに誇りを持っているんだ。）

The **view** from the top floor is just beautiful.（最上階からの眺めはただただ美しいよ。）

V[T] を（ある見方で）考える；を眺める

■ **view** sth in a certain light（〜に対してある見方をする）

If you **view** it **in a certain light**, Sapporo is a better place to live than Tokyo.
（見方によっては、札幌の方が東京よりも住みやすいよ。）

---

791 degree

[dɪgríː]

□□□□□□

N[C/U] 程度、度合い

I think you need a large **degree** of luck to become very successful in business.
（ビジネスで成功するにはかなりの程度の運が必要だと思うよ。）

a **degree** of sth（ある程度の〜）　　to what **degree** + question（どの程度〜なの？）

N[C] 学位

a bachelor's/master's/doctor's **degree**（学士号 / 修士号 / 博士号 = Ph.D.）

N[C]（温度や角度の）度

Akashi is on a longitude of 135 **degrees** east.（明石市は東経 135 度に位置している。）

The temperature topped 30 **degrees** in Osaka today.（今日大阪の最高気温は 30 度に達した。）

接尾語 **-gree, -grad, -gred** degree の -gree は古期フランス語 gradus（階段）が語源で、そのほか -grad, -gred も同じ語源を持ちます。他には graduate（卒業する）、degrade（位を下げる）があります。

792 **skepticism**
[sképtɪsɪzəm]

☐☐☐☐☐☐

N[U] 懐疑心、懐疑論

You can't be a good detective without a lot of **skepticism**.
(懐疑心がたくさんないと良い探偵にはなれないよ。)

▶ **skeptical** [sképtɪkəl] Adj. (〜に) 懐疑的な、疑い深い (about/of sth)

I really hate people who are negative, pessimistic, and **skeptical**.
(ネガティブで悲観的で疑い深い人、本当に嫌い。)

▶ **skeptically** [sképtɪkli] Adv. 懐疑的に、疑い深く

▶ **skeptic** [sképtɪk] N[C] 懐疑論者 (一般的に受け入れられている意見や考えに対してあえて疑問を投げかける人)

793 **communication**
[kəmjùːnəkéɪʃən]

☐☐☐☐☐☐

N[U] コミュニケーション、伝達

Lack of **communication** is often the cause of misunderstanding.
(誤解の原因は大体コミュニケーション不足からくるんだ。)

N[P] (パソコン、電話、ラジオなどの) 通信手段 【-s】

▶ **communicate** [kəmjúːnəkeɪt] V[I] (〜と) 連絡を取り合う (with sth/sb)

I normally use LINE to **communicate** with my friends.
(友達と連絡を取る時は基本 LINE 使ってるよ。)

▶ V[T] を (〜に) 伝達する (to sth/sb)

Can you **communicate** this to the client? (これクライアントに伝達してくれない？)

794 **work**
[wɜːrk]

☐☐☐☐☐☐

V[I] 機能する；うまくいく；働く、勤めている

I've finally figured out how the trains in Tokyo **work**.
(東京の電車がどう機能しているのか、ついに理解できたよ。)

N[U] 仕事、労働；職場；整形手術 **N[C]** 作品、著作物

at **work** (職場で)   go to **work** (出勤する)

Picasso has produced a number of astonishing **works**.
(ピカソは多くの驚くべき作品を生み出した。)

I'm pretty sure this singer's had some **work** done. (この歌手はきっと整形してるよ。)

▶ **worker** [wɜ́ːrkər] N[C] 働く人、労働者

795 **must-have**
[mʌ́sthæv]

☐☐☐☐☐☐

N[C] 必須のもの、必携のもの **Adj.** 必須の、必携の、マストな

A smartphone has become a **must-have** for everyone over the past decade.
(ここ 10 年でスマホはみんなのマストアイテムになったよね。)

▶ **nice-to-have** [náɪstəhæv] Adj. あった方がいい N[C] あった方がいいもの

796 **modern**
[mɑ́ːdərn]

☐☐☐☐☐☐

Adj. 現代の、最新の、モダンな

This restaurant's design is so **modern**. (このレストランのデザインはモダンだなぁ。)

Man Hey, you know that show we were chatting about that I thought sounded interesting? I just stumbled across some reviews online. They reminded me that I need to give it a shot before someone spoils the twist at the end for me. Can you send me a link to stream it?

Woman Sure. It's been a while, so I'll have to search for it. I've got it on DVD if you want to borrow it.

Man I don't think I have a DVD player anymore. It vanished at some point last year. I suspect we threw it out with the garbage. It's probably about time I got on board with new technology anyway.

Woman That's a pity, but I guess they are pretty much antiques. I also have to warn you, the stream doesn't have subtitles, so I hope you're fluent in Spanish.

男性 ねぇ、この前一緒に話してた番組で、俺が面白そうだと思ってたのあるじゃん？ちょうどネットでたまたまレビュー見つけたんだよね。ラストの意外な展開を誰かがネタバレする前に、そういえば試しに見とかなきゃなぁと思ってさぁ。ストリーミング用のリンク、送ってくれない？

女性 いいよ。でも結構前のだから、探さなきゃなぁ。DVDならあるよ。借りたければ。

男性 もうDVDプレイヤー持ってないと思う。去年のどっかで消えたよ。ごみと一緒に捨てたんじゃないかな。まぁ、いずれにせよきっとそろそろ新しいテクノロジーに乗っかる時期だろうしね。

女性 あら残念。でももうDVDはほぼアンティークみたいなもんだよね。あと、言っておかなきゃいけないんだけど、ストリーミングのやつ字幕ないから。あなたがスペイン語ペラペラだといいんだけど。

797 **chat**
[tʃæt]
☐☐☐☐☐☐

V[I]（〜について）話す、おしゃべりする、雑談する (about sth/sb)
N[C]（〜についての）おしゃべり、雑談 (about sth)　N[U] チャット
have a **chat** (with sb about sth)（(〜と〜について) 話す）
▶ **chatty** [tʃæṭi] Adj. おしゃべりな

798 **stumble**
[stʌ́mbəl]
☐☐☐☐☐☐

V[I]（〜に）つまずく (on/over sth)
stumble across sth/sb（偶然〜を見つける）

799 **review**
[rɪvjúː]
☐☐☐☐☐☐

N[C] レビュー、批評；復習　N[C/U] 再検討、再調査、見直し
V[T] をレビューする；を復習する；を再検討する、見直す；をチェックする
▶ **reviewer** [rɪvjúːər] N[C] 批評家；レビュー担当者

800 **remind**
[rɪmáɪnd]
☐☐☐☐☐☐

V[T] に（〜を）思い出させる、気づかせる (that + sentence/of sth)
These pictures **remind** me of my high school days.（この写真見ると高校時代思い出すなぁ。）
▶ **reminder** [rɪmáɪndər] N[C] 思い出させるもの、リマインダー

801 **give it a shot**
[gívɪţəʃɑ́ːt]
☐☐☐☐☐☐

Phr. 試してみる、やってみる
Just **give it a shot**. What's the worst that could happen?
（とりあえずやってみようよ。最悪どうなるっていうの？）

802 **spoil**
[spɔɪl]
☐☐☐☐☐☐

V[T]（ネタ）をばらす、台無しにする；を甘やかす　V[I] だめになる
N[P] 戦利品、（勝ち取った）利権【-s】
▶ **spoiled** [spɔɪld] Adj. 甘やかされた　▶ **spoiler** [spɔ́ɪlər] N[C] ネタバレする人・もの
a **spoiler** alert（ネタバレ注意 (の警告)）

803 **twist**
[twɪst]
☐☐☐☐☐☐

N[C]（意外な）話の展開；ねじれ　V[I/T]（体を）ひねる
▶ **twisted** [twɪstɪd] Adj. ねじれた；ひねくれた

804 **stream**
[striːm]
☐☐☐☐☐☐

V[T] をストリーミングする　V[I] 流れる
▶ **streaming** [stríːmɪŋ] N[U] ストリーミング

805 **search**
[sɜːrtʃ]
☐☐☐☐☐☐

V[I]（〜を求めて）探す、検索する (for sth)
V[T]（〜を求めて）を探す、検索する (for sth)　N[C] 捜索、検索
Why did you **search** my bag without asking?（なんで無断で私のバッグを漁ったの？）

806 **borrow**
[báːroʊ]
☐☐☐☐☐☐

V[T] を借りる　V[I] 借金する
Can I **borrow** you for a minute?（ちょっと助けを借りてもいい？）

234

807 vanish
[vǽnɪʃ]

V[I] 急に消える、突然なくなる

I thought my glasses **vanished**, but I was actually wearing them.
（メガネが急に消えたと思ったらつけてたわ。）

808 suspect
v. [səspékt]
N./Adj. [sʌ́spekt]

V[T]（〜ではないか）と思う（that + sentence）、に感づく
に（〜の）嫌疑をかける（of sth）　N[C] 容疑者　Adj. 疑わしい

▶ **suspicious** [səspíʃəs] Adj.（〜に）疑いを持った（about sth/sb）、疑わしい

▶ **suspiciously** [səspíʃəsli] Adv. 疑わしそうに

▶ **suspicion** [səspíʃən] N[C/U] 容疑 , 疑い

809 garbage
[gáːrbɪdʒ]

N[S/U] ごみ　= trash [træʃ]　= rubbish [rʌ́bɪʃ] <英>

Can you take out the **garbage** for me?（ごみ出ししてきてくれないかな？）

N[U] ばかばかしいこと

810 on board
[ɑːnbɔ́ːrd]

Phr.（流行等に）乗って、賛成して（with sth/sb）

Everyone is **on board** with the plan.（みんなその計画に賛成なんだ。）

811 pity
[píti]

N[S] 残念なこと　= shame [ʃeɪm]　N[U] 同情

■ it is a **pity** that + sentence（〜とは残念だ）

It's a **pity that** you weren't around for my birthday.
（僕の誕生日に君がいなくて残念だったよ。）

812 antique
[æntíːk]

N[C] アンティーク、骨董品　Adj. アンティークの

813 warn
[wɔːrn]

V[T] に（〜について）言っておく、警告する（about sth/that + sentence）

▶ **warning** [wɔ́ːrnɪŋ] N[C/U] 事前通告、警告

Chapter

18

刑法
Criminal Law

Due to the damaging consequences of breaching criminal law, violation often results in the imposition of harsh punishments such as fines, detainment in prison or juvenile centers, and even capital punishment in some countries.

This is because of the fact that failure to abide by these laws typically leads to the endangerment of people's property, health, safety, and welfare.

Although criminal law is characterized by the severity of its punishment, in many jurisdictions, there is a strong focus on permanent rehabilitation, with the intention of eventually transforming offenders into valuable members of society.

For example, Norway has been successful in keeping the recidivism rate extremely low by implementing rehabilitation-focused activities such as vocational training, including wood-working and assembly workshops, and accommodating inmates in spacious cells.

1 Due to the damaging consequences of breaching criminal law, violation often results in the imposition of harsh punishments such as fines, detainment in prison or juvenile centers, and even capital punishment in some countries.

刑法に違反すると悪影響がもたらされるため、違反行為にはしばしば罰金や、刑務所や少年院への収容、さらに一部の国では死刑という厳しい処罰が科される。

---

814 **criminal**
[krímənəl]
☐☐☐☐☐☐

Adj. 刑事上の、犯罪の　**N[C]** 犯罪者、犯人

Not bringing drinks to a house party is basically **criminal**.
（ハウスパーティするのに飲み物持ってこないとか犯罪レベルなんだけど。）

▶ **criminally** [krímənəli] Adv. 刑事上、犯罪的に　▶ **crime** [kraɪm] N[U] 犯罪　N[C] 犯罪行為

the **criminally** insane（（集合的に）触法精神障害者 *）
* 犯罪行為をしながら刑事責任を問われない精神障害者のこと

I want to let my kids do whatever they want to do as long as they don't commit **crimes**.
（犯罪さえしないんだったら自分の子供には何でも好きなことやらせたいんだ。）

---

815 **law**
[lɑ:]
☐☐☐☐☐☐

N[U] 法、法律 【the -】　**N[C]** （個々の）法律

I always abide by **the law**, even if it's a bit inconvenient.
（多少不都合であっても、私は法律はいつも遵守するよ。）

■ against **the law**（違法の、法律違反の）

Discrimination based on gender is **against the law**.（性別に基づく差別は違法だよ。）

▶ **lawyer** [lɑ́:jər] N[C] 弁護士　= **attorney** [ətə́:rni]

▶ **legal** [lí:gəl] Adj. 合法の

It is not **legal** to hack software.（ソフトウェアをハッキングするのは違法です。）

⇔ **illegal** [ɪlí:gəl] 違法の、非合法の

illegal activity/conduct（非合法活動 / 違法行為）

▶ **legally** [lí:gəli] Adv. 合法的に　⇔ **illegally** [ɪlí:gəli] 違法に、非合法に

▶ **lawsuit** [lɑ́:su:t] N[C] 訴訟　▶ **bylaw** [báɪlɑ:] N[C] （会社などの）規則

---

816 **imposition**
[ìmpəzíʃən]
☐☐☐☐☐☐

N[U] （罰則などを）科すこと、（税金などを）課すこと　**N[C]** 押し付け

The **imposition** of taxes does not necessarily benefit the country.
（課税は必ずしもその国にとって利益になるわけではないよ。）

▶ **impose** [ɪmpóʊz] V[T] を（〜に）科す、課す（on sth/sb）；(思想など) を押しつける

China decided to **impose** punitive tariffs on some U.S. imports.
（中国はアメリカからのいくつかの輸入品に報復関税 *を課すことを決めた。）　* 国の利益を守るために課される割増関税

---

817 **fine**
[faɪn]

N[C] 罰金 V[T] に罰金を科す

I can't believe they gave me a parking **fine** for being a minute over the time limit.
（時間制限を一分越しただけで駐車違反の罰金くらうとか信じらんない。）

Adj. 良い、大丈夫な；上質な；きめの細かい

I was a bit sick last week, but I feel **fine** now.
（先週はちょっと具合が悪かったんだけど、今はもう大丈夫だよ。）

the **finest** fabric（最も上質な生地）

---

818 **prison**
[prízən]

N[C/U] 刑務所、拘置所 = **jail** [dʒeɪl]

Surely you're not going to **prison** for stealing a chocolate bar.
（チョコバーを一個盗んだだけで刑務所行きはあり得ないよ。）

■ in **prison**（刑務所に入って）　　go to **prison** = be sent to **prison**（投獄される）

The cult leader is **in prison** now.（あのカルトの指導者は今刑務所だよ。）

▶ **prisoner** [prízənər] N[C] 囚人　　a political **prisoner**（政治犯）

▶ **imprison** V[T] を投獄する = **jail**　　▶ **imprisonment** N[U] 禁固、投獄
[ɪmprízən]　　　　　　　　　　　　　　　　　[ɪmprízənmənt]

prison vs **jail**　どちらも「刑務所」という意味で使われますが、prison は重犯罪などで長期的に拘束される場所であるのに対し、jail は軽犯罪などで短期的に拘束される場所というニュアンスがあります。

---

819 **juvenile**
[dʒúːvənəl]

Adj. 少年の、未成年者の；子供っぽい N[C] 未成年者

Playing video games at our age is a bit **juvenile**, isn't it?
（私たちの年齢でテレビゲームするってちょっと子供っぽいよね？）

juvenile delinquency/crimes（少年犯罪）

---

820 **capital**
[kǽpəṭl]

Adj. 死刑の；資本の；首都の；大文字の

Isn't it interesting that some countries have **capital** punishment, while others don't?
（死刑がある国と無い国があるって興味深くない？）

Please write your name in all **capital** letters.（お名前は全部大文字で書いてください。）

N[U] 資本、資金 N[C] 首都；中心地；大文字

The **capital** of Canada is Ottawa, not Toronto.　　raise **capital**　　in **capitals**
（カナダの首都はトロントじゃなくてオタワだよ。）　　　　（資金を集める）　　（大文字で）

▶ **capitalist** [kǽpəṭlɪst] N[C] 資本主義者；資本家　Adj. 資本主義の

a **capitalist** society（資本主義社会）

▶ **capitalism** N[U] 資本主義　　▶ **capitalize** V[T] を資本化する；を大文字で書く
[kǽpəṭlɪzəm]　　　　　　　　　　　　[kǽpəṭlaɪz]

2 This is because of the fact that failure to abide by these laws typically leads to the endangerment of people's property, health, safety, and welfare.

これは、刑法に従わなければ、一般的に人の財産や健康、安全、福祉が脅かされることになるからである。

821 failure
[féɪljər]

N[C/U] （〜）しないこと（to do）；失敗；倒産　N[C] 落ちこぼれ

Failure teaches success, so don't be afraid of making mistakes!
（失敗は成功のもとだから、ミスすることを恐れちゃいけないよ！）

I felt like a bit of a **failure** when I dropped out of university.
（大学を中退した時はちょっと落ちこぼれた感じがした。）

▶ **fail**　V[I]（〜）しない（to do）；失敗する；不合格になる
[feɪl]　V[T] で不合格になる

She never **fails** to email every week.（彼女は必ず毎週メールしてくるんだ。）

If you listen to my instructions, our plan won't **fail**.（私の指示を聞けば、計画が失敗することはないよ。）

Most people **fail** the exam.（ほとんどの人はその試験で不合格だ。）

822 abide by sth
[əbáɪd baɪ]

[PV]　〜に従う、順守する

We have to **abide by** John's rules when we're at his house.
（ジョンの家にいる時はジョンのルールに従わないとね。）

823 endangerment
[ɪndéɪndʒərmənt]

N[C/U]　脅かすこと、（存続などを）危うくすること

The arrival of Europeans on the North American continent led to the **endangerment** of many Native American languages.
（ヨーロッパの人たちが北アメリカ大陸に到着したことで、多くのアメリカ先住民の言葉が存亡の危機にさらされた。）

▶ **endanger** [ɪndéɪndʒər] V[T] を危険にさらす

Careless commercial development of this area would **endanger** the wildlife.
（この地域を何も考えないで商業開発したら野生動物を危険にさらすことになるよ。）

▶ **endangered** [ɪndéɪndʒərd] Adj. 絶滅寸前の、絶滅が危惧された

an **endangered** species（絶滅危惧種）

824 **property**
[prá:pərti]
☐☐☐☐☐☐

N[U] 財産、所有物 **N[C/U]** 不動産、物件 **N[C]** 属性、特性

Do you think it's a good time to buy **property**?
（不動産を買うのに良い時期だと思う？）

825 **health**
[helθ]
☐☐☐☐☐☐

N[U] 健康、健康状態

I know french fries aren't great for my **health**, but I just can't stop eating them.
（フライドポテトが健康にあんまり良くないのは分かってるんだけど、ただただ止められないんだよ。）

in good **health**（健康で）   damage sb's **health**（〜の健康を損なう）

▶ **healthy** [hélθi] Adj. 健康的な、健康に良い；健全な

↔ **unhealthy** [ʌnhélθi] 健康によくない；不健全な

I try to eat **healthy** food as much as possible because I know it will eventually make a big difference.
（できるだけ健康的な食事をするようにしてるんだ。最終的に大きな違いを生むことになるって分かってるからね。）

826 **safety**
[séɪfti]
☐☐☐☐☐☐

N[U] 安全、安全性

The in-flight **safety** video was so hilarious. I paid attention the whole time.
（あの機内の安全ビデオ、すごい面白くてずっと注目して見ちゃったよ。）

▶ **safe** [seɪf] Adj. 安全な、無事な

I don't want to live in that area. It's not very **safe**, is it?
（そのエリアには住みたくないなぁ。あんまり安全じゃないでしょ？）

▶ **safely** [séɪfli] Adv. 安全に、無事に

Make sure you drive **safely**, okay? You just got your driver's license.
（ちゃんと安全運転してよ？運転免許取ったばかりなんだから。）

827 **welfare**
[wélfer]
☐☐☐☐☐☐

N[U] 福祉；健康と幸せ；生活保護

Your **welfare** is the only thing that matters to me.
（私にとって重要なのはあなたの幸せだけだよ。）

on **welfare**（生活保護を受けて）   **welfare** services（福祉サービス）

3 Although criminal law is characterized by the severity of its punishment, in many jurisdictions, there is a strong focus on permanent rehabilitation, with the intention of eventually transforming offenders into valuable members of society.

刑法の特徴は処罰の厳しさにあるが、多くの法域では、いずれは犯罪者を社会の価値ある一員として生まれ変わらせることを目指し、永続的な社会復帰に重点が置かれている。

---

828 severity
[səvérəṭi]
☐☐☐☐☐☐

N[U] 厳しさ、（病気や問題などの）重大さ、深刻さ

To be honest, I don't think a 3-year sentence is harsh given the **severity** of the crimes that she committed.（正直な話、彼女が犯した犯罪の重大さを考えれば、3年の懲役が厳しいとは思わない。）

▶ **severe** Adj. 厳しい、重大な、深刻な
[səvír]

▶ **severely** Adv. 厳しく、ひどく
[səvírli]

A **severe** snowstorm blocked all the doors of my house.
（ひどい吹雪で家のドアが全部開かなくなった。）

---

829 permanent
[pə́:rmənənt]
☐☐☐☐☐☐

Adj. 永続的な、永久の、恒久の、終身の

How can I become a **permanent** resident of Australia?
（どうやったらオーストラリアの永住者になれるの？）

▶ **permanently** Adv. 永久に、一生
[pə́:rmənəntli]

▶ **permanence** N[U] 永久、永続性
[pə́:rmənəns]

---

830 intention
[ɪnténʃən]
☐☐☐☐☐☐

N[C/U] 意図、意向 = **intent** [ɪntént]

■ have no **intention** of doing（〜するつもりは一切ない）

Don't message me again because I **have no intention of** getting back together with you.
（あなたとよりを戻すつもりはないからもうメッセージしてこないで。）

by **intention**（意図的に、故意に） = on purpose [ɑ:npə́:rpəs]

with the **intention** of doing（〜することを目指して）

▶ **intend** [ɪnténd] V[T]（〜する）つもりである（to do）

▶ **intentional** [ɪnténʃənəl] Adj. 意図的な ⟷ **unintentional** [ʌnɪnténʃənəl] 故意でない

I know it's not **intentional**, but he always annoys people.
（意図的じゃないのは分かってるんだけど、彼はいつもみんなをイライラさせるんだ。）

▶ **intentionally** [ɪnténʃənəli] Adv. 意図的に

831 eventually
[ɪvéntʃuəli]
☐☐☐☐☐☐

Adv. いずれは、最終的には、結局は

Everyone will die **eventually**, so what's the meaning of life?
(みんな最終的には死ぬんだったら、人生の意味って何なんだろう?)

▶ **eventual** [ɪvéntʃuəl] Adj. 最終的な ▶ **eventuate** [ɪvéntʃueɪt] V[I] (最終的に)起こる

■ **eventuate** in sth (最終的に〜になる)

If you keep doing this shady business, I think it'll **eventuate in** a big loss.
(この怪しいビジネスし続けたら、最終的に大きな損失になると思うよ。)

---

832 transform
[trænsfɔ́:rm]
☐☐☐☐☐☐

V[T] を (〜に) 変貌させる、変身させる (into sth)

This 30-day program will **transform** you into a model.
(この30日プログラムでモデルに変身できますよ。)

▶ **transformation** [trænsfərméɪʃən] N[C/U] 変貌、変身

---

833 offender
[əféndər]
☐☐☐☐☐☐

N[C] 犯罪者

I think we should punish repeat **offenders** more severely.
(私は常習犯に対してはもっと厳しい処罰をするべきだと思うな。)

▶ **offend** [əfénd] V[I] 犯罪を犯す V[T] を嫌な気持ちにさせる、の気分を悪くさせる

▶ **offense** [əféns] N[C] 犯罪 N[U] 気を悪くさせること

■ take **offense** (at sth) ((〜で) 気を悪くする) ■ no **offense** (悪気はないんだけど)

He **took offense at** what I said. (彼は私が言ったことにムッとしたんだ。)

No offense, but I think you should get a haircut. (悪気はないんだけど、君は髪を切った方が良いよ。)

▶ **offensive** Adj. 不快な;攻撃的な   ▶ **offensively** Adv. 不快に
[əfénsɪv]   [əfénsɪvli]

---

834 valuable
[væljəbəl]
☐☐☐☐☐☐

Adj. 価値のある、貴重な、有益な

I keep getting told that I'm a **valuable** member of the team, but I don't get treated that way.
(チームにおいて価値のあるメンバーだってずっと言われ続けてるんだけど、そういう感じで扱われてないんだよね。)

▶ **valuation** [væljuéɪʃən] N[C/U] 査定、評価

▶ **value** [vælju:] N[C/U] 価値 N[P] 価値観【-s】 V[T] を大切に思う、尊重する

■ good **value** for money (値段の割に良い、コスパが良い、お買い得な)

This all-you-can-drink set is just 1,000 yen?! That's **good value for money**!
(この飲み放題セットたったの1,000円!?コスパいいね!)

Alice and I get along because we have similar **values**.
(アリスと私は価値観が似ているから仲が良いよ。)

I always **value** your time. (私はあなたの時間を大切に思ってるよ。)

▶ **invaluable** [ɪnvæljəbəl] Adj. 計り知れないほど価値を持つ、非常に貴重な

valuable に否定の意味を持つ接頭語 in- がついた形で、そこから「価値がつけられないほどの」、つまり「計り知れないほど価値を持つ」という意味になっています。

4 For example, Norway has been successful in keeping the recidivism rate extremely low by implementing rehabilitation-focused activities such as vocational training, including wood-working and assembly workshops, and accommodating inmates in spacious cells.

例えばノルウェーでは、木工や組み立て作業などの職業訓練を行ったり、広々とした監房に受刑者を収容したりして、社会復帰を重視した活動を実施することで、極めて低い再犯率を維持することに成功している。

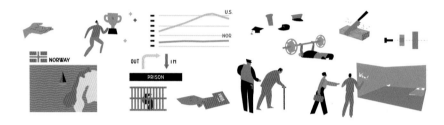

835 **successful**
[səksésfəl]
☐☐☐☐☐☐

Adj.（〜に）成功した（in sth）

You can't be **successful** without a lot of hard work.
（たくさんの努力なしに成功することはできないよ。）

↔ **unsuccessful** [ʌnsəksésfəl] 失敗した

▶ **successfully** [səksésfəli] Adv. 成功して、うまく、無事に

He **successfully** completed a master's degree.（彼は無事に修士号を取得した。）

▶ **success** [səksés] N[U] 成功　N[C] 成功したこと、うまくいったこと

▶ **succeed** [səksíːd] V[I]（〜で）成功する（in sth）　V[I/T]（〜の）後を継ぐ

Do you think the vice president will **succeed** the current president?
（あの副大統領って今の大統領の後を継ぐと思う？）

▶ **successor** N[C] 後任者
[səksésər]

▶ **succession** N[U] 継承　N[C] 連続
[səkséʃən]

a **succession** of sth（〜の連続）

836 **implement**
[ímpləmənt]
☐☐☐☐☐☐

V[T] を実施する、実行する

We'll **implement** this new software next week.（うちでは来週この新しいソフトを実装しますよ。）

▶ **implementation** [ìmpləmentéɪʃən] N[U] 実施、実行

837 **vocational**
[voʊkéɪʃənəl]
☐☐☐☐☐☐

Adj. 職業の、職業訓練の

I went to a **vocational** school after high school.（高校を卒業した後は専門学校に行ったんだ。）

▶ **vocation** [voʊkéɪʃən] N[C] 天職、職業　N[C/U] 使命

I've finally found a **vocation** that I'm passionate about.（ついに熱中できる天職を見つけたよ。）

vocation vs **occupation** vs **job**　どれも「職業」と訳されることがある単語ですが、job が最もカジュアルで一般的な形、occupation は若干フォーマルで公的書類等でよく見られる形、そして vocation は職業の中でも自分が適性や使命感をもってできる職、つまり「天職」というニュアンスが強くなります。

---

838 **training**
[tréɪnɪŋ]

N[U]　訓練、研修、トレーニング

■ in **training**（訓練中、研修中）　　　take **training**（訓練を受ける、研修を受ける）

I'm still in **training**, but I want to quit this job already.（まだ研修中だけどもうこの仕事辞めたい。）

▶ **train** [treɪn] V[T] を訓練する、教育する　V[I]（〜に向けた）訓練をする（for sth）

▶ **trainer** [tréɪnər] N[C] トレーナー、指導者　　▶ **trainee** [treɪníː] N[C] 訓練生、研修生

Go easy on him. He's still a **trainee**.（もうちょっと手加減しなよ。彼はまだ研修生なんだから。）

---

839 **assembly**
[əsémbli]

N[U]　組み立て　**N[C/U]**　集会、集まった人　**N[C]**　議会

Furniture **assembly** is ridiculously hard without instructions.
（家具の組み立てって説明書ないとあり得ないほど難しいなぁ。）

▶ **assemble** V[T] を組み立てる；を集合させる、招集する　V[I] 集合する
[əsémbəl]

I can't believe this 3-year-old kid **assembled** this gigantic castle from block toys.
（この3歳の子供がおもちゃのブロックからこんな巨大なお城を作ったなんて信じられない。）

If the fire alarm rings, staff should **assemble** outside the building.
（火災報知器が鳴ったら、スタッフは建物の外に集合してください。）

---

840 **accommodate**
[əkάːmədeɪt]

V[T]　を収容する；（要求など）を受け入れる；を（〜に）順応させる（to sth）

Do you have a conference room that can **accommodate** 50 people?
（50人収容できる会議室ってありますか？）

accommodate oneself to sth（〜に順応する）

▶ **accommodation** N[P] 宿泊施設【-s】 N[C/U] 和解、調停
[əkάːmədéɪʃən]

Have you booked your **accommodations** yet?（もう泊まるところは予約したの？）

▶ **accommodating** [əkάːmədeɪtɪŋ] Adj. 親切な、よく世話をする

---

841 **inmate**
[ínmeɪt]

N[C]　受刑者、囚人、（施設の）収容者

You look like an **inmate** in your driver's license photo.
（あんたの運転免許証の写真、受刑者みたいな顔してるわね。）

BCC NEWS **POLICE SEARCHING FOR BANK ROBBER SUSPECT**
CALL CRIME STOPPERS AT 1-100-8588-300 BCC

Now for an update on last week's big headline: the elusive bank robber that stole $5 million from BNA Bank.

To recap, a man held staff hostage for three hours at the L.A. branch on Friday afternoon of last week. During this ordeal, he physically assaulted employees before grabbing the money and fleeing from the scene of the crime in a van.

As a result of an anonymous tip-off, a man matching the description of the thief was glimpsed in the downtown district of Manhattan a couple of hours ago. He was last seen traveling with a companion and was wearing a black hoodie and sunglasses to disguise his identity.

As always, anybody with any information that could lead to the arrest of the suspect should contact the police immediately. The suspect is not to be approached under any circumstances.

先週、大きな話題を呼んだ事件の最新情報です。BNA銀行で500万ドルを盗んだ男が逃走した事件です。

おさらいすると、男は先週金曜日の午後、BNA銀行ロサンゼルス支店にて3時間にわたって従業員を人質に取り、その間、従業員に暴行を加えて現金を強奪。ワゴン車で犯行現場から逃走しました。

匿名の情報が寄せられ、強盗犯の特徴と一致する男が数時間前にマンハッタンの中心街で目撃されました。最後に目撃されたのは仲間との移動中、変装のために黒いパーカーとサングラスを着用していたとのことです。

いつも通り、容疑者逮捕につながる可能性のある情報を持っている方は、直ちに警察に連絡してください。また、どのような状況でも容疑者には近づかないようにしてください。

842 **headline**
[hédlaɪn]
☐☐☐☐☐☐

N[C] 見出し、ヘッドライン　V[I/T]（〜の）主役を務める

▶ **headliner** [hédlaɪnər] N[C] 主役を務める人

---

843 **robber**
[rá:bər]
☐☐☐☐☐☐

N[C] 強盗犯、強盗

▶ **robbery** [rá:bəri] N[C/U] 強盗、強盗事件

▶ **rob** [rɑːb] V[T] から（〜を）奪う（of sth）、（場所や人）から金を奪う

---

844 **steal**
[sti:l]
☐☐☐☐☐☐

V[I/T]（〜を）盗む；（〜を）盗塁する　N[S] お買い得なもの

Why would anyone **steal** my old textbooks?（何で俺の古い教科書なんか盗むんだろう。）

▶ **stealth** [stelθ] N[U] ひそかにやること

---

845 **recap**
V1. [ri:kǽp]
N./V2. [rí:kæp]
☐☐☐☐☐☐

V[I/T]（〜を）おさらいする、要約する　N[C] おさらい、要約

Let's quickly **recap** what we covered in the last class.

（前の授業でやったことを簡単におさらいしましょう。）

---

846 **staff**
[stæf]
☐☐☐☐☐☐

N[C/P]（集合的に）従業員、職員、スタッフ　V[T]（職員など）を配置する

staff の数え方 staff は働く人全員を集合的に指す言葉のため、1 人の staff を指すときに a staff とは言えません。代わりに a staff member と言うことができます。また、働く人全員を表す際、staff はアメリカ英語では基本単数扱いですが（例：The staff is...）、イギリス英語では基本複数扱いです（例：The staff are...）。

---

847 **hostage**
[hɑ:stɪ́dʒ]
☐☐☐☐☐☐

N[C] 人質

take sb **hostage**（〜を人質にとる）

---

848 **assault**
[əsá:lt]
☐☐☐☐☐☐

V[T] に暴行を加える、を攻撃する　N[C/U]（〜への）暴行、攻撃（on sth/sb）

sexually **assault** sb（〜に性的暴行を加える）

---

849 **grab**
[græb]
☐☐☐☐☐☐

V[T] を盗む；をつかむ、手に入れる

Do you want to **grab** a coffee?（コーヒー買いに行かない？）

---

850 **flee**
[fli:]
☐☐☐☐☐☐

V[I/T]（〜から）逃走する、逃げる（from sth）

---

851 **scene**
[si:n]
☐☐☐☐☐☐

N[C]（事故や犯罪の）現場；（映画などの）場面、シーン

▶ **scenic** [sí:nɪk] Adj. 景色の良い　▶ **scenery** [sí:nəri] N[U] 景色、景観

---

852 **anonymous**
[əná:nəməs]
☐☐☐☐☐☐

Adj. 匿名の、無名の、作者不明の

▶ **anonymously** [əná:nəməsli] Adv. 匿名で　▶ **anonymity** [ænəníməti] N[U] 匿名

853 **thief**
[θiːf]
☐☐☐☐☐

N[C] 泥棒（複数形：thieves）

▶ **thieve** [θiːv] V[I/T]（〜を）盗む　▶ **theft** [θeft] N[C/U] 盗み、窃盗

854 **glimpse**
[glɪmps]
☐☐☐☐☐

V[T] を一瞬目にする、ちらっと見る　N[C] 一瞬見ること
catch a **glimpse** of sth/sb（〜をちらっと見る）

855 **district**
[dístrɪkt]
☐☐☐☐☐

N[C] 地区、区域、地域

856 **companion**
[kəmpǽnjən]
☐☐☐☐☐

N[C] 仲間、友人、連れ；対の片方；ガイド、手引き
a travel **companion**（旅仲間）

857 **wear**
[wer]
☐☐☐☐☐

V[T] を着る、着ている；をすり減らす　V[I] すり減る　N[U] 摩耗
wear vs **put on**　どちらも「着る」を意味しますが、wear は衣服を着ている状態を表し、put on は衣服を身に着ける動作を表します。

858 **disguise**
[dɪsgáɪz]
☐☐☐☐☐

V[T] を変装させる、隠す　N[C/U] 変装
in **disguise**（変装して）

859 **arrest**
[ərést]
☐☐☐☐☐

N[C/U] 逮捕、勾留　V[T] を逮捕する、捕まえる

860 **contact**
[ká:ntækt]
☐☐☐☐☐

V[T] に連絡する　N[U] 連絡、接触、出会い　N[C] コネ
Feel free to **contact** me.（いつでも連絡してね。）

N[P] 良好な関係【-s】

861 **police**
[pəlí:s]
☐☐☐☐☐

N[P] 警察【the -】　V[T] を監視する
a **police** officer（警察官）　= a cop [ka:p]　a **police** station（交番、警察署）

▶ **policing** [pəlí:sɪŋ] N[U] 治安維持、警備

Chapter

19

知的財産法
Intellectual Property Law

Intellectual property law exists to encourage innovation and creativity and to protect copyright, patents, and trademarks.

Recently, with the advent of globalization of commerce, the law's fundamental principle that the scope of such rights is limited only to the state that grants them, and therefore that the rights granted by one state are independent of the rights granted by another, is being questioned.

As transborder digital transmissions of domestically produced content can occur instantly, it is not feasible to regulate intellectual property under the current system.

Some people advocate that this could potentially be solved by the harmonization of law, namely the creation of common international standards to address issues, but others disagree.

1 Intellectual **property law exists to** encourage innovation **and** creativity **and to** protect copyright, patents, **and trademarks.**

知的財産法は、イノベーションと創造性を促し、著作権や特許、登録商標を保護するために存在している。

---

862 intellectual
[ìntəléktʃuəl]

Adj. 知的な、知性の、理性的な　**N[C]**　知識人

It's pretty hard to have an **intellectual** conversation with somebody as stubborn as Warren.
(ウォーレンほど頑固なやつと知的な会話をするのは結構大変なんだよなぁ。)

▶ **intellectually** [ìntəléktʃuəli] Adv. 知的に、理性的に

This job is very easy and not that bad moneywise, but it's not that **intellectually** stimulating. (この仕事は簡単だし、お金的にも悪くないけど、あんまり知的な刺激がないんだよね。)

▶ **intellect** [íntəlekt] N[C/U] 知性、思考力　N[C] 知的な人

---

863 encourage
[ɪnkə́ːrɪdʒ]

V[T]　を促進する；に（〜するよう）勧める、奨励する（to do）

I love how my girlfriend always **encourages** me to try different things.
(彼女の、僕にいつもいろんなことに挑戦するように勧めてきてくれるところがすごい好きなんだ。)

◀▶ **discourage**（人）が（〜するのを）思いとどまらせる（from doing）；やる気を失わせる
[dɪskə́ːrɪdʒ]

My teacher never praises me no matter how hard I study. Her attitude has really **discouraged** me from studying. (僕の先生はどれだけ頑張って勉強しても褒めてくれなくて、勉強のやる気が完全に失せた。)

▶ **encouragement** N[U] 励まし　◀▶ **discouragement** 思いとどまらせること；落胆
[ɪnkə́ːrɪdʒmənt]　　　　　　　　　　　　　　　　　　[dɪskə́ːrɪdʒmənt]

▶ **encouraging** [ɪnkə́ːrɪdʒɪŋ] Adj. 励みになる、元気づける

I've achieved great results after following your advice for just a few days! This is so **encouraging!** (君の助言に従ってからたった数日でめちゃくちゃいい結果が出た！これはすごいやる気が出る！)

◀▶ **discouraging** [dɪskə́ːrɪdʒɪŋ] 落胆させるような、やる気をなくすような

接頭語 en-　「〜の状態にする」を意味する接頭語で、勇気（= courage）のある状態にすることから「元気づける」という意味になります。他には enable（できるようにする）、endanger（危険にさらす）があります。

---

864 innovation
[ìnəvéɪʃən]

N[U]　イノベーション、革新、刷新　**N[C]**　革新的な考え、新しい考え

There hasn't been any real **innovation** in smartphones for a few years now.
(ここ数年のスマホは本当の意味でのイノベーションが何もないなぁ。)

▶ **innovate** V[I/T] （〜を）革新する、刷新する   ▶ **innovator** N[C] 革新者
[ínəveɪt]   [ínəveɪtər]

▶ **innovative** Adj. 革新的な、刷新的な   ▶ **innovatively** Adv. 革新的に、刷新的に
[ínəveɪtɪv]   [ínəveɪtɪvli]

You need to be **innovative** if you want to stand out on social media.
（SNS で目立ちたいなら革新的じゃなきゃいけないよ。）

---

865 **creativity**
[kri:eɪtívəti]

□□□□□□

N[U] 創造性、創造力

I added Luke to the team to bring some **creativity** to this project.
（創造性をプロジェクトにもたらすためにルークをチームに追加したよ。）

▶ **create** [kriéɪt] V[T] を創る、創造する   ▶ **creator** [kriéɪtər] N[C] クリエイター

▶ **creative** Adj. 創造的な、クリエイティブな   ▶ **creatively** Adv. 創造的に、クリエイティブに
[kriéɪtɪv]   [kriéɪtɪvli]

Guys, let's think **creatively** here. （みんな、ここはクリエイティブに考えよう。）

---

866 **protect**
[prətékt]

□□□□□□

V[T] を保護する、守る   **V[I]** （〜を）防ぐ（against sth）

What's the best way to **protect** my computer from being hacked?
（パソコンをハッキングから守る一番良い方法って何かな？）

▶ **protection** [prətékʃən] N[U] 保護 N[C/U] （〜から）保護するもの（against sth）

▶ **protective** Adj. 保護する（of sth）   ▶ **protectively** Adv. 守ろうとして
[prətéktɪv]   [prətéktɪvli]

protective gloves （保護手袋）

▶ **over-protective** [òuvərprətéktɪv] Adj. 過保護の

My parents are way too **over-protective**. （うちの両親はあまりにも過保護なんだ。）

▶ **protector** [prətéktər] N[C] プロテクター

---

867 **copyright**
[kά:piraɪt]

□□□□□□

N[C/U] 著作権   **V[T]** を著作権で保護する

Are there any **copyright** issues with using images that we found on Google in our ad?
（私たちの広告にグーグルで見つけた画像を使うのって著作権的に何か問題あるかな？）

---

868 **patent**
[pǽtnt]

□□□□□□

N[C] 特許   **V[T]** の特許を取る

You should apply for a **patent** if you don't want your idea stolen.
（アイディアを盗まれたくないなら特許申請した方がいいよ。）

▶ **patented** [pǽtntɪd] Adj. 特許取得済みの

a **patented** technology （特許取得済み技術）

2

Recently, with the advent of globalization of commerce, the law's fundamental principle that the scope of such rights is limited only to the state that grants them, and therefore that the rights granted by one state are independent of the rights granted by another, is being questioned.

昨今、商取引のグローバル化が到来したことで、知的財産権が適用される範囲は権利が付与される国に限定され、ある国によって付与された権利は他国では通用しないという知的財産法の基本原則が問題視されている。

---

869 advent
[ǽdvent]
☐☐☐☐☐☐

N[S] （〜の）到来、出現 （of sth）【the -】

The **advent** of cheap flights over the last few years has really changed where I go on vacation. （ここ数年で格安航空が出てきたおかげで休みの時に行けるところが本当に変わったよ。）

---

870 commerce
[kɑ́:mɜːrs]
☐☐☐☐☐☐

N[U] 商取引、商業

Do you think the explosion in international **commerce** has to do with the Internet or something else?
（国際貿易が急激に活発化しているのってインターネットに関係しているのかな？それとも何か違うもの？）

▶ **commercial** [kəmɜ́ːrʃəl] Adj. 商取引の、商業の；商業的な　N[C] コマーシャル

This is just a prototype, so it'll have to be refined before it can go into **commercial** production.
（これはただの試作品だから、商業生産に入る前にもっと洗練させなきゃ。）

a **commercial** break （コマーシャルの時間）

▶ **commercially** [kəmɜ́ːrʃəli] Adv. 商業的に

---

871 fundamental
[fʌ̀ndəméntl]
☐☐☐☐☐☐

Adj. 基本的な、根本的な　**N[P]** 基本、基礎、原理 【-s】

Being able to swim is pretty **fundamental** in playing water polo.
（水球やるなら泳げることが結構基本になってくるよ。）

Most talented musicians understand the **fundamentals** of music thoroughly.
（大抵の優秀な音楽家は音楽の基礎を徹底的に理解してるよ。）

▶ **fundamentally** [fʌ̀ndəméntəli] Adv. 基本的に、根本的に

We broke up because we have **fundamentally** different views on marriage.
（僕たちは結婚に対する考え方が根本的に違ったから別れたんだ。）

872 **scope**
[skoʊp]
□□□□□□

N[U] 範囲、領域

We need to clearly define the **scope** of our work so that we can figure out how many people to put on to the project.
（プロジェクトに何人必要か理解するには、仕事の範囲を明確に決めてないといけないね。）

▶ **scope sth/sb out** [skóʊpáʊt] [PV] を（良し悪しを判断するために）よく見る

I'm going to go **scope out** the apartment over there tomorrow.
（明日あそこにあるアパートを見てくる予定なんだ。）

---

873 **limited**
[límɪtɪd]
□□□□□□

Adj. 限定された、限られた、制限された

I bought this snack straight away because it said it was **limited** edition.
（このお菓子期間限定だって書いてあったからすぐに買ったよ。）

▶ **limit** [límɪt] V[T] を（〜に）制限する（to sth） N[C] 制限、限度

There's a **limit** to the number of times you can download this data.
（このデータをダウンロードできる回数には制限があります。）

▶ **limitation** [lìmətéɪʃən] N[U] 制限すること N[C] 限界、弱点；制約

There are some **limitations** to this theory.（この理論にはいくつか限界があるんだ。）

---

874 **grant**
[grænt]
□□□□□□

V[T] を付与する、与える；を認める   N[C] 助成金、補助金

I have finally been **granted** a visa.（ビザがやっと下りたよ。）

■ take sth/sb for **granted**（〜を当たり前だと思う）

Don't **take** people's support **for granted**! You have to appreciate it.
（みんなのサポートを当たり前だと思っちゃだめだよ。感謝しなきゃ。）

▶ **granted** [grǽntɪd] Adv. 確かに   Cnj. 仮に（〜だとしたら）（that + sentence）

Granted, there is an opportunity to become a millionaire overnight on the stock market. However, that doesn't mean that this will happen to you.
（確かに、株式市場にはあっという間に大金持ちになるチャンスがある。でも、だからといってそれが君に起こるとは限らないんだよ。）

grant vs **give** どちらも「与える」という意味がありますが、grant は「正式に、法的に」というニュアンスが伴う一方、give はより一般的に何かを与えるという意味で使用することができます。

---

875 **independent**
[ìndɪpéndənt]
□□□□□□

Adj. （〜から）独立した、自立した（of sth/sb）

My son is 30, so it's about time he became **independent**.
（うちの息子は 30 歳だから、もう自立して良い頃なんですよね。）

◆▶ **dependent** [dɪpéndənt]（〜に）依存した（on/upon sth/sb）

▶ **independently** [ìndɪpéndəntli] Adv.（〜から）独立して、自立して（of sth/sb）

Look! I can move my chest muscles **independently** of each other.
（見てよ！俺、胸筋を片方ずつ別々に動かせるんだぜ！）

▶ **independence** [ìndɪpéndəns] N[U] 独立、独立性、自立

3 As transborder digital transmissions of domestically produced content can occur instantly, it is not feasible to regulate intellectual property under the current system.

国内で制作されたコンテンツが、デジタル伝送によって一瞬で国境をまたぐこともあるため、現行制度で知的財産を規制することは実現不可能なのだ。

---

876 transmission
[trænsmíʃən]
▢▢▢▢▢▢

N[C/U] 伝送、送信、伝達　**N[U]** （知識などの）伝承

Isn't it amazing that we can get live **transmissions** from Mars?
（火星から生中継できるってすごくない？）

▶ **transmit** [trænsmít] V[I/T]（〜を）送る、送信する；伝承する

SMS is the system used to **transmit** text messages.
（SMS はテキストメッセージを送るのに使われるシステムのことだよ。）

---

877 domestically
[dəméstɪkli]
▢▢▢▢▢▢

Adv. 国内で、家庭内で

Why did you bring a passport? We're flying **domestically**.
（なんでパスポート持ってきたの？国内線しか乗らないよ。）

▶ **domestic** [dəméstɪk] Adj. 国内の、家庭の

The **domestic** market in Japan is huge, so I don't think we need to think about selling overseas just yet. （日本の国内市場はものすごい大きいし、まだ海外に売る必要はないんじゃないかな。）

▶ **domesticate** [dəméstɪkeɪt] V[T] を飼い慣らす、家畜化する；を家庭的にする

My wife is really **domesticated**. She helps with a lot of the chores.
（僕の奥さんは本当に家庭的なんだよね。家事もたくさん手伝ってくれるし。）

---

878 produce
[prədú:s]
▢▢▢▢▢▢

V[T] を制作する、生産する；（結果など）を生む　**N[U]** 農産物

How much chocolate do you think this factory **produces** in a day?
（この工場、一日でどれくらいのチョコを作っていると思う？）

▶ **production** [prədʌ́kʃən] N[U] 制作、生産；生産量　N[C]（映画や娯楽の）制作物

I usually enjoy Ghibli **productions**. （基本的にジブリの作品は好きなんだ。）

▶ **product** [prá:dʌkt] N[C/U] 製品

879 instantly
[ínstəntli]
□□□□□□

Adv. 一瞬にして、即座に、すぐに

My friend's a bit of a celebrity, so he was **instantly** recognized when we went out together yesterday.
（俺の友達はちょっとした有名人だから、昨日一緒に出掛けたらすぐ気づかれてたよ。）

▶ **instant** [ínstənt] Adj. 一瞬の、即座の、すぐの　N[S] 一瞬

instant coffee（インスタントコーヒー（すぐに作れることから））

---

880 feasible
[fí:zəbəl]
□□□□□□

Adj. 実現可能な、実行可能な

Do you think it's **feasible** to do a day trip from Paris to London?
（パリからロンドンに日帰り旅行に行くって可能だと思う？）

▶ **feasibility** [fi:zəbíləti] N[U] 実現可能性、実行可能性

---

881 regulate
[régjəleɪt]
□□□□□□

V[T] を規制する、取り締まる；を調節する

I think the way social media companies use personal information should be more heavily **regulated**. （SNS系企業の個人情報の使用はもっと厳しく規制されるべきだと思うな。）

▶ **regulatory** [régjələtɔːri] Adj. 規制する

a **regulatory** authority（規制当局）

▶ **regulation** [règjəléɪʃən] N[C] 規則、規定　N[U] 規制

rules and **regulations**（規則）（しばしば rules と合わせて使用されます。）

▶ **regulator** [régjəleɪtər] N[C] 規制機関；調節装置

---

882 current
[kə́:rənt]
□□□□□□

Adj. 現在の、今の

How do you keep up with **current** events? （君はどうやって時事についていってるの？）

N[C]　（空気や水の）流れ

an ocean **current**（海流）

▶ **currently** [kə́:rəntli] Adv. 現在は、今は

I'm **currently** living in Thailand, but I'm moving to Germany next month.
（今はタイに住んでるけど、来月ドイツに引っ越すんだ。）

live in vs **be living in**　どちらもある場所に住んでいることを表しますが、live in はその場所にこれまでもずっと住んできたというニュアンスを持ち、be living in はその -ing の形から今現在そこに住んでいるというニュアンスが強くなります。そのため、例えば現在一年間の交換留学でアメリカに住んでいる場合、I'm living in the U.S. という方が、その状況をより正確に表す文章になります。

4 Some people advocate that this could potentially be solved by the harmonization of law, namely the creation of common international standards to address issues, but others disagree.

この問題は、各国で法律の統一を図る、つまり、問題解決に向けた共通の国際基準を設ければ解決され得るという意見もあれば、反対意見もある。

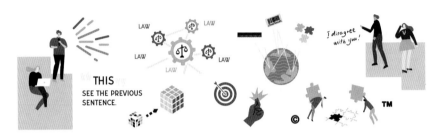

THIS
SEE THE PREVIOUS
SENTENCE.

---

883 advocate

v. [ǽdvəkeɪt]
n. [ǽdvəkət]

V[T] を主張する、支持する、擁護する　**N[C]**　支持者、擁護者

This professor is **advocating** a vegan diet. (この教授はヴィーガン食を支持しているんだ。)

▶ **advocacy** [ǽdvəkəsi] N[U] 支持、擁護

an **advocacy** group （支援団体）

語根 voc, vok 「呼ぶ」という意味の語根で、他には invoke（呼び出す）や evoke（呼び起こす）などがあります。

---

884 potentially

[pətén∫əli]

Adv. もしかすると〜かもしれない、潜在的に

Drone deliveries could **potentially** be life-changing in the next few years.
（これから数年の間にドローンによる配達で生活が変わるかもしれないね。）

▶ **potential** Adj. 潜在的な、可能性のある
[pətén∫əl]　N[U] 潜在性、可能性、ポテンシャル

My girlfriend was like, "If I'm not your **potential** wife, why are you dating me?"
（彼女が「私があなたの奥さんになる可能性がないなら、なんで私と付き合ってるわけ？」って。）

Let me give you some advice to unlock your full **potential**.
（ポテンシャルを十分に発揮するためにいくつかアドバイスをあげよう。）

---

885 solve

[sɑːlv]

V[T] を解決する、解く

I can't **solve** this issue by myself, so I might need your help brainstorming some ideas.
（この問題は自分では解決できないから、アイディアを思いつくのに君の助けが必要かも。）

▶ **solution** [səlúː∫ən] N[C] （〜に対する）解決策、答え （to/for sth）

I came up with a good **solution** to this problem! I'll walk you through it later.
（この問題の良い解決策を思いついたよ！後で一つ一つ説明してあげるね。）

886 **harmonization**
[hὰːrmənəzéɪʃən]
□□□□□□

N[U] 統一、調和、協調

The **harmonization** of all our different systems is taking a long time, but it will be worth it.
（異なる全てのシステムを統一するのにめちゃくちゃ時間かかってるんだけど、やる価値はあるよ。）

▶ **harmonize** [hάːrmənaɪz] V[T] （制度など）を統一する V[I]（～と）調和する（with sth）

Starbucks in Kyoto is designed to **harmonize** with the surrounding landscape.
（京都のスタバは周りの景観と調和するようなデザインになってるんだよ。）

---

887 **namely**
[néɪmli]
□□□□□□

Adv. つまり、すなわち、具体的に言うと = **specifically** [spəsífɪkli]

I've visited the biggest cities in Italy, **namely** Rome, Florence, and Venice.
（イタリアのいくつかの主要な街に行ったんです。具体的には、ローマ、フィレンツェ、ヴェネツィアに行きました。）

---

888 **standard**
[stǽndərd]
□□□□□□

N[C/U] 基準、標準、理想

You should surround yourself with people who have high **standards**.
（基準が高い人たちに囲まれるようにした方がいいよ。）

My high **standards** are keeping me single. （理想が高いせいでずっと独身なんだ。）

Adj. 標準的な；ありふれた

▶ **standardize** [stǽndərdaɪz] V[T] を標準化する、規格化する

▶ **standardization** [stǽndərdəzéɪʃən] N[U] 標準化、規格化

The **standardization** of replacement parts across all our products will make repairing them much easier.
（うちの全ての商品の取り換え部品を標準化すれば、修埋はずっと楽になるでしょう。）

---

889 **address**
V. [ədrés]
N. [ǽdres]
□□□□□□

V[T] （問題解決に向けて）に取り組む、対処する；に演説する

Can you please **address** this issue as soon as you can?
（この問題なる早で対処してくれる？）

V[T] を（～に）宛てて送る（to sb）

N[C] 住所、アドレス；演説

Colleague (M) My **editor** wants me to write an article about a **bunch** of **celebrities** that were popular in the 70s. Is it fine for me to use **pictures** of them that I find on the Internet? I don't want to be **blamed** for getting us into any legal **trouble** or have to **withdraw** my article from publication.

Colleague (W) It shouldn't be a problem if you **disclose** the source of the images. It might not **hurt** to **check** with the **owners** or administrators of the websites.

Colleague (M) I also want to use **quotes** from some of their movies or songs. Can I do that without **paying** them?

Colleague (W) I'll **admit** I'm not sure. Your concerns are **legitimate** though, so maybe send a **draft** to Emma to check when you're done. She works in the legal **department**, so she's pretty experienced and **diligent** about this sort of thing. I think you just want to be **careful** not to **annoy** anybody important.

同僚 (男性) 編集長が70年代に人気だった数多くの有名人について記事を書いてほしいみたいなんだけど、ネットで見けたそういう有名人の写真って使っても大丈夫かな？法律トラブルに巻き込まれて責められたり、記事を取下げなきゃいけなくなったりするのは嫌だし。

同僚 (女性) 画像のソースを開示すれば問題ないはずじゃないかな。サイトの所有者とか管理者に確認するといいかね。

同僚 (男性) 映画とか曲から引用もしたいんだけど、お金払わないでできるかな？

同僚 (女性) 正直分かんないなぁ。でもその心配はもっともだし、準備ができたらエマに下書きを送ってみたら？彼女は務部門で働いているから、こういうことに関してはかなり経験もあるし、よく勉強もしている。とにかく重人物をいらだたせるようなことだけはしないように注意した方がいいと思う。

890 **editor**
[édɪṭər]

N[C] 編集長、編集者

▶ **edit** [édɪt] V[T] を編集する、修正する   N[C] (原稿などの) 編集、手直し

▶ **editable** [édɪṭəbəl] Adj. 編集可能な   ▶ **editorial** [èdətɔ́:riəl] Adj. 編集の

891 **bunch**
[bʌntʃ]

N[C] 多数；集まり；(ブドウなどの) 房；(花などの) 束

a **bunch** of sth (数多くの〜、たくさんの〜)

892 **celebrity**
[səlébrəṭi]

N[C] 有名人、芸能人   **N[U]** 名声   = **celeb** [səléb]

Lots of **celebrities** are running their own YouTube channel these days.
(最近はたくさんの芸能人が自分の YouTube チャンネルを運営しているよ。)

893 **picture**
[píktʃər]

N[C] 写真、絵、画像   **N[S]** 状況   **V[T]** を想像する；を描写する

■ the big **picture** (全体像)

I just can't see **the big picture**. (全体像が見えないんだけど。)

894 **blame**
[bleɪm]

V[T] を (〜のことで) 責める、のせいにする (for sth)

don't **blame** me if/when + sentence (〜しても私を責めないでね)

N[U] (悪いことに対する) 責任

895 **trouble**
[trʌ́bəl]

N[C/U] トラブル、問題   **N[U]** 面倒

have **trouble** doing (〜するのに苦労する)   in **trouble** (困っている)

V[T] に面倒をかける；を心配させる

896 **withdraw**
[wɪðdrɑ́:]

V[T] を取り下げる；(お金を) 引き出す；を撤退させる；(支援を) 打ち切る

V[I] (〜から) 撤退する (from sth)

▶ **withdrawal** [wɪðdrɑ́:əl] N[U] 取り下げ、中止、撤回   N[C/U] (預金の) 引き出し；撤退

897 **disclose**
[dɪsklóʊz]

V[T] を開示する、公表する；を暴露する   ≒ **leak** [li:k] (情報など) を漏らす

▶ **disclosure** [dɪsklóʊʒər] N[U] 開示、(情報などの) 公開

898 **hurt**
[hɜːrt]

V[I] 痛い、つらい   **V[T]** を傷つける、けがさせる

Adj. 傷ついた、けがをした

might not **hurt** to do (〜してもいいかもしれない)

I'm sorry if I **hurt** you. (もし傷つけてたらごめん。)

899 **check**
[tʃek]

V[I] (〜に) 確認する (with sb)；(〜を) 調べる (for sth)

Let me quickly **check** and get back to you. (ちょっと確認してまた連絡するね。)

V[T] を確認する、調べる   **N[C]** 調査；勘定   **N[C]** 小切手 = **cheque** 〈英〉

900 owner
[óʊnər]

N[C] 所有者；飼い主

▶ **own** [oʊn] V[T] を所有する　Adj. 自分の；独特な

901 quote
[kwoʊt]

N[C] （～からの）引用文（from sth）；見積もり

V[I/T] （～を）引用する　V[T] を見積もる

▶ **quotation** [kwoʊtéɪʃən] N[C] 引用文；見積もり　N[U] 引用

902 pay
[peɪ]

V[I/T] （人に）支払う、（代金などを）支払う

pay (sb) for sth （（～に）～の代金を支払う）　**pay** well/badly （割に合う / 合わない）

▶ **payment** [péɪmənt] N[C/U] 支払い、支払額

903 admit
[ədmít]

V[T] を（正直に）認める、白状する；(場所に人など) を入れることを許す

▶ **admittedly** [ədmíṭɪdli] Adv. ～は確かだが

▶ **admittance** [ədmíṭəns] N[U] 入場許可、入学許可

904 legitimate
[lədʒíṭəmət]

Adj. もっともな、正当な；合法な　◆ **illegitimate** [ìlɪdʒíṭəmət] 非合法の

▶ **legitimately** [lədʒíṭəmətli] Adv. 合法的に　▶ **legitimacy** [lədʒíṭəməsi] N[U] 合法性

▶ **legitimize** [lədʒíṭəmaɪz] V[T] を正当化する、合法化する

905 draft
[dræft]

N[C] 下書き、草稿、ドラフト；隙間風

V[T] の下書きを書く；を徴兵する；をドラフトで獲得する　Adj. 下書きの

906 department
[dɪpáːrtmənt]

N[C] 部門、学科；売り場

907 diligent
[dílədʒənt]

Adj. よく勉強している、勤勉な；(調査などが) 入念な

▶ **diligently** [dílədʒəntli] Adv. 一生懸命に　▶ **diligence** [dílədʒəns] N[U] 勤勉

908 careful
[kérfəl]

Adj. 注意深い、慎重な；（～に / ～するよう）気を付けた (with sth/to do)

▶ **carefully** [kérfəli] Adv. 注意深く、慎重に；綿密に、丁寧に

▶ **care** [ker] V[I] （～を）気にする、気に掛ける (about sth/sb)

　　　　N[U] 世話；注意；手入れ

909 annoy
[ənɔ́ɪ]

V[T] をいらだたせる

▶ **annoying** [ənɔ́ɪɪŋ] Adj. いらいらさせる　▶ **annoyed** [ənɔ́ɪd] Adj. いらいらした

▶ **annoyingly** [ənɔ́ɪɪŋli] Adv. いらいらするほど

▶ **annoyance** [ənɔ́ɪəns] N[U] いらだち　N[C] いらだたせるもの

🔄 CH. 5, 9, 13, 16, 19

Chapter

20

国際法
International Law

International law mainly dictates the legal responsibilities of states in their conduct with each other and the treatment of people within their boundaries.

One of the long-standing problems in international law is the notion of state sovereignty, which is, simply put, the idea that all states are equal, and one nation cannot dictate the actions of another.

Because of this underlying concept, no universally accepted authority to enforce international law exists. Countries can therefore choose not to follow international law or even to breach their treaties.

In addition, international disputes can be submitted to the International Court of Justice only by mutual consent of the parties and can still be vetoed if the dispute is in relation to a permanent member of the Security Council.

1 International **law mainly** dictates **the legal** responsibilities **of** states **in their** conduct **with** each other and the treatment **of people within their** boundaries.

国際法は主に、国家間の行為や国境内の人々の処遇に対する国家の法的責任を定めたものである。

---

910 **international**
[ìntərnǽʃənəl]
☐☐☐☐☐☐

Adj. 国際的な

It's great that the check-in process for **international** flights is so much quicker than it used to be. (国際便のチェックイン、昔と比べてずっと素早くできるようになったから最高。)

international law（国際法）

▶ **internationally** [ìntərnǽʃənəli] Adv. 国際的に

IELTS is **internationally** recognized as one of the most reliable English tests.
(IELTS は一番信頼できる英語試験として国際的な認知がある。)

---

911 **dictate**
[díkteɪt]
☐☐☐☐☐☐

V[T] を規定する、決定する ; に命令する　**N[C]** 命令

What I have for dinner is usually **dictated** by what's in my fridge already.
(私の夜ごはんは基本冷蔵庫に何があるかによって決まるんだ。)

V[T] （口述して）を（〜に）書きとらせる（to sb）　**V[I]** 口述する

▶ **dictator** [díkteɪtər] N[C] 独裁者

Adolf Hitler was the **dictator** of Germany during World War II.
(第二次世界大戦中、アドルフ・ヒトラーはドイツの独裁者だった。)

▶ **dictatorship** [dɪktéɪtərʃɪp] N[C/U] 独裁（政治）、専制　N[C] 独裁国家

▶ **dictatorial** Adj. 独裁的な
[dìktətɔ́:riəl]

▶ **dictation** N[U] 書き取り、口述　N[C] 書き取りテスト
[dɪktéɪʃən]

a **dictatorial** government（独裁政治）　　take **dictation**（書き取る）

---

912 **responsibility**
[rɪspà:nsəbíləti]
☐☐☐☐☐☐

N[C/U] 責任、義務　**N[U]** （事故や過失に対する）責任

It may not be your fault, but it's your **responsibility**.
(君のせいじゃないかもしれないけど、君の責任だよ。)

have **responsibility** (for sth)（（〜に対する）責任がある）

take **responsibility** (for sth)（（〜に対して）責任を取る）

a sense of **responsibility**（責任感）

▶ **responsible** [rɪspάːnsəbəl] Adj. 責任のある、責任感のある

■ be **responsible** for sth（〜に責任がある）

You **are responsible for** your own actions.（君は自分の行動に責任があるんだよ。）

▶ **responsibly** [rɪspάːnsəbli] Adv. 責任を持って

---

913 state
[steɪt]
☐☐☐☐☐☐

N[C]　国家、国；州；状態　**N[U]**　（国の）政府

I knew Vatican City was a sovereign **state**, but I didn't know that the population was only about a thousand.
（バチカン市国が主権国家なのは知ってたけど、人口がたった 1000 人ほどだということは知らなかった。）

the **States**（アメリカ合衆国 (the United States の略)）　　a **state** of affairs（情勢、事態）

V[T]　だと言う、述べる　**Adj.**　国の；州の

state that + sentence（〜であると述べる）　　**state** education（公教育）

---

914 conduct
N. [kάːndʌkt]
V. [kəndʌ́kt]
☐☐☐☐☐☐

N[U]　行為、ふるまい、品行；（企業活動などの）運営方法

I wonder why her **conduct** at work has been so unprofessional lately.
（彼女の最近の職場での行動はなんであんなにプロフェッショナルらしくないんだろう。）

V[T]　を行う、実施する　**V[I/T]**　（楽団などを）指揮する　**V[T]**　を伝導する

Does this paper **conduct** electricity?! Who invented this?
（この紙、電気伝わるの !? 誰が発明したの ?）

▶ **conductor** [kəndʌ́ktər] N[C] 指揮者；伝導体

I'm a big fan of the **conductor** of this orchestra.（このオーケストラの指揮者、大好きなんだ。）

---

915 treatment
[tríːtmənt]
☐☐☐☐☐☐

N[U]　（人の）処遇、扱い；（けがなどの）治療　**N[C/U]**　（薬品による）処理

It's obvious that Fred gets special **treatment** from the boss just because they went to the same university.
（フレッドは上司と同じ大学に行ったというだけで明らかに特別扱いされてるんだ。）

medical **treatment**（治療）

▶ **treat** [triːt] V[T] を扱う；を治療する　N[C] ご褒美；特別な経験　N[U] おごり

How are foreigners **treated** in Japan?（日本で外国人はどういう扱いをされるの ?）

The performer gave the elephant an apple as a **treat** for balancing on a ball.
（そのパフォーマーは玉乗りをしたご褒美として象にリンゴをあげたんだ。）

It's my **treat**!（私がおごるよ！）

---

916 boundary
[bάʊndəri]
☐☐☐☐☐☐

N[C]　境界、境界線；（範囲などの）限界、限度

I enjoy my work so much that I don't really have **boundaries** between work and life.
（仕事がめちゃくちゃ楽しいから、私には仕事と生活の境界線が無いんだ。）

2 One of the long-standing problems in international law is the notion of state sovereignty, which is, simply put, the idea that all states are equal, and one nation cannot dictate the actions of another.

国際法における長年の問題として国家主権の概念がある。これは簡単に言えば、全ての国家は平等であり、ある国が他国の行動について命令することはできないという考えである。

---

917 problem

[prá:bləm]

☐☐☐☐☐☐

N[C] 問題、課題　Adj. 問題を起こす

I don't mind cooking, but the **problem** is I don't want to do the dishes.
（料理は別に嫌じゃないけど、問題は食器を洗いたくないってことなんだ。）

a **problem** child（問題児）

■ have a **problem** with sth/sb（〜に問題がある）

I **have a problem with** my computer.（パソコンに問題があるんだ。）

▶ **problematic** [prà:bləmǽṭɪk] Adj. 問題のある

The process to gain my permanent visa was a lot more **problematic** than I thought it would be.（永住ビザを取る過程は思ってたよりずっと問題だらけだったよ。）

---

918 notion

[nóʊʃən]

☐☐☐☐☐☐

N[C/U] 概念、考え

I think the **notion** that everything will be great after you get promoted is a bit unrealistic.
（昇進した後は何事も良くなるっていう考えはちょっと現実的じゃないんじゃないかな。）

▶ **notional** [nóʊʃənəl] Adj. 概念的な　▶ **notionally** [nóʊʃənəli] Adv. 概念的に

---

919 sovereignty

[sá:vrənti]

☐☐☐☐☐☐

N[U] 主権、統治権

A state is comprised of four elements: government, territory, population, and **sovereignty**.
（国家というのは 4 つの要素から成っているんだ。それは政府、領土、国民、そして主権だよ。）

▶ **sovereign** [sá:vrən] Adj. 主権のある、独立した　N[C] 国王、君主

a **sovereign** state/nation（主権国家）

---

920 simply put

[símpli put]

☐☐☐☐☐☐

Phr. 簡単に言えば　= to put it simply [tu pʊ́ṭɪt símpli]

Simply put, we just need to get everything done by the end of the day.
（簡単に言えば、今日中にとりあえず全部終わらせないといけないってことよ。）

921 **equal**
[íːkwəl]
☐☐☐☐☐☐

Adj.　平等な；（〜と）等しい、同じ（to sth）　**V[T]**　に等しい

We all have an **equal** chance of winning, so don't give up till it's over.
（全員平等に勝つチャンスがあるから、終わるまで諦めないでね。）

■ **equal** in number/size/value（数 / 大きさ / 価値が同じの）

This apple is roughly **equal in size** to this orange.
（このリンゴはこのオレンジと大きさが大体一緒だよ。）

20 plus 10 **equals** 30.（20 足す 10 は 30。）

N[C]　同等のもの・人

▶ **equally** [íːkwəli] Adv. 等しく、平等に、同じくらい

In this anime, all the characters are **equally** important.
（このアニメでは全てのキャラクターが同じくらい重要なんだ。）

▶ **equality** [ikwɑ́ːləti] N[U]　平等　⟷　**inequality** [ìnɪkwɑ́ːləti] N[C/U]　不平等

Despite it being the 21st century, gender **equality** still seems to be an issue.
（もう 21 世紀なのに、まだ男女平等が問題のようだね。）

922 **nation**
[néɪʃən]
☐☐☐☐☐☐

N[C]　国、国家　**N[S]**　国民【the -】

The future of this **nation** looks bright.（この国の未来は明るそうだ。）

a **nation**-state（国民国家）

▶ **national** [nǽʃənəl] Adj. 国の、国家の；全国的な　N[C] 国民

A lot of young people these days don't know the lyrics of the **national** anthem.
（最近の若者の多くは国歌の歌詞を知らないんだ。）

a **national** tour（全国ツアー）　　　　**national** news（全国ニュース）

▶ **nationally** [nǽʃənəli] Adv. 全国的に

923 **action**
[ǽkʃən]
☐☐☐☐☐☐

N[C]　（具体的な）行動、行為　**N[U]**　（問題などへの）行動、対処

He's all talk and no **action**.（あいつは口だけで行動しないよ。）

take **action**（行動する）

V[T]　を実行する、行う

The task we talked about yesterday has been **actioned** already.
（昨日話したあのタスクはもう実行しました。）

接尾語 -ion, -tion　動詞について単語を名詞化する役割があります。他には decision（決定）、relation（関係）などがあります。

3 Because of this underlying concept, no universally accepted authority to enforce international law exists. Countries can therefore choose not to follow international law or even to breach their treaties.

この基本的概念によって、国際法を遵守させる普遍的な権限というものが存在していない。それゆえ、各国は国際法に従わないどころか、条約違反すらできるのだ。

---

924 **concept**
[ká:nsept]

☐☐☐☐☐☐

N[C] 概念、考え

It's just a **concept** at this stage, but I'm confident that my online store is going to make a killing. (現段階ではただの考えなんだけど、私のオンラインストアめちゃくちゃ儲かる自信あるよ。)

■ have no **concept** of sth (〜について全く理解していない)

It was obvious that the politician **had no concept of** the U.S. economy.
(その政治家がアメリカ経済について全く理解していないのは明らかだった。)

▶ **conceptual** Adj. 概念的な、考え方の　　▶ **conceptually** Adv. 概念的に
[kənséptʃuəl]　　　　　　　　　　　　　　　　　 [kənséptʃuəli]

I understand what you're saying **conceptually**, but I'm having a hard time visualizing it.
(あなたの言っていることは概念的には理解できるんだけど、なかなかイメージできないでいるんだ。)

---

925 **universally**
[jù:nəvə́:rsəli]

☐☐☐☐☐☐

Adv. 普遍的に、広く、一般的に

Can you believe that climate change is still not **universally** accepted as fact?
(気候変動が未だに事実として広く受け入れられてないなんて信じられる？)

▶ **universal** [jù:nəvə́:rsəl] Adj. 普遍的な、世界共通の

Many people have attempted to make a **universal** language, but all have failed.
(たくさんの人が世界共通言語を作ろうとしてきたが、全て失敗に終わっている。)

▶ **universality** N[U] 普遍性　　▶ **universe** N[S] 宇宙【the -】
[jù:nəvɜ:rsǽləti]　　　　　　　　 [jú:nəvɜ:rs]

universe vs **space** どちらも「宇宙」という意味を持つことがありますが、若干ニュアンスが異なります。universe が地球を含めた万物全てを指す宇宙であるのに対し、space は大気圏外の宇宙空間を意味しています。

---

926 **authority**
[əθɔ́:rəti]

☐☐☐☐☐☐

N[U] 権限、権力、権威　　**N[P]** 当局【the -s】　　**N[C]** 権威者

You should be careful about what you say to him because he has the **authority** to fire you. (彼に対する発言には気を付けた方が良いよ、彼は君をクビにする権力があるからね。)

▶ **authoritarian** [əθɔ́ːrətériən] Adj. 権威主義の、独裁政治の　N[C] 独裁的な人

an **authoritarian** regime/government（独裁政権）

▶ **authoritarianism** [əθɔ́ːrətériənɪzəm] N[U] 権威主義、独裁主義

▶ **authoritative** [əθɔ́ːrətətɪv] Adj. 権威のある、信頼できる；命令的な

authoritative information（信頼できる情報）

▶ **authorize** [ɑ́ːθəraɪz] V[T] を承認する、許可する

My boss **authorized** this party, so don't worry about getting in trouble.
（このパーティはうちの上司に許可をもらってるし、面倒なことにはならないから心配しないで。）

▶ **authorization** [ɑ̀ːθərəzéɪʃən] N[C/U] 承認　N[C] 許可証

---

927 enforce
[ɪnfɔ́ːrs]
☐☐☐☐☐☐

V[T] を遵守させる、施行する、強制する

How can international law be law if it cannot be **enforced**?
（国際法が施行できないならどうやってそれは法律となり得るわけ？）

▶ **enforcement** [ɪnfɔ́ːrsmənt] N[U] 施行、実施、強制

▶ **enforceable** [ɪnfɔ́ːrsəbəl] Adj. 施行できる、実施できる、強制できる

Is an oral agreement legally **enforceable**?（口頭でした合意って法的に強制力あるの？）

---

928 exist
[ɪgzíst]
☐☐☐☐☐☐

V[I] 存在する；（逆境の中〜によって）生存する、生きていく

Do aliens really **exist**?（エイリアンって本当に存在するの？）

▶ **existence** [ɪgzístəns] N[U] 存在

Help me. My son is asking me to prove the **existence** of Santa Claus.
（ちょっと助けて。息子がサンタの存在を証明しろって言ってくるの。）

▶ **existing** [ɪgzístɪŋ] Adj. 存在する、現存する　= **existent** [ɪgzístənt]

Kinkaku-ji is a must-see in Kyoto. It's one of the few **existing** golden temples in the
world.（金閣寺は京都で絶対見た方がいいよ。世界に現存する数少ない金色のお寺の一つだから。）

---

929 breach
[briːtʃ]
☐☐☐☐☐☐

V[T] に違反する、(約束など) を破る　**N[C/U]** 違反、侵害　**N[C]** (関係の) 断絶

Selling counterfeit stuff on eBay is a **breach** of the terms and conditions.
（eBay で偽物を売るのは利用規約違反だよ。）

What happens when a **breach** of contract occurs?（契約違反が発生した時は何が起きるの？）

breach vs **violate**　どちらも「違反する」という意味の単語ですが、breach は契約や合意したこと
の違反を指して使われることが多い一方、violate は法律や規定の違反に対して使われることが多いです。

---

930 treaty
[tríːti]
☐☐☐☐☐☐

N[C] 条約、協定

The U.S. has tax **treaties** with a number of countries.
（アメリカはたくさんの国と租税条約を結んでいる。）

the Japan-U.S. Security **Treaty**（日米安全保障条約）

4 In addition, international disputes can be submitted to the International Court of Justice only by mutual consent of the parties and can still be vetoed if the dispute is in relation to a permanent member of the Security Council.

また、国際紛争に関しては国連の国際司法裁判所に提訴できるが、これは当事国同士が同意した場合に限られ、安全保障理事会の常任理事国が紛争当事国である場合は、拒否権を行使される可能性もある。

---

931 submit
[səbmít]

V[T] を提出する；を（〜に）服従させる（to sth/sb）

How is it possible to **submit** more than a hundred resumes without getting even a single response?（100通以上履歴書提出して一通も返信ないんだけどどうしたらそんなことあり得る？）

V[I] （〜に）服従する、おとなしく従う（to sth/sb）

My dad always **submits** to my mom.（うちのお父さんはお母さんにいつも服従してるよ。）

▶ **submission** N[U] 提出；服従 N[C] 提出物   ▶ **submissiveness** N[U] 従順さ
[səbmíʃən]   [səbmísɪvnəs]

The electronic **submission** of tax returns is becoming common in Japan.
（確定申告の電子提出は日本で一般的になってきている。）

▶ **submissive** Adj. 服従する、従順な   ▶ **submissively** Adv. 服従して、従順に
[səbmísɪv]   [səbmísɪvli]

My dogs are all very **submissive**.（うちの犬はみんなとても従順なんだ。）

---

932 court
[kɔːrt]

N[C/U] 裁判所、法廷；（スポーツの）コート   **N[C]** 中庭；宮廷

I don't really like going to **court**. Maybe I shouldn't have become a lawyer.
（私、裁判所に行くのがあんまり好きじゃないんだ。弁護士になるべきじゃなかったのかも。）

the International **Court** of Justice（国際司法裁判所（ICJ））

in **court**（法廷で）   take sb to **court**（〜を訴える）

▶ **courthouse** [kɔːrthaʊs] N[C] 裁判所（の建物）

---

933 mutual
[mjúːtʃuəl]

Adj. 相互の、お互いの

He doesn't like me, but it's fine because the feeling is **mutual**.
（彼は私のことが好きじゃないけど、お互いそう感じてるから別に良いんだ。）

▶ **mutually** Adv. 相互に、互いに
[mjúːtʃuəli]

▶ **mutuality** N[C/U] 相互関係、相互支援
[mjúːtʃuæləti]

Rika and Bob were **mutually** attracted to each other, so the love wasn't one-sided.
（リカとボブはお互いに惹かれてたから、どちらかが一方的に好きだったってわけじゃないよ。）

mutually exclusive and collectively exhaustive（モレなくダブりなく）

---

934 **party**
[páːrti]
☐☐☐☐☐☐

N[C] 当事者、関係者 ; 政党 ; パーティ   V[I]   パーティをする

I wish there were more than one **party** that I could vote for.
（二つ以上の政党に投票できたらいいんだけどなぁ。）

the Democratic **Party**（民主党）   the Republican **Party**（共和党）

Let's **party** tonight!（今夜パーティしようよ！）

---

935 **veto**
[víːtoʊ]
☐☐☐☐☐☐

V[T]   に拒否権を行使する   N[C/U]   拒否権（複数形：vetoes）

It's your birthday, so you can **veto** whatever venue we choose.
（君の誕生日なんだから、私たちが選ぶ場所を拒否してもいいんだよ。）

---

936 **security**
[səkjúrəti]
☐☐☐☐☐☐

N[U]   安全、セキュリティ   ⟷ **insecurity** [ìnsəkjúrəti] N[C/U] 不安

This **security** app is free but very effective.
（このセキュリティーアプリ無料だけどすごい効果あるよ。）

N[P]   有価証券 【-s】

▶ **secure** [səkjúr] Adj. 安全な、安定した   ⟷ **insecure** [ìnsəkjúr] 不安な

▶ **securely** Adv. 安全に、しっかりと ⟷ **insecurely** 危なっかしく、不安定に
[səkjúrli]   [ìnsɪkjúrli]

接尾語 **-ity** 形容詞について単語を「性質」や「状態」を表す名詞にする役割があります。他には ability（能力）、stability（安定性）などがあります。

---

937 **council**
[káʊnsəl]
☐☐☐☐☐☐

N[C]   理事会、評議会 ; 地方議会

What does the **Council** of the European Union do?
（欧州連合理事会って何するの？）

▶ **councilor** N[C] 評議員、（地方議会の）議員
[káʊnsələr]

the House of **Councilors**（参議院）   the House of Representatives（衆議院）

Interviewer (W)	The Paris Agreement limits countries to a maximum level of carbon emissions. Given the concrete evidence supporting the predicted adverse effects of global warming, and the fact that the U.S. negotiated and willingly adopted the terms of the Agreement, what do you think about the U.S. violation of the Agreement?
Expert (M)	To be frank, this violation is an act of utmost selfishness by the U.S. government. Every country has a duty to confront the implications of this catastrophe, as none of us are immune. However, it is difficult to enforce compliance. Moreover, it may be a moot point, as the U.S. has passed legislation that negates the Agreement.
Interviewer (W)	How difficult is it to abolish this legislation?
Expert (M)	While unlikely, appointing a new president is the most realistic way of amending these changes. It's a pressing concern, as the legislation could cause the Agreement's collapse.

インタビュアー (女性)	パリ協定は各国の二酸化炭素の最大排出量を制限するものですよね。地球温暖化によって予想される悪影響を裏付ける具体的な証拠がある中、アメリカは協定の条項の取り決めを行い、進んで採択しました。アメリカが協定違反したことについてどう思われますか?
専門家 (男性)	率直に言うと、この違反はアメリカ政府の極めて身勝手な行為です。全ての国には、この大惨事による影響に立ち向かう義務があります。影響を受けない国なんてないんですから。しかし、順守を強制することは難しいですね。加えて、アメリカが協定を否定する法案を可決しましたから、無意味な議論なのかもしれません。
インタビュアー (女性)	この法案を撤廃することは難しいのでしょうか?
専門家 (男性)	可能性は低いですが、今回の変更を修正する最も現実的な方法は、大統領を新たに任命することでしょうね。この法律はパリ協定の崩壊をも招きかねないので、これはかなり差し迫った問題です。

938 **concrete**
[ká:nkri:t]
☐☐☐☐☐☐

Adj. 具体的な ↔ **abstract** [æbstrækt] 抽象的な

Adj. コンクリートの　N[U] コンクリート

▶ **concretely** [ka:nkrí:tli] Adv. 具体的に

---

939 **adverse**
[ædvə́:rs]
☐☐☐☐☐☐

Adj. （都合の）悪い、不利な

▶ **adversely** [ædvə́:rsli] Adv. 不利に、逆行して　▶ **adversity** [ədvə́:rsəti] N[C/U] 逆境、困難

---

940 **negotiate**
[nəgóuʃieɪt]
☐☐☐☐☐☐

V[T] を取り決める　V[I]（～と）交渉する（with sb）

▶ **negotiation** [nəgòuʃiéɪʃən] N[C/U] 交渉、協議

▶ **negotiable** [nəgóuʃiəbəl] Adj. 交渉の余地がある

---

941 **adopt**
[ədá:pt]
☐☐☐☐☐☐

V[T] を採択する、採用する；を養子にする

▶ **adopted** [ədá:ptɪd] Adj. 養子の

▶ **adoption** [ədá:pʃən] N[U] 採択、採用　N[C/U] 養子縁組み

---

942 **frank**
[fræŋk]
☐☐☐☐☐☐

Adj. 率直な

to be **frank** (with you)（率直に言うと、はっきり言うと）

▶ **frankly** [fræŋkli] Adv. 率直に　▶ **frankness** [fræŋknəs] N[U] 率直さ

---

943 **utmost**
[ʌ́tmoust]
☐☐☐☐☐☐

Adj. 極度の、最大の　N[S] 極限、最大限

with **utmost** respect/gratitude（最大の敬意 / 謝意を持って）

---

944 **selfishness**
[sélfɪʃnəs]
☐☐☐☐☐☐

N[U] 身勝手

▶ **selfish** [sélfɪʃ] Adj. 利己的な、自分勝手な　↔ **unselfish** [ʌnsélfɪʃ] 利己的でない

▶ **selfishly** [sélfɪʃli] Adv. 利己的に

---

945 **duty**
[dú:t̬i]
☐☐☐☐☐☐

N[C/U] 義務；職務；関税

on **duty**（勤務中で）　↔ off **duty**（勤務時間外で）

---

946 **confront**
[kənfrʌ́nt]
☐☐☐☐☐☐

V[T] に立ち向かう、と対決する；に立ちはだかる

▶ **confrontation** [kà:nfrəntéɪʃən] N[C/U] 立ち向かうこと、対決

▶ **confrontational** [kà:nfrəntéɪʃənəl] Adj. 対立的な

---

947 **implication**
[ìmpləkéɪʃən]
☐☐☐☐☐☐

N[C] 影響　N[C/U] 暗示、含意

▶ **imply** [ɪmplái] V[T] をほのめかす　▶ **implicit** [ɪmplísɪt] Adj. 含意された、暗黙の

it is **implied** that + sentence（～ということがほのめかされている）

---

948 **catastrophe**
[kətǽstrəfi]
☐☐☐☐☐☐

N[C/U] 大惨事、大災害　N[C] 大失敗

▶ **catastrophic** [kæ̀t̬əstrá:fɪk] Adj. 悲惨な、最悪な

949 immune
[ɪmjúːn]

Adj. （〜に）影響を受けない（to sth）；免疫のある；
（〜を）免れる（from sth）

▶ **immunity** [ɪmjúːnəti] N[U]（〜に対する）免疫（to sth）；（責任や義務の）免除（from sth）

---

950 compliance
[kəmpláɪəns]

N[U]（〜の）順守、コンプライアンス（with sth）

in **compliance** with sth（（規則など）に従って）

▶ **comply** [kəmpláɪ] V[I]（〜に）従う（with sth）

▶ **compliant** [kəmpláɪənt] Adj. 準拠した；従順な

---

951 moreover
[mɔ̀ːróʊvər]

Adv. 加えて、その上　= furthermore [fə̀ːrðərmɔːr]

---

952 moot
[muːt]

Adj.（状況や行動がもはや）無意味な

---

953 abolish
[əbáːlɪʃ]

V[T] を撤廃する、廃止する

---

954 appoint
[əpɔ́ɪnt]

V[T] を（〜に）任命する（as sth）；を指定する

▶ **appointment** [əpɔ́ɪntmənt] N[C/U] 任命　N[C] 約束

▶ **appointed** [əpɔ́ɪntɪd] Adj. 任命された；指定された

---

955 amend
[əménd]

V[T] を修正する、改正する

▶ **amended** [əméndɪd] Adj. 修正された、改正された

▶ **amendment** [əméndmənt] N[U] 修正、改正　N[C] 修正箇所

---

956 pressing
[présɪŋ]

Adj. 差し迫った、緊急の　= urgent [ə́ːrdʒənt]

a **pressing** issue（差し迫った問題）

---

957 legislation
[lèdʒəsléɪʃən]

N[U] 法律；法律制定

▶ **legislative** [lédʒəslətɪv] Adj. 立法の　▶ **legislature** [lédʒəslətʃər] N[C] 議会、立法府

▶ **legislate** [lédʒəsleɪt] V[I/T]（法律を）制定する

---

958 collapse
[kəlǽps]

N[S/U] 崩壊、破綻　V[I] 崩壊する　V[T] を崩壊させる

There're still a lot of theories around why the Roman Empire **collapsed**.
（どうしてローマ帝国が崩壊したのかに関しては未だにたくさんの説があるんだ。）

↺ CH. 1, 6, 10, 14, 17, 20

開発学
Development Studies

Development studies is an extraordinarily broad field that has only relatively recently attained a high level of credibility and official status among colleges and universities, especially in regions with a colonial history.

The primary catalyst for its rise to prominence in the mid-twentieth century was scholars' and academics' leveraging it as a response to growing concerns about the economic outlook for poorer countries plagued by recession as a result of World War II.

There was a realization that economic policies in isolation could not eliminate issues such as malnutrition, poverty, and lack of education, and that a more interdisciplinary approach with greater breadth was required to resolve them.

The career prospects for graduates specializing in this area are similarly diverse. Many go on to careers in federal and municipal government, non-government organizations, development consulting firms, and educational institutions.

1

Development studies is an extraordinarily broad field that has only relatively recently attained a high level of credibility and official status among colleges and universities, especially in regions with a colonial history.

開発学は非常に幅広い分野で、比較的最近になって大学等で高いレベルの信頼と正式な地位を得た。特に昔は植民地だった地域ではその傾向が顕著である。

DEVELOPMENT STUDIES

7,753 ratings

← colonized

---

959 extraordinarily
[ɪkstrɔ́ːrdənerəli]
□□□□□□

Adv. 非常に、並外れて、異常に ⟷ ordinarily [ɔ́ːrdənerəli] 通常は、普通に

Dan remained **extraordinarily** calm even though everybody was very angry at him.
(みんなはダンに対してすごい怒ってたのに、彼は異常なくらい落ち着いてたよ。)

▶ **extraordinary** [ɪkstrɔ́ːrdəneri] Adj. 異常な、並外れた、とてつもない

The football match yesterday was **extraordinary**.
(昨日のフットボールの試合はとてつもなかったよ。)

⟷ **ordinary** [ɔ́ːrdəneri] 普通の、平凡な

---

960 attain
[ətéɪn]
□□□□□□

V[T] を獲得する、達成する

You can only **attain** your goals if you keep growing and developing.
(自分が成長して、発展し続けることで初めてゴールを達成することができるんだ。)

▶ **attainment** [ətéɪnmənt] N[U] 獲得、達成　N[C] 獲得したもの

▶ **attainable** [ətéɪnəbəl] Adj. 達成可能な

---

961 level
[lévəl]
□□□□□□

N[C] レベル、水準；高さ、高度；（組織などの）地位；階 = floor [flɔːr]

This band is on a completely different **level**. (このバンドは完全にレベルが違うよ。)

The bathroom is on **level** 2. (トイレは二階にありますよ。)

▶ **high-level** [hàɪlévəl] Adj. 大まかな、ざっくりした；高水準の

I just did a **high-level** check, so I can't guarantee that this calculation is absolutely correct.
(ざっくりしたチェックしかしてないから、この計算が絶対合ってるとは言えないや。)

high-level の意味　high-level は、日本語でよく使われる「高水準の」以外にも、「目線が高いところから見ている」という意味を持ち、そこから「大まかな、ざっくりした」という意味に派生しています。

V[T] を平らにする；（建物や街など）を破壊する

962 **credibility**
[krèdəbíləti]

N[U] 信頼、信頼性、信用

You won't be fired if you miss the deadline, but you'll lose a lot of **credibility**.
(締め切りを守らなくてもクビにはならないけど、自分への信頼はかなり失うだろうね。)

▶ **credible** Adj. 信頼できる、信用できる ⟷ **incredible** 信じられない、素晴らしい
[krédəbəl]   [ɪnkrédəbəl]

You can tell that this article is **credible** because of who wrote it.
(書いた人からこの記事は信用できるって分かるよ。)

▶ **credibly** Adv. 信用できるように ⟷ **incredibly** ものすごく、信じられないほど
[krédəbli]   [ɪnkrédəbli]

---

963 **official**
[əfíʃəl]

Adj. 正式な、公式な；表向きの   **N[C]** 役人、官僚、公務員

I'm not actually sure if our relationship is **official**.
(僕たちって正式に付き合ってるのかよく分からないんだよね。)

a government **official** (国家公務員、政府職員)

▶ **officially** [əfíʃəli] Adv. 正式に、公式に

I haven't been **officially** promoted yet, but my boss has told me that it's definitely happening.
(まだ正式に昇進したわけじゃないんだけど、上司には確実だって言われてるよ。)

---

964 **college**
[kɑ́:lɪdʒ]

N[C/U] 大学、カレッジ **N[C]** （大学の）学部

I don't know exactly what I want to study at **college**, but probably something related to new technologies. （大学で何を勉強したいかはっきりは分からないんだけど、たぶん新技術に関連したことをやりたいんだと思う。）

college vs **university** どちらも「大学」と訳されることがありますが、基本的にアメリカでは college は学士号やそれに準ずる学位を提供する学校で、二年制のコースを提供する学校も college と呼ばれることがあります。一方で、多くの場合 university は修士号や博士号も提供する学校を指します。しかし、会話では区別なく使われることもよくあります。イギリスでは college はより明確に区別されており、一般的に高卒資格を取得できる学校や専門学校を指します。

---

965 **colonial**
[kəlóuniəl]

Adj. 植民地の

There are still lots of **colonial** borders in Africa.
(アフリカにはまだ植民地時代にひかれた国境がたくさん残ってる。)

▶ **colony** [kɑ́:ləni] N[C] 植民地、植民地国家

▶ **colonize** [kɑ́:lənaɪz] V[T] を植民地化する

Do you think we'll **colonize** the Moon or Mars first?
(月の植民地化と火星の植民地化、どっちが先に起きると思う？)

▶ **colonialism** [kəlóuniəlɪzəm] N[U] 植民地主義、植民地化政策

▶ **colonizer** [kɑ́:lənaɪzər] N[C] 植民者、入植者

2 The primary catalyst for its rise to prominence in the mid-twentieth century was scholars' and academics' leveraging it as a response to growing concerns about the economic outlook for poorer countries plagued by recession as a result of World War II.

開発学が 20 世紀半ばに注目されるようになった主なきっかけは、第 2 次世界大戦の影響で不況に苦しむ貧困国の景気の先行きに懸念が高まったことを受け、学者や研究者らが開発学を活用するようになったことだった。

---

966 **catalyst**
[kǽṭlɪst]

N[C] （〜の）きっかけ、引き起こすもの（for sth）；触媒

- act as a **catalyst** for sth（〜のきっかけになる）

I think this injection of cash will **act as a catalyst for** our company really taking off.
（この資金注入はうちの会社の大きな成功のきっかけになると思うよ。）

▶ **catalysis** [kətǽləsɪs] N[U] 触媒作用   ▶ **catalytic** [kæ̀ṭəlíṭɪk] Adj. 触媒（作用）の

---

967 **prominence**
[prɑ́:mənəns]

N[U] 卓越、卓越性、著名、有名

- come/rise to **prominence**（卓越する、有名になる、注目されるようになる）

Although his channel currently has millions of subscribers, it **rose to prominence** due to the initial success of a couple of videos.
（彼のチャンネル、今では何百万も登録者がいるけど、有名になった理由は最初の2、3個の動画が成功したからなんだ。）

▶ **prominent** [prɑ́:mənənt] Adj. 著名な、目立った

▶ **prominently** [prɑ́:mənəntli] Adv. 目立つように

---

968 **response**
[rɪspɑ́:ns]

N[C/U] 対応、反応；返答、回答、応答

Thank you for your quick **response**.（迅速な回答ありがとうございます。）

in **response** (to sth)（（〜に）応じて）

▶ **respond** [rɪspɑ́:nd] V[I]（〜に）対応する、反応する (to sth)；（〜に）返答する (to sth)

How did the client **respond** to the proposal?
（お客さん、その提案に対してどういう反応だった？）

▶ **responsive** [rɪspɑ́:nsɪv] Adj.（〜に対して）対応が速い、反応が速い (to sth)

Sam is really **responsive** to messages.（サムはメッセージに対するレスが本当に速いんだ。）

▶ **responsiveness** ［rɪspáːnsɪvnəs］N[U] 対応の速さ、反応の速さ

---

969 **outlook**
［áʊtlʊk］

N[S]　（～の）先行き、見通し（for sth）

What's the employment **outlook** for Europe this year?
（今年のヨーロッパでの雇用はどんな見通し？）

N[C]　（物事に対する）見方、態度（on sth）

Having a positive **outlook** improves your health enormously.
（ポジティブな物事の見方を持っていると、健康状態がものすごい良くなるんだよ。）

---

970 **poor**
［pɔːr］

Adj. 貧困の、貧しい；（～が）乏しい（in sth）　N[P] 貧しい人々【the -】

Do you think the gap between the rich and **the poor** can't be helped, or is there something we can do to solve it?
（リッチな人と貧しい人のギャップって仕方ないのかな、それとも解決するためにできることがあるのかな？）

Japan is **poor** in natural resources, so its relationship with other countries is very critical.
（日本は天然資源に乏しいから、他国との関係がすごい重要なんだ。）

Adj. かわいそうな；（質や健康状態などが）悪い

Poor thing.（かわいそうに。）

▶ **poverty** ［páːvərţi］N[U] 貧困　N[S/U] 乏しいこと、欠如

■ live in **poverty**（貧しい暮らしをする）

When I was a student, my staple food was instant noodles because I was **living in** extreme **poverty**.（学生の時は極貧生活してたから、主食はインスタント・ラーメンだった。）

▶ **poorly** ［pɔ́ːrli］Adv. 下手に、ひどく、不十分に

This book was so **poorly** written that I couldn't keep reading after a few minutes.
（この本、わかりにくすぎて読んで数分でやめちゃった。）

---

971 **plague**
［pleɪg］

V[T]　を苦しめる、悩ます　N[C]　疫病、伝染病

My company is **plagued** by a lack of leadership.
（うちの会社はリーダーシップがなくて苦しんでるんだ。）

---

972 **recession**
［rɪséʃən］

N[C/U]　不況、不景気、景気後退

There hasn't been a **recession** in this country for a while. I hope it doesn't mean that the next one will be bad.
（この国はしばらく不況が来てないんだ。次来るのがひどいってことじゃなきゃいいけど。）

in **recession**（不況である）

▶ **recede** ［rɪsiːd］V[I]　（洪水などが）引く；（姿などが）遠くに消えていく

（感情や記憶が）薄れていく；（髪の生え際が）後退する

3 There was a realization that economic policies in isolation could not eliminate issues such as malnutrition, poverty, and lack of education, and that a more interdisciplinary approach with greater breadth was required to resolve them.

経済政策だけでは、栄養失調や貧困、教育不足といった問題を取り除くことができず、これらの問題を解決するには、より幅広く学際的なアプローチが必要であることが認識されたのだ。

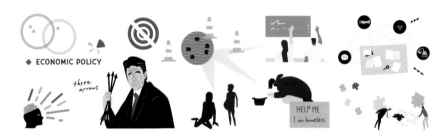

◆ ECONOMIC POLICY

three arrows

HELP ME I am homeless.

973 **realization**
[rì:ələzéɪʃən]
□□□□□□

N[S] 認識すること、気づくこと、悟ること

■ come to the **realization** that + sentence (〜だと悟る、気づく)

I finally **came to the realization that** spending more money on useless things isn't going to make me happy. (無駄なものにこれ以上お金を使っても自分は幸せになれないっていうついに気づいたよ。)

N[U] 実現；（資産の）現金化

▶ **realize** [rí:əlaɪz] V[T] に気づく、を理解している；を実現する

I've been making an effort to **realize** my dream of being a singer.
(歌手になる夢を実現するためにずっと努力してるんだ。)

▶ **realizable** [ríəlàɪzəbəl] Adj. 実現可能な

Financial independence is only **realizable** if you invest your time and money well when you're young. (若い時に時間とお金を上手に投資して初めて経済的自由を手に入れることができるんだ。)

▶ **realized** [rí:əlaɪzd] Adj. 実現された　⟷　**unrealized** [ʌ̀nrí:əlaɪzd] 未実現の

unrealized gains/losses (未実現利益 / 未実現損失)

974 **policy**
[pá:ləsi]
□□□□□□

N[C/U] 政策、方針；（個人の）主義、ポリシー　**N[C]** 保険証券

I wonder why our company has a **policy** that says employees can't have relationships with colleagues. (なんでうちの会社って、従業員が同僚と付き合っちゃいけないっていう方針があるんだろう。)

■ an insurance **policy** (万が一の保険)

I broke up with my girlfriend because I felt like I was just **an insurance policy** for her.
(自分がただの万が一の保険にされてるような気がしたから、彼女とは別れたよ。)

975 **isolation**
[àɪsəléɪʃən]
□□□□□□

N[U] 分離、孤立、隔離；孤独感

I enjoyed traveling across the Sahara Desert by myself, but the **isolation** got to me after a while. (一人でサハラ砂漠横断の旅して楽しかったんだけど、しばらくしてから孤独感に襲われたよ。)

in **isolation**（それだけで、他と切り離して、孤立して）

▶ **isolate** [áɪsəleɪt] V[T] を分離する、孤立させる

Why did the Tokugawa Shogunate try so hard to **isolate** Japan from the outside world?
（徳川幕府はどうしてあんなに頑張って日本を鎖国しようとしたの？）

▶ **isolated** [áɪsəleɪt̬ɪd] Adj. 孤立した、単独の；孤独な

I often feel **isolated** from other people.（よく自分が周りから孤立してるなぁって感じるんだ。）

---

976 **eliminate**
[ɪlíməneɪt]
☐☐☐☐☐☐

V[T] を取り除く；（チームや選手）を**敗退させる**；（敵など）を**抹殺する**

Relaxing in a stone sauna is one way I **eliminate** stress.
（岩盤浴でリラックスすることは私のストレス解消法の一つなんだ。）

▶ **elimination** [ɪlìmənéɪʃən] N[U] 除去、排除

---

977 **malnutrition**
[mæˈlnuːtríʃən]
☐☐☐☐☐☐

N[U] 栄養失調、栄養不良

I donate \$200 every month to children suffering from **malnutrition** around the world.
（私は栄養失調で苦しんでいる世界中の子供たちに毎月 200 ドル募金してるんだ。）

接頭語 mal-「悪い」という意味の接頭語で、悪い（= mal）栄養（= nutrition から）「栄養失調」という意味になります。他には malfunction（故障）や malaria（マラリア）、malicious（悪意のある）があります。

---

978 **breadth**
[bredθ]
☐☐☐☐☐☐

N[C/U] 幅、広がり

The **breadth** and depth of knowledge he has is just amazing.
（彼の持つ知識の幅と深さはただただ素晴らしいよ。）

---

979 **resolve**
[rɪzáːlv]
☐☐☐☐☐☐

V[T] を解決する；（〜しようと）**決心する**（to do/that + sentence）

If you have a problem with your neighbor, it's important to try to **resolve** it as soon as possible.
（もし近所の人と問題があったら、できるだけ早く解決しようとすることが重要だよ。）

▶ **resolution** [rèzəlúːʃən] N[S/U] 解決；解像度 N[U] 決意の固さ N[C] 決意、決心；決議

■ make a **resolution** (to do)（（〜しようと）決心する）

I've **made a resolution to** spend more time traveling overseas this year.
（今年は、もっと海外旅行に時間を使おうと決心したんだ。）

a New Year's **resolution**（新年の抱負）

4 The career prospects for graduates specializing in this area are similarly diverse. Many go on to careers in federal and municipal government, non-government organizations, development consulting firms, and educational institutions.

この分野で学位を取得した卒業生のキャリアの見通しも同じく多様で、多くは、連邦政府や地方自治体、非政府組織、開発コンサルティング会社、教育機関などのキャリアに進むことになる。

---

980 **career**
[kərír]

N[C] キャリア、仕事、経歴　Adj. キャリアの

I don't think there's anything wrong with changing **careers** many times because you only live once.（人生一回きりなんだし、別に何回もキャリアを変えても何の問題もないと思うよ。）

a **career** opportunity（キャリアの機会）　a **career** choice（キャリアの選択肢）

---

981 **prospect**
[prá:spekt]

N[P]　（仕事などの成功の）見通し【-s】

N[C/U]　可能性、見込み、展望　N[S]　予想

This player is definitely a great **prospect**, but it's going to be a few more years before he's the finished article.
（この選手がすごい有望なのは間違いないけど、完璧な選手になるにはあと数年必要だろうね。）

V[I]　（石油や金などを求めて）探査する（for sth）

▶ **prospective** Adj. 見込みのある、有望な　◀▶ **retrospective** 遡及的な
　[prəspéktɪv]　　　　　　　　　　　　　　　　　　[rètrəspéktɪv]

a **prospective** customer（見込みのある客）

▶ **prospectively** Adv. 先を見越して　◀▶ **retrospectively** 遡及的に、過去に遡って
　[prəspéktɪvli]　　　　　　　　　　　　　　　　　[rètrəspéktɪvli]

As a general rule, a law cannot be applied **retrospectively**.
（一般的に言って、法律は遡及して適用できないんだ。）

---

982 **graduate**
N./Adj. [grædʒuət]
V. [grædʒueɪt]

N[C]　卒業生　= **grad** [græd]

■ a new **graduate/grad**（新卒、新入社員）

He's **a new graduate**, so make sure you take plenty of time to coach him.
（彼はまだ新入社員だから、たっぷり時間を取ってコーチングしてあげてね。）

V[I/T] （～を）卒業する（from sth）

I **graduated** from university, but I don't remember what I studied at all.
（大学卒業したけど、何を勉強したか一切覚えてないよ。）

Adj. 大学院の　= grad [græd]

a **graduate/grad** school （大学院）

a **graduate/grad** student = a postgraduate < 英 > （大学院生）

▶ **graduation** [grædʒuéɪʃən] N[U] 卒業　N[C/U] 卒業式

---

983 **federal**
[fédərəl]
☐☐☐☐☐☐

Adj. 連邦の、連邦政府の

Should healthcare be a **federal** matter or managed locally?
（医療って連邦政府レベルの問題なのかな？それとも各地方で管理されるべき？）

the **federal** government （連邦政府）　　　**federal** laws （連邦法）

▶ **federation** [fèdəréɪʃən] N[C] 連邦、連合、連盟；連邦政府　N[U] 連邦化

---

984 **municipal**
[mju:nísəpəl]
☐☐☐☐☐☐

Adj. 地方自治の、市の

■ the **municipal** government （地方自治体（政府）、市政）

This report says job satisfaction among **municipal government** employees varies widely
depending on the region, but it doesn't explain why. （このレポートによると地方公務員の
仕事に対する満足度は地域によって大きく異なるらしいんだけど、それがなぜかは書いてないんだ。）

▶ **municipally** Adv. 地方自治体によって、市営で ▶ **municipality** N[C] 地方自治体
　[mju:nísəpəli]　　　　　　　　　　　　　　　　　　　　　[mju:nìsəpǽləti]

---

985 **government**
[gʌ́vərnmənt]
☐☐☐☐☐☐

N[C] 政府、政権　**N[U]** 行政（機構）、政治（体制）

The English level of Japanese people won't improve unless the **government** takes
action. （政府が行動を取らない限り、日本人の英語レベルが改善することはないよ。）

under the present **government** （現政権のもと）

▶ **governmental** [gʌ̀vərnméntl] Adj. 政府の

▶ **govern** [gʌ́vərn] V[I/T] （～を）統治する、治める；（～を）つかさどる、支配する

▶ **governance** [gʌ́vərnəns] N[U] 統治、（会社などの）ガバナンス

---

986 **consulting**
[kənsʌ́ltɪŋ]
☐☐☐☐☐☐

Adj. コンサルティングの、顧問の　**N[U]** コンサルティング業

I want to work at a **consulting** firm, but I'm a bit worried about the hours.
（コンサル会社で働きたいんだけど、ちょっと労働時間が心配なんだ。）

▶ **consult** V[I/T] （～に）相談する（with sb） ▶ **consultant** N[C] コンサルタント、顧問
　[kənsʌ́lt]　　　　　　　　　　　　　　　　　　　　　　[kənsʌ́ltənt]

Can I **consult** with my lawyer before I make a decision?
（決断する前に弁護士と相談してもいいですか？）

▶ **consultation** [kɑ:nsʌltéɪʃən] N[U] 助言　N[C/U] 協議　N[C] 診察

One of the most incredible economic developments of the last few decades is the rise of the Asian Tigers.

The Asian Tigers – made up of South Korea, Singapore, Taiwan, and Hong Kong – went through a virtually uninterrupted surge in economic growth between the 1960s and 1990s. This was marked by these countries posting average annual growth rates greater than 7 percent during this period. Hong Kong and Singapore are now world-leading financial hubs, while South Korea and Taiwan are renowned for their output of electronic devices.

While some believe that these countries owe their growth to minimal taxes and welfare, others at least partially credit government intervention with steering these nations around development obstacles. This was embodied by the Hong Kong government combatting, weathering, and eventually suppressing currency speculation during the perilous 1997 Asian financial crisis, which caused market crashes in other Asian countries and shattered their economies.

この数十年間における最も驚くべき経済成長の一つは「アジアの虎」の台頭だ。

韓国、シンガポール、台湾、香港から成るアジアの虎は、1960年代から1990年代にかけて、ほぼ途切れることなく急速に経済成長を遂げた。特に目立ったのは、これらの4地域がこの間に平均して7％を超える年間経済成長率を記録したことだ。そして今では香港とシンガポールは世界をリードする金融ハブとなり、韓国と台湾は電子機器の生産で有名である。

これらの国々の成長は、最小限の税金と福祉のおかげだと考える人もいるが、発展上の障害を回避できたのは、少なくとも部分的には政府介入の功績であるという人もいる。こうした見方は、大変危険な状態にあった1997年のアジア通貨危機のさなか、通貨投機と闘い、危機を切り抜け、最終的には抑制した香港政府によって具現化された。アジア通貨危機によって、アジアのそれ以外の地域や国々では株式市場が暴落し、経済は壊滅的な打撃を受けた。

987 **uninterrupted**
[ʌnìntərʌ́ptɪd]

Adj. 途切れない、中断なしの、連続した

▶ **uninterruptedly** [ʌnìntərʌ́ptɪdli] Adv. 途切れることなく

▶ **interrupt** [ìntərʌ́pt] V[T] を中断させる　V[I/T]（〜に）口を挟む

▶ **interruption** [ìntərʌ́pʃən] N[C/U] 妨害、中断

988 **surge**
[sɜːrdʒ]

N[C] 急増、殺到　V[I] 急増する、殺到する

a **surge** of anger（こみ上げる怒り）　a **surge** in stock prices（株価の急騰）

989 **mark**
[mɑːrk]

V[T] を目立たせる、特色づける；を示す　V[I/T]（〜に）印をつける

▶ **marked** [mɑːrkt] Adj. 著しい　▶ **markedly** [mɑ́ːrkɪdli] Adv. 著しく

990 **post**
[poʊst]

V[T]（利益や成長など）を記録する、計上する

（動画や記事）を投稿する、掲載する、掲示する

N[C]（ネットの）投稿；柱；職、地位

991 **average**
[ǽvərɪdʒ]

Adj. 平均の、平均的な　N[C] 平均　V[T] 平均〜になる、の平均値を求める

on **average**（平均で）

▶ **average out** [ǽvərɪdʒáʊt] [PV] 平均値に落ち着く

992 **hub**
[hʌb]

N[C] 中心地、拠点；（車輪の）ハブ

Paris is known as the fashion **hub** of the world.
（パリは世界的なファッションの中心地として知られている。）

993 **output**
[áʊtpʊt]

N[C/U] 生産、生産高

N[U] アウトプット、出力　V[T] を出力する、アウトプットする

↔ **input** [ìnpʊt] インプット / を入力する、インプットする

994 **electronic**
[ilèktrɑ́ːnɪk]

Adj. 電子の

an **electronic** device（電子機器）

▶ **electronically** [ilèktrɑ́ːnɪkli] Adv. 電子的に

995 **owe**
[oʊ]

V[T] は（〜の）おかげである (to sth/sb)　= owe A B（B は A のおかげである）

に（〜の）借りがある (to sb)　= owe A B（A に B の借りがある）

▶ **owing** [óʊɪŋ] Adj. 借りたままの

996 **partially**
[pɑ́ːrʃəli]

Adv. 部分的に　= **partly** [pɑ́ːrtli]

▶ **partial** [pɑ́ːrʃəl] Adj. 部分的な；不公平な　↔ **impartial** [ɪmpɑ́ːrʃəl] 公平な

▶ **partiality** [pɑ̀ːrʃiǽləti] N[U] 不公平　↔ **impartiality** [ɪmpɑ̀ːrʃiǽləti] 公平

997 credit
[krédɪt]
☐☐☐☐☐☐

V[T] を信用する；を入金する　N[U] 信用；功績　N[C] 履修単位

credit sb (with sth)（が〜の功績があることを) 信じる、認める)

■ give **credit** (to sb)（(功績を認めて〜を) ほめる)

You should **give credit to** Kathy for doing a great job.
(君は最高の仕事をしたキャシーをほめるべきだよ。)

---

998 steer
[stɪr]
☐☐☐☐☐☐

V[I/T]（〜を) 操縦する、運転する

steer sth/sb around sth（〜に〜を回避させる)

▶ **steering wheel** [stírɪŋ wi:l] N[C] (自動車の) ハンドル　= the wheel [ðəwí:l]

---

999 obstacle
[ά:bstəkəl]
☐☐☐☐☐☐

N[C] 妨げ、障害、障害物

overcome **obstacles**（障害を乗り越える)

1000 embody
[ɪmbá:di]
☐☐☐☐☐☐

V[T] を具現化する、体現する

▶ **embodiment** [ɪmbá:dimənt] N[U] 具現化；化身

1001 combat
V1./N. [kά:mbæt]
V2. [kəmbét]
☐☐☐☐☐☐

V[T] と戦う、に対抗する　N[C/U] 戦闘、戦い

▶ **combative** [kəmbætɪv] Adj. 好戦的な

▶ **combatively** [kəmbætɪvli] Adv. 好戦的に

1002 weather
[wéðər]
☐☐☐☐☐☐

V[T] を切り抜ける、乗り切る　N[U] 天気、天候

What's the **weather** like?（天気はどんな感じ？)　= How's the weather?

V[I] 変色する　V[T] を変色させる

1003 suppress
[səprés]
☐☐☐☐☐☐

V[T] を抑制する、鎮圧する

She's using diet pills to **suppress** her appetite.
(彼女は食欲を抑えるためにダイエットの薬飲んでるんだ。)

▶ **suppressed** [səprést] Adj. (感情などを) 抑えた　▶ **suppression** [səpréʃən] N[U] 抑制、鎮圧

1004 perilous
[pérələs]
☐☐☐☐☐☐

Adj. 危険の多い、非常に危険な

▶ **perilously** [pérələsli] Adv. 危険なほど　▶ **peril** [pérəl] N[C/U] 危険

1005 crash
[kræʃ]
☐☐☐☐☐☐

N[C] (株式市場の) 暴落；衝突、墜落

V[I] (市場が) 暴落する；衝突する；(人の家で) 寝る　V[T] をぶつける

Can I **crash** at your place tonight?（今晩家に泊まってもいい？)

1006 shatter
[ʃætər]
☐☐☐☐☐☐

V[T] を壊滅させる、打ち砕く、粉々にする　V[I] 粉々になる

▶ **shattered** [ʃætərd] Adj. 衝撃を受けた、ショックを受けた；粉々に砕けた

▶ **shattering** [ʃætərɪŋ] Adj. 衝撃的な、ショッキングな

⟲ CH. 2, 7, 11, 15, 18, 21

Chapter

22

戦争
Warfare

What constitutes a "just" war has been debated for thousands of years. Some assert that warfare is never justified in any scenario, while others, believing there are certain situations where it is undeniably warranted, reject this view.

Opponents of warfare under any circumstance typically argue that war is expensive and traumatic and causes unnecessary loss of life, so it must be avoided. They also claim it leads to social issues such as internally displaced people and refugees.

On the other hand, those of the opinion that war can be justified often cite provocation, infringement of a country's sovereignty, and another country abusing its power to commit crimes against its own citizens as just causes to wage war.

Both sides generally agree that there are rules and codes of ethics that should not be violated in times of war, such as bans on violence against civilians and vulnerable populations, including the elderly, injured, and sick.

1

What constitutes a "just" war has been debated for thousands of years. Some assert that warfare is never justified in any scenario, while others, believing there are certain situations where it is undeniably warranted, reject this view.

「正当な」戦争とは何を指すのかは何千年にもわたり議論されてきた。どのようなシナリオであっても戦争が正当化されることはないという意見もあれば、特定の状況によっては間違いなく正当化されるとして、その考えを否定する見方もある。

A "JUST" WAR?

1007 **war**

[wɔːr]

N[C/U] 戦争、闘争、戦い

What's the best way to win an armrest **war** when I'm sitting in the middle seat on a plane?
（飛行機で真ん中の席に座ってる時に肘掛けの取り合いに勝つ一番良い方法は何かな？）

declare **war** (on sth)（(〜に) 宣戦布告する）　　win/lose a **war**（戦争に勝つ / 負ける）

■ a tug of **war**（綱引き）

I think a relationship is like **a game of tug of war**.
（人間関係って綱引きゲームみたいなものだと思うんだよなぁ。）

▶ **warfare** [wɔ́ːrfer] N[U] 戦争、戦争行為、戦争状態

▶ **warrior** [wɔ́ːriər] N[C] 戦士、武士　　▶ **warring** [wɔ́ːrɪŋ] Adj. 交戦中の

warring countries（交戦中の国々）

war vs **warfare**　どちらも戦争という意味で使われることのある表現ですが、war は一般的な戦争を意味するのに対し、warfare はより具体的に戦争行為や戦争状態を表すことがあります。また、その具体的なイメージから、特定の兵器を使う戦争を表すときにもよく使われる傾向にあります（例：chemical warfare ＝化学兵器を使った戦争）。

1008 **justified**

[dʒʌ́stəfaɪd]

Adj. 正当化された

I know he was pretty rude to you, but I don't think slapping him was **justified**.
（彼がかなり失礼だったのは分かるけど、だからといって彼にビンタしたことを正当化できるわけじゃないと思う。）

▶ **justify** [dʒʌ́stəfaɪ] V[T] を正当化する　　▶ **just** [dʒʌst] Adj. 正しい、公平な

Don't try to **justify** every mistake you make.（自分のミスを全部正当化しようとしないで。）

▶ **justification** [dʒʌ̀stəfəkéɪʃən] N[C/U] 正当な理由

1009 **scenario**

[sənériou]

N[C] シナリオ、事態；脚本

I think experience and knowledge are the only textbooks that teach you how to draw a success **scenario** for your business.

（経験と知識こそがビジネス成功のシナリオを描く方法を教えてくれる唯一の教科書だと、私は思うよ。）

a worst case **scenario**（最悪のケース）

1010 **certain**
[sɜ́ːr̹tn̹]
☐☐☐☐☐☐

Adj. 特定の、ある一定の；（〜するのが）確実な、避けられない（to do）（〜を）確信している（of/about sth, that + sentence）

I'm **certain** that everything will be okay in the end.
（最終的にはきっと全部何とかなると確信してるよ。）

↔ **uncertain** [ʌnsɜ́ːr̹tn̹] 不確かな；確信がない

▶ **certainly** [sɜ́ːr̹tn̹li] Adv. 確かに、確実に；もちろん

▶ **certainty** N[C] 確実なこと　N[U] 確実性、確信　↔ **uncertainty** 不確実性
[sɜ́ːr̹tn̹ti]　　　　　　　　　　　　　　　　　　　　[ʌnsɜ́ːr̹tn̹ti]

I can't predict the score with **certainty**, but I'm fairly sure our team will win pretty easily.
（確実にスコアを予想するのは無理だけど、うちのチームが結構余裕で勝つのはほぼ間違いないと思う。）

1011 **undeniably**
[ʌndɪnáɪəbli]
☐☐☐☐☐☐

Adv. 間違いなく、確実に、紛れもなく

I admit he's **undeniably** charismatic, but to be honest with you, I don't really understand what he's trying to say half the time.
（彼が紛れもないカリスマだってことは認めるけど、正直、彼の言いたいことって半分くらいしか分からない。）

▶ **undeniable** [ʌndɪnáɪəbəl] Adj. 否定できない　↔ **deniable** [dɪnáɪəbəl] 否定できる

▶ **deny** [dɪnáɪ] V[T] を否定する、否認する、拒否する　▶ **denial** [dɪnáɪəl] N[C/U] 否定、否認

■ there's no **denying** sth/that + sentence（〜は否定できない、明らかだ）

There's no denying that this shirt is good quality, but it's a bit too pricey.
（このシャツの品質が良いのは明らかだけど、ちょっと高すぎるな。）

■ in **denial**（about sth）（（現実など）を受け入れられない）

He's still **in denial about** the break-up with his ex-girlfriend.
（彼は元カノとの別れをまだ受け入れられてないんだ。）

1012 **warranted**
[wɔ́ːrəntɪd]
☐☐☐☐☐☐

Adj. 正当な

Do you think capital punishment for littering is **warranted**?（ポイ捨てで死刑って正当だと思う？）

▶ **warrant** [wɔ́ːrənt] V[T] を正当化する；を保証する　N[C] 認可書；（捜索などの）令状

This movie definitely **warrants** a second viewing.（この映画はリピート確実だね。）

▶ **warranty** [wɔ́ːrənti] N[C/U] 保証、保証書

I paid an extra $200 for a three-year **warranty**.　　under **warranty**
（3年保証にするために追加で200ドル払ったよ。）　　（保証期間中の）

1013 **reject**
[rɪdʒékt]
☐☐☐☐☐☐

V[T] を否定する、拒絶する、断る

What should I do if I still love a boy who **has rejected** me before?
（前に断られてるのにその男の子のことがまだ好きな場合どうすればいいかな？）

▶ **rejection** [rɪdʒékʃən] N[C/U] 否定、拒絶、拒否、却下

2 **Opponents of warfare under any circumstance typically argue that war is
expensive and traumatic and causes unnecessary loss of life, so it must be
avoided. They also claim it leads to social issues such as internally displaced
people and refugees.**

戦争はどのような状況でも回避しなければならないとする人たちは、一般的に、戦争が高くつくことや、深い
傷を残すこと、そして人命が無駄に失われることをその理由に挙げている。そして、国内避難民や難民を生む
などの社会問題を招くということも主張している。

1014 expensive
[ɪkspénsɪv]
□□□□□□

Adj. （値段が）高い、高価な　= **pricey** [práɪsi]

Studying in the U.S. is very **expensive**, but there are a lot of scholarships you can apply for.
（アメリカで勉強するのはすごいお金がかかるけど、君が応募できる奨学金はたくさんあるよ。）

▶ **expensively** [ɪkspénsɪvli] Adv. 高いお金をかけて

▶ **expense** [ɪkspéns] N[C/U] 費用、支出　N[P] 経費【-s】

▶ **expend** [ɪkspénd] V[T] （時間・努力・お金など）を費やす

■ **at sb's expense** （〜の費用で、〜をだしにして）

John's jokes are always **at somebody's expense**.（ジョンはいつも人をだしにして笑いを取るんだ。）

▶ **expendable** Adj. 消耗品の、使い捨ての　　▶ **expenditure** N[C/U] 支出
　[ɪkspéndəbəl]　　　　　　　　　　　　　　　　　[ɪkspéndətʃər]

1015 traumatic
[trɑːmǽt̬ɪk]
□□□□□□

Adj. 心に傷を残すような、トラウマになる

My parents' divorce was a **traumatic** event for me, but I'm coping okay now.
（うちの両親が離婚したのは自分にとってトラウマになるような出来事だったけど、今はなんとか大丈夫。）

▶ **traumatically** Adv. 心に傷を負わせる形で　▶ **trauma** N[C/U] 心の傷、トラウマ
　[trɑːmǽt̬ɪkli]　　　　　　　　　　　　　　　　[trɑ́ːmə]

▶ **traumatize** V[T] にトラウマを負わせる　▶ **traumatized** Adj. トラウマを負った
　[trɑ́ːmətaɪz]　　　　　　　　　　　　　　　[trɑ́ːmətaɪzd]

1016 loss
[lɑːs]
□□□□□□

N[C/U] 失うこと、喪失、紛失；死、死去　**N[C]** （経済的な）損失

I'm very sorry for your **loss**.（お悔やみを申し上げます。）　**loss** of life（人命の喪失）

Your departure is going to be a great **loss** for the company, but as a friend, I wish you all
the best at your next job.

（君が辞めることは会社にとって大きな損失だけど、友達として、君が次の仕事で上手くいくことを願ってるよ。）

▶ **lose** [luːz] V[T] をなくす、失う；(体重) を減らす V[I/T]（試合などに）負ける

I don't know how, but I managed to **lose** both of my socks in the wash over the weekend.
（週末になぜか洗濯中に靴下両方失くしちゃったんだ。）

▶ **loser** [lúːzər] N[C] 敗者、負け犬、ダメ男 / 女

Why is she dating a **loser** like him?（あの子、なんで彼みたいなダメ男と付き合ってるの？）

1017 **avoid**
[əvɔ́ɪd]

V[T] を回避する、（〜することを）避ける (doing)

I'm trying to **avoid** my ex, but it's pretty hard since we work on the same floor.
（元カレのこと避けようとしてるんだけど、同じ階で働いてるから結構難しいんだよね。）

▶ **avoidance** [əvɔ́ɪdəns] N[U] 回避、避けること

▶ **avoidable** Adj. 回避できる、避けられる   ↔ **unavoidable** 避けられない
[əvɔ́ɪdəbəl]   [ʌnəvɔ́ɪdəbəl]

Most car accidents are entirely **avoidable**.（だいたいの車の事故は完全に避けられるものなんだ。）

1018 **internally**
[ɪntɜ́ːrnəli]

Adv. 内部で、内側で、体内で

We'll discuss this **internally** and get back to you.（これに関しては内部で話してからまた連絡しますね。）

The lecture was so boring that I was **internally** screaming.
（講義がつまんな過ぎて心の中で悲鳴を上げてたよ。）

↔ **externally** [ɪkstɜ́ːrnəli] 外部から、外面的に、対外的に

▶ **internal** Adj. 内部の、（心や身体の）内側にある   ↔ **external** 外部の、外付けの
[ɪntɜ́ːrnl]   [ɪkstɜ́ːrnl]

an **external** device （外付けデバイス）

1019 **displaced**
[dɪspléɪst]

Adj. 住む場所を奪われた、追放された

Thankfully, even though thousands of people were **displaced** by the tsunami, no lives
were lost.（何千もの人が津波によって住む場所を奪われたんだけど、幸い死者は出なかったんだ。）

internally **displaced** people （国内避難民（= IDPs））

▶ **displace** [dɪspléɪs] V[T] を強制的に立ち退かせる；に取って代わる

1020 **refugee**
[rèfjədʒíː]

N[C] 難民

My parents came to this country as **refugees** and managed to make a life for themselves.
（私の両親はこの国に難民として来て、それからなんとか自力で生活できるようになったんだ。）

▶ **refuge** [réfjuːdʒ] N[C] 避難所、保護施設、（野生動物などの）保護区 N[U] 避難

seek/take **refuge** （避難する）

refugees vs **internally displaced people** refugees（難民）は人種や国籍、宗教などの理由により迫害を受けることを恐れて国外に避難した人のことを指す表現です。一方、internally displaced people（国内避難民）は同様の理由により居住地を離れながらも、国外には逃げていない人たちのことを指します。

3 On the other hand, those of the opinion that war can be justified often cite provocation, infringement of a country's sovereignty, and another country abusing its power to commit crimes against its own citizens as just causes to wage war.

一方で、戦争は正当化され得るとする人たちはよく相手国からの挑発行為や国家主権の侵害、そして相手国が権力乱用によって自国民に罪を犯した場合などを、宣戦布告の大義名分として挙げている。

1021 **cite**
[saɪt]
☐☐☐☐☐☐

V[T] を（～として）挙げる、引用する（as sth）；を表彰する

It sucks that my report was turned down just because I forgot to **cite** references.
（参考文献の引用忘れただけで私のレポート却下されたんだけど。最悪。）

▶ **citation** [saɪtéɪʃən] N[U] 引用　N[C] 引用文；表彰（状）

1022 **provocation**
[prɑ̀:vəkéɪʃən]
☐☐☐☐☐☐

N[C/U] 挑発行為、挑発

He loses control at the slightest **provocation**.
（あいつってちょっと挑発されただけで自分のコントロールが効かなくなるんだよね。）

▶ **provoke** [prəvóuk] V[T] を挑発する、怒らせる；(感情や反応など) を引き起こす

This guy is always trying to **provoke** people on Twitter.
（この人いつもツイッターで人のこと挑発してるんだよ。）

▶ **provocative** [prəvɑ́:kəṭɪv] Adj. 挑発的な；(性的に) そそるような

▶ **provocatively** [prəvɑ́:kəṭɪvli] Adv. 挑発的に

1023 **infringement**
[ɪnfrínʤmənt]
☐☐☐☐☐☐

N[C/U] （～の）侵害、違反（of sth）

Uploading someone's LINE conversation onto Twitter is a complete **infringement** of their privacy, isn't it?　（人のLINEの会話をツイッターに上げるとか完全にプライバシーの侵害じゃない？）

copyright/patent **infringement**（著作権 / 特許権侵害）

▶ **infringe** [ɪnfrínʤ] V[T] を侵害する　V[I]（～を）侵害する（on/upon sth）

I didn't mean to **infringe** on copyright.（著作権を侵害するつもりはなかったんだ。）

1024 **abuse**
v. [əbjú:z]
N. [əbjú:s]
☐☐☐☐☐☐

V[T] を乱用する、悪用する；を虐待する；を罵る

N[C/U] 乱用、悪用；虐待　N[U] 悪い言葉、暴言

Isn't getting your secretary to pick up your dry cleaning an **abuse** of power?

（秘書にドライクリーニング取ってきてもらうのって、職権の乱用じゃないのかな？）

▶ **abusive** [əbjúːsɪv] Adj. 乱用された、悪用された；虐待的な；口の悪い

abusive words（ひどい言葉）

▶ **abuser** [əbjúːzər] N[C] 乱用者；虐待者

1025 **commit**
[kəmít]
□□□□□□

V[T] を犯す

■ **commit** a crime（犯罪を犯す）　　**commit** murder/suicide（殺人を犯す / 自殺する）

It's not like I **committed a crime** or something, so I don't know why she's so mad at me.
（別に犯罪を犯したわけでもないのに、なんで彼女が私にあんなに怒ってるのか分からないよ。）

V[T] に（～を）約束させる、を（～に）捧げる（to sth）

If you really want to pass the exam, you have to **commit** yourself to studying.
（本当に試験に合格したいなら、全力で勉強しないとね。）

V[I] （～を）約束する、（～に）本気で取り組む（to sth）

▶ **commitment** N[C/U] 約束、（責任などを伴う）やらないといけないこと
[kəmítmənt]　　N[U] コミットメント、献身

I have a lot of work **commitments** today.（今日仕事でやらないといけないことがたくさんあるんだ。）

■ make a **commitment** (to do)（（～すると）約束する、誓う）

He **made a commitment** not **to** touch his smartphone until he's done with the test, so he won't reply back anytime soon.
（彼はテストが終わるまでスマホに触らないって誓ったから、すぐには返信来ないと思うよ。）

▶ **committed** [kəmítɪd] Adj.（～に）献身的な、本気な（to sth）

You'll never find somebody more **committed** to the team than me.
（私以上にチームに献身的な人はきっと見つからないよ。）

The thought that my boyfriend may not be **committed** to our relationship is worrying me.
（もしかしたら彼氏が私たちの関係に本気じゃないんじゃないかって思ってずっと心配なんだよね。）

1026 **citizen**
[sítəzən]
□□□□□□

N[C] 国民、市民

Do you want to be a Canadian **citizen**, or just a permanent resident?
（カナダ人になりたいのか、ただ永住者になりたいのか、どっち？）

▶ **citizenship** [sítəzənʃɪp] N[U] 市民権　　Japanese **citizenship**（日本の市民権）

1027 **wage**
[weɪdʒ]
□□□□□□

V[T] （戦争や反対運動）を行う、を遂行する　　**N[C]** 賃金

■ **wage** (a) war (on/against sth)（（～に対して）戦争をする、宣戦布告する、解決に向けて取り組む）

The convenience store chain has decided to **wage a war on** waste by offering food that is close to expiration to homeless people.
（そのコンビニチェーンは食品ロスの解決に取り組むために消費期限切れ間近の食品をホームレスにあげることを決めたんだ。）

an hourly **wage**（時給）　　an average **wage**（平均賃金）

4 Both sides generally agree that there are rules and codes of ethics that should not be violated in times of war, such as bans on violence against civilians and vulnerable populations, including the elderly, injured, and sick.

どちらの意見でも概ね一致するのは、戦時下では一般市民や高齢者、負傷者、病人などを含む弱者に対する暴力行為の禁止など、侵害されるべきではないルールや倫理規定が存在するという点だ。

1028 rule
[ru:l]
☐☐☐☐☐☐

N[C]　ルール、規則

I generally obey the **rules** unless they don't make sense.
（不合理でない限りは、自分は基本的にルールには従うよ。）

a **rule** of thumb（目安、経験則）　　ground **rules**（基本的なルール）

N[U]　支配、統治　V[I/T]　（〜を）支配する、統治する

Do you think robots will **rule** the world in the future?
（将来ロボットが世界を支配することになると思う？）

▶ **ruler** [rú:lər] N[C] 支配者、統治者；定規

1029 violate
[váɪəleɪt]
☐☐☐☐☐☐

V[T]　を侵害する、に違反する

I hate how Tom **violates** my personal space all the time.
（トムがいつもわたしのパーソナルスペースを侵害してくるから嫌なんだけど。）

▶ **violation** N[C/U] 侵害、違反　　▶ **violator** N[C] 違反者
　[vàɪəléɪʃən]　　　　　　　　　　　　[váɪəleɪtər]

■ in **violation** of sth（〜を侵害して、〜に違反して）

If you quit, you'll be **in violation of** our agreement.
（辞めたら契約違反になりますよ。）

1030 civilian
[səvíljən]
☐☐☐☐☐☐

N[C]　一般市民　Adj.　一般市民の、一般人の

The main responsibility of the police is to protect **civilians**.
（警察の主な責任は一般市民を守ることだ。）　　▶ **civic** [sívɪk] Adj. 市の、都市の

▶ **civil** [sívəl] Adj. 市民の、民間の、民事の

▶ **civilize** [sívəlaɪz] V[T] を文明化する、近代化する

▶ **civilization** [sɪvələzéɪʃən] N[C/U]（特定の地域や時代の）文明　N[U] 文明、文明化

the Egyptian **civilization**（エジプト文明）

1031 **vulnerable**
[vʌlnərəbəl]
☐☐☐☐☐☐

Adj.（～に対して）弱い、傷つきやすい、脆弱な（to sth/sb）

Personally, I find boys who show their **vulnerable** side more attractive.
（個人的に、弱い面を見せてくれる男の子の方が魅力的に感じるんだ。）

▶ **vulnerability** [vʌlnərəbiləţi] N[U] 弱さ、脆弱性　N[C]（個々の）脆弱性

We need to make sure that we minimize **vulnerabilities** in our software.
（ソフトウェアの脆弱性を最小限にしないといけないね。）

1032 **elderly**
[éldərli]
☐☐☐☐☐☐

N[P] 高齢者【the -】　**Adj.** 年配の、年をとった

Don't you think **elderly** people these days are much healthier than they were 50 years ago?
（最近のお年寄りって 50 年前と比べてずっと健康だと思わない？）

▶ **elder** [éldər] N[C] お年寄り　Adj. 年配の、年上の

1033 **injured**
[índʒərd]
☐☐☐☐☐☐

N[P] 負傷者【the -】　**Adj.** 負傷した、けがをした

We have a lot of **injured** players on our team, but our performance hasn't been that bad so far.
（うちのチームはけがしてる選手が多いんだけど、これまでパフォーマンスはそんなに悪くないんだ。）

▶ **injure** [índʒər] V[T] にけがをさせる、を傷つける

Be careful not to **injure** yourself when you're using that chainsaw.
（そのチェーンソー使ってる時、けがしないように気を付けてね。）

▶ **injury** [índʒəri] N[C/U] けが、負傷

Make sure you stretch before exercising to prevent **injury**.
（けががしないように運動の前はちゃんとストレッチしてね。）

It looks like a nasty **injury**, but it's not too painful.（ひどいけがに見えるけど、そんなに痛くはないよ。）

injured vs **hurt**　どちらも「傷ついた」という意味で使うことのできる表現ですが、injured は基本的に事故やスポーツなどで物理的な身体のけがを負ったときに使う表現である一方、hurt はひどいことを言われた時などに感じる精神的な苦痛にも使えます。また、injured の方が hurt よりも重傷であるイメージが伴います。

1034 **sick**
[sɪk]
☐☐☐☐☐☐

N[P] 病人【the -】　**Adj.** 病気の、体調の悪い；うんざりした；カッコいい

I feel a bit **sick** today, so I'll work from home.（今日はちょっと体調が悪いので、家から仕事します。）

■ **sick** of sth/sb（～にうんざりした、飽きた）

I'm pretty **sick of** Sophie's negative attitude.
（ソフィーのネガティブな態度にはもううんざりしてる。）

▶ **sickness** [síknəs] N[U] 病気、吐き気　N[C]（特定の）病気

Student (W)　There's been an **obvious** increase in proliferation of **weapons**, **tyranny**, and **protests** and **riots** around the world over the last few years, which leads me to **conclude** that a full-scale war is **inevitable**. Where do you predict the next major war will happen?

Guest Speaker (M)　Given that we live in such a chaotic political **landscape**, I think it's really hard to **anticipate** where or when the next big war is going to **break out** with any real precision.

Student (W)　What do you think will cause the next major conflict? There are **hypotheses** that it could be due to a new **nuclear arms race** or a competition to colonize space, but what's your opinion?

Guest Speaker (M)　I'm certain that the next major **hostilities** will be over natural resources. They're becoming increasingly vital, but **diminishing** at a rapid pace, so less **affluent** countries will have **incentives** to **resort** to violence to get them. **Diplomatic** solutions such as economic **sanctions** are unlikely to be effective in these situations.

生徒 (女性)　ここ数年で、兵器の拡散、暴政、そして抗議デモや暴動が世界中で明らかに増えてきていて、それを踏まえて、私自身、大規模な戦争は避けられないという結論に達しています。次の大規模な戦争はどこで起きると予想していますか？

ゲストスピーカー (男性)　私たちはこれだけ混沌とした政治情勢の中にいるわけですし、どこでいつ次の大きな戦争が起きるのかを的確に予測することは、とても難しいと思います。

生徒 (女性)　では、何が次の大規模な争いを引き起こすと思いますか？新たな核軍備競争や、宇宙空間獲得競争が原因になり得るという仮説もあります。何か意見はありますか？

ゲストスピーカー (男性)　次の戦いは確実に天然資源をめぐるものになると思います。天然資源はますます不可欠なものになっていますが、ものすごいスピードで減少しています。なので、貧しい国々には、暴力をふるってでもそれを手に入れようとするインセンティブがあるでしょうね。経済制裁のような外交的な解決策がそうした状況で効果を発揮する可能性も低いですね。

1035 **obvious**
[á:bviəs]

Adj. 明らかな、明白な

▶ **obviously** [á:bviəsli] Adv. 明らかに　▶ **obviousness** [á:bviəsnəs] N[U] 明らかさ

If you're on a diet, the peanut butter donut you're eating now is **obviously** not a good choice.（ダイエット中なら、その今食べてるピーナッツバタードーナッツは明らかに間違ってると思う。）

1036 **weapon**
[wépən]

N[C] 兵器、武器

nuclear/chemical **weapons**（核 / 化学兵器）

1037 **tyranny**
[tírəni]

N[C/U] 暴政、専制政治

▶ **tyrant** [táɪrənt] N[C] 暴君、君主　▶ **tyrannical** [tɪrǽnɪkəl] Adj. 専制的な

1038 **protest**
N./V1. [próutest]
V2. [prətést]

N[C] 抗議デモ　**N[C/U]** 抗議、異議

V[I/T]（〜に）抗議する、異議を唱える（against sth/sb）

▶ **protester** [prətéstər] N[C] 抗議をする人

1039 **riot**
[ráɪət]

N[C] 暴動　**V[I]** 暴動を起こす

▶ **rioter** [ráɪətər] N[C] 暴徒　▶ **riotous** [ráɪətəs] Adj. 暴動の

1040 **conclude**
[kənklú:d]

V[T]（〜という）結論に至る（that + sentence）；（条約など）を締結する

V[I/T]（〜を）締めくくる

▶ **conclusion** [kənklú:ʒən] N[C] 結論；締結、終結

▶ **conclusive** [kənklú:sɪv] Adj. 決定的な

come to the **conclusion** that + sentence（〜という結論に達する）

1041 **inevitable**
[ìnévətəbəl]

Adj. 避けられない、不可避の

▶ **inevitability** [ɪnèvətəbíləti] N[U] 不可避、必然性　N[C] 不可避なこと

▶ **inevitably** [ɪnévətəbli] Adv. 必然的に

1042 **landscape**
[lǽndskeɪp]

N[C]（政治や社会の）状況；景色、風景、風景画　**V[T]** の景観を整える

the political/social **landscape**（政治的 / 社会的状況）

1043 **anticipate**
[æntísəpeɪt]

V[T] を予測する、予想する、予期する

I didn't **anticipate** my post would get so many likes.
（自分の投稿がそんなにいいねされるとは思わなかったよ。）

▶ **anticipation** [æntìsəpéɪʃən] N[U] 予想、期待

1044 **break out**
[bréɪkáʊt]

[PV]（戦争や病気が）起きる、発生する、勃発する

▶ **breakout** [bréɪkaʊt] N[C] 脱獄、脱走

1045 hypothesis
[haɪpá:θəsɪs]

N[C] 仮説

▶ **hypothetical** [hàɪpəθéṭɪkəl] Adj. 仮定の

▶ **hypothetically** [hàɪpəθéṭɪkli] Adv. 仮定の話として

1046 nuclear
[nú:kliːər]

Adj. 核の、原子力の

a **nuclear** reactor（原子炉） **nuclear** power（原子力）

1047 arms
[ɑːrmz]

N[P] 武器、兵器

▶ **armed** [ɑːrmd] Adj. 武装した ▶ **army** [ɑːrmi] N[U] 陸軍【the -】 N[C] 軍隊

1048 race
[reɪs]

N[C] 競争；競走、レース；人種

▶ **racial** [réɪʃəl] Adj. 人種の ▶ **racially** [réɪʃəli] Adv. 人種的に

▶ **racist** [réɪsɪst] N[C] 人種差別主義者 Adj. 人種差別的な

1049 hostility
[hɑːstíləṭi]

N[U] 敵意、反感

▶ **hostilities** [hɑːstíləṭiz] N[P] 争い、戦闘

▶ **hostile** [hɑ́ːstəl] Adj. 敵意のある、敵対する ◀▶ **friendly** [fréndli]

1050 diminish
[dɪmíniʃ]

V[I] 減少する、減る V[T] を減少させる、減らす；（評判など）を傷つける

▶ **diminished** [dɪmíniʃt] Adj. 減少した

1051 affluent
[ǽfluənt]

Adj. 豊かな、裕福な；豊富な

▶ **affluence** [ǽfluəns] N[U] 裕福さ、豊かさ

1052 incentive
[ɪnséntɪv]

N[C/U] インセンティブ、刺激、動機

give/have an **incentive** to do（〜するインセンティブを与える / がある）

▶ **incentivize** [ɪnséntəvaɪz] V[T] に動機を与える、インセンティブを与える

1053 resort
[rɪzɔ́ːrt]

V[I]（〜に）頼る、（〜を）当てにする（to sth） N[C] リゾート

resort to violence（暴力をふるう）

1054 diplomatic
[dìpləmǽṭɪk]

Adj. 外交的な、外交の

▶ **diplomat** [dípləmæt] N[C] 外交官 ▶ **diplomacy** [dɪplóʊməsi] N[U] 外交

▶ **diplomatically** [dìpləmǽṭɪkli] Adv. 外交的に

1055 sanction
[sǽŋkʃən]

N[C] 制裁 V[T] を認可する

impose **sanctions** on sth/sb（制裁を〜に課す）

Chapter

23

政治
Politics

As political systems and ideologies such as authoritarianism and totalitarianism typically deprive people of basic human rights, cause corruption and bribery, and do not reflect the will of citizens, democratic regimes have become the dominant form of government around the world.

However, the voter turnout rate in parliamentary elections has experienced rapid decline in recent times. Authorities have been constantly urging eligible voters to voice their opinions, with limited success.

For example, the political apathy and indifference of eligible voters in Japan can be attributed to several factors, including distrust of political institutions, voting not being compulsory, and the burden of traveling to the polls.

Although various solutions have been proposed to elevate the number of votes, such as increased penalties for non-voters, promotion through social media influencers, and absentee voting, which allows ballots to be cast prior to election day, no silver bullet has been found so far.

1

As political systems and ideologies such as authoritarianism and totalitarianism typically deprive people of basic human rights, cause corruption and bribery, and do not reflect the will of citizens, democratic regimes have become the dominant form of government around the world.

権威主義や全体主義といった政治体制やイデオロギーは通常、一般市民の基本的人権を剥奪し、汚職や賄賂を招き、民意を反映しないことから、民主主義政権が世界中で主流な政治形態になっている。

1056 deprive
[dɪpráɪv]
▢▢▢▢▢▢

V[T] から (〜を) 剥奪する、奪う (of sb)

I think it's really important that I don't let people **deprive** me of too much of my free time.
（自分の自由な時間を人に奪われ過ぎないようにすることはものすごい重要なことだと思うんだ。）

▶ **deprived** [dɪpráɪvd] Adj. 貧しい、恵まれない

▶ **deprivation** [dèprəvéɪʃən] N[C/U] 欠乏、欠如 N[U]（生活必需品の）不足状態

sleep **deprivation**（睡眠不足）

1057 corruption
[kərʌ́pʃən]
▢▢▢▢▢▢

N[U] 汚職；堕落、腐敗；（データなどの）破損 **N[C]** 言葉が訛って変化した形

I don't think **corruption** is a big issue in our country, but who knows?
（汚職は僕たちの国では大きな問題ではないと思うけど、でも実際どうなんだろうね？）

▶ **corrupt** Adj. 汚職の；腐敗した；（データなどが）破損した V[T] を堕落させる
[kərʌ́pt]

Oh God, I spent the whole week preparing this document, and it now says that the file is **corrupt**.（おいマジかよ。丸一週間かけてこの文書準備して、今になってファイルが破損してるってよ。）

1058 bribery
[bráɪbəri]
▢▢▢▢▢▢

N[U] 賄賂、収賄

It seems like there's a lot less **bribery** compared to when I was a kid.
（自分が子供のころと比べると賄賂はずっと減ったみたい。）

▶ **bribe** V[T] に（〜するために）賄賂を渡す (to do)；（子供など）を（〜で）釣る (with sth)
[braɪb] N[C] 賄賂；（子供などを釣るための）餌

My dad **bribed** me with money to make me study harder.
（お父さんが僕をもっと勉強させるためにお金で釣ってきたんだ。）

offer a **bribe**（賄賂を渡す）⟷ accept/take a **bribe**（賄賂を受け取る）

1059 **reflect**
[rɪflékt]
☐☐☐☐☐☐

V[T] を反映する、映す；（光などを）反射する

I'm pretty unmotivated to share my opinions during meetings because they've never been **reflected** in the final decision.
（会議中、あんまり意見を言う気にならないんだ。一回も自分の意見が最終的な決定に反映されたことないんだもん。）

I tried working on the beach, but the monitor on my laptop **reflected** too much light for me to see. （試しにビーチで仕事してみたんだけど、ノートパソコンのモニターが光を反射しすぎて何も見えなかった。）

V[I] （〜について）じっくり考える、振り返る（on sth）

While taking a shower, I often **reflect** on what I learned during the day.
（シャワーを浴びながらその日に何を学んだかをよく振り返るんだ。）

▶ **reflection** [rɪflékʃən] N[C] 反映、表れ；（鏡や水面に）映った姿 N[U] 反射；熟考

You might think it's strange, but I often practice speaking English to my **reflection** in the mirror.
（変だと思われるかもしれないけど、俺よく鏡に映ってる自分に向かって英語を話す練習をするんだ。）

▶ **reflective** Adj. （〜を）反映した（of sth）；考え深い ▶ **reflectively** Adv. 考え込んで
[rɪfléktɪv]   [rɪfléktɪvli]

1060 **will**
[wɪl]
☐☐☐☐☐☐

N[S] 意思、願望 **N[C/U]** 意志、決意 **N[C]** 遺書

■ against sb's **will** （意思に反して）

It's true I went out on a date with her, but believe me, it was **against my will**.
（彼女とデートに行ったのは本当だけど、信じて。あれは俺の意思じゃなかったから。）

He has a strong **will**. （彼は意志が強いよ。）

1061 **democratic**
[dèməkrǽtɪk]
☐☐☐☐☐☐

Adj. 民主主義の、民主的な

Isn't it kind of interesting that the **Democratic** People's Republic of Korea has "**democratic**" in its name, but its political system isn't?
（朝鮮民主主義人民共和国って名前に「民主主義」って入ってるのに、その政治体制はそうじゃないって、なんか面白くない？）

Liberal **Democratic** Party （自由民主党） Constitutional **Democratic** Party （立憲民主党）

▶ **democratically** [dèməkrǽtɪkli] Adv. 民主的に

Nothing is decided **democratically** in my family because my wife calls the shots on everything.
（うちの家庭では妻がなんでも決めるんで、何一つとして民主的に決められるものはないんです。）

▶ **democracy** [dɪmáːkrəsi] N[U] 民主主義、民主制 N[C] 民主主義国

the principles of **democracy** （民主主義の原則）

▶ **democratize** V[T] を民主化する ▶ **democratization** N[U] 民主化
[dɪmáːkrətaɪz]   [dɪmàːkrətəzéɪʃən]

1062 **regime**
[reɪʒíːm]
☐☐☐☐☐☐

N[C] 政権；制度

I swear there's a **regime** change every few years in this country.
（この国では数年に一回必ず政権交代があるんだよ。）

a tax **regime** （税制）

2 However, the voter turnout rate in parliamentary elections has experienced rapid decline in recent times. Authorities have been constantly urging eligible voters to voice their opinions, with limited success.

しかし近年、議会選挙の投票率は急激に低下してきている。当局は、有権者に意思表示をするよう絶えず呼び掛けてきているが、成果はあまり出ていない。

1063 voter
[vóu̯ṭər]
□□□□□□

N[C] 有権者、投票者

How do **voters** living abroad cast their votes?
(海外に住んでいる有権者はどうやって投票すればいいの？)

▶ **vote** V[I] （〜に）投票する (for sth/sb)　N[C] 票　N[S] 投票総数【the -】；投票権【the -】
[voʊt]

vote against sth/sb （〜に反対票を投じる）　　**vote** on sth （〜を投票で決める）

take a **vote** on sth （〜を投票で決める）

1064 turnout
[tɔ́ːrnaʊt]
□□□□□□

N[S/U] 投票率、投票者数；参加者数　**N[C]** 出足

■ voter **turnout** (rate) （投票率）　　a high/low **turnout** （高い / 低い投票率）

In recent years, **the voter turnout rate** in Japan has been falling.
(日本の投票率は最近ずっと下がってるんだ。)

■ a good/poor **turnout** （良い / 悪い出足）

We had **a** really **good turnout** at my event last week, so I'm hoping the next one will be just as good. （先週の僕のイベントはすごい出足が良かったから、次も同じくらい良いといいなぁ。）

1065 parliamentary
[pàːrləméntəri]
□□□□□□

Adj. 議会の、国会の、議員の

It's embarrassing to see a lot of Diet members dozing off during a **parliamentary** debate.
(国会討論中にうたた寝してる議員がたくさんいるのを見ると恥ずかしい気持ちになるよ。)

▶ **parliament** [pάːrləmənt] N[C] 国会、議会　N[C/U] 国会会期
　　　　　　　　　　　　 N[U] （イギリスの）国会【P-】

▶ **parliamentarian** [pὰːrləmentériən] N[C] 国会議員

国によって異なる「議会、国会」の呼び名　Parliament はイギリス・カナダ・フランスなどの議会を指す時に使われる単語で、アメリカの国会は Congress [kάːngres]、日本の国会は Diet [dάɪət] と呼ばれることが一般的です。

1066 **election**
[ilékʃən]
☐☐☐☐☐☐

N[C/U] 選挙 **N[U]** 選出、当選

The best part-time job that I've ever had was counting votes on **election** day.
(今までで最高のバイトは選挙の日に投票数を数えるバイトだよ。)

a parliamentary **election** (議会選挙)   a presidential **election** (大統領選挙)

▶ **elect** [ilékt] V[T] を（投票で）選ぶ；(〜すること) を選択する (to do)

■ **elect** sb to sth ((人) を〜の地位に選ぶ)   **elect** sb (as) sth ((人) を〜として選出する)

Barack Obama was the first African-American person **elected to** the presidency.
(バラク・オバマは大統領の地位に選出された初のアフリカ系アメリカ人だったんだ。)

▶ **elective** [iléktɪv] Adj. 選挙の、選挙で選ばれる；選択の、必修でない N[C] 選択科目

Is this course **elective** or compulsory? (このコースって選択科目？ それとも必修？)

1067 **decline**
[dɪkláɪn]
☐☐☐☐☐☐

N[C/U] 低下、減少、下落 **V[I]** 減少する、低下する **V[I/T]** (〜を) 断る

■ a **decline** in sth (〜の低下、下落)   a **decline** of sth ((量や数) の低下、下落)

I think the 80% **decline** in my Instagram followers was because I posted about 20 pictures of my face in a row.
(インスタのフォロワーが 80% 減った理由は、自分の顔の写真を 20 枚くらい連投したからだと思う。)

on the **decline**/in **decline** (減少して)

I've received offers from a few companies, so now I'm thinking about which ones to **decline**.
(いくつかの会社からオファーをもらったから、今はどれを断ろうか考えてるんだ。)

語根 cline 「傾く」という意味の語根で、「下に (= de) 傾く (= cline)」ことから「低下 (する)」という意味になります。他には recline (もたれる)、incline (〜したい気持ちにさせる) などがあります。

1068 **urge**
[ɜːrdʒ]
☐☐☐☐☐☐

V[T] に (〜するよう) 呼びかける、強く勧める (to do)；を主張する、力説する

I'd **urge** your kids to go to college as an insurance policy unless there's something that they're passionate about doing.
(何か夢中になってできるものでもない限り、私なら保険として子供に大学進学することを強く勧めるよ。)

N[C] 衝動、欲求

the **urge** to do (〜したいという衝動)

▶ **urgent** [ɜ́ːrdʒənt] Adj. 緊急の   ▶ **urgently** [ɜ́ːrdʒəntli] Adv. 緊急に、至急

It'd be great if you could finish this work today, but it's not **urgent**, so no stress.
(この仕事今日終わらせてくれたらすごく助かるけど、急ぎじゃないから、これでストレス抱えたりしないでね。)

▶ **urgency** [ɜ́ːrdʒənsi] N[S/U] 緊急

1069 **voice**
[vɔɪs]
☐☐☐☐☐☐

V[T] (意見など) を声に出す **N[C]** 意見 **N[C/U]** 声 **N[S]** 発言権

Feel free to **voice** your opinion. I promise you won't be judged.
(自由に意見言ってね。絶対それで君のことを判断したりしないから。)

You have a really good **voice**. (君は良い声してるね。)

make one's **voice** heard (自分の考えを聞いてもらう)

3 For example, the political apathy and indifference of eligible voters in Japan can be attributed to several factors, including distrust of political institutions, voting not being compulsory, and the burden of traveling to the polls.

例えば、日本の有権者が政治に対して無気力・無関心であることの裏には、政治制度への不信、投票が強制ではないこと、投票所まで足を運ぶのが負担であることなど、さまざまな要因があると考えられている。

1070 **apathy**
[ǽpəθi]
☐☐☐☐☐☐

N[U] 無気力、無感情、無関心

I think **apathy** in your relationship is a sign that it's over.
（無感情はもう関係が終わってるサインだと思うよ。）

▶ **apathetic** [æpəθétɪk] Adj. （〜について）無関心な（about sth/sb）

I thought he was quite **apathetic** about his life, but it turns out that he actually wants to become a millionaire and move to New York.
（あいつって結構人生どうでもいいみたいな感じだと思ってたけど、実際は大富豪になってニューヨークに引っ越したいんだって。）

1071 **indifference**
[ɪndífərəns]
☐☐☐☐☐☐

N[U] （〜に対する）無関心、無頓着、冷淡さ（to sth）

A little jealousy may be a positive thing because **indifference** can kill a relationship.
（ちょっとしたやきもちは良いことなのかも。無関心のせいで関係がダメになることもあるからね。）

▶ **indifferent** [ɪndífərənt] Adj. （〜に）無関心で（to sth/sb）

I'm **indifferent** to politics.（政治には無関心なんだ。）

▶ **indifferently** [ɪndífərəntli] Adv. 無関心に

1072 **attribute**
V. [ətríbjuːt]
N. [ǽtrəbjùːt]
☐☐☐☐☐☐

V[T] を（〜に）起因すると考える（to sth/sb）

I've had a lot of help throughout my life, but I **attribute** most of my success to my parents.
（これまで人生は色々と助けられて生きてきたけど、自分の成功の多くは両親のおかげだと思っているよ。）

N[C] 特性、特質、属性

What do you think are the main **attributes** of good managers?
（良い上司の主な特性って何だと思う？）

▶ **attribution** [ǽtrəbjúːʃən] N[U] （A を B に）起因すると考えること （of A to B）

The **attribution** of blame for the loss to the players is a bit unfair.
（試合に負けた責任を選手のせいにするのはちょっと不公平だよ。）

▶ **attributable** [ətríbjəṭəbəl] Adj. （〜に）起因する (to sth/sb)

1073 distrust
[dɪstrʌ́st]
☐☐☐☐☐☐

N[S/U] 不信感   V[T] を信用しない

I have a **distrust** of taxis in this country because I've been ripped off so many times.
（この国のタクシーは信頼してないよ。何回もぼったくられたことあるからね。）

▶ **distrustful** [dɪstrʌ́stfəl] Adj. 不信感を抱く、信用しない

distrust vs **mistrust** distrust と同じく「不信感（を抱く）」とよく訳される単語に mistrust がありますが、ニュアンスが少し異なります。distrust は自分の知識や経験をもとに生まれる不信感であるのに対し、mistrust はどちらかと言うと直感的な「なんとなく感じる不信感」という意味合いが強くなります（例：I mistrust strangers. 知らない人ってなんか信じられない）。

1074 compulsory
[kəmpʌ́lsəri]
☐☐☐☐☐☐

Adj. 強制的な、義務的な、必修の　= **mandatory** [mǽndətɔːri]

I'm not going to take the training if it's not **compulsory**.
（その研修、強制じゃないなら私は受けないよ。）

▶ **compulsive** [kəmpʌ́lsɪv] Adj. （行動などが）やめられない

I have a problem with **compulsive** snacking.（お菓子食べるのやめられなくて困ってるんだけど。）

compulsive gambling （ギャンブル依存症）

▶ **compulsively** [kəmpʌ́lsɪvli] Adv. やめられずに

▶ **compulsiveness** [kəmpʌ́lsɪvnəs] N[U] （とりつかれたように）やめられないこと

1075 burden
[bɚ́ːrdn]
☐☐☐☐☐☐

N[C] （〜にとっての）負担、重荷 (on sb)

Revolving payment reduces the monthly **burden**, but in the long run, interest adds up, so it's dangerous too.
（リボ払いにすると月々の負担が軽くなるけど、長期的に見ると利息がかさんでくるから危険でもある。）

V[T] に （〜の）負担をかける (with sth)

I've been really busy at work trying to wrap up everything before I go on vacation because I don't want to **burden** others with my work.
（休暇に入る前に仕事を全部片付けようとしててすごい忙しいんだ。自分の仕事で周りに負担をかけたくないから。）

▶ **burdensome** [bɚ́ːrdnsəm] Adj. 負担になる

1076 poll
[poʊl]
☐☐☐☐☐☐

N[P] 投票所【the -s】N[C] 世論調査　V[T] （票数）を獲得する；に世論調査をする

To avoid the crowds, I'm going to **the polls** before election day.
（混んでるのを避けるために、選挙日前に投票所に行く予定だよ。）

4 Although various solutions have been proposed to elevate the number of votes, such as increased penalties for non-voters, promotion through social media influencers, and absentee voting, which allows ballots to be cast prior to election day, no silver bullet has been found so far.

投票数を増やすために、投票に行かない有権者への罰則を強化する、SNS 上のインフルエンサーに投票を呼び掛けてもらう、選挙日前の投票を可能にする不在者投票などのさまざまな解決策が提案されてきたが、今のところ特効薬は見つかっていない。

1077 **elevate**
[élɪveɪt]

▢▢▢▢▢▢

V[T] を増やす、高く上げる、向上させる

I decided to change jobs because I realized that continuing to do the same thing won't **elevate** the quality of my life any further.
(同じことずっとしてても自分の人生の質がこれ以上向上しないって気づいたから、転職することにしたよ。)

▶ **elevated** [élɪveɪtɪd] Adj. (地位や高さが) 高い

▶ **elevation** [èlɪvéɪʃən] N[C] 海抜、標高

▶ **elevator** [élɪveɪtər] N[C] エレベーター　**= lift** [lɪft] <英>

1078 **penalty**
[pénəlti]

▢▢▢▢▢▢

N[C] (〜に対する) 罰則、処罰、罰金 (for sth)

It's surprising that Japan doesn't impose **penalties** for drinking alcohol on the street.
(日本では道端でお酒飲んでも罰則がないなんて驚きだよ。)

▶ **penalize** [pí:nəlaɪz] V[T] を罰する　▶ **penal** [pí:nl] Adj. 刑罰の、刑事上の

the **penal** system (刑罰制度)

1079 **absentee**
[ǽbsənti:]

▢▢▢▢▢▢

N[C] 不在者、欠席者

There're too many **absentees** today, so I'm going to cancel the dinner.
(今日のディナーは欠席者があまりにも多いから、キャンセルする予定だよ。)

absentee voting (不在者投票)

▶ **absent** [ǽbsənt] Adj. (〜を) 不在で、欠席して；(〜に) 欠けている (from sth)

He's **absent** from school today because he got the flu.
(彼はインフルエンザにかかったから、今日は学校を欠席してるよ。)

▶ **absent-minded** [æbsəntmáındıd] Adj. 忘れっぽい、うっかりした

Sorry, I forgot to pick up the groceries. I've been **absent-minded** lately.
(ごめん、食料品買って帰るの忘れちゃった。最近忘れっぽいんだよなぁ。)

▶ **absence** [æbsəns] N[C/U] 不在、欠席 N[U] 欠如

■ in sth's/sb's **absence**（〜がない場合）= in the **absence** of sth/sb

In the absence of further information, I can't make a decision.
(もっと情報がないと決断できないよ。)

▶ **absenteeism** [æbsənti:ızəm] N[U] サボり癖、長期欠席

Some think the high level of student **absenteeism** at college is the fault of students, but to play devil's advocate, is it possible that the root cause is the quality of lecturers?
(大学で学生の欠席が多いのを学生のせいにする人がいるけど、あえて批判的に考えてみて、根本的な原因は講師の質にあるっていう可能性ないかな。)

1080 **ballot**
[bǽlət]
☐☐☐☐☐☐

N[C] 投票用紙 **N[C/U]** 投票

Asking people whose name they wrote on their **ballot** is a big no-no.
(投票用紙に誰の名前を書いたか聞くのは絶対やっちゃいけないことだよ。)

a spoiled **ballot**（無効票） a secret **ballot**（無記名投票） a **ballot** box（投票箱）

1081 **cast**
[kæst]
☐☐☐☐☐☐

V[T] を投げる；を（〜に）キャスティングする（as sb） **N[C]** 出演者

■ **cast** doubt on sth（〜に疑問を投げかける） **cast** a vote/ballot（投票する）

I like that philosophy **casts doubt on** what's commonly believed to be true and presents new ways of thinking.
(哲学は一般に真実だと思われていることに疑問を投げかけて、新しい考え方を提示してくれるから好きなんだ。)

▶ **casting** [kǽstıŋ] N[U] キャスティング、配役

1082 **bullet**
[búlıt]
☐☐☐☐☐☐

N[C] 銃弾、弾丸

I would often play with a toy gun using plastic **bullets** when I was a little child.
(子どもの頃はよくプラスチックの銃弾を使うおもちゃの銃で遊んでたなぁ。)

■ a silver **bullet**（特効薬、簡単な解決策） a **bullet** point（（箇条書きに使う）黒丸）

There's no **silver bullet** that will improve your English overnight.
(一晩で英語力を上げられる特効薬なんて存在しないよ。)

silver bullet の語源 この表現は民話において werewolf（狼男）や witch（魔女）などを銀の弾丸（= silver bullet）で倒すことができると言われたことに由来しており、そこから「何にでも使える解決策=特効薬」という意味で比喩的に使用されるようになりました。

1083 **so far**
[soʊ fɑːr]
☐☐☐☐☐☐

Phr. 今のところ = **thus far** [ðʌs fɑːr]

Do you have any questions **so far**?（ここまでで何か質問ありますか？）

So far so good.（今のところ順調だよ。）

Politician (W)   I believe that free healthcare should be a basic human right for all, regardless of race, financial situation, or age. No matter how meticulously we plan, unforeseen circumstances can arise at any moment.

Politician (M)   Free healthcare is clearly an unsustainable fantasy, as most tax revenue is already pledged to vital long-term construction projects. To pretend otherwise insults the intelligence of our citizens. Further, healthcare for most citizens is funded privately through their employers. Universally-free healthcare therefore benefits only a minority of the population.

Politician (W)   Even so, many lack complementary health insurance and should not be abandoned. Regardless of your ideological beliefs, free healthcare is a fundamental human right which cannot be neglected for the sake of infrastructure.

Politician (M)   The fundamental issue here is that you are being stubborn and refuse to compromise. The obvious solution is a hybrid of the free and private models. Rationally, we should provide full state-funded healthcare to low income earners, and less to the wealthy.

政治家 (女性)   無料の医療サービスは、人種、財務状況、年齢などにかかわらず、全員に与えられる基本的人権であるべきです。どれだけ綿密に計画しても、予期せぬ状況はいつでも起きる可能性がありますからね。

政治家 (男性)   無料の医療サービスは、明らかに持続不可能な絵空事にすぎません。既に税収の大半が、極めて重要な長期建設プロジェクトに投入されているんですよ。できないことをできるみたいに言うのは、国民の知性をばかにするのと同じですよ。その上、ほとんどの国民医療はそれぞれの雇用主を通して民間資金で賄われています。よって、全国民を対象とした無料の医療サービスは、少数の国民の利益にしかなりません。

政治家 (女性)   だとしても、多くの国民は補完的な健康保険がないですし、見捨てられるべきではありません。あなたのイデオロギー的な信念にかかわらず、無料の医療サービスは基本的な人権であり、インフラのために無視することはできません。

政治家 (男性)   ここでの根本的な問題は、あなたが頑固で、妥協しないということです。明確な解決策は無料型と民間型のハイブリッドモデルです。合理的に考えて、低所得者向けには全額政府負担の医療サービスを提供し、富裕層に対してはもっと抑えるべきでしょう。

1084 **regardless**
[rɪgáːrdləs]

Adv.（〜に）かかわらず、関係なく（of sth）

Regardless of what others say, I'll work as hard as I can.

〈周りが何と言おうと、自分は精一杯頑張るよ。〉

1085 **age**
[eɪdʒ]

N[C/U] 年齢、年　　N[C] 時代　　N[P] 長い時間【-s】

at the **age** of sth（〜歳で）　with **age**（年齢とともに）　take **ages**（長い時間がかかる）

V[I] 年を取る、老ける；熟成する　　V[T] を老けさせる；を熟成させる

1086 **meticulously**
[mətíkjələsli]

Adv. 綿密に、細心の注意を払って

▶ **meticulous** [mətíkjələs] Adj. 綿密な、細心の

▶ **meticulousness** [mətíkjələsnəs] N[U] 綿密さ

1087 **arise**
[əráɪz]

V[I] 起きる、生じる

You need to be patient and keep putting in the effort until an opportunity **arises**.

〈機会が現れるまで、我慢強く努力をし続けないといけないよ。〉

1088 **fantasy**
[fǽntəsi]

N[C/U] 絵空事、空想、夢想　　N[S/U] 空論

▶ **fantastic** [fæntǽstɪk] Adj. 空想的な；素晴らしい

1089 **pledge**
[pledʒ]

V[T]（お金）を投入する、出資する、寄付する；を誓う、公約する

N[C]（約束された）拠出資金、寄付金；誓約、公約

1090 **pretend**
[prɪténd]

V[I/T]（〜という / 〜する）ふりをする（that + sentence/to do）

▶ **pretentious** [prɪténʃəs] Adj. 気取った、うぬぼれた

▶ **pretension** [prɪténʃən] N[C/U] 気取り

▶ **pretense** [prɪténs] N[S/U] ふり、見せかけ　▶ **pretended** [prɪténdɪd] Adj. 見せかけの

1091 **insult**
V. [ɪnsʌ́lt]
N. [ínsʌlt]

V[T] を侮辱する　　N[C] 侮辱的発言；侮辱となるもの

insult sb's intelligence（〜をばかにする）　= **insult** the intelligence of sb

▶ **insulting** [ɪnsʌ́ltɪŋ] Adj. 侮辱的な、無礼な

1092 **fund**
[fʌnd]

V[T] に出資する、資金提供する　　N[C] 資金、基金　　N[P] 財源【-s】

▶ **funding** [fʌ́ndɪŋ] N[U]（特定の目的のための）資金

▶ **fundraising** [fʌ́ndrèɪzɪŋ] N[U] 資金調達

1093 **privately**
[práɪvətli]

Adv. 民間で、個人で；こっそり、内緒で

▶ **private** [práɪvət] Adj. 民間の、個人の；内密の、私的な、私用の

▶ **privacy** [práɪvəsi] N[U] プライバシー、私生活

1094 minority
[maɪnɔ́:rəti]

N[S] 少数、少数派　N[U] 未成年　↔ **majority** [mədʒɑ́:rəti] 大部分、過半数；成人

▶ **minorities** [maɪnɔ́:rətiz] N[P] 少数民族

▶ **minor** [máɪnər] N[C] 未成年者；副専攻　Adj. あまり重要でない

1095 abandon
[əbǽndən]

V[T] を見捨てる、捨てる；を中止する；を去る；を置き去りにする

▶ **abandoned** [əbǽndənd] Adj. 捨てられた

an **abandoned** dog/cat（捨て犬 / 猫）

▶ **abandonment** [əbǽndənmənt] N[U] 中止；遺棄、放棄

1096 ideological
[àɪdiəlá:dʒɪkəl]

Adj. イデオロギー的な

▶ **ideologically** [àɪdiəlá:dʒɪkli] Adv. イデオロギー的に

▶ **ideology** [àɪdiá:lədʒi] N[C/U] イデオロギー

1097 neglect
[nɪglékt]

V[T] を無視する、軽視する；（～するのを）怠る（to do）

N[U] 無視、軽視；怠慢

▶ **neglected** [nɪgléktɪd] Adj. 無視された　▶ **neglectful** [nɪgléktfəl] Adj. 怠慢な

1098 sake
[seɪk]

N[U] 目的、ため

for the **sake** of sth/sb（～のために）　= for sth's/sb's own **sake**

for God's **sake**（お願いだから、頼むから）

1099 infrastructure
[ínfrəstrλktʃər]

N[C] インフラ、構造基盤

▶ **infrastructural** [ìnfrəstrλktʃərəl] Adj. インフラの、構造基盤の

1100 stubborn
[stλbərn]

Adj. 頑固な；（汚れなどが）しつこい

1101 refuse
[rɪfjúːz]

V[I] 拒む V[T]（～するのを）拒む（to do）、を断る　N[U] ごみ、廃棄物

▶ **refusal** [rɪfjúːzəl] N[C/U] 拒絶、拒否；却下

1102 compromise
[kά:mprəmaɪz]

V[I] 妥協する　V[T]（品質など）を損なう；（原則や信条）を曲げる

N[C/U] 妥協

▶ **compromising** [kά:mprəmaɪzɪŋ] Adj. 人に見られると困る、評判を汚すような

1103 wealthy
[wélθi]

N[P] 富裕層【the -】　Adj. 裕福な　= **rich** [rɪtʃ]

▶ **wealth** [welθ] N[U] 裕福、富

↻ CH. 4, 9, 13, 17, 20, 23

Chapter

24

経済学
Economics

Economics seeks to explain how people allocate finite resources to produce, distribute, and consume goods and services to satisfy desire. It can be divided into two branches: macroeconomics and microeconomics.

Macroeconomics is the study of the aggregate economy. Gross domestic product, inflation rates, and unemployment rates are considered key indicators in assessing the ability of fiscal and monetary policies to achieve the restoration and stable growth of economies.

The discipline of microeconomics, on the other hand, has to do with prices and the supply and demand of commodities that are sold and purchased by individuals, households, and firms.

Although some disagree, many assert that these two areas should be simultaneously considered, as the behavior of individual economic agents and their choices, examined as part of microeconomics, profoundly underpin macroeconomic phenomena.

1 **Economics seeks to** explain **how people** allocate finite resources **to produce, distribute, and** consume goods **and services to satisfy** desire. **It can be divided into two branches: macroeconomics and microeconomics.**

経済学は、人の欲求を満たすために、限りある資源をどのように配分して財やサービスを生産・分配・消費するかを説明しようとする学問である。これは、マクロ経済学とミクロ経済学の 2 つの分野に分けられる。

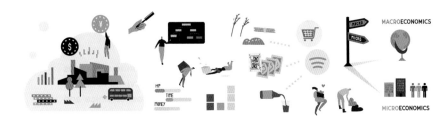

1104 **explain**
[ɪkspléɪn]
☐☐☐☐☐☐

V[I/T] （〜を）説明する；の理由となる

There are a lot of teachers who can't **explain** to their students why they have to study, and I think that's an issue.
（生徒になぜ勉強しなきゃいけないか説明できない先生って結構いて、それって問題だと思うんだよね。）

That **explains** it. （そういうことか。）

▶ **explanation** [èksplənéɪʃən] N[C/U] 説明

Leo turns up late so often that he doesn't even bother giving **explanations** anymore.
（レオは遅刻しすぎて、もうなんで遅刻したか説明すらしなくなったんだ。）

▶ **explanatory** [ɪksplǽnətɔːri] Adj. 説明のための、注釈的な

Without **explanatory** comments, I wouldn't really be able to understand Shakespeare's writing. （注釈が付いてないとシェイクスピアの書いたことはあんまり理解できないんだよね。）

▶ **self-explanatory** [sèlfɪksplǽnətɔːri] Adj. 説明不要の、自明の

1105 **allocate**
[ǽləkeɪt]
☐☐☐☐☐☐

V[T] を（〜に）配分する、割り当てる（to sth/sb）

You should **allocate** this task to the new graduate because it's pretty straightforward.
（この仕事はあの新卒に任せたらいいよ。結構簡単だから。）

▶ **allocation** [æləkéɪʃən] N[U] 割り当て、配分 N[C] 配分量、配給額

This new database will let us more accurately track the **allocation** of staff to projects.
（この新しいデータベースを使えば、プロジェクトごとのスタッフの割り当てをより正確に追跡することができるよ。）

1106 **finite**
[fáɪnaɪt]
☐☐☐☐☐☐

Adj. 限りある、有限の

We only have a **finite** amount of time, so we should make sure we spend it wisely.
（時間は有限なんだから、賢く使うようにしないとね。）

⟷ **infinite** [ínfənət] 無限の、果てしない、計り知れないほどの

1107 resource
[rí:sɔːrs]

N[C] 資源、資金、人手

■ have the **resources** to do（〜する資源がある）

I have big ambitions, but I don't **have the resources to** realize them.
（大きな野望はあるんだけど、実現するための資金がないんだよね。）

▶ **resourceful** Adj. 機転が利く、臨機応変な
[rɪsɔ́ːrsfəl]

▶ **resourcefully** Adv. 機転を利かして
[rɪsɔ́ːrsfəli]

I'm glad Bill's summitting Everest with me because he's one of the most **resourceful** people I know.
（私がエベレストに登る時ビルも来てくれるみたいで良かった。彼は知ってる中でも一番臨機応変に行動できる人だから。）

▶ **resourced** [rí:sɔːrst] Adj.（資源や人手などが）足りている

The company's planning to recruit more people because it's under-**resourced** right now.
（その会社は今人手不足だからもっと人を雇う予定なんだ。）

1108 consume
[kənsúːm]

V[T] を消費する；を摂取する；を（炎が）破壊する

I feel super hungry after studying because my brain **consumes** so much energy when I concentrate.（集中すると脳がエネルギーめっちゃ使うから、勉強した後は超お腹空くんだよなぁ。）

▶ **consumption** [kənsʌ́mpʃən] N[U] 消費；摂取

energy **consumption**（エネルギー消費）

unfit for human **consumption**（人が飲食するのに適していない）

▶ **consumer** [kənsúːmər] N[C] 消費者

1109 goods
[gʊdz]

N[P] 財、商品、品物

The prices of household **goods** have increased like crazy since last year.
（家庭用品の値段が去年からヤバいくらい上がってるんだ。）

1110 desire
[dɪzáɪr]

N[C/U] 欲求、欲望 V[T] を強く望む

The author of this book says letting go of **desires** brings us to the next stage of our lives, but I think that's impossible for humans to do.
（この本の著者は欲を捨てることで人生の次のステージに行けるって書いてるんだけど、人間がこれをやるのは不可能だと思うよ。）

sexual **desire**（性欲）　　　**desire** to do（〜したいと強く思う）

▶ **desirable** [dɪzáɪrəbəl] Adj. 望ましい、好ましい、価値のある

Slick advertising can make anything look **desirable**.
（広告がカッコいいと何でも価値がありそうに見えちゃうんだよね。）

▶ **desired** Adj. 望ましい
[dɪzáɪrd]

▶ **desirably** Adv. 望ましく
[dɪzáɪrəbli]

2 Macroeconomics is the study of the aggregate economy. Gross domestic product, inflation rates, and unemployment rates are considered key indicators in assessing the ability of fiscal and monetary policies to achieve the restoration and stable growth of economies.

マクロ経済学は、経済全体についての研究である。国内総生産やインフレ率、失業率は、景気回復と安定した経済成長を実現するための財政・金融政策を評価する際の重要な指標と見なされている。

1111 **aggregate**
[ǽgrəgət]
☐☐☐☐☐☐

Adj. 全体としての、総計の　**N[C/U]** 合計、集合体

The winner of this competition will be decided through an **aggregate** score of home and away games. （この大会の勝者はホームとアウェイの試合の総得点で決定されます。）

1112 **gross**
[groʊs]
☐☐☐☐☐☐

Adj. 総計の；（見た目などが）気持ち悪い　**Adv.** 総計で

■ **gross** profit（総利益、粗利）

Why is our **gross profit** looking so bad this month?
（今月の総利益なんでこんな悪いの？）

That's so **gross**. （それめっちゃキモい。）

1113 **inflation**
[ɪnfléɪʃən]
☐☐☐☐☐☐

N[U] インフレ、物価上昇　↔ **deflation** [dɪfléɪʃən] デフレーション

I can't believe my pay raise was less than **inflation**.
（昇給がインフレ以下だったとかあり得ないわ。）

▶ **inflationary** [ɪnfléɪʃəneri] Adj. インフレの　↔ **deflationary** [dɪfléɪʃəneri] デフレの

inflationary policies（インフレ政策）

▶ **inflate** [ɪnfléɪt] V[T] を膨らませる、（価格など）をつり上げる　V[I] 膨らむ

Do we need a pump to **inflate** the balloons?
（その風船膨らませるのにポンプ必要かな？）

1114 **fiscal**
[fískəl]
☐☐☐☐☐☐

Adj. 財政の、会計の、国家歳入の

Apple's **fiscal** year* always ends on the last Saturday of September.
(アップルの会計年度はいつも 9 月の最後の土曜日が終わりなんだ。) *英豪では a financial year とも言います。

▶ **fiscally** [fískəli] Adv. 財政上、財政的に、国家歳入上

1115 **monetary**
[mʌ́nətri]
☐☐☐☐☐☐

Adj. 金融の、通貨の、貨幣の

Monetary incentives are good tools to motivate people, but non-monetary ones are also important.
(お金のインセンティブはモチベを上げる良いツールだけど、お金以外の動機も重要だよ。)

1116 **restoration**
[rèstəréɪʃən]
☐☐☐☐☐☐

N[C/U] 回復、修復、復元、復旧

The **restoration** of the building is taking ages, but it's going to look awesome once it's done.
(建物の復旧にはめちゃくちゃ時間がかかってるけど、終わったらすごいいい感じになるはずだよ。)

▶ **restore** [rɪstɔ́ːr] V[T] を回復する、修復する、復元する

Do you know how I can **restore** my files?
(どうやったらファイルを復旧できるか知ってる？)

1117 **growth**
[groʊθ]
☐☐☐☐☐☐

N[U] 成長、発展、発育、増加

At work, I take advantage of all opportunities that help my **growth** and development.
(職場では自分の成長と発展に繋がる機会は全て掴み取るようにしてるよ。)

▶ **grow** V[I] 成長する、育つ、増加する V[T] を成長させる、育てる、増加させる
[groʊ]

You've **grown** since the last time I saw you!（前会った時よりも大きくなったね！）

■ **grow** up（（人が）育つ）

I **grew up** in Japan.（私は日本育ちなんだ。）

▶ **growing** [gróʊɪŋ] Adj. 成長している、増加している

There's a **growing** demand for digital marketing skills in the job market.
(求人市場ではデジタルマーケティングのスキルに対する需要が高まっているよ。)

3 The discipline of microeconomics, on the other hand, has to do with prices and the supply and demand of commodities that are sold and purchased by individuals, households, and firms.

一方、ミクロ経済学は、個人や家計、そして企業によって売買される商品の価格や需給に関係したものである。

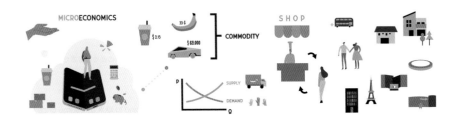

1118 have to do with sth/sb

[hǽvtʊduwɪð]

☐☐☐☐☐☐

Phr. 〜と関係がある

So, what does that **have to do with** me? （で、それって私に何の関係があるの？）

■ **have** something/nothing **to do with** sth/sb （〜に関係している／関係していない）

Removing these videos **has nothing to do with** copyright infringement.
（この動画を消したのは著作権侵害とは一切関係ないよ。）

1119 price

[praɪs]

☐☐☐☐☐☐

N[C] 価格、値段　**V[T]** に値段を付ける

What's the **price** for this? （これの値段はいくらですか？）

▶ **pricey** [práɪsi] Adj. (値段が) 高い　= **expensive** [ɪkspénsɪv]

My suit was a little bit **pricey**, but I think I'll be wearing it for a long time.
（私のスーツはちょっと高かったけど、長く着ると思うんだ。）

1120 supply

[səplái]

☐☐☐☐☐☐

N[C/U] 供給、提供　**V[T]** を供給する、提供する

OPEC sometimes reduces oil **supplies** to increase oil prices.
（OPEC は石油価格を上げるために石油の供給を減らすことがあるんだ。）

supply A with B/B to A （B を A に供給する）

▶ **supplies** [səpláɪz] N[P] 必需品、物資

▶ **supplier** [səpláɪər] N[C] サプライヤー、供給者

1121 commodity

[kəmá:dəṭi]

☐☐☐☐☐☐

N[C] 商品、売買品

The prices of **commodities** are mainly determined by supply and demand.
（商品の価格は主に供給と需要によって決まるんだ。）

1122 **sell**
[sel]
□□□□□□

V[I/T] （〜を）売る、販売する；（数量が）売れる

Stock trading sounds so easy. I just need to buy low and **sell** high, right?
（株取引って簡単そうだよね。安く買って高く売れば良いだけでしょ？）

■ be **sold** on sth（〜にしっくりきた、信じた）

I'm not **sold on** what this ad is saying.
（この広告が言ってることなんかしっくりこないんだよなぁ。）

▶ **selling** [séliŋ] Adj. 売れている N[U] 販売

This handbag is one of the best **selling** items this year.
（このハンドバッグは今年一番売れてるアイテムの一つなんです。）

▶ **seller** [sélər] N[C] 売り手、販売者

▶ **sale** [seil] N[C/U] 販売 N[P] 売上、販売数【-s】

■ for **sale**（売り物の）   ■ on **sale**（売られている；セール品の）

Is this scarf* **for sale** or just on display?
（このマフラーって売り物ですか？それともディスプレー用ですか？）

*scarfは首に巻くもの全般を指す単語で、その中にはマフラーも含まれます。

Is this **on sale**?（これってセール品ですか？）

make a **sale**（販売する、売る）   have a **sale**（セールをする）

▶ **salable** [séiləbəl] Adj. 売り物になる、売れる

I can't afford a delay in my pay because I don't have any **salable** assets right now.
（給料の支払いが遅れると困るんだよなぁ。今は別に売れるようなものも持ってないしさぁ。）

1123 **purchase**
[pə́:rtʃəs]
□□□□□□

V[T] を買う、購入する **N[C/U]** 購入 **N[C]** 購入品

You can **purchase** anything online nowadays.（最近は何でもオンラインで買えるよ。）

▶ **purchaser** [pə́:rtʃəsər] N[C] 買い手、購買者

I'm having a hard time finding a **purchaser** for my old phones.
（私の古い携帯を買ってくれる人が中々見つからないんだよね。）

purchase vs **buy** どちらも「買う」という意味を持ち、日常会話においてこれらは同義語として使われます。しかし、purchase の方が若干フォーマルなニュアンスを持ち、ゆえに契約書や、土地の購入など値段の高いものの購入においては purchase が好まれる傾向があります。

1124 **household**
[háʊshoʊld]
□□□□□□

N[C] 家計、世帯 **Adj.** 家庭の

I think it's amazing that women are now the primary breadwinners in more and more **households**.（女性がますます多くの世帯において主な稼ぎ手になってきているのは素晴らしいことだと思う。）

household debt（家計負債）

▶ **householder** [háʊshòʊldər] N[C] 世帯主

4 Although some disagree, many assert that these two areas should be simultaneously considered, as the behavior of individual economic agents and their choices, examined as part of microeconomics, profoundly underpin macroeconomic phenomena.

異論はあるが、多くはこれら2つの学問分野を同時に考慮する必要があると主張している。ミクロ経済学の一部として考察される個々の経済主体の行為とその選択がマクロ経済学における現象を大きく支えているからだ。

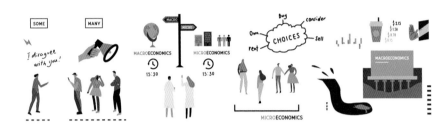

1125 **disagree**
[dìsəgríː]

V[I] （〜に）異議を唱える（with sth/sb）

I don't **disagree** with your idea, but I still feel like there's a better one.
（君の考えに反対というわけじゃないんだけど、もっと良いのがある気がするんだ。）

↔ **agree** [əgríː]（〜に）同意する（with sth/sb）

▶ **disagreement** N[C/U]（意見の）相違、不一致　　↔ **agreement** 同意
[dìsəgríːmənt]　　　　　　　　　　　　　　　　　　　　　[əgríːmənt]

I had a **disagreement** with my boyfriend last night, but we're all good now.
（昨日の夜、彼氏とちょっと意見の食い違いがあったんだけど、今はもう大丈夫。）

▶ **disagreeable** Adj. 嫌な、不愛想な　　↔ **agreeable** 心地の良い、愛想の良い
[dìsəgríːəbəl]　　　　　　　　　　　　　　　　　　[əgríːəbəl]

I'm surprised that you don't get along with Jean, because she's not really a **disagreeable** sort of person.（ジーンって別に感じが悪いような人じゃないから、君が仲良くないなんて驚きだよ。）

1126 **assert**
[əsə́ːrt]

V[T] だと主張する、断言する（that + sentence）

■ **assert** oneself（自己主張する）

You should **assert yourself** more in the workplace.
（職場ではもっと自己主張した方がいいよ。）

▶ **assertion** [əsə́ːrʃən] N[C] 主張、断言

▶ **assertive** Adj. 主張の強い　　▶ **assertively** Adv.（発言や要求を）はっきりと
[əsə́ːrṭɪv]　　　　　　　　　　　　　[əsə́ːrṭɪvli]

I've had a successful career mainly because I'm **assertive** in everything that I do.
（私がキャリアで成功できた理由は、自分がやること全てにおいて主張が強いからだと思う。）

1127 **simultaneously**
[sàimǝltéɪnɪǝsli]
▢▢▢▢▢▢

Adv. 同時に

I can't do two things **simultaneously**, so let me focus on one thing at a time.
(二つのこと同時にできないから、一度に一つのことに集中させて。)

▶ **simultaneous** [sàimǝltéɪnɪǝs] Adj. 同時の、同時に起こる

1128 **agent**
[éɪdʒǝnt]
▢▢▢▢▢▢

N[C] 行動主体；代理人、代理店；スパイ；薬剤、薬品

What's the easiest way to become a CIA **agent**?
(CIA のスパイになる一番簡単な方法って何かな？)

a travel **agent**（旅行代理店） a secret **agent**（スパイ） chemical **agents**（化学薬品）

▶ **agency** [éɪdʒǝnsi] N[C] 代理店；機関、局

the Central Intelligence **Agency**（中央情報局（CIA））

1129 **choice**
[tʃɔɪs]
▢▢▢▢▢▢

N[C] 選択、選ぶこと N[S] 選択する権利 N[S/U] 選択の幅

I personally think studying abroad gives you better options, but the **choice** is yours.
(個人的には日本にいるよりも留学した方が良い選択肢が増えると思うけど、決めるのは君だからね。)

have no **choice** but to do（〜するしか選択肢がない）

▶ **choose** [tʃuːz] V[I/T]（〜を）選択する、選ぶ

It was really hard to **choose** between the two, but I went with the red shirt instead of the pink one.（めっちゃ迷ったけど、結局ピンクじゃなくて赤のシャツにしたわ。）

▶ **choosy** Adj. よく選ぶ、こだわりが強い、好みのうるさい = **picky**   = **fussy**
     [tʃúːzi]   [píki]   [fʌ́si]

I'm a very **choosy** person when it comes to making friends.
(私は友達はちゃんと選ぶタイプなんだ。)

choose vs **select** vs **pick** どれも「選ぶ」という意味を持ちますが、choose は「よく考えた上で自ら望んで選ぶ」というニュアンスを持ち、ゆえに I chose to live abroad. と言えば、「色々考えた結果、自らが望んで海外で住むことに決めた」という意味合いに。select はより一般的に選択肢の中から「選ぶ」という意味。pick は 3 つの中で一番インフォーマルで、ランダムに選ぶような状況でもよく使われます。

1130 **profoundly**
[prǝfáʊndli]
▢▢▢▢▢▢

Adv. 大きく、非常に；深く、心から

I'm **profoundly** thankful for all your support.（たくさんのサポートを心より感謝します。）

▶ **profound** [prǝfáʊnd] Adj. 重大な、多大な；深い、心からの

I'm not sure if what he says is actually **profound**, or whether it just sounds that way because he uses big words.
(彼って本当に深いこと言ってるのか、難しい言葉を使うからそう聞こえるだけなのかどっちなんだろう。)

1131 **underpin**
[ʌ̀ndǝrpín]
▢▢▢▢▢▢

V[T] を支える、支持する、裏付ける

Do you have any statistical data to **underpin** your theory?
(君の理論を裏付ける統計データはあるの？)

▶ **underpinning** [ʌ̀ndǝrpìnɪŋ] N[C/U] 基礎、土台、根拠

THE ECONOMIC REVIEW

No. 39,422   NEW YORK, MONDAY, APRIL 14 $3.25

Is the U.S. Trade Deficit Actually Becoming a Problem?

By JEAN WINGFIELD (EXCLUSIVE)

The U.S. has been notorious for its trade deficit (i.e., imports exceeding exports) since the 1970s. Some claim that it exposes the country to the risk of bankruptcy and blame countries such as China for causing trade friction that leads to this deficit. If true, curbing imports by creating trade barriers (e.g., tariffs) to shift to a surplus position may be valid.

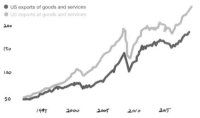

● US exports of goods and services
● US imports of goods and services

▲ Monthly U.S. International Trade in Goods and Services

However, many economists argue that the negative image of deficits is an illusion, as trade deficits are equivalent to investments from abroad. For example, if a U.S. wholesaler imports shoes from China, they trade dollars for Chinese yuan. The entity earning those dollars then invests in U.S. assets, such as Treasury bills, corporate stocks, and real estate. Overall, this foreign investment has a positive impact on the U.S. economy.

米国の貿易赤字は本当に問題になっているのか？

米国は1970年代以降、貿易赤字（つまり輸入額が輸出額を上回った）状態にあることでよく知られている。これにより米国は破綻のリスクにさらされ、こうした赤字につながる貿易摩擦を引き起こしているとして、中国などの国を非難する人もいる。これが本当であれば、貿易障壁（関税など）を設けることで輸入品を制限し、黒字転換することが有効かもしれない。

しかし、多くの経済学者たちは、貿易赤字は海外からの投資と等しく、ゆえに赤字の持つマイナスイメージは幻想であると主張している。例えば、米国の卸売業者が中国から靴を輸入する際、卸売業者はドルを人民元と交換する。そのドルを稼いだ者は、短期国債や会社株式、不動産などの米国資産に投資する。全体として見れば、この外国からの投資は、米国経済にプラスの影響を及ぼしているというわけだ。

1132 notorious
[noʊtɔ́:riəs]

Adj.（悪いことで）良く知られた、悪名高い

▶ **notoriously** [noʊtɔ́:riəsli] Adv. 悪名高くも

1133 trade
[treɪd]

N[U] 貿易、取引　N[S] 交換　N[C]（金融）取引

a **trade** surplus/deficit（貿易黒字 / 赤字）

V[T] を貿易する、取引する　V[I/T]（〜を）交換する

1134 deficit
[défəsɪt]

N[C] 赤字、（財政の）不足

in **deficit**（赤字で）

▶ **deficiency** [dɪfíʃənsi] N[C/U] 不足、欠乏

1135 import
N/V1. [ímpɔ:rt]
V2. [ɪmpɔ́:rt]

N[U] 輸入；重要性　N[C] 輸入品

V[T] を（〜へ / 〜から）輸入する（into/from sth）

▶ **importer** [ɪmpɔ́:rtər] N[C] 輸入者、輸入国

1136 export
N/V1. [ékspɔ:rt]
V2. [ɪkspɔ́:rt]

N[U] 輸出　N[C] 輸出品

V[T] を（〜へ / 〜から）輸出する（to/from sth）

▶ **exporter** [ɪkspɔ́:rtər] N[C] 輸出者、輸出国

1137 expose
[ɪkspóʊz]

V[T] を（〜に）さらす、触れさせる（to sth）

▶ **exposed** [ɪkspóʊzd] Adj.（〜に）さらされた（to sth）

▶ **exposure** [ɪkspóʊʒər] N[U]（〜に）さらすこと、さらされること、触れること（to sth）

1138 bankruptcy
[bǽŋkrəptsi]

N[C/U] 破綻、破産、倒産

▶ **bankrupt** [bǽŋkrʌpt] Adj. 破産した　≒ **broke** [broʊk] お金が一切ない、金欠の

go **bankrupt**（破産する）

1139 friction
[fríkʃən]

N[U] 摩擦　N[C/U] あつれき

▶ **frictional** [fríkʃənəl] Adj. 摩擦の　↔ **frictionless** [fríkʃənləs] 摩擦のない

1140 curb
[kɜ:rb]

V[T] を制限する、抑える

N[C] 制限、抑制；（歩道の）縁石　= **kerb**〈英・同音〉

▶ **curbstone** [kɜ́:rbstoʊn] N[C]（歩道の）縁石　= **kerbstone**〈英・同音〉

1141 barrier
[bériər]

N[C] 障壁、壁；障害物

At the end of the day, I think language learning comes down to removing mental **barriers**.（結局のところ、言語学習は心理的障壁を取り除くことにかかっていると思う。）

1142 tariff
[térɪf]
⬜⬜⬜⬜⬜

N[C]（〜にかかる）関税（on sth）

impose **tariffs** on sth（〜に関税をかける）

1143 surplus
[sə́:rpləs]
⬜⬜⬜⬜⬜

N[C/U] 黒字、余剰、超過

a budget **surplus**（財政黒字）

1144 illusion
[ɪlúːʒən]
⬜⬜⬜⬜⬜

N[C] 幻想、勘違い、錯覚

I think job security is just an **illusion**.（雇用保障なんてただの幻想だと思うよ。）

▶ **illusory** [ɪlúːsəri] Adj. 幻想の、錯覚の　= **illusive** [ɪlúːsɪv]

1145 equivalent
[ɪkwívələnt]
⬜⬜⬜⬜⬜

Adj.（〜と）等しい、同等の（to sth）

N[C]（〜と）同等のもの、（〜に）相当するもの（to/of sth）

▶ **equivalently** [ɪkwívələntli] Adv. 等しく、同等に

▶ **equivalence** [ɪkwívələns] N[U] 同等

1146 earn
[ɜːrn]
⬜⬜⬜⬜⬜

V[I/T]（お金や利益を）稼ぐ

▶ **earnings** [ɜ́ːrnɪŋz] N[P] 所得、収入、利益

1147 asset
[ǽset]
⬜⬜⬜⬜⬜

N[C] 資産、財産

↔ **liability** [làɪəbíləṭi] 負債　≒ **debt** [det] 負債、借金

1148 bill
[bɪl]
⬜⬜⬜⬜⬜

N[C] 証券、証書、手形；勘定、請求書；紙幣；法案

V[T] に請求書を送付する

a Treasury **bill**/T-**bill**（（米国財務省が発行する）短期国債、T ビル）

▶ **billable** [bíləbl] Adj. 請求可能な

1149 stock
[stɑːk]
⬜⬜⬜⬜⬜

N[C/U] 株式、株；在庫；（肉や魚などの）だし　N[C] 蓄え、備蓄

V[T] を仕入れる

in **stock**（在庫のある）　■ out of **stock**（在庫切れの）

I'm sorry, it's **out of stock** already.（ごめんなさい、もう在庫切れなんです。）

1150 real estate
[ríːəl ɪstèɪt]
⬜⬜⬜⬜⬜

N[U] 不動産

a **real estate** agency（不動産屋）

▶ **estate** [ɪstéɪt] N[C] 私有地　N[U] 財産

1151 overall
[òʊvərɔ́ːl]
⬜⬜⬜⬜⬜

Adv. 全体として、全体的に見て　Adj. 全体的な、総合的な

↻ CH. 5, 10, 14, 18, 21, 24

Chapter

25

ビジネス・経営
Business & Management

Many argue that successful corporations share common traits such as solid financial management practices, appropriate budgeting processes, sound investments, and dedicated employees, but having these does not necessarily guarantee a company's success.

In fact, most of the world's highly profitable and fastest-growing companies foster innovation by encouraging employees to take the initiative to implement changes. This "innovation competency" is far more critical than any other in establishing a competitive edge.

Google, for example, has explicitly focused on breeding a relaxed rather than stringent culture to prioritize novel ideas over instant perfection in order to remain ahead of the curve.

As a result, not only has this strategy played an absolutely vital role in making the company's business sustainable, it has also boosted its revenue and profit margin exponentially.

1 Many argue that successful corporations share common traits such as solid financial management practices, appropriate budgeting processes, sound investments, and dedicated employees, but having these does not necessarily guarantee a company's success.

成功している会社が持つ共通項としては、堅実な財務管理手法、適切な予算編成プロセス、手堅い投資、献身的な従業員などがよく挙げられるが、こうした条件さえそろえば、会社の成功が必ず保証されるわけでもない。

1152 corporation
[kɔ̀ːrpəréɪʃən]
☐☐☐☐☐☐

N[C] 会社、大企業、法人（= Corp.）

He only built this **corporation** two years ago, and he's already making a ridiculous amount of money. (彼は2年前に会社を立ち上げたばかりなのに、もうヤバいくらい儲かってるんだ。)

▶ **corporate** [kɔ́ːrpərət] Adj. 会社の、企業の、法人の

My favorite **corporate** slogan is Nike's "Just do it."
(僕の好きな企業スローガンはナイキの "Just do it" だな。)

1153 management
[mǽnədʒmənt]
☐☐☐☐☐☐

N[U] 管理、経営、マネジメント　**N[S/U]** 経営陣

The results of his department's employee survey make me doubt his **management** abilities.
(彼の部署の社員アンケートの結果を見た感じだと、彼の管理能力が疑わしいと言わざるを得ないな。)

Management has taken action to turn it around.
(経営者たちは状況を好転させるためにアクションを取った。)

▶ **manage** V[T] を管理する、経営する、運営する
[mǽnədʒ] V[I/T]（〜を）うまくやる、やりくりする

■ **manage** to do（どうにかして〜する、なんとか〜する）

I **managed to** graduate from my university, even though my grades weren't great.
(成績はそんなに良くなかったけど、なんとか大学を卒業できたよ。)

▶ **manager** [mǽnədʒər] N[C] 管理者、部長、経営者、マネージャー；監督

▶ **managerial** [mæ̀nədʒíriəl] Adj. 管理の、経営の

Previous **managerial** experience is required for this job post.
(この求人は過去に経営経験があることが要件です。)

1154 budgeting
[bʌ́dʒətɪŋ]
☐☐☐☐☐☐

N[U] 予算編成

The CFO implemented a more efficient **budgeting** system to save the financial team time.
(CFOは財務チームの時間を節約するために、より効率のいい予算編成システムを導入したんだ。)

さあ、次世代の単語学習を。

アプリなら、できることがほかにもたくさん。

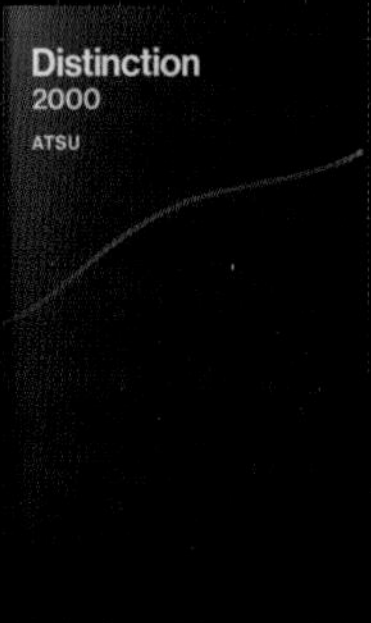

Distinction
2000
ATSU

Web なら
割引価格で
購入できます。

詳しくはコチラ →

スタディモード 📖
覚えられない単語を
繰り返し出題。
サクサク覚えられる。

ストリーク＆XP 🎮
ゲーム感覚で
楽しいから
ずーっと続く。

検索機能 🔍
驚異的な検索力で
アプリ中を
素早くサーチ。

音声認識 ᴸᵗ
発音のチェックも
サクッと完了。

ネイティブ音声 ᵠ
10,000 以上の
ナチュラル音声も
すべてこのアプリで。

音声再生 ▶ᴵᴵ
絞り込み、シャッフル、
連続再生。
すべて思い通り。

▶ **budget**　N[C] 予算　Adj. 格安の、お買い得の
[bʌ́dʒɪt]　V[I/T]（〜の）予算を組む（for sth）

a **budget** airline/hotel（格安航空 / ホテル）

1155 **investment**
[ɪnvéstmənt]
☐☐☐☐☐☐

N[C/U]　（〜に対する）投資（in sth）

The best **investment** you'll ever make is in your own education.
（自分自身の教育こそ最高の投資だよ。）

▶ **invest** V[I]（〜に）投資する（in sth）　V[T] を（〜に）投資する（in sth）
[ɪnvést]

I'd rather **invest** money in property than spend it on drinking.
（僕はお金を飲み会に使うくらいなら、不動産投資に使いたいな。）

▶ **investor** [ɪnvéstər] N[C] 投資家　▶ **investee** [ɪnvestí:] N[C] 投資を受ける側

1156 **necessarily**
[nesəsérɪli]
☐☐☐☐☐☐

Adv.（否定文で）必ずしも〜ない；必然的に

Getting a full score on TOEIC doesn't **necessarily** mean that you write, speak, and understand English as well as a native English speaker.
（TOEIC で満点取ったからといって、ネイティブと同じくらい上手に英語を書いたり、話したり、理解したりできるとは限らないよ。）

▶ **necessary** [nésəseri] Adj. 必要な、必須の

What ingredients would you say are absolutely **necessary** for making curry?
（カレー作るのに絶対必要な材料って何かな？）

▶ **necessity** [nəsésəti] N[U] 必要（性）　N[C] 必需品、必要なもの

▶ **necessitate** [nəsésəteɪt] V[T] を必要とする

1157 **guarantee**
[gèrəntí:]
☐☐☐☐☐☐

V[T]　を保証する、確実にする　N[C/U]　保証

I **guarantee** that this will be the best book you'll ever read.
（この本が君の人生において最高の一冊になること間違いなしだよ！）

1158 **company**
[kʌ́mpəni]
☐☐☐☐☐☐

N[C]　会社、企業、法人　N[U]　同伴；来客；一団

There are rumors that his **company** is affiliated with the mafia.
（彼の会社はマフィアと関わりがあると噂されてるんだ。）

Do you want some **company**?（一緒に行こうか？）

■ keep sb **company**（〜に付き合う、〜と一緒にいる）

I'll **keep** you **company** until your cab comes.（タクシーが来るまで一緒にいてあげるよ。）

▶ **accompany** [əkʌ́mpəni] V[T] と一緒に行く、に同伴する

company vs **corporation**　どちらも「会社」と訳されることが多いですが、普段の会話では company はそのサイズに関係なく一般的な「会社」を意味し、一方で corporation は「大企業」を指すときに使われることが多い単語です。ゆえに、company という言葉の中に corporation という言葉が含まれているというイメージがあります。

2

In fact, most of the world's highly profitable and fastest-growing companies foster innovation by encouraging employees to take the initiative to implement changes. This "innovation competency" is far more critical than any other in establishing a competitive edge.

実際、世界で高い利益を上げて急成長している企業の大半は、従業員がイニシアティブを取って改革を行うよう奨励してイノベーションを促進している。この「イノベーションを引き起こす能力」は、競争力を確立する上で何にもまして重要である。

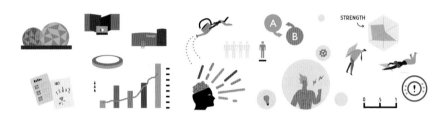

1159 profitable
[prá:fɪṭəbəl]

Adj. 利益になる、儲かる；有益な

We need to determine if adopting the new system is really **profitable** for our company.
(この新しいシステムを導入することが本当に会社にとって有益なのか、ちゃんと判断する必要があるね。)

▶ **profitably** Adv. 利益を出して
[prá:fɪṭəbli]

▶ **profitability** N[U] 収益性、利益率
[prà:fɪṭəbíləṭi]

▶ **profit** [prá:fɪt] N[C/U] 利益　V[T] の利益になる，　V[I] 利益を得る

make a **profit** (利益を得る)　　**profit** from sth (〜から利益を得る)

profit vs **benefit**　どちらも「利益」という意味ですが、基本的には profit は金銭的な利益 (売上−費用) のことで、benefit は社会に対する利益など、金銭的でない利益に使用されます。

1160 foster
[fá:stər]

V[T] を促進する、育む；を (里子として) 育てる　**Adj.** 里親の、里子の

I need a strict coach to **foster** my talent. (僕には才能を育むための厳しいコーチが必要なんだ。)

a **foster** family (里親の家族)

1161 initiative
[ɪníʃəṭɪv]

N[S] イニシアティブ、主導権【the -】　**N[U]** 率先、自発性　**N[C]** 構想

■ take the **initiative** to do (率先して〜する)

He **took the initiative to** help out the victims of the earthquake in Japan.
(彼は率先して日本の地震による被災者を助ける活動をしたんだ。)

1162 competency
[ká:mpəṭənsi]

N[C/U] 能力、力量　= **competence** [ká:mpəṭəns]

How much English **competency** is needed to study abroad at an Ivy League school?
(アメリカのアイビーリーグに留学するためには、どれくらいの英語力が必要なんだろう？)

▶ **competent** Adj. 有能な；まずまずの　⬌ **incompetent** 無能な
[kɑ́:mpəṭənt]　　　　　　　　　　　　　[ɪnkɑ́:mpəṭənt]

▶ **competently** [kɑ́:mpəṭəntli] Adv. 有能に

1163 **far**
[fɑːr]
☐☐☐☐☐☐

Adv. (比較級を強調して) はるかに；遠くに　**Adj.** (〜から) 遠い (from sth)

I'm jealous of you because you're **far** more intelligent than I am.
(君は僕よりもはるかに賢いから本当に羨ましいよ。)

by **far** ((最上級を強調して) はるかに、断然)

■ as **far** as I know (私の知ってる限り)　■ as **far** as I'm concerned (私的には)

As far as I know, he hasn't finished his work yet.
(僕の知る限りでは、彼はまだ仕事終わってないみたいだよ。)

As far as I'm concerned, Freddie Mercury is the greatest singer of all time.
(私の意見としては、フレディー・マーキュリーは歴史上最も偉大な歌手だと思います。)

so **far** (今までのところ)

▶ **farther** [fɑ́:rðər] Adj. もっと遠い　Adv. もっと遠くに

How much **farther** is it to our hotel? (ホテルまであと距離はどれくらい？)

▶ **farthest** [fɑ́:rðɪst] Adj. もっとも遠い　Adv. もっとも遠く

1164 **competitive**
[kəmpéṭəṭɪv]
☐☐☐☐☐☐

Adj. 競争力のある、競争の激しい；勝ちにこだわる

Why is everybody so **competitive**? I thought it was supposed to be a warm-up game.
(なんでみんなそんなに勝ちにこだわってるの？ ただのウォーミングアップのための試合だと思ってたんだけど。)

▶ **competitiveness** [kəmpéṭəṭɪvnəs] N[U] 競争力；競争心

▶ **competition** [kɑ̀:mpətíʃən] N[U] 競争；競走相手；競技会

▶ **competitor** [kəmpéṭəṭər] N[C] 競争者、競争相手

▶ **compete** [kəmpíːt] V[I] (〜と) 競争する (with/against sb)

I hate how we're made to **compete** against each other. I prefer to improve myself so that I can help others.
(僕、競争させられるのが嫌いなんだ。周りを助けられるように自分を向上させる方が好きだな。)

1165 **edge**
[edʒ]
☐☐☐☐☐☐

N[S] 強み、優位性；(声などの) 鋭さ　**N[C]** 端、へり；刃

Having an extra day of rest will give our team a bit of an **edge** over the opposition.
(休みが一日多いから、うちのチームは相手よりも少し有利だろうね。)

a competitive **edge** (競争力)

■ have an/the **edge** (over/on sth/sb) ((〜より) 優位に立つ)

Since you can speak English, I think you **have the edge** in this company.
(君は英語が話せるし、この会社では優位に立てると思うよ。)

▶ **edgy** [édʒi] Adj. 緊張した、いらいらした；流行の先端を行く

3 Google, for example, has explicitly focused on breeding a relaxed rather than stringent culture to prioritize novel ideas over instant perfection in order to remain ahead of the curve.

例えばグーグルは、厳格な文化よりも、のびのびとした文化を生み出すことに明確に力を入れてきたが、それは、時代を先取りし続けるために、完璧さを安直に求めることよりも斬新なアイディアを優先しているからである。

1166 explicitly
[ɪksplísɪtli]
☐☐☐☐☐☐

Adv. 明確に、明白に、はっきりと；露骨に

Even though the teacher **explicitly** explained the details of the activity, several students still had no clue what to do.
(先生は活動内容について明確に説明したんだけど、まだ何人かの生徒はどうすれば良いか分かってなかったんだ。)

▶ **explicit** [ɪksplísɪt] Adj. 明確な、明白な；露骨な

↔ **implicit** [ɪmplísɪt] 含意された、暗黙の

I like how my boss always gives me very **explicit** instructions on how he wants something done. (僕の上司は作業をどうこなして欲しいのか、いつも明確な指示をくれるから好きなんだ。)

▶ **explicitness** [ɪksplísɪtnəs] N[U] 明確さ、明白さ；露骨さ

1167 breed
[bri:d]
☐☐☐☐☐☐

V[T] を生み出す；を飼育する、繁殖させる；を引き起こす

Politicians need to be careful what they say in public so that they don't **breed** discrimination against certain groups.
(政治家はある特定の層に対する差別を生まないために、人前での発言には気をつける必要がある。)

V[I] 繁殖する　N[C] 品種、種

▶ **breeding** [bri:dɪŋ] N[U] 繁殖、飼育；品種改良；育ち

■ a **breeding** ground (温床；繁殖地、飼育場)

Dark web forums are **breeding grounds** for crime.
(ダークウェブの掲示板は犯罪の温床なんだ。)

▶ **breeder** [bri:dər] N[C] ブリーダー、飼育者

1168 relaxed
[rɪlǽkst]
☐☐☐☐☐☐

Adj. のびのびとした、リラックスした、（規制などが）緩やかな

I spent a **relaxed** weekend in Hawaii with my girlfriend.
(彼女とハワイでゆっくり週末を過ごすことができたよ。)

▶ **relax** [rɪlǽks] V[T] をリラックスさせる、緩める　V[I] リラックスする、緩む

This yoga pose will help you **relax** your back muscles.
（このヨガのポーズをすると背中の筋肉をほぐすことができるよ。）

Relax, this test isn't that hard. （まぁそんな緊張すんなよ、この試験そんな難しくないよ。）

▶ **relaxing** [rɪlǽksɪŋ] Adj. リラックスさせるような

Reading a book on a hammock is very **relaxing**. （ハンモックの上で本を読むと本当に落ち着く。）

▶ **relaxation** [rìːlækséɪʃən] N[U] くつろぎ、息抜き

1169 **stringent**
[stríndʒənt]
☐☐☐☐☐☐

Adj. 厳格な、厳しい

In the U.S., there are **stringent** laws governing underage drinking.
（アメリカでは未成年の飲酒が法律によって厳しく禁止されてるんだ。）

▶ **stringently** [stríndʒəntli] Adv. 厳しく   ▶ **stringency** [stríndʒənsi] N[U] 厳しさ

1170 **novel**
[nάːvəl]
☐☐☐☐☐☐

Adj. 斬新な、画期的な、目新しい   **N[C]** 小説

I heard our professor was awarded the Nobel Prize in Chemistry for discovering a
novel antibiotic. （うちの教授、新しい抗生物質を発見してノーベル化学賞受賞したらしいよ。）

a romantic **novel** （恋愛小説）

▶ **novelist** [nάːvəlɪst] N[C] 小説家

▶ **novelty** [nάːvəlt̬i] N[U] 珍しさ、目新しさ   N[C] 珍しいもの、目新しいこと

Tourists are still a **novelty** in this country.
（この国では観光客はまだ珍しい存在なんだ。）

1171 **perfection**
[pərfékʃən]
☐☐☐☐☐☐

N[U] 完璧さ、完全さ

He always demands **perfection** from his teammates.   to **perfection**
（彼はいつもチームメイトに完璧を求めるんだ。）   （完璧に）

▶ **perfect** [pə́ːrfekt] Adj. 完璧な、完全な；（用途や目的に）ぴったりの （for sth）

Even though this car is three years old, it's in **perfect** condition because it's been
serviced regularly.（この車を買ってからもう3年経つけど、定期的に車両点検を行っているから状態は完璧。）

▶ **perfectly** Adv. 完璧に、完全に   ▶ **perfectionist** N[C] 完璧主義者
[pə́ːrfektli]   [pərfékʃənɪst]

1172 **curve**
[kɜːrv]
☐☐☐☐☐☐

N[C] 曲線、カーブ   **V[I]** 曲がる   **V[T]** を曲げる

I love the **curves** on this building. （この建物の曲線がすごい好きなんだよなぁ。）

ahead of the **curve** （時代を先取りした）

▶ **curved** [kɜːrvd] Adj. 曲がった、曲線状の   ⟷ **straight** [streɪt] 真っすぐの

▶ **curveball** [kɜ́ːrvbɑːl] N[C] （野球などの）変化球；予期せぬ出来事・質問

■ throw sb a **curveball** （（予期せぬ出来事や質問で）～を驚かせる）

She **threw** me **a curveball** during the interview.
（彼女は面接中に予想もしなかった質問を投げかけてきた。）

4 As a result, not only has this strategy played an absolutely vital role in making the company's business sustainable, it has also boosted its revenue and profit margin exponentially.

結果として、この戦略はグーグルの事業を持続可能にする上で絶対に重要な役割を果たしただけでなく、収益と利益率を飛躍的に伸ばすことにもつながった。

1173 **absolutely**
[æbsəlúːtli]

Adv. 絶対に、間違いなく、確実に；（返答として）もちろん；どういたしまして

Since last week, she's been **absolutely** addicted to bubble tea and drinks it twice a day!
（先週から彼女はすっかりタピオカティーにはまっちゃって、一日二回も飲んでるんだ！）

▶ **absolute** [æbsəluːt] Adj. 絶対的な、完全な、まったくの

How can you work like that? Your office is an **absolute** mess.
（どうやってこんなんで仕事できるの？オフィス超散らかってんじゃん。）

会話の返答としても使える absolutely
absolutely は相手の質問に対して賛成する際や、共感を示したい時によく使用される表現です。
"Do you think you can finish this tonight?"（これ今晩終わらせられると思う？）
"Yeah, absolutely!"（もちろん！）
また「絶対にダメ、全くそうじゃない」という意味で absolutely not という形もよく使われます。
"Do you have a crush on him?"（彼のこと好きになっちゃったの？）
"Absolutely not!"（全然！）

1174 **business**
[bíznɪs]

N[U] 事業、ビジネス、商売

I heard his **business** is going well and that he'll be opening a second store in Osaka next month.（彼のビジネスはうまくいっているみたいで、来月には大阪で二店舗目を開くらしいよ。）

■ in/out of **business**（営業中の / 廃業した、潰れた）　■ **business** as usual（いつものこと）

The store went **out of business** last year.（あのお店は去年潰れたよ。）

He got super drunk and crashed at my place yesterday. **Business as usual**.
（あいつ昨日超酔っ払って、俺ん家で寝やがってさ。まぁ、いつものことか。）

1175 **sustainable**
[səstéɪnəbəl]

Adj. 持続可能な

We need to stop relying on power plants and instead look for more **sustainable** energy sources.（発電所に頼るのをやめて、別のより持続可能なエネルギー資源を探す必要があるね。）

sustainable growth（持続可能な成長）

▶ **sustainably** [səstéɪnəbli] Adv. 持続的に、持続可能な方法で

He traveled around to a few organic farms to learn how to live **sustainably**.
（彼は持続可能な暮らし方について学ぶためにいくつか有機農園をまわったんだ。）

▶ **sustainability** N[U] 持続可能性　　▶ **sustain** V[T] を持続させる、維持する
[səstèɪnəbíləti]　　　　　　　　　　　　　　　[səstéɪn]

1176 **boost**
[buːst]
☐☐☐☐☐☐

V[T] を伸ばす、高める、増大させる　N[C] 起爆剤；上昇、増加

His seminar on studying English **boosted** my confidence.
（彼の英語学習セミナーで自信が高まったよ。）

▶ **booster** [búːstər] N[C]（自信などを）高めるもの；後援者

Red Bull is a good **booster** for me.（レッドブル飲むとテンション上がるわ。）

1177 **revenue**
[révənuː]
☐☐☐☐☐☐

N[U] 収益、収入、歳入　= **revenues** [révənuːz]

The annual **revenues** of the largest companies in Australia are pretty small compared to those of Japanese companies.
（オーストラリアで一番大きい企業の収益は日本と比べると結構少ない。）

1178 **margin**
[máːrdʒɪn]
☐☐☐☐☐☐

N[C] 利益、マージン；余白；余裕；周辺部；（得点などの）差

■ profit **margin**（利益率）

Do coffee shops have good **profit margins**?（コーヒー屋さんって利益率良いの？）

There's no **margin** for error here, so I have to make sure it's a good shot.
（ここでミスる余裕はないから、ちゃんとやらないとな。）

▶ **marginal** [máːrdʒɪnəl] Adj. わずかな；余白に書かれた；周辺部の

I was only making **marginal** improvements each month, so I stopped going to painting lessons.（毎月ちょっとずつしか上達しなかったから、絵のレッスン受けるのやめちゃったよ。）

▶ **marginally** [máːrdʒɪnəli] Adv. わずかに

Interestingly, your happiness increases a lot when your personal income rises from 4 million to 6 million yen, but happiness only grows **marginally** when your personal income rises from 10 million to 12 million yen.
（面白いことに、年収が400万円から600万円に上がると幸福度がすごい上がるんだけど、1,000万円から1,200万円に上がる場合、幸福度はわずかにしか上昇しないんだ。）

1179 **exponentially**
[èkspənénʃəli]
☐☐☐☐☐☐

Adv. 飛躍的に、急激に、指数関数的に、幾何級数的に

Once he immersed himself in the culture, his Spanish improved **exponentially**.
（スペイン文化に浸るようになって、彼のスペイン語力は急激に伸びたんだ。）

▶ **exponential** [èkspənénʃəl] Adj. 急激な、指数関数的な

There has been **exponential** growth in the number of TikTok users over the last three years.
（ここ3年で、TikTokのユーザー数は急激に増えているよね。）

▶ **exponent** [ɪkspóʊnənt] [ékspoʊnənt] N[C] 指数

Details

We have a great opportunity for an experienced Sales Manager who can lead and organize our sales representatives to deliver consistent results and provide outstanding customer service to our clients. The successful candidate will exhibit professional behavior and possess the following qualifications and qualities:

- Minimum of 3 years of work experience relevant to the occupation
- Excellent verbal and written communication skills
- Ability to direct and coach a sales team to operate in the most productive and cost-efficient manner
- Dedication to providing great customer service.

An MBA would be an advantage. This position reports directly to the executives.

We also offer amazing perks including:

- Fully covered medical insurance plan
- Competitive compensation + commissions
- Free tax return services
- Retirement pension

If this sounds like you, please send an email to robert@davidretail.com with your resume attached.

Robert Gordon
Recruitment Manager

Sales Manager
Los Angeles, CA 22 hours ago

Apply

詳細

弊社の営業担当者を率いてまとめ上げ、着実に成果を出し、優れた顧客サービスをクライアントに提供できる経験豊富なセールスマネージャーを募集しています。適任者はプロフェッショナルとしての行動を示す、以下の能力と資質がある方です。

- 同職に関連した最低3年の実務経験
- 口頭でのやり取りや文書における高いコミュニケーション能力
- 生産的かつ費用対効果の高い方法で営業チームを指揮し、指導できる
- 優れた顧客サービスの提供に尽力できる

MBA取得者は有利です。幹部に直接報告を行う役職です。

また、以下のような充実した手当も用意しています。

- 医療保険の全面適用
- 他社に引けを取らない給与+歩合給
- 無料の確定申告サービス
- 退職年金

適任と思われた方は、**robert@davidretail.com** まで履歴書を添付の上メールをお送りください。

ロバート・ゴードン 採用マネージャー

Dear Robert,

My name is Charlie, and I'm very interested in the job posting for the role of Sales Manager for David Retail. I believe my experience is a great match for the job vacancy.

I am currently the Sales Manager for IT Solutions Enterprises but have been seeking an opportunity to work in the retail industry.

In my current role, I have had over five years of experience managing a large sales team (100+ reps) to achieve outstanding sales results. I was also in charge of running multiple sales campaigns and loyalty programs. For example, I led the creation of an Instagram promotion campaign to market our new accounting software, which boosted quarterly sales by more than 30%. In addition to my practical work experience, I also have an MBA from Cornell University.

My work experience and skills will allow me to provide in-depth analytics and actionable insights to greatly improve the marketing and sales of your merchandise, which makes me the ideal candidate for this role.

Thank you for your consideration. I look forward to hearing from you.

Regards,

Charlie

ロバート様

チャーリーと申します。David Retailのセールスマネージャーの求人に非常に興味を持っております。私の経験は、貴社の求人にとてもふさわしいと思っております。

私は現在、ITソリューションエンタープライズのセールスマネージャーを務めていますが、小売業界で働く機会を求めています。

現在の役職で5年以上の経験を持ち、大人数の営業チーム（担当者は100人以上）のマネジメントを行いながら素晴らしい販売実績を上げてきました。また、販促キャンペーンとロイヤリティプログラムも複数担当しました。例えば、弊社の新しい会計ソフトを売り出す際にはインスタグラムを利用した販促キャンペーンの開発を指揮し、その結果、四半期売上の30％増を達成しました。実務経験に加え、コーネル大学でMBAも取得しています。

私の実務経験とスキルによって、綿密な分析と実現性の高い見識を提供し、貴社商品のマーケティングと販売を大幅に改善できるはずです。私はこの役職にまさに適任と言えるでしょう。

ご検討いただければ幸いです。ご連絡をお待ちしております。

よろしくお願いいたします。

チャーリー

1180 representative
[rèprɪzéntətɪv]
☐☐☐☐☐☐

N[C] 担当者、係員　= rep [rep]　N[C] 代表者；下院議員【R-】

a sales **representative**（販売員、営業担当者）= a sales **rep**

Adj.（〜を）表している（of sth）；代表的な

▶ **represent** [rèprɪzént] V[T] を代表する；を表現する

▶ **representation** [rèprɪzentéɪʃən] N[C/U]（〜を）表すもの（of sth）

1181 consistent
[kənsístənt]
☐☐☐☐☐☐

Adj. 着実な；一貫した、矛盾のない

↔ **inconsistent** [ìnkənsístənt] 一貫性のない、矛盾した

▶ **consistently** [kənsístəntli] Adv. 一貫して　↔ **inconsistently** [ìnkənsístəntli] 矛盾して

▶ **consistency** [kənsístənsi] N[C/U] 一貫性

↔ **inconsistency** [ìnkənsístənsi] 一貫性のなさ

1182 customer
[kʌ́stəmər]
☐☐☐☐☐☐

N[C] 顧客、客

I really hate when **customers** behave like they're God.

（客が自分は神様みたいな感じでふるまうの本当嫌なんだけど。）

1183 service
[sɝ́ːrvɪs]
☐☐☐☐☐☐

N[C/U] サービス　N[C] 公共事業　N[U] 奉仕；勤務（期間）

customer **service**（顧客サービス）

1184 candidate
[kǽndɪdət]
☐☐☐☐☐☐

N[C]（就職の）志望者；候補者

▶ **candidacy** [kǽndɪdəsi] N[U] 立候補

1185 exhibit
[ɪgzíbɪt]
☐☐☐☐☐☐

V[T]（性質や感情）を示す、見せる

V[I/T]（〜を）展示する　N[C] 展示会、展示品

▶ **exhibition** [èksəbíʃən] N[C] 展示会、展覧会　N[U] 展示

1186 qualification
[kwὰːləfəkéɪʃən]
☐☐☐☐☐☐

N[C/U] 能力、資格、適性　N[U] 資格取得　N[C/U]（規則などの）制限

▶ **qualified** [kwάːləfaɪd] Adj.（〜に必要な / 〜する）能力のある（for sth/to do）；資格のある

▶ **qualify** [kwάːləfaɪ] V[I]（〜の）資格がある（for sth）

V[T] に（〜の）資格を与える（for sth）；（言葉）を修飾する

▶ **qualifier** [kwάːləfaɪər] N[C] 予選通過者、予選通過；出場決定戦

1187 occupation
[ὰːkjəpéɪʃən]
☐☐☐☐☐☐

N[C] 職業　N[C/U] 占拠

What's your **occupation**?（職業は何ですか？）

1188 verbal
[vɝ́ːrbəl]
☐☐☐☐☐☐

Adj. 口頭による、言葉による　↔ **written** [rítn] 書面による

▶ **verbally** [vɝ́ːrbəli] Adv. 言葉で、口頭で　▶ **verbalize** [vɝ́ːrbəlaɪz] V[I/T]（〜を）言葉で表す

1189 productive
[prədʌ́ktɪv]

Adj. 生産的な；有意義な

I feel guilty when I'm not **productive**.（僕は生産的でいないと罪悪感にかられるんだ。）

▶ **productively** [prədʌ́ktɪvli] Adv. 生産的に ▶ **productivity** [pròʊdəktívəti] N[U] 生産性

1190 advantage
[ədvǽnṭɪdʒ]

N[C/U] 有利；強み、長所 ↔ **disadvantage** [dìsədvǽnṭɪdʒ] 不利；デメリット

take **advantage** of sth/sb（～をうまく利用する）

▶ **advantageous** [ædvæntéɪdʒəs] Adj. 有利な、都合の良い

1191 executive
[ɪgzékjəṭɪv]

N[C] 幹部、役員、重役 **Adj.** 幹部の；（幹部の人が購入するような）高級な

▶ **execute** [éksəkju:t] V[T]（計画など）を実行する；を処刑する

▶ **execution** [èksəkjú:ʃən] N[U] 実行、実施 N[C/U] 処刑

1192 insurance
[ɪnʃárəns]

N[U] 保険、保険料 **N[S/U]** 対策、保険

▶ **insure** [ɪnʃúr] V[T] に保険をかける ▶ **insured** [ɪnʃúrd] Adj. 保険をかけられた

▶ **insurer** [ɪnʃúrər] N[C] 保険業者

1193 compensation
[kɑ̀:mpenséɪʃən]

N[U] 給与、報酬；賠償金 **N[C/U]** 償い、補償

▶ **compensate** [kɑ́:mpənseɪt] V[I]（～を）補う（for sth） V[T] に賠償する、補償する

1194 commission
[kəmíʃən]

N[C/U] 歩合給、コミッション；手数料 **N[C]** 委員会

1195 tax
[tæks]

N[C/U] 税、税金 **V[T]** に課税する

a **tax** return（確定申告）

▶ **taxpayer** [tǽkspèɪər] N[C] 納税者

1196 retirement
[rɪtáɪrmənt]

N[C/U] 退職、引退

▶ **retire** [rɪtáɪr] V[I]（～を）退職する、引退する（from sth） V[T] を退職させる

▶ **retired** [rɪtáɪrd] Adj. 退職した、引退した

1197 pension
[pénʃən]

N[C] 年金

▶ **pensioner** [pénʃənər] N[C] 年金受給者

1198 resume
N. [rézəmèɪ]
V. [rɪzú:m]

N[C] 履歴書 **V[I/T]**（～を）再開する

1199 recruitment
[rɪkrú:tmənt]

N[U] 採用、新人募集

▶ **recruit** [rɪkrú:t] V[I/T]（～を）採用する；（～を）徴兵する N[C] 新人；新兵

▶ **recruiting** [rɪkrú:tɪŋ] N[U] 採用活動 ▶ **recruiter** [rɪkrú:tər] N[C] 採用担当者

1200 match
[mætʃ]

N[C] 適合する人・もの；試合；マッチ

V[I/T] （〜と）調和する、マッチする；（〜と）一致する　V[T] に匹敵する

Do you think my belt and shoes have to **match**?
（ベルトと靴って合ってないといけないと思う？）

1201 vacancy
[véɪkənsi]

N[C] 空席、欠員、空室

a job **vacancy**（求人）

▶ **vacant** [véɪkənt] Adj. 空いている

1202 enterprise
[énṭərpraɪz]

N[C] 会社、企業　N[U] 事業

▶ **enterprising** [énṭərpraɪzɪŋ] Adj. 積極的な、野心的な

1203 retail
[rí:teɪl]

N[U] 小売り　Adv. 小売りで　V[I] 小売りされる　V[T] を小売りする

▶ **retailer** [rí:teɪlər] N[C] 小売店、小売業者　▶ **retailing** [rí:teɪlɪŋ] N[U] 小売業

1204 charge
[tʃɑ:rdʒ]

N[U] 責任、義務　N[C/U] 料金、使用料；充電

be in **charge** of sth（〜を担当している、〜の責任者である）

N[C] 告訴、告発、容疑；非難

V[I/T] （〜を）請求する　V[I] 充電される

V[T] を充電する；を告発する、非難する

My phone won't **charge** properly.（私のスマホ、ちゃんと充電されないんだ。）

▶ **charger** [tʃá:rdʒər] N[C] 充電器

1205 campaign
[kæmpéɪn]

N[C] キャンペーン、運動　V[I] キャンペーンを行う、運動を行う

1206 quarterly
[kwɔ́:rṭərli]

Adj. 四半期の、年4回の　Adv. 四半期ごとに、年4回　N[C] 季刊誌

▶ **quarter** [kwɔ́:rṭər] N[C] 四半期；4分の1

1207 merchandise
N1. [mə́:rtʃəndaɪs]
N2./V. [mə́:rtʃəndaɪz]

N[U] 商品、製品　V[T] を販促する

▶ **merchandiser** [mə́:rtʃəndaɪzər] N[C] 小売業者

▶ **merchandising** [mə́:rtʃəndaɪzɪŋ] N[U] 販売方法、販売計画、販売促進

1208 look forward to sth
[lʊk fɔ́:rwərtə]

[PV] を楽しみにする

I'm **looking forward to** seeing you.（会えるの楽しみにしてるよ。）

↻ CH. 6, 11, 15, 19, 22, 25

Chapter

26

教育
Education

In recent times, what constitutes an appropriate teaching method has been debated intensely. Also under discussion is whether prevailing methods must be totally overhauled or merely refined incrementally.

Many believe that traditional teaching methods, such as lectures, classes in formal settings, and cramming in preparation for tests and exams have been rendered obsolete by modern technology and recent changes in student attitudes.

For example, the younger generation is said to have shorter attention spans due to the ubiquity of new technologies and gadgets, and they therefore find traditional knowledge transfer methods unstimulating, rigid, and inflexible.

In response, educators are trying to reverse teaching stereotypes in various ways, such as shortening classroom sessions and modifying the pace of learning to suit the needs of struggling students.

1

In recent times, what constitutes an appropriate teaching method has been debated intensely. Also under discussion is whether prevailing methods must be totally overhauled or merely refined incrementally.

近年、適切な教授法をめぐる議論が激しさを増している。同様に、一般的に普及している教授法を全面的に見直す必要があるのか、あるいは単に少しずつ改良するだけで良いのか、という議論も行われている。

1209 appropriate
Adj. [əpróupriət]
V. [əpróuprieɪt]
☐☐☐☐☐☐

Adj. 適切な、適した、ふさわしい　**V[T]** (資金など) を充てる

I don't think it's **appropriate** to ask so many personal questions at work.
(職場であんなにたくさんプライベートな質問をするのは適切じゃないと思うな。)

▶ **appropriately** [əpróupriətli] Adv. 適切に、ふさわしく

You can't really complain about the cold if you're not dressed **appropriately**.
(ちゃんとした服装してないのに寒いとか言っちゃだめでしょ。)

▶ **appropriateness** [əpróupriətnəs] N[U] 適切さ

I question the **appropriateness** of this movie for children.
(この映画が子供にとって適切かどうかは疑問だな。)

1210 intensely
[ɪnténsli]
☐☐☐☐☐☐

Adv. 激しく、強烈に；まじめに、熱心に

I prefer to work **intensely** for five or six hours a day rather than take it easy for 12 hours.
(ダラダラ12時間仕事するよりも、一日5、6時間まじめに仕事する方が好きだな。)

▶ **intense** [ɪnténs] Adj. 激しい、強烈な；まじめな、真剣な

The exam was really **intense**, but I managed to pass it, thanks to all my preparation.
(試験はめちゃくちゃきつかったけど、ちゃんと準備したおかげでなんとか受かることができたよ。)

intense heat/cold (強烈な暑さ / 寒さ)　　an **intense** taste (とても濃い味)

▶ **intensity** [ɪnténsəti] N[U] 激しさ　N[C/U] (光や音の) 強さ

The **intensity** of the job was driving me crazy last week, but everything's done and dusted now.
(先週はあの仕事がめちゃくちゃきつくて頭がおかしくなりそうだったけど、もう全部終了したよ。)

1211 totally
[tóuṭli]
☐☐☐☐☐☐

Adv. 全面的に、完全に、まったく

I **totally** agree with you. (君に完全に同意だよ。)

▶ **total**　Adj. 全面的な、完全な、まったくの　N[C] 合計
[tóʊtl̩]　V[T] を合計する、（合計で〜）になる

I thought the **total** price would be $100, but I forgot to include tax.
（合計金額は 100 ドルだと思ってたんだけど、税金のこと忘れてた。）

■ **in total**（合計で）

My trip to Japan cost about $4000 **in total**.（日本旅行は合計で 4000 ドルくらいかかったよ。）

▶ **totality** [toʊtǽləti] N[U] 全体、全体性

■ **in totality**（全体を通して見ると、全体的に）

You can't really grasp the meaning of this book from just the first few chapters. You have to consider the work **in totality**.
（この本は最初の数チャプターだけ読んでもあんまり意味が分からないと思うから、作品全体を通して見た方がいいよ。）

1212 **overhaul**
V. [oʊvərhɔ́ːl]
N. [óʊvərhɔːl]

V[T] を徹底的に見直す；（機械など）を総点検する　N[C] 見直し；総点検

My watch needs to be **overhauled**, but I don't know where to get it done.
（腕時計の総点検をしてもらわないといけないんだけど、どこでやってもらえば良いのか分からないんだよね。）

1213 **merely**
[mírli]

Adv. 単に　= only [óʊnli]

Ken is **merely** an acquaintance. I've never hung out with him outside of work.
（ケンはただの知り合いだよ。職場以外での付き合いもないしね。）

▶ **mere** [mɪr] Adj. 単なる、ほんの

I was **mere** seconds away from breaking the marathon record.
（マラソンの記録更新まであとほんの数秒だったんだ。）

1214 **refine**
[rɪfáɪn]

V[T] を改良する、洗練する；を精製する

I've decided to try yoga to **refine** my posture.（姿勢を良くするためにヨガやることにしたよ。）

▶ **refinement** [rɪfáɪnmənt] N[U] 改良、洗練；精製　N[C] 改良点、改良品

Your report could do with some **refinement**.
（あなたのレポートはもうちょっと改善した方が良いね。）

▶ **refined** Adj. 改良された、洗練された；精製された　▶ **refinery** N[C] 精製所
[rɪfáɪnd]　[rɪfáɪnəri]

1215 **incrementally**
[ìnkrəméntəli]

Adv. 少しずつ、徐々に、次第に

My hometown's developed **incrementally** over the last few years.
（私の地元はここ数年でちょっとずつ発展したんだ。）

▶ **incremental** Adj. 徐々に増加する　▶ **increment** N[C] 増加、増加量
[ìnkrəméntl̩]　[ínkrəmənt]

in small **increments**（少しずつ）

2 Many believe that traditional teaching methods, such as lectures, classes in formal settings, and cramming in preparation for tests and exams have been rendered obsolete by modern technology and recent changes in student attitudes.

多くの人は、講義や型通りの授業、試験に備えた詰め込み学習といった従来型の教授法は、現代の技術や、今どきの生徒の態度における変化から、時代遅れになっていると考えている。

1216 lecture
[léktʃər]

N[C] （〜の）講義（on/about sth）；説教

His **lecture** on Classical Japanese was so boring that I started drawing a picture on the corner of my textbook.
（あの人の古文の講義つまんなすぎて途中で教科書の隅に絵描き始めちゃったよ。）

V[I] （〜の）講義をする（on/about sth）；説教をする

Duncan **lectures** at a few colleges but spends most of his time here.
（ダンカンはいくつかの大学で教えてるけど、大体はこの大学にいるよ。）

V[T] に（〜の）講義をする（on/about sth）；に説教をする

My mom started **lecturing** me again on how dangerous it is to travel overseas by myself.
（お母さんが私に一人で海外旅行するのがどれだけ危険かについてまたあーだこーだ言い出したんだ。）

▶ **lecturer** [léktʃərər] N[C] 講師、講演者

1217 class
[klæs]

N[C/U] 授業　N[C] 学級、クラス；（社会の）階級　N[U] 階級制

■ **in class**（授業中に、授業で）

It's becoming more and more common to use tablets **in class**.
（授業でタブレットを使うのはどんどん一般的になってきてるよ。）

1218 cram
[kræm]

V[I] （〜に向けて）詰め込み学習をする（for sth）　V[T] を詰め込む

Yesterday, I pulled an all-nighter to **cram** for the exam, but I've just realized that the exam is actually tomorrow.
（昨日試験に向けて徹夜して色々詰め込んだんだけど、試験明日だったわ。）

▶ **crammed** [kræmd] Adj. （〜が）ぎっしり詰まった、（〜で）いっぱいの（with sth/sb）

■ **crammed full of sth/sb**（〜でいっぱいの）

The train was **crammed full of** passengers.（電車は乗客でいっぱいだったよ。）

1219 preparation
[prèpəréɪʃən]
▢▢▢▢▢▢

N[U]　準備、用意　N[P]　（将来に向けた）準備計画、準備行為　【-s】

The best **preparation** that you can do the night before an exam is to get a good night's sleep. （試験前夜にできる最高の準備はしっかり寝ることだよ。）

do some **preparation** for sth
（〜に向けて準備をする）

in **preparation** for sth
（〜に備えて、〜の準備中で）

■ make **preparations** for sth（〜に向けて色々と準備をする）

I need to **make** some **preparations for** the party tonight.
（今晩のパーティに向けて色々と準備しないと。）

▶ **prepare**　V[I]（〜に向けて）準備をする（for sth）**= prep**［ prep ］
［ prɪpér ］　　V[T] を準備する；を（〜に向けて）準備させる（for sth）

Give me five minutes to **prepare**. （準備するから5分ちょうだい。）

▶ **prepared**［ prɪpérd ］Adj. 準備ができた　　▶ **preparatory**［ prɪpérətɔːri ］Adj. 準備の

I wasn't really **prepared** for the exam when I took it.
（あんまり準備せずに受験しちゃったんだよね。）

a **preparatory** phase
（準備段階）

1220 test
[test]
▢▢▢▢▢▢

N[C]　試験、テスト、検査　V[T]　を試験する、テストする、検査する

I'm so sick of having to take all these pointless **tests** at school.
（意味のないテストを学校で受けさせられるのもう本当に嫌なんだけど。）

1221 render
[réndər]
▢▢▢▢▢▢

V[T]　をある状態にする；を提供する、与える；を翻訳する

■ **render** A B（A を B の状態にする）

YouTube and Netflix have **rendered** my DVD player useless.
（YouTube と Netflix があるから DVD プレイヤーはもう要らないよ。）

It's really hard to **render** English poetry into other languages.
（英語の詩を他の言語に翻訳するのは本当に難しいよ。）

render services（サービスを提供する）

▶ **rendering**［ réndərɪŋ ］N[C]（演劇などの）表現、演出

1222 obsolete
[àːbsəliːt]
▢▢▢▢▢▢

Adj.　時代遅れの、廃れた、（古くなって）使われなくなった

The concept of physically going to school to take lessons is a bit **obsolete** given the number of quality lectures online.
（オンラインで質の良い授業はたくさんあるし、授業を受けるために実際に学校に行くっていう考えはちょっと時代遅れだよね。）

▶ **obsolescence**［ àːbsəlésəns ］N[U] 陳腐化、老朽化

▶ **obsolescent**［ àːbsəlésənt ］Adj. 時代遅れになってきている、廃れつつある

How are you going to clear out **obsolescent** inventory?
（古くなってきた在庫はどうやって処分するの？）

obsolete vs **obsolescent**　どちらも似ていますが、obsolete はもうすでに古くなっていることを意味し、obsolescent は完全に古くなっているわけではないが、現在進行形で古くなってきている様子を表す形容詞です。

3

For example, the younger generation is said to have shorter attention spans due to the ubiquity of new technologies and gadgets, and they therefore find traditional knowledge transfer methods unstimulating, rigid, and inflexible.

例えば、若い世代は、新しいテクノロジーやガジェットが至るところにあるため集中力の持続時間が短くなったと言われており、そのせいで、彼らは知識を伝達する従来の方法を退屈でかたい、そして柔軟性に欠けると感じている。

1223 generation
[dʒènəréɪʃən]
□□□□□□

N[C] 世代　N[U] （エネルギーの）発生、生成

I didn't really hit it off with my boss because of the **generation** gap.
（上司とはジェネレーションギャップがあるから中々意気投合しなかったんだよね。）

the older/younger **generation**　　the new/next **generation**
（昔の世代 / 若い世代）　　　　　　（新世代 / 次世代）

▶ **generate** [dʒénəreɪt] V[T] を生み出す、もたらす

The best way to **generate** more page views on your website is through social media.
（サイトのページビュー数をもっと増やすには、SNS を活用するのが一番良いよ。）

▶ **generational** [dʒènəréɪʃənəl] Adj. 世代間の　▶ **generator** [dʒénəreɪtər] N[C] 発生機

an electricity **generator** （発電機）

1224 short
[ʃɔːrt]
□□□□□□

Adj. 短い ;（背が）低い ; 足りない、不足して

My daughter didn't stop crying for hours because I accidentally cut her hair too **short**.
（うちの娘、私が間違って髪を短く切りすぎたせいで何時間も泣き止まなかったの。）

be **short** (of sth) （（～が）不足している、足りない）

▶ **shortly** [ʃɔːrtli] Adv. 間もなく、すぐに ; 手短に

▶ **shorten** [ʃɔːrtn] V[T] を短くする　V[I] 短くなる

▶ **shortage** [ʃɔːrtɪdʒ] N[C/U] 不足

1225 span
[spæn]
□□□□□□

N[C] （注意や集中力などの）持続時間 ; 期間 ; 全長

We were able to get to the top of the mountain in a relatively short **span** of time.
（山頂には比較的短い時間でたどり着くことができたよ。）

■ an attention/concentration **span** （集中力が続く時間）

His English is great, but his TOEIC scores are never good because his **attention span** is so short. （彼は英語が上手なんだけど集中力が続かないから TOEIC ではいつも点数が微妙なんだ。）

V[T] （ある期間）にわたる ;（橋などが川など）に架かる

1226 transfer
[trǽnsfɜ:r]
☐☐☐☐☐☐

N[U] 伝達、移動　**N[C/U]** 送金；転送；転勤、異動　**N[C]** 乗り換え

It's just a guess, but gesturing may be very important in information **transfer**.
（もしかしたら、ジェスチャーって情報伝達においてめちゃくちゃ重要なのかもしれない。）

V[T] を移動させる；を送金する；を転勤させる；を乗り換える
V[I] 転勤する；乗り換える

I'm going to **transfer** my data to an external hard disc because my SD card is out of space.
（SD カードの容量がないからデータを外付けハードディスクに移すね。）

I'll give you my bank details so that you can **transfer** me the money.
（送金できるように銀行口座教えるね。）

I had to **transfer** flights twice to get to London.
（ロンドン行くまでに2回乗り継ぎしないといけなかったんだ。）

▶ **transferable** [trænsfɜ́:rəbəl] Adj. （スキルなどが）他でも使える、；譲渡可能な

transferable skills （他でも使えるようなスキル）

1227 unstimulating
[ʌnstímjələr̀ɪt̬ɪŋ]
☐☐☐☐☐☐

Adj. 退屈な、刺激的でない

My current job is very stable, but intellectually **unstimulating**.
（今の仕事はすごい安定してるけど、頭を使わないからつまらないんだ。）

↔ **stimulating** [stímjəleɪt̬ɪŋ] 刺激的な

▶ **stimulate** [stímjəleɪt] V[T] を刺激する、かき立てる

▶ **stimulation** [stìmjəléɪʃən] N[U] 刺激　▶ **stimulant** [stímjələnt] N[C] 刺激物

▶ **stimulus** [stímjələs] N[C] 刺激、励み（複数形：stimuli [stímjəlaɪ]）

1228 rigid
[rídʒɪd]
☐☐☐☐☐☐

Adj. （考えなどが）かたい、柔軟でない、厳格な

The way he talks is so **rigid**. It's as if he were reading from a dictionary.
（彼の話し方ってすごいかたくて、まるで辞書を読んでいるかのようなんだ。）

▶ **rigidly** [rídʒɪdli] Adv. かた苦しく、厳格に　▶ **rigidity** [rɪdʒídət̬i] N[U] かた苦しさ

1229 inflexible
[ɪnfléksəbəl]
☐☐☐☐☐☐

Adj. 柔軟でない、融通の利かない

My boss is super **inflexible**. （私の上司って全然融通利かないんだよね。）

↔ **flexible** [fléksəbəl] 柔軟な、融通の利く、曲げやすい

My schedule is pretty **flexible**, so let me know what time works for you.
（私のスケジュールはかなり柔軟だから、何時が一番都合いいか教えてよ。）

▶ **flexibly** [fléksəbli] Adv. 柔軟に　▶ **flexibility** [flèksəbílət̬i] N[U] 柔軟性

▶ **flex** [fleks] V[T] （手足など）を曲げる、（筋肉）を収縮させる

I was **flexing** my abs all day yesterday and my six-pack is unbelievably beautiful now.
（昨日ずっと腹筋してたから、私のシックスパック今ビビるほど美しいよ。）

4 In response, educators are trying to reverse teaching stereotypes in various ways, such as shortening classroom sessions and modifying the pace of learning to suit the needs of struggling students.

これに対応するために、教育者たちは授業についていけない生徒のニーズに合わせて授業時間を短縮したり、学習ペースを変えたりと、さまざまな方法で教えることに関する固定観念を覆そうとしている。

1230 **reverse**
[rɪváːrs]
☐☐☐☐☐☐

V[T] を覆す、逆転させる、裏返す **V[I]** （車で）バックする、後進する

We need to **reverse** this negative trend in sales.
（この売上のネガティブなトレンドを覆さないとね。）

Adj. 反対の、逆の **N[S]** 逆、反対、裏側【the -】

▶ **reversal** [rɪváːrsəl] N[C/U] 逆転、覆すこと

▶ **reversible** [rɪváːrsəbl] Adj. （服などが）リバーシブルの；元に戻すことができる

a **reversible** jacket （リバーシブルのジャケット）

1231 **stereotype**
[stériətàɪp]
☐☐☐☐☐☐

N[C] 固定観念 **V[T]** （固定観念に基づいて）を（〜だと）決めつける（as sth）

There's a **stereotype** that we have to start working after graduating from college, but I think we should just do whatever we want to.
（大学卒業後は仕事し始めないといけないって固定観念があるけど、別に好きなことすればいいじゃんって思うよ。）

▶ **stereotypical** [stèriətípɪkl] Adj. 固定観念的な、型にはまった

stereotypical views （型にはまった考え方）

▶ **stereotypically** [stèriətípɪkli] Adv. 固定観念的に、型どおりに

接頭語 stereo- 元々「固い」という意味を持ち、立体的な固体のイメージから派生して「立体的な」という意味も持ちます。ゆえに、stereotype は固い（＝ stereo）型（＝ type）から「固定観念」という意味になります。また、日本語でもよく耳にする stereo sound（ステレオサウンド）はその音が立体的な様子に由来しています。

1232 **session**
[séʃən]
☐☐☐☐☐☐

N[C] （ある活動を行う）時間、授業、会；（大学の）学期；（議会などの）会議

We'll have a Q&A **session** at the end of this workshop, so please bear with me.
（質疑応答の時間はこのワークショップの最後に設けていますので、少しお付き合いください。）

1233 **modify**
[mάːdəfaɪ]
□□□□□□

V[T] を変更する、修正する；を修飾する

Now that you've signed the contract, we can't **modify** it from this point on unless we both agree.
(もう契約書にご署名頂いたので、ここからはお互いの合意なしに契約の修正はできません。)

▶ **modification** [mὰːdəfəkéɪʃən] N[C/U] 変更、修正

▶ **modified** Adj. 変更された、修正された ▶ **modifiable** Adj. 変更可能な、修正可能な
[mάːdəfaɪd]   [mάːdəfàɪəbl]

genetically **modified** (遺伝子組み換えの)

1234 **pace**
[peɪs]
□□□□□□

N[S/U] ペース、速度、勢い **N[C]** (人の) 1歩、歩幅

You can do things at your own **pace**, so don't worry about how others are doing.
(自分のペースで色々やれば良いんだから、他の人がどうしてるかなんて気にしなくていいんだよ。)

keep **pace** with sth/sb (〜と同じスピードで進む、ついていく)

V[I] (不安な様子で) 行ったり来たりする **V[T]** のペースを調節する

■ **pace** oneself (ペース配分を考えてやる、ほどほどにする)

It's been only 10 minutes, and you've already had three glasses of wine. You should
pace yourself. (まだ10分しか経ってないのにもうワイン3杯飲んでるよ。ペース考えた方が良いよ。)

▶ **fast-paced** [fæstpéɪst] Adj. ペースの速い、スピード感のある

I like working in a **fast-paced** environment. (スピード感のある環境で働くのが好きなんだ。)

1235 **suit**
[suːt]
□□□□□□

V[T] (要求や都合など) に合う；に (服や色などが) 似合う

We can't make products that **suit** the needs of every customer, so we should first
decide who we're targeting.
(お客さん全員のニーズに合った商品を作るのは無理だから、まず誰をターゲットにするのかを決めた方がいいね。)

What time **suits** your schedule? (いつが都合良いですか？)

This beige coat **suits** you very well! (このベージュのコート、すごい似合うよ！)

N[C] スーツ；訴訟 = lawsuit [lɔ́ːsuːt] ；(トランプの) スート*、組札

* スペード (spades)、クラブ (clubs)、ハート (hearts)、ダイヤ (diamonds) の4種類のこと

▶ **suitable** Adj. (〜に) ふさわしい、適した (for sth/sb) ↔ **unsuitable** 不適切な
[súːtəbl]   [ʌnsúːtəbl]

Is this app **suitable** for children? (このアプリって子供が使っても大丈夫かな？)

1236 **struggling**
[strʌ́glɪŋ]
□□□□□□

Adj. 苦労している、苦戦している

He was a **struggling** artist once, but now he's famous all over the world.
(彼はかつては苦労してたけど、今では世界的に有名なアーティストなんだ。)

▶ **struggle** V[I] (〜を求めて / 〜するのに) 奮闘する、苦労する (for sth/to do)
[strʌ́gəl]   N[C] 奮闘、争い

I'm **struggling** to finish my lunch, so feel free to help yourself to some of it.
(ランチ全部食べられそうにないから、ちょっと食べたかったら食べて良いよ。)

03 FRI　From Passive Disinterest To Active Learning （Teaching）

Struggling for active student participation in your class? Keen to persuade students to concentrate and improve their knowledge retention and satisfaction? Active learning may be the answer, based on numerous studies performed as well as robust testimony from many teachers that swear by the method. We will briefly summarize the basics of active learning and illustrate with some examples of techniques that can be applied in your class.

What is active learning?

Active learning refers to any learning activity in which participants interact with each other, as opposed to listening passively.

Think-pair-share

The most common active learning method is think-pair-share. This is a peer-to-peer discussion strategy where the lecture is paused, and students are given sufficient time to think. Students are then given the cue to pair up and discuss the topic and are instructed to share their thoughts with the class. Time allocation is fundamental to avoiding awkward and tense moments during this period.

Flipped classrooms

In a flipped classroom, media consumed at home, such as videos, accomplish the same goal as traditional, monotonous classes. Students then proceed to the classroom where a large portion of their time is spent on active learning.

受動的で関心の低い学習からアクティブ・ラーニングへ

自分の授業に生徒たちを積極的に参加させることに苦労していませんか？生徒たちに集中するよう説得して、知識の定着と満足度を向上させたいですか？アクティブ・ラーニングがその答えかもしれません。これは、数々の研究報告と、そのメソッドに信頼を置く多くの教師たちによる確かな証言を基にしています。アクティブ・ラーニングの基本を簡単に要約し、みなさんの授業で適用できるテクニックの例をいくつかご紹介します。

アクティブ・ラーニングとは？
アクティブ・ラーニングとは、授業を受動的に聞くのではなく、参加者が互いに交流し合う学習活動を指します。

シンク-ペア-シェア
最も一般的なアクティブ・ラーニングのメソッドは、シンク-ペア-シェアです。これは、生徒同士でディスカッションさせる戦略で、ここでは講義は一時中断され、生徒たちは考えるための十分な時間が与えられます。その後、生徒たちは2人1組になりトピックを議論するよう合図され、クラス全員に自分たちの考えを共有するよう指示されます。ここでの時間配分は、この間に気まずい、緊張した時間が流れないようにするための基本になります。

反転授業
反転授業では、生徒たちに自宅で動画などのメディアを視聴させることで、従来の単調な授業と同じ目的を達成するものです。その後、生徒たちは教室へ行き、そこで大部分の時間を能動的な学習に使用します。

1237 participation
[pɑ:rtìsəpéɪʃən]

N[U] 参加

▶ **participate** [pɑ:rtísəpeɪt] V[I] (〜に) 参加する (in sth)

▶ **participant** [pɑ:rtísəpənt] N[C] 参加者

1238 keen
[ki:n]

Adj. (〜を) したい、熱望した (to do/on doing) ; (感覚などが) 鋭い

▶ **keenly** [kí:nli] Adv. 熱心に、鋭く   ▶ **keenness** [kí:nnəs] N[U] 熱望、熱心 ; 鋭さ

1239 persuade
[pərswéɪd]

V[T] を (〜するよう) 説得する (to do)、に (〜を) 納得させる (of sth)

▶ **persuasion** [pərswéɪʒən] N[U] 説得 ; 信念   ▶ **persuasive** [pərswéɪsɪv] Adj. 説得力のある

▶ **persuasively** [pərswéɪsɪvli] Adv. 説得力を持って

▶ **persuasiveness** [pərswéɪsɪvnəs] N[U] 説得力

1240 satisfaction
[sæṭɪsfǽkʃən]

N[C/U] 満足度、満足感、満足 ; (希望や要望の) 充足

▶ **satisfy** [sǽṭɪsfaɪ] V[T] を満足させる ; (要件や条件) を満たす

▶ **satisfied** [sǽṭɪsfaɪd] Adj. (〜に) 満足した (with sth)

◆▶ **dissatisfied** [dìssǽṭəsfaɪd] 不満足な

▶ **satisfying** [sǽṭɪsfaɪɪŋ] Adj. 満足感を与えるような

▶ **satisfactory** [sæṭɪsfǽktəri] Adj. 満足のいく

1241 testimony
[téstəmoʊni]

N[C/U] 証言 ; (努力などの) 証 (of/to sth)

▶ **testimonial** [tèstəmóʊniəl] N[C] 証明書、推薦状 ; 表彰状

1242 swear
[swer]

V[I/T] (本当に〜だと) 誓う (that + sentence)   V[I] 汚い言葉を使う

swear by sth (〜 (の効果) に信頼を置く   a **swear** word (汚い言葉)

My dog can talk like a human. I **swear**. (私の犬、人間みたいに話せるんだ。マジだよ。)

1243 summarize
[sʌ́məraɪz]

V[I/T] (〜を) 要約する、まとめる

▶ **summary** [sʌ́məri] N[C] (〜の) 要約、概要 (of sth)

1244 apply
[əplái]

V[T] を適用する、応用する ; (化粧品や塗料) を塗る

V[I] (〜に) 当てはまる (to sth) ; (物に / 人や組織に) 申し込む (for sth/to sb)

▶ **applicant** [ǽpləkənt] N[C] 申込者、応募者

▶ **application** [æpləkéɪʃən] N[C/U] 申し込み、出願

▶ **applicable** [əplíkəbəl] Adj. 適用可能な   ▶ **applicability** [æplɪkəbíləṭi] N[U] 適用可能性

1245 opposed
[əpóʊzd]

Adj. (〜に) 反対している (to sth)

as **opposed** to sth (〜とは違って、〜とは対照的に)

▶ **oppose** [əpóʊz] V[T] に反対する

▶ **opposition** [à:pəzíʃən] N[U] 反対 ; 対戦相手、敵 【the -】

▶ **opponent** [əpóʊnənt] N[C] 反対者 ; (競技などの) 対戦相手、敵

1246 passively
[pǽsɪvli]

Adv. 受動的に、受け身で、消極的に ⟷ **actively** [ǽktɪvli] 積極的に

▶ **passive** [pǽsɪv] Adj. 受動的な、受け身の、消極的な ⟷ **active** [ǽktɪv] 積極的な

1247 peer
[pɪr]

N[C] 同級生、同僚、同業者、仲間

peer-to-**peer**（同級生同士の）

V[I]（～の中を / ～を通して）のぞき込む（into/through sth）

1248 sufficient
[səfíʃənt]

Adj. 十分な ＝ **enough** [ənʌ́f] ⟷ **insufficient** [ìnsəfíʃənt] 不十分な

▶ **sufficiently** [səfíʃəntli] Adv. 十分に ▶ **sufficiency** [səfíʃənsi] N[U] 十分

▶ **suffice** [səfáɪs] V[I] 十分である

1249 instruct
[ɪnstrʌ́kt]

V[T] に（～するよう）指示する（to do）；を指導する

▶ **instruction** [ɪnstrʌ́kʃən] N[P] 指示 N[P] 取扱説明書【-s】 N[U] 指導

▶ **instructor** [ɪnstrʌ́ktər] N[C] インストラクター

1250 awkward
[ɑ́:kwərd]

Adj. 気まずい、落ち着かない；不器用な

▶ **awkwardly** [ɑ́:kwərdli] Adv. 気まずい感じで；不器用に

▶ **awkwardness** [ɑ́:kwərdnəs] N[U] 気まずさ；不器用さ

1251 tense
[tens]

Adj. 緊張した、張り詰めた；(筋肉などが) 張った N[C/U]（動詞の）時制

▶ **tensely** [ténsli] Adv. 緊張して、張り詰めて

▶ **tension** [ténʃən] N[U] 緊張 N[C/U] 緊張状態

1252 period
[píriəd]

N[C] 期間；時代、時期；(授業などの) 時間；生理；ピリオド

＝ **full stop** [fʊl stɑ́:p]〈英〉 have a **period**（生理中である）

▶ **periodic** [pìriá:dɪk] Adj. 定期的な、周期的な

▶ **periodically** [pìriá:dɪkli] Adv. 定期的に、周期的に

1253 accomplish
[əká:mplɪʃ]

V[T] を達成する

▶ **accomplishment** [əká:mplɪʃmənt] N[U] 達成 N[C/U] 成果、業績

a sense of **accomplishment**（達成感）

1254 monotonous
[məná:t̬ənəs]

Adj. 単調な

▶ **monotonously** [məná:t̬ənəsli] Adv. 単調に ▶ **monotony** [məná:t̬əni] N[U] 単調さ

This work is pretty **monotonous** but necessary.（この仕事はかなり単調だけど必要なんだ。）

1255 proceed
[proʊsí:d]

V[I]（～に）進む（to sth）；（～を）続行する（with sth） N[P] 収益【-s】

1256 portion
[pɔ́:rʃən]

N[C] 部分、一部；(食事などの) 一人分の量、一人前

a large/small **portion**（of sth）（（～の）大部分 / ごく一部）

Chapter

27

医学史
History of Medicine

While modern medical professionals are highly educated and formally trained, and the practice of medicine is now thoroughly controlled and standardized, this was not the case until the 20th century.

Prior to this, doctors acquired and accumulated their skills and wisdom through word of mouth, as well as trial and error, leading to huge differences among medical professionals.

However, since the beginning of the 20th century, the rapid rate of improvement and reform in medicine has been largely driven and fueled by breakthroughs in medical theory and equipment.

Inventions such as antibiotics and flu vaccines, together with developments in the fields of chemistry, genetics, and radiography, accelerated these improvements and the transition to modern medicine.

1

While modern medical professionals are highly educated and formally trained, and the practice of medicine is now thoroughly controlled and standardized, this was not the case until the 20th century.

現代の医療専門家は高度な教育と正式な訓練を受け、現在、医療行為は徹底的に管理・標準化されているが、これは 20 世紀になってからのことである。

1257 **professional**
[prəféʃənəl]

N[C] 専門家、プロ　**Adj.** 専門家の、専門職の；仕事上の

As a finance **professional**, you should have at least a basic understanding of accounting.
(金融専門家として、最低でも会計についての基本的な理解は持っていた方がいいよ。)

▶ **professionally** Adv. 専門的に、プロとして；仕事上　▶ **profession** N[C] 専門職
[prəféʃənəli]　　　　　　　　　　　　　　　　　　　　　[prəféʃən]

It's important to always behave **professionally** at work if you want to get promoted.
(昇進したいなら職場で常にプロフェッショナルにふさわしいふるまいをすることが重要だよ。)

1258 **formally**
[fɔ́:rməli]

Adv. 正式に、公式に；形式的に、形式上；礼儀正しく

I've been acting as store manager for a few weeks now, so it'll be good to finally be **formally** promoted next month. (今や数週間も店長代理してるから、来月遂に正式に昇進になって嬉しい。)

⟷ **informally** [ɪnfɔ́:rməli] 非公式に；形式ばらないで

▶ **formal** Adj. 正式な；堅苦しい；フォーマルな　⟷ **informal** 非公式の；形式ばらない
[fɔ́:rməl]　　　　　　　　　　　　　　　　　　　　　　[ɪnfɔ́:rməl]

This is a **formal** event, so please make sure you wear a tie.
(これはフォーマルなイベントなので、必ずネクタイをするようにして下さい。)

▶ **formality** [fɔ:rmǽləṭi] N[C] 形式的なこと　N[U] フォーマルさ

⟷ **informality** [ɪnfɔ:rmǽləṭi] N[U] 形式ばらないこと；略装

1259 **practice**
[prǽktɪs]

N[U]（専門職の）業務、仕事、開業　**V[I/T]**（〜に）従事する

I've just set up my own **practice** as a lawyer. (ちょうど弁護士として独立開業したところなんだ。)

N[U] 練習、訓練　**N[C]** 練習期間　**V[I/T]**（〜を）練習する

Practice makes perfect. (継続は力なり。)

N[U] 実践　**N[C/U]** 習慣的に行われていること

put sth into **practice**（〜を実践する、実施する）　　in **practice**（実践では、実際には）

▶ **practical** Adj. 実践的な、実用的な   ↔ **impractical** 非実用的な、非現実的な
[prǽktɪkəl]   [ɪmprǽktɪkəl]

Don't you think what we learn at this college is just not **practical** enough? It's too focused on theory. （この大学で学ぶことって実用性に欠けてると思わない？理論ばっかり。）

▶ **practically** [prǽktɪkli] Adv. 現実的に；事実上

▶ **practicality** [præ̀ktɪkǽləṭi] N[U] 実用性

▶ **practicable** [prǽktɪkəbəl] Adj. 実行可能な

1260 medicine
[médɪsən]
☐☐☐☐☐☐

N[U]　医療、医学　N[C/U]　薬、医薬品

Why are there so many different types of cold and flu **medicine** if they all do the same thing? （なんでこんなに風邪薬に種類あるの。全部効果は一緒でしょ？）

▶ **medical** [médɪkəl] Adj. 医療の、医学の

▶ **medicate** V[T] を薬で治療する   ▶ **medication** N[C/U] 薬物、薬剤
[médɪkèɪt]   [mèdəkéɪʃən]

take **medication** （薬を服用する）   on **medication** （薬を服用中の）

▶ **medicinal** Adj. 薬効のある、薬の   ▶ **medicinally** Adv. 医薬的に
[mədísɪnəl]   [mədísɪnəli]

1261 thoroughly
[θə́:roʊli]
[θə́:rəli]
☐☐☐☐☐☐

Adv. 徹底的に、すっかり、完全に

I've checked this pretty **thoroughly**, so there shouldn't be any mistakes.
（これは僕がかなり徹底的にチェックしたから、ミスは無いはずだよ。）

▶ **thorough** Adj. 徹底的な、完全な   ▶ **thoroughness** N[U] 徹底していること
[θə́:rə] [θə́:roʊ]   [θə́:rənəs] [θə́:roʊnəs]

The **thoroughness** of the janitor is just amazing.（あの清掃員の徹底っぷりはただただ素晴らしい。）

1262 control
[kəntróʊl]
☐☐☐☐☐☐

V[T]　を管理する、制御する、規制する

I broke up with my girlfriend because she was always trying to **control** every aspect of my life. （いつも僕の生活全てをコントロールしようとしてきたから、彼女とは別れたんだ。）

under **control** （上手くいっている；制御されて） have **control** over sth/sb （〜を支配している）

▶ **controller** [kəntróʊlər] N[C] 管理者；制御装置

1263 case
[keɪs]
☐☐☐☐☐☐

N[S] （特定の）状況、事実【the -】　N[C] 事例；訴訟、申し立て；犯罪事件

For some reason, everybody seems to think I love baseball, but that's really not **the case**.
（なぜかみんな僕がめっちゃ野球好きだと思ってるみたいなんだけど、実際はそうじゃないんだよ。）

■ in sb's **case** （〜の場合）   ■ (just) in **case** （万が一、念のため）

Saying that your job is rewarding sounds a bit of a cliché, but **in my case**, it's true.
（仕事にやりがいを感じるってちょっと決まり文句っぽいけど、僕の場合は本当にそう思ってるよ。）

I'm pretty sure this information is correct, but can you double-check it **just in case**?
（この情報きっと正しいと思うんだけど、念のためもう一度確認してくれない？）

2 Prior to this, doctors acquired and accumulated their skills and wisdom through word of mouth, as well as trial and error, leading to huge differences among medical professionals.

それ以前は、医師たちは技術と知恵を口伝えで試行錯誤しながら身に付け、蓄積していたため、医療専門家の質には非常に大きなばらつきがあったのだ。

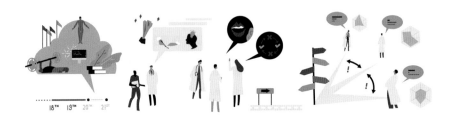

1264 **prior**

[praɪr]

□□□□□□

Adj. 前の、事前の

■ **prior** to sth（〜の前に、〜に先立って）

Prior to studying here, I spent a couple of years traveling around Asia.
（ここで勉強する前は、2年ほどアジアを旅していたんです。）

prior to vs **before** 後に名詞を取る場合、どちらも「〜の前」という同様の意味を持ちます。しかし、prior to はラテン語にルーツを持つ表現で、before の方がより一般的な表現として受け入れられているため、会話では before を使用することが多いです。

1265 **acquire**

[əkwáɪər]

□□□□□□

V[T] を身に付ける、習得する；を獲得する；を買収する

It's not too difficult for a child to **acquire** two or more languages at the same time.
（子供にとって2つ以上の言語を同時に習得するのはものすごい難しいっていうわけじゃないんだ。）

■ an **acquired** taste（だんだんと好きになる味、大人の味）

Do you hate the bitter taste of coffee? It's **an acquired taste**, so just keep drinking it, and you'll appreciate it eventually.
（コーヒーの苦いのが嫌いだって？だんだん好きになるものだから、とりあえず飲み続けてたら最終的に分かるよ。）

▶ **acquisition** [ækwəzíʃən] N[U]（知識などの）習得　N[C/U] 買収

mergers and **acquisitions**（合併と買収、M&A）

1266 **accumulate**

[əkjú:mjəleɪt]

□□□□□□

V[T] を蓄積する、貯める　V[I] 蓄積する、貯まる

What's the best way to **accumulate** miles as quickly as possible?
（マイルをできるだけ早く貯めるのに一番良い方法って何かな？）

▶ **accumulation** [əkjù:mjəléɪʃən] N[C/U] 蓄積、積み重ね

The **accumulation** of knowledge takes both time and focus.
（知識を蓄えるには時間と労力が必要だよ。）

1267 wisdom
[wízdəm]
▢▢▢▢▢▢

N[U]　知恵、分別、賢明さ

I always enjoy hanging out with my grandpa because he shares so much **wisdom** with me.
（おじいちゃんはものすごいたくさんの知恵をシェアしてくれるから、一緒に時間を過ごすといつも楽しいんだ。）

▶ **wise** [waɪz] Adj. 賢い、賢明な、分別のある　　▶ **wisely** [wáɪzli] Adv. 賢く

「親知らず」は「知恵の歯」？　親知らずは英語で wisdom tooth（複数形：wisdom teeth）と言います。これは、人が知恵が付き賢くなった頃に生えてくることに由来しています。

接尾語としての -wise　wise は接尾語としても使われることがあり、その場合は「〜の方向に」もしくは「〜の点では」という意味を持ちます。
- 「〜の方向に」の例：clockwise（時計回りに）、lengthwise（縦に、長く）
- 「〜の点では」の例：moneywise（お金の点では）、timewise（時間の点では）

1268 word
[wɜːrd]
▢▢▢▢▢▢

N[C]　単語、語

I love reading everything he writes because he just has a way with **words**.
（彼の執筆するものは本当に全部好きなんだ。とにかく言葉の使い方が上手いんだよね。）

have a **word** (with sb)（（〜と）少し話す）　　have **words** (with sb)（（〜と）口論する）

word of mouth（口伝え、口コミ）　　the F-**word**, the C-**word**（汚い言葉）

▶ **wordy** [wɜ́ːrdi] Adj.（文章などが）とても長い、くどい

His Facebook posts are always **wordy**.（あいつの Facebook の投稿いつもめちゃくちゃ長いんだよ。）

▶ **wording** [wɜ́ːrdɪŋ] N[U] 言い回し、言葉遣い

I think you should change your **wording** a bit in the report.
（報告書の言い回し、もうちょっと変えた方が良いと思うよ。）

1269 trial
[traɪəl]
▢▢▢▢▢▢

N[C/U]　試行；試用、トライアル；（効果や安全性を試す）試験；裁判

My free Netflix **trial** expires tomorrow, but I'm still not sure if I want to pay for a subscription.　（Netflix の無料お試し明日で切れるけど、登録にお金払いたいかどうかはまだ微妙なんだ。）

trial and error（試行錯誤）

I can't help watching when celebs go on **trial**.
（芸能人が裁判にかけられると、どうしても見ちゃうんだよなぁ。）

▶ **try** [traɪ] V[I/T]（〜を）試みる、試す　N[C] 試み

■ give sth a **try**（〜を試す）　**try** doing（試しに〜する）　**try** to do（〜しようとする）

Just **give** it **a try** and see what happens.（とりあえずやってみてどうなるか見てみなよ。）

1270 huge
[hjuːdʒ]
▢▢▢▢▢▢

Adj.　非常に大きな、巨大な　⟷ **tiny** [táɪni] とても小さい

I know she has a **huge** ego, but she is one of the best singers in the world.
（彼女のエゴがものすごい大きいのは知ってるけど、世界最高の歌手の一人だよ。）

▶ **hugely** [hjúːdʒli] Adv. 非常に、大いに

3 However, since the beginning of the 20th century, the rapid rate of improvement and reform in medicine has been largely driven and fueled by breakthroughs in medical theory and equipment.

しかし、20世紀に入ると、医学は主に医学理論と医療機器の飛躍的進歩により、急速な改善と改革が強く推し進められていった。

1271 rapid
[rǽpɪd]
☐☐☐☐☐☐

Adj. 急速な、速い

I think we should build more infrastructure to deal with this **rapid** population growth.
(この急速な人口増加を何とかするにはもっとインフラを整えないといけないと思うよ。)

▶ **rapidly** [rǽpɪdli] Adv. 急速に、速く

1272 rate
[reɪt]
☐☐☐☐☐☐

N[C] 速度、ペース

At this **rate**, we're never going to get to Osaka, so no more toilet breaks for the rest of the trip. (このペースだと絶対大阪に着かないから、これ以上途中でトイレ休憩するのは無しね。)

■ at a fast/slow **rate**（速い / 遅い速度で）

Why is the cost of living in Australia increasing **at such a fast rate**?
(なんでオーストラリアの生活費ってこんなに速いスピードで上がってるの？)

N[C] 割合、率；料金、価格

an interest **rate**（利率）   the birth/divorce **rate**（出生率 / 離婚率）

the exchange **rate**（為替レート）

▶ **rating** [réɪtɪŋ] N[C] 評価、格付け   N[P] 視聴率【-s】   ▶ **ratio** [réɪʃioʊ] N[C] 割合

You should check its reviews and **ratings** before you buy.
(買う前にレビューと評価見た方が良いよ。)

at the **ratio** of five to one（5対1の割合で）

1273 reform
[rɪfɔ́ːrm]
☐☐☐☐☐☐

N[C/U] 改革、（法律などの）改正

I'm not sure if this economic **reform** will work, but we have to try something.
(この経済改革がうまくいくかは分からないけど、とりあえず何かやってみなきゃ。)

V[T] を改革する、改正する；を改心させる   V[I] 改心する

▶ **reformation** N[C/U] 改革；改心   ▶ **reformed** Adj. 改良された；改心した
[rèfərméɪʃən]   [rɪfɔ́ːrmd]

1274 **drive**

[draɪv]

☐☐☐☐☐☐

V[T]　を推進する、活発にする；を駆り立てる

The widespread usage of mobile devices is **driving** the digital banking boom in Latin America.
（モバイル端末が広く使われるようになり、ラテンアメリカではデジタルバンキングブームが活発化しているんだ。）

V[T]　を（〜に）追い込む（to sth）　**V[I/T]**　（〜を）運転する

■ **drive** sb crazy（〜の頭をおかしくさせる）

This math problem is **driving** me **crazy**.（この数学の問題、頭がおかしくなるよ。）

N[U]　意欲、やる気　**N[C]**　ドライブ、運転；車道；欲望、衝動

▶ **driver** [dráɪvər] N[C] ドライバー、運転手；原動力

■ a slave **driver**（人使いの荒い人）

My boss is such **a slave driver**.（俺の上司は本当に人使いが荒い。）

▶ **driving** [dráɪvɪŋ] Adj. 推進する、猛烈な　N[U] 運転

a **driving** force（原動力）

drive のコアイメージ　drive には運転する、活発にする、駆り立てるなど様々な意味がありますが、コアとなるイメージは「力で突き動かす」ことです。これさえ覚えれば、複数の意味を一つ一つ丸暗記しなくても、この英単語を実践的に使うことができます。英単語学習では常にコアイメージを意識しましょう。

1275 **fuel**

[fjúːəl]

☐☐☐☐☐☐

V[T]　（活動など）を推進する；に燃料を供給する　**V[I/T]**　（〜に）給油する

I accidentally **fueled** the argument by opening old wounds.
（昔の嫌なことを思い出させて喧嘩をヒートアップさせちゃった。）

N[C/U]　燃料

nuclear **fuel**（核燃料）　　　fossil **fuels**（化石燃料）

■ add **fuel** to the fire（火に油を注ぐ）

Mocking the teacher while she is angry is just **adding fuel to the fire**.
（先生が怒ってる時にからかうなんて火に油を注ぐようなものだよ。）

1276 **breakthrough**

[bréɪkθruː]

☐☐☐☐☐☐

N[C]　飛躍的進歩、躍進、（難関の）突破

■ make a **breakthrough**（飛躍的な進歩を遂げる、突破口を開く）

My gut tells me that we're about to **make a breakthrough**, so don't give up just yet.
（もう少しで突破口を開ける予感がするんだ。だからまだ諦めないで。）

1277 **equipment**

[ɪkwípmənt]

☐☐☐☐☐☐

N[U]　機器、機材、設備、用品

I've been focusing more on practicing my photography rather than buying more **equipment**.
（俺は機材を増やすよりも写真撮影の練習に重点的に取り組んでるよ。）

office/kitchen **equipment**（オフィス / キッチン用品）

▶ **equip** [ɪkwíp] V[T] に（〜を）備え付ける、装備する（with sth）

▶ **equipped** [ɪkwípt] Adj.（設備などが）備え付けられた、装備された（with sth）

fully **equipped** with sth（〜が完備された）

4 Inventions such as antibiotics and flu vaccines, together with developments in the fields of chemistry, genetics, and radiography, accelerated these improvements and the transition to modern medicine.

抗生物質やインフルエンザワクチンなどが発明され、さらに化学や遺伝学、X 線撮影の分野が発展したことで、こうした改善と現代医学への移行は、いっそう加速していった。

1278 **antibiotic**
[æn̩ṭɪbaɪɑ́:t̬ɪk]
☐☐☐☐☐☐

N[C]　抗生物質

I feel better already, so do I really need to take these **antibiotics** for another week?
（もう良くなっている感じがするんですけど、この抗生物質、本当にあと一週間飲まないといけないんですか？）

↔ **probiotic** [pròʊbaɪɑ́:t̬ɪk] プロバイオティクス、善玉菌

1279 **flu**
[fluː]
☐☐☐☐☐☐

N[U]　インフルエンザ　= influenza [ɪnfluénzə]

It's so annoying how I seem to get the **flu** every couple of weeks during the winter.
（冬の間は 2 週間に一回インフルかかってるっぽくて本当辛い。）

Sorry, but I can't come to the party tonight. I'm almost dying from the **flu** right now.
（ごめん、今夜のパーティ行けない。今インフルエンザで死にそう。）

1280 **vaccine**
[væksiːn]
☐☐☐☐☐☐

N[C/U]　ワクチン

I know how important **vaccines** are, but it doesn't stop them from being painful.
（ワクチンがどれだけ重要かは分かってるけどさ、痛いことには変わりないでしょ。）

▶ **vaccinate** [vǽksəneɪt] V[T] にワクチンを接種をする、予防接種をする

You should get **vaccinated** before you travel to any tropical country.
（熱帯の国に旅行する前は予防接種受けた方が良いよ。）

▶ **vaccination** [væksənéɪʃən] N[C/U] ワクチン接種、予防接種

1281 **chemistry**
[kéməstri]
☐☐☐☐☐☐

N[U]　化学、化学反応；（恋愛などにおける）相性

The most annoying thing about **chemistry** is having to memorize the periodic table.
（化学の一番嫌いなところは周期表を暗記しなきゃいけないことなんだ。）

▶ **chemical** [kémɪkəl] Adj. 化学的な　N[C] 化学物質

I'm worried that this hair dye has dangerous **chemicals** in it.
（このヘアカラー剤、危険な化学物質が入ってるんじゃないかって心配してるんだ。）

▶ **chemist** [kémɪst] N[C] 化学者

1282 **genetics**
[dʒənétɪks]

☐☐☐☐☐☐

N[U] 遺伝学、遺伝的特徴

I don't know if it's **genetics** or something else, but I never gain any weight no matter what I eat.（遺伝なのか、他に理由があるのかよく分からないけど、僕は何食べても絶対に太らないんだ。）

▶ **genetic** [dʒənétɪk] Adj. 遺伝的な、遺伝の ▶ **genetically** [dʒənétɪkli] Adv. 遺伝的に

You know how cilantro tastes like soap to some people? That's **genetic**.
（人によってパクチーが石けんみたいな味するってやつあるじゃん？あれ遺伝なんだって。）

genetically modified （遺伝子組み換えの）

▶ **gene** [dʒiːn] N[C] 遺伝子 ▶ **geneticist** [dʒənétəsɪst] N[C] 遺伝学者

1283 **accelerate**
[əkséləreɪt]

☐☐☐☐☐☐

V[T] を加速させる、促進する **V[I]** 加速する

I decided to attend the workshop to **accelerate** my career.
（キャリアを加速させるためにそのワークショップに参加することに決めたんだ。）

▶ **acceleration** [əksèləréɪʃən] N[S/U] 加速、促進

The **acceleration** on Emma's new car is insane. Riding in it feels like being in a video game. （エマの新車の加速はヤバい。乗ったらまるでテレビゲームの世界にいるような感じがするよ。）

▶ **accelerator** [əkséləreɪtər] N[C] アクセル、加速装置

1284 **transition**
[trænzíʃən]

☐☐☐☐☐☐

N[C/U] 移行、推移、変化、転換

I'm finding the **transition** from working life to retirement pretty strange, but I'm sure I'll get used to it.
（仕事の日々から定年後の生活に変化してそこそこ違和感はあるけど、まぁきっと慣れると思うよ。）

in **transition** （移行中の、転換期にある）

▶ **transitional** [trænzíʃənəl] Adj. 移行の、過渡期の

When changing jobs, it's natural to experience a **transitional** period before you become comfortable. （仕事を変える時、慣れるまでの転換期を経験するのは自然なことだよ。）

▶ **transit** [trænzɪt] N[U] 通過；輸送；乗り継ぎ

■ in **transit** （輸送中の）

Your package is still **in transit**.（あなたの荷物はまだ輸送中です。）

接頭語 trans- 「向こう側へ」という意味の接頭語で、「trans（向こう側へ）ition（行くこと）」から「移行、推移」という意味になります。他には transfer（〜を移す）や transport（〜を運ぶ）などがあります。

Doctor (M) You know how we look at medical practices of the past and think that they're terribly crude and primitive? Do you think future generations will look at our modern techniques, which we consider the peak of human ingenuity, and think that we're brutal barbarians using inferior methods?

Doctor (W) I certainly hope not. In our defense, it's not like we're cutting people up alive to study their hearts or letting their blood to observe how blood flows. Besides, technological advancements continue to help us improve.

Doctor (M) I guess that's true. Innovations like nanobots should aid us in reducing the need for invasive, uncomfortable procedures such as surgery. Augmented reality should also minimize commutes for patients.

Doctor (W) Yeah, I'm sure that we will devise substitutes for these uncomfortable procedures. In the meantime, we need to continue to demonstrate compassion and due diligence in treating patients.

医者 (男性) 昔の医療行為を見ると、とても粗悪で原始的だと思わない？僕たちが人間の創意工夫の最高峰と考えている現代技術を将来の世代が見たら、僕らのことを劣悪な手法を使う残忍で野蛮な人たちだと思うのかな？

医者 (女性) それは本当に勘弁ね。言い訳じゃないけど、別に私たちは心臓を調べるために人を生きたまま切ったり、血液がどのように流れるか観察するために流血させたりしているわけではないじゃない。それに、技術進歩のおかげで私たちは改善し続けてるわ。

医者 (男性) そうかもしれないね。ナノボットのようなイノベーションが、手術みたいな切開を伴う不快な医療処置の必要性を減らす手助けとなるはずだしね。拡張現実も、患者の通院を最小限にしてくれるはずだし。

医者 (女性) うん、きっと私たちは、こういう嫌な医療処置の代わりになるものを発明するわ。それまで、私たちは患者さんを扱う際に、思いやりと十分な配慮を示し続ける必要があるわね。

1285 **terribly**
[térəbli]

Adv. とても、ひどく、本当に

I'm **terribly** sorry.（本当に申し訳ございません。）

▶ **terrible** [térəbəl] Adj. とんでもない、ひどい、最悪な

1286 **crude**
[kru:d]

Adj. 粗悪な；下品な；未加工の

▶ **crudely** [krúːdli] Adv. 粗く、大まかに

▶ **crudeness** [krúːdnəs] N[U] 粗さ；下品さ

1287 **primitive**
[prímətɪv]

Adj. 原始的な、初期の、旧式の

▶ **primitively** [prímətɪvli] Adv. 原始的に

1288 **peak**
[pi:k]

N[C] 最高点、最高潮、最盛期 V[I] ピークに達する Adj. 最高峰の、最高の

He's a good player, but I think he's past his **peak**.

（あの選手は良いけど、全盛期は過ぎてると思う。）

1289 **ingenuity**
[ìndʒənjúːəti]

N[U] 創意工夫、発明の才

▶ **ingenious** [ɪndʒíːniəs] Adj. 独創的な、巧妙な、精巧な

▶ **ingeniously** [ɪndʒíːniəsli] Adv. 巧みに

1290 **brutal**
[brúːtl]

Adj. 残忍な、残酷な

▶ **brutally** [brúːtəli] Adv. 残忍に、残酷に ▶ **brutality** [bruːtæləti] N[U] 残忍さ、残酷さ

▶ **brutalities** [bruːtælətiz] N[P] 残虐行為 ▶ **brute** [bruːt] N[C] 野蛮人；野獣

1291 **barbarian**
[bɑːrbériən]

N[C] 野蛮人；教養のない人

▶ **barbaric** [bɑːrbérɪk] Adj. 野蛮な ▶ **barbarism** [bɑ́ːrbərɪzəm] N[U] 野蛮な行為

1292 **inferior**
[ɪnfíriər]

Adj.（〜よりも）劣悪な、劣った、劣等感を持った（to sth/sb）

↔ **superior** [səpíriər] 優れた；上質の

▶ **inferiority** [ɪnfìrió:rəti] N[U] 劣っていること、劣等、粗悪

↔ **superiority** [səpìrió:rəti] 優れていること

1293 **defense**
[dɪféns]

N[S/U] 弁護、擁護 N[U] 防衛、防御；守備 N[C] 防衛手段、防御策；守備陣

in sb's **defense**（言い訳じゃないけど、自己弁護をさせてもらうと）

▶ **defensive** [dɪfénsɪv] Adj. 身構えた；防御的な、防衛の

▶ **defend** [dɪfénd] V[T] を弁護する V[I/T]（〜を）守る、防御する

1294 **blood**
[blʌd]

N[U] 血液、血

▶ **bleed** [bliːd] V[I]（〜が）出血する ▶ **bloody** [blʌ́di] Adj. 血まみれの

Your nose is **bleeding**.（鼻血出てるよ。）

1295 flow
[floʊ]
□□□□□□

V[I]（〜から / 〜に）流れる（from/into sth）　N[C] 流れ

Stop overthinking. Just go with the **flow**. (考えすぎないで、流れに任せなよ。)

1296 besides
[bɪsáɪdz]
□□□□□□

Adv. それに、そのうえ　Prep. 〜以外に、〜に加えて

▶ **beside** [bɪsáɪd] Prep. 〜のそばに

1297 aid
[eɪd]
□□□□□□

V[T] の手助けとなる、を（〜に関して）援助する（in/with sth）

N[U] 援助、助け　N[C] 補助となるもの

1298 procedure
[prəsíːdʒər]
□□□□□□

N[C] 医療処置　N[C/U] 手続き、手順

1299 surgery
[sə́ːrdʒəri]
□□□□□□

N[C/U] 手術、外科、外科手術

have a **surgery** (手術を受ける)

▶ **surgical** [sə́ːrdʒɪkəl] Adj. 手術の、外科の　▶ **surgically** [sə́ːrdʒɪkli] Adv. 手術で

▶ **surgeon** [sə́ːrdʒən] N[C] 外科医

1300 commute
[kəmjúːt]
□□□□□□

N[C] 通勤　V[I]（〜に）通勤する（to sth）

▶ **commuter** [kəmjúːt/ər] N[C] 通勤客　▶ **commuting** [kəmjúːtɪŋ] N[U] 通勤

1301 substitute
[sʌ́bstətuːt]
□□□□□□

N[C]（〜の）代わりになるもの、代用品（for sth/sb）；控えの選手

V[T] を（〜の）代わりに使う（for sth/sb）

▶ **substitution** [sʌ̀bstətúːʃən] N[C/U] 代用；選手交代

1302 demonstrate
[démənstreɪt]
□□□□□□

V[T] をはっきり示す、明確に示す；を実演する

▶ **demonstration** [dèmənstréɪʃən] N[C] 示すこと、表現；実演；デモ

▶ **demonstrator** [démənstreɪtər] N[C] 実演者；デモ参加者

1303 compassion
[kəmpǽʃən]
□□□□□□

N[U] 思いやり、同情

▶ **compassionate** [kəmpǽʃənət] Adj. 思いやりのある

▶ **compassionately** [kəmpǽʃənətli] Adv. 思いやりを持って

1304 due
[duː]
□□□□□□

Adj. 十分な、しかるべき；到着予定である；（〜する）予定である（to do）

due diligence (注意義務、相当な注意)　**due** care (十分な注意)

Adj.（支払いや提出の）期限が来た

⟳ CH. 8, 13, 17, 21, 24, 27

医療倫理
Medical Ethics

Medical ethics is a set of moral principles that serve to guide how medical professionals act in confusing decision-making situations where conflicting ideas are in play.

For example, euthanasia, or death with dignity, the deliberate termination of a terminally ill person's life in order to relieve them of their suffering, is one of the most frequently debated areas in medical ethics.

There have been numerous landmark legal precedents, as well as codes of conduct such as the Declaration of Helsinki, that have contributed to the molding of modern medical ethics.

However, as medical ethics is not an exact science, it remains difficult to create comprehensive and fair standards that are relevant irrespective of an individual's culture or background.

1 Medical ethics is a set of moral principles that serve to guide how medical professionals act in confusing decision-making situations where conflicting ideas are in play.

医療倫理とは、対立した考えによって意思決定に混乱が生じる状況において、医療専門家の行動の指針となる道徳原則のことである。

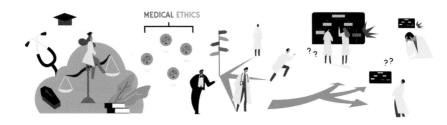

MEDICAL ETHICS

1305 **ethics**
[éθɪks]
□□□□□□

N[U]　倫理学、道徳哲学

I know we need to make money, but we can't lose sight of our **ethics**.
(お金を稼がないといけないのは分かるけど、倫理観を見失ってはいけないよ。)

▶ **ethic** [éθɪk] N[C] 倫理、道徳　　▶ **ethically** [éθɪkli] Adv. 倫理的に、道徳的に

▶ **ethical** [éθɪkəl] Adj. 倫理的な、道徳的な　↔ **unethical** [ʌnéθɪkəl] 非倫理的な

ethics は単数扱い or 複数扱い？　一般的に ethics は ethic の複数形として扱われ、複数扱いとなることがほとんどですが、学問分野としての ethics は複数形でも単数扱いになります。economics（経済学）、mathematics（数学）、physics（物理学）なども同様に単数扱いです。

1306 **moral**
[mɔ́:rəl]
□□□□□□

Adj.　道徳的な　N[P] 道徳、モラル【-s】

My number one requirement in a partner is that they are a **moral** person.
(パートナーに求めるもの第一位は道徳的な人であるってことかな。)

↔ **immoral** [ɪmɔ́:rəl] Adj. 道徳に反した　　**amoral** [èɪmɔ́:rəl] Adj. 道徳観念のない

▶ **morally** [mɔ́:rəli] Adv. 道徳的に

1307 **serve**
[sɜːrv]
□□□□□□

V[I/T]　（役割や目的を）果たす

I don't need an expensive watch because my phone **serves** the same purpose.
(携帯が同じ目的を果たしてくれるし、高い時計は要らないよ。)

serve to do（〜するのに役立つ）

V[I/T]　（客に）注文を聞く、対応する；（店が食事などを）出す

Have you been **served**? (もうご注文お伺いしてますか？)

We were **served** a beautiful wine with different kinds of delicious cheese at the restaurant.
(レストランでは最高のワインと色んな種類の美味しいチーズを出してくれたよ。)

V[T]　（ある期間）を務める；を服役する

He **served** seven years in prison for robbery. (彼は強盗で 7 年間服役したんだ。)

▶ **serving** [sə́ːrvɪŋ] N[C]（食事などの）ひとり分、一人前

Mapo tofu has about 300 calories per **serving**.（麻婆豆腐は一人前300カロリーくらいだよ。）

1308 **act**
[ækt]
□□□□□□

V[I] 行動する、ふるまう；ふりをする V[I/T]（～を）演じる N[C] 行動

Even when I'm stressed, I try to **act** calm so that others don't panic.
（イライラしているときでも、他の人がパニックにならないように冷静にふるまうようにしているんだ。）

Girls who **act** dumb so that they look cute are really scary.
（可愛く見せるためにバカなふりする女の子ってめちゃくちゃ怖い。）

▶ **acting** [ǽktɪŋ] Adj. 代理の N[U] 演技

Sam is going to be the **acting** manager while Andrew is away.
（アンドリューが休んでる間はサムが代理マネージャーになるよ。）

1309 **confusing**
[kənfjúːzɪŋ]
□□□□□□

Adj. 混乱を招く、混乱しやすい

What I just explained is pretty **confusing**, so I'll give you a moment to think about it.
（今説明したことはややこしいから、すこし考える時間をあげるね。）

▶ **confused** [kənfjúːzd] Adj. 混乱した ▶ **confusion** [kənfjúːʒən] N[C/U] 混乱；混同

Wait, I'm **confused**. Can you explain that again?（待って、どういうこと？もう一回説明して？）

▶ **confuse** [kənfjúːz] V[T] を混乱させる；を（～と）混同する（with sth）

1310 **decision**
[dɪsíʒən]
□□□□□□

N[C] 決定、決断 N[U] 決断力；決定すること

It was a really tough **decision** to make, but we decided to have the steak instead of the fish.（かなり決めるの大変だったんだけど、魚じゃなくてステーキを食べることにしたよ。）

■ **make a decision**（決定する）

Sorry, it always takes me forever to **make a decision**.
（ごめん、いつも決めるのにものすごい時間がかかるんだ。）

▶ **decide** [dɪsáɪd] V[I/T]（～を）決定する、決める

I can't **decide** where to eat.（どこで食事するか決められないよ。）

■ **decide** to do（～することを決める）

I've **decided to** study abroad.（留学することに決めたよ。）

▶ **decisive** [dɪsáɪsɪv] Adj. 決断力のある ↔ **indecisive** [ìndɪsáɪsɪv] 優柔不断な

I'm so **indecisive**.（私、すごい優柔不断なんだ。）

1311 **conflicting**
[kənflíktɪŋ]
□□□□□□

Adj. 対立する、矛盾する

My boyfriend and I have some **conflicting** opinions, but we agree on the important things.
（彼は私と意見が対立する部分もあるけど、大事なことでは意見が一致するんだ。）

▶ **conflict** N[C/U] 対立、衝突；紛争；葛藤 V[I]（～と）対立する、矛盾する（with sth）
N. [kɑ́ːnflɪkt] **V.** [kənflíkt]

▶ **conflicted** [kənflíktɪd] Adj.（～について）葛藤した（about sth）

2 For example, euthanasia, or death with dignity, the deliberate termination of a terminally ill person's life in order to relieve them of their suffering, is one of the most frequently debated areas in medical ethics.

例えば、末期患者を苦痛から解放するために意図的に命を絶つ安楽死や尊厳死は、医療倫理で最もよく議論される領域の一つである。

1312 euthanasia
[jùːθənéɪʒə]

N[U] 安楽死 = mercy killing [mɜ́ːrsikilɪŋ]

Is **euthanasia** legal in Japan?（安楽死って日本で合法なの？）

▶ **euthanize** [júːθənaɪz] V[T] を安楽死させる

1313 death
[deθ]

N[C/U] 死、死亡；（〜の）消滅、終わり（of sth）

It took me a while to get over the **death** of my dog, but I'm fine now.
（犬が死んでから立ち直るのにしばらく時間がかかったけど、今はもう大丈夫。）

■ to **death**（死ぬほど）

You scared me **to death**!（死ぬほど驚いたよ！）

▶ **deathly** [déθli] Adj. 死んだような　Adv. 死んだように

You are **deathly** pale.（あなた死んだような顔色してるわよ。）

▶ **die** [daɪ] V[I] 死ぬ；（バッテリーなどが）切れる；（機械などが）作動しなくなる

My fridge just **died**, so I'm going to buy a new one tomorrow.
（冷蔵庫が壊れちゃったから、明日新しいのを買いに行くよ。）

▶ **dead** [ded] Adj. 死んだ；切れた；作動していない

My phone is **dead**, so I need to recharge the battery.（携帯の電池切れたから充電しなきゃ。）

1314 dignity
[dígnəti]

N[U] 威厳、尊厳

I respect this tennis player so much because even when he loses, he loses with **dignity**.
（このテニス選手、本当に尊敬してる。負けた時ですら威厳があるんだ。）

death with **dignity**（尊厳死）

▶ **dignify** V[T] に威厳をつける
[dígnəfaɪ]

▶ **dignified** Adj. 威厳のある、堂々とした
[dígnəfaɪd]

You look so **dignified** in that cosplay court dress! (その宮廷服のコスプレ、すごい威厳ある感じ！)

1315 termination
[tɜ̀:rmənéɪʃən]
☐☐☐☐☐☐

N[C/U] 停止、終了

The **termination** of my employment contract took ages.
(雇用契約の終了にめちゃくちゃ時間かかったよ。)

▶ **terminate** [tɜ́:rməneɪt] V[T] を終わらせる、打ち切る V[I] 終了する

I heard some religions strictly prohibit **terminating** pregnancies.
(宗教によっては中絶を厳しく禁止してるらしいね。)

▶ **terminal** [tɜ́:rmənəl] Adj. 末期の；最後の N[C] 終着駅、終点、ターミナル

▶ **terminally** [tɜ́:rmənəli] Adv. 末期的に

1316 ill
[ɪl]
☐☐☐☐☐☐

Adj. 病気の、具合が悪い

I'm a bit **ill** today, so I'm going to stay at home. (ちょっと今日は具合が悪いから、家にいるね。)

terminally **ill**（末期症状の）

▶ **illness** [ílnəs] N[C/U] 病気

ill vs **sick** どちらも「病気の、具合が悪い」と訳されることが多いですが、用法には違いがあります。ill は短期的な病気（例：インフルエンザ等）から長期的な病気（例：がん等）までを表すことができ、状況によって程度が異なります。一方、sick は基本的に短期的な病気に対してのみ使われます。また、ill の方がよりフォーマルな表現です。

1317 relieve
[rɪlí:v]
☐☐☐☐☐☐

V[T] （重荷や心配などから）を**解放する** (of sth)；（痛みや苦しみなど）を**和らげる**

I'm going to have a few drinks after work today to **relieve** some stress.
(ストレス発散のために今日は仕事が終わったら何杯か飲みに行くよ。)

▶ **relieved** Adj. 安心した、ほっとした   ▶ **relief** N[S/U] 安堵；緩和
[rɪlí:vd]   [rɪlí:f]

I'm **relieved** to hear that. (それを聞いて安心したよ。)   That's a **relief**. (ホッとした。)

▶ **reliever** [rɪlí:vər] N[C] 和らげるもの；（野球の）リリーフ投手

a pain **reliever**（鎮痛薬）

1318 suffering
[sʌ́fərɪŋ]
☐☐☐☐☐☐

N[C/U] 苦痛、苦しみ

I think medical marijuana should be legal because it can ease the **suffering** of people who are dying in pain. (医療大麻は合法で良いと思う。痛みを感じながら亡くなる人の苦しみを和らげられるから。)

▶ **suffer** [sʌ́fər] V[I] （〜に）苦しむ (from sth)
                       V[T] （苦痛など）を受ける；（困難など）を経験する

I'm **suffering** from a fever now, so I don't think I can make it tomorrow.
(今熱出て苦しいから、明日は行けないと思う。)

My team **suffered** a massive defeat last night. (昨晩うちのチームはぼろ負けしたんだ。)

▶ **sufferer** [sʌ́fərər] N[C] （病気などで）苦しんでいる人

3 There have been numerous landmark legal precedents, as well as codes of conduct such as the Declaration of Helsinki, that have contributed to the molding of modern medical ethics.

ヘルシンキ宣言などの行動規範だけでなく、現代の医療倫理の形成に寄与した画期的な判例も数多くある。

1319 landmark
[lǽndmɑːrk]
☐☐☐☐☐☐

Adj. 画期的な　**N[C]** 目印；歴史的建造物；画期的な出来事

I think this has the potential to be a **landmark** case.（これは画期的な事件になる可能性があると思う。）

The Pantheon is one of the most famous **landmarks** in Rome.
（パンテオンはローマで最も有名な歴史的建造物の一つだよ。）

1320 precedent
[présədent]
☐☐☐☐☐☐

N[C/U] 判例、先例、前例

I'm sorry, I can't let you submit this assignment after the deadline because of the **precedent** it would set.
（申し訳ないんだけど、締め切り後はこの課題の提出は許可できません。前例を作ることになってしまうので。）

▶ **precede** [priːsíːd] V[T] よりも先に起こる、に先立つ

A huge lightning bolt **preceded** the thunder.（ものすごい稲妻が雷の前に起こったんだよ。）

▶ **preceding** [priːsíːdɪŋ] Adj. 先立つ

the **preceding** chapter（前章）

1321 as well as
[æzwélæz]
☐☐☐☐☐☐

Phr.（A as well as B の形で）B だけでなく A も、B も A も

I got a treatment **as well as** a haircut when I was at the hair salon.
（美容室では髪を切るだけじゃなくて、トリートメントもしたんだ。）

1322 code
[koʊd]
☐☐☐☐☐☐

N[C] 規範、規則、法；コード、記号

I think the company didn't succeed because it didn't have a **code** of ethics.
（あの会社は倫理規範が無かったから成功しなかったんだと思う。）

N[C/U] 暗号、コード

Your handwriting looks like some kind of secret **code** that nobody can read.
（君の手書き、なんか誰も読めない暗号みたいだね。）

V[T] を暗号化する ⟷ **decode** [di:kóʊd] (暗号など) を解読する

▶ **coded** [kóʊdɪd] Adj. 暗号化された、コード化された

▶ **coding** [kóʊdɪŋ] N[U] (サイトなどの) コーディング

1323 **declaration**
[dèkləréɪʃən]
☐☐☐☐☐☐

N[C/U] 宣言、声明、布告 **N[C]** (考えなどの)告白；申告書 **N[U]** 申告

When was the American **Declaration** of Independence written?
(アメリカの独立宣言っていつ書かれたの？)

▶ **declare** [dɪklér] V[T] を宣言する、布告する、だと断言する；を申告する

■ **declare** war on sth (〜に宣戦布告する)

In 2003, the United States and its allies **declared war on** Iraq.
(2003 年に、アメリカとその同盟国はイラクに宣戦布告した。)

You need to **declare** any food you have in your luggage when you arrive at the airport in Australia. (オーストラリアの空港に着いたら荷物に入っている食品は全部申告しないといけないよ。)

1324 **contribute**
[kəntríbju:t]
☐☐☐☐☐☐

V[I] (〜に) 寄与する、貢献する (to sth)

V[T] を (〜に) 寄付する (to sth)

I don't know what Carl **contributes** exactly, but he's fun to have around.
(具体的にカールが何を貢献してくれてるかは分かんないけど、居たら楽しいんじゃない。)

▶ **contribution** [kà:ntrɪbjú:ʃən] N[C] 貢献、寄与；寄付金

■ make a **contribution** (to sth) ((〜に) 貢献する)

Steve has **made a** significant **contribution to** the creation of this beautiful building.
(スティーブはこの美しい建物の建築に多大な貢献をしてくれた。)

▶ **contributory** [kəntríbjətɔːri] Adj. (〜に) 寄与する (to sth)

▶ **contributor** [kəntríbjətər] N[C] 寄付者、貢献者

1325 **mold**
[moʊld]
☐☐☐☐☐☐

V[T] を形成する、育て上げる；を型に入れて作る **N[C]** 型

■ **mold** A into B (A を B にする、A を B の形にする)

I think I'll be able to **mold** you **into** a fantastic basketballer.
(私なら君を最高のバスケ選手にすることができると思うよ。)

N[U] カビ

How can I remove this ugly black **mold** from the wall?
(どうやったら壁からこの気持ち悪い黒カビ取り除けるの？)

4

However, as medical ethics is not an exact science, it remains difficult to create comprehensive and fair standards that are relevant irrespective of an individual's culture or background.

しかし、医療倫理は厳密な科学ではないため、包括的かつ公正な基準を、個人の文化や背景を問わず適切となるようにつくり上げることは依然として難しいままである。

1326 **exact**
[ɪgzǽkt]
☐☐☐☐☐☐

Adj. 厳密な、正確な

I can't remember Greg's **exact** words, but he said something about going shopping this weekend.
（グレッグの言った正確な言葉は思い出せないけど、週末にショッピングに行くとか言ってた。）

▶ **exactly** [ɪgzǽktli] Adv. 厳密に、正確に、まさに

This is **exactly** what I was after!（これこそまさに私が求めていたものだ！）

▶ **exacting** [ɪgzǽktɪŋ] Adj. 厳格な；つらい

1327 **remain**
[rɪméɪn]
☐☐☐☐☐☐

V[I]（～の）ままである（adjective/sth）、残っている

Only two candidates **remain**, so I have a pretty good chance of winning this election.
（候補者は二人しか残ってないし、私がこの選挙に勝てる可能性は結構ある。）

▶ **remaining** [rɪméɪnɪŋ] Adj. 残りの、残った

You need to mix in one cup of the chocolate now and keep anything **remaining** for the final step.（ここでチョコレートを1カップ混ぜて、あと残っているものは最後に取っておきましょう。）

▶ **remainder** [rɪméɪndər] N[S]（～の）残り（of sth）【the -】

1328 **comprehensive**
[kɑ̀:mprəhénsɪv]
☐☐☐☐☐☐

Adj. 包括的な、広範囲にわたる

I've done some pretty **comprehensive** research into Frank's background, and some weird things caught my attention.
（フランクの経歴について結構広く調べたんだけど、そしたらちょっと奇妙なことに気が付いたんだ。）

▶ **comprehensively** [kɑ̀:mprəhénsɪvli] Adv. 包括的に

▶ **comprehensible** Adj. 理解できる ⟷ **incomprehensible** 理解できない
　[kɑ̀:mprəhénsəbəl]　　　　　　　　　　　[ɪnkɑ̀:mprəhénsəbəl]

▶ **comprehend** [kɑ̀:mprəhénd] V[I/T]（～を）理解する

▶ **comprehension** [kà:mprəhénʃən] N[U] 理解力

■ beyond sb's **comprehension**（理解できない）

How you can study for more than eight hours a day is just **beyond my comprehension**.
（一日 8 時間以上勉強するとか本当理解不能。）

1329 **fair**
[fer]
☐☐☐☐☐☐

Adj. 公正な、公平な、適正な　◆ **unfair** [ʌnfér] 不公平な、不正な、不適切な

Bill Gates said, "Life is not **fair**, get used to it." So true.
（ビル・ゲイツが「人生は公平じゃない。それに慣れろ」って言ったんだ。本当そうだよね。）

■ it's only **fair**（そうするのが正しい）　■ to be **fair**（公平な立場から言うと、客観的に）

I think **it's only fair** that the girl pays half the cost on a date. What do you think?
（デートの時は女性も半分払うのが正しいと思うんだけど、どう思う？）

To be fair, you can't expect Kelly to get to like you if you never talk to her.
（客観的に言うけど、あなたはケリーに全然話しかけないのに、それで好きになってもらおうなんて無理よ。）

Adj. 白い；（量や程度が）かなりの、相当の

fair skin　　Thank God we have a **fair** number of volunteers today.
（白い肌）　　（ありがたいことに、今日はかなりの数のボランティアがいるよ。）

▶ **fairly** [férli] Adv. 公平に、公正に；（量や程度が）まずまず、かなり、結構

I'm **fairly** confident that I passed the exam.（試験に受かった自信結構あるんだ。）

▶ **fairness** [férnəs] N[U] 公平さ、公正さ

The **fairness** of the election process is questionable.（あの選挙プロセスの公平性は疑問だね。）

1330 **relevant**
[réləvənt]
☐☐☐☐☐☐

Adj.（～に）適切な、関連のある（to sth）

I want to get a law degree, but I don't think it's really **relevant** to my job.
（法律の学位を取りたいんだけど、自分の仕事にあんまり関連性があると思えないんだよなぁ。）

◆ **irrelevant** [ɪréləvənt]（～に）無関係な（to sth）

▶ **relevance** N[U] 関連性、関係性　◆ **irrelevance** 無関連、無関係
　[réləvəns]　　　　　　　　　　　　　　　[ɪréləvəns]

1331 **irrespective**
[ɪrəspéktɪv]
☐☐☐☐☐☐

Adj.（～を）問わず、（～と）関係なく（of sth）

Irrespective of how busy you are, you should always be polite to customers.
（どれだけ忙しくても、接客はいつも丁寧にした方が良いよ。）

1332 **background**
[bǽkgraʊnd]
☐☐☐☐☐☐

N[C] 背景、経歴、生い立ち　N[C/U]（事の）背景、経緯

Even though I have a **background** in engineering, I decided to work in marketing.
（私はエンジニアリングの経験があるけど、マーケティングの仕事をすることに決めたよ。）

background information（背景知識）

Patient (W) Is it a good idea for my children or me to take a DNA test? I've heard that they're really good at detecting hidden diseases. After all, prevention is better than cure.

Doctor (M) True, they are useful in alerting us to defects in our DNA. Nonetheless, there are other issues that need to be considered. For example, if results indicate the presence of something chronic, could you bear that burden for the rest of your life, having it potentially dictate or restrict your actions?

Patient (W) That's a good point. I wouldn't want to be a slave to the results. I'd also want my children to undertake the assessment voluntarily. That way, they can keep the results confidential as well.

Doctor (M) I'm reluctant to make a recommendation, but I agree that you should spare them from making a decision until they're adults.

患者 (女性) うちの子たちや私自身がDNA検査を受けるのは良いことなんでしょうか？隠れた病気を見つけるのにすごい良いって聞いたんですけど。やはり、予防は治療にまさると言いますし。

医者 (男性) そうですね。DNA検査は、DNAの欠陥についての注意喚起においては役に立ちますね。ただ、考えておかなければならない問題が他にあります。例えば、もし結果が何か慢性的な病気の存在を示した場合、残りの人生、その重荷に耐えられますか？もしかするとそのせいで、あなたの行動が影響を受けたり、制限されたりするかもしれませんよ？

患者 (女性) なるほど。検査結果の奴隷にはなりたくないですね。うちの子たちにも、自発的に検査を受けてほしいし。そうすることで、結果を秘密にすることもできますしね。

医者 (男性) あまり助言はしたくないんですが、私も子供たちが大人になるまでは決断させない方が良いと思います。

1333 **detect**
[dɪtékt]
☐☐☐☐☐☐

V[T] を見つける、発見する、に気づく

▶ **detection** [dɪtékʃən] N[U] 発見、探知　▶ **detectable** [dɪtéktəbəl] Adj. 発見できる

▶ **detector** [dɪtéktər] N[C] 探知機　▶ **detective** [dɪtéktɪv] N[C] 探偵、刑事

1334 **cure**
[kjʊr]
☐☐☐☐☐☐

N[C] 治療、治療法　**V[T]** を治療する、治す

Prevention is better than **cure**. (予防は治療にまさる。)

▶ **curable** [kjʊ́rəbəl] Adj. 治療できる　↔ **incurable** [ɪnkjʊ́rəbəl] 治療できない

1335 **alert**
[əlɚ́ːrt]
☐☐☐☐☐☐

V[T] に（～について）注意を喚起する、警告する（to sth）

N[C/U] 警報　**Adj.** （～に対して）油断のない、警戒した（to sth）

on the **alert** (for sth/sb) ((～に対して) 警戒態勢で、用心して)

1336 **defect**
N. [díːfekt]
v. [dɪfékt]
☐☐☐☐☐☐

N[C] 欠陥、不備　**V[I]** （～から／～に）亡命する、離脱する (from sth/to sth)

▶ **defective** [dɪféktɪv] Adj. 欠陥のある　▶ **defectively** [dɪféktɪvli] Adv. 欠陥があって

▶ **defection** [dɪfékʃən] N[C/U] 亡命、離脱　▶ **defector** [dɪféktər] N[C] 亡命者、離脱者

1337 **nonetheless**
[nʌ̀nðəlés]
☐☐☐☐☐☐

Adv. ただ、とはいえ　= **nevertheless** [nèvərðəlés]

1338 **presence**
[prézəns]
☐☐☐☐☐☐

N[U] 存在、いること、存在感

China's **presence** in Africa has grown rapidly over the past decade.
(ここ十年でアフリカでの中国の存在感は急速に増してきているんだ。)

1339 **chronic**
[krάːnɪk]
☐☐☐☐☐☐

Adj. 慢性的な

▶ **chronically** [krάːnɪkli] Adv. 慢性的に

1340 **bear**
[ber]
☐☐☐☐☐☐

V[T] に耐える、を負う、負担する　**N[C]** クマ

bear the burden (of sth) ((～の) 重荷に耐える、負担に耐える)

▶ **bearable** [bérəbəl] Adj. 耐えられる　↔ **unbearable** [ʌnbérəbəl] 耐えられない

1341 **rest**
[rest]
☐☐☐☐☐☐

N[U] （～の）残り（of sth）【the -】　**N[C/U]** 休み

get some **rest** (少し休む)

V[I] 休む　**V[T]** を休ませる；(手や腕) を（～の上に）置く（on sth）

1342 **restrict**
[rɪstríkt]
☐☐☐☐☐☐

V[T] を制限する、限定する

▶ **restricted** [rɪstríktɪd] Adj. 制限された、限られた

▶ **restriction** [rɪstríkʃən] N[C/U] 制限、規制

▶ **restrictive** [rɪstríktɪv] Adj. 制限の、限定的な

1343 slave
[sleɪv]

N[C] 奴隷

Do it yourself! I'm not your **slave**.（自分でやってよ。あんたの奴隷じゃないんだから。）

a **slave** driver（人使いの荒い人）

▶ **slavery** [sléɪvəri] N[U] 奴隷制度、奴隷の身分

1344 undertake
[ʌndərtéɪk]

V[T] を引き受ける、開始する

▶ **undertaking** [ʌndərtèɪkɪŋ] N[C]（引き受けた）事業、仕事

1345 assessment
[əsésmənt]

N[C/U] 評価、査定、アセスメント

▶ **assess** [əsés] V[T] を評価する、査定する

▶ **self-assessment** [sèlfəsésmənt] N[C/U] 自己評価

1346 voluntarily
[vá:lənterəli]

Adv. 自発的に

▶ **voluntary** [vá:lənteri] Adj. 自発的な、ボランティアの

▶ **volunteer** [và:ləntír] N[C] ボランティア
　　　　　　　　　V[I] ボランティアをする　V[T] を自発的に提供する

1347 confidential
[kà:nfədénʃəl]

Adj. 秘密の、機密の

▶ **confidentially** [kà:nfədénʃəli] Adv. 内緒で

▶ **confidentiality** [kà:nfədenʃiǽləṭi] N[U] 機密性

1348 reluctant
[rɪlʌ́ktənt]

Adj.（〜するのに）気が進まない、しぶしぶの（to do）

▶ **reluctantly** [rɪlʌ́ktəntli] Adv. しぶしぶ

▶ **reluctance** [rɪlʌ́ktəns] N[S/U] 気が進まないこと

with **reluctance**（しぶしぶ）

1349 spare
[sper]

V[T] に（〜を）免れさせる（from sth）；（時間やお金など）を割く

Adj. 予備の、余っている　N[C] 予備品、スペア

1350 adult
[ədʌ́lt]

N[C] 大人、成人　Adj. 大人の、成人の、成人向けの

Just because they're **adults** doesn't mean they're smarter than you.
（彼らが大人だからと言って、君より頭が良いとは限らないよ。）

Chapter

29

公衆衛生
Public Health

Public health aims to strategically prevent the spread of disease, promote health, and prolong human life through the coordinated efforts of societies, organizations, communities, and individuals making informed decisions.

The foundation of public health is the prevention of epidemics of infectious diseases through the monitoring and tracking of the potential threats to health a population faces.

This foundation has close links to the historical roots of public health and stems from the reaction of the English government to the risk of disease becoming widespread during the Industrial Revolution.

Due to rapid urbanization caused by the Industrial Revolution, overly concentrated and unsanitary living conditions became serious social problems, prompting the government to recognize a wider social problem and take action to halt the outbreak of disease.

1 **Public health** aims to strategically **prevent the** spread **of** disease, promote health, and prolong **human life through the** coordinated efforts **of societies, organizations, communities, and individuals making informed decisions.**

公衆衛生は、社会や組織、地域、個人が、十分な情報を得た上で意思決定をする努力を組織的に行うことで、病気の蔓延を戦略的に防ぎ、健康を増進し、人の寿命を延ばそうとするものである。

1351 aim
[eɪm]
☐☐☐☐☐☐

V[I] （〜することを / 〜を）目指す（to do, at doing/at, for sth）

I'm **aiming** to have an early night. I'm exhausted.
（夜は早めに寝ることを目指してるよ。ヘトヘトなんだ。）

V[I] （標的などを）狙う（at sth）　V[T] を（〜に）向ける（at sth）

N[C] 目標、目的　N[U] （射撃などの）腕前、標準

1352 strategically
[strəti:dʒɪkli]
☐☐☐☐☐☐

Adv. 戦略的に

We need to plan and act **strategically** rather than always react to what's happening in front of us.
（目の前で起きることにいちいち対応するんじゃなくて、戦略的に計画を立てて行動しないといけないよ。）

▶ **strategy** [strǽtədʒi] N[C] 戦略　N[U] 計画　▶ **strategic** [strəti:dʒɪk] Adj. 戦略的な

1353 spread
[spred]
☐☐☐☐☐☐

N[S] 蔓延、広まり

Delaying the **spread** of this bad news isn't fair to anybody.
（この悪いニュースの拡散を遅らせるのは誰にとっても公正なことじゃないよ。）

V[I] 広がる、広まる　V[T] を広げる、広める、（広げて）塗る

Rumors **spread** very quickly in this company.（この会社では噂はすぐに広まるんだ。）

I **spread** the butter first, and then the jam.
（俺は最初にバターを塗って、それからジャムじゃないとだめなんだ。）

N[C/U] （マーガリンなどの）パンに塗るもの

1354 disease
[dɪzíːz]
☐☐☐☐☐☐

N[C/U] 病気　N[C] （社会などの）病、不健全な状態

I wonder if we'll ever get to a stage where we can prevent all **diseases** with vaccinations.
（いつかワクチン接種で全ての病気が防げるような段階までたどり着けるのかなぁ。）

▶ **diseased** [dɪzíːzd] Adj. 病気にかかった、病的な

1355 **prolong**
[prəlάːŋ]

V[T] を延ばす、長引かせる

Do you think drinking green tea every day will really **prolong** your life?
（毎日緑茶を飲んだら寿命が延びるって本当だと思う？）

▶ **prolonged** [prəlάːŋd] Adj. 長期にわたる、長引く

Prolonged use of medicine is not good for anyone's health.
（長期にわたる薬の使用は誰の健康にも良くないよ。）

1356 **coordinated**
[koʊɔ́ːrdəneɪt̬ɪd]

Adj. 組織的な、協調的な

I'm not great at sports, mainly because I'm not very **coordinated**.
（スポーツはあんまり得意じゃないんだ。僕、あまり協調的じゃないからね。）

▶ **coordinate** *V.* [koʊɔ́ːrdəneɪt] V[T]（活動など）をまとめる、調整する
    N./Adj. [koʊɔ́ːrdənət] N[C] 座標　Adj. 座標の

I wish I could have someone **coordinate** my schedule for me. I don't want to do this kind of admin work anymore.
（誰かが自分のスケジュールを調整してくれたらいいのになぁ。もうこういう事務的な作業はしたくないよ。）

an x-**coordinate**（x座標）

▶ **coordination** N[U] 協調、連携　　▶ **coordinator** N[C] コーディネーター、まとめ役
    [koʊɔ̀ːrdənéɪʃən]　　　　　　　　　　[koʊɔ́ːrdəneɪt̬ər]

1357 **effort**
[éfərt]

N[C/U] 努力

My marks were pretty bad this time around, so I'm going to put in way more **effort** next semester.（今回成績があんまり良くなかったから、次の学期ではもっともっと努力するつもり。）

■ make an **effort** (to do)（（〜する）努力をする）

You can achieve whatever you want if you **make an effort** with the right mindset.
（正しいマインドセットを持って努力すれば何だって達成できるよ。）

■ in an **effort** to do（〜しようと（努力）して）

I've been exercising every day **in an effort to** lose some weight.
（ちょっと体重を落とそうと毎日エクササイズしているんだ。）

▶ **effortless** [éfərtləs] Adj. 努力不要の、楽な、簡単そうな

▶ **effortlessly** [éfərtləsli] Adv. 楽々と、いとも簡単に

Professional figure skaters seem to jump **effortlessly**, but it's actually extremely difficult.
（プロのフィギュアスケート選手はいとも簡単そうに跳ぶんだけど、実際はものすごい難しいんだ。）

2 The foundation of public health is the prevention of epidemics of infectious diseases through the monitoring and tracking of the potential threats to health a population faces.

公衆衛生の基礎は、住民が直面する健康への潜在的な脅威を監視・追跡することで感染症の流行を防止することにある。

1358 **foundation**
[faʊndéɪʃən]
☐☐☐☐☐☐

N[C] 基礎、基盤、土台　**N[P]** 建物の土台【-s】

Having a strong **foundation** in math is really helpful for doing well in physics.
（数学の基礎がしっかりあると物理を理解するのにめちゃくちゃ役立つよ。）

N[U] 創立、設立　**N[C]** 財団　**N[C/U]**（化粧の）ファンデーション

▶ **foundational** [faʊndéɪʃənəl] Adj. 基礎となる、基盤となる

▶ **found** [faʊnd] V[T] を（〜に）基づかせる（on sth）；を創立する、設立する

He **founded** this NPO to provide quality education to children from poor families.
（彼は良質な教育を貧しい家庭に生まれた子供たちに提供するためにこの NPO を設立したんだ。）

▶ **founder** [fáʊndər] N[C] 創業者、創設者

1359 **epidemic**
[èpədémɪk]
☐☐☐☐☐☐

N[C]（病気の）流行、蔓延；（犯罪などの）急増　**Adj.** 蔓延している

Social media addiction is an **epidemic**, and I don't think there's a cure.
（ソーシャルメディア中毒が蔓延してるけど、俺は治す方法は無いと思うな。）

▶ **epidemiology** [èpədi:miɑ́:lədʒi] N[U] 疫学、伝染病学

1360 **infectious**
[ɪnfékʃəs]
☐☐☐☐☐☐

Adj. 伝染性の、感染性の

You should take a few days off if you think you're **infectious**.　an **infectious** disease
（うつる可能性があると思うなら、数日休んだ方がいいよ。）　（伝染病）

▶ **infection** [ɪnfékʃən] N[U] 感染　N[C] 感染症　▶ **infected** [ɪnféktɪd] Adj. 感染した

You should clean that cut if you don't want to get a bad **infection**.
（ひどい感染症を起こしたくないなら傷口は綺麗にした方がいいよ。）

1361 **monitor**
[mɑ́:nətər]
☐☐☐☐☐☐

V[T] を監視する　**N[C]** モニター

I swear these social media sites **monitor** what I say and read, because their ads are just way too relevant.

（この SNS サイトの広告、関連性ありすぎだろ。マジで俺の発言とか読んでるもの監視してるだろ。）

1362 **track**
[træk]
☐☐☐☐☐☐

V[T]　を追跡する

It's really cool how you can **track** the progress of a plane online now.
（今は飛行機の航路をオンラインで追跡できるなんてすごいよな。）

track sth/sb down（〜を見つけ出す、追跡して探し出す）

N[C/U]　線路　**N[C]**　小道；（陸上の）トラック；（通った）跡

■ go off **track**（脱線する）　　on the right **track**（順調に進んでいる）

Sorry I **went off track** a bit during the meeting.（ごめん、ミーティング中ちょっと脱線しちゃったね。）

N[U]　トラック競技

track and field（陸上競技）

▶ **tracker** [trǽkər] N[C] 追跡するもの

スペルと発音注意！　車のトラックは truck [trʌk] で、発音も違うので注意して下さい。

1363 **threat**
[θret]
☐☐☐☐☐☐

N[C/U]　脅威；脅し、脅迫

I think every guy that talks to my girlfriend is a **threat**.
（俺、自分の彼女に話しかけてくる男は全員脅威だと思ってる。）

pose a **threat** to sth/sb（〜に脅威を与える）

▶ **threaten** [θrétn] V[T] を脅す、脅迫する；の前兆となる　V[I]（悪いことなどが）差し迫る

The robber **threatened** the staff with a knife.（その強盗はスタッフをナイフで脅した。）

■ **threaten** to do（〜すると言って脅す）

The country **threatened to** use nuclear weapons.（その国は核兵器を使うと言って脅した。）

▶ **threatening** [θrétnɪŋ] Adj. 脅迫的な；（雲行きなどが）怪しい

The sky looks **threatening**. Maybe a storm is coming.
（雲行きが怪しそうだな。嵐が来るかもね。）

▶ **threateningly** [θrétnɪŋli] Adv. 脅迫的に

1364 **face**
[feɪs]
☐☐☐☐☐☐

V[T]　に直面する；（現実など）を受け入れる　**V[I/T]**　（〜に）向く、面する

Sometimes you **face** difficulties not because you're doing something wrong, but because you're doing something right.
（時には、間違ったことをしているからではなく、正しいことをしているからこそ困難に直面するということもあるんだ。）

I bought an apartment with a balcony **facing** south.
（バルコニーが南向きのアパートを買ったんだ。）

N[C]　顔；外観、面

a smug **face**（ドヤ顔）　　　　a smirking **face**（にやにやした顔）

3 This foundation has close links to the historical roots of public health and stems from the reaction of the English government to the risk of disease becoming widespread during the Industrial Revolution.

この基礎は、公衆衛生の歴史的起源と密接に関係しており、産業革命当時、英政府が病気の蔓延リスクに反応したことに由来している。

1365 **close**
Adj. [kloʊs]
V. [kloʊz]
☐☐☐☐☐☐

Adj. 密接な、近い；仲が良い

Tracy and I used to be **close**, but we haven't spoken much since her boyfriend came back from the UK.
（トレイシーと僕は仲良かったけど、彼女の彼氏がイギリスから帰ってきてからあんまり話してないんだ。）

That was **close**! (惜しかった！/ 危なかった！)

V[I] 閉じる、閉まる；終わる　**V[T]** を閉じる；を終える；を結ぶ

■ **close** a deal（契約を結ぶ）

We **closed a deal** with a large company based in the U.S.
（アメリカに本社を置く大企業と契約を結びました。）

▶ **closely** [klóʊsli] Adv. 密接に、近く；念入りに

I think intelligence and education are **closely** related. (知能と教育は密接に関わっていると思う。)

▶ **closeness** [klóʊsnəs] N[U] 近さ；親密さ　▶ **closure** [klóʊʒər] N[C/U] 閉鎖

1366 **root**
[ru:t]
☐☐☐☐☐☐

N[C] 起源；根源；（植物の）根　**V[I]** 根付く　**V[T]** を根付かせる

Did you know that German and English have the same **roots**?
（ドイツ語と英語ってルーツが一緒だって知ってた？）

the **root** cause (of sth) ((〜の) 根本的な原因)

1367 **stem**
[stem]
☐☐☐☐☐☐

V[I] （〜に）由来する、（〜から）生じる (from sth)　**N[C]** 茎、幹

Where do you think Saki's hatred toward me **stems** from?
（サキが俺のこと大嫌いなのはどこから来ているんだろう？）

a **stem** cell
（幹細胞）

1368 **reaction**
[riǽkʃən]

N[C/U] （〜に対する）反応（to sth）；（〜に対する）反発（against sth）

Your **reaction** when you ran into that glass door was hilarious.
（お前がガラスのドアにぶつかったときの反応、超ウケた。）

▶ **react** [riǽkt] V[I] （〜に）反応する（to sth）

How would you **react** if someone said, "I love you," but you felt nothing?
（誰かに「好きです」って言われても、何も感じなかったら、どう反応する？）

▶ **reactionary** [riǽkʃəneri] Adj. 反動的な   N[C] 反動主義者

▶ **reactive** [riǽktɪv] Adj. 後手後手の   ↔ **proactive** [pròʊǽktɪv] 先手先手の、前向きな

We should always be **proactive** rather than **reactive**.
（僕らは常に後手後手ではなくて先手先手で行くべきだ。）

1369 **risk**
[rɪsk]

N[C/U] リスク、危険、（悪いことが起きる）可能性

I know I'm taking a **risk** by buying a house right now, but I really like this place.
（今家を買うのはリスクなのは分かってるけど、この家すごく好きなんだ。）

at **risk** (of sth) （（〜の）危険がある）

V[T] を危険にさらす；の危険を冒す；を危険覚悟で行う

■ **risk** it （リスクを冒す、リスクをかける）

We could try to get into the restaurant without booking, but I don't want to **risk** it.
（あのレストランは予約なしで入れるかもしれないけど、リスクは冒したくないな。）

▶ **risky** [rɪ́ski] Adj. 危険な   ▶ **riskiness** [rɪ́skinəs] N[U] 危険度

1370 **widespread**
[wàɪdspréd]

Adj. 蔓延した、普及した、広まった、広範囲にわたる

Homelessness is a pretty **widespread** and serious issue.
（ホームレスはかなり広範で深刻な問題だ。）

1371 **revolution**
[rèvəlúːʃən]

N[C/U] （政治・社会的な）革命   N[C] （技術や考え方などの）革命

The smartphone **revolution** has changed the world.（スマホ革命は世界を変えたよ。）

N[C/U] 回転運動、公転 ↔ **rotation** [roʊtéɪʃən] 自転   N[C] 回転数

▶ **revolutionary** [rèvəlúːʃəneri] Adj. 革命的な   N[C] 革命家、革命児

a **revolutionary** movement （革命運動）

▶ **revolutionize** [rèvəlúːʃənaɪz] V[T] に革命をもたらす

Online English conversation services **revolutionized** the way people practice speaking.
（オンライン英会話サービスはスピーキングの練習方法に革命をもたらしたんだ。）

▶ **revolve** V[I] （〜の周りを）回転する、公転する（around sth/sb）
[rɪvɑ́ːlv] V[T] を回転させる

The Earth **revolves** around the Sun. （地球は太陽の周りを公転する。）

↔ **rotate** [róʊteɪt] 自転する / を交替制にする

4 Due to rapid urbanization caused by the Industrial Revolution, overly concentrated and unsanitary living conditions became serious social problems, prompting the government to recognize a wider social problem and take action to halt the outbreak of disease.

産業革命によって急速な都市化が起こり、人口の過密化と不衛生な生活環境が深刻な社会問題となったことから、英政府はより広範な社会問題を認識し、病気の発生を食い止める措置を講じるようになったのだ。

1372 concentrated
[kάːnsəntreɪṭɪd]
☐☐☐☐☐☐

Adj. 密集した、集中した；（液体が）濃縮した

It's important to make a **concentrated** effort if you really want to achieve what you're after.
（自分が求めているものを本当に手に入れたいなら、集中的に努力することが重要だよ。）

▶ **concentrate** V[I] （〜に）集中する (on sth)
[kάːnsəntreɪt] V[T] を（〜に）集中させる (on sth)　N[C/U] 濃縮物

I can't **concentrate** on my studies in a noisy environment.
（うるさい環境だと勉強に集中できないんだ。）

Let's **concentrate** all our efforts on this important project.（この重要なプロジェクトに全力を注ごう。）

▶ **concentration** N[U] 集中、集中力　N[C/U] （場所などへの）集中、密集
[kὰːnsəntréɪʃən]

1373 unsanitary
[ʌnsǽnəteri]
☐☐☐☐☐☐

Adj. 不衛生な　⟷ **sanitary** [sǽnəteri] 衛生的な

I avoid using public bathrooms because they're so **unsanitary**.
（公衆トイレはすごい不衛生だから使わないようにしてる。）

▶ **sanitization** N[U] 消毒、浄化　　▶ **sanitizer** N[C] 消毒液、消毒剤
[sǽnətəzéɪʃən]　　　　　　　　　　　[sǽnətaɪzər]

▶ **sanitize** [sǽnətaɪz] V[T] を消毒する；(都合が悪い部分) を削除する

I think this video is a highly **sanitized** version of what he really wanted to say.
（この動画では彼が本当に言いたかったことはかなりカットされてると思う。）

1374 condition
[kəndíʃən]
☐☐☐☐☐☐

N[P] （仕事や生活などの）環境、状況【-s】　**N[S/U]** 状態；体調

I want to check what **condition** the used laptop's in before I pay for it.
（その中古ノートパソコン、お金払う前に状態をチェックしておきたいな。）

working **conditions**（労働環境）

N[C] 条件

- on the **condition** that + sentence（〜という条件で）

I can give you some internship opportunities **on the condition that** you work hard.
（一生懸命働くことを条件として、インターンの機会をあげてもいいよ。）

under the **condition** that + sentence（〜という条件下で）

▶ **conditional** Adj. 条件付きの
  [kəndíʃənəl]

▶ **conditionally** Adv. 条件付きで
  [kəndíʃənəli]

I received a **conditional** offer from one of the universities I applied to.
（出願した大学の一つから条件付きのオファーをもらったんだ。）

1375 **prompt**
[prɑːmpt]
☐☐☐☐☐☐

V[T] を（〜するよう）促す、駆り立てる（to do）；に思い出させる

What **prompted** you to look for a new job?（どうして新しく仕事を探すことになったの？）

Can you please **prompt** me when my time is up?（時間切れになったら教えてくれますか？）

Adj. 迅速な、素早い、すぐの

Thank you for your **prompt** reply.（迅速な返信ありがとうございます。）

▶ **promptly** [prɑ́ːmptli] Adv. 迅速に、素早く、すぐに

Tom has been **promptly** responding to all my messages.
（トムはメッセージに全部すぐ返信してくれてるよ。）

1376 **recognize**
[rékəgnaɪz]
☐☐☐☐☐☐

V[T] を認識する、認める；に見覚えがある、を（それと）分かる

Wow, I didn't **recognize** you with that haircut.（おぉ、その髪型のせいで分からなかったよ。）

Do you **recognize** that guy?（あの人のこと見覚えある？）

▶ **recognition** [rèkəgníʃən] N[S/U] 認識   N[U] 見てそれと分かること、見覚え

1377 **halt**
[hɑːlt]
☐☐☐☐☐☐

V[T] を食い止める、中止する   **V[I]** 止まる、停止する

We had to **halt** production last night because something went wrong with the machinery.
（昨晩は機械の調子がおかしかったので、生産を中止しなければいけなかった。）

N[S] 停止、中止

come to a **halt**（止まる）   bring sth to a **halt**（〜を止める、〜を中止する）

1378 **outbreak**
[áʊtbreɪk]
☐☐☐☐☐☐

N[C] （病気などの突発的な）発生；（戦争などの）勃発

I don't really like how there's always an **outbreak** of extreme nationalism whenever the Olympics are on.（僕はオリンピック開催中にいつも極端な愛国心が生まれることがあまり好きじゃない。）

Man	I've noticed that you've been eating a lot more greens and fiber recently. Have you suddenly decided to ban meat and grains from your diet, or have you gotten on this nutrition fad?
Woman	I've been doing it for a while. I just didn't announce it to the world. I haven't quit meat entirely, but being on a plant-based diet helps me control my weight and stay fit without having to starve myself, especially if I exercise regularly. Besides, I feel less fatigued and more alert. Cooking tasty meals using less meat was initially a chore, but now it's just part of my routine.
Man	I'm glad that vegetables satisfy your appetite. Are you worried about your protein intake?
Woman	Not really. The protein from nuts is an adequate replacement. I was quite worried about cutting out essential minerals and vitamins, but I remedy that through eating fruit.

男性	そういえば最近、前よりも青野菜とか食物繊維、結構食べてるよね。急に肉と穀物を食べるの禁止にでもしたの？それとも流行りの栄養摂取方法に乗ってるの？
女性	もう始めてから結構経つよ。ただみんなに言わなかっただけ。完全にお肉をやめたわけじゃないけど、野菜中心の食事にすると、腹ペコにならないで体重をコントロールしたり、健康を維持したりできるんだよね。定期的にエクササイズしてればなおさらね。それに、あんまり疲れなくなったし、頭も前より冴えてる気がするの。お肉をあんまり使わないでおいしい料理を作るのは最初はおっくうだったけど、今ではもう日常の一部になったよ。
男性	野菜で食欲が満たされるのは良いよね。でもたんぱく質の摂取とか心配じゃない？
女性	別に心配じゃないよ。ナッツのたんぱく質で十分代わりになるし。必要なミネラルやビタミンが減るのは結構心配だったけど、フルーツを食べて解決してるよ。

1379 fiber
[fáɪbər]

N[U] 食物繊維　N[C/U] 繊維

▶ **fibrous** [fáɪbrəs] Adj. 繊維の、繊維質の

1380 ban
[bæn]

V[T] を禁止する　= **prohibit** [prəhíbɪt]　= **forbid** [fərbíd]　N[C] 禁止令

ban sb from doing（〜が〜するのを禁止する）

▶ **banned** [bænd] Adj. 禁止された

1381 grain
[greɪn]

N[C/U] 穀物　N[C]（米や麦の）一粒

▶ **grainy** [gréɪni] Adj. ざらざらした、粒々の

1382 nutrition
[nuːtríʃən]

N[U] 栄養摂取、栄養学

▶ **nutritious** [nuːtríʃəs] Adj. 栄養のある　▶ **nutrient** [núːtriənt] N[C] 栄養、栄養素

▶ **nutritional** [nuːtríʃənəl] Adj. 栄養の　▶ **nutritionally** [nuːtríʃənəli] Adv. 栄養的に、栄養学的に

1383 fad
[fæd]

N[C] 流行り、流行

I think the man bun is just a **fad**.（男性のお団子ヘアーはただの流行りだと思うよ。）

1384 announce
[ənáʊns]

V[T] と言う、を発表する、公表する、知らせる

▶ **announcement** [ənáʊnsmənt] N[C] 発表、公表、告知

▶ **announcer** [ənáʊnsər] N[C] アナウンサー

1385 quit
[kwɪt]

V[I/T]（〜を）やめる、辞める

quit doing（〜するのをやめる）

I **quit** my job, and I feel great now.（仕事辞めて今は最高の気分だよ。）

1386 weight
[weɪt]

N[C/U] 体重、重さ　N[C] おもり　N[U]（言葉などの）重み、重要性

put on/gain **weight**（太る）　lose **weight**（痩せる）

▶ **weigh** [weɪ] V[I] 重さがある

　　　　　V[T] の重さをはかる；を（〜と）比較検討する（against sth）

1387 fit
[fɪt]

Adj. 健康な、体調が良い；（〜に）適した、ふさわしい（for sth）

V[I] 収まる　V[T] に（サイズなどが）合う；を収める　N[C] 適合；激怒

have a **fit**（激怒する、キレる）

▶ **fit in** [fɪtɪn] [PV]（環境など）になじむ、溶け込む

1388 starve
[stɑːrv]

V[I] とてもお腹が空く、飢える、餓死する　V[T] を飢えさせる

starve to death（餓死する）

▶ **starved** [stɑːrvd] Adj. お腹の空いた、飢えた　▶ **starvation** [stɑːrvéɪʃən] N[U] 飢餓、餓死

▶ **starving** [stɑ́ːrvɪŋ] Adj. お腹の空いている、飢えている

1389 fatigued
[fətíːgd]

Adj. 疲れた、疲れ切った

▶ **fatigue** [fətíːg] N[U] 疲労、疲れ　V[T] を疲れさせる

chronic **fatigue**（慢性疲労）

1390 cook
[kʊk]

V[I] 料理する、火が通る　V[T] を料理する、調理する、に火を通す
N[C] 料理をする人、料理人

My mom is a great **cook**.（僕のお母さんはすごい料理が上手なんだよ。）

1391 chore
[tʃɔːr]

N[C] 面倒なこと、退屈なこと；(日常的にやらないといけない) 仕事、雑務

do household **chores**（家事をする）

1392 routine
[ruːtíːn]

N[C/U] 日常的なこと、習慣　Adj. 日常的な、定期的な、退屈な

You should make your studies part of your daily **routine**.
（勉強は毎日の習慣の一部にした方がいいよ。）

▶ **routinely** [ruːtíːnli] Adv. 日常的に、定期的に　▶ **routinize** [rúːṭənaɪz] V[T] を習慣化する

1393 appetite
[ǽpətaɪt]

N[C/U] 食欲

▶ **appetizer** [ǽpətaɪzər] N[C] 前菜　▶ **appetizing** [ǽpətaɪzɪŋ] Adj. 食欲をそそる

1394 protein
[próʊtiːn]

N[C/U] たんぱく質

I eat a **protein** bar after I work out to support muscle recovery.
（筋肉の回復を助けるために、運動した後はプロテインバーを食べるんだ。）

1395 intake
[ínteɪk]

N[C/U] 摂取量　N[C] 採用者 (数)、入学者 (数)

This app is very useful for keeping track of my calorie **intake**.
（このアプリ、カロリー摂取量を把握するのにすごい便利。）

1396 replacement
[rɪpléɪsmənt]

N[C] 代わりになるもの・人　N[U] 取り替え

▶ **replace** [rɪpléɪs] V[T] を (〜と) 取り替える (with sth/sb)；に取って代わる

▶ **replaceable** [rɪpléɪsəbəl] Adj. 取り替え可能な

↔ **irreplaceable** [ìrəpléɪsəbəl] Adj. 替えがきかない

1397 vitamin
[váɪṭəmɪn]

N[C] ビタミン

a **vitamin** pill（ビタミン剤）

1398 remedy
[rémədi]

V[T] を解決する、改善する　N[C] 解決策、改善策；治療薬

▶ **remedial** [rɪmíːdiəl] Adj. 解決の、改善の；治療の

▶ **remediable** [rɪmíːdiəbəl] Adj. 治療可能な

Chapter

30

精神医学
Psychiatry

Psychiatry is the field of medicine devoted specifically to the diagnosis, prevention, and treatment of mental disorders.

Patients seeking psychiatric help exhibit symptoms such as panic attacks, hallucinations, thoughts of suicide, extreme mood swings, significant tiredness, and excessive worrying.

Even though there are numerous treatments that can be applied to alleviate mental disorders, disorders are divided into only five categories: mood, anxiety, personality, psychotic, and substance-induced disorders.

Intriguingly, this categorization has remained largely unchanged for many years. This is despite the fact that psychiatric treatments have developed drastically over the last several decades, corresponding with a sharp reduction in the volume of hospitalizations for psychiatric patients.

1 Psychiatry **is the field of medicine** devoted specifically **to the** diagnosis, prevention, **and treatment of** mental disorders.

精神医学は、精神障害の診断、予防、治療に特化した医学の分野である。

1399 psychiatry
[saɪkáɪətri]

N[U] 精神医学

This may sound a bit dumb, but I often confuse psychology with **psychiatry**.
（ちょっとバカっぽく聞こえるかもしれないけど、よく心理学と精神医学をごっちゃにしちゃうんだよね。）

▶ **psychiatric** Adj. 精神医学の、精神科の
[sàɪkiǽtrɪk]

▶ **psychiatrist** N[C] 精神科医
[saɪkáɪətrɪst]

1400 devoted
[dɪvóʊt̮ɪd]

Adj. （〜を）専門に扱った（to sth）；（〜に）献身的な（to sth/sb）

Hey, how do I know if my boyfriend will still be **devoted** to me in the future?
（ねぇ、どうやったら彼氏が将来的にも愛してくれるか分かるかな？）

▶ **devote** [dɪvóʊt] V[T] を（〜に）捧げる、専念させる（to sth）

My dad **devoted** a lot of time to teaching me how to read and write.
（お父さんは私に読み書きを教えることにたくさん時間を割いてくれたんだ。）

devote oneself to sth（〜に専念する、身を捧げる）

▶ **devotion** [dɪvóʊʃən] N[U] 献身；信仰心
▶ **devotional** [dɪvóʊʃənəl] Adj. 信仰の

1401 specifically
[spəsífɪkli]

Adv. 特に；明確に、具体的に

I came back to this restaurant **specifically** for the garlic bread.
（あのガーリックパンが特に食べたくてまたこのレストランに来ちゃった。）

▶ **specific** [spəsífɪk] Adj. 特定の；明確な、具体的な

Can you be more **specific**?（もうちょっと具体的に説明してくれる？）

▶ **specify** [spésəfaɪ] V[T] を明記する、具体的に述べる

▶ **specification** [spèsəfəkéɪʃən] N[C/U] 仕様　N[P] 仕様書【-s】

1402 diagnosis
[dàɪəgnóʊsɪs]

N[C/U] 診断、診断結果；（原因などの）分析

What was the doctor's **diagnosis**?（お医者さんの診断は何だったの？）

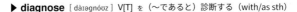

▶ **diagnose** [dàɪəgnóʊz] V[T] を（〜であると）診断する（with/as sth）

She was **diagnosed** with diabetes.（彼女は糖尿病だと診断された。）

▶ **diagnostic** [dàɪəgná:stɪk] Adj. 診断の、分析のための

diagnostic equipment（診断装置）

1403 **prevention**
[prɪvénʃən]
☐☐☐☐☐☐

N[U] 予防、防止

What's the best **prevention** of diabetes?（糖尿病予防に一番良いのは何かな？）

▶ **prevent** [prɪvént] V[T] を防ぐ、防止する

■ **prevent** sth/sb from doing（〜が〜するのを防ぐ）

Eating well and exercising daily will **prevent** you **from** getting sick.
（しっかり食べて、毎日運動することで病気を予防できるよ。）

▶ **preventable** [prɪvéntəbəl] Adj. 予防可能な

a **preventable** disease（予防可能な病気）

▶ **preventive** [prɪvéntɪv] Adj. 予防の　= **preventative** [prɪvéntətɪv]

a **preventive** measure（予防措置）

preventive vs **preventative**　どちらも全く同じ意味を持ちニュアンスなども特に違いはありませんが、一般的に preventive の方が頻繁に使用されると言われています。

1404 **mental**
[méntl]
☐☐☐☐☐☐

Adj. 精神的な　⟷　**physical** [fízɪkəl] 身体の

I really don't have the **mental** capacity to discuss it.
（そのことについて話すこころの余裕は本当に無い。）

▶ **mentally** [méntəli] Adv. 精神的に、気持ち的に　⟷　**physically** [fízɪkli] 身体的に

English studies can be a long journey, so you need to be **mentally** prepared.
（英語学習は長い道のりになることもあるから、気持ちの準備ができてなきゃいけないよ。）

▶ **mentality** [mentǽləti] N[C] 精神的な部分、物の考え方

At the end of the day, whether you can succeed largely depends on your **mentality**.
（結局、成功できるかどうかっていうのは精神的な部分によるところが大きいよ。）

1405 **disorder**
[dɪsɔ́:rdər]
☐☐☐☐☐☐

N[C] 障害、疾患　**N[U]** 混乱、無秩序、暴動

What's the best way to help people with mental **disorders**?
（精神障害の人を助ける一番良い方法って何だろう？）

▶ **disorderly** [dɪsɔ́:rdərli] Adj. 無秩序の、乱暴な

■ **disorderly** conduct（秩序を乱す行動、迷惑行為）

I can't believe he got charged with **disorderly conduct**. He's usually such a nice guy.
（彼が迷惑行為で訴えられたなんて信じられないよ。基本的にめっちゃ良い奴なんだけどな。）

2 Patients **seeking psychiatric help exhibit** symptoms **such as panic** attacks, hallucinations, **thoughts of** suicide, **extreme mood swings, significant** tiredness, **and excessive** worrying.

精神科の助けを求める患者は、パニック発作、幻覚、自殺願望、激しい気分変動、極度の疲労、過度の不安などの症状を示す。

1406 **patient**
[péɪʃənt]
☐☐☐☐☐☐

N[C] 患者、病人　**Adj.** 我慢強い、忍耐強い

I don't know why, but I get a lot more **patients** on weekdays compared to weekends.
(なんか謎なんだけど、週末よりも平日の方がたくさん患者さんが来るんだよね。)

Be **patient**. Good things take time.（我慢しなよ。良いことが起きるには時間がかかるからさ。）

⟷ impatient [ɪmpéɪʃənt] 我慢できない、（待ちきれずに）すぐイライラする

Why are you so **impatient**? Your order is coming.
(なんでそんなにイライラしてるの？注文したものはすぐ来るよ。)

▶ inpatient [ínpeɪʃənt] N[C] 入院患者　**⟷ outpatient** [áʊtpeɪʃənt] 外来患者

1407 **symptom**
[símptəm]
☐☐☐☐☐☐

N[C] 症状、兆候

The volatility in the stock market is a **symptom** of deeper economic issues.
(株式市場の不安定さはより深刻な経済問題を表している。)

▶ symptomatic [sìmptəmǽṭɪk] Adj. (〜の) 症状を示す (of sth)

1408 **attack**
[ətǽk]
☐☐☐☐☐☐

N[C] 発作　**N[C/U]** 攻撃　**V[I/T]** （〜を）攻撃する

Every time I think about the deadline, I have a bit of a panic **attack**.
(締め切りについて考えるたびにちょっとパニックになっちゃうんだ。)

a heart **attack**
(心臓発作)

make an **attack** (on sth/sb) ((〜を) 攻撃する)

1409 **hallucination**
[həlù:sənéɪʃən]
☐☐☐☐☐☐

N[C/U] 幻覚

I thought I saw Yukari on the train, but it must have been a **hallucination**.
(ユカリのこと電車でみたと思ったけど、幻覚だったに違いないよね。)

▶ hallucinate [həlú:səneɪt] V[I] 幻覚を起こす

▶ **hallucinatory** [həlú:sɪnətɔːri] Adj. 幻覚の、幻覚を引き起こす

▶ **hallucinogenic** [həlù:sɪnoʊdʒénɪk] Adj. 幻覚を引き起こす

hallucinatory side effects
（副作用として起きる幻覚）

a **hallucinogenic** drug
（幻覚を引き起こすドラッグ）

1410 **suicide**
[súːəsaɪd]
▢▢▢▢▢▢

N[C/U] 自殺   **N[C]** 自殺者

The **suicide** rate has dropped dramatically over the last few decades, but it's still too high.
（自殺率はここ数十年でものすごく減少したけど、それでもまだ高すぎるよ。）

■ commit **suicide**（自殺する）

Yukio Mishima was Japan's most famous postwar novelist, but he publicly **committed suicide** after failing to overthrow the government.
（三島由紀夫は戦後日本で最も有名な小説家だったが、政府の転覆に失敗し公開自殺を行った。）

▶ **suicidal** Adj. 自殺の、自殺行為の
[sùːəsáɪdl]

▶ **suicidally** Adv. 自殺したくなるほど
[sùːəsáɪdəli]

なぜ commit が使われるのか？　commit は犯罪などを犯すという意味の動詞で、suicide と合わせて使用されるのは、昔自殺が罪であると考えられていた名残りです。今は自殺は犯罪ではないという理由から、die by/from suicide、end one's life、take one's life という表現を好む人もいます。

1411 **tiredness**
[táɪrdnəs]
▢▢▢▢▢▢

N[U] 疲労、疲労感

I don't know if it's **tiredness** or hunger, but I feel a bit grumpy right now.
（疲れてるのかお腹すいてるのかわからないけど、ちょっと今機嫌悪い。）

▶ **tired** [taɪrd] Adj.（〜で）疲れた（from sth）

▶ **tiredly** [táɪrdli] Adv. 疲れて

■ **tired** of sth/sb（〜にうんざりした、飽きた）

I'm so **tired of** fighting with my boyfriend.（彼氏と喧嘩するのもううんざりなんだけど。）

▶ **tire**　V[I] 疲れる　V[T] を疲れさせる
[taɪr]　　N[C]（自動車などの）タイヤ

▶ **tiring** Adj. 疲れる、だるい
[táɪrɪŋ]

1412 **worry**
[wə́ːri]
▢▢▢▢▢▢

V[I]（〜を）心配する（about sth/sb）　**V[T]** を心配させる

I try not to **worry** too much about things that I can't control.
（自分でコントロールできないことに関しては心配しすぎないようにしてるよ。）

▶ **worried** [wə́ːrid] Adj.（〜について）心配した（about sth/sb）

I'm **worried** about you.（君のこと心配してるよ。）

▶ **worrying** [wə́ːriɪŋ] Adj. 心配させるような = **worrisome** [wə́ːrisəm]

▶ **worrier** [wə́ːriər] N[C] 心配性の人

worry about vs **be worried about**　どちらも「〜を心配している」という意味ですが、若干ニュアンスが異なります。worry about sth/sb はより一般的で、何かに対して基本的に心配していることを意味します（例：I worry about you because you are my best friend.）。一方で、be worried about sth/sb は今現在、この発言をしている時、まさに心配しているというニュアンスがあります（例：I'm worried about you because you look sick.）。

3 **Even though there are numerous treatments that can be applied to** alleviate **mental disorders, disorders are divided into only five** categories: mood, anxiety, personality, psychotic, and substance-induced **disorders.**

精神障害を和らげるために適用できる治療法はたくさんあるが、精神障害のカテゴリーは、気分障害、不安障害、パーソナリティ障害、精神病性障害、そして物質誘発性障害の 5 つしかない。

1413 alleviate
[əlíːvieɪt]
□□□□□□

V[T] を和らげる、緩和する、軽減する

Drinking more won't **alleviate** your heartbreak.（もっと飲んだからと言って失恋の傷は癒えないよ。）

▶ **alleviation** [əliːviéɪʃən] N[U] 緩和、軽減

the **alleviation** of pain（痛みの軽減）

1414 category
[kǽṭəgri]
□□□□□□

N[C] カテゴリー、部類、区分

Do you think we should sort these books by **category** or by age?
（ここにある本、カテゴリーと年代どっちで分けた方が良いと思う？）

▶ **categorize** [kǽṭəgəraɪz] V[T] を（～に）分類する（into sth）

I don't know why, but I've **categorized** my apps by color.
（なんとなくアプリを色別に分類してみたんだ。）

▶ **categorization** [kǽṭəgərəzéɪʃən] N[U] カテゴリー化、分類

▶ **categorical** [kæṭəgóːrɪkəl] Adj. 断定的な、はっきりした

▶ **categorically** [kæṭəgóːrɪkli] Adv. 断定的に、はっきりと

I can **categorically** say that this information is not correct.
（この情報が正しくないって断言できるよ。）

1415 mood
[muːd]
□□□□□□

N[C] 気分、機嫌　**N[S]** 雰囲気

I've been in a great **mood** lately because I'm getting married soon.
（もうちょっとで結婚するから最近すごい機嫌良いんだよね。）

in a good/bad **mood**（機嫌が良い / 悪い）　　　**mood** swings（感情の起伏）

▶ **moody** [múːdi] Adj. 機嫌が変わりやすい、気分屋の；不機嫌な

She is just too **moody**. One second she's happy, the next second she's grumpy.
（彼女はただただ気分屋すぎるんだよ。機嫌良さそうだと思ったら、急に不機嫌になったりするんだ。）

1416 **anxiety**
[æŋzáɪəti]

▢▢▢▢▢▢

N[U]　不安、心配、懸念　N[C]　不安の種、心配事

My **anxiety** about public speaking comes from a lack of practice.
（私が人前で話すとき不安になるのは練習不足が原因なんだ。）

▶ **anxious** [æŋkʃəs] Adj. （〜のことが）不安な、心配した（about sth/sb）

She is **anxious** about everything. She thinks about the worst scenario for each and every situation. （彼女は全てのことに対して不安なんだ。全部の状況に対して最悪のケースを考えるからね。）

▶ **anxiously** [æŋkʃəsli] Adv. 心配そうに

1417 **personality**
[pɜ̀ːrsənǽləti]

▢▢▢▢▢▢

N[C/U]　パーソナリティ、個性、性格　N[U]　人間としての魅力

I like meeting people with **personalities** that are different from my own because it broadens my perspective. （自分と違う個性を持ってる人に会うのが好きなんだ。視野が広がるからね。）

N[C]　有名人、タレント

a TV **personality** （テレビタレント）

▶ **personal** [pɜ́ːrsənəl] Adj. 個人の、私的な ▶ **personally** [pɜ́ːrsənəli] Adv. 個人的に

I don't think we should do it, but that's just my **personal** opinion.
（それやんない方が良くない？ただの個人的な意見だけど。）

Personally, I don't care who he's dating. （個人的に、彼が誰と付き合ってるかなんてどうでもいいん。）

▶ **person** [pɜ́ːrsən] N[C] 人 ▶ **people** [píːpəl] N[P] 人々；国民、庶民【the -】

persons は正しい？ persons は法的文書など、フォーマルな場面で稀に使われるもので、あまり一般的ではないため、複数形は基本的に people を使用しましょう。

peoples はいつ使う？ peoples は基本的に複数の民族のグループのまとまりを指すときに使用する表現です（例：indigenous peoples＝複数の民族グループから構成される先住民の人たち）。

1418 **substance**
[sʌ́bstəns]

▢▢▢▢▢▢

N[C]　物質　N[U]　本質、実質；（発言や考えの）内容、中身

Shane's a good speaker, but what he says usually doesn't have a lot of **substance**.
（シェーンは喋りが上手いけど、基本あんまり内容がないんだよな。）

▶ **substantial** [səbstǽnʃəl] Adj. （量や程度が）かなりの、相当の；実体がある、本質的な

▶ **substantiate** V[T] を立証する
[səbstǽnʃieɪt]

▶ **substantiation** N[U] 立証
[səbstænʃiéɪʃən]

1419 **induce**
[ɪndúːs]

▢▢▢▢▢▢

V[T]　を誘発する、（〜するように）し向ける（to do）

Telling our customers about how their details have been leaked will only **induce** panic, so we should delay the announcement until we find out who's responsible.
（個人情報が流出したことを顧客に漏らせばパニックを誘発するだけなので、誰に責任があるか分かるまでは告知を遅らせるべきじゃないかな。）

▶ **inducement** [ɪndúːsmənt] N[C/U] 誘因

4 Intriguingly, this categorization has remained largely unchanged for many years. This is despite the fact that psychiatric treatments have developed drastically over the last several decades, corresponding with a sharp reduction in the volume of hospitalizations for psychiatric patients.

興味深いことに、この分類は長年ほとんど変わっていない。この数十年間で精神科の治療が大幅に進歩し、患者数が急減しているにもかかわらずだ。

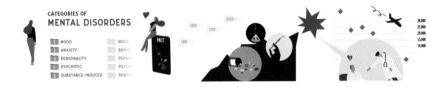

1420 intriguingly
[ɪntríːɡɪŋli]
☐☐☐☐☐☐

Adv. 興味深いことに

Intriguingly, most people don't know Facebook owns Instagram and WhatsApp.
(興味深いことに、大体の人は Facebook が Instagram と WhatsApp を所有していることを知らないんだ。)

▶ **intriguing** Adj. 興味深い
[ɪntriːɡɪŋ]

▶ **intrigue** V[T] の興味を引く、好奇心をそそる
[ɪntriːɡ]

I can't tell where you're from, but your accent is **intriguing**.
(君、どこ出身か分からないけど面白いアクセントがあるね。)

1421 unchanged
[ʌntʃéɪndʒd]
☐☐☐☐☐☐

Adj. 変わっていない、変わらない

The best thing about my neighborhood is that it's remained **unchanged** since I moved here. (うちの近所の一番いいところは、ここに引っ越してから何も変わってないことなんだ。)

▶ **change** V[T] を変化させる、変える V[I] 変化する、変わる N[C/U] 変化、変更
[tʃeɪndʒ] N[U] 小銭、お釣り

for a **change** (気分転換に、息抜きに)

I always give **change** to homeless people when I can.
(できる時はいつもホームレスの人に小銭をあげるようにしてる。)

▶ **changing** [tʃéɪndʒɪŋ] Adj. 変わりつつある

▶ **game-changer** [ɡéɪm tʃèɪndʒər] N[C] 革新的なもの、人生を変えるもの

Hair transplant surgery was a total **game-changer** for my dad.
(植毛手術は父さんの人生を完全に変えたんだ。)

1422 drastically
[dræstɪkli]
☐☐☐☐☐☐

Adv. 大幅に、思い切って

Her hairstyle has changed **drastically** since I last saw her.
(彼女の髪型前見た時からものすごい変わったなぁ。)

▶ **drastic** [dræstɪk] Adj. 大幅な、思い切った

I started my own company as a high school student. It was a pretty **drastic** decision, but I'm glad I did it. (高校生の時に自分の会社を始めたんだ。結構思い切った決断だったけど、やって良かったよ。)

1423 **correspond**
[kɔ̀:rəspá:nd]
☐☐☐☐☐☐

V[I] （〜と）一致する（with/to sth）；（〜と）文通する（with sb）

Sadly, my Snapchat views don't **correspond** with my Twitter followers.
（悲しいことに、スナップチャットのビュー数がツイッターのフォロワー数と一致しないんだよ。）

▶ **correspondence** [kɔ̀:rəspá:ndəns] N[C/U] 一致；手紙のやり取り

I think confidentiality in prisoner **correspondence** with legal counsel is important.
（受刑者が弁護士と行う手紙のやり取りを秘密にするのは重要だと思うな。）

▶ **corresponding** Adj. 一致する、類似する ▶ **correspondent** N[C] 担当記者、通信員
[kɔ̀:rəspá:ndɪŋ]   [kɔ̀:rəspá:ndənt]

1424 **sharp**
[ʃa:rp]
☐☐☐☐☐☐

Adj. 急激な；鋭い；鮮明な；（味が）ピリッとした；賢い **Adv.** ちょうどに

There was a **sharp** increase in our sales thanks to a popular YouTuber talking about our products.
（人気の YouTuber が私たちの商品について話してくれたおかげで、売上が急激に伸びたんだ。）

Let's meet at 5 o'clock **sharp**. (5時ちょうどに会おう。)

▶ **sharply** [ʃá:rpli] Adv. 急激に；鋭く

The number of robberies has decreased **sharply** since the introduction of these new laws. （この新しい法律が導入されてから強盗の数が急速に減ったんだ。）

▶ **sharpness** N[U] 鋭さ；鮮明さ   ▶ **sharpener** N[C] 鉛筆削り、研ぎ道具
[ʃá:rpnəs]   [ʃá:rpənər]

1425 **reduction**
[rɪdʌ́kʃən]
☐☐☐☐☐☐

N[C/U] 減少、削減

It says here that this drug is effective in belly fat **reduction**, but it still sounds a bit fishy to me.
（この薬はお腹の脂肪を減らすのに効果的ってここに書いてるけど、それでも私にはちょっと怪しい気がするな。）

▶ **reduce** [rɪdú:s] V[T] を減らす、縮小する；を煮詰める V[I] 痩せる；煮詰まる

There are many ways to **reduce** our impact on the environment, so there's really no excuse to do nothing. （環境への影響を少なくする方法はたくさんあるんだから、何もしないことに対する言い訳なんて本当にできないよ。）

▶ **reduced** Adj. 減った、削減された   ▶ **reducible** Adj. 単純化できる
[rɪdú:st]   [rɪdú:səbəl]

I have a **reduced** income now because I work a lot less, but my life is so much better.
（今は前より働く時間がずっと少ないから所得は減ったんだけど、生活はずっと良くなったよ。）

1426 **volume**
[vá:lju:m]
☐☐☐☐☐☐

N[C/U] 数量；容量 **N[U]** 体積；音量 **N[C]** （本などの）巻

We can either increase sales **volumes** or increase prices, but we won't be able to do both.
（売上数量を上げるか、値段を上げるかのどちらかはできるけど、両方はできないよ。）

▶ **voluminous** Adj. 容積の大きい；（服などが）ゆったりした、だぶだぶの；巻数の多い
[vəlú:mənəs]

For the ceremony, I'm going to wear a **voluminous** silk dress.
（セレモニーにはゆったりしたシルクのドレスを着て行くつもりなんだ。）

Emotional adjectives

感情を表す形容詞

I'm + 程度の副詞 + 感情を表す形容詞

英語で自分の感情を表したいときは「I'm + 程度の副詞 + 感情を表す形容詞」の形で表現することができます。

感情を表す形容詞 (emotional adjectives) というのは happy (幸せな) や sad (悲しい) といった、自分の感情を表現するために使われる形容詞のことです。程度の副詞 (adverbs of degree) というのは、a bit (ちょっと) や very (とても) のような、自分の感情の程度を表すもので、ネイティブが頻繁に使用します。これを使わずに「I'm + 感情を表す形容詞」だけで表現することもできますが、少し硬く、無味乾燥な英文になってしまう傾向にあるため、最初は程度の副詞と合わせて感情を英語で表現する練習をしておきましょう。

程度の副詞

really (本当に) / very, so (とても) /
pretty, quite (かなり) / a bit (少し) etc.

感情を表す形容詞

happy (幸せな) / angry (怒った) /
sad (悲しい) / scared (怖い) / surprised (驚いた) etc.

テンプレートに当てはめて、実際に感情を込めて発音することで覚えていきましょう!

😊 Happy（幸せ・喜び）

1427 **thrilled**
[θrɪld]

Adj. （〜に／〜することに）わくわくした、興奮した（with sth/to do）

▶ **thrilling** [θrílɪŋ] Adj. わくわくするような、スリル満点の

▶ **thrill** [θrɪl] V[T] をわくわくさせる　N[C] わくわく感、スリル

1428 **excited**
[ɪksáɪt̬ɪd]

Adj. （〜に）わくわくした、興奮した（by/about sth）

▶ **exciting** [ɪksáɪt̬ɪŋ] Adj. わくわくする　▶ **excite** [ɪksáɪt] V[T] をわくわくさせる

▶ **excitement** [ɪksáɪtmənt] N[U] わくわく、興奮

1429 **ecstatic**
[ekstæt̬ɪk]

Adj. （〜に）有頂天になった（about sth）

▶ **ecstasy** [ékstəsi] N[C/U] エクスタシー、恍惚、有頂天

1430 **pleased**
[pli:zd]

Adj. （〜のことが）嬉しい、満足した（about/with sth）

pleased to do（〜できて嬉しい）

▶ **pleasure** [pléʒər] N[U] 楽しさ、喜び　N[C] 楽しいこと

1431 **delighted**
[dɪláɪt̬ɪd]

Adj. （〜のことが）とても嬉しい（with/by/at sth）

delighted to do（〜してとても嬉しい）

▶ **delight** [dɪláɪt] N[U] 大喜び　N[C] 楽しみ　V[T] を大喜びさせる

▶ **delightful** [dɪláɪtfəl] Adj. 素晴らしい、感じのいい

1432 **glad**
[glæd]

Adj. （〜のことが／〜して）嬉しい（about sth/to do）

▶ **gladly** [glǽdli] Adv. 喜んで

1433 **chill**
[tʃɪl]

Adj. （〜に関して）気楽な、リラックスした（about sth）

= **relaxed** [rɪlǽkst]

V[I] のんびりする；落ち着く　= **chill out** [tʃɪláʊt]

V[T] を冷やす　N[C] 寒気、悪寒

1434 **amused**
[əmjú:zd]

Adj. （〜を）面白がった（by/at sth）

▶ **amuse** [əmjú:z] V[T] を楽しませる　▶ **amusing** [əmjú:zɪŋ] Adj. 面白い

▶ **amusement** [əmjú:zmənt] N[U] 楽しさ、おかしさ　N[P] 娯楽【-s】

1435 **eager**
[í:gər]

Adj. （〜を）しきりに求めて、熱望して（for sth）

eager to do（しきりに〜したがる）

▶ **eagerly** [í:gərli] Adv. 熱心に　▶ **eagerness** [í:gərnəs] N[U] 熱心さ、熱望

1436 **inspired**
[ɪnspáɪrd]
☐☐☐☐☐☐

Adj. （〜に）やる気にさせられた（by sth）

▶ **inspire** [ɪnspáɪr] V[T] を（〜する）気にさせる（to do）、鼓舞する

▶ **inspiring** [ɪnspáɪrɪŋ] Adj. やる気にさせるような

▶ **inspiration** [ìnspəréɪʃən] N[C/U] インスピレーション、着想

1437 **grateful**
[gréɪtfəl]
☐☐☐☐☐☐

Adj. （〜に）感謝している（for sth/to sb）

↔ **ungrateful** [ʌngréɪtfəl] 感謝しない

▶ **gratitude** [grǽtətu:d] N[U] 感謝　↔ **ingratitude** [ɪngrǽtətu:d] 恩知らず

😠 **Angry（怒り・いら立ち）**

1438 **resentful**
[rɪzéntfəl]
☐☐☐☐☐☐

Adj. （〜に）腹を立てた、憤慨した（of/at/about sth/sb）

▶ **resent** [rɪzént] V[T] に腹を立てる、憤る

▶ **resentment** [rɪzéntmənt] N[U] 腹立たしさ、恨み

1439 **mad**
[mæd]
☐☐☐☐☐☐

Adj. （〜に / 〜に関して）ものすごく怒った（about sth, at sb）

▶ **madly** [mǽdli] Adv. 狂ったように　▶ **madness** [mǽdnəs] N[U] 激怒、狂気

1440 **furious**
[fúriəs]
☐☐☐☐☐☐

Adj. （〜に）ものすごく怒った（at/about sth/sb, with sb）

▶ **fury** [fjúri] N[S/U] 激怒

1441 **envious**
[énviəs]
☐☐☐☐☐☐

Adj. （〜を）うらやんで（of sth/sb）

▶ **enviously** [énviəsli] Adv. うらやましげに　▶ **envy** [énvi] N[U] うらやましさ

1442 **jealous**
[dʒéləs]
☐☐☐☐☐☐

Adj. （〜を）嫉妬した、ねたんだ、うらやましい（of sth/sb）

Did you get a new computer? I'm so **jealous**!（新しいパソコン手に入れたの？いいなぁ。）

▶ **jealousy** [dʒéləsi] N[U] 嫉妬、やきもち

1443 **annoyed**
[ənɔ́ɪd]
☐☐☐☐☐☐

Adj. （〜に）いらいらした（at/about sth, with sb）　= angry [ǽngri]

▶ **annoy** [ənɔ́ɪ] V[T] をいらいらさせる　▶ **annoying** [ənɔ́ɪɪŋ] Adj. いらいらさせる

▶ **annoyance** [ənɔ́ɪəns] N[U] いらいら　N[C] 困ること

1444 **enraged**
[ɪnréɪdʒd]
☐☐☐☐☐☐

Adj. （〜に）かんかんに怒った（at sth）

▶ **enrage** [ɪnréɪdʒ] V[T] を激怒させる

▶ **rage** [reɪdʒ] N[C/U] 激怒　V[I] （〜に）激怒する、怒鳴る（at sth/sb）

1445 **irritated**
[írəteɪtɪd]
☐☐☐☐☐☐

Adj. （〜に）いらいらした（by/at sth, with sb）　= annoyed [ənɔ́ɪd]

▶ **irritate** [írəteɪt] V[T] をいらいらさせる；をひりひりさせる

▶ **irritating** [írəteɪtɪŋ] Adj. いらいらさせる

1446 fed up
[fèd ʌ́p]
☐☐☐☐☐☐

Adj.（〜に）うんざりした（with sth）

1447 disgusted
[dɪsɡʌ́stɪd]
☐☐☐☐☐☐

Adj.（〜に）嫌悪感を持っている、むかついた（at/by/with sth/sb）

▶ **disgust** [dɪsɡʌ́st] N[U] 嫌悪、反感

▶ **disgusting** [dɪsɡʌ́stɪŋ] Adj. 気持ち悪い、不快な、むかつかせる

1448 bothered
[bɑ́:ðərd]
☐☐☐☐☐☐

Adj.（〜のことが）気になる（about/by sth/sb）

▶ **bother** [bɑ́:ðər] V[T] を（〜で）心配させる（with sth）；のじゃまをする

V[I] わざわざ（〜）する（to do/doing）

1449 cheated
[tʃíː‌tɪd]
☐☐☐☐☐☐

Adj.（〜に）だまされた（by sth/sb）　= tricked [trɪkt]

▶ **cheat** [tʃíːt] V[I]（〜に隠れて）浮気をする（on sb）；カンニングをする、不正をする

V[T] をだます　N[C] いんちき（をする人）

※ cheated の場合は基本的に I'm ではなく I feel を使います（例：I feel a bit cheated.）。

1450 betrayed
[bɪtréɪd]
☐☐☐☐☐☐

Adj.（〜に）裏切られた（by sth/sb）

▶ **betray** [bɪtréɪ] V[T] を裏切る、密告する；(本心など) を示す

▶ **betrayal** [bɪtréɪəl] N[C/U] 裏切り　▶ **betrayer** [bɪtréɪər] N[C] 裏切り者

※ betrayed の場合、基本的には I'm ではなく I feel を使います（例：I feel so betrayed.）。

1451 scornful
[skɔ́:rnfəl]
☐☐☐☐☐☐

Adj.（〜を）軽蔑した（of sth/sb）

▶ **scorn** [skɔ:rn] N[U] 軽蔑　V[T] を軽蔑する

☹ Sad（悲しみ・苦しみ）

1452 lonely
[lóʊnli]
☐☐☐☐☐☐

Adj. さびしい、孤独な

▶ **loneliness** [lóʊnlinəs] N[U] さびしさ、孤独

▶ **alone** [əlóʊn] Adv. 一人で；独力で；孤独で

1453 guilty
[ɡílti]
☐☐☐☐☐☐

Adj.（悪いことをして）申し訳なく感じた、

うしろめたい（about sth）；（〜で）有罪の（of sth）

feel **guilty** about sth（〜を申し訳ないと思う）= feel bad about sth

▶ **guilt** [ɡɪlt] N[U] 罪悪感；有罪　≒ **sin** [sɪn] N[C/U]（道徳や宗教上の）罪

1454 embarrassed
[ɪmbérəst]
☐☐☐☐☐☐

Adj.（褒められたり失敗したりしたことが）恥ずかしい（about/at sth）

▶ **embarrass** [ɪmbérəs] V[T] に恥をかかせる

▶ **embarrassing** [ɪmbérəsɪŋ] Adj. 恥ずかしい

▶ **embarrassment** [ɪmbérəsmənt] N[U] 恥ずかしさ　N[C] 厄介なもの

1455 ashamed
[əʃéɪmd]
☐☐☐☐☐☐

Adj.（自分の言動などについて）恥ずかしい（of/at sth）

1456 humiliated
[hju:mílieɪt̬ɪd]
☐☐☐☐☐☐

Adj. 恥をかいた

▶ **humiliate** [hju:mílieɪt] V[T] に恥をかかせる、の自尊心を傷つける

▶ **humiliating** [hju:mílieɪt̬ɪŋ] Adj. 恥をかかせるような

▶ **humiliation** [hju:miliéɪʃən] N[U] 恥、屈辱

※ humiliated の場合、基本的には I'm ではなく I feel を使います（例：I feel humiliated.）。

1457 depressed
[dɪprést]
☐☐☐☐☐☐

Adj.（〜で）落ち込んだ（about/over sth）；うつの

▶ **depress** [dɪprés] V[T] を落ち込ませる；(価値) を下げる；(景気) を低迷させる

▶ **depression** [dɪpréʃən] N[C/U] 憂鬱、うつ；恐慌、不況

1458 empty
[émpti]
☐☐☐☐☐☐

Adj. むなしい；空の、（場所や席が）空いている、誰もいない
V[T] を空にする　V[I] 誰もいなくなる

1459 disappointed
[dìsəpɔ́ɪnt̬ɪd]
☐☐☐☐☐☐

Adj.（〜に）がっかりした、落胆した（at/by/about sth, in sb）

▶ **disappoint** [dìsəpɔ́ɪnt] V[T] をがっかりさせる

▶ **disappointing** [dìsəpɔ́ɪnt̬ɪŋ] Adj. がっかりさせるような

▶ **disappointment** [dìsəpɔ́ɪntmənt] N[U] がっかりすること、落胆　N[C] がっかりさせるもの

1460 pessimistic
[pèsəmístɪk]
☐☐☐☐☐☐

Adj.（〜について）悲観的な（about sth）

⟷ **optimistic** [à:ptəmístɪk] 楽観的な

▶ **pessimist** [pésəmɪst] N[C] 悲観的な人、悲観主義者

▶ **pessimism** [pésəmɪzəm] N[U] 悲観

1461 regretful
[rɪgrétfəl]
☐☐☐☐☐☐

Adj.（〜を）後悔した（about sth）

▶ **regret** [rɪgrét] V[T] を後悔する；を残念に思う　N[C/U] 後悔

regret doing（〜したことを後悔する）　**regret** to do（残念ながら〜する）

▶ **regrettable** [rɪgrét̬əbəl] Adj. 残念な　▶ **regrettably** [rɪgrét̬əbli] Adv. 残念ながら

Scared（恐怖・不安）

1462 uneasy
[ʌníːzi]
☐☐☐☐☐☐

Adj.（～のことが）不安な、心配な（about sth）
▶ **uneasily** [ʌníːzəli] Adv. 不安そうに、心配して

1463 upset
[ʌpsét]
☐☐☐☐☐☐

Adj.（～に）動揺した、気落ちした（at/with/by/about sth）；（胃が）不調の
V[T] を動揺させる；を不調にする；をひっくり返す
▶ **upsetting** [ʌpséţɪŋ] Adj. 動揺させる

1464 distressed
[dɪstrést]
☐☐☐☐☐☐

Adj.（～に）動揺した、心を痛めた（at/by/about sth）
▶ **distress** [dɪstrés] V[T] を苦しめる、悲しませる　N[U] 苦悩、悲しみ
▶ **distressing** [dɪstrésɪŋ] Adj. 苦痛な　= **distressful** [dɪstrésfəl]

1465 shocked
[ʃɑːkt]
☐☐☐☐☐☐

Adj.（～に）びっくりした、衝撃を受けた（by/at sth）
▶ **shock** [ʃɑːk] V[T] に衝撃を与える、びっくりさせる
N[C/U] ショック、衝撃　N[C] 電撃　N[U] ショック症
▶ **shocking** [ʃɑːkɪŋ] Adj. 衝撃的な

1466 cautious
[kɑ́ːʃəs]
☐☐☐☐☐☐

Adj.（～に）慎重な（about sth）
▶ **caution** [kɑ́ːʃən] N[U] 慎重さ、注意、用心　N[C] 警告
with **caution**（注意して、用心して）

1467 hesitant
[hézətənt]
☐☐☐☐☐☐

Adj.（～するのを）ためらって（about doing）
▶ **hesitate** [hézəteɪt] V[I]（～するのを）ためらう（to do）
Don't **hesitate** to ask questions.（遠慮なく質問してね。）
▶ **hesitation** [hèzətéɪʃən] N[C/U] ためらい

1468 scared
[skerd]
☐☐☐☐☐☐

Adj.（～を）怖がった（of sth/sb）
▶ **scary** [skéri] Adj. 怖い、恐ろしい
▶ **scare** [sker] V[T] を怖がらせる　V[I] 怖がる　N[C] 恐怖

1469 alarmed
[əlɑ́ːrmd]
☐☐☐☐☐☐

Adj.（～のことが）不安で、恐れて（by/at sth）
▶ **alarm** [əlɑ́ːrm] V[T] を不安にさせる、恐れさせる、に警鐘をならす
N[U] 不安、恐怖　N[C] 警報器；アラーム、目覚まし時計
▶ **alarming** [əlɑ́ːrmɪŋ] Adj. 不安にさせるような

Surprised（驚き）

1470 startled
[stάːrt̬ld]
☐☐☐☐☐☐

Adj. （〜に）びっくりした（at sth）　= surprised [sərpráɪzd]

▶ **startle** [stάːrt̬l] V[T] をびっくりさせる

▶ **startling** [stάːrt̬lɪŋ] Adj. びっくりさせるような

1471 speechless
[spíːtʃləs]
☐☐☐☐☐☐

Adj. （驚きや怒りで）言葉を失って

▶ **speechlessness** [spíːtʃləsnəs] N[U] 言葉もないこと

1472 flustered
[flʌ́stərd]
☐☐☐☐☐☐

Adj. 動揺した

▶ **fluster** [flʌ́stər] V[T] を動揺させる　N[S] 動揺

1473 panicked
[pǽnɪkt]
☐☐☐☐☐☐

Adj. （〜で）パニックになった（about sth）

▶ **panic** [pǽnɪk] V[I] パニックになる　V[T] をパニックにする　N[C/U] パニック

▶ **panicky** [pǽnɪki] Adj. パニック状態の、びくびくした

1474 shaken
[ʃéɪkən]
☐☐☐☐☐☐

Adj. 動揺した、ショックを受けた

▶ **shake** [ʃeɪk] V[I] 震える、揺れる　V[T] を振る、揺らす　N[C] 揺れ；シェーク

1475 rattled
[rǽt̬ld]
☐☐☐☐☐☐

Adj. （〜に）動揺した、慌てた（about sth）

▶ **rattle** [rǽt̬l] V[T] を動揺させる；（ドアなど）をガタガタ揺らす　V[I] ガタガタ揺れる

1476 spooked
[spuːkt]
☐☐☐☐☐☐

Adj. （〜に）驚いた（by sth）

▶ **spook** [spuːk] V[T] を怖がらせる、おびえさせる　V[I] （〜に）おびえる（at sth）
　　　　　　 N[C] お化け、幽霊

▶ **spooky** [spúːki] Adj. 幽霊が出そうな、薄気味悪い

⟳ CH. 11, 16, 20, 24, 27, 30

Chapter

31

数学
Mathematics

The world of mathematics expanded from simple counting, calculation, and measurement to modern mathematics, thanks to fundamental developments in fields such as arithmetic, geometry, and algebra.

While its underlying nature relates to the study of abstract objects, the practical applications derived from it have exerted a massive positive influence on human activity throughout history.

In fact, mathematics has become a vital tool for logically establishing solutions to problems in quite a few areas, including manufacturing, chemistry, probability, and statistics.

Against this backdrop, it has also become an educational imperative and therefore a mandatory subject in many approved school curricula, where various approaches, such as recreational mathematics and rote learning, are used to teach the subject.

1 The world of mathematics expanded from simple counting, calculation, and measurement to modern mathematics, thanks to fundamental developments in fields such as arithmetic, geometry, and algebra.

数学の世界は、算術、幾何学、代数などの分野が根本的な発展を遂げたおかげで、単純な集計や計算、測定から現代数学に広がった。

1477 **expand**
[ɪkspǽnd]
□□□□□□

V[I] 拡大する、増える　V[T] を拡大させる、広げる、増やす

Our company has **expanded** from three employees to a hundred over the past few years.
（ここ数年でうちの会社は従業員が 3 人から 100 人にまで拡大したんだ。）

■ **expand** on sth（〜をより細かく説明する）

Can you **expand** on that?（もう少し細かく説明してくれる？）

▶ **expansion** [ɪkspǽnʃən] N[C/U] 拡大、拡張、発展

My hometown is currently experiencing a rapid **expansion** in the number of tourists visiting.　（私の地元では現在、観光客の数が急速な勢いで拡大しています。）

▶ **expansionary** [ɪkspǽnʃənèri] Adj. 拡張的な、（金融政策などが）緩和的な

expansionary monetary policy（金融緩和政策）

1478 **count**
[kaʊnt]
□□□□□□

V[I/T]（〜を）数える　V[T] を含める

Does **counting** sheep really help you sleep?（羊を数えると本当に寝やすくなるの？）

count heads（人数を数える）　　　**count** sth/sb in/out（〜を計算に入れる / 計算から外す）

■ **count** on/upon sb（〜を頼る）

I'm **counting** on you!（君のこと頼りにしてるよ！）

V[T] を（〜だと）みなす（as sth）　V[I]（〜の）価値がある (for sth)

■ **count** for nothing（価値がない、無駄である）

Having all this money **counts for nothing** if you never have any time to enjoy yourself.（こんなにお金があっても楽しむ時間が全然ないなら無駄じゃん。）

N[C] 数えること、計算；総数、総計

Let's do a quick **count**.（ササっと数えよう。）

▶ **countable** [káʊnṭəbəl] Adj. 可算の ◀▶ **uncountable** [ʌnkáʊnṭəbəl] 不可算の

The hardest part of English is differentiating between **countable** and **uncountable** nouns.
(英語で一番難しいのは可算名詞と不可算名詞を区別することなんだ。)

▶ **countless** [káʊntləs] Adj. 数えきれないほどの

1479 calculation
[kælkjəléɪʃən]
☐☐☐☐☐☐

N[C/U] 計算、算定

Wow, how did you do that **calculation** so quickly?（えっ、どうやってそんな速く計算したの？）

▶ **calculate** [kælkjəleɪt] V[T] を計算する；を予測する

Let's **calculate** our income and expenses so that we can manage our money.
(お金をちゃんと管理できるように所得と費用の計算をしよう。)

▶ **calculator** N[C] 計算機   ▶ **calculating** Adj. 計算高い、損得勘定で動く
[kælkjəleɪtər]   [kælkjəleɪtɪŋ]

I decided to stop hanging out with her because she's such a **calculating** person.
(彼女は損得勘定で動く人だからもう付き合うのはやめるって決めたんだよね。)

1480 measurement
[méʒərmənt]
☐☐☐☐☐☐

N[U] 測定、測量   N[C] （測定して分かる）寸法、サイズ

You should check the **measurement** guide when buying clothes online.
(服をオンラインで買うときは測定ガイドをチェックした方が良いよ。)

▶ **measure** [méʒər] V[T] を測定する   N[C] 対策、手段；(評価) 基準   N[C/U] 単位

take **measures**（対策を取る）

▶ **measurable** [méʒərəbəl] Adj. 測定可能な；目に見える

I get demotivated when I can't see **measurable** improvements.
(目に見えるような伸びがないとモチベが下がっちゃうんだよね。)

▶ **measurably** [méʒərəbli] Adv. 測定できるほど；目に見えて

1481 arithmetic
[əríθmətɪk]
☐☐☐☐☐☐

N[U] 算術、算数

It looks like pretty basic **arithmetic**, but it's actually really complicated for most people.
(結構基本的な算数っぽい感じなんだけど、実際多くの人にとってはすごい複雑みたいね。)

1482 geometry
[dʒiɑ́ːmətri]
☐☐☐☐☐☐

N[U] 幾何学

Billiards is all about **geometry** and composure.（ビリヤードは幾何学と冷静さが全てだよ。）

▶ **geometric** Adj. 幾何学的な   ▶ **geometrically** Adv. 幾何学的に
[dʒiːəmétrɪk]   [dʒiːəmétrɪkli]

1483 algebra
[ǽldʒəbrə]
☐☐☐☐☐☐

N[U] 代数

You can't really do any advanced math without having a strong understanding of **algebra**.
(代数のことをよく理解しないで高等数学をやるのはちょっと厳しいよ。)

2 While its underlying nature relates to the study of abstract objects, the practical applications derived from it have exerted a massive positive influence on human activity throughout history.

数学の根本的な性質は抽象的な対象の研究に関連しているが、そこから得られる実践的な応用は、歴史を通じて人の活動に多大なプラスの影響を及ぼしてきた。

1484 underlying
[ˌʌndərláɪɪŋ]

Adj. 根本的な、根底にある、基礎をなす

What are the **underlying** causes of poverty?（貧困の根本的な原因って何だろう？）

▶ **underlie** [ˌʌndərláɪ] V[T] の根底にある、基礎にある

1485 object
[ɑ́:bdʒɪkt]

N[C] 対象；物体；目的、目標；目的語

Lately, I've been consciously spending more money on experiences rather than on **objects**.（最近は意識的に物じゃなくて経験にもっとお金を使うようにしているんだ。）

an unidentified flying **object**（未確認飛行物体、UFO）

1486 derive
[dɪráɪv]

V[T] を（〜から）得る、導き出す（from sth）

■ be **derived** from sth（〜に由来する、〜から得られる）

What kind of plants **are** these ingredients **derived from**?
（この材料ってどういう植物から得られるの？）

V[I] （〜に）由来する（from sth）

▶ **derivative** [dɪrívəţɪv] Adj. 派生的な；独創的でない、模倣的な
N[C] 派生物；デリバティブ

His ideas are very **derivative**. It's pretty obvious that he has nothing original.
（彼のアイディアってすごい模倣的なんだよね。自分で考えたものなんて明らかになさそうだし。）

1487 exert

[ɪgzə́:rt]

☐☐☐☐☐☐

V[T] （影響など）**を及ぼす**、（能力や力）**を発揮する**、（権力など）**を行使する**

We've been negotiating for months with no progress, so I think it's time for me to **exert** some pressure. (何か月も交渉して進展がないから、そろそろプレッシャーをかける時かなと思ってる。)

exert oneself （努力する、張り切る、頑張る）

▶ **exertion** [ɪgzə́:rʃən] N[C/U] 努力、尽力；行使、発揮

■ mental **exertion** （頭を使うこと）

Our brains often get tired after prolonged periods of **mental exertion**.
（私たちの脳は、長時間使うと疲労してしまうことが多い。）

1488 massive

[mǽsɪv]

☐☐☐☐☐☐

Adj. 多大な、膨大な、大幅な

I know moving to the U.S. is a **massive** risk, but I want to do it while I'm still young.
（アメリカに移ることが大きなリスクなのは分かってるけど、まだ若いうちにやってみたいんだ。）

▶ **massively** [mǽsɪvli] Adv. ものすごく、大幅に、非常に

Her account has been growing **massively** ever since she took that online Instagram course.
（彼女のアカウント、オンラインのインスタコースを取ってからものすごい成長してるんだよ。）

▶ **massiveness** [mǽsɪvnəs] N[U] 大量さ、膨大さ

1489 positive

[pá:zət̬ɪv]

☐☐☐☐☐☐

Adj. （効果などが）**プラスの**；**積極的な**；**肯定的な**；**正の**；**陽性の**

My favorite thing about Fiona is that she always seems so **positive**.
（フィオナっていつもすごいポジティブそうで好きなんだ。）

↔ **negative** [négətɪv] ネガティブな、否定的な；負の；陰性の

▶ **positively** [pá:zət̬ɪvli] Adv. ポジティブに、積極的に

It's always better to face problems **positively** because stressing about them doesn't help.
（どんな時も問題にはポジティブに向き合うのが良いよ。ストレスを抱えても何にもならないから。）

↔ **negatively** [négətɪvli] ネガティブに、否定的に

▶ **positivity** [pɑ:zətívəti] N[U] ポジティブさ

I love people who spread **positivity**. （ポジティブさを振りまく人めっちゃ好きだなぁ。）

↔ **negativity** [nègətívəti] ネガティブさ

1490 throughout

[θru:áʊt]

☐☐☐☐☐☐

Prep. ～を通じて、～の間ずっと　**Adv.** 至るところ；最初から最後まで

James has been really helpful **throughout** the whole process.
（ジェームズは全過程を通じて本当に役に立っているよ。）

3 In fact, mathematics has become a vital tool for logically establishing solutions to problems in quite a few areas, including manufacturing, chemistry, probability, and statistics.

実際、数学は、製造、化学、確率、統計など、かなり多くの分野において、問題に対する解決策を論理的に確立する上で極めて重要なツールになっている。

1491 vital
[váɪṭl]
☐☐☐☐☐☐

Adj. （〜にとって）極めて重要な、不可欠な（to sth/sb）

Music is a **vital** part of my life. （音楽は僕の人生に不可欠なものだよ。）

Adj. 活気のある、生き生きした

▶ **vitally** [váɪṭli] Adv. 極めて；命に関わるほどに

vitally important （極めて重要な）

▶ **vitality** [vaɪtǽləṭi] N[U] 活力、バイタリティー

I'm taking some supplements to restore my **vitality**.
（活力を取り戻すためにいくつかサプリを飲んでるんだ。）

▶ **revitalize** [ri:váɪṭəlaɪz] V[T] を生き返らせる、活性化する

1492 logically
[lá:dʒɪkli]
☐☐☐☐☐☐

Adv. 論理的に

I know it **logically** doesn't make any sense, but part of me still believes in Santa Claus.
（論理的に理解できないのは分かってるんだけど、ちょっとまだサンタクロースを信じてる部分があるんだ。）

▶ **logical** [lá:dʒɪkəl] Adj. 論理的な ▶ **logic** [lá:dʒɪk] N[U] 論理

You should understand that not everyone is **logical** like you.
（全員が君みたいに論理的じゃないってことを理解した方が良いと思う。）

1493 establish
[ɪstǽblɪʃ]
☐☐☐☐☐☐

V[T] を確立する；を設立する；を立証する

I finally **established** my own company! （ついに自分の会社を設立したんだ！）

establish oneself (as sth) （（〜としての）地位を確立する）

▶ **establishment** [ɪstǽblɪʃmənt] N[U] 確立；設立　N[C] 機関、組織

The **establishment** of healthy routines is the key to a happy life.
（健康的な習慣を確立することが幸せな生活を送る上でのカギだよ。）

an educational **establishment**（教育機関）

▶ **established**［ɪstǽblɪʃt］Adj. 確立された；定評のある

1494 **quite a few**
［kwáɪt̬ə fjúː］
☐☐☐☐☐☐

Phr. かなり多くの

We recruited **quite a few** people last month, so I don't think we'll be hiring any new people for a while.（先月かなりたくさんの人を雇ったから、しばらく新しい人は雇わないと思うよ。）

quite a few は可算名詞に対してのみ使用可能で、不可算名詞には quite a little を使用します。

1495 **manufacturing**
［mǽnjəfæ̀ktʃərɪŋ］
☐☐☐☐☐☐

N[U] 製造、製造業

I find the jeans **manufacturing** process so fascinating.
（僕はジーンズの製造過程ってものすごい面白いなぁって思うんだ。）

▶ **manufacture**［mǽnjəfæ̀ktʃər］V[T] を製造する、（大量）生産する
　　　　　　　　　　　　　　　　　N[U] 製造、（大量）生産

China **manufactures** and exports products in massive quantities to Western countries.
（中国はものすごい量の商品を製造してヨーロッパの国に輸出してるよ。）

▶ **manufacturer**［mǽnjəfæ̀ktʃərər］N[C] 製造会社、メーカー

1496 **probability**
［prɑ̀:bəbílət̬i］
☐☐☐☐☐☐

N[C/U] 確率、見込み　**N[C]** 起こりそうなこと

There's a low **probability** of my team winning tonight, but I still need to watch the game.
（今晩うちのチームが勝つ可能性は低いけど、それでも試合を見る必要はある。）

in all **probability**（きっと、おそらく）

▶ **probable**［prɑ́:bəbəl］Adj. 可能性の高い、ほぼ確実な

Looking at the sky, it's quite **probable** that it's going to rain in the next few minutes.
（空を見る限り、数分後にはかなりの確率で雨が降りそう。）

▶ **probably**［prɑ́:bəbli］Adv. きっと、おそらく

1497 **statistics**
［stətístɪks］
☐☐☐☐☐☐

N[U] 統計学　**N[P]** 統計、統計データ

I find **statistics** very boring because it involves a lot of calculation.
（統計学って計算がいっぱいでめちゃくちゃつまんない。）

statistics show that + sentence（統計によると～である）

▶ **statistical**［stətístɪkəl］Adj. 統計の、統計学の、統計上の

statistical evidence（統計学的な証拠）　　a **statistical** analysis（統計分析）

▶ **statistically**［stətístɪkli］Adv. 統計学的に、統計上

Statistically speaking, you're more likely to die on the way to the airport than on the plane.（統計学的に言うと、空港に行く途中に死ぬ可能性の方が飛行機で死ぬ可能性より高いんだよ。）

4 Against this backdrop, it has also become an educational imperative and therefore a mandatory subject in many approved school curricula, where various approaches, such as recreational mathematics and rote learning, are used to teach the subject.

こうした背景から、数学は教育においても差し迫って必要なものとなり、その結果、多くの承認された学校のカリキュラムで必須科目になっている。そうした学校では、レクリエーション数学や暗記学習などのさまざまなアプローチで数学を教えている。

1498 backdrop
[bǽkdrɑːp]
☐☐☐☐☐☐

N[C] 背景；（舞台の）背景幕

■ against a/the **backdrop** of sth （〜を背景にして）

Most things look beautiful **against a backdrop of** gray walls.
（大体のものは灰色の壁を背景にすると美しく見えるんだ。）

1499 imperative
[ɪmpérətɪv]
☐☐☐☐☐☐

N[C] 差し迫って必要なもの；義務、責務　**N[S]** 命令形【the -】

■ a moral **imperative** （人としてやるべきこと、道徳的義務）

I think saving money for my son to go to university in the future is **a moral imperative**.
（息子が将来大学に行くためのお金を貯めるのは、人としてやるべきことだと思う。）

Adj. 必須の、緊急の；威厳のある；命令形の

It's **imperative** that you get used to driving on the right side of the road before you head to the U.S. （アメリカに行く前に右側通行の運転に慣れておく必要があるよ。）

1500 mandatory
[mǽndətɔːri]
☐☐☐☐☐☐

Adj. 必須の、義務的な、強制的な　= **compulsory** [kəmpʌ́lsəri]

If this training isn't **mandatory**, I'd prefer not to waste my time on it.
（この研修、強制じゃないんだったらできればそれで時間を無駄にしたくないな。）

▶ **mandate** [mǽndeɪt] V[T] を命令する、義務付ける；に権限を与える
　　　　　　　　　N[C] （有権者などが議員に与える）権限

1501 approved
[əprúːvd]
☐☐☐☐☐☐

Adj. 承認された、認可された、公認の

The staff at this hotel is required to wear the **approved** uniform.
（このホテルのスタッフは認められた制服を着ないといけないんだ。）

◆ **unapproved** [ʌnəprúːvd] 承認されていない

▶ **approve** [əprúːv] V[T] を承認する、認可する　V[I]（〜に）賛成する（of sth）

My boss always **approves** my request to take annual leave.
(私の上司はいつも有給申請を承認してくれるんだ。)

My fiancé's father doesn't **approve** of me. What can I do to get him to like me?
(僕のフィアンセのお父さんが僕のことを認めてくれないんだ。好きになってもらうにはどうしたら良いかな？)

▶ **approval** [əprúːvəl] N[U] 承認、認可；賛成　◆ **disapproval** [dìsəprúːvəl] 不賛成

She is the kind of person that always needs the **approval** of others before doing anything.
(彼女は何をするにもいつも他人の賛成が必要なタイプなんだ。)

▶ **approving** Adj. 賛成する、満足げな　◆ **disapproving** 不賛成の、非難するような
　　[əprúːvɪŋ]　　　　　　　　　　　　　　　　　　[dìsəprúːvɪŋ]

▶ **approvingly** Adv. 賛成して　◆ **disapprovingly** 賛成できない様子で
　　[əprúːvɪŋli]　　　　　　　　　　　　　　　[dìsəprúːvɪŋli]

1502 **curriculum**　　N[C]　カリキュラム、教育課程（複数形：curricula/curriculums）
[kəríkjələm]

I actually like studying this subject because the **curriculum** is so interesting.
(実際この科目勉強するの好きなんだよね。カリキュラムがすごい面白くてさぁ。)

1503 **recreational**　　Adj. レクリエーションとしての、娯楽的な、休養の
[rèkriéɪʃənəl]

Only **recreational** fishing is allowed here, so we won't be able to use your ship.
(ここでは娯楽的な釣りしか許されてないから、君の船は使えないよ。)

▶ **recreation** [rèkriéɪʃən] N[U] 娯楽、気晴らし；再現　N[C]（個々の）娯楽；再現したもの

▶ **recreate** [rìːkriéɪt] V[T] を再現する

These Japanese students have been producing a virtual reality video to **recreate** the sights and sounds of the first Moon landing.
(この日本の学生たちは最初の月面着陸の様子や音を再現する VR 動画を作成しています。)

1504 **rote**　　N[U]　丸暗記
[roʊt]

■ **rote** learning（丸暗記学習）

I think the only way to learn how to write in Chinese is through **rote learning**.
(中国語の書き方を習得する方法は丸暗記しかないと思うな。)

learn sth by **rote**（〜を丸暗記する）

learn sth by rote ≒ learn sth by heart ？　「丸暗記する」と頻繁に訳される表現には他に learn sth by heart があります。しかし、これら二つにはニュアンスの違いがあります。by rote は特に何も考えずに機械的に暗記作業を繰り返し行うことで覚えることを意味するのに対し、by heart は学習の結果いつでも何も見ずに思い出せる状態になることを意味しています。つまり、rote は「学習方法」、heart は「結果」に焦点があります。

Numbers 数字

1, 3, 5, 7...	Odd numbers (奇数)	2, 4, 6, 8...	Even numbers (偶数)

How to read numbers (数字の読み方)

1　　2　　3　　4　　5

689,754,132,501,026

Trillion　Billion　Million　Thousand
兆　　　10億　　100万　　千

1. six hundred eighty-nine trillion
2. seven hundred fifty-four billion
3. one hundred thirty-two million
4. five hundred one thousand
5. twenty-six

689兆7541億3250万1026

The four basic arithmetic operations (四則演算)

Addition ＋	Subtraction ー	Multiplication ×	Division ÷
add A and B / AとBを足す	subtract A from B / BからAを引く	multiply A and B / AとBをかける	divide A by B / AをBで割る

How to read an equation (式の読み方)

1+2=3	**6-4=2**	**5×3=15**	**9÷3=3**
One plus two equals/is three.	Six minus four equals/is two.	Five times three equals/is fifteen.	Nine divided by three equals/is three.

Decimals (小数)

15.29

(a) decimal point (小数点)　　　読み方: fifteen point two nine

小数点は point と読み、小数点以降は two nine のように数字を一つずつ読みます。
※$15.29 は fifteen dollars and twenty-nine cents と読みます。

Fractions (分数)

$\dfrac{1}{3}$	$\dfrac{2}{5}$	$\dfrac{113}{310}$
読み方: one-third/a third	two-fifths*	one hundred thirteen over three hundred ten**

*分子が2以上の場合は分母の序数にsを付けます。　　**複雑な分数は「分子 over 分母」の形で読みます。

two-fifths of sth/sb は単数 or 複数扱い？

分子が2以上の場合、分母の序数には必ず s が付きますが、それ全体が複数扱いになるかどうかは、その後に続く名詞に左右されます。
例えば、two-fifths of a cake (ケーキの5分の2) という場合、a cakeは単数のため、それ全体も単数扱いになります (例：two-fifths of a cake is...)。一方、two-fifths of students という場合、studentsは複数形なので、全体も複数扱いになります (例：two-fifths of students are...)。

1505 **odd**
[ɑːd]
□□□□□□

Adj. 奇数の；変な、奇妙な；時々の

▶ **odds** [ɑːdz] N[P] 可能性、見込み、勝ち目

the **odds** are that + sentence （ほぼ間違いなく～だろう）

1506 **even**
[íːvən]
□□□□□□

Adj. 偶数の；平らな、均等な；一定の；互角の

Adv. ～でさえ、～ですら；（比較級を強めて）いっそう、さらに

1507 **trillion**
[tríljən]
□□□□□□

N[C] 兆

1508 **billion**
[bíljən]
□□□□□□

N[C] 十億

▶ **billionaire** [bìljənér] N[C] 億万長者

1509 **million**
[míljən]
□□□□□□

N[C] 百万

▶ **millionaire** [mìljənér] N[C] 百万長者、大金持ち、大富豪

1510 **thousand**
[θáʊzənd]
□□□□□□

N[C] 千

thousands of sth/sb （何千もの～）

1511 **addition**
[ədíʃən]
□□□□□□

N[U] 足し算；追加　N[C]（～への）追加分（to sth）

in **addition** (to sth) （（～に）加えて）

▶ **add** [æd] V[T] を足す；を（～に）加える（to sth）　V[I]（～を）増やす（to sth）

1512 **subtraction**
[səbtrækʃən]
□□□□□□

N[C/U] 引き算、（金額などを）引くこと

▶ **subtract** [səbtrækt] V[T] を（～から）引く（from sth）

▶ **subtractive** [səbtræktɪv] Adj. 引き算の

1513 **equation**
[ɪkwéɪʒən]
□□□□□□

N[C] 方程式、等式

▶ **equate** [ɪkwéɪt] V[I]（～に）等しい（to sth）

1514 **decimal**
[désəməl]
□□□□□□

N[C] 小数、十進数　Adj. 小数の、十進法の

1515 **fraction**
[frækʃən]
□□□□□□

N[C] 分数；ごく一部

▶ **fractional** [frækʃənəl] Adj. 分数の；わずかな

▶ **fractionally** [frækʃənəli] Adv. わずかに

Algebra – Linear equations (代数・一次方程式)

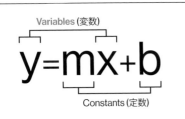 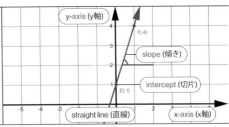

Geometry – 2D & 3D shapes (幾何学・平面図形と立体図形)

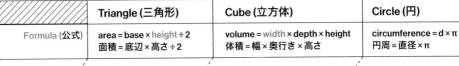

	Triangle (三角形)	Cube (立方体)	Circle (円)
Formula (公式)	area = base × height ÷ 2 面積 = 底辺 × 高さ ÷ 2	volume = width × depth × height 体積 = 幅 × 奥行き × 高さ	circumference = d × π 円周 = 直径 × π

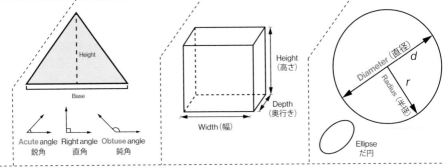

2D shapes (平面図形)

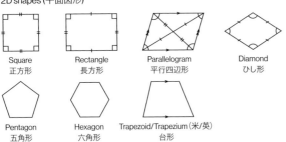

3D shapes (立体図形)

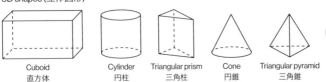

1516 **variable**
[vériəbəl]

N[C] 変数；要因　**Adj.** 変わりやすい

a **variable** cost（変動費）　⟷　a fixed cost（固定費）

▶ **variability** [vèriəbíləṭi] N[U] ばらつき、変わりやすさ

▶ **variably** [vériəbli] Adv. 変わりやすく

1517 **axis**
[ǽksɪs]

N[C] 軸；枢軸

▶ **axial** [ǽksiəl] Adj. 軸の

1518 **slope**
[sloʊp]

N[C] 傾き、傾斜；坂、斜面　**V[I]** 傾く

▶ **sloping** [slóʊpɪŋ] Adj. 傾斜した

1519 **intercept**
[ìnṭərsépt]

N[C] 切片　**V[T]** を妨害する、傍受する

▶ **interception** [ìnṭərsépʃən] N[C/U] 妨害、傍受

1520 **formula**
[fɔ́:rmjələ]

N[C] 公式；化学式；製法；（〜を達成するための）手段（for sth）

▶ **formulate** [fɔ́:rmjəleɪt] V[T] を公式化する；を処方する、調合する

▶ **formulation** [fɔ̀:rmjəléɪʃən] N[C/U] 策定、公式化、調合

1521 **height**
[haɪt]

N[C/U] 高さ、身長

▶ **heighten** [háɪṭn] V[I] 高まる　V[T] を高める

▶ **high** [haɪ] Adj. 高い　▶ **highly** [háɪli] Adj. 高く

1522 **width**
[wɪtθ]

N[C/U] 幅

▶ **wide** [waɪd] Adj. 幅の広い　▶ **widely** [wáɪdli] Adv. 幅広く

▶ **widen** [wáɪdən] V[I]（幅が）広がる　V[T]（幅）を広げる

1523 **acute**
[əkjú:t]

Adj. 鋭角の、鋭い；（痛みが）激しい；（問題が）深刻な

▶ **acutely** [əkjú:tli] Adv. 鋭く、激しく

▶ **acuteness** [əkjú:tnəs] N[U] 鋭さ；激しさ；深刻さ

1524 **obtuse**
[ɑ:btú:s]

Adj. 鈍角の、鈍感な、鈍い

▶ **obtusely** [ɑ:btú:sli] Adv. 鈍感な様子で　▶ **obtuseness** [ɑ:btú:snəs] N[U] 鈍感さ

1525 **diameter**
[daɪǽməṭər]

N[C/U] 直径

The **diameter** of the Sun is 109 times the size of the Earth's.
（太陽の直径は地球の直径の 109 倍なんだよ。）

1526 **radius**
[réɪdiəs]

N[C] 半径（複数形：radii）

Adverbs of frequency (頻度を表す副詞)

Frequency % （頻度*）	Adverbs of frequency （頻度の副詞）	Pronunciation （発音）	Meaning （意味）
100 %	always	[ɑ́ːlweɪz]	いつも
90 %	usually	[júːʒuəli]	ふつうは
80 %	normally	[nɔ́ːrməli]	
70 %	frequently	[fríːkwəntli]	よく、頻繁に
	often	[ɑ́ːfən][ɑ́ːftən]	
50 %	sometimes	[sʌ́mtaɪmz]	たまに、時々
30 %	occasionally	[əkéɪʒənəli]	
10 %	seldom	[séldəm]	めったに〜しない
5%	rarely	[rérli]	
	hardly ever	[hɑ́ːrdli évər]	
0%	never	[névər]	絶対に〜しない

*あくまで目安です。

Adverbs of probability (可能性を表す副詞)

Probability % （可能性*）	Adverbs of probability （可能性の副詞）	Pronunciation （発音）	Meaning （意味）
100 %	absolutely	[æbsəlúːtli]	確実に
	definitely	[défənətli]	
	surely	[ʃúrli]	
	certainly	[sə́ːrtṇli]	
80 %	probably	[prɑ́ːbəbli]	おそらく
50 %	maybe	[méɪbi]	たぶん
	perhaps	[pərhǽps]	
40 %	possibly	[pɑ́ːsəbli]	もしかすると

*あくまで目安です。

1527 **usually**
[júːʒuəli]
☐☐☐☐☐☐

Adv. ふつうは、普段は、通常は

▶ **usual** [júːʒuəl] Adj. いつもの、通常の

■ **as usual** （いつも通りの）

As usual, I went to Starbucks and studied for about five hours.
（いつも通り、スタバに行って 5 時間くらい勉強したよ。）

1528 **frequently**
[fríːkwəntli]
☐☐☐☐☐☐

Adv. よく、頻繁に

frequently asked questions （よくある質問）　**= FAQ**

▶ **frequent** [fríːkwənt] Adj. よくある、頻繁な

▶ **frequency** [fríːkwənsi] N[U] 頻度　N[C/U] 周波数

1529 **sometimes**
[sʌ́mtaɪmz]
☐☐☐☐☐☐

Adv. たまに、時々

Sometimes I feel like a genius. （たまに俺って天才だなぁって思うんだよね。）

▶ **sometime** [sʌ́mtaɪm] Adv. いつか、そのうち

1530 **occasionally**
[əkéɪʒənəli]
☐☐☐☐☐☐

Adv. たまに、時々

▶ **occasional** [əkéɪʒənəl] Adj. たまの

▶ **occasion** [əkéɪʒən] N[C] 特別な行事；特定の時；好機

I have a luxury watch, but I only wear it on special **occasions**.
（高級時計持ってるけど、特別な行事の時にしか着けないんだ。）

1531 **seldom**
[séldəm]
☐☐☐☐☐☐

Adv. めったに〜しない

He's a **seldom**-used bench player, but his performance on Saturday was really
good. （彼はめったに使われないベンチ選手なんだけど、土曜日のパフォーマンスはすごい良かったよ。）

1532 **rarely**
[rérli]
☐☐☐☐☐☐

Adv. めったに〜しない

I **rarely** drink alcohol, but I'll make an exception today.
（アルコールはめったに飲まないんだけど、今日は例外。）

▶ **rare** [rer] Adj. まれな、珍しい；生焼けの　　▶ **rareness** [rérnəs] N[U] 希少性

▶ **rarity** [rérəti] N[U] 希少性

rarely vs **hardly ever** vs **seldom**　どれも「めったに〜しない」という意味ですが、hardly ever は
rarely よりもカジュアルな表現です（どちらも会話で使用可能）。また、seldom は文章に用いられるこ
とが多く、会話ではあまり使用されません。

1533 **surely**
[ʃúrli]
☐☐☐☐☐☐

Adv. 確実に、きっと、間違いなく

Surely not. （（言われたことを真実だと信じられず）ウソだろ。）

▶ **sure** [ʃur] Adj. 確かな、確信した　　▶ **sureness** [ʃúrnəs] N[U] 確信

1534 **possibly**
[páːsəbli]
☐☐☐☐☐☐

Adv. もしかすると

▶ **possible** [páːsəbəl] Adj. 可能な、可能性のある　　▶ **possibility** [pɑːsəbíləti] N[C/U] 可能性

if **possible** （できれば、可能なら）　it's **possible** (for sb) to do （（〜が）〜するのは可能だ）

How to tell the time　時間の伝え方

What time is it? / What's the time? (今何時ですか?)　　It's... (今は…)

時計	読み方	時計	読み方
(6:00)	six o'clock	(12:05)	twelve oh five / five past twelve
(8:15)	eight fifteen / quarter past eight	(2:50)	two fifty / ten to three
(9:30)	nine thirty / half past nine	(6:45)	six forty-five / quarter to seven

quarter = 15分、half = 30分

past と to の使い方

「何時何分」と言いたい時、「分＋past＋時（〜時を〜分過ぎている）」と「分＋to＋時（＝〜時まであと〜分）」という言い方をすることができ、ネイティブがよく使用する表現です。

例1：twelve past six ＝ 6時を12分過ぎている＝6時12分

例2：twenty to five ＝ 5時まであと20分＝4時40分

また、一般的にデジタル時計を読むときは、past/to を使わず、数字をそのまま読みます（例：six twelve, four forty）。

How to say the date（日付の言い方）

アメリカ式

September 25, 2003　　　　　September twenty-fifth, two thousand three
September 25th, 2003

イギリス式

25 September 2003　　　　　twenty-fifth September two thousand and three
25th September, 2003
the 25th of September, 2003　　the twenty-fifth of September, two thousand and three

Chapter

32

物理学
Physics

The definition of physics is fluid and constantly changing, but broadly it is the study of matter, energy, motion, and force. Physics attempts to explain natural phenomena through observations and experiments.

Albert Einstein's general theory of relativity, for instance, determined that gravity is brought about by objects distorting and bending space and time, which are considered to be on the same fabric.

Although this appears intimidating at face value, many domains of physics have been exploited to trigger generous leaps forward in technologies that are now part of our daily lives.

A good example of this is the integrated circuit, pioneered by a winner of the Nobel Prize in Physics 2000, Jack Kilby. It has been deployed in virtually all smart devices, including tablets and smart appliances.

1 The definition of physics is fluid and constantly changing, but broadly it is the study of matter, energy, motion, and force. Physics attempts to explain natural phenomena through observations and experiments.

物理学の定義は流動的であり、絶えず変化しているが、広義では物質やエネルギー、運動、力の研究を言う。物理学は、観察と実験を通して自然現象の説明を試みるものである。

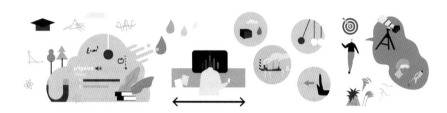

1535 fluid
[flúːɪd]
☐☐☐☐☐☐

Adj. 流動的な、変わりやすい **N[C/U]** 流体、液体

I can't really take anything he says seriously because his opinions are so **fluid**.
（彼の意見はコロコロ変わるから何も真面目に受け取れないんだよね。）

1536 constantly
[káːnstəntli]
☐☐☐☐☐☐

Adv. 絶えず、常に

Is it normal that I **constantly** feel like going on vacation?
（私、常に休暇に出かけたいと思ってるんだけど、普通かな？）

▶ **constant** [káːnstənt] Adj. 絶え間ない、一定の

Where's this **constant** creepy noise coming from?
（このずっと鳴ってる薄気味悪い音はどっから来てんのかな？）

1537 motion
[móʊʃən]
☐☐☐☐☐☐

N[S/U] 運動、動き **N[C]** 動作

My car looks even more beautiful when it's in **motion**.
（私の車、動いてる時はもっと綺麗だよ。）

1538 force
[fɔːrs]
☐☐☐☐☐☐

N[U] 力；武力、暴力 **N[C]** 影響力を持つもの・人；軍隊

For a skinny guy, he manages to hit the ball with a lot of **force**.
（彼、線が細い割には強い打球を打つよなぁ。）

V[T] に（〜するよう）強制する（to do）

Don't **force** yourself if you don't want to come.（来たくなかったら無理しないでね。）

▶ **forced** [fɔːrst] Adj. 強制の、無理やりの

Forced marriage is a big problem in many countries.
（多くの国で強制結婚は大きな問題になっているよ。）

▶ **forceful** [fɔ́:rsfəl] Adj. 力強い、強気な ▶ **forcefully** [fɔ́:rsfəli] Adv. 力強く、強引に

▶ **forcefulness** [fɔ́:rsfəlnəs] N[U] 力強さ

1539 **attempt**
[ətémpt]
☐☐☐☐☐☐

V[T] を試みる、に挑戦する **N[C]** 試み

I've done a marathon before, but I've never **attempted** a triathlon.
(私、マラソンはやったことあるけど、トライアスロンは挑戦したことないなぁ。)

attempt to do（〜しようとする、試みる）

▶ **attempted** [ətémptɪd] Adj. 未遂の

attempted murder（殺人未遂）

1540 **observation**
[àːbzərvéɪʃən]
☐☐☐☐☐☐

N[C/U] 観察 **N[C]** （気づいたことに関する）意見

One of my favorite science classes this semester was the **observation** of plants doing photosynthesis.
(今学期私が好きだった理科の授業の一つは、光合成してる植物の観察だったよ。)

Your **observation** is very interesting. （あなたの意見はとても興味深いですね。）

▶ **observe** [əbzə́:rv] V[I/T] （〜を）観察する V[T] に気づく；（規則など）に従う

I love **observing** how people behave when they think their boss is watching.
(上司に見られていると感じている時、人がどういう行動をするのか観察するのが大好きなんだ。)

▶ **observable** [əbzə́:rvəbəl] Adj. 目に見える、観察可能な

According to this research, CO_2 has no **observable** effect on global warming.
(この研究によると、二酸化炭素が地球温暖化に与える観察可能な影響はなかったんだ。)

1541 **experiment**
N. [ɪkspérəmənt]
v. [ɪkspérəmènt]
☐☐☐☐☐☐

N[C/U] （〜の）実験（on sth）

Please make sure you wear eye protection and gloves when doing chemistry **experiments**.
(化学実験する時は必ず保護めがねと手袋をして下さいね。)

V[I] （〜の）実験をする（on/with sth）；（〜を）試す（with sth）

■ **experiment** with sth（〜を使って実験する）

We are **experimenting with** new English teaching methods at our school.
(私たちの学校では新しい英語の教え方を実験してるんです。)

▶ **experimental** Adj. 実験の、実験的な ▶ **experimentally** Adv. 実験的に
[ɪkspèrəméntḷ]   [ɪkspèrəméntḷi]

We are developing a new app, but it's still at the **experimental** stage.
(新しいアプリを開発中なんだけど、まだ実験段階なんだ。)

▶ **experimentation** [ɪkspèrəmentéɪʃən] N[U] 実験すること；試すこと

experiment on sth vs **experiment with sth** experiment on sth の場合、sth には実験を行う対象（例：a mouse）が来る一方で、with の後には実験で使う手段（例：new techniques）が来ます。

2 Albert Einstein's general theory of relativity, for instance, determined that gravity is brought about by objects distorting and bending space and time, which are considered to be on the same fabric.

例えば、アルベルト・アインシュタインの一般相対性理論は、重力は、同一の構造上にあると考えられる時空が物体により歪曲して生じることを明らかにした。

ALBERT EINSTEIN

1542 general
[dʒénərəl]

Adj. 一般的な、通常の；大まかな、全体的な

I really hate **general** education courses. They're so boring.
（一般教養科目本当に嫌い。めっちゃつまんないよ。）

as a **general** rule （一般に、通常は）

▶ **generally** [dʒénərəli] Adv. 一般的に、通常

▶ **generalize** [dʒénərəlaɪz] V[I]（〜を）一般化する（about sth）

Why do you always **generalize** about people from other cultures?
（なんであなたはいつも他の文化から来た人を一括りにして考えちゃうわけ？）

▶ **generalization** [dʒènərəlɪzéɪʃən] N[U] 一般化　N[C] 一般論

1543 theory
[θíəri]

N[U] 理論、原理　**N[C]**（個々の）理論、論、説

There's a conspiracy **theory** that says that the Apollo 11 astronauts never really went to the Moon. （アポロ11号の宇宙飛行士は実際には月に行ってないっていう陰謀論があるんだ。）

in **theory** （理論的に）　　**theory** and practice （理論と実践）

▶ **theoretical** Adj. 理論的な　　▶ **theoretically** Adv. 理論的に
　[θiːərétɪkəl]　　　　　　　　　　　　 [θiːərétɪkli]

What you're saying is **theoretically** correct, but it's not going to work in practice.
（君の言っていることは理論的には正しいけど、実践ではそうはいかないよ。）

1544 determine
[dɪtɜ́ːrmɪn]

V[T] を明らかにする、特定する；を決定する、確定する

What I have for dinner is generally **determined** by how lazy I'm feeling.
（大体の場合、夜ごはんに何を食べるかは自分がどれくらい面倒くさいかによって決まるんだ。）

determine to do （〜すると決心する）

▶ **determined** [dɪtə́:rmɪnd] Adj. 意志の強い、断固とした、(〜すると) 決心した (to do)

I'm **determined** to study hard and pass the exam.
(一生懸命勉強して試験に受かるって決めたんだ。)

▶ **determination** N[U] 決定、決意、決心
[dɪtə̀:rmɪnéɪʃən]

▶ **determinant** N[C] 決定要因
[dɪtə́:rmɪnənt]

Supply and demand are the main **determinants** of price.
(需給こそが価格を決定する主な要因だよ。)

語根 term 「終わり」という意味の語根で、determine は悩んでいる状態を終わらせることから来ています。他には exterminate (絶滅させる) や terminate (終わらせる) などがあります。

1545 **gravity**
[grǽvəṭi]
▢▢▢▢▢▢

N[U]　重力、引力；重大さ；真剣さ

I love how when I'm swimming it feels like **gravity** doesn't exist.
(泳いでる時に重力が無いような感覚になるのがすごい好きなんだよね。)

▶ **gravitate** [grǽvɪtèɪt] V[I] (〜に) 引き付けられる (to sth)

Everyone **gravitates** to her smile. (誰もが彼女の笑顔に引き付けられるんだ。)

▶ **gravitation** [græ̀vətéɪʃən] N[U] 重力、引力

▶ **gravitational** [græ̀vətéɪʃənəl] Adj. 重力の、引力の

1546 **distort**
[dɪstɔ́:rt]
▢▢▢▢▢▢

V[T]　を歪める、歪曲させる

I think social media has a tendency to **distort** the truth.
(SNS って真実を歪める傾向があると思うんだよね。)

▶ **distortion** N[C/U] 歪み、歪曲
[dɪstɔ́:rʃən]

▶ **distorted** Adj. 歪んだ、歪曲した
[dɪstɔ́:rṭɪd]

I can't trust information on this forum because it's obvious how **distorted** it is.
(この掲示板の情報は信用できないよ。明らかに歪められてるからね。)

1547 **bend**
[bend]
▢▢▢▢▢▢

V[T]　を曲げる　　V[I]　曲がる

I accidentally **bent** my credit card where it says my name.
(クレジットカードの自分の名前書いてるところ間違って曲げちゃった。)

bend down/over/forward (かがむ)

bend one's knees (ひざを曲げる)　　　　on **bended** knee (ひざまずいて)

▶ **bendable** [béndəbəl] Adj. 曲げられる

Look! My glasses are **bendable**, so I can put them in my pocket.
(見て！私のメガネは曲げられるから、ポケットにしまっておけるんだ。)

1548 **fabric**
[fǽbrɪk]
▢▢▢▢▢▢

N[S]　構造、基盤　　N[C/U]　生地、布、織物

I know this jacket costs a lot, but the **fabric** is so nice.
(このジャケット確かに高いけど、生地が最高なんだよなぁ。)

3 Although this appears intimidating at face value, many domains of physics have been exploited to trigger generous leaps forward in technologies that are now part of our daily lives.

これだけみると圧倒されてしまいそうだが、これまで物理学の多くの分野が大幅な技術的躍進を引き起こすために利用され、そうした技術は今の私たちの日常生活の一部になっている。

1549 intimidating
[ɪntímədeɪtɪŋ]

Adj. 威圧的な、びくびくさせるような

Do you find Connie **intimidating** because she's tall, or because she's loud?
(コニーが威圧的だと感じる理由って背が高いからなのか、声が大きいからなのかどっち？)

▶ **intimidate** [ɪntímədeɪt] V[T] を脅す、怖がらせる

■ **intimidate** sb into doing（〜を脅して〜させる）

My boss is the worst. He **intimidated** me **into** keeping silent about his mistakes.
(私の上司最悪だよ。自分のミスについて黙ってるように私のこと脅してくるの。)

▶ **intimidated** Adj.（威圧されて）怖い　　▶ **intimidation** N[U] 脅し、脅迫
　　[ɪntímədeɪtɪd]　　　　　　　　　　　　　　　[ɪntìmədéɪʃən]

I sometimes feel **intimidated** by smart people.（たまに頭いい人って怖い感じするんだよね。）

1550 domain
[douméɪn]

N[C] 分野、領域；領土

■ in the public **domain**（公の領域にある、公開されている）

These reports are **in the public domain**, so you can download them anytime.
(このレポートは公開されてるから、いつでもダウンロードできるよ。)

1551 exploit
[ɪksplɔ́ɪt]

V[T] を利用する、搾取する；(資源など) を開発する

Japan were incredible at **exploiting** the weaknesses of the opponent.
(日本代表は敵の弱みをうまく利用するのが驚くほど上手かった。)

▶ **exploitation** [èksplɔɪtéɪʃən] N[U] 利用、搾取；開発

the **exploitation** of natural resources　　the **exploitation** of labor
(天然資源の利用)　　　　　　　　　　　　　　(労働者の搾取)

▶ **exploitable** [ɪksplɔ́ɪtəbəl] Adj. 利用できる、搾取できる

▶ **exploiter** [ɪksplɔ́ɪṭər] N[C] 利用者、搾取者

▶ **exploitative** [ɪksplɔ́ɪṭəṭɪv] Adj. 搾取的な

He has a very **exploitative** nature. He is always trying to scam money out of his friends.
（あいつはめちゃくちゃ搾取的なところがあるんだ。いつも友達からお金をだまし取ろうとしてるし。）

1552 trigger
[trɪ́gər]

V[T]　を引き起こす、の引き金となる　N[C]　引き金、要因

I'm worried that increasing prices will **trigger** a lot of unforeseen consequences.
（値段を上げたら予期せぬ結果をあれこれ引き起こしちゃうんじゃないかと心配なんだ。）

■ pull the **trigger**（（思い切って）決断を下す）

I **pulled the trigger** and deleted all the photos I took with my ex-boyfriend.
（思い切って元彼と撮った写真全部消したよ。）

▶ **triggering** [trɪ́gərɪŋ] Adj. 引き金となる

1553 generous
[dʒénərəs]

Adj.　大幅な；気前が良い、親切な

My boyfriend is a really **generous** person, and a lot of people take advantage of that.
（私の彼氏、親切すぎるから色んな人に利用されちゃうんだ。）

▶ **generously** [dʒénərəsli] Adv. たっぷり；気前よく

Sam **generously** paid for our lunch today.
（今日はサムが気前よく私たちのランチ代を払ってくれたんだ。）

▶ **generosity** [dʒènərá:səṭi] N[U] たっぷり；気前のよさ、寛容さ、寛大さ

You shouldn't take people's **generosity** for granted.
（人の寛容さを当たり前と思っちゃダメだよ。）

1554 leap
[liːp]

N[C]　跳躍、飛躍；急激な変化

There has been a big **leap** in sales since we launched the new product.
（新商品を発売してから売り上げが飛躍的に伸びたんだ。）

leap year（うるう年）

V[I]　（勢いよく）跳ぶ、跳ね上がる　V[T]　を跳び越える

1555 daily
[déɪli]

Adj.　日常の、毎日の　Adv.　毎日　N[C]　日刊新聞

I used to read the newspaper **daily**, but there's no real point anymore because everything's online.
（昔は新聞毎日読んでたんだけど、もう全部オンラインだからあんま意味ないなと思ってね。）

4 A good example of this is the integrated circuit, pioneered by a winner of the Nobel Prize in Physics 2000, Jack Kilby. It has been deployed in virtually all smart devices, including tablets and smart appliances.

好例は、2000 年度ノーベル物理学賞を受賞したジャック・キルビーによって開発された集積回路だ。集積回路は、タブレットやスマート家電など、ほぼ全てのスマートデバイスで利用されている。

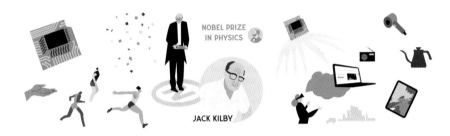

1556 integrated
[íntəgreı̯t ɪd]
☐☐☐☐☐☐

Adj. 統合された、融合した

I think we should take a more **integrated** approach to environmental protection.
（環境保護に対してはもっと統合的なアプローチを取るべきだと思うよ。）

an **integrated** circuit（集積回路）

▶ **integrate** V[T] を（〜の中に /〜と）統合する、組み込む（into/with sth）
[íntəgreıt] V[I] 統合する、融合する

Whether or not you can **integrate** studies into your normal life is the key to success.
（勉強を普段の生活に組み込めるかが成功のカギだよ。）

▶ **integration** [íntəgréıʃən] N[U] 統合、溶け込むこと

▶ **integral** [íntəgrəl] Adj.（〜に）不可欠な（to sth）

An insurance policy is **integral** to safe traveling, so you should definitely get one.
（安全な旅に保険は不可欠だから、絶対に入った方がいいよ。）

1557 pioneer
[pàɪənír]
☐☐☐☐☐☐

V[T] を（先駆的に）開発する、開拓する **N[C]** 先駆者、開拓者

This AI tool was **pioneered** by Australian scientists.
（この AI ツールはオーストラリアの科学者たちによって開発されたんだ。）

▶ **pioneering** [pàɪənírɪŋ] Adj. 先駆的な、開拓者の

This **pioneering** platform is so impressive. I can chat with a native speaker anytime, anywhere.（この最先端プラットフォームすごいなぁ。いつでもどこでもネイティブと会話ができるんだよ。）

1558 prize
[praɪz]
☐☐☐☐☐☐

N[C] 賞、賞金、賞品 **V[T]** を重んじる

There's no **prize** for coming second, so we have to win this thing.
（二位になっても賞金はないから、これは勝たなきゃいけないよ。）

award vs **prize** どちらも「賞、賞金」という意味ですが、award は功績や業績をたたえて授与されるものを指すのに対し、prize は競争やコンテストで与えられる賞や賞金を指します。

▶ **prized** [praɪzd] 大切な、貴重な

■ a **prized** possession（大切な持ち物、宝物）

That watch is his most **prized possession**.（あの時計は彼の一番の宝物なんだ。）

1559 **deploy**
[dɪplɔ́ɪ]

⬚⬚⬚⬚⬚⬚

V[T] を（効果的に）利用する；(部隊など) を**配置する、展開させる**

The U.S. recently **deployed** an additional two thousand soldiers to Syria.
（アメリカは最近 2,000 人の兵士を追加でシリアに配置した。）

V[I] （装備などが）うまく作動する

The news about an airbag accidentally **deploying** was really scary.
（エアバッグが誤作動したってニュース怖すぎた。）

▶ **deployment** N[C/U] 装備、(部隊などの) 配置、展開　N[U]（人や資源などの）活用
[dɪplɔ́ɪmənt]

the **deployment** of troops（部隊の配置）

1560 **virtually**
[vɚ́ːrtʃuəli]

⬚⬚⬚⬚⬚⬚

Adv. ほとんど、事実上、実質的には

I'm starting to get a bit lonely because **virtually** all my friends are married.
（友達がほぼ全員結婚しちゃったからちょっと寂しくなってきた。）

▶ **virtual** [vɚ́ːrtʃuəl] Adj. 事実上の、実質的な；仮想の

This **virtual** reality thing is awesome. This is much more fun than real life.
（この仮想現実（VR）のやつ最高か。現実より全然楽しいじゃん。）

1561 **smart**
[smɑːrt]

⬚⬚⬚⬚⬚⬚

Adj. スマートな、賢い、頭の良い

Sam just sounds **smart** because he has a deep voice and uses really big words.
（サムは低い声で大げさで難しい言葉使うから頭良さそうに聞こえるだけだよ。）

▶ **smartly** [smɑ́ːrtli] Adv. 賢く

▶ **smartness** [smɑ́ːrtnəs] N[U] 頭の良さ、賢さ

1562 **appliance**
[əpláɪəns]

⬚⬚⬚⬚⬚⬚

N[C] 家電、器具、装置

My mom's addicted to buying electrical **appliances** on Amazon.
（私のお母さんは Amazon で電化製品を買うのに夢中になってる。）

How do Hummingbirds Hover?

The mechanics through which hummingbirds hover, fly backward, and wander through the air over tiny distances has been a source of fascination for centuries. The flying ability boasted by these dainty, timid creatures is unique among birds. Simplistically speaking, this flight is achieved through the rapid and vigorous rotation of their wings in a figure-eight motion. The force generated by this motion, coupled with the hummingbird's light and hollow skeleton, allows it to float between flowers to search for nourishment and feed, seemingly defying the laws of physics.

The application of the theoretical physics behind their flight led to the design and construction of machinery that resembles hummingbirds, such as helicopters. The spinning of the helicopter blades mimics this miracle of physics, allowing the helicopter to soar vertically to extremely high altitudes and to float and move in any direction.

ハチドリはどうやって空中にとどまりながら飛んでいるのか？

ハチドリが空中で停止し、後方に飛び、わずかな距離を空中で飛び回るメカニズムは、何世紀にもわたって人々を魅了し続けてきた。きゃしゃで臆病なハチドリという生き物が誇るこの飛行能力は、鳥の中でも独特だ。簡単に言えば、ハチドリの飛行は、翼を急速かつ活発に8の字の形に回転させることによってもたらされる。この動きから生まれる力によってハチドリは、骨格が軽量で中が空洞であることもあり、花の間を浮遊しながら栄養と餌を探すことができるが、そうした動きは物理の法則に反しているように見える。

ハチドリの飛行を可能にしている理論物理学の応用は、ヘリコプターなどのハチドリに似た機械類の設計や構築につながった。ヘリコプターのブレードの回転はこの奇蹟の物理学を模倣したもので、これによって、ヘリコプターは非常に高い高度まで垂直に上昇し、浮遊し、どの方向にでも移動できるようになっている。

1563 backward
[bǽkwərd]
☐☐☐☐☐☐

Adv. 後方に、後ろ向きに；逆に、反対に　　Adj. 後ろ向きの、逆の

⟷ **forward** [fɔ́:rwərd] 前へ / 前向きの、前方への

work **backward** (逆算する)

1564 wander
[wá:ndər]
☐☐☐☐☐☐

V[I/T] （〜を）歩き回る、ぶらつく

wander through/around sth (〜中を歩き回る、ぶらつく)

▶ **wanderer** [wá:ndərər] N[C] 放浪者

1565 distance
[dístəns]
☐☐☐☐☐☐

N[C/U] 距離

from a **distance** (遠くから)　　in the **distance** (遠くに)

▶ **distant** [dístənt] Adj. 遠い　= **far away** [fá:rəwéɪ]

▶ **distantly** [dístəntli] Adv. 遠くに

1566 boast
[boʊst]
☐☐☐☐☐☐

V[T] を誇りにする、自慢とする (that + sentence)

V[I] （〜を）自慢する (about sth)　= **brag** [bræg]

▶ **boastful** [bóʊstfəl] Adj. 自慢げな　▶ **boastfully** [bóʊstfəli] Adv. 自慢げに

▶ **boastfulness** [bóʊstfəlnəs] N[U] 自慢げであること

1567 dainty
[déɪnṭi]
☐☐☐☐☐☐

Adj. きゃしゃな；上品な、優美な

▶ **daintiness** [déɪntinəs] N[U] きゃしゃであること；上品さ

▶ **daintily** [déɪnṭəli] Adv. 上品に、優美に

1568 timid
[tímɪd]
☐☐☐☐☐☐

Adj. 臆病な、気弱な

▶ **timidly** [tímɪdli] Adv. 気弱に、臆病に　▶ **timidity** [tɪmídəṭi] N[U] 気弱さ、臆病さ

1569 creature
[krí:tʃər]
☐☐☐☐☐☐

N[C] 生き物、動物

a bizarre **creature** (変な生き物)

1570 vigorous
[vígərəs]
☐☐☐☐☐☐

Adj. 活発な、元気な

▶ **vigorously** [vígərəsli] Adv. 活発に、元気に　▶ **vigor** [vígər] N[U] 活力、元気

1571 hollow
[há:loʊ]
☐☐☐☐☐☐

Adj. 中が空洞の；価値のない　　N[C] 空洞　　V[T] をへこませる

▶ **hollow sth out** [há:loʊ(w)áʊt] [PV] 〜をくり抜く

1572 skeleton
[skéləṭən]
☐☐☐☐☐☐

N[C] 骨格、骸骨

▶ **skeletal** [skéləṭəl] Adj. 骨格の、骸骨の　▶ **skull** [skʌl] N[C] 頭蓋骨

1573 nourishment
[nə́ːrɪʃmənt]

N[U]（生命維持に必要な）栄養、食物

▶ **nourish** [nə́ːrɪʃ] V[T] に栄養を与える、を養う

▶ **nourishing** [nə́ːrɪʃɪŋ] Adj. 栄養の多い

1574 feed
[fiːd]

N[U] 飼料、餌　　N[C] 供給

V[I] 餌を食べる

V[T] に食べ物を与える、餌を与える；を供給する

Please don't **feed** the pigeons.（ハトに餌をあげないでください。）

▶ **feeding** [fiːdɪŋ] N[C] 授乳

▶ **breast-feed** [bréstfiːd] V[I] 授乳する　　V[T] を母乳で育てる

1575 defy
[dɪfáɪ]

V[T]（法則や慣習）に反する、逆らう

▶ **defiance** [dɪfáɪəns] N[U] 反抗的な態度、抵抗

▶ **defiant** [dɪfáɪənt] Adj. 反抗的な　　▶ **defiantly** [dɪfáɪəntli] Adv. 反抗的に

1576 resemble
[rɪzémbəl]

V[T] と似ている

▶ **resemblance** [rɪzémbləns] N[C/U] 類似、似ていること

1577 spinning
[spínɪŋ]

N[U] 回転；紡績

▶ **spin** [spɪn] V[I] 回転する；糸を紡ぐ

　　V[T] を回転させる；（毛糸など）を糸に紡ぐ N[C/U] 回転

1578 blade
[bleɪd]

N[C]（プロペラの）羽根、回転翼；刃

1579 mimic
[mímɪk]

V[T] を模倣する、まねる、のものまねをする

Stop **mimicking** me!（僕のまねするのやめてよ！）

1580 soar
[sɔːr]

V[I] 上昇する、急増する、（気分などが）高揚する

Bitcoin prices are **soaring** today.（今日はビットコインの値段が急騰している。）

1581 altitude
[ǽltətuːd]

N[C/U] 高度、標高

at an **altitude** of sth（高度〜で）

1582 float
[floʊt]

V[I]（〜に）浮かぶ（in/on sth）　V[T] を浮かべる

▶ **floating** [flóʊtɪŋ] Adj. 浮いている；流動的な

天文学
Astronomy

Astronomy is the study of celestial objects, such as planetary systems, galaxies, asteroids, and star clusters. It also examines astronomical phenomena such as shooting stars and solar and lunar eclipses.

Among various topics within astronomy, the enigma of extraterrestrial life is likely one of the most fascinating. Indeed, interest in extraterrestrial life has attracted increased attention to Saturn's largest moon, Titan.

Scientists speculate that, except for Earth, Titan is the only celestial body in the solar system likely to contain the essential ingredients for life, including stable liquid on its surface, a dense atmosphere containing carbon compounds, and possibly water lurking beneath the frozen crust.

To confirm this hypothesis, NASA is planning to launch an autonomous drone to probe this alien world, which could pave the way for further exploration of this utterly uncharted frontier.

1 Astronomy is the study of celestial objects, such as planetary systems, galaxies, asteroids, and star clusters. It also examines astronomical phenomena such as shooting stars and solar and lunar eclipses.

天文学は、惑星系、銀河、小惑星、星団などの天体の研究である。それには、流星、日食、そして月食といった、天文現象の調査も含まれる。

1583 astronomy
[əstrɑ́:nəmi]
□□□□□□

N[U] 天文学

I majored in **astronomy** because I've always wanted to know if there's another planet like ours out there.
（どこか他に地球みたいな惑星があるのかずっと知りたいと思ってて、それで天文学専攻にしたよ。）

▶ **astronomical** [æstrənɑ́:mɪkəl] Adj. 天文学の；（数字などが）天文学的な

▶ **astronomically** [æstrənɑ́:mɪkli] Adv. 天文学的に

Isn't your iPhone white? I think there's an **astronomically** low chance of you finding it in this snow.
（君のiPhone白色じゃなかったっけ？この雪の中であれを見つけられる可能性は天文学的に低いと思うよ。）

▶ **astronomer** [əstrɑ́:nəmər] N[C] 天文学者 ▶ **astronaut** [æstrənɑ:t] N[C] 宇宙飛行士

1584 celestial
[sɪléstʃəl]
□□□□□□

Adj. 天体の、宇宙の

■ a **celestial** body/object （天体）

You can take a virtual reality tour of different sorts of **celestial bodies** using this cutting-edge VR headset. (この最先端のVRヘッドセットを使えば、色んな天体をまわる仮想現実ツアーができるんだ。)

1585 galaxy
[gǽləksi]
□□□□□□

N[C] 銀河 N[S] 銀河系【the G-】 = the Milky Way* [ðə mɪ́lki wéɪ]
*the Milky Wayは天の川と訳されることもあります。

It seems there are several kinds of **galaxies**, like elliptical and spiral ones, but they all look the same to me.
（楕円銀河とかうずまき銀河とか、銀河にはいくつか種類があるようなんだけど、俺には全部一緒に見える。）

■ a **galaxy** of sth/sb （〜の勢ぞろい）

The music festival brought together **a galaxy of** famous singers.
（あの音楽フェスには有名なシンガーたちが勢ぞろいした。）

1586 asteroid
[ǽstərɔɪd]

N[C] 小惑星

It's often said the dinosaurs went extinct due to an **asteroid**, but nobody knows for sure.
（恐竜は小惑星のせいで絶滅したとよく言われているけど、誰もはっきりとは分からないんだ。）

接頭語 astro-, aster- 「星の、天体の」を意味する接頭語で、他には astrology（占星術）や asterisk（アスタリスク（*））があります。

1587 cluster
[klʌ́stər]

N[C] 集団、集まり；（果物などの）房

The triple-lens **cluster** on the back of this smartphone is starting to look like tapioca pearls.　（このスマホの裏にある3つのレンズ、なんかタピオカに見えてきた。）

V[I] （〜の周りに）群がる、集まる（around sth）

Try not to **cluster** around the same table and spread out a bit.
（同じテーブルに集まらないで少し散らばってください。）

1588 lunar
[lúːnər]

Adj. 月の

What's the difference between the **lunar** and solar calendars?
（太陰暦と太陽暦の違いって何？）

1589 eclipse
[ɪklíps]

N[C] 食、日食、月食　　N[S/U] 輝きを失うこと、衰退

■ a solar/lunar **eclipse**（日食 / 月食）

a total solar/lunar **eclipse**（皆既日食 / 皆既月食）

a partial solar/lunar **eclipse**（部分日食 / 部分月食）

I learned how solar **eclipse**s work when I was in junior high school, but I don't remember the exact details now.
（中学の時に日食の仕組みについて習ったけど、今はあんまり細かいこと覚えてないなぁ。）

V[T] （天体）を食する；を凌駕する

Older people in the company often fear their skills will be **eclipsed** by the knowledge and ability of new hires.
（社内にいる年齢の高い人たちは、新入社員の持つ知識や能力が自分たちのスキルを凌駕することを恐れている。）

2 Among various topics within astronomy, the enigma of extraterrestrial life is likely one of the most fascinating. Indeed, interest in extraterrestrial life has attracted increased attention to Saturn's largest moon, Titan.

天文学に関するさまざまなトピックの中で、地球外生命の謎はおそらく最も魅力的なものの一つだろう。実際、地球外生命への関心から、土星最大の衛星であるタイタンにますます注目が集まっている。

1590 **enigma**
[ənígmə]
☐☐☐☐☐☐

N[C] 謎、謎めいたもの・人

She just quit social media without telling anybody. She's such an **enigma**.
(彼女は誰にも言わずに SNS をやめたんだ。本当に謎だなぁ。)

▶ **enigmatic** Adj. 謎めいた
[ènɪgmǽṭɪk]

▶ **enigmatically** Adv. 謎めいて
[ènɪgmǽṭɪkli]

1591 **extraterrestrial**
[èkstrətəréstriəl]
☐☐☐☐☐☐

Adj. 地球外の　**N[C]** 地球外生物、宇宙人

■ **extraterrestrial** life（地球外生命体）

It's difficult to believe that there's no **extraterrestrial life** in a universe this vast.
(こんなに広大な宇宙に地球外生命体が居ないと信じることの方が難しいよ。)

1592 **likely**
[láɪkli]
☐☐☐☐☐☐

Adv. おそらく、多分

■ most/very **likely**（きっと、ほぼ間違いなく）

I'll **most likely** be heading to the pool after work.
(仕事終わりはきっとプールに行くよ。)

Adj. ありえそうな、もっともらしい

be **likely** to do（～しそうだ）　■ be more/less **likely** to do（～する可能性の方が高い / 低い）

After graduating from high school, I'm **more likely to** go to a university than search for a job.　(高校卒業後は仕事を探すよりも大学行く可能性の方が高いかな。)

▶ **unlikely** [ʌnláɪkli] Adj. ありそうもない、可能性の低い

It's very **unlikely** that my parents will let me go to your party tonight, but I'll ask anyway.
(今晩の君のパーティ、俺の親はきっと行かせてくれないと思うんだけど、とりあえず聞いてみるよ。)

That collaboration between the American pop star and the Chinese table tennis player is great because it's so **unlikely**.
（あのアメリカのポップスターと中国の卓球選手のコラボは最高。めっちゃ意外だよね。）

▶ **likelihood** [láɪklihʊd] N[U] 可能性、見込み

I think there's little **likelihood** that our team will win this game, but I'll still cheer for them.
（うちのチームがこの試合に勝つ可能性はほぼないけど、それでも応援するよ。）

1593 **fascinating**
[fǽsəneɪtɪŋ]
☐☐☐☐☐☐

Adj. 魅力的な、魅惑的な、とても興味深い

One of the most **fascinating** things about Japan is you can buy pretty much anything from a vending machine. （日本の最も魅力的なことの一つは自販機でほぼ何でも買うことができることなんだ。）

▶ **fascinatingly** [fǽsəneɪtɪŋli] Adv. 魅力的に、興味深く

▶ **fascinate** [fǽsəneɪt] V[T] を魅了する、の興味をそそる

▶ **fascinated** [fǽsəneɪtɪd] Adj. (〜に) 魅了された、興味をそそられた （with/by sth）

▶ **fascination** [fæsənéɪʃən] N[S/U] 魅了、魅力

1594 **attention**
[əténʃən]
☐☐☐☐☐☐

N[U] 注目、関心；注意；世話、配慮

■ pay **attention** (to sth/sb) ((〜に) 注意を払う、(〜を) 注意して聞く / 見る)

You should **pay** more **attention** when your coach is talking.
（監督が話してる時はもっと集中した方が良いよ。）

■ **attention**-seeking（注目されたがる）　get/attract **attention** (注目を集める)

She's a bit **attention-seeking**. （彼女ってちょっと注目されるのが好きな感じあるんだよな。）

▶ **attend** [əténd] V[I/T] (〜に) 出席する、(学校などに) 通う

▶ **attentive** [əténtɪv] Adj. 注意深く聞いている / 見ている；(〜に) 気を配った (to sth/sb)

I wasn't really **attentive** in class when I was a kid. （子供の時はあんまり授業聞いてなかったんだ。）

▶ **attentively** Adv. 注意深く；気を配って ▶ **attentiveness** N[U] 注意深さ；気配り
　　[əténtɪvli]　　　　　　　　　　　　　　　　　　[əténtɪvnəs]

1595 **Saturn**
[sǽtən]
☐☐☐☐☐☐

N[Prop.] 土星

Did you know that you can't land on **Saturn** because it's just a ball of gas?
（土星はただのガスのかたまりだから、着陸はできないって知ってた？）

1596 **moon**
[mu:n]
☐☐☐☐☐☐

N[C] 衛星 (惑星の周りを公転する天体のこと)

Mercury and Venus are the only planets in our solar system that don't have a **moon**.
（この太陽系の中で水星と金星にだけは衛星が無いんだよ。）

N[S] （天体としての）月【the M/m-】；（空にかかる）月

The Earth looks beautiful from the **Moon**.
（月から見える地球は美しいんだ。）

a crescent/full/new **moon** (三日月 / 満月 / 新月)

3 Scientists speculate that, except for Earth, Titan is the only celestial body in the solar system likely to contain the essential ingredients for life, including stable liquid on its surface, a dense atmosphere containing carbon compounds, and possibly water lurking beneath the frozen crust.

科学者らは、タイタンは太陽系では地球以外で唯一、生命に不可欠な材料が存在する天体なのではないかと推測している。それには、地表の安定した液体や炭素化合物を含む高密度の大気、そして凍った地殻の下に隠れているかもしれない水などが含まれる。

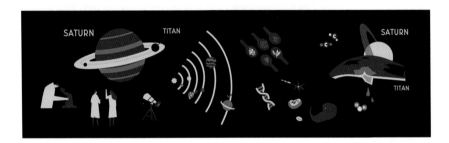

1597 speculate
[spékjəleɪt]
☐☐☐☐☐☐

V[I/T]　（〜について）推測する（on/about sth）
V[I]　（〜に）投機する（in sth）

People can **speculate** about the future, but nobody knows for sure what's going to happen.
（人は自分の未来について推測することはできても、何が起きるのか確実に分かる人はいないよ。）

▶ **speculation** [spèkjəléɪʃən] N[C/U] 推測、憶測；投機

▶ **speculative** Adj. 推測の；投機の　　▶ **speculatively** Adv. 推測で；投機的に
　[spékjələtɪv]　　　　　　　　　　　　　　　[spékjələtɪvli]

highly **speculative**（推測による部分が大きい）

▶ **speculator** [spékjəleɪtər] N[C] 投機家

1598 except
[ɪksépt]
☐☐☐☐☐☐

Prep. 〜以外は、〜を除いて　**Cnj.** 〜という点以外は (that + sentence)

I can eat anything **except** green peas.（グリーンピース以外は何でも食べられるよ。）

■ **except** for sth（〜以外は、〜を除いて）

Everyone came to the meeting **except for** John because he was on a business trip.
（ミーティングにはジョン以外みんな来たよ。彼は出張中だったからね。）

I like him **except** he's always late.（いつも遅刻してくること以外、彼のことは好きだよ。）

1599 ingredient
[ɪngríːdiənt]
☐☐☐☐☐☐

N[C]　材料、具、成分；（成功などの）要素

■ a secret **ingredient**（秘密の食材、隠し味）

Dark chocolate is the **secret ingredient** that I add when I make curry.
（カレーを作る時はダークチョコを隠し味として入れるんだ。）

There are so many weird **ingredients** in this sports drink.
（このスポーツドリンク、なんか変な原料がめちゃくちゃたくさん入ってるなぁ。）

1600 liquid
[líkwɪd]

N[C/U]　液体、水分　Adj.　液体の；流動的な

I like how sand in a desert moves like **liquid** when the wind blows.
（僕は風が吹いた時に砂漠の砂がまるで液体のように動くのが好きなんだ。）

liquid nitrogen（液体窒素）

Cash is the most **liquid** asset.（現金が一番流動性の高い資産だよ。）

▶ **liquidity** [lɪkwídəţi] N[U]　流動性

People in Japan are finding it really hard to change jobs because of low **liquidity** in the labor market.（労働市場の流動性がすごい低いせいで、日本ではみんな転職しにくいと感じているよ。）

▶ **liquidate** [líkwədeɪt] V[I/T]（～を）清算する ▶ **liquidation** [lìkwədéɪʃən] N[C/U]　清算

1601 dense
[dens]

Adj.　高密度の、濃い；密集した；頭の鈍い

I think we should call off the hike today because there's going to be **dense** fog in the mountains throughout the whole day.
（一日中山に濃い霧が出るみたいだから、今日のハイキングはやめたほうがいいんじゃないかな。）

Do you think she's just bad at expressing herself, or really **dense**?
（彼女ってただ自己表現が下手なのか、本当に頭が弱いのか、どっちだろう？）

▶ **densely** [dénsli] Adv.　濃く；密集して ↔ **sparsely** [spáːrsli] まばらに

I feel that the quality of life in Tokyo is made lower by how **densely** populated it is.
（東京は人が密集しすぎているせいで生活の質が下がっている気がする。）

▶ **density** [dénsəţi] N[C/U]　密度　= **denseness** [dénsnəs]

population **density**（人口密度）

1602 lurk
[lɜːrk]

V[I]　隠れる、潜む、待ち伏せする

I freaked out when I found my friend **lurking** under my bed.
（友達が俺のベッドの下で待ち伏せしてたって分かった時はめっちゃビビったよ。）

1603 crust
[krʌst]

N[C/U]　地殻；（パンやピザの）耳、（パイなどの）皮

Earth's **crust** is very thin compared to its other layers. My teacher said it's like the peel of an apple.
（地球の地殻は他の層と比べるとものすごい薄いから、先生はリンゴでいう皮みたいなもんだって言ってた。）

The **crust** on this bread makes it delicious but also really hard to cut.
（このパン、皮があるからまた美味しいんだけど、切るのがすごい大変なんだよね。）

▶ **crusty** [krʌ́sti] Adj.（パンなどの）皮がかたい

crusty baguette（皮がかたいバゲット）

4 To confirm this hypothesis, NASA is planning to launch an autonomous drone to probe this alien world, which could pave the way for further exploration of this utterly uncharted frontier.

この仮説を確かめるため、NASA は自律飛行型ドローンを打ち上げてこの異世界を調査する計画を進めている。それによって、全く未知のフロンティアをよりいっそう探索する道が開かれることになるかもしれない。

1604 **launch**
[lɑːntʃ]
□□□□□□

V[T] を打ち上げる；を始める；を発売する

How many fireworks can we **launch** at once?（花火は一回に何発打ち上げることができるの？）

We're going to **launch** a new service next month.
（私たちは来月から新サービスを開始します。）

N[C] 発射、打ち上げ；開始；発売

I look forward to every Apple **launch** event.（アップルの新製品発表は毎回楽しみにしています。）

▶ **launcher** [lɑːntʃər] N[C] 発射装置

1605 **autonomous**
[ɑːtɑːnəməs]
□□□□□□

Adj. 自律的な、自立した、自主的な、自動の；自治の

I'm very excited about the launch of **autonomous** taxis, but I'm also a bit worried about how safe they are.（自動運転タクシーの開始はすごい楽しみなんだけど、安全性がちょっと心配かな。）

an **autonomous** vehicle = a self-driving car（自動運転車）

an **autonomous** body（自治体）

▶ **autonomously** [ɑːtɑːnəməsli] Adv. 自主的に、自立して、自動で

I'm slowly programming all my appliances at home to work **autonomously**.
（うちの家電が全部自動化されるようにちょっとずつプログラミングしてるんだ。）

▶ **autonomy** [ɑːtɑːnəmi] N[U] 自立性、自主性；自治（権）

1606 **probe**
[proʊb]
□□□□□□

V[T] を調査する、探査する

I'll need more time to **probe** this data if you want me to get any proper insights from it.
（もっとデータを徹底的に調べるための時間が必要だよ。きちんとした洞察を得て欲しいならね。）

V[I] （〜を）詮索する（into sth）

N[C] 調査；探査機

a space **probe**（宇宙探査機）

▶ **probing**［próʊbɪŋ］Adj. 探りを入れる

Asking effective **probing** questions is the key to solving customers' problems.
（顧客の問題を解消するには、効果的に探りの質問をすることが鍵だよ。）

1607 alien
［éɪliən］
☐☐☐☐☐☐

Adj. 異質の、未知の；外国の　　N[C] 在留外国人；エイリアン

We studied trigonometry last week, so it shouldn't be an **alien** concept to you.
（三角法は先週勉強したし、全然分からないってことは無いと思うよ。）

▶ **alienate**［éɪliəneɪt］V[T] を（〜から）遠ざける、仲間外れにする（from sth/sb）

We'll **alienate** our fans if we increase the ticket prices more than we already have.
（チケットの値段を今よりも上げたらファンを遠ざけることになっちゃうよ。）

▶ **alienation**［èɪliənéɪʃən］N[U] 疎外感

1608 pave
［peɪv］
☐☐☐☐☐☐

V[T] を舗装する

■ **pave** the way (for sth)（（〜への）道を切り開く）

It's completely up to you to **pave the way for** your own career.
（キャリアで自分自身の道を切り開けるかは完全に自分次第だよ。）

▶ **paved**［peɪvd］Adj. 舗装された

▶ **pavement**　N[C] 舗道；歩道 <英> = **sidewalk**［sáɪdwɑ:k］<米>
　［péɪvmənt］　N[C/U] 舗装部分 = **paving**［péɪvɪŋ］

1609 utterly
［ʌ́tərli］
☐☐☐☐☐☐

Adv. 全く、完全に　= **completely**［kəmplí:tli］

My computer is **utterly** broken, but I have no money, so I'll have to make do.
（俺のパソコン、完全に壊れてるんだけど、お金ないからこのまま何とかしないといけないんだ。）

▶ **utter**［ʌ́tər］Adj. 全くの、完全な　V[T] を言う、（音など）を発する

I feel **utter** despair at the moment, but I think I'll be fine by tomorrow.
（今は絶望のどん底にいるけど、明日には大丈夫になってると思う。）

▶ **utterance**［ʌ́tərəns］N[C] 発言　N[U] 口に出すこと

I try not to give **utterance** to my work problems when I get home.
（家に帰ったら仕事の問題については口に出さないようにしてるよ。）

utterly vs **completely** どちらも「完全に」と訳されることが多い単語ですが、utterly は主にネガティブな状況で使われるのに対して、completely はポジティブでもネガティブでもどちらでも使われるという違いがあります。

1610 frontier
［frʌntír］
☐☐☐☐☐☐

N[C] フロンティア、未開拓の領域、最先端；国境

I became an AI engineer because I wanted to be at the **frontier** of AI technology.
（AI 技術の最先端にいたかったから、AI エンジニアになったんだ。）

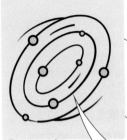

The Milky Way

The Milky Way is the galaxy that contains our Solar System and is one of billions of galaxies in the universe. The name comes from its appearance as a faint, dimly glowing band that stretches across and illuminates the sky. Many elite astronomers have made it their sole mission to get a sense of the scale of the Milky Way. Using modern apparatus and laboratory equipment, they have been able to estimate that there are 100 to 400 billion stars and over 100 billion planets in the galaxy.

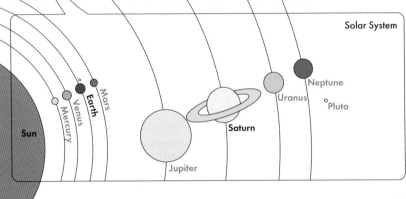

Solar System

Sun

Mercury

Venus

Earth

Mars

Jupiter

Saturn

Uranus

Neptune

Pluto

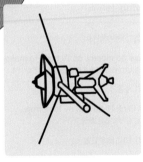

Artificial Satellites

An artificial satellite is an object that is deliberately launched into orbit. There are a variety of satellites used for different purposes, including navigation and broadcasting.

Astronomical satellites, in particular, are helpful in making a sensational amount of data available for astronomers to scrutinize.

天の川　天の川は私たちの太陽系を含む銀河で、宇宙に無数に存在する銀河の一つです。この名前は、ぼんやりとした、かすかに光る帯が、空を横切り、明るく照らす様子に由来しています。多くのエリート天文学者たちは、天の川の規模を把握することを自らの唯一の使命とし、最新の装置や実験機器を使って、銀河には1,000〜4,000億の星と1,000億以上の惑星があると推定してきました。

人工衛星　人工衛星は、軌道に意図的に打ち上げられる物体で、ナビゲーションや衛星放送など、その用途は多岐にわたります。中でも天文衛星は、天文学者が膨大な量のデータを精査する際に役立っています。

1611 faint
[feɪnt]
□□□□□□

Adj. かすかな、弱々しい **V[I]** 気絶する、気を失う **N[S]** 気絶、失神

faint from anemia（貧血で倒れる）

▶ **faintly** [féɪntli] Adv. かすかに

1612 dimly
[dímli]
□□□□□□

Adv. ぼんやりと、薄暗く

▶ **dim** [dɪm] Adj. ぼんやりした、薄暗い ▶ **dimness** [dímnəs] N[U] 薄暗さ

1613 glowing
[glóʊɪŋ]
□□□□□□

Adj. 光を放った、（光が）燃えるような；（評価が）非常に好意的な

▶ **glow** [gloʊ] N[S] ほのかな光；血色 V[I] 光を放つ、輝く

▶ **glowingly** [glóʊɪŋli] Adv. 絶賛して

1614 stretch
[stretʃ]
□□□□□□

V[I] 伸びる、伸縮する；ストレッチをする **V[T]** を伸ばす

stretch across（横切る）

N[C] 伸びたもの；ストレッチ；無理があること；（一続きの）期間

▶ **stretchy** [strétʃi] Adj. 伸縮性のある ▶ **stretcher** [strétʃər] N[C] 担架

1615 illuminate
[ɪlú:məneɪt]
□□□□□□

V[T] を照らす、に光を当てる；（問題など）を明らかにする

▶ **illuminated** [ɪlú:məneɪ̯tɪd] Adj. 照明で照らされた

▶ **illuminating** [ɪlú:məneɪ̯tɪŋ] Adj. 啓発的な

▶ **illumination** [ɪlù:mənéɪʃən] N[U] 照明、明るくすること

1616 elite
[ɪlí:t]
□□□□□□

Adj. エリートの、精鋭の **N[C]** エリート

1617 sole
[soʊl]
□□□□□□

Adj. 唯一の、たった一つの、単独の **N[C]** 足の裏、靴底

▶ **solely** [sóʊlli] Adv. 単に、もっぱら

1618 mission
[míʃən]
□□□□□□

N[C] 使命、任務、理念；使節団

▶ **missionary** [míʃəneri] N[C] 宣教師 Adj. 布教の、伝道の

1619 sense
[sens]
□□□□□□

N[C/U]（漠然とした）感覚 **N[C]**（五感の）感覚；意味 **N[U]** 分別

V[T] を感じる

get a **sense**（of sth）（（～の）感覚を理解する、（～を）感じ取る）

make **sense**（意味がわかる、理解できる） in a **sense**（ある意味）

▶ **sensory** [sénsəri] Adj. 感覚の ▶ **sensitivity** [sènsətívəti] N[U] 敏感さ、気配り

▶ **sensitive** [sénsətɪv] Adj.（～に）敏感な、気配りのある（to sth）

▶ **sensitively** [sénsətɪvli] Adv. 敏感に

1620 apparatus
[ˌæpərǽṭəs]
☐☐☐☐☐☐

N[C/U] 装置、器具、機器；機関、組織

1621 laboratory
[lǽbrətɔːri]
☐☐☐☐☐☐

N[C] 実験室、実習室、研究室　= lab [læb]

1622 estimate
v. [éstəmeɪt]
N. [éstəmət]
☐☐☐☐☐☐

V[T] を推定する、見積もる　N[C] 見積もり、推定

▶ **estimated** [éstəmeɪṭɪd] Adj. 見積もられた

▶ **estimation** [èstəméɪʃən] N[C/U] 見積もり　N[U] 意見

1623 planet
[plǽnɪt]
☐☐☐☐☐☐

N[C] 惑星

▶ **planetary** [plǽnɪteri] Adj. 惑星の

1624 Mercury
[mə́ːrkjəri]
☐☐☐☐☐☐

N[Prop.] 水星　N[U] 水銀【m-】

1625 Venus
[víːnəs]
☐☐☐☐☐☐

N[Prop.] 金星

1626 Mars
[mɑːrz]
☐☐☐☐☐☐

N[Prop.] 火星

1627 Jupiter
[dʒúːpəṭər]
☐☐☐☐☐☐

N[Prop.] 木星

1628 Uranus
[júrənəs]
☐☐☐☐☐☐

N[Prop.] 天王星

1629 Neptune
[néptuːn]
☐☐☐☐☐☐

N[Prop.] 海王星

1630 Pluto
[plúːṭoʊ]
☐☐☐☐☐☐

N[Prop.] 冥王星

1631 **satellite**
[sǽṭəlaɪt]
□□□□□□

N[C] 衛星；衛星国

1632 **navigation**
[nævəɡéɪʃən]
□□□□□□

N[U] ナビゲーション、航行、航海

▶ **navigate** [nǽvəɡeɪt] V[I/T]（～を）誘導する、航行する、航海する

1633 **broadcast**
[brɑ́:dkæst]
□□□□□□

V[I/T]（～を）放送する；（～を）言う、広める　　N[C] 放送、番組

It's not exactly a secret, but try not to **broadcast** it to everyone.
（別に秘密ってわけでもないけど、みんなには言わないでおこう。）

▶ **broadcaster** [brɑ́:dkæstər] N[C] アナウンサー、キャスター

▶ **broadcasting** [brɑ́:dkæstɪŋ] N[U]（テレビやラジオの）放送

1634 **sensational**
[senséɪʃənəl]
□□□□□□

Adj. 驚くべき、素晴らしい；世間を驚かせる

▶ **sensationally** [senséɪʃənəli] Adv. ものすごく；世間を驚かせるような

▶ **sensation** [senséɪʃən] N[C/U] 感覚、知覚

1635 **available**
[əvéɪləbəl]
□□□□□□

Adj. 利用できる、入手できる；（人が）空いている、都合がつく

I'm not **available** this week, so can we catch up next week?
（今週は空いてないから、来週会うのはどう？）

▶ **availability** [əvèɪləbíləti] N[U] 利用できること、入手可能性、空き状況

1636 **scrutinize**
[skrú:ṭənaɪz]
□□□□□□

V[T] を精査する、詳しく調べる

▶ **scrutiny** [skrú:ṭəni] N[U] 精査、詳細な調査

↻ CH. 14, 19, 23, 27, 30, 33

Chapter

34

化学
Chemistry

Chemistry is the study of matter, which is composed of pure substances and mixtures. Pure substances can be broken down into elements, which contain only one kind of atom, and compounds, which contain two or more different atoms bonded together to form molecules.

Atoms consist of three types of particles: protons and neutrons, which make up the nucleus, and electrons, which surround them. The majority of the field focuses on these particles, particularly with respect to how they behave.

For instance, carbon dioxide and water molecules are formed through carbon and hydrogen, respectively, overlapping their orbitals with oxygen orbitals and sharing their electrons to bond firmly.

Given that it occupies an intersection of multiple scientific realms, chemistry has the deserved reputation of being the central science that is capable of accommodating many fields.

1 Chemistry is the study of matter, which is composed of pure substances and mixtures. Pure substances can be broken down into elements, which contain only one kind of atom, and compounds, which contain two or more different atoms bonded together to form molecules.

化学は、物質についての研究であり、物質は純物質と混合物から構成されている。純物質は、一種類の原子のみでできている単体と、2つ以上の異なる原子が結合して分子を形成している化合物に分けられる。

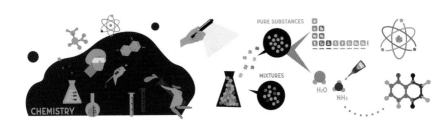

1637 matter
[mǽṭər]
☐☐☐☐☐☐

N[U] 物質　**N[C]** 事柄、問題

■ gray **matter**（頭脳；(脳や脊髄の) 灰白質）

My grandma solves crossword puzzles every day to exercise her **gray matter**.
（私のおばあちゃんは、頭の体操のために毎日クロスワードを解いてるんだ。）

■ it's (only) just a **matter** of time (before/until + sentence)（〜するのは時間の問題だよ）

It's just a matter of time before he gets fired.（彼がクビになるのは時間の問題だよ。）

■ the **matter**（(〜に関する) 困った問題（with sth/sb））

What's **the matter**?（何かあったの？）

V[I] 重要である、問題である

It doesn't **matter**. Forget about it.（大丈夫。忘れて。）

1638 compose
[kəmpóʊz]
☐☐☐☐☐☐

V[T] を構成する　**V[I/T]**（〜を）作曲する

■ be **composed** of sth（〜から成る、構成される）

This book **is composed of** many different topics, so it's hard to figure out where to start.（この本はたくさんの違うトピックから構成されてるからどこから始めていいか分からないよ。）

V[T] を落ち着かせる

■ **compose** oneself（落ち着く）

I'm trying to **compose myself**, but I just can't!（頑張って落ち着こうとしてるんだけど、無理だよ！）

▶ **component** [kəmpóʊnənt] N[C] 構成要素

Every language is made up of three **components**: vocabulary, grammar, and pronunciation.
（全ての言語は単語、文法、発音という主に3つの構成要素からできているんだ。）

▶ **composed** Adj. 落ち着いた
[kəmpóʊzd]

▶ **composedly** Adv. 落ち着いて
[kəmpóʊzɪdli]

My greatest strength is that I can remain **composed** in any situation.
（私の最大の強みは、どんな状況でも落ち着いていられることなんだ。）

▶ **composer** [kəmpóʊzər] N[C]　作曲家

1639 **pure**
[pjʊr]
☐☐☐☐☐☐

Adj. 純粋な、ピュアな；澄んだ；完全な

The water at the beach was so **pure** you could see the bottom without even trying.
（ビーチの水がものすごい澄んでて、底の方まで簡単に見ることができたよ。）

I got this job just by **pure** luck.（この仕事は完全に運だけで手に入れたよ。）

▶ **purely** [pjʊ́rli] Adv. 純粋に、単に

He married her **purely** because he loves her.
（彼は純粋に彼女のことを愛しているから結婚したんだ。）

▶ **purity** [pjʊ́rəṭi] N[U]　純粋、純度

1640 **break (sth) down**
[breɪk daʊn]
☐☐☐☐☐☐

[PV]　（〜を）分解する

You really need to **break** his talk **down** into smaller parts to fully get what he's talking about.
（彼の言ってることを完全に理解するには、話を細かく分解しないといけない。）

1641 **atom**
[ǽṭəm]
☐☐☐☐☐☐

N[C]　原子

Isn't it fascinating that a tiny uranium **atom** can generate so much power?
（小さなウラン原子があれだけのパワーを生み出せるってすごくない？）

▶ **atomic** [ətá:mɪk] Adj. 原子の

an **atomic** bomb（原子爆弾）

1642 **compound**
N./Adj. [ká:mpaʊnd]
V. [kəmpáʊnd]
☐☐☐☐☐☐

N[C]　化合物、混合物；（壁や塀で囲まれた）敷地、構内

Mixing tree sap with mud in the right way creates a **compound** that you can use as glue.
（樹液を泥と良い感じで混ぜると接着剤として使える化合物になるんだ。）

V[T]　（問題など）を悪化させる；を（〜と）混ぜる、調合する（with sth）

Adj.　複合の　　**V[T]**　を複利で計算する

This term deposit interest is **compounded** annually.
（この定期預金の利息は毎年複利で計算されます。）

1643 **molecule**
[má:lɪkju:l]
☐☐☐☐☐☐

N[C]　分子

I've been crushing these herbs for so long that they're going to turn into **molecules** soon.
（このハーブ長時間すりつぶしすぎてもはや分子になってしまいそうだわ。）

▶ **molecular** [məlékjələr] Adj. 分子の

2 **Atoms consist of three types of** particles: protons **and** neutrons, **which make up the** nucleus, **and** electrons, **which** surround **them. The majority of the field focuses on these particles, particularly with respect to how they** behave.

原子は 3 種類の粒子から成る。それらは、原子核を構成する陽子と中性子、そしてそれをとり囲む電子だ。化学分野の大半は、これらの粒子、特にその反応に関する研究を中心に行っている。

1644 **particle**
[pά:rʈəkəl]
☐☐☐☐☐☐

N[C] 粒子；助詞

I think I keep sneezing because there are so many dust **particles** in the air.
（くしゃみが止まらないのは空気中にホコリの粒子が超たくさん舞ってるからだと思う。）

Particles like "ga," "wo," and "de" are the most difficult part of Japanese.
（が、を、で等の助詞が日本語で一番難しい部分なんだ。）

接頭語 part- 「部分」という意味の接頭語で、そこに「一つのもの」という意味の接尾語 -icle がついて「粒子」という意味に。他には particular（特定の）、participate（参加する）などがあります。

1645 **proton**
[próuʈɑ:n]
☐☐☐☐☐☐

N[C] 陽子

How do **protons** fired from the Sun manage to reach Earth over all that distance?
（太陽から放出される陽子ってあんな遠いところからどうやって地球に到達するの？）

1646 **neutron**
[nú:trɑ:n]
☐☐☐☐☐☐

N[C] 中性子

My textbook says our sun doesn't actually have enough mass to become a **neutron** star. To be honest, I don't know what that means.
（テキストによると、太陽って実は中性子星になれるほどの質量は無いんだって。正直言って、意味不明。）

1647 **nucleus**
[nú:kliəs]
☐☐☐☐☐☐

N[C] 原子核（複数形：nuclei/nucleuses）

Humans have 23 pairs of chromosomes within the **nucleus** of a cell.
（人間は細胞の核の中に 23 対の染色体があるんだ。）

1648 **electron**
[iléktrɑ:n]
☐☐☐☐☐☐

N[C] 電子

Electrons play an essential role in many phenomena such as electricity and magnetism.
（電子は電気や磁気といった多くの現象で欠かせない役割を果たしているよ。）

1649 **surround**
[səráʊnd]

▢▢▢▢▢▢

V[T] を囲む、包囲する **N[P]** 周囲、環境【-s】

I'm never worried about anything because I **surround** myself with people I trust.
（信頼できる人に囲まれるようにしているから何かに不安になったりしたことは一度もないよ。）

We enjoyed exploring both the city and the **surrounds** of Sydney.
（シドニーは街中もその周りの地域もどっちも楽しかったよ。）

▶ **surrounding** [səráʊndɪŋ] Adj. 周囲の、周辺の **N[P]** 環境【-s】

a **surrounding** area （周辺地域）

Chameleons change color to blend in with their **surroundings**.
（カメレオンは色を変えて周りの環境と同化するんだ。）

1650 **behave**
[bɪhéɪv]

▢▢▢▢▢▢

V[I] （物質などが）反応をする；ふるまう；行儀を良くする

The way Bob **behaved** with the customer was very impressive.
（ボブのそのお客さんへの対応の仕方は素晴らしかった。）

behave well/badly (to sb) （（〜に対して）行儀良く / 悪くふるまう）

■ **behave** as if + sentence （まるで〜かのようにふるまう）

Sarah **behaved as if** the world was going to end when a tiny fly landed on her croissant.
（サラはクロワッサンに小さいハエが止まった時、まるで世界の終わりみたいな反応をしたんだよ。）

■ **behave**＊ oneself （行儀良くする） ＊この用法では他動詞扱いですが、基本的には自動詞で使われる単語です。

Behave yourself while I'm away, okay? （私がいない間行儀良くするのよ、分かった？）

▶ **behavior** [bɪhéɪvjər] N[U] 反応；ふるまい、態度 N[C/U] 行動

The intern always comes in late, lacks concentration, and isn't motivated. His **behavior** is clearly not up to scratch.
（あのインターンは遅刻するし、集中力も無いし、やる気もない。あの態度は明らかに水準には達してないね。）

▶ **behavioral** [bɪhéɪvjərəl] Adj. 行動の

That student is really smart, but he has a bit of a **behavioral** problem.
（あの生徒はめちゃくちゃ頭が良いんだけど、ちょっとだけ行動に問題があるんだ。）

3 For instance, carbon dioxide and water molecules are formed through carbon and hydrogen, respectively, overlapping their orbitals with oxygen orbitals and sharing their electrons to bond firmly.

例えば、二酸化炭素分子と水分子はそれぞれ、炭素と水素の軌道が酸素の軌道と重なり合い、互いの電子が共有され、しっかりと結合することによって形成される。

1651 **carbon dioxide**
[kɑ́:rbən daɪɑ́:ksaɪd]
☐☐☐☐☐☐

N[U] 二酸化炭素、CO_2

How do **carbon dioxide** emissions cause global warming?
（どうやって二酸化炭素の排出は地球温暖化を引き起こすの？）

▶ **carbon** [kɑ́:rbən] N[U] 炭素

1652 **hydrogen**
[háɪdrədʒən]
☐☐☐☐☐☐

N[U] 水素

Is **hydrogen** water actually better than regular water?
（水素水って実際普通の水より良いの？）

1653 **overlap**
v. [òʊvərlǽp]
N. [óʊvərlæp]
☐☐☐☐☐☐

V[T] を（〜と）重ね合わせる（with sth）、と重複する

I made a cool song by **overlapping** different audio track files with each other.
（異なるオーディオトラックを重ね合わせてカッコいい曲作ったよ。）

V[I] （〜と）重なり合う、重複する（with sth） **N[C/U]** 重複

1654 **orbital**
[ɔ́:rbɪtl]
☐☐☐☐☐☐

N[C] （電子が通る）軌道 **Adj.** 軌道の

Electrons and their **orbitals** determine which reactions can take place between molecules.
（電子とその軌道が分子間においてどんな反応が起こり得るのかを決めているんだ。）

▶ **orbit** N[C/U] 軌道
[ɔ́:rbət] V[I/T] （〜の周りを）軌道を描いて回る

The moon **orbits** Earth and not the other way around.
（地球が月の周りを回ってるんじゃなくて、月が地球の周りを回ってるんだよ。）

1655 **oxygen**
[άːksɪdʒən]

□□□□□□

N[U] 酸素

Make sure there's enough **oxygen** in your tank before you go diving.
（ダイビングをする前は必ずタンクに十分酸素が入ってるか確認してね。）

▶ **oxidize** [άːksədaɪz] V[I] 酸化する V[T] を酸化させる

You should wrap the half-eaten banana because it'll **oxidize** really quickly.
（その食べかけのバナナ、すぐ酸化しちゃうからラップした方が良いよ。）

▶ **oxidation** [ὰːksədéɪʃən] N[U] 酸化 = **oxidization** [ὰːksədəzéɪʃən]

How can I prevent the **oxidation** of my silver jewelry?
（私のシルバージュエリー、どうやったら酸化するのを防げるかな？）

1656 **bond**
[bɑːnd]

□□□□□□

V[I] 結合する、接着する；（～と）絆を結ぶ（with sb）

Always being yourself is the best way to **bond** with your friends.
（ありのままの自分で居続けることが、友達との絆を深める一番の方法だよ。）

V[T] を（～と）結合させる、接着させる（to sth）

Using glue and heat is the best way to **bond** these two pieces of wood together.
（この二つの木をくっつけるには接着剤と熱を使うのが一番だね。）

N[C] 絆；債権；結合、接着

There has always been a strong **bond** between my kids.
（うちの子たちの間にはいつも強い絆があるのよ。）

N[P] （ロープやチェーンなどの）束縛するもの【-s】

▶ **bondage** [bάːndɪdʒ] N[U] 束縛

1657 **firmly**
[fɜ́ːrmli]

□□□□□□

Adv. しっかりと、かたく；確固として；毅然と

I'm **firmly** of the belief that Bitcoin is the way of the future.
（私はビットコインにかなり将来性を感じる。）

▶ **firm** [fɜːrm] Adj. しっかりした、かたい

I usually prefer to sleep on **firm** mattresses.
（基本的に、私はかためのマットレスで寝る方が好きだな。）

take a **firm** attitude (toward sth/sb)（（～に対して）強硬な態度を取る）

▶ N[C] 会社、（組織としての）事務所

an accounting **firm**（会計事務所）

▶ **firmness** [fɜ́ːrmnəs] N[U] かたさ

At this ramen place, you can choose the **firmness** of the noodles.
（このラーメン屋では麺のかたさが選べるよ。）

hard vs **firm**　どちらも「かたい」という意味を持ちますが、hard は貫通できないくらいカチカチであるという感覚があるのに対し、firm は程よい弾力性があり、しっかりしているというニュアンスを持ちます。

4 Given that it occupies an intersection of multiple scientific realms, chemistry has the deserved reputation of being the central science that is capable of accommodating many fields.

化学は、複数の科学分野が交差した共通領域を占めていることから、多くの分野に対応できる「セントラルサイエンス」として、当然の評価を得てきた。

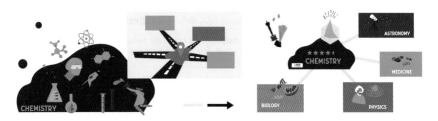

1658 occupy
[á:kjəpaɪ]
☐☐☐☐☐☐

V[T] を占める、占領する、に居住する

What do you do when your mind is **occupied** by negative thoughts?
（心がネガティブな考えで埋め尽くされてる時ってどうしてる？）

▶ **occupied** [á:kjəpaɪd] Adj. 忙しい；（トイレや部屋が）使用中の；占領された

That room is **occupied**, so let's use that one in the corner.
（あの部屋は使われてるから、あの角の部屋使おうよ。）

1659 intersection
[ìntərsékʃən]
☐☐☐☐☐☐

N[C] （集合の）共通部分；交差点　**N[U]** 交差

Is engineering really the **intersection** between physics and math?
（工学って本当に物理と数学が交わったところにあるものなの？）

▶ **intersect** [ìntərsékt] V[I/T] （〜と）交わる、交差する（with sth）

Flinders Street **intersects** Elizabeth Street.
（フリンダース・ストリートはエリザベス・ストリートと交差してるよ。）

1660 multiple
[mʌ́ltəpəl]
☐☐☐☐☐☐

Adj. 複数の、多数の

It was pretty hard working **multiple** jobs at once, but I definitely learned a lot.
（複数の仕事を掛け持ちするのは結構大変だったけど、確実にたくさん学びがあったよ。）

▶ **multiply** V[I] 増える、増殖する　V[T] に（〜を）かける、掛け合わせる（by sth）
[mʌ́ltəplaɪ]

▶ **multiplication** [mʌ̀ltəplɪkéɪʃən] N[U] 掛け算；増殖

1661 realm
[relm]
☐☐☐☐☐☐

N[C] 領域、分野；王国

■ within/beyond the **realm** of possibility（可能で / 不可能で）

Re-writing the entire program from scratch is not **beyond the realm of possibility**, but I'd prefer not to do it.
（プログラムを一から書き直すのは不可能ではないけど、やりたくはないなぁ。）

1662 deserved
[dɪzɜ́:rvd]
☐☐☐☐☐☐

Adj. 当然の、ふさわしい

■ well-**deserved**（（賞や昇進などに）ふさわしい、当然の）

Congratulations on your promotion! **Well-deserved**.（昇進おめでとう！当然の結果だね。）

▶ **deserve** [dɪzɜ́:rv] V[T] に値する、ふさわしい

I think you **deserve** a nice meal because you've been studying so hard.
（すごい勉強頑張ってるんだし、おいしいごはんくらい食べても良いんじゃないかな。）

deserve to do（〜するのにふさわしい）

1663 reputation
[rèpjətéɪʃən]
☐☐☐☐☐☐

N[C] 評判、評価、名声

■ have a good/bad **reputation**（良い / 悪い評判がある）

Greg's been nothing but nice to me, so I don't understand why he **has** such **a bad reputation**.（グレッグは私にとって良い人でしかないから、なんであんなに悪評が立ってるのか理解できない。）

▶ **reputed** [rɪpjú:ṭɪd] Adj. 評判の良い；（〜すると）言われている（to do）

This Shibuya crossing is **reputed** to be the busiest intersection in the world.
（この渋谷の交差点は世界で最も人が多い横断歩道だと言われているんだ。）

▶ **reputedly** [rɪpjú:ṭɪdli] Adv. 評判では、噂では

1664 capable
[kéɪpəbəl]
☐☐☐☐☐☐

Adj. 有能な、能力がある

■ be **capable** of sth/doing（〜できる、する能力がある）

At the age of three, he **was** already **capable of** speaking two languages.
（三歳の時に彼はもう二つの言語を話すことができたんだ。）

▶ **capably** [kéɪpəbli] Adv. うまく、上手に

▶ **capability** [kèɪpəbíləṭi] N[C/U] 能力

■ have the **capability** to do（〜する能力がある）

I find people who **have the capability to** keep growing really attractive.
（成長し続けることができる人って魅力的だなぁって思う。）

be able to do vs **be capable of doing** どちらも「できる」という意味を持ちますが、capable は特に「〜する能力やスキルがある」という意味で使われます。例えば、「彼は英語が話せる」というのは能力に関する話のため He's able to speak English. と He's capable of speaking English. はどちらも可能ですが、「明日来られない」というのは能力ではなく状況的な話のため、I won't be able to come tomorrow. が正しく、I won't be capable of coming tomorrow. とは言えません。

1

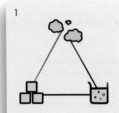

States of Matter

There are three states of matter: solid, liquid, and gas. The states are determined by the way tiny particles are bonded together. For instance, a solid object has a fixed volume and shape, with every particle tightly connected to its neighbors. The changing of states is mainly driven by temperature and pressure changes .....

Continue

2

Chemical Reactions: Fire

Chemical reactions are processes in which substances are converted into different substances. The first chemical reaction that humans learned to control was fire, which is a sequence of reactions that cause explosions and flames.

The fire triangle is very helpful in understanding how best to extinguish a fire, as interfering with or removing one of these components will stop a fire .....

Continue

3

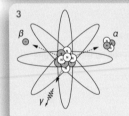

Radioactivity

Radioactivity or radioactive decay can be both useful and dangerous. For example, moderate doses of gamma ray radiation are used to destroy cancer cells, as it can penetrate human tissues. On the other hand, over-exposure to radiation can be harmful, as it can damage DNA .....

Continue

物質の状態

物質には、固体、液体、気体の3つの状態がある。その状態は、小さな粒子の結合の仕方によって決まる。例えば、固体は一定の体積と形を持ち、すべての粒子は隣接する粒子としっかりと結び付いている。状態変化は、主に温度と圧力の変化によって起こる。

化学反応：火

化学反応は、物質が別の物質に変化する過程のことである。人間が最初に操ることを覚えた化学反応は火で、これは爆発と炎を引き起こす、一連の反応である。火のトライアングルは、これらの要素のいずれかを防ぐ、もしくは取り除くことで火が消えるため、消火の最善の方法を理解するのに非常に役に立つ。

放射能

放射能または放射性崩壊は有用かつ危険でもある。例えば、中線量のガンマ線放射はがん細胞を破壊するのに利用される。ヒトの組織に侵入できるからだ。一方、放射線に当たりすぎると有害となる。DNAに損傷を与える恐れがあるためだ。

1665 solid
[sá:lɪd]
▢▢▢▢▢▢

N[C] 固体　Adj. 固体の；（金や銀が）純粋の；しっかりとした；堅実な

solid gold/silver（純金 / 銀）　**solid** evidence（しっかりとした証拠）　**solid** advice（堅実なアドバイス）

Adj. 中身の詰まった　⟷ hollow [há:loʊ] 中が空洞の

▶ **solidly** [sá:lɪdli] Adv. 固く；堅実に　▶ **solidify** [səlídəfaɪ] V[I] 固まる　V[T] を固める

▶ **solidness** [sá:lɪdnəs] N[U] 固さ　= **solidity** [səlídəṭi]

1666 tiny
[táɪni]
▢▢▢▢▢▢

Adj. とても小さい

make a **tiny** mistake（とても小さいミスをする）

▶ **tininess** [táɪninəs] N[U] とても小さいこと

1667 fixed
[fɪkst]
▢▢▢▢▢▢

Adj. 一定の、固定した；確固たる

▶ **fix** [fɪks] V[T] を固定する、決定する；（問題）を解決する、修理する

My laptop never turns on. Can you **fix** it?（ラップトップの電源が全然つかないんだけど、直せる？）

1668 neighbor
[néɪbər]
▢▢▢▢▢▢

N[C] 隣のもの、隣人、近所の人

▶ **neighborhood** [néɪbərhʊd] N[C] 近所　▶ **neighboring** [néɪbərɪŋ] Adj. 近くの

1669 temperature
[témpərətʃər]
▢▢▢▢▢▢

N[C/U] 温度、気温、体温

What's the **temperature** today?（今日って気温何度？）

▶ **temperate** [témpərət] Adj. 温帯の、温暖な　▶ **temper** [témpər] N[C/U] 気性、気質；短気さ

lose one's **temper**（怒りだす）

1670 convert
[kənvə́:rt]
▢▢▢▢▢▢

V[T] を変える、転換する；を改宗させる　V[I] 変わる、変換する

▶ **conversion** [kənvə́:rʒən] N[C/U] 変換、転換；改宗

▶ **converter** [kənvə́:rṭər] N[C] 変換器

1671 sequence
[sí:kwəns]
▢▢▢▢▢▢

N[C] 順番　N[C/U] 順序

a **sequence** of sth（一連の〜、〜の連続）

▶ **sequential** [sɪkwénʃəl] Adj. 連続的な　▶ **sequentially** [sɪkwénʃəli] Adv. 連続して

▶ **sequel** [sí:kwəl] N[C] 続編

1672 explosion
[ɪksplóʊʒən]
▢▢▢▢▢▢

N[C/U] 爆発

▶ **explode** [ɪksplóʊd] V[I] 爆発する　V[T] を爆発させる

▶ **explosiveness** [ɪksplóʊsɪvnəs] N[U] 爆発性

▶ **explosive** [ɪksplóʊsɪv] Adj. 爆発性の　N[C/U] 爆発物

1673 flame
[fleɪm]
▢▢▢▢▢▢

N[C/U] 炎　V[I]（炎を上げて）燃える　= **flame up** [fleɪmʌ́p]

1674 extinguish
[ɪkstíŋgwɪʃ]

V[T] （火や炎）を消す

▶ **extinguisher** [ɪkstíŋgwɪʃər] N[C] 消火器　= a fire extinguisher

---

1675 interfere
[ìntərfír]

V[I] （〜を）妨害する、妨げる（with sth）；（〜に）干渉する（in sth）

I don't think parents should **interfere** with their children's decisions.
（親は子供の決めたことに口出ししない方が良いと思う。）

▶ **interference** [ìntərfírəns] N[U] 干渉

1676 radioactivity
[rèɪdiouæktívəti]

N[U] 放射能

▶ **radioactive** [rèɪdiouæktɪv] Adj. 放射能の　▶ **radiation** [rèɪdiéɪʃən] N[U] 放射線

▶ **radiate** [réɪdieɪt] V[I/T] （〜を）放射する、発する

1677 decay
[dɪkéɪ]

N[U] 崩壊、腐敗、衰退　V[I] 腐敗する、衰退する

tooth **decay**（虫歯）　= **cavity** [kævəti]

1678 dangerous
[déɪndʒərəs]

Adj. 危険な

▶ **dangerously** [déɪndʒərəsli] Adv. 危険に　▶ **danger** [déɪndʒər] N[C/U] 危険

in **danger**（危険にさらされた）

1679 moderate
[má:dərət]

Adj. 中くらいの、適度な、穏やかな　V[I] 穏やかになる

V[T] を穏やかにする

▶ **moderately** [má:dərətli] Adv. 適度に　▶ **moderation** [mà:dəréɪʃən] N[U] 適度

1680 ray
[reɪ]

N[C] 光線；（魚の）エイ

▶ **X-ray** [éksreɪ] N[C] エックス線

1681 destroy
[dɪstrɔ́ɪ]

V[T] を破壊する、壊す

▶ **destroyed** [dɪstrɔ́ɪd] Adj. 破壊された；腹を立てた

1682 penetrate
[pénətreɪt]

V[T] に侵入する；を通り抜ける、貫通する

V[I] （〜に）しみ込む、入り込む（into sth）

▶ **penetration** [pènətréɪʃən] N[C/U] 貫通；侵入

1683 tissue
[tíʃu:]

N[U] （細胞の）組織　N[C] ティッシュ（ペーパー）

blow one's nose with a **tissue**（ティッシュで鼻をかむ）

1684 harmful
[há:rmfəl]

Adj. （〜に）有害な（to sth/sb）　↔ **harmless** [há:rmləs] 無害の

▶ **harmfully** [há:rmfəli] Adv. 有害に　▶ **harm** [hɑːrm] N[U] 害

do **harm**（害を及ぼす）　do more **harm** than good（有害無益だ）

↺ CH. *15, 20, 24, 28, 31, 34*

Chapter

35

生物学
Biology

Biology is the field of science involving the study of living organisms, including their physical structure, chemical processes, and physiological mechanisms.

Although biology comprises a variety of complicated aspects of living organisms, there are a large number of unifying concepts which combine and synthesize them into a coherent, rational field.

These concepts include, for example, that cells are the basic building blocks of organisms, genes are the fundamental units of heredity, and evolution is the engine that spurs and disrupts the creation of different species and contributes to their extinction.

Out of these, evolution and the connected notion of natural selection are among the endlessly contentious areas of biology, as they contradict the basic doctrines of many major religions.

1 Biology **is the** field **of science** involving **the study of living** organisms, **including their** physical **structure, chemical processes, and** physiological mechanisms.

生物学は、生物を研究する科学の分野で、生物の物理的構造、化学プロセス、生理学的なメカニズムなどが含まれる。

1685 **biology**
[baɪɑ́:lədʒi]
□□□□□□

N[U]　生物学

I find plant **biology** so much more interesting than human **biology**.
(僕は植物生物学の方がヒューマンバイオロジーよりもずっと面白いと思うんだよなぁ。)

▶ **biological** [bàɪəlɑ́:dʒɪkəl] Adj. 生物学の

a **biological** clock （体内時計）　　▶ **biologically** [bàɪəlɑ́:dʒɪkli] Adv. 生物学的に

▶ **biologist** [baɪɑ́:lədʒɪst] N[C] 生物学者

1686 **field**
[fi:ld]
□□□□□□

N[C]　分野、領域；農地、田畑；競技場

I want to study commerce, but I don't know what to specialize in because it's such a broad **field**. （商学を勉強したいんだけど、すごい広い分野だから何を専攻すれば良いか分かんないや。)

V[I]　（野球などで）守備につく

V[T]　（質問など）を対処する；（ボール）を処理する

1687 **involve**
[ɪnvɑ́:lv]
□□□□□□

V[T]　を含む；を（〜に）巻き込む、参加させる（in sth）

I'm only going to attend this workshop if it **involves** free food.
(このワークショップにはタダ飯が含まれるんだったら行くよ。)

V[T]　を（〜と）関わらせる（with sth/sb）

Please don't **involve** me with Tom. I really hate him.
(頼むからトムと関わらせようとしないで。彼のことは本当に嫌いなんだ。)

▶ **involvement** [ɪnvɑ́:lvmənt] N[U] 参加、関与　N[C] 活動

The suspect denied his **involvement** in the crime.
(容疑者はその犯罪への関与を否定したんだ。)

▶ **involved** Adj. (〜に) 巻き込まれた、参加した (in sth) ; (〜と) 関わりを持った (with sth/sb)
[ɪnvάːlvd] 複雑な、込み入った

I got **involved** in their fight again. (あいつらの喧嘩にまた巻き込まれたんだ。)

I stopped using Facebook because I found I was getting way too emotionally
involved in trivial matters.
(どうでもいいことにめちゃくちゃ感情移入するようになってきたから、Facebook 使うの止めたんだ。)

1688 **organism**
[ɔ́ːrgənɪzəm]
□□□□□□

N[C]　生物、有機体

■ a living **organism** (生物)

I feel like this company is like **a living organism** because it's so fast-paced and
complex. (この会社ってなんか生き物みたいな感じがする。展開がものすごい速いし、とても複雑なんだ。)

▶ **organic** Adj. 有機体の ; 有機栽培の　　　▶ **organically** Adv. 有機的に ; 有機栽培で
[ɔ́ːrgǽnɪk]　　　　　　　　　　　　　　　　　　[ɔ́ːrgǽnɪkli]

1689 **physical**
[fízɪkəl]
□□□□□□

Adj.　物理的な ; 物質の ; 身体の

They say mental health and **physical** health are strongly connected.
(こころと身体の健康は強く関連していると言われているんだ。)

a **physical** examination (健康診断)

▶ **physically** [fízɪkli] Adv. 物理的に ; 物質的に ; 身体的に

▶ **physics** [fízɪks] N[U] 物理学　　　▶ **physicist** [fízɪsɪst] N[C] 物理学者

▶ **physician** [fɪzíʃən] N[C] 内科医

1690 **physiological**
[fɪ̀ziəlάːdʒɪkəl]
□□□□□□

Adj.　生理学的な

My **physiological** responses to public speaking are breathing quickly and sweating,
so it's really obvious when I'm nervous.
(人前で話す時は息が荒くなったり汗かいたり生理的な反応が出るから、緊張してるとすぐバレちゃうんだ。)

▶ **physiologically** [fɪ̀ziəlάːdʒɪkli] Adv. 生理学的に

▶ **physiology** [fɪ̀ziάːlədʒi] N[U] 生理学　　▶ **physiologist** [fɪ̀ziάːlədʒɪst] N[C] 生理学者

1691 **mechanism**
[mékənɪzəm]
□□□□□□

N[C]　メカニズム、仕組み、構造

There are a few **mechanisms** that we can leverage to fix the economy, but the
longer we wait, the less effective they'll be.
(この悪い経済を立て直すのに使えるメカニズムはいくつかあるけど、待てば待つほど効果はなくなっていくよ。)

2 Although biology comprises a variety of complicated aspects of living organisms, there are a large number of unifying concepts which combine and synthesize them into a coherent, rational field.

生物学は、生物に関するさまざまな複雑な側面から成るが、そうした側面を結び付け統合し、まとまりのある合理的な分野にする統一概念が多数存在する。

1692 complicated
[kάːmpləkeɪ̯t̬ɪd]
□□□□□□

Adj. 複雑な

My relationship with Tomoki is pretty **complicated** at the moment, but hopefully it will sort itself out. （トモキと俺の関係は今結構複雑なんだけど、そのうち何とかなるといいな。）

▶ **complicate** [kάːmpləkeɪt] V[T] を複雑にする、面倒にする

I'll just keep quiet because I don't want to **complicate** things.
（物事を複雑にしたくないから僕はただ静かにしてるよ。）

▶ **complication** [kὰːmpləkéɪʃən] N[C/U] 面倒なこと

1693 aspect
[æspekt]
□□□□□□

N[C] 側面、局面、見方；（部屋や窓の）向き

There are so many interesting **aspects** to Georgia's personality.
（ジョージアの性格には面白いところがたくさんあるよ。）

1694 unify
[júːnəfaɪ]
□□□□□□

V[T] を統一する、統合する；一つになる

I wish somebody would **unify** all these different streaming services into one product.
（誰かこのバラバラのストリーミング配信サービス、一つに統合してくれないかなぁ。）

▶ **unification** [jùːnəfəkéɪʃən] N[U] 統一、統合

▶ **unity** [júːnət̬i] N[U] 団結；統合、統一性

The researcher said Korean **unification** could cost trillions of dollars.
（朝鮮統一には何兆ドルもかかる可能性があるってその研究者が言ってたよ。）

接頭語 uni- 「一つの」という意味の接頭語で、一つに（＝ uni）作る（＝ fy）から「〜を統一する」という意味になり、他には uniform（ユニフォーム）や union（連合）があります。

1695 combine
v. [kəmbáɪn]
N. [kάːmbaɪn]
□□□□□□

V[T] を（〜と）混ぜ合わせる、組み合わせる（with sth）

I really like how this chef **combines** different herbs and spices to make unique flavors.
（このシェフ、色んなハーブとスパイスを混ぜ合わせて独特な味を作り出すんだ。最高だよ。）

V[I] 結びつく、混じり合う　N[C] 企業連合

▶ **combination** N[C/U] 組み合わせ　N[C]（数字や文字の）組み合わせ
[kɑ̀:mbənéɪʃən]

■ in **combination** with sth（〜と組み合わせて）

Chemotherapy, **in combination with** other types of treatment, can contribute significantly to curing cancer.（化学療法はその他の種類の治療と組み合わせることで、がんの治療に大きく役立つよ。）

1696 **synthesize**
[sínθəsaɪz]
☐☐☐☐☐☐

V[T] を統合する、合成する

We have a lot of great ideas already, so it shouldn't take us long to **synthesize** them into a plan of attack.
（もう最高のアイディアがたくさんあるから、戦略に落とし込んでいくのにそんなに時間はかからないはずだよ。）

▶ **synthesis** [sínθəsɪs] N[U]（化学の）合成　N[C/U] 統合、総合

▶ **synthetic** [sɪnθétɪk] Adj. 合成の

▶ **synthesizer** [sínθəsaɪzər] N[C] シンセサイザー

▶ **photosynthesis** [fòʊt̬oʊsínθəsɪs] N[U] 光合成

1697 **coherent**
[koʊhírənt]
☐☐☐☐☐☐

Adj. まとまりのある、首尾一貫した、理路整然とした

Kevin's always really **coherent**, so I'm a bit surprised that you found him unclear.
（ケヴィンっていつも理路整然としてるから、君が彼の言うことがはっきり分からなかっただなんてちょっと驚き。）

▶ **coherently** [koʊhírəntli] Adv. 首尾一貫して、理路整然と

▶ **coherence** [koʊhírəns] N[U] 一貫性

I can't believe you anymore. There is no **coherence** between what you're saying and what you're doing.（君のことはもう信じられない。言ってることとやってることに一貫性がないもん。）

1698 **rational**
[rǽʃənəl]
☐☐☐☐☐☐

Adj. 合理的な、理性的な

Tony's decisions are always **rational** and logical, but sometimes I think they're a bit harsh.
（トニーの決断はいつも合理的で論理的なんだけど、たまにちょっとキツい感じがあると思う。）

▶ **rationally** [rǽʃənəli] Adv. 合理的に、理性的に

▶ **rationalize** [rǽʃənəlaɪz] V[I/T]（〜を）正当化する、合理化する

I can't believe that you're still trying to **rationalize** your decision to plagiarize my essay.
（お前が俺のエッセイを盗作しようと思ったことを未だに正当化しようとしてるなんて信じられないよ。）

▶ **rationalization** [rǽʃənələzéɪʃən] N[C/U] 正当化、合理化

▶ **rationale** [rǽʃənǽl] N[C/U] 論理的根拠

What's the **rationale** behind it?（その論理的根拠は何？）

3 These concepts include, for example, that cells are the basic building blocks of organisms, genes are the fundamental units of heredity, and evolution is the engine that spurs and disrupts the creation of different species and contributes to their extinction.

こうした概念には、例えば、細胞は生物の基本的な構成要素であること、遺伝子は遺伝に関する基本単位であること、進化はさまざまな種の誕生を促進・妨害する一方で種の絶滅に寄与する原動力になっていることなどが含まれる。

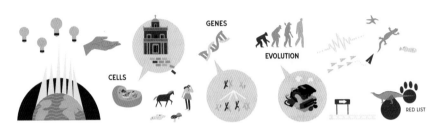

1699 cell
[sel]
☐☐☐☐☐☐

N[C] 細胞；独房、小部屋；携帯電話　= mobile [móʊbəl] <英>

That video bored me so much that I think I lost brain **cells** watching it.
(あの動画つまんなすぎて見てる間に脳細胞死んだわ。)

▶ **cellular** [séljələr] Adj. 細胞の；携帯電話の

The biologist is studying the genetic qualities of bees at a **cellular** level.
(その生物学者は蜂の遺伝形質を細胞レベルで研究しているんだ。)

1700 building block
[bíldɪŋ blɑ́ːk]
☐☐☐☐☐☐

N[C] 構成単位；積み木

Your marks at university are a **building block** towards you having a successful career.
(大学での成績は思い通りのキャリアを築く上での要素になるよ。)

1701 unit
[júːnɪt]
☐☐☐☐☐☐

N[C] 単位；単元；部隊；部門

Why are there so many different **units** of measurement? So confusing.
(なんでこんなに色んな測定の単位があるの？めっちゃこんがらがる。)

A calorie is a **unit** of energy.（カロリーはエネルギーの単位だよ。）

an intensive care **unit**（集中治療室）

1702 **heredity**
[hərédəti]

N[U]　遺伝、遺伝的形質

Do you think we'll ever figure out if **heredity** or nurture has more influence over what somebody becomes?
(遺伝と教育のどっちの方が人格に影響するのか、いつか分かるようになると思う？)

heredity vs **genetics**　どちらも「遺伝」という意味ですが、厳密に言うと heredity は親から子へと受け継がれる性質のことを意味し、これを研究する学問分野のことを genetics と呼びます。

▶ **hereditary** [hərédəteri] Adj. (次の世代に) 遺伝する、遺伝性の

Some genetic disorders are not **hereditary**.
(遺伝性疾患には次の世代に遺伝しないものもある。)

1703 **spur**
[spɜːr]

V[T]　を促進する、に拍車をかける　N[C]　拍車；(行動の) 刺激

I think a corporate tax cut is needed in Japan to **spur** corporate investment.
(私は、日本の法人税削減は会社の投資の促進のために必要だと思うな。)

1704 **disrupt**
[dɪsrʌ́pt]

V[T]　を妨害する、中断させる、混乱させる

Drinking tea at night seems to **disrupt** my sleep, so I've started drinking milk instead.
(夜にお茶飲むと睡眠に良くなさそうだから、代わりに牛乳を飲み始めたんだ。)

Some people say that manufacturing is one of the industries that will soon be **disrupted** by artificial intelligence.
(製造業は人工知能によって真っ先に混乱が起きる産業の一つだと言う人もいるんだ。)

▶ **disruption** [dɪsrʌ́pʃən] N[C/U] 妨害、中断、混乱

▶ **disruptive** [dɪsrʌ́ptɪv] Adj. 破壊的な、混乱をもたらす、
　　　　　　　　　　　　　　　　(既存の技術などを打ち砕くほど) 革命的な

The iPhone was **disruptive** to the entire world of technology when it was first released.
(iPhone は初めてリリースされた時、世界のテクノロジー業界全体に破壊的革命を引き起こしたんだ。)

a **disruptive** technology (破壊的技術 (従来の技術に取って代わり、産業を激しく動かすような新技術のこと))

▶ **disruptively** [dɪsrʌ́ptɪvli] Adv. 支障をきたすほど、破壊的に

▶ **disruptor** [dɪsrʌ́ptər] N[C] 破壊するもの・人

1705 **species**
[spíːʃiːz]

N[C]　(生物の) 種 (複数形も species)

I wonder how many **species** of birds there are.
(鳥って何種類くらいいるんだろうなぁ。)

4 Out of these, evolution and the connected notion of natural selection are among the endlessly contentious areas of biology, as they contradict the basic doctrines of many major religions.

この中で、進化とそれに関連した自然選択の概念は、多くの主要宗教の基本的教義と矛盾していることから、生物学の中でも論争が尽きない分野の一つになっている。

NATURAL SELECTION

HOLY BIBLE

1706 **evolution**
[evəlúːʃən]
☐☐☐☐☐☐

N[U]　進化；発展、進展

It's been a privilege to witness the **evolution** and growth of this team over the last few years.（ここ数年、このチームの進化と成長を見させていただいて光栄です。）

Darwin's theory of **evolution**（ダーウィンの進化論）

▶ **evolve**　V[I]（～から / ～に）進化する、発展する（from/into sth）
[ɪvɑːlv]　　V[T] を進化させる、発展させる

Did humans **evolve** from apes, or did we get here some other way?
（人間って類人猿から進化したの？それとも何か違う形でこうなったのかな？）

▶ **evolutionary** [evəlúːʃəneri] Adj. 進化の、進化論的な

1707 **connected**
[kənéktɪd]
☐☐☐☐☐☐

Adj.（～と）関連した、結びついた、関係している（with/to sth）

It says my laptop is **connected** to Wi-Fi, but I have no internet access. What's going on?
（僕のノートパソコン、Wi-Fi に繋がってるって出るんだけど、ネット繋がんないんだよね。どうなってんだろ？）

▶ **connect**　V[I] 結びつく、繋がる
[kənékt]　　V[T] を（～と）結び付ける、繋ぐ（with/to sth）

▶ **connection** [kənékʃən] N[C] 関連、関係；接続便　N[U] 接続　N[P] コネ【-s】

■ **in connection with** sth（～に関連して）

The police arrested a 22-year-old man **in connection with** the murder.
（警察は殺人に関わったとして 22 歳の男を逮捕した。）

▶ **connective** [kənéktɪv] Adj. 連結した

connected vs **linked**　どちらも「関連した、結び付いた」という意味で、状況に応じて一方が好まれることはありますが、基本的に同じ意味を持ち、大きな違いはありません。

1708 **endlessly**
[éndləsli]
☐☐☐☐☐☐

Adv. 果てしなく、終わりなく

Brian has a tendency to talk **endlessly** about really pointless stuff.
（ブライアンってどうでもいいことをずっと話す傾向があるよな。）

▶ **endless** [éndləs] Adj. 果てしない、終わりのない

I have an **endless** number of emails that I need to reply to today.
（今日は果てしない量の返信しないといけないメールがあるんだ。）

1709 **contentious**
[kənténʃəs]
☐☐☐☐☐☐

Adj. 議論を引き起こす；論争好きな

We had a **contentious** relationship, so we decided to break up.
（付き合ってるとき喧嘩が多かったから別れることにしたんだ。）

▶ **contend**   V[I]（〜のために）争う（for sth）
[kənténd]   V[T] だと主張する（that + sentence）

I've applied for the graduate position, but I'm not too confident about it because I'm **contending** with a lot of highly qualified people.
（その新卒用のポジションに応募したんだけど、すごい有能な人たちと競争してるからそんなに自信ないよ。）

▶ **contention** [kənténʃən] N[U] 論争、議論 N[C] 主張

1710 **area**
[ériə]
☐☐☐☐☐☐

N[C] 分野、領域；地域、地区 **N[C/U]** 面積

You should be humble when you are outside your **area** of expertise.
（自分の専門分野外にいるときは謙虚にしてた方がいいよ。）

1711 **contradict**
[kὰ:ntrədíkt]
☐☐☐☐☐☐

V[I/T]（〜と）矛盾する；（〜に）反論する、逆らう

■ **contradict** oneself（前と矛盾したことを言う）

You've just **contradicted yourself**.（前に言ってたことと矛盾してるよ。）

You shouldn't **contradict** your boss.（上司に逆らわない方がいいよ。）

▶ **contradiction** N[C/U] 矛盾 ▶ **contradictory** Adj. 矛盾した
[kὰ:ntrədíkʃən]   [kὰ:ntrədíktəri]

His explanations were full of **contradictions**, so I could easily tell he was lying.
（彼の説明は矛盾だらけだったから、嘘ついてるって簡単に分かったよ。）

You want to be famous, but you don't want to do social media? That's a bit **contradictory**.（有名になりたいけど、SNS はやりたくないって？ちょっと矛盾してるよ。）

1712 **doctrine**
[dá:ktrɪn]
☐☐☐☐☐☐

N[C/U]（宗教の）教義、（政治や学問の）主義、学説；（外交などの）政策

The Monroe **Doctrine** is an old U.S. policy opposing European colonialism.
（モンロー主義はヨーロッパ諸国の植民地主義に反対する昔のアメリカの政策のことだよ。）

laissez-faire **doctrine**（自由競争主義）

▶ **doctrinal** [dá:ktrɪnəl] Adj. 教義に関する

▶ **indoctrinate** [ɪndá:ktrəneɪt] V[T] に（〜を）教えこむ、洗脳する（in/with sth）

I really hate teachers who try to **indoctrinate** their students with their personal beliefs.
（自分の個人的な信条を学生に教えこもうとする先生本当に嫌いだわ。）

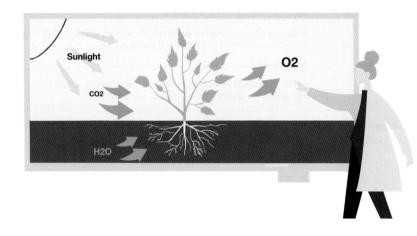

Teacher (W) Your assignment this semester is to devise a relatively straightforward experiment to test how sensitive different types of plants are to sunlight. The experiment should therefore test the quantity of byproducts that are generated from plants absorbing sunlight. The deadline for the first draft is the end of next month.

Student (M) Just to clarify, we should test the efficiency of photosynthesis in different plants?

Teacher (W) Correct. You'll also need to be able to reproduce the results in order to form conclusions free of bias, so use the enclosed greenhouse area. Also, if you manage to develop methods to measure the impact of sunlight, pollination, and fertilization on plants blooming, you might even receive an award in the science competition.

Student (M) Haha. First and foremost, I'll try to make sure the plants survive. I hope they can tolerate some pretty harsh treatment.

教師 (女性) みなさんの今学期の課題は、異なる種類の植物が日光に対してどれくらい敏感であるかをテストする、比較的簡単な実験を考案してもらうことです。なので、実験は日光を吸収している植物から生まれる副産物の量を調べるものになりますよ。最初の下書きの締め切りは来月末です。

生徒 (男性) ちょっと明確にしておきたいんですけど、それって異なる植物の光合成の効率性をテストするってことですか?

教師 (女性) その通りです。加えて、偏りのない結論に達するために、結果は再現性のあるものでなければなりません。なので、あの密閉された温室エリアを使用するようにしてくださいね。あと、もし日光、受粉、そして受精が植物の開花に与える影響の測定方法を考え出せたら、科学コンテストで賞をもらうことだってできるかもしれませんよ。

生徒 (男性) はは。まずは植物が枯れずにちゃんと生き残るように頑張ります。かなり厳しい扱いに耐えられると良いですけどね。

1713 **semester**
[səméstər]

N[C] 学期　= **term** [tɜːrm]

the first/second **semester**（前 / 後期）

1714 **straightforward**
[strèɪtfɔ́ːrwərd]

Adj. 簡単な、明快な；率直な、正直な

▶ **straightforwardly** [strèɪtfɔ́ːrwərdli] Adv. 簡単に；率直に

▶ **straightforwardness** [strèɪtfɔ́ːrwərdnəs] N[U] 簡単さ；率直さ

1715 **plant**
[plænt]

N[C] 植物、苗；工場　V[T] を植える

▶ **planting** [plǽntɪŋ] N[C/U] 植え付け、種まき

1716 **byproduct**
[báɪprʌ̀dəkt]

N[C] 副産物

Molasses is a **byproduct** of sugarcane refinement.
（糖蜜はサトウキビの精製から作られる副産物なんだ。）

1717 **absorb**
[əbzɔ́ːrb]

V[T] を吸収する；をとりこにする、没頭させる

▶ **absorbed** [əbzɔ́ːrbd] Adj.（～に）没頭した（in sth）

My children are so **absorbed** in their iPads.（うちの子たち、iPad にものすごく夢中なの。）

▶ **absorption** [əbzɔ́ːrpʃən] N[U] 吸収；没頭

1718 **deadline**
[dédlaɪn]

N[C] 締め切り、期日　= **due date** [dúːdeɪt]

What's the **deadline**?（締め切りいつ？）　= When's the **deadline**?

1719 **clarify**
[klérəfaɪ]

V[T] を明確にする、はっきりさせる

just to **clarify**（ちょっと明確にしておきたいんだけど）

▶ **clarification** [klèrəfəkéɪʃən] N[C/U]（話を明確にするための）説明、明確化

1720 **photosynthesis**
[fòʊṭoʊsínθəsɪs]

N[U] 光合成

▶ **photosynthetic** [fòʊṭoʊsɪnθéṭɪk] Adj. 光合成の

▶ **photosynthesize** [fòʊṭoʊsínθəsaɪz] V[I/T]（～を）光合成する

1721 **reproduce**
[rìːprədúːs]

V[T]（実験結果など）を再現する；（デザインなど）を複製する　V[I] 繁殖する

▶ **reproducible** [rìːprədúːsəbəl] Adj. 再現性のある　▶ **reproductive** [rìːprədʌ́ktɪv] Adj. 繁殖の

▶ **reproduction** [rìːprədʌ́kʃən] N[U] 複製；繁殖 N[C] 複製品

1722 **bias**
[báɪəs]

N[S/U] 偏り、偏見、バイアス　V[T] に偏見を持たせる

≒ **prejudice** [prédʒədɪs] 偏見、先入観 / に偏見を持たせる

▶ **biased** [báɪəst] Adj. 偏った、偏見のある　↔ **unbiased** [ʌnbáɪəst] 偏りのない、公平な

bias vs **prejudice**　どちらも「偏見」という意味がありますが、bias は必ずしもネガティブではないのに対し、prejudice はほとんどの場合にネガティブなイメージがあります。

1723 enclosed
[ɪnklóʊzd]

Adj. 密閉された、囲まれた；同封された

▶ **enclose** [ɪnklóʊz] V[T] を囲む；を同封する

▶ **enclosure** [ɪnklóʊʒər] N[C] 囲まれた場所　N[U] 囲むこと

1724 pollination
[pà:lənéɪʃən]

N[U] 受粉、授粉

▶ **pollen** [pá:lən] N[U] 花粉　▶ **pollinate** [pá:ləneɪt] V[T] に授粉する

1725 fertilization
[fɜ:rt̬ələzéɪʃən]

N[U] 受精；（土壌の）肥沃化

▶ **fertilize** [fɜ́:rt̬əlaɪz] V[T] を受精させる；を肥沃にする

▶ **fertilizer** [fɜ́:rt̬əlaɪzər] N[C/U] 肥料

▶ **fertile** [fɜ́:rt̬əl] Adj. 繁殖力のある；肥沃な　▶ **fertility** [fərtíləti] N[U] 繁殖力；肥沃さ

1726 bloom
[blu:m]

V[I] 開花する、咲く　N[C/U] 花

come into **bloom**（花が咲き始める）　in full **bloom**（満開の）

▶ **blossom** [blá:səm] N[C/U] 花　V[I]（大規模に）開花する

1727 receive
[rɪsíːv]

V[T] をもらう、受け取る；を迎え入れる

▶ **received** [rɪsíːvd] Adj.（考えなどが）一般に受け入れられた

▶ **reception** [rɪsépʃən] N[S] 反応　N[U] 歓迎　N[C] 歓迎会

▶ **receipt** [rɪsíːt] N[U] 受け取ること、受領　N[C] レシート、領収書

1728 award
[əwɔ́:rd]

N[C] 賞、賞品；賠償金　V[T]（賞など）を与える、授与する

an **award** ceremony（授賞式）

V[T]（競技でペナルティなど）を与える

1729 survive
[sərváɪv]

V[I/T]（〜を）生き残る、生き抜く

Barely **surviving**.（（忙しさなどの中）ぎりぎり生きてるよ。）

1730 tolerate
[tá:ləreɪt]

V[T] に耐える、を許容する、大目に見る

▶ **tolerance** [tá:lərəns] N[U] 寛大さ　▶ **tolerantly** [tá:lərəntli] Adv. 寛大に

▶ **tolerable** [tá:lərəbəl] Adj. 耐えられる、我慢できる

↔ **intolerable** [ɪntá:lərəbəl] Adj. 耐えられない

▶ **tolerant** [tá:lərənt] Adj. 耐性のある；寛大な　↔ **intolerant** [ɪntá:lərənt] Adj. 寛容でない

1731 harsh
[hɑ:rʃ]

Adj. 厳しい、過酷な

■ be **harsh** on sb（〜に厳しい、きつく当たる）　= be **hard** on sb

Don't **be** so **harsh** on me.（私にそんなに強く当たらないで。）

▶ **harshly** [hɑ́:rʃli] Adv. 厳しく　▶ **harshness** [hɑ́:rʃnəs] N[U] 厳しさ、過酷さ

⟳ CH. 16, 21, 25, 29, 32, 35

神経科学
Neuroscience

Neuroscience is the study of the nervous system consisting of the brain, spinal cord, and peripheral nerves. This field helps us better understand learning, memory retention, cognition, behavior, and consciousness.

Initially, the heart was viewed as the seat of consciousness and intelligence due to a lack of adequate means to obtain and enlarge knowledge of how the brain functions.

However, this kind of misunderstanding dissipated with the passage of time, and over the past two centuries, great strides have been made in neuroscience owing to the enhancement of research techniques and understanding of nerve impulses.

As a consequence, neuroscience today plays a pivotal role both clinically and academically, yet further research is required to comprehend the intricate world of the nervous system in its entirety.

1 Neuroscience **is the study of the** nervous **system consisting of the** brain, spinal **cord, and** peripheral **nerves. This field helps us better understand learning, memory** retention, cognition, **behavior, and** consciousness.

神経科学は、脳、脊髄、および末梢神経から成る神経系の研究である。この分野は、学習、記憶維持、認知、行動、意識についての理解を深めるのに役立っている。

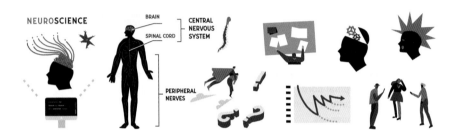

1732 neuroscience
[nùroʊsáɪəns]
☐☐☐☐☐☐

N[U] 神経科学

I started studying **neuroscience** to understand the brain a bit better.
(脳のことをもうちょっとよく理解したくて、神経科学の勉強を始めたんだ。)

▶ **neuroscientist** [nùroʊsáɪəntəst] N[C] 神経科学者

1733 nervous
[nə́:rvəs]
☐☐☐☐☐☐

Adj. 神経の；神経質な；緊張した、不安な

I'm only **nervous** around Noah because I really like him.
(ノアのこと本当に好きだから彼のそばにいるときだけは緊張するんだ。)

the **nervous** system（神経系）　　have a **nervous** breakdown（精神的に病む）

▶ **nervously** [nə́:rvəsli] Adv. 緊張して、不安な様子で

I was **nervously** waiting for him because I've been stood up so many times.
(これまで何回もドタキャンされてるから不安な気持ちで彼のこと待ってたよ。)

▶ **nerve** [nɜ:rv] N[C] 神経　N[U] 勇気

the optic **nerve**（視神経）　　**nerve** palsy/paralysis（神経麻痺）

■ get on sb's **nerves**（〜をイラっとさせる、〜の気に障る）

Stop shaking your legs! It**'s getting on my nerves**.
(貧乏ゆすりやめて。イラっとするから。)

■ have a/the **nerve** to do（〜する勇気がある）

I don't **have the nerve to** tell her that she has a nose hair sticking out.
(彼女に鼻毛が出てるなんて言う勇気ないよ。)

1734 brain
[breɪn]
☐☐☐☐☐☐

N[C] 脳、頭脳　N[S]（組織における）頭脳的な存在【the -s】

My **brain** hurts from all this thinking, so I'm going to take a break.
(色々考えて頭が痛いから、ちょっと休むよ。)

He's the **brains** of this organization. （彼はこの組織の頭脳的な存在なんだ。）

have **brains**/a good **brain**
（頭が良い、知能が高い）

pick sb's **brain** (about sth)
（〜に（〜について）聞く、知恵を借りる）

▶ **no-brainer** [nòʊbréɪnər] N[S] 考えるまでもないこと、当たり前のこと

Of course I'm coming to lunch. It's a **no-brainer**.
（もちろんランチには行くよ。当たり前じゃん。）

1735 **spinal**
[spáɪnl]
☐☐☐☐☐☐

Adj. 脊柱の、脊髄の

■ the **spinal** cord （脊髄）

It's not easy to find a cure for **spinal cord** injuries.
（脊髄損傷の治し方を見つけるのは簡単じゃないよ。）

▶ **spine** [spaɪn] N[C] 脊柱、背骨；とげ

cactus **spines** （サボテンのとげ）

1736 **peripheral**
[pərífərəl]
☐☐☐☐☐☐

Adj. 末梢の、周辺の；重要でない **N[C]** 周辺機器

He used to be crucial to the team, but he's become a bit **peripheral** over the last year or so.
（昔は彼はチームにとって不可欠な存在だったんだけど、最近はあんまり重要じゃなくなってきたんだよなぁ。）

▶ **periphery** [pərífəri] N[C] 周辺；末梢

There are so many homeless people on the **periphery** of this town.
（この街の周辺にはホームレスがものすごいたくさんいるんだ。）

1737 **retention**
[rɪténʃən]
☐☐☐☐☐☐

N[U] 維持、保持；（水分や熱の）保持力；記憶力

My memory **retention** is really bad late at night, so I try to study more during the day.
（夜遅くになると記憶の定着がすごい悪くなるから、昼に多く勉強するようにしてるよ。）

▶ **retain** [rɪtéɪn] V[T] を維持する、保つ

How do you **retain** so much knowledge? I can never remember anything the lecturer says.
（どうやってそんなに知識を維持してるの？私は講師の言ってること全然覚えられないんだけど。）

1738 **cognition**
[kɑːgníʃən]
☐☐☐☐☐☐

N[U] 認知、認識

I'm not sure if coffee actually improves my **cognition**, or whether it's just a placebo.
（コーヒーって本当に認知力をアップしてくれるのか、それともただのプラシーボ効果なのか、どっちなんだろう。）

▶ **cognitive** [kɑːgnəṭɪv] Adj. 認知の、認識の

cognitive functions （認知機能）

▶ **cognizant** [kɑːgnɪzənt] Adj. (〜を) 認知して、気付いて (of sth)

Not many people are **cognizant** of the fact that we're going to face a huge economic crisis.
（私たちがものすごい経済危機に直面しようとしていることに気付いている人はあんまりいないんだ。）

2

Initially, the heart was viewed as the seat of consciousness and intelligence due to a lack of adequate means to obtain and enlarge knowledge of how the brain functions.

最初の頃は、脳機能に関する知識を獲得・拡大するための適切な手段が不足していたため、心臓が意識と知性の源であると考えられていた。

1739 initially

[ɪníʃəli]

☐☐☐☐☐☐

Adv. 最初は、当初は

I didn't realize it **initially**, but I think I started falling in love with Lucas pretty soon after meeting him. (最初は気づかなかったけど、会ってわりとすぐルーカスのこと好きになり始めてたと思う。)

▶ **initial** [ɪníʃəl] Adj. 最初の、初めの　N[C] イニシャル

The **initial** growth of my subscriber numbers was fast, but it slowed down all of a sudden. (最初の方は登録者数が勢いよく成長してたんだけど、急にそれがゆっくりになっちゃったんだ。)

▶ **initiate** [ɪníʃieɪt] V[T] を開始する；に（初歩的なこと）を教える（into sth）

I was **initiated** into swimming when I was two years old. (私は2歳の時に水泳を教わったんだ。)

1740 seat

[siːt]

☐☐☐☐☐☐

N[C] （活動の）中心地、所在地；席；議席　**V[T]** を座らせる

The Australian **seat** of government is in Canberra. (オーストラリアの政府の中心地はキャンベラだよ。)

Please be **seated**. (どうぞお掛けください。)　**seat** oneself (座る)

1741 consciousness

[kɑ́ːnʃəsnəs]

☐☐☐☐☐☐

N[U] 意識　⟷ **unconsciousness** [ʌnkɑ́ːnʃəsnəs] 無意識

James lost **consciousness** after only one drink yesterday. (ジェームスは昨日たった一杯飲んだだけで意識飛んじゃったんだよ。)

▶ **conscious** Adj. 意識のある、意識的な；（〜に）気付いている（of sth）
[kɑ́ːnʃəs]

She's **conscious** of the fact that her intelligence makes her intimidating. (彼女は頭の良さが自分を威圧的に見せていることを自覚してるよ。)

⟷ **unconscious** [ʌnkɑ́ːnʃəs] 意識不明の、無意識的な；気付いていない

He was **unconscious** for a few days, but he's completely fine now.
（彼は数日間意識不明だったんだけど、今は全然大丈夫。）

▶ **consciously** [ká:nʃəsli] Adv. 意識的に、意図的に

Friendship generally isn't something you can **consciously** make happen.
（友情って普通は意識的に作れるものじゃないよ。）

↔ **unconsciously** [ʌnká:nʃəsli] 無意識的に

1742 **adequate**
[ǽdəkwət]
☐☐☐☐☐☐

Adj. 適切な、十分な；まずまずの

Cindy's work is **adequate**, but I think it has the potential to be exceptional.
（シンディーの仕事は十分ではあるんだけど、格別なものにできるポテンシャルはあると思うんだ。）

↔ **inadequate** [ɪnǽdəkwət] 不適切な、不十分な

▶ **adequately** Adv. 適切に、十分に   ↔ **inadequately** 不十分に
  [ǽdəkwətli]   [ɪnǽdəkwətli]

▶ **adequacy** [ǽdəkwəsi] N[U] 適切さ、十分であること、妥当性

adequate vs **sufficient** adequate は「かろうじて十分である、なんとか足りている」というニュアンスを持つことがありますが、どちらも「十分な」という意味で、基本的には普段の使用で大きな違いはありません。

1743 **means**
[mi:nz]
☐☐☐☐☐☐

N[C] 手段、方法（複数形も means）

I don't have the financial **means** to buy a new computer right now.
（今は新しいパソコンを買うようなお金は無いんだ。）

a **means** of communication   by **means** of sth
（コミュニケーションの手段）   （～によって、～を用いて）

1744 **obtain**
[əbtéɪn]
☐☐☐☐☐☐

V[T] を獲得する、手に入れる、得る

I need to **obtain** a copy of my birth certificate, but I don't really know how.
（出生証明書を手に入れないといけないんだけど、どうやって手に入れるかよく分かんないんだよね。）

▶ **obtainable** [əbtéɪnəbəl] Adj. 手に入れることができる、得られる

↔ **unobtainable** [ʌnəbtéɪnəbəl] 入手不可能な

Australian visas are **obtainable** online. （オーストラリアのビザはオンラインで手に入るよ。）

1745 **enlarge**
[ɪnlá:rdʒ]
☐☐☐☐☐☐

V[T] を拡大する、大きくする   V[I] 拡大する

It cost a lot to **enlarge** all my wedding photos, but it was worth it.
（結婚式の写真を拡大するのにはすごいお金がかかったけど、その価値はあったよ。）

▶ **enlargement** [ɪnlá:rdʒmənt] N[S/U] 拡大、増大 N[C] 引き伸ばし写真

3 However, this kind of misunderstanding dissipated with the passage of time, and over the past two centuries, great strides have been made in neuroscience owing to the enhancement of research techniques and understanding of nerve impulses.

しかし、こうした誤解は時間がたつとともになくなり、この2世紀で研究技術が向上し、神経衝撃の働きが分かってきたことで、神経科学は飛躍的に進歩した。

THIS KIND OF
MISUNDERSTANDING

1746 misunderstanding [mìsʌndərstǽndɪŋ] □□□□□□
N[C/U] 誤解　**N[C]** （小さな）意見の相違、揉め事

It's obvious that it was just a big **misunderstanding**, so I don't understand why we're still arguing about it.
（あれは明らかにただの大きな誤解だったんだし、なんでまだ喧嘩してるのか理解できない。）

▶ **misunderstand** [mìsʌndərstǽnd] V[I/T] （〜を）誤解する

Sorry, I bought flour instead of flowers because I completely **misunderstood** what you wanted.　（ごめん、お花じゃなくて小麦粉買っちゃった。欲しいもの完全に誤解してた。）

1747 dissipate [dísəpeɪt] □□□□□□
V[I] （煙や感情などが）消える、散る　**V[T]** を散らす

I'm going to wait for the crowds to **dissipate** before I line up for a drink.
（ドリンクの列に並ぶ前に人がいなくなるの待つことにする。）

▶ **dissipated** [dísəpeɪtɪd] Adj. 道楽にふける

▶ **dissipation** [dìsəpéɪʃən] N[U] 消散；道楽

1748 stride [straɪd] □□□□□□
N[C] 進歩、向上；大股の一歩、歩幅　**V[I]** 大股で歩く

Making your **stride** shorter when you run might improve your speed.
（走る時の歩幅を短くするとスピードが上がるかもしれないよ。）

■ take sth in **stride** （〜を難なく切り抜ける）

I admire how he just **takes** everything **in stride**.
（彼って何でも難なく切り抜けるからすごいよなぁ。）

make **strides** in sth/to do （〜において大躍進を遂げる）

1749 owing to
[óʊɪŋ tù:]
☐☐☐☐☐☐

Prep. 〜のために、〜のおかげで

I worked hard, but my success is also **owing to** a lot of luck and support from others.
（自分でも一生懸命頑張ったけど、私の成功はたくさんの運と周りからのサポートのおかげでもあるんだ。）

1750 enhancement
[ɪnhǽnsmənt]
☐☐☐☐☐☐

N[U] 向上、改善　**N[C]** 改良

Let's make some **enhancements** to our website to increase the number of visitors.
（訪問者を増やすために私たちのウェブサイトをいくらか改良しようよ。）

▶ **enhance** [ɪnhǽns] V[T] を高める

This course helped me **enhance** my ability to think logically.
（このコースは論理的に考える能力を高めるのに役立ったよ。）

1751 technique
[tekníːk]
☐☐☐☐☐☐

N[C] 技術、技法　**N[U]** テクニック、技量

Messi's dribbling **technique** is incredible!（メッシのドリブルテクニックすごいな。）

▶ **technical** [téknɪkəl] Adj. 技術的な、専門的な

Stop using so many **technical** terms! You're just showing off, aren't you?
（そんなに専門用語ばっかり使わないでよ。見せびらかしたいだけでしょ？）

▶ **technically** [téknɪkli] Adv. 技術的に、専門的に；厳密に（言えば）

■ **technically** speaking（厳密に言えば）

Technically speaking, watermelons are not fruit.
（厳密に言えばスイカは果物じゃないよ。）

▶ **technician** [tekníʃən] N[C] 技術者、技師

1752 impulse
[ímpʌls]
☐☐☐☐☐☐

N[C/U] （物理的な）衝撃；衝動

■ **on impulse**（衝動的に）　　**impulse** buying（衝動買い）

This shirt was 80% off, so I bought it **on impulse**.
（このシャツは 80% オフだったから、衝動買いしちゃった。）

▶ **impulsive** [ɪmpʌ́lsɪv] Adj. 衝動的な

▶ **impulsively** [ɪmpʌ́lsɪvli] Adv. 衝動的に

Acting **impulsively** without a plan is often a bad idea.
（大体の場合、計画無しで衝動的な行動をするのは良くない。）

▶ **impulsiveness** [ɪmpʌ́lsɪvnəs] N[U] 衝動性

4 As a consequence, neuroscience today plays a pivotal role both clinically and academically, yet further research is required to comprehend the intricate world of the nervous system in its entirety.

その結果、今日、神経科学は臨床的にも学術的にも重要な役割を果たしているが、複雑に入り組んだ神経系の世界を全て理解するには、さらなる研究が必要だ。

YET

NERVOUS SYSTEM

1753 **consequence**
[ká:nsəkwəns]
☐☐☐☐☐☐

N[C] 結果 **N[U]** 重要性

I lost a lot of money as a **consequence** of speculative trading.
(投機的なトレードの結果ものすごく大損した。)

as a **consequence** (of sth) ((〜の) 結果として)

▶ **consequent** Adj. 結果として起こる ▶ **consequently** Adv. 結果として、したがって
[ká:nsəkwənt]   [ká:nsəkwəntli]

1754 **pivotal**
[pívətəl]
☐☐☐☐☐☐

Adj. 極めて重要な、中心的な、中枢の

You're really **pivotal** to the team, so you need to look after yourself.
(君はチームにとって本当に中心的な存在なんだから、自分のことちゃんと大事にしないとだめだよ。)

a **pivotal** moment (極めて重要な時)

▶ **pivot** N[C] 中枢；旋回軸 V[I] (〜を中心に) 回る (on/upon sth) V[T] を回転させる
[pívət]

1755 **clinically**
[klínɪkli]
☐☐☐☐☐☐

Adv. 臨床的に

Some doctors say that a person's brain continues to work for a few hours even after they are declared **clinically** dead.
(医者の中には人の脳は医学的に死亡していると宣言された後でも数時間は動き続けているという人もいるんだ。)

▶ **clinical** [klínɪkəl] Adj. 臨床の、病床の

■ a **clinical** trial (治験)

I joined a **clinical trial** to help discover a cure for cancer.
(がんの治療法発見に役立ちたくて治験に参加したんだ。)

▶ **clinic** [klínɪk] N[C] 診療所、クリニック

1756 yet
[jet]
☐☐☐☐☐☐

Cnj. しかし、それにもかかわらず、それでも

I like most kinds of seafood, **yet** I hate scallops.
（大体のシーフードは好きなんですけど、ホタテは嫌いなんです。）

Adv. まだ；（疑問文で）もう；いっそう

Don't give up. We may **yet** win.（あきらめないで。まだ勝つ可能性はあるよ。）

■ have **yet** to do（まだ〜していない）

I **have yet to** book my flight.（まだ飛行機は予約していません。）

■ **yet** again（またしても、またまた）

My laptop has frozen **yet again**.（パソコンがまたまたフリーズしたんだけど。）

not **yet**（まだだよ、まだです）

yet vs **but** どちらも「しかし」という意味ですが、yet の方がフォーマルな表現です。また、yet の方が意外性を強調する傾向があります。

1757 required
[rɪkwáɪərd]
☐☐☐☐☐☐

Adj. 必要とされる、必須の

Can I leave this meeting a bit earlier if I'm not **required**?
（もし私のこと必要ないならこのミーティングちょっと早く出てもいいかな？）

▶ **require** [rɪkwáɪr] V[T] を必要とする、要求する

■ **require** sth/sb to do（〜に〜することを要求する）

Living abroad **requires** you **to** make a lot of effort in many ways, but it's worth it.
（海外に住むと色んな意味で多くの努力が必要になるけど、それだけの価値があるよ。）

▶ **requirement** [rɪkwáɪrmənt] N[C] 必要条件、要件、要求

Being CPA qualified is one of the **requirements** for working at an accounting firm in Japan.
（日本では公認会計士資格を持っていることが会計事務所で働く上での要件の一つなんだ。）

1758 intricate
[íntrəkət]
☐☐☐☐☐☐

Adj. 複雑な、込み入った

I love how **intricate** the patterns are on this shirt.
（このシャツ、柄がすごい複雑なところが大好きなんだよね。）

▶ **intricately** [íntrəkətli] Adv. 複雑に

You can find **intricately** carved pieces of art everywhere in Bali.
（バリ島のあちこちで複雑な彫刻作品を見つけることができるよ。）

▶ **intricacy** [íntrəkəsi] N[U] 複雑さ

1759 entirety
[ɪntáɪrəti]
☐☐☐☐☐☐

N[S] 全体、全部

■ in its **entirety**（全部、そっくりそのまま）

You can't judge the series without seeing it **in its entirety**.
（全部見ないでシリーズものを判断しちゃだめだよ。）

▶ **entire** [ɪntáɪr] Adj. 全体の、全部の　　▶ **entirely** [ɪntáɪrli] Adv. 完全に、まったく

What?! Have you eaten the **entire** cake already?（え!?ケーキもう全部食べたの？）

Sensory words 5 senses
感覚を表す単語　　五感

Taste

Smell

Touch

Hearing

Vision

1760 taste
[teɪst]
☐☐☐☐☐☐

N[U] 味覚；（ファッションなどの）センス　　N[C/U] 味；好み、テイスト
V[I] （〜の）味がする (adjective)、（〜のような）味がする (like sth)
It **tastes** good!（おいしい！）　This **tastes** like chicken.（これ鶏肉みたいな味がするね。）
V[T] の味を感じる；を味見する；を味わう

▶ **tasty** [téɪsti] Adj. おいしい

1761 smell
[smel]
☐☐☐☐☐☐

N[U] 嗅覚　　N[C] におい　　V[I] （〜の）においがする (adjective/of sth)、
（〜のような）においがする (like sth)
You **smell** nice.（君、良いにおいするね。）
I **smell** of cigarettes because John wouldn't stop smoking next to me.
（ジョンが隣でタバコを吸うのをやめないから、僕までタバコのにおいがするんだ。）
These candles **smell** like freshly-baked cookies.
（このろうそく、焼き立てのクッキーみたいなにおいがするんだ。）

▶ **smelly** [sméli] Adj. とても臭い

1762 touch
[tʌtʃ]
☐☐☐☐☐☐

N[U] 触覚　　N[C] 軽く触れること；（細部の）仕上げ　　N[S] 感触
V[I/T] （〜に）さわる、触れる　　V[T] を感動させる

▶ **touchy** [tʌ́tʃi] Adj. タブーな、デリケートな
a **touchy** subject（タブーな話、触れられたくない話）

▶ **touching** [tʌ́tʃɪŋ] Adj. 感動的な

1763 hearing
[híːrɪŋ]
☐☐☐☐☐☐

N[U] 聴覚、聴力　　N[C] 公聴会

▶ **hear** [hɪr] V[I/T] （〜が）聞こえる、（〜を）聞く、耳にする
hear from sb（〜から連絡がある）

■ **hear** of sth/sb（〜のことを聞く）
Have you **heard of** Atsueigo?（Atsueigo って聞いたことある？）

■ **hear** about sth/sb（（ニュースや出来事などについて）〜のことを聞く）
Have you **heard about** the restaurant?（あのレストランのこと聞いた？）

hear of vs **hear about**　Have you heard of/about Atsu? はどちらも文法的には正しいですが、意味合いが違います。of の場合、「Atsu って人、聞いたことある？」という感じで、その人の存在を認知しているかを聞く表現です。一方 about を使うと、「Atsu のこと聞いた？」というように、その人に関する情報やニュースについて聞いたかを問う表現になります。

1764 vision
[víʒən]
□□□□□□

N[U] 視覚、視力   = sight [saɪt]   = eyesight [áɪsaɪt]

N[C] 展望、ビジョン

I have blurry **vision**. My eyes may be tired.（視界がぼやけてるんだ。目が疲れてるのかも。）

have good/bad **eyesight**（視力が良い / 悪い）

▶ **envision** [ɪnvíʒən] V[T] を心に描く、想像する

▶ **visionary** [víʒəneri] N[C] 先見の明のある人   Adj. 先見の明のある、洞察力のある

 Taste and smell（味覚と嗅覚）

This is + (really/very/so/pretty/quite/a bit) + sensory word

1765 sweet
[swi:t]
□□□□□□

Adj. 甘い；親切な、優しい

▶ **sweetness** [swí:tnəs] N[U] 甘さ、甘味   ▶ **sweetener** [swí:tnər] N[C/U] 甘味料

▶ **sweetheart** [swí:tha:rt] N[C] 良い人、親切な人   ▶ **sweeten** [swí:tn] V[T] を甘くする

1766 sugary
[ʃúɡəri]
□□□□□□

Adj. 甘い、甘ったるい、砂糖を含んだ

▶ **sugarcoat** [ʃúɡərkoʊt] V[T] をオブラートに包む   ▶ **sugar** [ʃúɡər] N[C/U] 砂糖

Please don't **sugarcoat** it. Just tell me what you actually think about me!
（オブラートに包まないで、僕のこと実際どう思ってるか教えてよ！）

1767 sour
[saʊr]
□□□□□□

Adj. すっぱい；不機嫌な V[I]（関係などが）悪化する V[T] を悪化させる

▶ **sourness** [sáʊrnəs] N[U] すっぱさ；不機嫌さ

1768 salty
[sá:lt̬i]
□□□□□□

Adj. しょっぱい、塩辛い

▶ **salt** [sa:lt] N[U] 塩   V[T] に塩を振る、塩味をつける

▶ **salted** [sá:ltɪd] Adj. 塩味の、塩漬けの

salted caramel（塩キャラメル）

▶ **saltiness** [sá:ltinəs] N[U] しょっぱさ

1769 savory
[séɪvəri]
□□□□□□

Adj. しょっぱい、塩味の ⟷ **sweet** [swi:t] 甘い

Do you want something sweet or **savory**?（甘いものとしょっぱいもの、どっちがいい？）

▶ **savor** [séɪvər] V[T] を味わう

savory を使用するときは、程度を表す副詞（really や very など）を伴いません。

1770 bitter
[bít̬ər]
□□□□□□

Adj. 苦い；（経験などが）つらい；（言動や寒さが）厳しい

▶ **bitterness** [bít̬ərnəs] N[U] 苦さ；つらさ

1771 burnt
[bɜːrnt]

Adj. 焦げた

▶ **burn** [bɜːrn] V[I] 焦げる、燃える　V[T] を焦がす、燃やす；をやけどする

▶ **burning** [bɜ́ːrnɪŋ] Adj. 燃えるような、燃えている

▶ **burned out** [bɜ̀ːrndáʊt] Adj.（仕事などで）燃え尽きた、とても疲れた

1772 spicy
[spáɪsi]

Adj.（香辛料がきいて）辛い

≒ **hot** [hɑːt]（唐辛子などがきいて）辛い、ヒリヒリする

≒ **spice** [spaɪs] N[C/U] 香辛料、スパイス　[U] 刺激　V[T] にスパイスを加える

= **spice sth up** [spaɪsʌ́p]

1773 rich
[rɪtʃ]

Adj. コクのある、濃厚な、こってりした　⟷ **light** [laɪt] あっさりした

金持ちの、裕福な　⟷ **poor** [pɔːr] 貧しい；（〜を）豊富に含む（in sth）

1774 smoky
[smóʊki]

Adj. スモーキーな；煙たい

▶ **smoke** [smoʊk] V[T] を燻製にする；（たばこなど）を吸う

V[I] 喫煙する　N[C] 喫煙　N[U] 煙

1775 bland
[blænd]

Adj. 味が薄い、味気ない

▶ **blandness** [blǽndnəs] N[U] 味気なさ、淡白な味付け

1776 fresh
[freʃ]

Adj. 新鮮な、できたての；さわやかな；新しい；淡水の

▶ **freshness** [fréʃnəs] N[U] 新鮮さ；さわやかさ；斬新さ

▶ **freshly** [fréʃli] Adv. 新しく

freshly ground coffee（ひきたてのコーヒー）

1777 rotten
[rɑ́ːtn]

Adj. 腐った

▶ **rot** [rɑːt] V[I] 腐る　V[T] を腐らせる　N[U] 腐敗、腐敗物

1778 stale
[steɪl]

Adj. 新鮮でない、古くなった；よどんだ、いやなにおいの

▶ **staleness** N[U] [stéɪlnəs] 新鮮でないこと、古くなっていること；よどみ、いやなにおい

1779 stinky
[stíŋki]

Adj. 臭い

▶ **stink** [stɪŋk] V[I] 悪臭がする　N[C] 悪臭

▶ **stinkbug** [stíŋkbʌg] N[C] カメムシ

1780 ripe
[raɪp]

Adj. 熟成した、熟した、食べごろの

▶ **ripeness** [ráɪpnəs] N[U] 成熟、熟成

▶ **ripen** [ráɪpən] V[I] 熟成する、熟す　V[T] を熟させる、熟成させる

Touch（触覚）

This is + (really/very/so/pretty/quite/a bit) + sensory word

1781 **chewy**
[tʃúːi]

Adj. 噛み応えのある、モチモチした、コシの強い

▶ **chew** [tʃuː] V[I] （〜を）噛む （on/at sth）　V[T] を噛む

1782 **moist**
[mɔ́ɪst]

Adj. しっとりした　⟷ **dry** [draɪ] 乾燥した、ぱさぱさした；（お酒が）辛口の、辛い

▶ **moisture** [mɔ́ɪstʃər] N[U] 湿気、水分

▶ **moisturize** [mɔ́ɪstʃəraɪz] V[I/T] （〜に）潤いを与える

▶ **moisten** [mɔ́ɪsən] V[I] 湿る、ぬれる　V[T] を湿らす、ぬらす

▶ **moistness** [mɔ́ɪstnəs] N[U] しっとりしていること、湿り気

1783 **tender**
[téndər]

Adj. （肉などが）柔らかい　⟷ **rubbery** [rʌ́bəri] 硬い　= **tough** [tʌf]
優しい、思いやりのある　V[T] を提出する、申し出る

▶ **tenderize** [téndəraɪz] V[T] (肉など) を柔らかくする

▶ **tenderness** [téndərnəs] N[U] 柔らかさ；優しさ

1784 **fluffy**
[flʌ́fi]

Adj. ふわふわした

▶ **fluff** [flʌf] N[U] 糸くず、綿毛　V[T] (枕や髪など) をふわっとさせる、膨らませる

1785 **jiggly**
[dʒígli]

Adj. ぷるぷるした

▶ **jiggle** [dʒígəl] V[I] 軽く揺れる　V[T] を軽く揺らす

1786 **brittle**
[brítl̩]

Adj. サクサクした、砕けやすい、もろい

1787 **crunchy**
[krʌ́ntʃi]

Adj. バリバリした、ボリボリした

≒ **crispy** [kríspi] パリパリした、サクサクした

▶ **crunch** [krʌntʃ] N[S] バリバリという音；危機、ピンチ　N[C] 腹筋運動
V[I] バリバリという音を立てる　V[I/T] （〜を）バリバリ食べる （on sth）
V[T] (データなど) を大量に処理する

▶ **crunchiness** [krʌ́ntʃinəs] N[U] バリバリした食感

1788 **mushy**
[mʌ́ʃi]

Adj. ドロドロした、トロトロした

▶ **mush** [mʌʃ] N[U] ドロドロしたもの

1789 smooth
[smuːð]

Adj. なめらかな、すべすべした　　↔ **grainy** [gréɪni] ざらざらした

▶ **smoothly** [smúːðli] Adv. なめらかに、スムーズに、順調に

1790 greasy
[gríːsi]

Adj. 油っこい、べたつく　　= **oily** [ɔ́ɪli]

▶ **grease** [griːs] N[U] 油、脂肪　　V[T] に油を塗る

1791 chunky
[tʃʌ́ŋki]

Adj. 具が大きい；分厚い

▶ **chunk** [tʃʌŋk] N[C] 大きな塊；かなりの量

1792 watery
[wɔ́ːṭəri]

Adj. 水っぽい；涙ぐんだ

▶ **water** [wɔ́ːṭər] N[U] 水　　V[I] よだれを出す；(痛みなどで) 涙を出す
V[T] (動物や植物) に水をやる

1793 gooey
[gúːi]

Adj. べたべたした、ねばねばした　　= **sticky** [stíki]

▶ **goo** [guː] N[U] べたべたしたもの

1794 slimy
[sláɪmi]

Adj. ねばねばした、ぬるぬるした

▶ **slime** [slaɪm] N[U] ぬるぬるするもの

1795 prickly
[príkli]

Adj. とげとげの、ちくちくする

▶ **prickle** [príkəl] N[C] とげ；ちくちくすること　　V[I] ちくちくする　　V[T] をちくちくさせる

1796 bumpy
[bʌ́mpi]

Adj. でこぼこした、がたがたした；浮き沈みの多い

▶ **bump** [bʌmp] N[C] こぶ、はれ；衝突　　V[I] ぶつかる　　V[T] (体の部分) をぶつける
bump into sb (〜に偶然出会う)　　= **run into sb**

1797 coarse
[kɔːrs]

Adj. ざらざらした、粗い；(話し方が) 下品な、汚い

▶ **coarseness** [kɔ́ːrsnəs] N[U] 粗さ；下品さ

1798 slick
[slɪk]

Adj. つるつるの、てかてかの；(スポーツなどで動きが) なめらかな

▶ **slickness** [slíknəs] N[U] つるつるしていること

Hearing（聴覚）

It's + (really/very/so/pretty/quite/a bit) + sensory word

1799 noisy
[nɔ́ɪzi]

Adj.（騒音などが）うるさい

▶ **noisily** [nɔ́ɪzəli] Adv. うるさく   ▶ **noise** [nɔɪz] N[C/U] 騒音、雑音

1800 loud
[laʊd]

Adj.（音が）大きい、騒々しい；（服が）派手な　Adv. 大声で、大音量で

= **loudly** [láʊdli]

▶ **loudness** [láʊdnəs] N[U] 音の大きさ、騒々しさ

1801 deafening
[défənɪŋ]

Adj.（音が）ものすごく大きい、（耳が聞こえなくなるくらい）うるさい

▶ **deaf** [def] Adj. 耳が聞こえない、聴覚障害の

▶ **deafness** [défnəs] N[U] 耳が聞こえないこと、難聴

1802 silent
[sáɪlənt]

Adj. 静かな、しんとした、音のない、無言の、黙った

▶ **silence** [sáɪləns] N[U] 静けさ　N[C/U] 沈黙、無言　▶ **silently** [sáɪləntli] Adv. 静かに

1803 peaceful
[píːsfəl]

Adj. 静かな、安らかな；平和的な、穏やかな

▶ **peace** [piːs] N[U] 静けさ、安らぎ；平和、穏やかさ

▶ **peacefully** [píːsfəli] Adv. 安らかに；平和的に

Vision（視覚）

It's + (really/very/so/pretty/quite/a bit) + sensory word

1804 tidy
[táɪdi]

Adj. きちんとした、整頓された；きれい好きな

↔ **untidy** [ʌntáɪdi] 散らかった　= **messy** [mési]

V[I/T]（～を）整頓する、片付ける　= **tidy up** [taɪdi(y)ʌ́p]

▶ **tidiness** [táɪdinəs] N[U] 整頓されていること

1805 messy
[mési]

Adj. 散らかった

▶ **mess** [mes] V[T] をぐちゃぐちゃにする

▶ **mess up** [mesʌ́p]　N[S/U] 散らかった状態

1806 crowded
[kráʊdɪd]

Adj. 混雑した、込んでいる

▶ **crowd** [kraʊd] V[I/T]（～に）押し寄せる、（～に）群がる　N[C] 人込み、民衆、観衆

1807 **dazzling**
[dǽzəlɪŋ]
☐☐☐☐☐☐

Adj. まぶしい、輝かしい　= **flashy** [flǽʃi]
▶ **dazzle** [dǽzəl] V[T] の目をくらませる　N[U] まぶしさ

1808 **hazy**
[héɪzi]
☐☐☐☐☐☐

Adj. かすんだ、ぼんやりした
▶ **haze** [heɪz] N[C/U] かすみ、ぼんやりした状態　V[I] かすむ　V[T] をかすませる

1809 **blurry**
[bláːri]
☐☐☐☐☐☐

Adj. ぼんやりした、かすんだ
▶ **blur** [blɜːr] V[I] ぼんやりする　V[T] をぼんやりさせる　N[C] ぼんやりしているもの
▶ **blurred** [blɜːrd] Adj. ぼんやりとした

↺ CH. 17, 22, 26, 30, 33, 36

環境
Environment

Various issues afflict the environment, including the depletion of the ozone layer, acid rain, and desertification, but above all, global warming is expected to have the most far-reaching and damaging consequences.

The impact of global warming is immeasurable. Observable consequences include the disappearance of animal habitats due to the melting of Arctic ice and sinking of islands such as Tuvalu in the South Pacific.

Thankfully, there is growing consensus that this phenomenon is caused by a rapid increase in greenhouse gas emissions since the Industrial Revolution. Since the cause of excess heat being trapped on the Earth's surface is understood, it is possible to predict future impacts more accurately.

As we now know the drivers and future impacts of global warming, it is critical to take swift mitigation action, including increasing the use of renewable energy such as solar power, and to improve housing, water, hygiene, and waste management to adapt to the inevitable future consequences.

1

Various issues **afflict** the environment, including the depletion of the ozone layer, acid rain, and desertification, but above all, global warming is expected to have the most far-reaching and damaging consequences.

オゾン層の破壊や酸性雨、砂漠化など、さまざまな問題が環境を苦しめているが、何よりも、地球温暖化は最も広範囲で有害な影響を及ぼすと考えられている。

1810 **afflict**
[əflíkt]

V[T] を苦しめる、悩ませる

A lot of poor countries are **afflicted** by corruption.
（多くの貧しい国は汚職に苦しんでいるんだ。）

▶ **affliction** [əflíkʃən] N[C/U] 苦悩、苦痛

1811 **depletion**
[dɪpliːʃən]

N[U] 破壊、減少、枯渇

I wonder what's causing the **depletion** of my money.
（なんで俺のお金、枯渇してきてるんだろ。）

the **depletion** of natural resources（天然資源の枯渇）

▶ **deplete** [dɪpliːt] V[T] を減少させる、枯渇させる

I love tuna sashimi, but it's getting more and more expensive because overfishing over the last few years has **depleted** the tuna population.
（マグロの刺身大好きなんだけど、ここ数年、乱獲のせいで生息量が減ってきて、どんどん値段が高騰してるんだ。）

▶ **depleted** [dɪpliːtɪd] Adj. 消耗した、枯渇した

Is it true that you should only charge your phone when the battery is fully **depleted**?
（携帯のバッテリーって完全に消耗してからチャージした方が良いって本当なの？）

1812 **ozone**
[óʊzoʊn]

N[U] オゾン

■ the **ozone** layer（オゾン層）

I read in the newspaper that the massive hole in **the ozone layer** over Antarctica is gradually becoming smaller.
（南極大陸上空のオゾン層にあいた巨大な穴が徐々に小さくなってきてるって新聞で読んだ。）

1813 layer
[léɪər]
☐☐☐☐☐☐

N[C] 層、重なり V[T] を層にする

How many **layers** should a proper lasagna have?
（ちゃんとしたラザニアって何枚層があるべきなんだろう？）

in **layers**
（重ねて、層にして）

▶ **layered** [léɪərd] Adj. 層になった

1814 acid
[ǽsɪd]
☐☐☐☐☐☐

Adj. 酸性の；辛辣な；酸味のある = acidic [əsídɪk] **N[C/U] 酸**

This scientist is denying the harmful effects of **acid** rain, but he has no evidence to support his claims.
（この科学者は酸性雨の有害な影響を否定しているんだけど、それを裏付ける証拠は一切無いんだ。）

■ the **acid** test （（成功などを判断するための）厳しい試練）

The real **acid test** for our products is how well they sell.
（僕らの商品にとっての本当の試練は、それがどれだけ売れるかなんだ。）

▶ **acidity** [əsídəti] N[U] 酸性度；酸味

I don't really like the **acidity** of this coffee.
（このコーヒーの酸味があんまり好きじゃないんです。）

▶ **acidify** [əsídəfaɪ] V[T] を酸性にする V[I] 酸性になる

1815 desertification
[dɪzɜ̀ːrtəfəkéɪʃən]
☐☐☐☐☐☐

N[U] 砂漠化

It's so green here that it's hard to believe that **desertification** might be an issue in a few years.
（ここは緑も多いし、あと数年で砂漠化が問題になる可能性があるなんて信じられないね。）

▶ **desert** N[C/U] 砂漠 V[T] （配偶者など）を見捨てる V[I/T] （～から）脱走する
  N [dézərt] *V,* [dɪzɜ́ːrt]

the Sahara **Desert** （サハラ砂漠）

I can't believe you **deserted** me when I needed you the most.
（君を一番必要としていた時に僕のことを見捨てるなんて信じられないよ。）

▶ **deserted** [dɪzɜ́ːrtɪd] Adj. 人けのない；見捨てられた

The restaurant was completely **deserted** when I visited last time.
（あのレストラン、前行ったときはガラッガラだった。）

デザートのスペルは違う？　お菓子などのデザートは砂漠の意味の desert よりも s が一つ多く、dessert となります。また、発音とアクセントも以下のように異なるので注意してください。
・desert [dézərt] 砂漠　・dessert [dɪzɜ́ːrt] デザート

1816 above all
[əbʌvɑ́ːl]
☐☐☐☐☐☐

Phr. 何よりも、とりわけ

Above all, we need to remember to focus on our game plan, rather than react to what our opponents do.
（何より重要なのは、相手の動きに反応するんじゃなくて、忘れずに自分たちのゲームプランに集中することです。）

2 The impact of global warming is immeasurable. Observable consequences include the disappearance of animal habitats due to the melting of Arctic ice and sinking of islands such as Tuvalu in the South Pacific.

地球温暖化の影響は計り知れない。観測できる影響としては、北極で氷が融解して動物の生息地が失われていることや、南太平洋に浮かぶツバルなどの島々が海に沈みつつあることなどが挙げられる。

1817 **global warming** [glòubəl wɔ́:rmɪŋ] **N[U]** 地球温暖化

Do you think all this rain is due to **global warming**?
（この雨って全部地球温暖化のせいだと思う？）

1818 **disappearance** [dìsəpíərəns] **N[C/U]** 消滅、消失、失踪

Your **disappearance** was pretty sudden, so we were a bit worried.
（お前急に消えたから俺ら結構心配してたんだぞ。）

↔ **appearance** [əpírəns] N[C/U] 見た目、外見　N[C] 出現、登場

■ **in appearance**（見た目は）

This watch is luxurious not only **in appearance** but also in craftsmanship.
（この時計は見た目が高級なだけじゃなくて、込められた職人魂もまた贅沢なんだよ。）

▶ **disappear** [dìsəpír] V[I] 消える、消滅する

↔ **appear** [əpír] 現れる、世に出る、出演する；（〜のように）見える（adjective）

■ **appear** to do（〜するように見える）　■ it **appears** that + sentence（〜ということのようだ）

I saw my teacher walking with a woman who **appeared to** be his girlfriend, so I secretly followed them.（うちの先生が彼女らしき女性と歩いてるの見かけたから、こっそりついて行ったんだ。）

Oh my god, **it appears** my YouTube account has been permanently deleted.
（ウソだろ、俺の YouTube アカウント、永久に削除されたっぽい。）

1819 **melting** [méltɪŋ] **N[U]** 融解　**Adj.** 溶けていく；（声や表情が）なごませるような

You may think the **melting** point and freezing point of a substance are the same, but sometimes they are not.（物質の融点と氷点は同じだと思うかもしれないけど、たまに違うことがあるんだ。）

▶ **melt** [melt] V[I] 溶ける；（気持ちなどが）和らぐ　V[T] を溶かす；（気持ちなど）を和らげる

I wish they made ice cream that didn't **melt**. I eat too slowly.
（溶けないアイスクリームがあったらいいのになぁ。僕、食べるのすごい遅いからさぁ。）

Let's microwave this pizza a bit to **melt** the cheese.
（このピザ、チーズを溶かすためにちょっと電子レンジでチンしようよ。）

I don't know why, but my heart **melts** every time I see my grandma.
（なんでか分からないけど、おばあちゃんに会うたびに気持ちが和らぐんだ。）

▶ **melted** [méltɪd] Adj. 溶けた

Is it okay to use **melted** butter instead of vegetable oil?
（サラダ油の代わりに溶けたバター使っても大丈夫かな？）

1820 **Arctic**
[ɑ́ːrktɪk]
☐☐☐☐☐☐

Adj. 北極（圏）の；凍えるような、極寒の　N[S] 北極、北極圏【the -】

I can't believe that **Arctic** foxes don't start to shiver until the temperature goes below negative 70 degrees. （ホッキョクギツネはマイナス70度を下回らないと震えださないなんて信じられない。）

↔ **Antarctic** [æntɑ́ːrktɪk] 南極の / 南極【the -】

▶ **Antarctica** [æntɑ́ːrktɪkə] N[Prop.] 南極大陸

1821 **sink**
[sɪŋk]
☐☐☐☐☐☐

V[I] 沈む；（価値や数量が）低下する　V[T] を沈ませる

I think the scene where the ship **sinks** is the best part of *Titanic*.
（船が沈んでいくシーンは映画『タイタニック』の最高の場面だと思う。）

■ **sink** in（実感が湧く）　　■ **sink** or swim（死ぬか生きるかの）

At the time, I didn't understand why she gave me that advice, but it's slowly **sinking in** now.
（当時はなんで彼女がそんなアドバイスをくれたのか理解できなかったけど、今少しずつ分かってきたよ。）

Working in a **sink or swim** environment causes me a lot of stress, but this kind of workplace offers many learning opportunities as well.
（死ぬか生きるかの環境で働くとストレスも多いけど、こうした職場環境では多くの学習機会も得られるんだ。）

▶ **sinking** [sɪ́ŋkɪŋ] Adj. 沈みつつある

混同注意！ sink vs **think**　どちらもカタカナで書くとシンクですが、発音はそれぞれ [sɪŋk]、[θɪŋk] と異なります。think の th は舌の先を上下の歯に軽く当て、その隙間から息を出す音です。

1822 **island**
[áɪlənd]
☐☐☐☐☐☐

N[C] 島

If you could only take three things, what would you take with you to a deserted **island**?
（無人島に何か3つだけ持っていけるとしたら、何持ってく？）

1823 **Pacific**
[pəsífɪk]
☐☐☐☐☐☐

N[S] 太平洋【the -】= the Pacific Ocean　Adj. 太平洋の；平和的な【p-】

What do you think of my idea to swim across **the Pacific** to attempt a Guinness World Record?
（ギネス世界記録に挑戦するために太平洋を泳いで横断するっていうアイディア、どう思う？）

▶ **pacify** [pǽsəfaɪ] V[T] をなだめる；に平和をもたらす

There are some useful phrases I often use to **pacify** irate customers.
（めっちゃ怒ってるお客をなだめるために僕がよく使ってる良い表現がいくつかあるんだ。）

▶ **pacifism** [pǽsəfɪzəm] N[U] 平和主義　▶ **pacifist** [pǽsəfɪst] N[C] 平和主義者

3 Thankfully, there is growing consensus that this phenomenon is caused by a rapid increase in greenhouse gas emissions since the Industrial Revolution. Since the cause of excess heat being trapped on the Earth's surface is understood, it is possible to predict future impacts more accurately.

幸いにも、地球温暖化は産業革命以降、温室効果ガスの排出量が急増したことで引き起こされるという合意ができつつある。地表に過剰な熱がたまっている理由が分かったことで、将来の影響をより正確に予測することも可能になった。

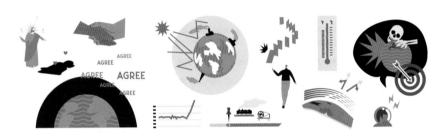

1824 **thankfully**
[θǽŋkfəli]
☐☐☐☐☐☐

Adv. 幸いなことに、ありがたいことに

Thankfully, the girl I have a crush on hasn't been taken yet.
(幸い俺の好きな子はまだ誰にも取られてないんだ。)

▶ **thankful** [θǽŋkfəl] Adj.（〜を）ありがたく思って、感謝して (for sth/to sb)

I'm **thankful** to my parents for everything they've done for me.
(両親には自分にしてくれた全てのことに対して感謝しているよ。)

1825 **greenhouse**
[grí:nhaʊs]
☐☐☐☐☐☐

N[C] 温室、ビニールハウス

I want to build a **greenhouse** in my backyard, but I don't think there's enough space there.
(裏庭にビニールハウスを建てたいんだけど、十分なスペースがなさそうなんだよね。)

the **greenhouse** effect（温室効果）   a **greenhouse** gas（温室効果ガス）

1826 **gas**
[gæs]
☐☐☐☐☐☐

N[C/U] ガス、気体　N[U] ガソリン = gasoline [gǽsəli:n]；アクセル【the -】

Why does inhaling helium **gas** change your voice?
(なんでヘリウムガス吸ったら声が変わるのかな？)

Step on the **gas**.（スピード上げてよ。）

1827 **emission**
[imíʃən]
☐☐☐☐☐☐

N[C] 排出量　N[U] 排出

This report says that carpooling just once a week can reduce our carbon **emissions** by 15 percent.（このレポートによると、週一で相乗りするだけで炭素排出量を15%も減らせるんだって。）

▶ **emit** [imit] V[T] を放出する、放射する

The radiation **emitted** from cell phones and computers is very small, so I don't think it will damage our health.
（携帯電話とかパソコンから放出される放射線はすごい少ない量だから、健康を害することはないと思うよ。）

語根 mit　「送る」という意味の語根で、外に（＝ e）送る（＝ mit）ことから「放射する」となります。
他には transmit（送信する）や submit（提出する）などがあります。

1828 **excess**
[ɪksés]
☐☐☐☐☐☐

Adj. 過剰な、超過の、余分な　**N[S/U]** 余分なもの、超過、過剰

Charging $200 for just one kilogram of **excess** baggage is a bit ridiculous, isn't it?
（超過手荷物たった1キロで200ドルも請求するってちょっとバカげてない？）

▶ **excessive** [eksésɪv] Adj. 過度な、（値段などが）法外な

Sometimes I feel like Japanese customer service is a bit **excessive**.
（日本の顧客サービスってたまにちょっとやりすぎなんじゃないかなぁって感じるんだよね。）

▶ **excessively** [eksésɪvli] Adv. 過度に

▶ **exceed** [ɪksíːd] V[T] を超える、超過する

I think I deserve a promotion because I consistently **exceed** expectations.
（私はいつも期待を上回ってるし、昇進に値すると思うんだよね。）

1829 **heat**
[hiːt]
☐☐☐☐☐☐

N[U] 熱、熱さ、暑さ　**N[S/U]** （コンロなどの）火

I'm going to burn if I don't get out of this **heat** soon.
（そろそろこの暑さから抜け出さないと燃えちまうよ。）

a low/medium/high **heat**（弱火 / 中火 / 強火）

▶ **heated** [híːtɪd] Adj. 白熱した、激しい；温水の、暖められた

They're having a **heated** debate about whether or not cash should be abolished.
（現金を廃止すべきかどうかに関して、ずっと激しい議論が続いてるよ。）

a **heated** (swimming) pool（温水（水泳）プール）

▶ **heatedly** [híːtɪdli] Adv. 白熱して、激しく

1830 **trap**
[træp]
☐☐☐☐☐☐

V[T] （熱など）をためる；を閉じ込める；をわなで捕まえる

Sorry, I'm running a bit late because I was **trapped** in a conversation that I couldn't get out of.
（ごめん、話してたら抜け出せなくなっちゃって、ちょっと遅れてる。）

V[T] （サッカーでボール）をトラップする

N[C] わな、落とし穴；策略

4 As we now know the drivers and future impacts of global warming, it is critical to take swift mitigation action, including increasing the use of renewable energy such as solar power, and to improve housing, water, hygiene, and waste management to adapt to the inevitable future consequences.

地球温暖化の原因と将来の影響が分かった今、太陽エネルギーなどの再生可能エネルギーの活用を増やすといった迅速な緩和措置を講じること、そして住宅や水、衛生、廃棄物管理を改善して、将来の避けられない影響に適応することが極めて重要だ。

1831 swift
[swíft]
▢▢▢▢▢▢

Adj. 迅速な、速やかな、即座の

I appreciate your **swift** reply. (迅速に回答していただきありがとうございます。)

▶ **swiftly** [swíftli] Adv. 迅速に、速やかに　　▶ **swiftness** [swíftnəs] N[U] 迅速さ

1832 renewable
[rɪnúːəbəl]
▢▢▢▢▢▢

Adj. 再生可能な；更新可能な

There are actually a lot of companies that invest in **renewable** energy just for the sake of getting grants from the government.
(政府から助成金をもらうためだけに再生可能エネルギーに投資している会社、実際たくさんあるよ。)

This working holiday visa is for a maximum of 12 months and is not **renewable**.
(このワーホリビザは最大 12 か月で、更新はできません。)

▶ **renew** [rɪnúː] V[T] を更新する；を再開する

What types of identification should I bring to **renew** my membership?
(会員の更新ってどんな身分証を持っていけば良いのかな？)

▶ **renewal** [rɪnúːəl] N[C/U] 更新、再開

1833 solar
[sóʊlər]
▢▢▢▢▢▢

Adj. 太陽の、太陽光の

Is it possible to power a household entirely by **solar** power?
(太陽エネルギーで家庭が必要なエネルギーを全て供給することって可能？)

1834 power
[páʊər]
▢▢▢▢▢▢

N[U] エネルギー、電力、電気

The German public remains strongly opposed to nuclear **power**.
(ドイツ国民は核エネルギーに対して今も強く反対してるよ。)

■ a **power** outlet（コンセント）

Excuse me, do you guys have **power outlets** here?（すいません、ここってコンセントあります？）

N[U]　力；権力；影響力　N[C/U]　能力

I really want to employ you at our company, but I just don't have the **power** to make that decision.（君をうちの会社で雇いたいと本当に思うんだけど、ちょっと僕にはその決定をする権限がないんだ。）

N[C]　大国、強国　▶ **superpower**［súːpərpàʊər］N[C] 超大国

V[T]　に動力を供給する　V[I]　力強く突き進む

▶ **powerful**［páʊərfəl］Adj. 力強い　　▶ **powerfully**［páʊərfəli］Adv. 力強く

1835 **hygiene**
［háɪdʒiːn］
□□□□□□

N[U]　衛生、清潔

■ personal **hygiene**（個人の衛生）　dental **hygiene**（歯科衛生）　food **hygiene**（食品衛生）

I can't share a room with somebody that has poor **personal hygiene**.
（不衛生な人と部屋をシェアするとか無理。）

▶ **hygienic**［haɪdʒénɪk］Adj. 衛生的な、清潔な

▶ **hygienically**［haɪdʒénɪkli］Adv. 衛生的に、清潔に

1836 **waste**
［weɪst］
□□□□□□

N[U]　廃棄物、ごみ　N[S/U]　無駄遣い、浪費

Going paperless will significantly reduce the amount of **waste** that our company produces.
（ペーパーレス化を実現すれば、うちの会社のごみの量がぐっと減るね。）

industrial **waste**（産業廃棄物）　　nuclear **waste**（核廃棄物）

This is a **waste** of time.（これは時間の無駄だよ。）　　go to **waste**（無駄になる）

V[T]　を無駄にする、浪費する　Adj. 廃物の

You should stop **wasting** your money on drinking every night.
（毎晩飲むためにお金を無駄にするの、やめた方が良いよ。）

▶ **wasted**［wéɪstɪd］Adj. 無駄な；衰弱した；酔っぱらった

Nick got so **wasted** last night that he ended up sleeping on the street.
（ニックは昨日の夜めちゃくちゃ酔っぱらってそのまま道で寝ちゃったんだ。）

▶ **wasteful**［wéɪstfəl］Adj. 無駄の多い

1837 **adapt**
［ədæpt］
□□□□□□

V[I]　（〜に）適応する、順応する（to sth）

My daughter was struggling to **adapt** to her new school at first, but she's fine now.
（うちの娘は最初は新しい学校に馴染むのに苦労してたんだけど、今はもう大丈夫だよ。）

V[T]　を（〜に）順応させる（to sth）；を改造する

▶ **adaptive** Adj. 順応性のある　　▶ **adaptable** Adj.（〜に）順応できる（to sth）
　［ədæptɪv］　　　　　　　　　　　　　　［ədæptəbəl］

▶ **adaptability** N[U] 順応性　　▶ **adaptation** N[U] 順応、適応　N[C] 変更；改作
　［ədæptəbíləti］　　　　　　　　　　［ædəptéɪʃən］

Interviewer (W) With the increasing number of **devastating** disasters, it's difficult to know where we should direct our attention. Which **crises** most **concern** you?

Expert (M) The **ecological** disaster that I find most horrific is the **pollution** generated by the use of **fossil** fuels. As you may know, the **deterioration** of air quality is closely linked to **rising** global temperatures. This climate change **manifests** itself in a myriad of **damaging** environmental phenomena, such as **drought**, **storms** of increased severity, **erosion**, and **ecosystem destruction**.

Interviewer (W) What do you think is the quickest way to **mitigate** these impacts?

Expert (M) A great start would be to increase the use of **alternative** power sources. We also need to reduce activities that are exacerbating these disasters, such as the **contamination** of waterways due to **deforestation** and **discarding** of **hazardous** waste.

インタビュアー（女性） 壊滅的な災害がどんどん増えて、もうどこに注意を向けるべきなのか分からなくなってきました。一番懸念されている危機は何でしょうか？

専門家（男性） 私が一番恐ろしいと感じている生態学的な災害は、化石燃料の使用によって生じる汚染ですね。ご存知かもしれませんが、大気質の悪化は地球温暖化と密接に関係しているんです。こうした気候変動は、干ばつや、年々深刻になっている暴風雨、浸食、生態系破壊など、数多くの有害な環境現象として現れています。

インタビュアー（女性） そうした影響を緩和する最も簡単な方法は何だと思われますか？

専門家（男性） 大きな第一歩となるのは代替エネルギー源の使用を増やすことです。また、森林破壊や有害廃棄物の処分による水路の汚染といった、災害を悪化させるような行為も減らしていく必要がありますね。

1838 devastating
[dévəsteɪtɪŋ]

Adj. 壊滅的な、ひどい

▶ **devastate** [dévəstert] V[T] を壊滅させる ▶ **devastation** [dèvəstéɪʃən] N[U] 破壊、荒廃

▶ **devastated** [dévəsteɪtɪd] Adj. 壊滅状態の；非常にショックを受けた

1839 crisis
[kráɪsɪs]

N[C/U] 危機

the global financial **crisis**（世界金融危機） = the GFC

1840 concern
[kənsə́:rn]

V[T] を不安にさせる、心配させる；に関係する

N[C] 不安にさせるもの、心配事、関心事   N[U] 不安、心配、関心

▶ **concerned** [kənsə́:rnd] Adj. (〜を) 心配した (about sth/sb)；(〜と) 関係した (with sth/sb)

▶ **concerning** [kənsə́:rnɪŋ] Prep. 〜に関して

1841 ecological
[i:kəlá:dʒɪkəl]

Adj. 生態的学な、生態学の

▶ **ecologically** [i:kəlá:dʒɪkli] Adv. 生態学的に ▶ **ecology** [iká:lədʒi] N[U] 生態学

1842 pollution
[pəlú:ʃən]

N[U] 汚染、公害

▶ **pollute** [pəlú:t] V[T] を (〜で) 汚染する (with sth)

▶ **polluted** [pəlú:tɪd] Adj. 汚染された ▶ **pollutant** [pəlú:tənt] N[C/U] 汚染物質

▶ **polluter** [pəlú:tər] N[C] 汚染を引き起こすもの

1843 fossil
[fá:səl]

N[C] 化石

▶ **fossilize** [fá:səlaɪz] V[I] 化石化する V[T] を化石化する

▶ **fossilization** [fà:sələzéɪʃən] N[U] 化石化 ▶ **fossilized** [fá:səlaɪzd] Adj. 化石化した

1844 deterioration
[dɪtɪ̀rɪəréɪʃən]

N[U] （破壊状態や環境の）悪化、劣化

▶ **deteriorate** [dɪtiriəreɪt] V[I] 悪化する

1845 rising
[ráɪzɪŋ]

Adj. 上昇する

▶ **rise** [raɪz] V[I] 上昇する、増加する、起きる

Rise and shine!（朝だから起きて！）

1846 manifest
[mǽnəfest]

V[T] を明示する、表明する   Adj. 明らかな

manifest itself (in sth)（（問題や症状が〜に）現れる）

▶ **manifestly** [mǽnəfestli] Adv. 明らかに ▶ **manifestation** [mǽnəfestéɪʃən] N[C/U] 表明、表れ

▶ **manifesto** [mǽnəféstoʊ] N[C] マニフェスト

1847 damaging
[dǽmɪdʒɪŋ]

Adj. 有害な、被害を与えるような

▶ **damage** [dǽmɪdʒ] N[U] 被害、損害 V[T] に被害を与える

1848 drought N[C/U] 干ばつ

[draʊt]

Australia is going through a severe **drought** this year.
（オーストラリアは今年厳しい干ばつを経験している。）

1849 storm N[C] 暴風雨、嵐　V[T] を襲撃する

[stɔːrm]

a **storm** of criticism（批判の嵐）

1850 erosion N[U] 浸食

[ɪróʊʒən]

▶ **erosive** [ɪróʊsɪv] Adj. 浸食性の　▶ **erode** [ɪróʊd] V[I/T]（～を）浸食する

1851 ecosystem N[C] 生態系；（経済などの）エコシステム

[íːkoʊsɪstəm]

1852 destruction N[U] 破壊

[dɪstrʌ́kʃən]

▶ **destructive** [dɪstrʌ́ktɪv] Adj. 破壊的な　▶ **destructively** [dɪstrʌ́ktɪvli] Adv. 破壊的に

▶ **destructiveness** [dɪstrʌ́ktɪvnəs] N[U] 破壊的なこと

▶ **self-destruct** [sèlfdɪstrʌ́kt] V[I] 自爆する

1853 mitigate V[T] を緩和する、軽減する

[mítəɡeɪt]

▶ **mitigation** [mìtəɡéɪʃən] N[U] 緩和、軽減

1854 alternative Adj. 代替の、代わりの　N[C] 代替案、代わりになるもの

[ɑːltə́ːrnətɪv]

▶ **alternatively** [ɑːltə́ːrnətɪvli] Adv. 代わりに　▶ **alter** [ɑ́ːltər] V[I] 変わる　V[T] を変える

▶ **alternate** *Adj.* [ɑ́ːltərnət] *V.* [ɑ́ːltərneɪt] Adj. 交互の　V[I] 交互に起こる　V[T] を交互に行う

1855 contamination N[U] 汚染

[kəntæ̀mənéɪʃən]

▶ **contaminate** [kəntǽməneɪt] V[T] を汚染する

▶ **contaminated** [kəntǽməneɪtɪd] Adj. 汚染された

▶ **contaminant** [kəntǽmənənt] N[C] 汚染物質

1856 deforestation N[U] 森林破壊、森林伐採

[diːfɔ̀ːrəstéɪʃən]

▶ **deforest** [diːfɔ́ːrɪst] V[T]（森林）を伐採する　▶ **deforested** [diːfɔ́ːrɪstɪd] Adj. 森林伐採された

1857 discard V[T] を処分する、捨てる　= **throw sth away** [θróʊ(w)əwéɪ]

[dɪskɑ́ːrd]

▶ **discarded** [dɪskɑ́ːrdɪd] Adj. 捨てられた　N[C] 捨てられたもの；捨て札

1858 hazardous Adj.（～にとって）有害な、危険な（to sth）

[hǽzərdəs]

▶ **hazard** [hǽzərd] V[T] を思い切って言ってみる　N[C] 危険

hazard a guess (that + sentence)（（～だと）推測する）

Chapter

38

工学
Engineering

Engineers are people who hold specialized skills and knowledge in devising and constructing machinery and structures. Archaeological discovery of tools such as the lever, wheel, and pulley suggests that engineering already existed in the Ancient era.

During the Middle Ages, new inventions such as automated musical instruments, developed in the Muslim world, and watermills driven by the rise and fall of tides, began appearing, which coincided with the beginning of mathematics being used by artisans.

Following on from this, during the Renaissance, British engineer Thomas Savery invented the first steam engine based on the pressure cooker developed by French inventor Denis Papin. The invention was subsequently refined and became an enormous impetus for the Industrial Revolution.

In modern times, the term "engineer" is ubiquitous. The term encapsulates vastly different specializations, including aerospace and marine engineers, who mainly handle vehicles, mining engineers who focus on mineral extraction, and software engineers who design and develop software.

1 Engineers are people who hold specialized skills and knowledge in devising and constructing machinery and structures. Archaeological discovery of tools such as the lever, wheel, and pulley suggests that engineering already existed in the Ancient era.

エンジニアは、機械や構造物の考案と組み立てについての専門的な技術と知識を持つ人のことを言う。てこや車輪、滑車といった道具の考古学的発見により、工学は古代から既に存在していたことが分かる。

1859 **hold**
[hoʊld]

V[T] を持つ；を支える；を抱き締める；(イベントなど) を開く

This tablet is too big for me to **hold** in one hand.
(このタブレットデカすぎて片手じゃ持てないよ。)

■ **hold** on to sth (〜を持ち続ける、〜をしっかり持つ)

Can you **hold on to** my backpack? I'll be back in a sec.
(私のリュック持っててくれない？すぐ戻るから。)

Hold me tight!　　We're going to **hold** an event in Sapporo next week.
(ぎゅっと抱きしめて！)　(来週札幌でイベントを開く予定なんだ。)

hold one's nose (鼻をつまむ)　　**hold** hands (手を握る)

■ **hold** sth/sb up (〜を遅らせる、〜の時間を取らせる)

Sorry for **holding** you **up** from going home.
(家に帰るところだったのに時間取らせてごめんね。)

1860 **devise**
[dɪváɪz]

V[T] を考案する、発明する

I've **devised** a strategy to win us this game.
(このゲームで私たちが勝つための戦略を考案したんだ。)

▶ **device** [dɪváɪs] N[C] 機器、装置、デバイス；爆発物；手段；策略

1861 **tool**
[tu:l]

N[C] 道具、工具、ツール

There are so many study **tools** that you can download for free.
(無料でダウンロードできる勉強ツールはたくさんあるよ。)

1862 **lever**
[lévər]
☐☐☐☐☐☐

N[C] てこ、レバー **V[T]** をてこで動かす

It's really easy to get the lid off the bottle if you use a **lever**.
（ボトルのフタはてこを使えば本当に簡単に開けることができるよ。）

▶ **leverage** [lévərɪdʒ] N[U] てこの力；影響力 V[T] （すでにあるもの）を利用する、使う

I don't have enough **leverage** to guarantee you a job at my workplace, but I can at least try to get you an interview.
（あなたをうちの職場で雇えるって保証できるほど影響力はもってないけど、面接を設けようとすることぐらいはできるかも。）

I think you can **leverage** the skills you have to make more money in a different field.
（君は今あるスキルを利用して違う分野でもっと稼げると思うよ。）

1863 **wheel**
[wiːl]
☐☐☐☐☐☐

N[C] 車輪；（車などの）ハンドル【the -】

I can't believe the front **wheel** of my new bike is already bent.
（新しい自転車の前輪、もう曲がっちゃってるとかあり得ないんだけど。）

■ reinvent the **wheel** （（無駄に）一からやり直す）

Let's use what we've got rather than **reinvent the wheel**.
（一からやり直すんじゃなくて、もうすでにできてるものを活用しようよ。）

V[I] くるくる回る

I saw a giant flock of birds **wheeling** in the sky this morning, and it was kind of scary.
（今朝鳥の大群が空をぐるぐる飛びまわってるの見たんだけど、なんか怖かったよ。）

reinvent the wheel（車輪の再発明）の由来 車輪（＝ wheel）は最古の最重要な発明とも言われており、それを再発明することは「無駄に一からやり直す」ことであると考えられることに由来しています。

1864 **pulley**
[púli]
☐☐☐☐☐☐

N[C] 滑車

This **pulley** system makes moving these crates onto the ship so much easier.
（この滑車システムがあると、ここにある木箱を船まで移動するのがずっと楽になるんだ。）

1865 **era**
[írə]
☐☐☐☐☐☐

N[C] 時代、時期、年代

Japan introduced a constitution for the first time in its history during the Meiji **era**.
（日本は明治時代に歴史上初の憲法を導入した。）

2 During the Middle Ages, new inventions such as automated musical instruments, developed in the Muslim world, and watermills driven by the rise and fall of tides, began appearing, which coincided with the beginning of mathematics being used by artisans.

中世になると、イスラム世界で開発された自動演奏楽器や、潮の満ち引きで動く水車などの新しい発明品が登場するが、職人が数学を扱うようになったのもこれと同じ時期である。

ANCIENT   MODERN

1866 middle
[mídl]
☐☐☐☐☐☐

Adj. 中央の、中間の

How well-off is China's **middle** class?（中国の中流階級ってどれくらい裕福なのかな？）

the **Middle** Ages（中世）　　**middle** age（中年（45〜60歳くらいのこと））

N[C] 真ん中、中央、中間、最中【the -】

■ in the **middle** of sth（〜の最中）

Sorry, I'm **in the middle of** something. Can I give you a call later?
（ごめん、今取り込み中なんだ。後で電話かけ直して良い？）

■ in the **middle** of nowhere（何もないところに）

How did we get lost **in the middle of nowhere**?
（私たちなんでこんな何もないところに迷い込んじゃったんだろ。）

1867 instrument
[ínstrəmənt]
☐☐☐☐☐☐

N[C] 楽器；器具；（金融の）商品

Do you play any musical **instruments**?（なんか楽器弾くの？）

a musical **instrument**（楽器）　a surgical **instrument**（手術器具）　a financial **instrument**（金融商品）

▶ **instrumental** Adj.（〜の）役に立つ、助けになる（in sth）
[ìnstrəméntl]　　N[C] 器楽曲（歌のない楽器のみで演奏された曲のこと）

This online conversation platform has been **instrumental** in improving students' English.
（このオンライン英会話プラットフォームは学生の英語力を高める上で役立っているんです。）

1868 Muslim
[mázlɪm]
☐☐☐☐☐☐

Adj. イスラムの、イスラム教徒の

Europe's **Muslim** population has been rising year after year.
（年々ヨーロッパでのイスラム人口は増えてきているんだ。）

the **Muslim** world = the Islamic world（イスラム世界）

N[C] イスラム教徒

▶ **Islamic** [ɪzlæmɪk] Adj. イスラムの、イスラム教の   ▶ **Islam** [ízlɑːm] N[U] イスラム教

an **Islamic** state（イスラム国家）

▶ **Islamism** N[U] イスラム主義   ▶ **Islamist** N[C] イスラム教徒
  [ízləmɪzəm]   [ízləmɪst]

1869 fall
[fɑːl]
☐☐☐☐☐☐

N[C] 落下、低下   **N[S]** 失脚、陥落   **N[P]** 滝【-s】   **N[C/U]** 秋

There was a bit of a **fall** in sales, but our profit actually increased thanks to the new product line.（ちょっと売り上げは落ちたけど、実は新しい製品ラインのおかげで利益は上がったんだ。）

the rise and **fall** (of sth)（(〜の) 上下、(〜の) 増減、(〜の) 盛衰）

V[I] 落ちる、低下する；転ぶ；(雨や雪などが) 降る；崩壊する

The man was really drunk and **fell** from the balcony, but he somehow didn't get hurt.
（その男性はめちゃくちゃ酔っててバルコニーから落ちたんだけど、なぜかけがをしなかったんだ。）

V[I] （〜の範囲に）入る（into sth）

1870 tide
[taɪd]
☐☐☐☐☐☐

N[C/U] 潮、潮の満ち引き

Did you know that **tides** are caused by the gravitational interaction between Earth and the Moon?（潮の満ち引きって地球と月の重力の関係で起きてるって知ってた？）

▶ **tidal** [táɪdl] Adj. 潮の、干満の

1871 coincide
[kòʊɪnsáɪd]
☐☐☐☐☐☐

V[I] （〜と）同時に起こる（with sth）；(考えなどが) 一致する

The rain always seems to **coincide** with the weekends.
（いつも週末に合わせて雨が降ってる感じがする。）

▶ **coincidence** [koʊínsɪdəns] N[C/U] 偶然   N[S] 一致

What a **coincidence**!（偶然だね！）

▶ **coincidental** Adj. 偶然の   ▶ **coincidentally** Adv. 偶然にも
  [koʊìnsədéntl]   [koʊìnsədéntəli]

1872 artisan
[ɑ́ːrtəzən]
☐☐☐☐☐☐

N[C] 職人

Japanese **artisans** are admired all over the world for their outstanding craftsmanship.
（日本の職人はそのずばぬけた職人魂のおかげで世界で賞賛を受けている。）

3 Following on from this, during the Renaissance, British engineer Thomas Savery invented the first steam engine based on the pressure cooker developed by French inventor Denis Papin. The invention was subsequently refined and became an enormous impetus for the Industrial Revolution.

その後、ルネサンス期には英国のエンジニア、トーマス・セイヴァリが、フランスの発明家ドニ・パパンが開発した圧力鍋を基に蒸気エンジンを発明した。その発明は、その後改良され、産業革命の大きな推進力となった。

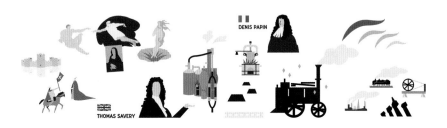

DENIS PAPIN

THOMAS SAVERY

1873 **follow**
[fá:lou]
☐☐☐☐☐☐

V[I] 後に続く、後に起きる

More information will **follow** soon!（詳細はまた近々お知らせします！）

follow on (from sth)（（〜の）後に続く）

■ as **follows**（以下の通り）

The details are **as follows**.（詳細は以下の通りです。）

■ **follow** up (on sth/with sb)（（〜について / 〜に）フォローアップする）

Can you **follow up on** this with the client?
（お客さんにこのことについてフォローアップしてくれない？）

V[T] に続く；の後について行く；（足跡や道など）をたどる；（規則など）に従う

Just **follow** me! I'll show you where my office is.
（私についてきて！　私のオフィスの場所、案内してあげるから。）

follow the rules（ルールに従う）

V[I/T] （〜を）理解する

His explanation was a bit difficult to **follow**.（彼の説明はちょっと理解するのが難しかった。）

▶ **following** Prep. 〜の後に
[fá:louɪŋ]　　Adj. 次の、以下の　N[S/P] 以下、下記【the -】

I ran into the interviewer at the station **following** the interview.
（面接の後、駅でばったり面接官に会ったんだ。）

▶ **follower** [fá:louər] N[C] フォロワー、支持者、信者

1874 **renaissance**
[rénəsɑːns]
☐☐☐☐☐☐

N[S] ルネサンス期（中世と近代の間の時代）【the R-】；復興、再興

Gothic architecture is experiencing a bit of a **renaissance** right now.
（ゴシック建築は今少しだけ再興しつつあるんだ。）

1875 **engine**
[éndʒɪn]
☐☐☐☐☐☐

N[C] エンジン、機関；機関車；原動力

Content is like a growth **engine** for your blog, so you should try to write useful posts, rather than increase the number of articles.
（コンテンツはブログを成長させるエンジンみたいなものだから、記事数を増やすよりも役立つ記事を書こうとした方がいいよ。）

a steam **engine**（蒸気エンジン、蒸気機関）

1876 **pressure**
[préʃər]
☐☐☐☐☐☐

N[U] 圧力；強要　**N[C/U]** （精神的な）プレッシャー；気圧

Even when he's under a lot of **pressure**, he's great at controlling his emotions.
（彼はプレッシャーを感じてる時でもとても上手に感情をコントロールできるんだ。）

■ no **pressure**（無理なら大丈夫、無理しないで）

Do you want to come to my party tonight? It's a bit last minute, so **no pressure**.
（今夜うちのパーティ来ない？あ、でもちょっといきなりだし、強制じゃないから。）

V[T] に（〜するよう）プレッシャーをかける（to do）

pressure sb into doing（〜にプレッシャーをかけて〜させる）

語根 press それ単体でも「押す」という意味があり、語根として使われる時も同様のイメージを持ちます。他には depress（下に押す＝憂鬱にする）や express（外に押し出す＝表現する）などがあります。

1877 **subsequently**
[sʌ́bsɪkwəntli]
☐☐☐☐☐☐

Adv. その後、後に

I bought some new golf balls just last week but **subsequently** lost all of them over the weekend.
（先週新しいゴルフボールをいくつか買ったんだけど、その後週末に全部失くしちゃったよ。）

▶ **subsequent** [sʌ́bsɪkwənt] Adj. その後の、（〜に）続いて（to sth）

1878 **enormous**
[ənɔ́ːrməs]
☐☐☐☐☐☐

Adj. 非常に大きな、巨大な、膨大な

The restaurant always serves an **enormous** amount of food.
（あのレストランはいつもものすごい量の食事を出してくるんだ。）

▶ **enormously** [ənɔ́ːrməsli] Adv. ものすごく、非常に、膨大に

▶ **enormity** [ənɔ́ːrməti] N[U] 巨大さ、膨大さ

1879 **impetus**
[ímpətəs]
☐☐☐☐☐☐

N[S/U] 推進力、原動力、勢い、弾み

■ give **impetus** to sth（〜を勢いづける、〜に拍車をかける）

This vocabulary book will surely **give impetus to** your English studies.
（この単語帳は確実に英語学習に拍車をかけてくれると思うよ。）

4 In modern times, the term "engineer" is ubiquitous. The term encapsulates vastly different specializations, including aerospace and marine engineers, who mainly handle vehicles, mining engineers who focus on mineral extraction, and software engineers who design and develop software.

現代では、「エンジニア」という用語はどこにでも見られるようになった。この用語は、主に乗り物を扱う航空宇宙技師や造船技師、鉱物の採掘を専門とする鉱山技師、ソフトウェアの設計・開発を手掛けるソフトウェアエンジニアなど、非常にさまざまな分野をカバーしている。

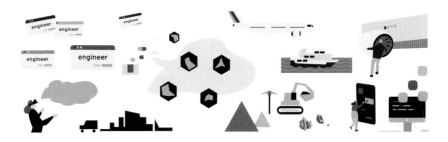

1880 ubiquitous
[ju:bíkwəṭəs]
☐☐☐☐☐☐

Adj. どこにでもある、いたるところにある

Cashless payment is so **ubiquitous** in China, some places don't even accept cash.
(中国はキャッシュレス決済がいたるところにあって、場所によっては現金が使えないところすらあるんだ。)

▶ **ubiquitously** [ju:bíkwəṭəsli] Adv. どこにでも、いたるところに

This Christmas song is heard **ubiquitously** in November and December.
(このクリスマスソングは 11 月と 12 月にあちこちで流れます。)

▶ **ubiquity** [ju:bíkwəṭi] N[U] どこにでもあること、いたるところにあること

I think the **ubiquity** of knowledge is making people with good memories less valuable.
(知識ってもうどこにでもあるから、記憶力の良い人の価値ってどんどん低くなっていると思うんだ。)

1881 vastly
[væstli]
☐☐☐☐☐☐

Adv. 非常に、大いに

He's **vastly** experienced in a lot of different industries, so I think he'll be a great addition to the team. (彼は色んな業界で幅広く経験を積んでるから、チームにとってすごいプラスになると思うよ。)

▶ **vast** Adj. ものすごい大きい、広大な、膨大な ▶ **vastness** N[U] 広大さ
[væst]　[væstnəs]

It's true that she has a **vast** amount of money, but that doesn't mean she'll never run out.
(確かに彼女はものすごい額のお金を持ってるけど、だからと言ってそれがずっとなくならないわけじゃないよ。)

the **vastness** of the universe (宇宙の広大さ)

1882 marine
[mərí:n]
☐☐☐☐☐☐

Adj. 海の、航海の、海軍の　**N[C]** 海兵隊員

I'm really interested in **marine** life, so it's a shame that I never learned how to swim.
(海の生き物にとても興味があるんだけど、お恥ずかしいことに泳ぎ方を習ったことがないんだよね。)

a **marine** biologist（海洋生物学者） a **marine** engineer（造船技師）

1883 **handle**
[hǽndl]
☐☐☐☐☐☐

V[T] を扱う、操作する；に（手で）触れる；(問題など) に対処する

You should delete your browsing history before you let someone else **handle** your smartphone, just in case.（誰かに自分のスマホを操作させる前は、閲覧履歴消しといた方がいいよ。万が一のために。）

Wash your hands before you **handle** food, okay?
（食べ物に触れる前にちゃんと手を洗わないとだめだよ？）

Handling customer complaints is the last thing I want to do at work.
（客のクレーム対応とか職場で一番やりたくないことだよ。）

▶ **handling** [hǽndlɪŋ] N[U] 取り扱い、対応、対処

N[C] （ドアなどの）取っ手

車のハンドルは和製英語？ 日本語ではハンドルという言葉を使いますが、英語で handle はドアなどの取っ手を意味する単語です。英語で車のハンドルは the (steering) wheel と言います。

1884 **vehicle**
[víːəkəl]
☐☐☐☐☐☐

N[C] 乗り物、車両；達成手段；（伝達や表現のための）媒体、手段

This driver's license lets me drive all kinds of **vehicles**.
（この運転免許証があればどんな種類の乗り物も運転できるんだ。）

You should use your company as a **vehicle** for growing yourself.
（会社は自分を成長させるための達成手段として使った方がいいよ。）

1885 **mining**
[máɪnɪŋ]
☐☐☐☐☐☐

N[U] 鉱業、採掘、採鉱

Our electricity bill this month was ridiculous, and we found out that it was because my brother was doing Bitcoin **mining** in his room!
（今月の電気代がヤバかったんだけど、その原因はお兄ちゃんが部屋でビットコインの採掘をしてたからだって分かったんだ。）

▶ **mine** [maɪn] V[I/T]（〜を）採掘する (for sth) N[C] 鉱山；地雷

What are those people **mining** for? I don't think there's anything there.
（あの人たちは何を採掘してるんだろう？あそこには何もないと思うんだけど。）

▶ **miner** [máɪnər] N[C] 鉱山労働者、採鉱者

1886 **mineral**
[mínərəl]
☐☐☐☐☐☐

N[C] 鉱物、鉱石；ミネラル、無機物 **Adj.** ミネラルを含んだ

I heard that this water has **minerals** in it that are great for your health.
（この水には身体に良いミネラルが含まれてるらしいよ。）

mineral water（ミネラルウォーター）

Student (W)	During my research for this assignment, I found these marvelous instructions that captured my attention. They detail how to build a catapult. Can we build a functioning prototype using these instructions, or are they forged?
Professor (M)	I don't think they're fake. However, let's consider a few factors before we rush ahead and start construction. Any thoughts?
Student (W)	Well, there's a risk that it won't be able to take as much strain as the diagram suggests. To negate this, I'll build a model with smaller proportions and test it in a supervised facility. I'll clear the area near the catapult as well during the test phase, in case its expected flight range is exaggerated.
Professor (M)	Also, you could streamline the building process by removing the superfluous gears. Check with the faculty head as well to make sure they have no objections and that we haven't overlooked anything.

生徒 (女性)	今回の課題の研究中、この素敵な説明書を見つけて、興味を引かれたんです。これ、投石機の作り方について詳しく説明してるものなんですけど、この説明書で、実際に動く試作品とか作れますか？それとも、この説明書って偽物だったりします？
教授 (男性)	偽物とは思わないな。でも、急いで作り始める前に、いくつかの要素について考えてみよう。どう思う？
生徒 (女性)	えーっと、この図が示しているだけの力に耐えられないっていうリスクはありますよね。このリスクを否定するために、もっと小さい比率のモデルを作って、管理された施設の中でテストしてみますね。テスト段階では投石機の近くにも何も無いようにしておきます。投石機の予想飛行範囲が誇張されている場合も考えて。
教授 (男性)	あと、余分なギアを取り除いて、作るプロセスを簡素化できるかもしれないね。学部長にも確認して、確実に異議がないように、そして何かしらの見落しもないようにしてね。

1887 **assignment**
[əsáɪnmənt]
☐☐☐☐☐☐

N[C] 課題　N[C/U] 仕事、任務　N[U] 割り当て
▶ **assign** [əsáɪn] V[T] を割り当てる、配属する
assign sb sth（(人) に〜を割り当てる）　be **assigned** to sth（〜に配属される）

1888 **marvelous**
[márvələs]
☐☐☐☐☐☐

Adj. 素敵な、最高の、素晴らしい
▶ **marvel** [máːrvəl] V[I]（〜に）驚く（at sth）　N[C] 驚くべきこと

1889 **capture**
[kǽptʃər]
☐☐☐☐☐☐

V[T] を引きつける；をとらえる、捕まえる　N[U] 捕獲、捕虜にすること
capture sb's attention（〜の注意を引きつける）
▶ **captive** [kǽptɪv] Adj. 捕虜になった N[C] 捕虜
▶ **captivity** [kæptívəti] N[U] 捕らわれた状態

1890 **forge**
[fɔːrdʒ]
☐☐☐☐☐☐

V[T] を偽造する；を鍛造する；(関係など) を構築する
▶ **forgery** [fɔ́ːrdʒəri] N[C] 偽造品　N[U] 偽造罪

1891 **fake**
[feɪk]
☐☐☐☐☐☐

Adj. 偽物の、偽造の　V[I/T]（〜の）ふりをする、（〜を）偽る　N[C] 偽物
a **fake** smile（愛想笑い、作り笑い）

1892 **rush**
[rʌʃ]
☐☐☐☐☐☐

V[I]（〜しようと）急ぐ（to do）
V[T] を大急ぎで行う；をせかす　N[S] 殺到；急ぐこと
[PV] **rush into** sth [rʌʃíntuː] 〜を急いで行う　in a **rush**（急いで）

1893 **thought**
[θɑːt]
☐☐☐☐☐☐

N[C/U] 考え、意見
Any **thoughts**?（どう思う？）
▶ **thoughtful** [θɔ́ːtfəl] Adj. 思いやりのある；考え込んだ
▶ **thoughtfully** [θɔ́ːtfəli] Adv. 思いやって；考え込んで
▶ **thoughtfulness** [θɔ́ːtfəlnəs] N[U] 思いやりのあること；考え込むこと

1894 **strain**
[streɪn]
☐☐☐☐☐☐

N[U] かかる力、荷重
N[C/U] 重圧、重荷、重い負担；(筋肉などを) 痛めること
V[T] (体の一部) を痛める、疲れさせる；(関係) に緊張をもたらす
strain one's ears（耳を澄ます）
▶ **strained** [streɪnd] Adj. 緊張した、張り詰めた

1895 **negate**
[nɪgéɪt]
☐☐☐☐☐☐

V[T] を否定する、無効にする
▶ **negation** [nɪgéɪʃən] N[U] 否定すること
self-**negation**（自己否定）

1896 proportion
[prəpɔ́ːrʃən]

N[C/U] 比率、割合　N[C]（全体の中で占める）部分

in **proportion** to sth（〜とバランスが取れて）

▶ **proportional** [prəpɔ́ːrʃənəl] Adj.（〜と）比例した (to sth)　= **proportionate** [prəpɔ́ːrʃənət]

▶ **proportionally** [prəpɔ́ːrʃənəli] Adv.（〜と）比例して (to sth)

= **proportionately** [prəpɔ́ːrʃənətli]

1897 supervise
[súːpərvaɪz]

V[I/T]（〜を）管理する、監督する、指揮する

▶ **supervision** [sùːpərvíʒən] N[U] 管理、監督、指揮

▶ **supervisory** [sùːpərváɪzəri] Adj. 監督の　▶ **supervisor** [súːpərvaɪzər] N[C] 管理者、監督者

1898 facility
[fəsíləti]

N[C] 施設　N[U] 容易さ

▶ **facilities** [fəsílətiz] N[P] 設備

1899 phase
[feɪz]

N[C] 段階、局面　V[T] を段階的に行う

phases of the moon（月の満ち欠け、月相）

▶ **phase** sth **in** [feɪzín] [PV] 〜を段階的に導入する

↔ **phase** sth **out** [feɪzáut] [PV] 〜を段階的に廃止する

1900 exaggerated
[ɪgzǽdʒəreɪtɪd]

Adj. 誇張された、大げさな

▶ **exaggeration** [ɪgzædʒəréɪʃən] N[U] 誇張、大げさに言うこと　N[C] 誇張された表現・話

▶ **exaggerate** [ɪgzǽdʒəreɪt] V[I/T]（〜を）誇張する、大げさに言う

1901 superfluous
[suːpɝ́ːrfluəs]

Adj. 余分な、不必要な　= **unnecessary** [ʌnnésəseri]

I think including James on our team is a bit **superfluous**.
（僕らのチームにジェームズは余計だと思うんだ。）

1902 gear
[gɪr]

N[C/U] ギア、歯車　N[U] 道具（一式）、用具（一式）

fishing/camping **gear**（釣り / キャンプ道具）

1903 faculty
[fǽkəlti]

N[C] 学部；能力　N[C/U] 教授陣

the **Faculty** of Economics/Law/Engineering（経済 / 法 / 工学部）

1904 objection
[əbdʒékʃən]

N[C] 異議、反対

▶ **object** V[I]（〜に）反対する (to sth/sb)　N[C] 物、物体；目的語；目的、目標
V. [əbdʒékt] N. [áːbdʒɪkt]

1905 overlook
V. [oʊvərlʊ́k]
N. [óʊvərlʊk]

V[T] を見落とす、見逃す　= **miss** [mɪs]；を大目に見る；を見渡す

We stayed at a hotel room that **overlooks** a river and some mountains. It was amazing.（川や山を見渡せるホテルに泊まったんだ。最高だったよ。）

N[C] 見晴らしのよい場所

↻ CH. 19, 24, 28, 32, 35, 38

Chapter

39

コンピューターサイエンス
Computer Science

Computer science is the study of computer theory, engineering, and applications. These three fields use algorithms to extract, manipulate, store, harvest, and communicate digital data to help facilitate interactions between computers and humans.

Theoretical computer science is a rather abstract field which strives to achieve more efficient, optimized, and sophisticated ways to perform computation.

Computer engineering is a dynamic area that often combines knowledge of electrical engineering to design and develop operating systems, networks, robots, and related machinery.

Applications utilize computer theory and engineering to tackle real-world problems. For example, such applications are seen in the field of artificial intelligence, which is gaining momentum at an incredibly rapid rate.

1 Computer **science is the study of computer theory, engineering, and applications. These three fields use algorithms to** extract, manipulate, store, harvest, **and communicate digital** data **to help** facilitate **interactions between computers and humans.**

コンピューターサイエンスは、コンピューターの理論、工学、および応用に関する研究である。この3つの分野では、デジタルデータの抽出・操作・保存・収集・伝達のためにアルゴリズムを使用し、コンピューターと人間の相互作用を容易なものにする。

COMPUTER SCIENCE

1906 **computer**
[kəmpjúːṭər]

N[C] コンピューター、パソコン

My **computer**'s pretty laggy, so I think it's time for a new one.
(俺のパソコン結構遅くなってるから、そろそろ新しいの買い時だと思うんだよね。)

▶ **compute** [kəmpjúːt] V[I/T] (〜を) 計算する

I use a Google app to **compute** how many views my blog has.
(僕は自分のブログの閲覧数を計算するのにグーグルのアプリを使ってるよ。)

▶ **computation** [kàːmpjətéɪʃən] N[C/U] 計算

▶ **computable** [kəmpjúːṭəbəl] Adj. 計算可能な

The universe is so vast that its size and complexity are not yet **computable** by current means.
(宇宙ってめちゃくちゃ広大だからその大きさとか複雑さはまだ現在存在する方法では計算しきれないんだ。)

1907 **extract**
v. [ɪkstrǽkt]
N. [ékstrækt]

V[T] を (〜から) 抽出する、抜く (from sth)

I'm going to try and **extract** some more details from Dave.
(デイヴからもっと詳細を引き出してみるね。)

N[C/U] 抽出物、エキス N[C] 引用

▶ **extraction** [ɪkstrǽkʃən] N[C/U] 抽出、採取；抜歯 N[C] 抜歯

The **extraction** process of aluminum using electrolysis is so interesting.
(アルミニウムを電気分解で抽出する過程ってすごい面白いよなぁ。)

I had two wisdom teeth **extractions** today. (今日親知らずを二本抜きました。)

▶ **extractor** [ɪkstrǽktər] N[C] 抽出する機械

a juice **extractor**（（果物などの）ジューサー）

1908 manipulate
[mənípjəleɪt]
▢▢▢▢▢▢

V[T] を操作する、操る、加工する；を改ざんする

This photo has been **manipulated** way too much.（この写真さすがに加工されすぎでしょ。）

▶ **manipulation** [mənìpjəléɪʃən] N[C/U] 操作、加工；改ざん

media **manipulation**（情報操作）

▶ **manipulative** [mənípjələţɪv] Adj.（都合よく）人の行動を操る

He's smart and intelligent, but sometimes he's a bit **manipulative**.
（彼って賢くて知的なんだけど、たまにちょっと都合よく人を使うことがあるんだ。）

▶ **manipulator** [mənípjəleɪtər] N[C]（都合よく）他人の行動を操る人

1909 store
[stɔ:r]
▢▢▢▢▢▢

V[T] を保存する、保管する；を蓄える　**N[C]** 貯蔵、蓄え；店

I'd love to get a bike, but I don't really have anywhere in my apartment to **store** it.
（自転車欲しいんだけど、うちのマンションには置く場所が無いんだ。）

▶ **storage** [stɔ́:rɪdʒ] N[U] 保存、保管；貯蔵

1910 harvest
[hɑ́:rvəst]
▢▢▢▢▢▢

V[T] を収集する；を収穫する　**N[C/U]** 収穫、収穫期　**N[C]** 収穫高

I think that all these loyalty cards are just being used to **harvest** our personal information.
（ポイントカードってただ個人情報を収集するために使われてると思うんだけど。）

The **harvest** of vegetables was huge this year.（今年は野菜の収穫がすごかったんだ。）

▶ **harvesting** [hɑ́:rvəstɪŋ] N[U]（データの）収集；収穫

Lately there has been a big debate about the unauthorized data **harvesting** happening through social media.（最近は SNS 上で無断で行われるデータ収集が大きな議論になっているよ。）

1911 data
[déɪţə]
▢▢▢▢▢▢

N[U] データ

I need more **data** on the demographics of this city before I can decide if I want to start a business there.
（ここでビジネスを始めるかどうか決める前に、この街の人口統計のデータがもっと必要なんだ。）

データは元々複数形？　data は元々 datum という名詞の複数形として使われていましたが、現在では不可算名詞として扱われることがほとんどです。

1912 facilitate
[fəsíləteɪt]
▢▢▢▢▢▢

V[T] を容易にする、楽にする、円滑に進める

I've been asked to **facilitate** the meeting, but I'm not sure what I need to do.
（私は会議の進行役をするように言われたんだけど、何をすれば良いのかよく分からないんだ。）

▶ **facilitation** N[U] 容易にすること
[fəsìlɪtéɪʃən]

▶ **facilitator** N[C] 司会者、進行役
[fəsíləteɪtər]

2 **Theoretical computer science is a** rather abstract **field which** strives **to** achieve **more** efficient, optimized, **and** sophisticated **ways to perform computation.**

理論計算機科学はかなり抽象的な分野であるが、より効率的で、最適で、洗練された計算方法の達成を目指すものである。

THEORETICAL
COMPUTER SCIENCE

1913 **rather**
[rǽðər]
□□□□□□

Adv. かなり、結構；どちらかと言えば；（～よりも）むしろ (than sth)

Would you **rather** travel to the Moon or explore more of Earth?
（月に旅行に行くのと地球をもっと探検するの、どちらかと言えばどっちがいい？）

■ I'd **rather** do (than do)（（～するよりも）～したい）

I'd rather have coffee **than** tea.（お茶よりコーヒーの方が飲みたい。）

■ I'd **rather** not do（できれば～したくない）

I'd rather not talk about it.（できればその話はしたくないな。）

1914 **abstract**
[ǽbstrækt]
□□□□□□

Adj. 抽象的な

What you're talking about is pretty **abstract**, so can you give me some concrete examples?
（言ってることがかなり抽象的なんだけど、もうちょっと具体例とか出してくれない？）

▶ **abstractly** [ǽbstræktli] Adv. 抽象的に

Thinking **abstractly** basically means thinking about things that are not actually present.
（抽象的に考えるっていうのは、基本的には実際に存在していない物事について考えるっていう意味だよ。）

▶ **abstraction** [æbstrǽkʃən] N[C] 抽象概念　N[U] 抽象化

1915 **strive**
[straɪv]
□□□□□□

V[I] （～のために / ～を目指して）努力する (for sth/to do)

Rather than accept things the way they are, we should always **strive** to do better.
（現状に甘んじるんじゃなくて、常によりよいものを目指していかないとね。）

▶ **strife** [straɪf] N[U] 争い、戦い、紛争

What do you think I can do to resolve this **strife** in my family?
（この家族内で起きてる争いってどうやって解決すれば良いと思う？）

1916 **achieve**
[ətʃíːv]
▢▢▢▢▢▢

V[T]　を達成する、成し遂げる、勝ち取る

It's crazy how much our team has **achieved** already this year.
（うちのチーム、今年もうこんなに色々達成してめちゃくちゃすごいよなぁ。）

achieve a goal/objective（目的 / 目標を達成する）

▶ **achievement** [ətʃíːvmənt] N[U] 達成　N[C] 業績、成果、偉業

a sense of **achievement**（達成感）

▶ **achievable** [ətʃíːvəbəl] Adj. 達成できる

You should make sure that the goals you set for yourself are challenging but also **achievable**.（自分に対して設定するゴールはやりがいがあると同時に達成可能なものにした方がいいよ。）

▶ **achiever** [ətʃíːvər] N[C] 達成者、成功者

1917 **efficient**
[ɪfíʃənt]
▢▢▢▢▢▢

Adj. 効率的な　⟷ **inefficient** [ìnɪfíʃənt] 非効率な

There's a fine line between being **efficient** and being sloppy.
（効率的にやるっていうことと、雑にやることの差は紙一重だよ。）

effective and **efficient**（効果的で効率的な）

▶ **efficiently** [ɪfíʃəntli] Adv. 効率的に　⟷ **inefficiently** [ìnɪfíʃəntli] 非効率に

Planning your day ahead will help you work more **efficiently**.
（事前に一日の計画を立てておくともっと効率的に仕事ができるよ。）

▶ **efficiency** [ɪfíʃənsi] N[U] 効率　⟷ **inefficiency** [ìnɪfíʃənsi] 非効率

▶ **efficiencies** [ɪfíʃənsiz] N[P] コスト削減

1918 **optimize**
[ɑ́ːptəmaɪz]
▢▢▢▢▢▢

V[T]　を最適化する；を最大限に利用する

I don't have a lot of free time, so I have to **optimize** my workout routine.
（そんなに自由に使える時間無いし、運動習慣を最適化しないといけないなぁって。）

▶ **optimization** [ɑ̀ːptəməzéɪʃən] N[U] 最適化

▶ **optimum** [ɑ́ːptəməm] N[S] 最適（条件）【the -】　Adj. 最適な　= **optimal** [ɑ́ːptəməl]

Do you know what the **optimum** level of daily protein intake is?
（一日の最適なプロテイン摂取量ってどれくらいか知ってる？）

1919 **sophisticated**
[səfístəkeɪtɪd]
▢▢▢▢▢▢

Adj. 洗練された、精巧な、教養のある

My taste buds have become more **sophisticated** since I started eating out more often.　（頻繁に外食し始めて以来、味覚が洗練されてきたんだ。）

▶ **sophisticate** V[T] を洗練させる　N[C] あか抜けた人、教養人
　　V. [səfístəkeɪt]　*N.* [səfístəkət]

The **sophisticates** of the city taught me how to enjoy the nightlife of Tokyo.
（街のあか抜けた人たちが東京での夜遊びの楽しみ方を教えてくれたんだ。）

▶ **sophistication** [səfìstəkéɪʃən] N[U] 精巧さ、洗練されていること

3 **Computer** engineering **is a** dynamic **area that often combines knowledge of** electrical **engineering to** design **and develop** operating **systems,** networks, **robots, and** related **machinery.**

コンピューター工学は絶えず変化する分野で、しばしば電気工学の知識を組み合わせてオペレーティングシステムやネットワーク、ロボット、および関連機器の設計・開発を行うものである。

1920 **engineering**
[ènʤɪnírɪŋ]
☐☐☐☐☐☐

N[U] 工学、エンジニアリング

I often confuse software **engineering** with computer science.
（よくソフトウェア工学とコンピューターサイエンスを混同しちゃうんだよね。）

▶ **engineer** [ènʤɪnír] V[T] を設計する；をたくらむ　N[C] エンジニア、技術者、技師

He's trying to **engineer** a move away from the club.
（彼は別のクラブに移籍しようとたくらんでいるんだ。）

a software **engineer**（ソフトウェアエンジニア）

1921 **dynamic**
[daɪnǽmɪk]
☐☐☐☐☐☐

Adj. 絶えず変化する；活発な；動的な　⟷ static [stǽtɪk] 静的な

I love working in a **dynamic** and exciting environment.
（僕はダイナミックでワクワクするような環境で働くのが大好きなんだ。）

N[P] （組織や集団内での）力関係【-s】　N[U] 力学【-s】　N[S] 原動力

▶ **dynamically** [daɪnǽmɪkli] Adv. 精力的に

I decided to move to New York because I wanted to work **dynamically**.
（精力的に仕事したかったからニューヨークに引っ越すことに決めたよ。）

1922 **electrical**
[iléktrɪkəl]
☐☐☐☐☐☐

Adj. 電気の、電動の

You shouldn't do **electrical** work yourself. It's too dangerous.
（電気工事は自分でしない方が良いよ。危険すぎる。）

an **electrical** car（電気自動車）

▶ **electrically** [iléktrɪkli] Adv. 電気によって

This sports car is 100% **electrically** powered.（このスポーツカー、100%電気で動くんですよ。）

▶ **electricity** [ilèktrísəti] N[U] 電気、電力

The **electricity** was out for quite a while after the huge thunderstorm.
（激しい雷雨の後しばらく電気がつかなかったんだ。）

1923 **design**
[dɪzáɪn]

▢▢▢▢▢▢

V[I/T]（〜を）設計する、デザインする　N[C/U] 設計、デザイン

■ be **designed** to do/for sth（〜することを目的に / 〜のために設計されている）

This course **is designed to** provide students with a big-picture view of programming.
（このコースはプログラミングの全体像を学生に理解させることを目的に設計されています。）

1924 **operating**
[á:pəreɪtɪŋ]

▢▢▢▢▢▢

Adj.（PC の）オペレーションに関する；経営上の、営業上の

Our **operating** costs are way too high, so we need to do something about them immediately.
（うちの営業コストが高すぎるから、今すぐ何かしないとダメなんだ。）

operating income（営業利益）

▶ **operate** 　V[T] を操作する；を経営する、運営する
　[á:pəreɪt] 　V[I] 動く、営業する；（〜を）手術する（on sth/sb）

If you don't like the restaurant that you're working at now, you should open and **operate** your own restaurant.
（今働いてるレストランが好きじゃないなら、自分のレストランを開いて経営するのが良いと思うよ。）

If he doesn't improve with the treatment, we'll have to **operate** on him.
（その治療で良くならなかったら、手術しないといけないですね。）

▶ **operation** [à:pəréɪʃən] N[U] 操作、運転　N[C] 手術；作戦　N[C/U] 経営、営業

a military **operation**（軍事作戦）　　a business **operation**（ビジネスの運営）

in **operation**（動いている）

1925 **network**
[nétwɜːrk]

▢▢▢▢▢▢

N[C]　ネットワーク、繋がり、人脈

You should expand your professional **network** if you want to advance in your career.
（キャリアで上に行きたいなら仕事のネットワークを広げた方が良いよ。）

▶ **networking** [nétwɜːrkɪŋ] N[U] ネットワーキング、人と繋がること

1926 **related**
[rɪléɪt̬ɪd]

▢▢▢▢▢▢

Adj.（〜と）関連した（to sth/sb）；（〜と）親戚の（to sb）

↔ **unrelated** [ʌnrɪléɪt̬ɪd] 関連のない、無関係の

I hate when people ask me work-**related** questions after hours.
（勤務時間後に仕事関連の質問してくる人無理。）

▶ **relate** [rɪléɪt] V[I]（〜と）関連がある（to sth/sb）；（〜に）共感する（to sb）
　　　　　　　　　V[T] を（〜と）関連づける、関係づける（to sth）

I can totally **relate** to that.（それ本当に共感できる。）

▶ **relatable** [rɪléɪt̬əbəl] Adj. 関係づけられる；共感できる

▶ **relation** [rɪléɪʃən] N[C/U] 関連、関係　N[P]（国家や団体間の）関係【-s】

▶ **relationship** [rɪléɪʃənʃɪp] N[C] 関係、結びつき

relations vs **relationship**　relations は relationship よりもフォーマルで、国家間や団体間の関係を表すときによく使用されます（例：relations between Japan and the U.S.）。一方で relationship はより広く一般的に人と人の関係を表すときに使われることが多く、比較的カジュアルな表現です（例：my relationship with my girlfriend）。

4 Applications utilize computer theory and engineering to tackle real-world problems. For example, such applications are seen in the field of artificial intelligence, which is gaining momentum at an incredibly rapid rate.

そして応用分野では、コンピューターの理論や工学を利用し、実社会の問題への取り組みが行われている。 例えば、こうした応用は、極めて急速に勢いを増している人工知能分野において見ることができる。

APPLICATION

1927 **utilize**
[júːṭəlaɪz]
☐☐☐☐☐☐

V[T] を利用する、活用する

How can I **utilize** my time more effectively?
（どうやったら自分の時間をもっと効果的に使えるかな？）

▶ **utilization** [jùːṭələzéɪʃən] N[U] 利用、活用

Through improved **utilization** of social media, we can definitely increase our sales.
（SNSをもっとうまく使えば、確実に売り上げは上がると思うよ。）

▶ **utility** [juːtíləṭi] N[C]（電気やガスなどの）公共サービス　N[U] 効用、有用性

My rent includes all **utilities** costs.（私の家の家賃は公共料金全部含まれてるんだ。）

1928 **tackle**
[tǽkəl]
☐☐☐☐☐☐

V[T] に取り組む　**V[I/T]**（〜に）タックルする　**N[C]** タックル

I don't really have the energy to **tackle** this problem right now. I'm so tired.
（今この問題に取り組むようなエネルギーは僕にはないよ。すごい疲れちゃった。）

tackle vs address どちらも「（問題などに）取り組む」と訳されることが多い動詞ですが、若干ニュアンスの違いがあります。tackle はスポーツのタックルから想像できるように、多くの努力を要して、その問題を倒すイメージですが、address は単純にその問題に取り組むというニュアンスがあります。

1929 **real-world**
[ríəl wɜːrld]
☐☐☐☐☐☐

Adj. 実社会の、現実世界の

Many economists are trying to solve **real-world** problems by applying outdated theories.
（多くの経済学者は時代遅れの経済理論を使って現実世界の問題を解決しようとしているんだ。）

▶ **real world** [ríəl wɜːrld] N[S] 実社会、現実世界【the -】

1930 **intelligence**
[ɪntélədʒəns]
☐☐☐☐☐☐

N[S] 知能、知力；機密情報

What do you think is the best way to measure the **intelligence** of our students?
（学生の知能を測るのに一番良い方法って何だと思う？）

high/average/low **intelligence**（高い / 平均的な / 低い知能）

▶ **intelligent** [ɪntélədʒənt] Adj. 頭の良い、知的な

Several studies now prove how **intelligent** dolphins really are.
（イルカが実際どれほど頭が良いかはもういくつかの研究によって証明されてるよ。）

▶ **intelligently** [ɪntélədʒəntli] Adv. 知的に

He speaks very **intelligently**, but he's actually just all talk.
（彼はすごく知的に話すんだけど、実際は口先だけだよ。）

1931 **gain**
[geɪn]

V[I/T]（〜を）得る；増やす；稼ぐ　N[C/U]　益、利益

How do I **gain** more followers on Twitter?
（ツイッターでもっとフォロワーを増やすにはどうすれば良いの？）

■ **gain**/lose weight（体重が増える / 減る）

Oh no, I **gained weight*** again.（あぁ、また体重増えちゃった。）
* gain five kilos（5 キロ体重が増えた）のように具体的な重さを続けることもできます。

1932 **momentum**
[məméntəm]

N[U]　勢い、弾み

I don't think that the **momentum** behind Bitcoin will continue indefinitely.
（僕はビットコインの勢いがずっと続くとは思えないな。）

gain/lose **momentum**（勢いを増す / 失う）

1933 **incredibly**
[ɪnkrédəbli]

Adv.　極めて、非常に、信じられないほど

His knowledge of the TV industry is **incredibly** vast.
（彼はテレビ業界に関する知識が極めて豊富なんだ。）

▶ **incredible** [ɪnkrédəbəl] Adj. 信じられない；素晴らしい

Did you start your own company? That's **incredible**!（起業したの？素晴らしい！）

⬅➡ **credible** [krédəbəl] 信じられる、信頼できる

I think politicians need to be **credible** and held clearly accountable.
（僕は政治家というのは信頼できて、かつ明確な説明責任を持つ必要があると思うよ。）

*My **Preliminary** Thoughts on the Latest **Edition** of Grapefruit's Flagship **Tablet**, the X9*

💬 56 Comments | ⤸ 259 Shares

Design

The X9 has an ultra-thin form factor, which is much-improved over its predecessor, and comes in a variety of sizes to cater to different customer needs. It inherits the X8's stunning screen. The X9 comes in a dizzying array of colors. While there are a number of interesting options on offer, including 'Peach Pink,' my favorite is 'Classic black.'

Performance

Grapefruit claims that the X9, which comes installed with xOS 5.1, is '20 times faster' than the X8 and has significantly extended battery life. However, anecdotal evidence, confirmed by my own testing, indicates negligible performance gains.

Price

While robust and capable, at a starting RRP of $1,500, the price of the X9 is too steep for casual users, and, to a certain extent, it is likely to seem like an indulgence even to power users. However, given Grapefruit's virtual monopoly on the high-end tablet market, the X9 will likely be a success.

グレープフルーツ社の主力タブレットの最新エディションX9について、私のとりあえずの意見

デザイン

X9には超薄型のフォームファクタが搭載されていて、前作よりも大幅に改善されています。顧客の異なるニーズに応えるさまざまなサイズも出ています。X8のものすごく美しい画面もそのまま継承されています。
X9では目まぐるしい数のカラーが展開されています。「ピーチピンク」のようないくつもの面白い選択肢が提供されていますが、私のお気に入りは「クラシックブラック」です。

性能

グレープフルーツ社は、xOS 5.1がインストールされているX9は、X8より「20倍速く」、バッテリー寿命も大幅に延びたとうたっています。しかし、これが確かな証拠になるというわけではないのですが、私が自分で行ったテストでは、この性能向上は取るに足りないレベルであるということが確認されています。

価格

頑丈で有能ですが、希望小売価格が1,500ドルからというのはライトユーザーには高すぎますし、ある程度はヘビーユーザーにとっても贅沢品のように思えるかもしれません。ただし、ハイエンドタブレット市場がグレープフルーツ社の実質的な独占状態にあることを考えれば、X9はおそらくヒット商品になるでしょう。

1934 preliminary
[prɪlímɪnəri]

Adj. とりあえずの、予備的な　N[C] 下準備

1935 edition
[ɪdíʃən]

N[C] エディション、版、号

1936 tablet
[tˈæblət]

N[C] タブレット端末；錠剤　= **pill** [pɪl]

1937 predecessor
[prédəsesər]

N[C] 前作、旧型；前任者

↔ **successor** [səksésər] N[C] 後任者、後継者

1938 cater
[kéɪţər]

V[I] （〜の要求に）応える (to sth/sb)　V[I/T]（〜に）料理を提供する

▶ **catering** [kéɪţərɪŋ] N[U] (料理の) ケータリング

▶ **caterer** [kéɪţərər] N[C] ケータリング業者

1939 inherit
[ɪnhérɪt]

V[T] を引き継ぐ、受け継ぐ；を相続する

▶ **inheritance** [ɪnhérɪtəns] N[C] 相続遺産　N[U] 相続　N[C/U] 遺伝的形質

▶ **inherited** [ɪnhérɪtɪd] Adj. 受け継がれた、相続された；遺伝の

▶ **heir** [er] N[C] 相続人

1940 stunning
[stˈʌnɪŋ]

Adj. ものすごく美しい、素晴らしい、驚くような

▶ **stunningly** [stˈʌnɪŋli] Adv. 驚くほど

▶ **stun** [stʌn] V[T] を気絶させる、驚かせる

▶ **stunned** [stʌnd] Adj. あぜんとした

1941 screen
[skri:n]

N[C] 画面、スクリーン；網戸

V[T] を検査する；を選抜する；を上映する

▶ **screening** [skri:nɪŋ] N[C/U] 検査　N[C] 上映

1942 dizzying
[dízɪŋ]

Adj. 目まぐるしいほどの、目まいがするような

▶ **dizzy** [dízi] Adj. (目まいで) ふらふらする　V[T] をふらふらさせる

▶ **dizzily** [dízəli] Adv. (目まいで) ふらふらして　▶ **dizziness** [dízinəs] N[U] 目まい

1943 install
[ɪnstˈɔ:l]

V[T] をインストールする；を設置する、取り付ける；を就任させる

▶ **installation** [ɪnstəléɪʃən] N[U] インストール；設置；就任　N[C] 施設；設備

▶ **installment** [ɪnstˈɔlmənt] N[C] 分割払い、分割一回分の支払い

pay in **installments**（分割払いで支払う）

1944 battery
[bǽṭəri]
⬜⬜⬜⬜⬜⬜

N[C] バッテリー、電池　**N[U]** 暴行

run out of **battery** （バッテリーが切れる）

1945 anecdotal
[æ̀nɪkdóʊṭl]
⬜⬜⬜⬜⬜⬜

Adj. 事例に基づく；逸話の

anecdotal evidence （確かな証拠となるわけではないもの、事例証拠）

▶ **anecdote** [ǽnɪkdoʊt] N[C] 逸話

1946 confirm
[kənfɝ́ːrm]
⬜⬜⬜⬜⬜⬜

V[T] を確認する、裏付ける

▶ **confirmation** [kὰːnfərméɪʃən] N[U] 裏付け、確認

▶ **confirmed** [kənfɝ́ːrmd] Adj. 確認済みの；筋金入りの

1947 negligible
[néɡlədʒəbəl]
⬜⬜⬜⬜⬜⬜

Adj. 取るに足りない、無視できるほどの

▶ **negligibly** [néɡlədʒəbli] Adv. 無視できるほどに

▶ **negligence** [néɡlədʒəns] N[U] 過失、怠慢

▶ **negligent** [néɡlədʒənt] Adj. 怠慢な　▶ **negligently** [néɡlədʒəntli] Adv. 怠慢で

1948 robust
[roʊbʌ́st]
⬜⬜⬜⬜⬜⬜

Adj. 頑丈な、丈夫な、しっかりした

▶ **robustly** [roʊbʌ́stli] Adv. 頑丈で、丈夫に、しっかりと

▶ **robustness** [roʊbʌ́stnəs] N[U] しっかりしていること、（経済などの）健全さ

1949 steep
[stiːp]
⬜⬜⬜⬜⬜⬜

Adj. （値段が）高すぎる；険しい、急な

▶ **steeply** [stíːpli] Adv. 急に、急激に　▶ **steepness** [stíːpnəs] N[U] 険しさ、急勾配

▶ **steepen** [stíːpən] V[I] 険しくなる　V[T] を急勾配にする

1950 casual
[kǽʒuːəl]
⬜⬜⬜⬜⬜⬜

Adj. 普段使いの、形式ばらない、カジュアルな、気軽な；（仕事が）短期の

▶ **casually** [kǽʒuːəli] Adv. カジュアルに、気軽に

▶ **casualness** [kǽʒuːəlnəs] N[U] カジュアルさ、気軽さ

1951 extent
[ɪkstént]
⬜⬜⬜⬜⬜⬜

N[S/U] 範囲、程度

to a certain **extent**/to some **extent** （ある程度）　to a large/small **extent** （大いに / 少しは）

the **extent** to which + sentence （どの程度〜か）

1952 indulgence
[ɪndʌ́ldʒəns]
⬜⬜⬜⬜⬜⬜

N[C] 贅沢品、贅沢、道楽　**N[U]** （悪い習慣などに）ふけること

▶ **indulge** [ɪndʌ́ldʒ] V[I] （〜に）ふける (in sth)　V[T] を甘やかす

▶ **indulgent** [ɪndʌ́ldʒənt] Adj. 甘い、寛大な　▶ **indulgently** [ɪndʌ́ldʒəntli] Adv. 寛大に

1953 monopoly
[mənάːpəli]
⬜⬜⬜⬜⬜⬜

N[C] 独占、独占事業、独占企業

▶ **monopolize** [mənάːpəlaɪz] V[T] を独占する

▶ **monopolization** [mənὰːpəlɪzéɪʃən] N[U] 独占化

▶ **monopolistic** [mənὰːpəlístɪk] Adj. 独占的な　▶ **monopolist** [mənάːpəlɪst] N[C] 独占者

Chapter

40

人工知能（AI）
Artificial Intelligence

In a nutshell, artificial intelligence (AI) is a system that simulates human intelligence using specific algorithms. Deep learning, a subset of machine learning, has taken center stage in recent years.

Deep learning utilizes neural networks that imitate the human brain to interpret enormous amounts of data. It is already being used in many areas such as automatic language translation, cancer detection, fraud identification, and YouTube recommendations.

As deep learning has the potential to radically disrupt existing industries, it is currently a buzzword creating a stir in the field of AI. In fact, it is predicted that almost 50% of human jobs will soon be taken over by this state-of-the-art technology.

Given that this technology will remove the need for many current jobs, particularly clerical and administrative work, and create in parallel new jobs pertaining to AI and robotics, having diverse and relevant skills will be essential to overcoming the challenges that result from these changes.

1

In a nutshell, artificial intelligence (AI) is a system that simulates human intelligence using specific algorithms. Deep learning, a subset of machine learning, has taken center stage in recent years.

簡単に言えば、人工知能（AI）は、特定のアルゴリズムを使って人の知能を模倣したシステムを言う。中でも近年は、機械学習の一部であるディープラーニングが注目を集めている。

---

¹⁹⁵⁴ **in a nutshell**
[ɪnə nʌ́tʃel]
☐☐☐☐☐☐

Phr. 簡単に言えば、簡潔に

This three-minute video explains the history of America **in a nutshell**, so it's definitely worth a watch even if you don't have much time.
（この 3 分動画はアメリカの歴史を簡潔に説明してくれてるから、時間がなくても絶対見た方が良いよ。）

---

¹⁹⁵⁵ **simulate**
[símjəleɪt]
☐☐☐☐☐☐

V[T] を模倣する、シミュレーションする

I often cuddle my body pillow at night just to **simulate** having a boyfriend because I've never had one. （彼氏いたことないから、よく夜に抱き枕抱いて彼氏いることをシミュレーションしてるんだ。）

▶ **simulation** [sìmjəléɪʃən] N[C/U] シミュレーション、模擬実験

I saw a computer **simulation** of a magnitude 8.0 earthquake, and it was quite graphic.
（マグニチュード 8.0 の地震のコンピューターシミュレーションを見たんだけど、結構生々しかったよ。）

▶ **simulated** Adj. シミュレーションによる、模擬の ▶ **simulator** N[C] シミュレーター
[símjəleɪtɪd]   [símjəleɪtər]

---

¹⁹⁵⁶ **algorithm**
[ǽlgərɪðəm]
☐☐☐☐☐☐

N[C] アルゴリズム

YouTube often changes its **algorithm**, so what gets recommended to you to watch might not always appeal.
（YouTube はアルゴリズムをよく変えるから、別に見たいと思わない動画がおすすめされることもあるかも。）

---

¹⁹⁵⁷ **deep**
[di:p]
☐☐☐☐☐☐

Adj. 深い；奥行きのある

My friend and I had a really **deep** conversation about the meaning of life.
（友達と人生の目的に関してものすごい深い話をしたんだ。）

deep learning （ディープラーニング、深層学習）

This cupboard is so **deep** I can't reach the mugs in the back.
（この食器棚、奥行きがありすぎて後ろのマグカップに届かないんだ。）

■ **deep** inside one's heart （心の奥底で）

My mom acts like she doesn't care about me, but I know **deep inside her heart** she loves me.
（お母さんは私のことなんて気にしてないみたいにふるまうけど、心の奥底では私のことを愛してくれてるの知ってるんだ。）

▶ **deeply** [díːpli] Adv. 深く

I can't concentrate **deeply** when there is background noise, so I normally go to the library to study.（周りに雑音があると深く集中できないから、基本勉強するときは図書館に行くんだ。）

▶ **depth** [depθ] N[C/U] 深さ、奥行き；（問題などの）深刻さ

The more I get to know Bill, the more I'm impressed by the **depth** of his knowledge.
（ビルのことを知れば知るほど、彼の知識の深さに感心するよ。）

1958 **subset**
[sʌ́bset]

N[C] 一部、部分集合

A large **subset** of the patients trialed responded positively to the medication.
（治験を受けた人の大部分が、その薬に対して良好な反応を示したんです。）

▶ **set** [set] N[C] 集合；セット V[T] を置く；を定める Adj. 固定された；準備ができた

■ **all set** (for sth/to do) （（〜の／〜する）準備ができた） a universal **set** （全体集合）

Are you **all set to** go?（行く準備できた？） = Are you ready to go?

We're **all set for** tomorrow's event. Excited!（明日のイベントの準備は万全。楽しみ！）

1959 **machine**
[məʃíːn]

N[C] 機械；コンピューター

Our office installed a really expensive coffee **machine**, but the beans are super cheap, so the coffee ends up being terrible.
（うちのオフィスにめちゃくちゃ高いコーヒーマシンが設置されたんだけど、豆を超ケチってるから結局コーヒーはめっちゃ不味いんだ。）

a vending **machine** （自動販売機）

▶ **machinery** [məʃíːnəri] N[U] 機械類、（機械内部の）部品、仕組み

1960 **take center stage**
[teɪk séntər steɪdʒ]

Phr. 注目を集める

This new phone will definitely **take center stage** at the tech expo next month.
（この新しい携帯は来月のテックエクスポで間違いなく注目を集めると思うよ。）

直訳すると「舞台の中央（= center stage）を取る（= take）」となり、ステージの中央に立つと注目を集めることに由来する比喩的な表現です。

2 Deep learning utilizes neural networks that imitate the human brain to interpret enormous amounts of data. It is already being used in many areas such as automatic language translation, cancer detection, fraud identification, and YouTube recommendations.

ディープラーニングは、人の脳を模倣したニューラルネットワークを利用して膨大な量のデータを解釈する。既に自動翻訳、がんの発見、不正行為の検出、YouTube のおすすめ機能など、多くの分野で活用されている。

1961 **neural**
[nʊ́rəl]
☐☐☐☐☐☐

Adj. 神経の、神経系の

Neural bypass technology could help people with paralyzed limbs regain control of movement.
(神経バイパス技術を使えば、手足が麻痺してる人の動きを取り戻すことができるかもしれない。)

▶ **neuron** [nʊ́rɑːn] N[C] ニューロン、神経細胞　**= a nerve cell** [ə nɜ́ːrvsel]

1962 **imitate**
[íməteɪt]
☐☐☐☐☐☐

V[T] を模倣する、まねる；の物まねをする

In the past, China was criticized for always **imitating** products from other countries, but these days there's so much innovation happening there. (中国は他の国の商品をまねてばかりで昔は批判を受けてたけど、最近ではものすごいイノベーションが巻き起こってるよ。)

▶ **imitation** [ìmətéɪʃən] N[U] 模倣、まね　N[C] 模倣品；物まね　Adj. 模造の

They say "**imitation** is the sincerest form of flattery," but it's still annoying when people copy my ideas.
(「模倣は最も誠実な褒め言葉」ってよく言うけど、それでもやっぱり自分のアイディアがコピーされたら嫌だなぁ。)

imitation is the sincerest form of flattery　flattery は「お世辞」という意味で、人が誰かをまねすることは、その人に対する敬意の裏返しであるという意味のことわざで、皮肉っぽく使われることもあります。

1963 **automatic**
[ɑ̀ːtəmǽtɪk]
☐☐☐☐☐☐

Adj. 自動的な；無意識な

I couldn't help punching him in the face. It was an **automatic** reaction.
(彼の顔をパンチせずにはいられなかった。あれは条件反射だった。)

▶ **automatically** [ɑ̀ːtəmǽtɪkli] Adv. 自動的に；無意識に

▶ **automation** [ɑ̀ːtəméɪʃən] N[U] 自動化　▶ **automated** [ɑ́ːtəmeɪtɪd] Adj. 自動の

I made an **automated** stock trading system, so I don't have to be in front of monitors all the time anymore. I'm a genius.
(自動株取引システムを作ったから、もうモニターの前にずっといる必要がないんだ。私って天才。)

1964 translation
[trænsléɪʃən]
☐☐☐☐☐☐

N[U] 翻訳 ;（別形態への）転換　**N[C]** 翻訳本、翻訳物 ; 訳語

This **translation** app helped me a lot when I was traveling through Mongolia.
（モンゴル旅行中はこの翻訳アプリがめっちゃ役に立ったよ。）

▶ **translate** [trænslért] V[T] を（〜に）翻訳する、訳す（to sth）　V[I] 翻訳する

Can you help me **translate** this article from Japanese to English?
（この記事を日本語から英語に訳すの手伝ってくれない？）

▶ V[I]（〜に）つながる（into sth）　V[T] を（〜に）つなげる（into sth）

Effort **translates** into success.（努力は成功につながるんだ。）

▶ **translator** [trænsléɪtər] N[C] 翻訳家、翻訳機

1965 cancer
[kǽnsər]
☐☐☐☐☐☐

N[C/U] がん　**N[S]** 害悪　**N[U]** かに座【C-】　**N[C]** かに座の人【C-】

■ have **cancer**（がんにかかっている）　lung/breast/skin **cancer**（肺 / 乳 / 皮膚がん）

My dad **had cancer** three years ago, but after going through chemo treatment he's back to his normal life now.
（私のお父さんは 3 年前にがんが見つかったんだけど、何回か抗がん剤治療をして、今は普通の生活ができてるんだ。）

a **cancer** on society（社会における害悪）

▶ **cancerous** [kǽnsərəs] Adj. がんの　▶ **carcinogenic** [kà:rsənoʊdʒénɪk] Adj. 発がん性の

I try to avoid food additives as much as possible because some of them are **carcinogenic**.
（食品添加物には発がん性があるものもあるからできるだけ避けるようにしてるよ。）

▶ **carcinogen** [ka:rsínədʒən] N[C] 発がん物質

1966 fraud
[frɑ:d]
☐☐☐☐☐☐

N[C/U] 不正行為、詐欺　**N[C]** 詐欺師

I've installed a surveillance camera to prevent employee **fraud** like the theft of money.
（お金の窃盗みたいな従業員による不正を防ぐために監視カメラを設置したよ。）

credit card **fraud**（クレジットカード詐欺）

▶ **fraudulent** Adj. 不正の、詐欺の　▶ **fraudulently** Adv. 不正に、騙して
[frɑ́:dʒələnt]　　　　　　　　　　　　　[frɑ́:dʒələntli]

▶ **fraudulence** [frɑ́:dʒələns] N[U] 不正、詐欺

1967 recommendation
[rèkəmendéɪʃən]
☐☐☐☐☐☐

N[C/U] おすすめ、推薦　**N[C]** 助言、勧告 ; 推薦状

What's your **recommendation**?（おすすめは何ですか？）

■ make a **recommendation**（助言をする、提案をする）

We **made a recommendation** to the client today.（今日はお客さんに提案をしたんだ。）

▶ **recommend** [rèkəménd] V[T] を推薦する、勧める

If you have the chance to visit Sapporo during your Japan trip, I highly **recommend** eating sushi and miso ramen.
（日本旅行中に札幌に行く機会があるなら、お寿司と味噌ラーメンを食べることを強くおすすめするよ。）

3

As deep learning has the potential to radically disrupt existing industries, it is currently a buzzword creating a stir in the field of AI. In fact, it is predicted that almost 50% of human jobs will soon be taken over by this state-of-the-art technology.

ディープラーニングは、既存の産業を根本から崩壊させる可能性があるため、現在、AI の分野で話題沸騰の流行語になっている。実際、人の仕事のほぼ 50%は近いうちにこの最先端技術に取って代わられるという予測もある。

1968 **radically**
[rǽdɪkli]
☐☐☐☐☐☐

Adv. 根本的に、抜本的に；急進的に

My TOEIC score improved immediately after I **radically** changed the way I studied for it.
（勉強の仕方を根本から変えたらすぐに TOEIC の点数が上がったんだ。）

▶ **radical** [rǽdɪkəl] Adj. 根本的な；急進的な

▶ **radicalize** [rǽdɪkəlaɪz] V[T] を抜本的に変える；を急進的にする

▶ **radicalism** [rǽdɪkəlɪzəm] N[U] 急進主義

1969 **industry**
[índəstri]
☐☐☐☐☐☐

N[C] （特定の）産業、業界　**N[U]** 産業、工業

What kind of **industry** do you want to work in in the long-term?
（長期的にはどんな業界で働きたい？）

▶ **industrial** Adj. 産業の、工業の　　▶ **industrially** Adv. 産業上、工業的に
[ɪndʌ́striəl]　　　　　　　　　　　　[ɪndʌ́striəli]

an **industrial** city（産業都市）

▶ **industrious** Adj. 勤勉な、よく働く　▶ **industriously** Adv. 勤勉に
[ɪndʌ́striəs]　　　　　　　　　　　　[ɪndʌ́striəsli]

Although you may think that all ants are **industrious**, the reality is that the majority of them are doing absolutely nothing.
（アリはみんなよく働いていると思ってるかもしれないけど、実際のところ大部分のアリは全く何もしてないんだよ。）

▶ **industriousness** [ɪndʌ́striəsnəs] N[U] 勤勉さ

1970 **buzzword**
[bʌ́zwɜ:rd]
☐☐☐☐☐☐

N[C] 流行語、業界用語、バズワード

Consultants use way too many **buzzwords**. I can never understand what they're talking about. （コンサルの人って業界用語使い過ぎてて何話してるのか意味不明。）

1971 stir
[stɜːr]
▢▢▢▢▢▢

N[S]　騒ぎ、興奮　N[C]　かき混ぜること

- create/cause a **stir**（話題を呼ぶ、騒ぎを起こす、物議をかもす）　give sth a **stir**（〜をかき混ぜる）

His tweets often **cause a stir**.（彼のツイートはよく物議をかもすんだ。）

V[T]　をかき混ぜる；（感情）をかき立てる；を揺れ動かす　V[I]　揺れ動く

I never **stir** my espresso because I want to enjoy the way it changes flavor as I drink.
（私はエスプレッソは絶対にかき混ぜないよ。飲み進める中で味が変わるのを楽しみたいからね。）

▶ **stirring** Adj. 感動的な、刺激的な　　▶ **stirringly** Adv. 感動的に、刺激的に
[stɜ́ːrɪŋ]　N[C] 兆し、芽生え　　　　[stɜ́ːrɪŋli]

make/deliver a **stirring** speech（感動的なスピーチをする）

▶ **stirrer** [stɜ́ːrər] N[C] マドラー

Excuse me, can I get a **stirrer** for my coffee?
（すいません、コーヒー用にマドラーをもらえますか？）

▶ **stir-fry** V[T] をさっと炒める　N[C] 炒め料理　　▶ **stir-fried** Adj. さっと炒めた
[stɜ́ːrfraɪ]　　　　　　　　　　　　　　　[stɜ́ːrfraɪd]

1972 soon
[suːn]
▢▢▢▢▢▢

Adv.　近いうちに、もうすぐ

Sorry, I'm running a bit late, but I'll be there **soon**.
（遅れててごめん、でももうすぐ着くよ。）

- as **soon** as possible（できるだけ早く）

I want to leave this company get-together **as soon as possible**.
（この会社の飲み会できるだけ早く出たい。）

- **sooner** or later（いつかは、遅かれ早かれ）　　- **sooner** rather than later（すぐに）

I want to marry **sooner or later**, but I think it's also okay for people not to marry. It's their choice.
（私はいつかは結婚したいけど、他の人が結婚しないのは、それはそれでいいと思う。それぞれの選択だからね。）

I need to book my flight **sooner rather than later** because the prices keep going up.
（すぐにフライト予約しなきゃ。じゃないと値段がどんどん上がっていっちゃうから。）

1973 take (sth) over
[teɪkóʊvər]
▢▢▢▢▢▢

[PV]　（〜に）取って代わる；（〜を）引き継ぐ；（〜を）買収する

He's going to **take over** as CEO of his relative's business, so he has nothing to worry about moneywise.（彼は親戚のビジネスを継いで CEO になる予定だからお金に関して何も心配することがないんだ。）

▶ **takeover** [téɪkòʊvər] N[C] 買収、乗っ取り

1974 state-of-the-art
[stèɪṭəvðiːáːrt]
▢▢▢▢▢▢

Adj.　最先端の、最新鋭の

Massachusetts Institute of Technology provides all the equipment you need to learn about **state-of-the-art** technology.
（マサチューセッツ工科大学は、最先端技術を学ぶのに必要な設備を全て提供してくれるんだ。）

state-of-the-art の語源　art には「技術」という意味があり、state には「状態」という意味があるため、直訳すると「技術の状態」、つまり「技術水準」となります。これは、20 世紀初頭に、ある技術マニュアルにおいて in the present state of the art this is all that can be done（現在の技術水準ではこれができることの限界）という文章があり、そこから一般に使われるようになったと言われています。

4 Given that this technology will remove the need for many current jobs, particularly clerical and administrative work, and create in parallel new jobs pertaining to AI and robotics, having diverse and relevant skills will be essential to overcoming the challenges that result from these changes.

この技術によって、現存する多くの仕事、特に事務・管理業務が不要になり、それに合わせて AI およびロボット工学に関連する仕事が新しく創造されることを考えると、こうした変化で生じる問題を乗り越えるには、さまざまな関連スキルを身に付けることが不可欠になってくるだろう。

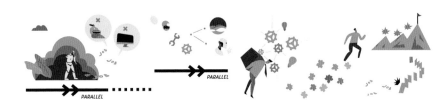

1975 technology
[teknάːlədʒi]
☐☐☐☐☐☐

N[C/U] 技術、テクノロジー

How accurate is this lie-detection **technology**?　　modern **technology**
（このうそ発見技術ってどれくらい正確なの？）　　（現代技術）

▶ **technological** Adj. 技術的な　　▶ **technologically** Adv. 技術的に
[tèknəlάːdʒɪkəl]　　　　　　　　　[tèknəlάːdʒɪkli]

Nowadays, the pace of **technological** change is so fast that it's not easy to predict what the world is going to look like even just a few years from now.
（最近では技術変化の速度がものすごい速いから今から数年後の世界がどうなっているかさえ予想するのが難しいんだ。）

▶ **technologist** [teknάːlədʒɪst] N[C] 科学技術者

1976 clerical
[klérɪkəl]
☐☐☐☐☐☐

Adj. 事務の、事務的な

I'll send you a new copy of the contract later because I found a **clerical** error.
（事務的なミスを見つけちゃったから、新しい契約書をまた後で送るね。）

a **clerical** job （事務的な仕事）

1977 administrative
[ədmínəstrətˌɪv]
☐☐☐☐☐☐

Adj. 管理の、経営の、行政の；事務の、総務の　　= admin [ǽdmɪn]

I spend so much time on **administrative** tasks during the day that I usually don't get around to doing actual work until I get home.
（日中は事務的な仕事に時間を取られすぎるから、大抵は家に帰るまで実際の仕事にとりかかれないんだ。）

▶ **administer** V[T] を管理する、運営する、統治する
[ədmínəstər]　　　　を（〜に）受けさせる、実施する (to sth)

The test will be **administered** to all primary school students across the country.
（そのテストは全国の小学生に対して実施される予定です。）

▶ **administration** [ədmìnəstréɪʃən] N[U] 管理；経営陣、当局；政権

the Trump **administration**（トランプ政権）

▶ **administratively** [ədmínəstrəṭɪvli] Adv. 管理的に、経営的に、行政的に

1978 **parallel**
[pérəlel]
☐☐☐☐☐☐

N[C] （A と B の / ～との）類似点（between A and B/with sth）

■ draw a **parallel** between A and B（(類似点を探すために) A と B を比較する）

While there are many specialists who **draw a parallel between** Japan a few decades ago **and** China today, I think they are actually quite different.
（数十年前の日本と今の中国を比較する専門家はたくさんいるけど、実際二つは結構違うと思うんだよね。）

in **parallel** (with sth)（（～と）並行して、同時に）

Adj. （～と）平行な（with/to sth）；類似の；同時の

The trainer had me do squats by bending my knees until my thighs were **parallel** with the floor.
（トレーナーにスクワットさせられたんだけど、太ももと床が平行になるまで膝を曲げさせられたんだ。）

parallel lines（平行線）

▶ **unparalleled** [ʌnpérəleld] Adj. 比類ない、並ぶもののない

接頭語 **para-** 「並んで、越えて、近くに」という意味の接頭語で、他には paraphrase（言い換え＝近い意味で言い表す）や paradox（逆説＝予想を越えたもの）などがあります。

1979 **pertain**
[pɜːrtéɪn]
☐☐☐☐☐☐

V[I] （～に）関連する、関係する（to sth/sb）

I'm not sure your question **pertains** to the topic being discussed, so we can chat about that later.（君の質問は議論のトピックとは関係ないかもしれないから、後で話そう。）

▶ **pertinence** [pɜ́ːrṭənəns] N[U] 関連性 ▶ **pertinent** [pɜ́ːrṭənənt] Adj. 関連のある

1980 **robotics**
[roʊbάːṭɪks]
☐☐☐☐☐☐

N[U] ロボット工学、ロボティクス

Some people say advancements in **robotics** could exterminate the human race, but I don't think that will happen during my lifetime.
（ロボティクスの発展によって人類が滅びるかも知れないって言ってる人もいるけど、自分が生きている間にはそれは起きないと思うな。）

▶ **robot** [róʊbɑːt] N[C] ロボット

The hotel tried to utilize **robots** to make its operations more efficient but ended up removing most of them because they kept malfunctioning.
（あのホテルはロボットを使って運営をもっと効率的にしようとしたんだけど、ロボットが何度も故障したから結局ほとんど撤去しちゃったんだ。）

▶ **robotic** [roʊbάːṭɪk] Adj. ロボットのような

I'm not sure if it's because he's super logical, but he sounds a bit **robotic**.
（彼が超ロジカルだからか分からないけど、彼ってちょっとロボットっぽく聞こえるんだ。）

1981 **overcome**
[òʊvərkʌ́m]
☐☐☐☐☐☐

V[T] （困難や問題など）を乗り越える、克服する

You need to **overcome** your fear of criticism if you want to be famous on social media.
（SNS 上で有名になりたいなら、まず批判されることへの恐怖を克服しないといけないよ。）

MeTube Live | Impact of Artificial Intelligence

Woman What's your view on artificial intelligence?

Man I'm excited by AI, but I also dread it.

Woman What frightens you about AI?

Man The prospect of evil machines scheming to seize control of the world is quite remote at this point in time, given the technology is still in its infancy. I'm mainly concerned that they'll overtake humans, leading to innocent people losing their jobs through no fault of their own.

Woman It's really admirable that you feel that way. However, history shows us that although undergoing significant technological disruption condemns segments of the population to short-term hardship, in the long-term, unemployment returns to its former level. People will get training and be utilized in jobs compatible with their new skills. Even so, it's important for governments not to dismiss this transition period as trivial and to help people through the adaptation period and to withstand these changes.

女性 人工知能についてはどういった考えをお持ちですか？

男性 AIにはワクワクもしてるんですけど、怖いと思う部分もありますね。

女性 AIの何が怖いんですか？

男性 邪悪なマシンが世界の掌握をたくらむっていう可能性は、現時点ではかなり低いと思うんですよ。技術もまだ初期段階ですし。私が懸念してるのは、主に、AIが人間を追い越すことによって、罪の無い人たちが、別に自分に過失があるわけではないのに、仕事を失うことになるという点ですね。

女性 そんな風に感じるなんてさすがですね。でも、歴史を見ると、大きな破壊的な技術革命を受けると、一部の人たちは短期的な苦難を余儀なくされますが、長期的には、失業率も前のレベルに戻るんですよね。人はトレーニングを受けて、その新しいスキルと相性の良い仕事で活用されるようになるんでしょうね。だとしても、各国政府がこの過渡期を些細なものとして退けるのではなく、その適応期間を切り抜け、変化に耐えられるよう、人々を手助けしていくことが重要ですよね。

1982 **dread**
[dred]

V[T] を怖いと思う、恐れる　N[S/U] 恐怖、恐れ

dread doing（〜することを考えるだけで怖くなる）

▶ **dreadful** [drédfəl] Adj. ひどい　　▶ **dreadfully** [drédfəli] Adv. ひどく、恐ろしく

▶ **dreaded** [drédɪd] Adj. 恐ろしい

1983 **frighten**
[fráɪtn]

V[T] を怖がらせる、ギクッとさせる　= scare [sker]

▶ **frightened** [fráɪtnd] Adj.（〜を）怖がった（of sth）

▶ **frightening** [fráɪtnɪŋ] Adj. 怖い　　▶ **frighteningly** [fráɪtnɪŋli] Adv. 怖いほど

1984 **evil**
[íːvəl]

Adj. 邪悪な、悪の、悪い　N[C] 悪いこと　N[U] 悪、邪悪

⟺ **good** [gʊd] 善、美徳

good and **evil**（善悪）

▶ **evilly** [íːvəli] Adv. 悪意を持って、邪悪に

1985 **scheme**
[skiːm]

V[I]（〜することを）たくらむ（to do）　N[C] たくらみ、計画

▶ **schematize** [skíːmətaɪz] V[T] を体系化する　　▶ **schemer** [skíːmər] N[C] 策略家

▶ **schematic** [skiːmǽtɪk] Adj. 図式の　　▶ **schematically** [skiːmǽtɪkəli] Adv. 図式的に

1986 **seize**
[siːz]

V[T] を（強く）つかむ、奪う、手に入れる；を押収する

seize control (of sth)（（〜を）掌握する、（〜の）支配権を握る）

▶ **seizure** [síːʒər] N[C/U] 奪取、掌握、差し押さえ　N[C] 発作

1987 **remote**
[rɪmóʊt]

Adj.（可能性や見込みが）低い；遠隔の、遠い　N[C] リモコン

▶ **remotely** [rɪmóʊtli] Adv. 遠隔で；（否定文で）これっぽちも

▶ **remoteness** [rɪmóʊtnəs] N[U] 遠く離れていること

1988 **infancy**
[ínfənsi]

N[U] 初期段階；幼児期、乳児期

in its **infancy**（初期段階にある）

▶ **infant** [ínfənt] N[C] 幼児、乳児　　▶ **infantile** [ínfəntaɪl] Adj. 幼児の、乳児の；幼稚な

1989 **overtake**
[òʊvərtéɪk]

V[I/T]（〜を）追い越す　V[T] を上回る

We're going to be **overtaken** by the competitors if we don't improve.

（私たち、もっと良くならないと競合他社に追い越されちゃうよ。）

1990 **innocent**
[ínəsənt]

Adj. 無罪の、潔白な；悪気のない、無邪気な　N[C] 素朴な人、お人よし

▶ **innocently** [ínəsəntli] Adv. 罪を犯さず；悪意なく、無邪気に

▶ **innocence** [ínəsəns] N[U] 無罪；無邪気

1991 fault
[fɑ:lt]

N[U] 過失、責任　N[C] 欠陥、故障；欠点、短所；断層
V[T] を責める
- ▶ **faulty** [fɔ́:lt̬i] Adj. 欠陥のある　↔ **faultless** [fɔ́:ltləs] 完璧な、ミスのない

1992 admirable
[ǽdmərəbəl]

Adj. さすがの、称賛に値する、立派な、見事な
- ▶ **admirably** [ǽdmərəbli] Adv. 立派に、見事に　▶ **admiration** [æ̀dməréɪʃən] N[U] 称賛
- ▶ **admire** [ədmáɪr] V[T] をすごいと思う、称賛する；を鑑賞する

1993 undergo
[ʌ̀ndərɡóʊ]

V[T] （変化や試練）を受ける、経験する
I'm going to **undergo** an operation next week. （来週手術を受ける予定なんだ。）

1994 condemn
[kəndém]

V[T] に（〜を / 〜することを）余儀なくする (to sth/to do)；を非難する
- ▶ **condemnation** [kɑ̀:ndəmnéɪʃən] N[C/U] 厳しい非難
- ▶ **condemnatory** [kəndémnətɔːri] Adj. 非難的な
- ▶ **condemned** [kəndémd] Adj. 死刑を宣告された

1995 hardship
[hɑ́:rdʃɪp]

N[C/U] 苦難、困難、苦労
Going through **hardship** makes you stronger. （苦難を経験することで、もっと強くなれる。）

1996 former
[fɔ́:rmər]

Adj. 前の、昔の　N[U] 前者【the -】　↔ **latter** [lǽtər] 後者【the -】
a **former** president （元大統領）
- ▶ **formerly** [fɔ́:rmərli] Adv. 前は、昔は、以前は

1997 compatible
[kəmpǽt̬əbəl]

Adj. （〜と）相性の良い、気の合った、互換性のある （with sth/sb）
Do you know if this speaker is **compatible** with my phone?
（このスピーカー、僕のスマホと互換性あるか分かる？）
- ▶ **compatibility** [kəmpæ̀t̬əbíləti] N[U] 相性、互換性

1998 dismiss
[dɪsmís]

V[T] を退ける、に取り合おうとしない；を解雇する、解任する
- ▶ **dismissal** [dɪsmísəl] N[U] （考えの）放棄、排除　N[C/U] 解雇、免職；（訴訟の）却下

1999 trivial
[tríviəl]

Adj. 些細な、取るに足りない
- ▶ **trivia** [tríviə] N[U] 雑学、豆知識

2000 withstand
[wɪðstǽnd]

V[T] に耐える、抵抗する
I'm impressed with how you can **withstand** all that abuse from customers.
（あんなにお客さんから悪態をつかれても耐えられるとかすごいわ。）

 **Active** Recall

Final Review
最終レビュー

もうすこしです！ここからは、以下の復習プランに沿って英単語学習を進めていきましょう。このプラン通りに学習すれば、すべての英単語に対して6回も取り組むことができ、英単語の定着率をいっそう向上させることができます。最後まで走り抜けましょう！

DAY *1*　CH. 21, 26, 30, 34, 37, 40

DAY *2*　CH. 22, 27, 31, 35, 38

DAY *3*　CH. 23, 28, 32, 36, 39

DAY *4*　CH. 24, 29, 33, 37, 40

DAY *5*　CH. 25, 30, 34, 38

DAY *6*　CH. 26, 31, 35, 39

DAY *7*　CH. 27, 32, 36, 40

DAY *8*　CH. 28, 33, 37

DAY *9*　CH. 29, 34, 38

DAY *10*　CH. 30, 35, 39

DAY *11*　CH. 31, 36, 40

DAY *12*　CH. 32, 37

DAY *13*　CH. 33, 38

DAY *14*　CH. 34, 39

DAY *15*　CH. 35, 40

DAY *16*　CH. 36

DAY *17*　CH. 37

DAY *18*　CH. 38

DAY *19*　CH. 39

DAY *20*　CH. 40

528

INDEX（索引）

1）　黒太字＝見出し語（番号つきの語）

　　黒細字＝反意語、同義語など見出し語以外の単語

2）　数字はページ数を表します。

534

536

548

554

Distinction 2000

Acknowledgments

The Distinction 2000 team embarked on this massive and ambitious project to get ahead of the curve and set the new gold standard for vocabulary books and English education in Japan. Each and every team member constantly collaborated closely and bounced creative ideas off each other to make the very best, innovative, picture-perfect book. All this time and effort invested have borne fruit magnificently, culminating in the gorgeous book that you now hold in your hands.

I wish to express my gratitude to Andrew Huang, Micah Judish, Kino Tsumori, Colin O'Brien, Brooke Lathram-Abe, Nick Norton, Mark Welch, Ann Lethin, Vinay Murthy, and Karen Headrich for playing a pivotal role in creating and proofreading English passages and screening vocabulary, and Misako Nagao for providing invaluable advice with respect to English-Japanese translation.

I sincerely thank Yuki Aihara and Ryo Sakamoto for drawing the ineffably beautiful cover and illustrations and bringing the words to life.

I am very grateful to Jiei Kuroyanagi, Misato Nakahara, Kenta Hara, and Shugo Miura, who have helped me in many ways throughout this project.

I extend my appreciation to Ryoji Yamaguchi for always responding to my requests promptly and flexibly to perfect the DTP design, the Ouraidou team for checking the draft repeatedly for quality, and Yuta Tashiro and KADOKAWA for giving me this great opportunity to publish this book.

Last but not least, I would also like to express my gratitude, with a deep sense of reverence, towards my parents and followers, who have always supported me in many aspects. This publication would not have been possible without your unwavering belief.

音声について

本書に収録されている英語をネイティブがスピード別に読み上げた音声を聞くことができます。記載されている注意事項をよくお読みになり、下記のサイトから無料でダウンロードページへお進みください。

https://www.kadokawa.co.jp/product/321907000333

上記のURLへパソコンからアクセスいただくと、mp3形式の音声データをダウンロードできます。
「Distinction 2000」のダウンロードボタンをクリックしてダウンロードし、ご利用ください。

スマートフォンに対応した再生方法もご用意しています。詳細は上記URLへアクセスの上、ご確認ください（ご使用の機種によっては、ご利用いただけない可能性もございます。あらかじめご了承ください）。

【注意事項】

- 音声のダウンロードはパソコンからのみとなります（再生はスマートフォンでも可能です）。携帯電話・スマートフォンからはダウンロードできません。
- 音声はmp3形式で保存されています。お聞きいただくにはmp3ファイルを再生できる環境が必要です。
- ダウンロードページへのアクセスがうまくいかない場合は、お使いのブラウザが最新であるかどうかご確認ください。
- フォルダは圧縮されていますので、解凍したうえでご利用ください。
- なお、本サービスは予告なく終了する場合がございます。あらかじめご了承ください。

著者／ATSU
英文執筆・校正／Andrew Huang, Micah Judish, Kino Tsumori,
Colin O'Brien, Brooke Lathram-Abe, Nick Norton, Mark Welch,
Ann Lethin, Vinay Murthy, Karen Headrich
装丁・デザイン／相原 ユーキ、Ryo Sakamoto
イラスト／相原 ユーキ、Ryo Sakamoto
翻訳協力／Kino Tsumori、長尾 実佐子
編集協力／黒柳 慈永、中原 美里、原 健太、三浦 柊吾、
山中 清太朗、三國 憲太郎、Timothy Way、河源社
音声収録／ELEC
校正／鷗来堂
DTP／相原 ユーキ、山口 良二

ディスティンクション
Distinction 2000

2020年 3 月28日　初版発行
2024年 8 月 5 日　23版発行

著者／ATSU
アツ

発行者／山下 直久

発行／株式会社KADOKAWA
〒102-8177　東京都千代田区富士見2-13-3
電話 0570-002-301(ナビダイヤル)

印刷所／株式会社加藤文明社印刷所

●お問い合わせ
https://www.kadokawa.co.jp/ (「お問い合わせ」へお進みください)
※内容によっては、お答えできない場合があります。
※サポートは日本国内のみとさせていただきます。
※Japanese text only

定価はカバーに表示してあります。